THE SEEKER'S GLOSSARY: BUDDHISM

SUTRA
TRANSLATION
Committee of the U.S. & Canada
New York - San Francisco - Niagara Falls - Toronto

Other works by the Committee

1. *The Buddhist Liturgy*

2. *The Sutra of Bodhisattva Ksitigarbha's Fundamental Vows*

3. *The Dharma of Mind Transmission*

4. *The Practice of Bodhisattva Dharma*

5. *An Exhortation to Be Alert to the Dharma*

6. *A Composition Urging the Generation of the Bodhi Mind*

7. *Practice and Attain Sudden Enlightenment*

8. *Pure Land Buddhism: Dialogues with Ancient Masters*

9. *Pure-Land Zen, Zen Pure-Land*

10. *Pure Land of the Patriarchs*

11. *Horizontal Escape: Pure Land Buddhism in Theory and Practice*

12. *Mind Transmission Seals*

13. *The Prajna Paramita Heart Sutra*

14. *Pure Land, Pure Mind*

15. *Bouddhisme, Sagesse et Foi*

16. *Entering the Tao of Sudden Enlightenment*

17. *The Direct Approach to Buddhadharma*

18. *Three Sutras on Complete Enlightenment*

19. *Terre Pure des Patriarches*

20. *Samantabhadra: Supreme Vows / Voeux Suprêmes*

21. *Zen & Sukhavati: Lettres du Maître Yin-kouang*

22. *Mind-Seal of the Buddhas*

23. *Samantabhadra: Votos Supremos*

In entering Buddha Dharma, there are generally three approaches: teaching, interpretation and practice. Teachings are shallow, interpretation is profound, but practice is supreme. (Elder Master Ching-yin Hui-yuan, 6th c.). According to Buddhist Teaching, all people possess an inherently enlightened True Nature that is their real identity. By becoming mindful of Buddha [through reciting the Buddha's name], therefore, people are just regaining their own real identity. They are remembering their own Buddha-nature. (*Pure Land, Pure Mind* / Introduction by Dr. J.C.Cleary)

2nd Edition
Updated and Enlarged
1998
●

**Sutra Translation Committee of the
United States and Canada**
Dharma Master Lok To, Director
2611 Davidson Ave.
Bronx, New York 10468 (USA)
Tel. (718) 584-0621

Reprinted and Donated by
**The Corporate Body of
the Buddha Educational Foundation**
11F., 55 Hang Chow South Road Sec 1,
Taipei, Taiwan, R.O.C.
Tel: 886-2-23951198 , Fax: 886-2-23913415

Contents

.Note to the Second Edition　　　　　　　　　i
.Preface　　　　　　　　　　　　　　　　　iii
.Note on Language/Abbreviations　　　　　　vi

Glossary　　　　　　　　　　　　　1-725

APPENDICES:

Avatamsaka Sutra, chapter 40:　　　　　　727
　"Practices and Vows of the
　Bodhisattva Samantabhadra"

Note on Pure Land Buddhism　　　　　　　745
　(Dr. J.C. Cleary)

The Last Rites　　　　　　　　　　　　　765
　(Dharma Master Thích Thiền Tâm)

◉ Mudras of Rebirth　　　　　　　　　　800

The supreme and endless blessings
of Samantabhadra's deeds,
I now universally transfer.
May every living being, drowning
and adrift,
Soon return to the Land of Limitless
Light!

The Vows of Samantabhadra
Avatamsaka Sutra

Note to the Second Edition

This is a revised and expanded edition of *The Seeker's Glossary of Buddhism*, which first appeared a year ago. The text is a compendium of excerpts and quotations from some 350 works by monks, nuns, professors, scholars and other laypersons from nine different countries, in their own words or in translation. The editors have merely organized the material, adding a few connecting thoughts of their own for ease in reading.

How to use the Glossary: This book can be used in three ways: to find the definition of unfamiliar terms; to gain a broader understanding of specific Buddhist concepts; and also as an introduction to Buddhism. In the last instance, we suggest that readers begin with the entry on *Parables*, then move on to *Practice, Obstacles to Cultivation* and *Ten Non-Seeking Practices*. Other entries of a more contemporary interest can be read with benefit by all. These include: *Birth Control, Organ Transplants, Vegetarianism, Universe, Immortality.*

Realms of worlds in empty space might reach an end,
And living beings, karma and afflictions be extinguished;
But they will never be exhausted, and neither will my vows.
(Vows of Bodhisattva Samantabhadra: **Avatamsaka Sutra***)*

Amitabha Festival
16 Dec. 1997
Rye Brook, NY

Minh Thành, MA, MBA
Bodhisattva-in-Precepts
P.D. Leigh, MS

With bad advisors forever left behind,
From paths of evil he departs for eternity,
Soon to see the Buddha of Limitless Light
And perfect Samantabhadra's Supreme Vows.

The Vows of Samantabhadra
Avatamsaka Sutra

Preface

In the vast corpus of the Mahayana tradition, one text, the *Avatamsaka Sutra*, stands supreme. Described by Dr. D.T. Suzuki as the "epitome of Buddhist thought, Buddhist sentiment and Buddhist experience", the sutra recounts the story of the youth Sudhana, the perennial seeker of the Way, who toward the end of the sutra sought entrance into Maitreya's Tower -- his own Self-Nature and Mind.

The present *Seeker's Glossary of Buddhism* is devoted to this inner pilgrimage, as it attempts to make the treasures of Maitreya's Tower accessible *to the greatest number*. Thus, over the last several years, the editors have canvassed some 30 Buddhist dictionaries and encyclopedias and over 350 books on Buddhism, published in different languages, extracting what they believe are key terms and concepts useful to the average student of Buddhism. Although the whole range of

Buddhist thought is covered, special emphasis is placed on the Pure Land and Hua-yen (Avatamsaka) world views, the so-called *Schools of Existence (q.v.)*. An important aspect of this Glossary is its extensive cross-referencing of key Buddhist terms, a feature which we believe is particularly useful at this stage of development of Buddhist terminology in the West.

Perceptive readers will no doubt find errors and omissions as well as (intentional) repetitions and (unintentional) redundancies. For these and other lapses, we request their indulgence and encourage them to write to the Sutra Translation Committee, 2611 Davidson Avenue, Bronx, NY 10468, USA. Tel./Fax: (718) 584-0621.

☼ ☼ ☼

To those pressed for time and hungry for solace, the Buddha bequeathed "countless" teachings leading to enlightenment -- 84,000 paths corresponding to the 84,000 afflictions of sentient beings. The most *pervasive* and most *accessible* in East Asia for the past millennium[*] has been the Pure Land tradition and its practice of Buddha Recitation -- the invocation and/or visualization of Buddha Amitabha. Whether a seeker chooses the Pure Land path or any other of the 84,000, however, the main condition for success, indeed the *sine qua non*, is the development of the Bodhi Mind -- the aspiration to achieve Buddhahood for the benefit of all sentient beings. To quote the *Avatamsaka Sutra* (ch. 39):

Just as a diamond, even if cracked, relieves poverty and want, in the same way the diamond of the Bodhi-mind, even if split, relieves the poverty of the mundane whirl.

As this book was being readied for publication, two of the editors' close family members, bà Nguyễn Thị Hoàng and Mrs. Lily Dickstein, unexpectedly passed away. Their sudden departure brought home to us, as never before, the transitory nature of human existence -- the Truth of Impermanence. To *Má* and Lily and to all sentient beings throughout the worlds of the Ten Directions, this Glossary is respectfully dedicated. May they all develop the Bodhi Mind and swiftly return to the Pure Land of Amitabha Buddha -- to the Pure Land of their Self-Nature and Mind.

Just as when a lamp is lit in a darkened room, a thousand years of darkness immediately vanishes, in the same way when the lamp of the Bodhi-mind illuminates sentient beings, countless eons of darkness are immediately dispelled (*Avatamsaka Sutra/ Hua-yen ching/Kinh Hoa Nghiêm*).

Rye Brook, NY
Winter 1997

Minh Thành
P.D. Leigh

---

*The Pure Land School is presently the school of Buddhism in China and Japan that has the most followers. (*The Shambhala Dictionary of Buddhism*, p. 174.) Given its popular appeal, [Pure Land] quickly became the object of the most dominant form of Buddhist devotion in East Asia. (M. Eliade, ed., *Encyclopedia of Religions*, vol. 12.)

Note on Language
& Abbreviations

Following the precedent of the foundation Bukkyo Dendo Kyokai (which is sponsoring the translation into English of the *Mahayana Tripitaka*), editing of quoted texts has been kept to a minimum, with no systematic attempt to standardize variant spelling, transliteration, capitalization or punctuation (e.g., Asvagosa/Asvaghosha/Ashvaghosha; Chan/Ch'an; Dharma/Dhamma; realize/realise; eon/aeon). Wade-Giles is the preferred transliteration system for Chinese.

Please note the following abbreviations:

Chin:	Chinese	*q.v.*:	see separate entry
Jpn:	Japanese	sect.:	section
Skt:	Sanskrit	tr.:	translator
Vn:	Vietnamese	C.E.	Common era (A.D.)

Acknowledgements

We respectfully acknowledge the following Good Spiritual Advisors, without whose advice, assistance and support this book could not have come to fruition. Special thanks go first and foremost to Dharma Master Lok To, *Sutra Translation Committee of the United States and Canada*, who gave us his full encouragement and backing; Ven. Kurunegoda Piyatissa, the distinguished head of the *New York Buddhist Vihara*, who graciously and speedily provided the Pali and Sanskrit versions of key terms (which, given the constraints of space and time, will appear only in a forthcoming expanded edition); Rev. Shan Kwang of Niagara Falls, Canada, who, upon hearing of this Glossary project, graciously donated a multi-volume set of the annotated *Lotus Sutra*; the Vietnamese Buddhist community of Wichita, Kansas, who originally requested the editors to recommend a Buddhist dictionary, on the occasion of their visit to the local slaughterhouses (see *Vegetarianism, Animal slaughter*); Mr. Ed Brandon of Ottawa, Canada, who obligingly designed a special program for automatic generation of cross-references (see *Preface*!); Mr. Do Huu Trach, *le doyen des terminologues bouddhistes au Canada*, who provided advice on entries in various languages; Mr. Ngo Van Hoa of Ottawa, co-author of a Zen dictionary, who went through the Glossary and steered us away from a number of mistakes; Mr. Nguyen Van Phu, a distinguished former school principal, who called our attention to several questionable points, between trips out of town to see his extended family; Messrs. Vu Van Thai and Huynh Huu Hong, of Ville Anjou (Quebec), Buddhist scholars in their own right, who between them lent us three sets of rare Buddhist dictionaries, unavailable for purchase anywhere in the US; Messrs. Steven Lane and Dave Kuzminski, who consented to the editors hauling away several huge cartons of Dharma books from their respective apartments and keeping them for an extended period of time; Mr. Pram Nguyen, who valiantly tried to steer us away from substantive errors, all the while educating us on the little-known Esoteric tradition of Vietnam; Mr. Dương Đình Hỷ, who gallantly plowed through the manuscript, despite his busy schedule and the imminent approach of the Lunar New Year; Mr. Thomas Leung, who kindly drew our attention to several questionable points of Dharma; Mr. Trang Le, who for the sake of correct Dharma, never declined to meet with the principal editor on the shortest notice, in the most unlikely places, at the saddest times; Messrs. Sang Lam and Richard Chau, who wordprocessed this seemingly never-ending Glossary, sometimes sleeping over at the editors' house -- many times catching the midnight local back to the West Bronx; the late Ms. Ada B. Taylor of Stratford, Connecticut, whose thoughtful gift of a Japanese art book more than a decade ago graces this Glossary; and Prof. Forrest G. Smith and Dr. Ellen B. Dickstein, whose discerning review of the content and ever-vigilant editing of the language of Shakespeare added depth to the text and gave it a scholarly imprint. Last but certainly not least, we would like to mention here a number of teachers and Kalyanamitras whom our principal editor had the good fortune to meet on his recent visit to India, to fulfill his mother's wish to rest in the sacred site of *Vulture Peak*: Ven. M. Wimalasara Thero (Maha Bodhi Society in Bodhgaya); Ven. M. Suddhammalankara Thero (Maha Bodhi Society of India, Calcutta); Ven. Dr. B. Khemanando of Thailand; Ven. Thích Chơn Minh (New Delhi University); Prof. Kazuo Azuma of Chiba Ken, Japan; and Dr. Sukamal Chowdhury of Calcutta. Each was kind enough to go over certain sections of the manuscript, and through these fruitful interactions, some twenty entries were revised and amended. *Whatever errors remain are, of course, the responsibility of the editors alone*. To all these Kalyanamitras, we say "Thank you, Cám-ơn, Arigato Gozaimasu" ... All merits and virtues deriving from this work, which is freely distributed to all seekers, are respectfully dedicated to sentient beings throughout the Dharma Realm.

Second Edition: We acknowledge the following good spiritual advisors and friends who took part in the updating of this Glossary (*in the order of our temporal association with them*): *Masters/Bhikshus* Lok To, Thich Phuoc Bon, Thich Tri Hoang and K. Watanabe; *Upasaka/upasika* Duong Dinh Hy, Do Huu Trach, David Cushman, Marilyn Isler, Steven Lane, Ngo Van Hoa, John Ironmount, Vu Van Thai and Forrest G. Smith. Special acknowledgement is also due to the late *upasika* N.T. Hoang/Dieu Phung, who as a senior editor and benefactor of the VHSG, indirectly contributed to this second edition.

vhsg: 1/1998

Dictionaries and Encyclopedias
(quoted and/or consulted,
in order of relevance to the present Glossary)
●

1 - *Dictionary of Beliefs and Religions*, Larousse: 1994.

2 - *A Dictionary of Japanese Buddhist Terms*, Hisao Inagaki: 1988.

3 - *Historical Dictionary of Buddhism*, Charles S. Prebish: 1993.

4 - *A Dictionary of Buddhism: Chinese - Sanskrit - English - Thai*, The Chinese Buddhist Order of Sangha in Thailand: 1976.

5 - *The Perennial Dictionary of World Religions*, K. Crim, ed.: 1981.

6 - *Phật Học Từ Điển*, Đoàn Trung Còn: 1963. (3 volumes)

7 - *Handbook of Chinese Buddhism*, Ernest J. Eitel: 1888.

8 - *Zen Dictionary*, Ernest Wood: 1957.

9 - *Buddhist Dictionary*, Nyanatiloka and Nyanaponika. (revised 1980)

10 - *A Glossary of Buddhist Terms*, A. C. March: 1937.

11 - *A Dictionary of Buddhist Terms and Terminologies*, K. K. Murthy: 1991.

12 - *Dictionnaire du Bouddhisme, René de Berval*, tr.: 1991.

13 - *A Dictionary of Chinese Buddhist Terms*, William Edward Soothill: 1934.

14 - *Từ Điển Phật Học Vietnam*, Thích Minh Châu: 1991.

15 - *Từ Điển Phật Học Hán Việt*, Kim Cương Tử and Thích Thanh Minh: 1992 (2 volumes).

16 - *World Scripture*, International Religious Foundation: 1991.

17 - *A Dictionary of Buddhist Terms and Concepts*, Nichiren Shoshu International Center, Tokyo: 1983.

18 - *A Popular Dictionary of Buddhism*, Christmas Humphrey: 1962.

19 - *Encyclopedia Britannica*: 1995.

20 - *Encyclopedia of Religions*, M. Eliade, chief editor: 1987.

21 - *A Dictionary of Buddhism*, T.O. Ling: 1972.

22 - *The Shambala Dictionary of Buddhism and Zen* : 1991.

23 - *Le Petit Dictionnaire D'Esotérisme*, Jean Darles, M. S. T. (No date of publication).

24 - *The Encyclopedia of Eastern Philosophy and Religion*, Ingrid Fischer-Schreiber, et al: 1994.

25 - *Encyclopedia of Buddhism*, Dr. G. P. Malalasekera: 1956--.

26 - *A Dictionary of Pali Proper Names*, Dr. G. P. Malalasekera.

27 - *A Handbook of Living Religions*, John R. Hinnells, ed.: 1984.

28 - *World Religions: Eastern Traditions*, G. Oxtoby: 1996.

29 - *The Dictionary of Global Culture*, K.A. Appiah & Gates: 1997.

30 - *The Oxford Dictionary of World Religions* : 1997. ▲

अ

◉ A (SYLLABLE)

See also: Dual Birth; Buddha Recitation Samadhi

▶"The Sanskrit prefix 'A' means 'not', the negative. Before another vowel a consonant may be added. (Humphrey)." The meditation on the Sanskrit letter "A" is the most important meditation in Esoteric Buddhism. "The entire system of doctrine and practice set forth in the *Mahavairocana Sutra* (key text in Esoteric Buddhism) is symbolized in concentrated form in the single seed syllable 'A'. The commentary on the *Mahavairocana Sutra* says, 'The 'A' syllable gate is the king of all mantras.' (T. Yamasaki, *Shingon*)." Yama: 192

"The sound 'A' is regarded as the source from which all words are produced. It is therefore termed the 'mother of all sounds'. It exemplifies the Mahayana doctrine that the world of change is immediately the realm of ultimate reality or, in other words, Samsara is identical with Nirvana. 'A' is also employed to suggest the idea of the evolution of all phenomena from [thusness]. In Esoteric Buddhism, it symbolizes the unity of the whole world. Thence it is identified with Vairocana, [the primordial] Buddha." Dait: 5

Buddhism of Wisdom & Faith/ excerpts:
"If the mind is very unsettled and we cannot use [Buddha Recitation], we should, with each utterance, concentrate firmly on the letter 'A' in *Amitabha Buddha.* When the letter 'A' is present, all the other letters are also present. If, because of delusion and forgetfulness, the letter 'A' is lost, all the other letters are also lost. Moreover, the letter 'A' is the key and fundamental letter of the alphabet and is therefore considered the mother of all other letters. Through concentration on reciting the Buddha's name while

simultaneously holding fast to the letter 'A', eventually mind and environment both dissolve and amalgamate into one bloc, as great as space itself. Buddha Amitabha and the practitioner will then both disappear. At that time, naturally, the letter 'A' will have ceased to exist as well. However, it was lost earlier because the mind was unsettled and scattered, while it no longer exists now precisely because of the harmonious state of 'perpetual concentration.' This is the manifestation of emptiness of Mind and environment -- the entry point into the *Buddha Recitation Samadhi* (q.v.)."
Thich: 239-240 #0001

◙ **A DI ĐÀ**
see Amitabha Buddha

◙ **ABHIDHARMA**
See also: Tripitaka; Sastra

▶"Lit. Higher Dhamma (Dharma). The third division of the canon of the Theravada and Mahayana Schools. It is largely a commentary on the sermons or sutras, and subjects them to analysis. Philosophical and psychological, it contains an entire system of mind training."
Hump: 25

In Buddhism, commentaries and treatises are of two types: (1) the *Abhidharma* contains mainly, though not exclusively, the commentaries expounded by Buddha Sakyamuni and recited at the First Council, held in 483 B.C., the year of the Buddha's passing. Maha-Kasyapa, the President of the Council, is believed to have recited the Abhidharma personally. It is codified in the third basket of both the Theravada and Mahayana canons; (2) *Sastras* are later commentaries and treatises, written by Mahayana patriarchs such as Nagarjuna (2nd/3rd B.C.), Asangha and Vasabandu (5th century) to explain important points in the teachings of the Buddha. (An important sastra, for example, is the *Awakening of the Faith Treatise*.) The sastras constitute a major part of the Mahayana Tripitaka.
Editor: na #0166

◙ **ABORTION**
See also: Birth Control; Kalala; Ksitigarbha

▶"Act of abortion, i.e., terminating life of a fetus, is explicitly mentioned in Buddhist canonical scriptures, in the Vinaya-Pitaka, as a grave

offence. If abortion is brought about by a Buddhist monk, or if he is in any way a party to the procuring of an abortion by offering advice as to the methods or supplying abortive medicine, penalty is expulsion from monkhood. This is in accordance with Buddhist view that destruction of life is a moral transgression."

Ling: 7

"According to Buddhist tenets, the life cycle of a sentient being begins when the consciousness enters the womb, and traditionally this has been considered the moment of conception. Therefore, there is no objection to contraception which interferes with conception without damaging sentient life. Termination of pregnancy, on the other hand, necessarily occurs after conception, so it is not advised."

Tsomo/1995: 101

"As a scholar, Dr. R. Thurman (q.v.) is especially critical of fuzzy thinking in popular Buddhism. As an example, he cites a 1992 article in *Tricycle* by Helen Tworkov, the magazine's editor, in which Tworkov acknowledges strong anti-abortion teachings in Buddhism but also writes that 'Dharma teachings can be used to validate either pro-choice or anti-abortion politics.' To Thurman, 'that's simply incorrect. It's the taking of life. The fundamentalists do have it emotionally right -- the killing of fetuses is a mass massacre from the Buddhist point of view. It is not a fuzzy issue in Buddhism.' (R. Kamenetz)"

NY Times Magazine:5/5/96 #1109

◉ **ACADEMIC STUDY**
See also: North America (Buddhism in); Europe (Buddhism in)

►"Early interest in the Mahayana, stimulated by the discovery of Sankrit texts from Nepal and the work of Eugene Burnouf and other scholars, had rather weakened by the end of the nineteenth century. This was due to the natural enthusiasm at the discovery of the Pali literature. A number of scholars active during the first half of the twentieth century sought to re-emphasize the value of works available in Chinese and Tibetan translation. Many of these represent North Indian traditions just as ancient as those from Sri Lanka. One group of scholars working in Russia was especially associated with the name of T. Shcherbatsky. Influenced by contact with the living tradition of Northern Buddhism, they sought to comprehend Buddhist thought in terms of European philosophical development. A second group, composed mainly of Belgian and French scholars, was more interested in the Mahayana as a religion and in the history of Buddhism. The most influential writer of this group was probably Louis de La Vallée Poussin... The period [following] the Second World War has seen a strong c o n t i n u a n c e   o f   t h i s Franco-Belgian school, most notably with the work of E. Lamotte. Moreover the researches in Tibet of the Italian scholar, G. Tucci, have given a new impetus to studies of Northern Buddhism. Important contributions have been made by scholars from India, especially in the study of Buddhist philosophy and history, and by Japanese scholars notably in the field of Eastern Buddhism. At the same time new discoveries from the sands of Central Asia, the caves of Tun-huang, Gilgit in Kashmir and from the libraries of Nepal and Tibet have recovered lost Buddhist literature and opened up new fields for research. Text-critical and historical studies using these new materials have been developed, especially in Germany. The recent expansion of Buddhist studies in North America seems likely to develop new approaches [Tantric school, Pure Land school, Women Studies, etc.]."

Hinn: 321-322

Pure Land School

Unlike Zen or Tibetan Buddhism, Pure Land Buddhism is still little known in the West. However, it is the most popular school in Asia. Although Pure Land is sometimes looked upon as a basically popular form of Buddhism, it actually covers all strata of practitioners. For some practitioners, Pure Land is synonymous with complete reliance on other-power, the power of Amitabha Buddha. For others, Pure Land is Mind -- it is Mind created, Mind-only. (see Pure Land School).

Editor: na   1929

◙ **ACARYA/ACHARYA**

See also: Ajahn

▸"Teacher or master. Applied to an eminent priest who guides the student in conduct and sets an example for him."   Dait: 5

"One of the two kinds of spiritual leaders known in Buddhism; the second type of teacher is the upadhyaya. Originally acharya was understood to mean a master of the Dharma, whereas the upadhyaya taught discipline and adherence to the rules."
Sham: 2 #0002

◙ **ACTS OF GOD**
Syn: Natural Disasters
See also: Cause and Effect

▸(A legal term.) "From the Buddhist point of view, earthquakes and similar phenomena are neither Acts of God nor caprices of nature; they are causally related to the thoughts and actions primarily of human beings. Man and his environment are not separate; they are mutually conditioning -- two aspects of one reality. Each of our thoughts pulsates with the heartbeat of the cosmos, and the universe in turn is affected by and reflects our thoughts and actions. We cannot ravage and pollute the earth, upsetting the balance of the forces of nature -- our own nature -- without repercussions from the earth. C.G. Jung was quoted in a 1971 article in the *New York Times* as saying (following an earthquake that destroyed many Chilian cities), 'Even though today's scientists may reject the idea, the earth seems to be in tune with the destructive fury of mankind.' But this is only half the equation. Through man's pollution of the atmosphere and the soil, the very air he breathes and the food he eats poison him, eliciting from his body a similar protest in the form of pollution diseases, the foremost of which may be cancer. Thus the circle of destruction is complete."
Kapl/80: 252 #1189

◙ **ADAMANTINE MOUNTAINS**
See also: Cosmology (Buddhist); Billion-World Universe

▸"In Buddhism, the outermost mountain-range made of iron which encircles a world-system."
Inag: 399
According to Buddhist teachings, there is an infinite number of world systems in the cosmos and our earth is one infinitesimal part of one such system.
Editor: na #0699

◙ **ADI-BUDDHA**
See also: Vairocana Buddha; Esoteric School

▸"Term used in Mahayana

Buddhism, especially in Nepal and Tibet, for the 'primordial Buddha,' the Buddha without beginning."
Ling: 8
"The primordial Buddha. Although the concept itself can be traced to early Buddhism, it is widely acknowledged that the notion of the Adi-Buddha was fully developed in esoteric Buddhism. In early Tibetan Vajrayana Buddhism, the Adi-Buddha is often associated with Samantabhadra who represents the Dharma-kaya. In later Tibetan Vajrayana, it is Vajradhara who represents the Dharma-kaya. In [traditional Mahayana] Buddhism, the Adi-Buddha is represented by Mahavairocana."
Preb: 38 #0482

◙ ADORNMENT

▸"The action and effect of creating the beauties of a purified field [such as the Pure Land of Amitabha Buddha]."
Gomez: 281 #1694

◙ ADULTERY
See also: Precepts

▸"Adultery is mentioned in Buddhist texts as one of a number of forms of similar sexual misconduct. Thus, a monk who is guilty of adultery is to be excommunicated from the Order; but this is so in any case of sexual intercourse in which a monk is willfully involved, irrespective of whether the woman is married or not. For laymen, sexual intercourse is forbidden with any woman who is under any form of protection -- whether that of parents, guardians, or husband."
Ling: 9 #1111

◙ ADVERSITY
See Enemies

◙ AFFLICTIONS
See also: Afflictions are Bodhi; Emotions; Delusion; Evil; Love-attachment
----
▸"The passions and ignorance that cause one to wander in Samsara and hinder one from reaching enlightenment. The word 'afflictions' emphasizes the effects of defilements. One list of the basic defilements names six: greed, hatred (or anger), ignorance (or delusion), arrogance, doubt, and wrong (evil) views."
Chan: 472-473
The basic goal of Buddhist

teachings is to keep the mind empty and still so that our innate wisdom can manifest itself. (A Buddha is all wisdom at all times.) Thus, Buddhism fosters practices and habits that subdue passions and simplify life, freeing the cultivator for spiritual pursuits. It is in this context that sexual desire, excessive rest and sleep, etc. are considered afflictions. Editor: na Buddha Sakyamuni compared human beings chasing after the fleeting pleasures of this world to a child licking honey off a sharp knife. There is no way they can avoid hurting themselves. "They are like men who carry torches against a strong wind; the flame will surely burn their hands and faces."

Subduing Afflictions

Buddhism of Wisdom & Faith/excerpts:

"The karmas of greed, anger and delusion manifest themselves in many forms, which are impossible to describe fully. I will discuss, in general, four basic ways to subdue them.

I. *SUPPRESSING AFFLICTIONS WITH THE MIND.* There are only two points of divergence between the deluded and the enlightened (i.e., Buddhas and Bodhisattvas): purity is Buddhahood, defilement is the state of sentient beings. Because the Buddhas are in accord with the Pure Mind, they are enlightened, fully endowed with spiritual powers and wisdom. Because sentient beings are attached to worldly Dusts, they are deluded and revolve in the cycle of Birth and Death. To practice Pure Land is to go deep into the Buddha Recitation Samadhi, awakening to the Original Mind and attaining Buddhahood. Therefore, if any deluded, agitated thought develops during Buddha Recitation, it should be severed immediately, allowing us to return to the state of the Pure Mind. This is counteracting afflictions with the mind.

II. *SUPPRESSING AFFLICTIONS WITH NOUMENON.* When deluded thoughts arise which cannot be suppressed with the mind, we should move to the second stage and 'visualize principles.' For example, whenever the affliction of greed develops, we should visualize the principles of impurity, suffering, impermanence, No-Self. Whenever the affliction of anger arises, we should visualize the principles of compassion, forgiveness and emptiness of all dharmas.

III. *SUPPRESSING AFFLICTIONS WITH PHENOMENA.* Persons with heavy karma who cannot suppress their afflictions by visualizing principles alone should use 'phenomena,' that is, external forms. For example, individuals who are prone to anger and delusion and are aware of their shortcomings, should, when they are on the verge of bursting into a quarrel, immediately leave the scene and slowly sip a glass of cold water. Those heavily afflicted with the karma of lust-attachment who cannot suppress their afflictions through 'visualization of principle,' should arrange to be near virtuous Elders and concentrate on Buddhist activities or distant travel, to overcome lust and memories gradually. The saying 'absence makes the heart grow fonder,' should really read 'out of sight, out of mind.' This is because sentient beings' minds closely parallel their surroundings and environment. If the surroundings disappear, the mind loses its anchor, and, gradually, all memories fade.

IV. *SUPPRESSING AFFLICTIONS WITH REPENTANCE AND RECITATION.* In addition to the above three methods, which range from the subtle to the gross, there is a fourth: repentance and the recitation of sutras, mantras and Amitabha Buddha's name. If performed regularly, repentance and recitation eradicate bad karma and generate merit and wisdom... Depending on circumstances, the practitioner can use any of these four methods to counteract the karma of greed, anger and delusion in a general way. If these methods are practiced patiently and in earnest, there is nothing that cannot be accomplished."

Tam: 167-170 #1383

◙ **AFFLICTIONS ARE BODHI**
Syn: Samsara is Nirvana
See also: Ultimatism

►A Mahayana teaching of the *highest* level, for those already awakened / enlightened (see *Ultimatism* for explanation).

"A basic Zen teaching. Afflictions are inseparable from Buddhahood. *[At the noumenon or the theoretical level]*, afflictions and Buddhahood are considered to be two sides of the same coin. Since all existence has the tathata (thusness) as its underlying essence, afflictions too must rest on this tathata. Enlightenment, i.e., identity with

the tathata, is achieved only when one realizes that afflictions in themselves can have no real, independent existence. The doctrine is considered to *express the ultimate teaching of Mahayana*."
Dait: 21

Turn Afflictions into Bodhi
This is a key Mahayana concept. As an example, supposing a woman returns home, only to discover that her only child has suddenly died. This is the worst affliction imaginable. Yet, if through this affliction she understands that disease and death are the common lot of all sentient beings, she will have realized the truth of impermanence. She will have turned an affliction (loss of a loved one) into Bodhi (Enlightenment).
Editor: na   #0081

◙ **AGADA**
syn: Panacea
See also: Pure Land Buddhism

▸A panacea, a "cure-all", a remedy for all diseases and evils. All methods and schools of Buddhism are best -- best for a particular group, at a particular time. This is why the Buddha extolled all sutras as being foremost, as being kings of the Dharma. Of all these methods and schools, the one that is considered foremost and at the same time a panacea is Pure Land. Pure Land is a cure-all because it applies to people of all capacities and walks of life.
Editor: na

◙ **AGAMA**

▸"Often used as a generic term for the Theravada sutras."
Dait: 4
"Lit., tradition. The Agamas are Chinese translations of the Sutras or Sermons as collected by the Sarvastivadin School (q.v.). They vary little from the corresponding Sutta Pitaka (Sutra Pitaka) of the Theravada Canon of today."
Hump: 27 #0006

◙ **AGE OF MONKS AND NUNS**
see   Sacerdotal age

◙ **AGGREGATES**
see   Skandhas

◙ **AGNOSTICISM**
See also: Atheism

▸"The doctrine that man can never know the nature of Ultimate Reality. Buddhism differs from agnosticism in that it

asserts an innate transcendental faculty in man (buddhi) that by elimination of all elements of 'defilement' allows one to attain perfect knowledge and enlightenment."
Hump: 27 #0481

◙ **AHIMSA**
Syn: Non-killing; Non-harming
See also: Compassion; Vegetarianism; Killing

▸"Skt., lit. 'non-harming.' In Buddhism non-harming of living beings is considered one of the most important aspects of the Buddhist spiritual attitude. The rule of vegetarianism for monks and nuns in most Buddhist cultures is based on this principle of ahimsa."
Sham: 2 #0317

◙ **AJAHN**
See also: Acarya

▸"Thai pronunciation for the Sanskrit Acharya ('teacher'). Can denote a senior school or college teacher; in the Thai (Buddhist Order), a meditation master."
Snel: 261 #0719

◙ **AJANTA**
See also: Pilgrimage sites (India); Tun-huang

▸"City in the western part of central India, famous for Buddhist grottoes dating from 200 to 700 C.E. The twenty-nine caves, which extend over a distance of 5.6 kilometers, hold the best-preserved Buddhist frescoes in the world. They represent the greatest monument to Buddhist painting in India. The frescoes illustrate in part the life of the historical Buddha (Siddartha Gautama), as it is known from the sutras (Prince Siddartha at the four gates, the temptation of Mara, entry into Parinirvana, etc.), and in part stories from the previous existences of the Buddha (Jataka). They give a detailed picture of life in India at the beginning of historical times. Four caves are so-called chaityas and contain stupas."
Sham: 3 #0318

◙ **AJATASATRU / AJATASATTU**
See also: Meditation Sutra; Bimbisara; Longer Amitabha Sutra; Jivaka
----
▸"A king of Magadha in Shakyamuni's day. While still a prince, he became friendly with Devadatta, who incited him to have his father Bimbisara killed and become king in his stead. He

made Magadha into the most powerful kingdom in India. Later he converted to Buddhism and supported the First Buddhist Council for the compilation of Buddha Shakyamuni's teachings. According to the *Nirvana Sutra*, since King Bimbisara had no heir by his wife Vaidehi, he consulted a diviner, who said that there was a hermit presently living in the mountains who, after he died, would be reborn as Bimbisara's son. Bimbisara was so impatient for the birth of an heir that he had the hermit killed. Shortly after, Vaidehi conceived, but the diviner foretold that the child would become the king's enemy.' In fear of this child, the king dropped him from atop a tower [but the child survived the fall]... It is said that as a young man Ajatasatru was persuaded to rebel against his father by Devadatta, who told him the story of his birth."
Sokk: 7-8

"Ajatasattu's name means 'enemy before birth,' which according to the legend, derives from his mother's wish to drink blood from the knee of her husband [when she was pregnant with him]. This was interpreted by the astrologers to mean that her child would kill his father.

Ajatasattu is described as an ambitious prince who wanted to become ruler of the kingdom as quickly as possible and could not wait for the death of his father. Together with Devadatta, he contrived a double conspiracy: since Devadatta was eager to take over the leadership of the Buddhist order, he was to murder the Buddha, and Ajatasattu was to kill his own father. The plot was discovered. Bimbisara pardoned his son and ceded him the throne. Ajatasattu, nevertheless, did not feel secure with his father still alive and had him incarcerated and starved together with his wife, Queen Vaidehi."
Sham: 3

"After Bimbisara's death, Ajatasatru came to regret his conduct deeply. Tormented by guilt over the death of his father, he broke out in virulent sores during the second month of his fiftieth year, and it was predicted that he would die in the third month. At the advice of his physician and minister Jivaka, he sought out Shakyamuni Buddha who taught him the doctrines of the *Nirvana Sutra*, enabling him to eradicate his evil karma and prolong his life."
Sokk: 7-8

NOTE: The story of Ajatasatru has been immortalized in the prologue of the *Meditation Sutra*, one of the three core texts of the Pure Land school.
Editor: na   #0008

◎ **AJITA**
see Maitreya

◎ **AKASAGARBHA BODHISATTVA**
Syn: Kokuzo Bodhisattva; Empty Store Bodhisattva
See also: True Emptiness/ Wonderful Existence; Wish-fulfilling Gem
----
►*"Jpn/* Kokuzo; A deity of wisdom, virtue, and good fortune, whose activity is to fulfill all wishes. [Her] direction is south. The esoteric tradition considers this the direction from which all treasures come, and south is also associated with the Buddha Ratnasambhava (Hosho), whose name means 'giving birth to treasure'. Kokuzo's name literally means 'repository of the void,' void here indicating not merely nothingness, but the mysterious potentiality that gives rise to all phenomena. The *samaya* (principal, essential) form of Kokuzo is the wish-fulfilling gem. The samadhi of the Morning Star

meditation focuses on this magical jewel, symbol of 'void potentiality'. The wish-fulfilling gem embodies Kokuzo's enlightened energy, the universe itself which evolves eternally in perfect freedom..."
Yama: 185
"The name of Akasagarbha (Kokuzo) Bodhisattva literally means 'repository of the void,' void here indicating not merely nothingness, but the mysterious potentiality that gives rise to all phenomena."
Yama: 185   #2172

◎ **AKSOBHYA BUDDHA**

►"The immovable Buddha. Aksobhya is one of the five [primordial] Buddhas. His left hand is in the shape of a fist, his right hand touches the ground, and he is of golden complexion."
Dait: 12   #0010

◎ **ALAYA CONSCIOUSNESS**
Syn: Alaya Vijnana; Eighth Consciousness; Store Consciousness; Karma Repository.
See also: Consciousnesses; Scriptural Recital.

►"All karma created in the present and previous lifetimes is

stored in the Alaya Consciousness. This is regarded as that which undergoes the cycle of birth and death ... All the actions and experiences of life that take place through the first seven consciousness are accumulated as karma in this Alaya Consciousness, which at the same time exerts an influence on the workings of the seven consciousnesses."
Sokk: 9

"The concept of Alaya-Vijnana constitutes the basis of the 'mind-only' doctrine of the Yogachara and stands at the center of this school's theory of individualization, according to which past karmic seeds ... enter into the Alaya-Vijnana, whence they arise again to occasion thought activity. This individuated thinking is ridden with ignorance and egotism, which instigate the notion that it constitutes a real person in the real world."
Sham: 4 #0011

◎ ALAYA VIJNANA
see Alaya Consciousness

◎ ALL IN ALL
see "One is all, All is one"

◎ ALL IN ONE
see "One is All, All is One"

◎ ALL-KNOWING
Syn: Lion among Men; Light of the Worlds; Light of the Future
See also: Buddha

▶"All knowing [sarvajna]. This is a common epithet of Buddhas, who are regarded as 'all-knowing' because they know all the paths that lead to liberation, and because they know the causes and effects of all events and all things."
Gomez: 281-282 #1696

◎ ALMS
see Dana

◎ ALMSROUND
see Takahatsu

◎ AMBEDKAR, DR. B.R. (1891-1956)
See also: India (Buddhism in); Hinduism/Buddhism

▶"Founder of the Indian movement for converting Harijans (untouchables) from Hinduism to Buddhism. Member of Bombay Legislative Assembly, later Law Minister in the Central Government at Indian independence. 1956: at Nagpur, he and his wife along with 500,000 followers [mostly composed of Harijans

(Untouchables)] formally renounced the Hindu religion and espoused Buddhism. Work carried on by Indian Buddhist Society, which he founded. Author of book: *The Buddha and His Dhamma*."
Snel: 311 #0752

◙ **AMBROSIA**
Syn: Amrta

▸"A drink which gives immortality."
Luk/1970: 231
An epithet of Nirvana. Note the expression "Sweat Dew of the Dharma."

◙ **AMIDA (Jpn)**
see   Amitabha Buddha

◙ **AMIDA KYO (Jpn)**
see   *Amitabha Sutra*

◙ **AMIDABUTSU SETSURIN**

▸"A Japanese work (translated as *Encyclopedia of Amitabha Buddha*) composed by Zensho Keijo in the 13th century. It is composed of seven fascicles and is a collection of references to Amitabha Buddha and his Pure Land (Sukhavati) found in various Buddhist sutras and sastras. More than two hundred

texts are mentioned by name. It is of great value for materials dealing with Pure Land Buddhism."
(*Encyclopedia of Buddhism*, v. I: p.425)

◙ **AMIDA-JI**

▸One of the most common names of the temples in Japan, especially those of Pure Land Buddhism. *Amida* is the Japanese transcription of the word *Amitabha* who is the primary Buddha of this school.
[Five of the most popular Amida-Ji are:]
(1) The Amida-ji in Suo Prefecture (presently Yamaguchi prefecture). It is in Mure village, Saha-gun, Yamaguchi of western Japan. Its full name is Keguzan Amidaji. It belongs to the Kogi Shingon-shu (or orthodox Mantrayana school), the main temple of which is Koyasan. This temple shows a good example of the relation of Buddhism and the state. The temple was founded in 1180 A. D. by Shun-jobo Chogen who was the reconstructor of Daibutsu in Nara. The history of this temple during the middle ages is not quite clear. But in the Kanbun period (1661-1673 A.D.), it was reconstructed just as it is

seen now, and converted to the Shingon-shu from the Jodo-shu. (Festival: July 14-15.)

(2) The Amida-ji in Yamashiro Prefecture (presently Kyoto Prefecture). It is in Kochiya, Atago-gun, Kyoto of central Japan. It was founded by Tanzei in the early 17th century along with the other Amida-jis founded by him in many districts of Japan. Of them this is the largest and most famous; its full name is Isshinki-myoketsujo Komyozan. It belongs to the Jodo sect. This is a very silent and quiet place with many old and big pine trees in its park. Some of these trees are especially famous because of their legends connected with the founder, Tanzei. The 25th of May is the festival day of this temple.

(3) The Amida-ji in Sagami Prefecture (presently Kanagawa Prefecture). It is in Tonosawa village. Ashigara-gun, Kanagawa Prefecture of eastern Japan. This also was founded (1632 A. C.) by Tanzei and was supported by the count of Sagami.In the park there is the so-called Asoka stupa.

(4) The Amida-ji in Kyoto, viz., Rendaizan Amida-ji. It belongs to the Jodo sect and was founded in the Tenmon period (1532-1555.) by Seigyoku. Formerly it was in Omi Prefecture (presently Shiga Prefecture) and transferred here in 1585.

(5) The Amida-ji in Nagato Prefecture. It is in Shimonoseki city, Yamaguchi Prefecture, western Japan. It was built for the delight of the young emperor Antoku, who died in the last battle between the Taira an Minamoto clans. It became popular after Lafcadio Hearn wrote about it. It first belonged to the Tendai sect, but was later converted into Shingon and then into Jodo. After the separation of Buddhism and Shintoism in 1875. The temple was forcibly converted into a Shinto shrine (current name of temple is Akamanomiya).

(Encyclopedia of Buddhism, v. I: p. 430)

◙ **AMIDISM**
see Pure Land Buddhism (Summary)

◙ **AMIS DU BOUDDHISME, LES**
See France (Buddhism in) #0478

◙ **AMITA**
see Amitabha Buddha

◙ **AMITABHA** *BUDDHA*
Syn: Amida; Amita; Amitayus
See also: Pure Land Buddhism (S u m m a r y); E x i s t e n c e

(Amitabha/Pure Land); Buddha Recitation; Pure Land School; Mind; Immortality; Raigo

----

▸*Chin*/ O-Mi-T'o-Fo; *Jpn*/ Amida; *Vn*/ A-Di-Đà. The word Amitabha is used in English to represent two Sanskrit terms, "Amitabha" ("Infinite Light") and "Amitayus" ("Infinite Life"). Amitabha is the most commonly used name for the Buddha of Infinite Light and Infinite Life, "the archetype of cosmic compassion" (T. Cleary). A transhistorical Buddha venerated by all Mahayana schools (T'ien-T'ai, Esoteric, Zen ...) and, particularly, Pure Land. Presides over the Western Pure Land (Land of Ultimate Bliss) or Sukhavati, where anyone can be reborn through utterly sincere (i.e., singleminded) recitation of his name, particularly at the time of death.
Editor/Tam: 141
"About the middle of the 7th century in China, Amitabha replaced Shakyamuni and Maitreya as the supreme object of popular devotion. Associated with Amitabha were the two g r e a t   B o d h i s a t t v a s , M a h a s t h a m a p r a p t a   a n d Avalokitesvara (Kuan Yin)."
Ling: 16

"Although [Amitabha] Buddha figures prominently in a very large number of Mahayana sutras, the three principal sutras (in terms of later Buddhism) of the Pure Land school are the two *Amitabha Sutras* and the *Meditation Sutra*. The religious faith within Buddhism that is oriented to the personality of this particular Buddha is known as 'the Pure Land teaching'. It is generally believed that both Nagarjuna (2nd-3rd c.) and Vasubandhu (5th-6th c.) in India held to this faith."
Dait: 7
"The Fourth of the Dhyani (Esoteric) Buddhas. The personification of Compassion. In the Pure Land schools of China and Japan, Amitabha is the intermediary between Supreme Reality and mankind, and faith in him ensures rebirth in his Paradise (Sukhavati). Symbolically, Amitabha is Higher Self (or Self-Nature)."
Hump: 30
Amitabha Buddha at the higher or noumenon level represents the True Mind, the Self-Nature common to the Buddhas and sentient beings -- infinitely bright and everlasting. This deeper understanding provides the rationale for the harmonization

of Zen and Pure Land, two of the most popular schools of Mahayana Buddhism.

Editor: na

I. *BUDDHA vs. CREATOR-GOD*
"Although the tone of Pure Land Buddhist devotion may be theistic... its content is clearly Buddhist. Amita Buddha is both like and unlike a Supreme Being or God in the following respects: 1) He is unique in his own realm (the Pure Land), but he is not unique in the universe as a whole, being only one of many Buddhas, each unique in his own realm (Buddha-land) and each having distinctive properties. (2) He is the creator of his realm, the source of all good in it, and the parent-like protector and helper (or savior) of its inhabitants, but he does not create, sustain, or destroy the universe as a whole, nor is he the ontological support (a 'Ground of Being') for the universe as a whole. (3) He is omniscient and all-seeing within and outside of his realm and is especially concerned with knowing human activity, so that he may remove ignorance; but he does not judge or punish. (4) He is outside 'this world'; he is visualized as living in a paradise in the sky and is 'Other Power'--that is, other than the passionate, defiled mind of the practitioner; but he does not stand above the worshiper as an ontologically 'Higher Power.' (5) His life is immeasurably long, but his life is not infinite, since there was a time when he was not a Buddha."

Yoshi/Corless: 247

II. *PURE LAND IN THE TRIPITAKA*
In the *Encyclopedia of Buddhism*, Vol. I, Dr. G.P. Malalasekera, founding president of the World Fellowship of Buddhists, quotes a Japanese author who found in the Tripitaka two hundred texts referring to Amitabha Buddha and His Pure Land (thirty-one of the texts are in Sanskrit).

Editor/Dia: 168

"Thirty-one Sanskrit texts and over [two] hundred Chinese and Tibetan translations refer to Amitabha and/or Sukhavati. For example, the author of the *Treatise on the Buddha-womb Theory* concludes his highly technical work on the tathagatagarbha (Buddha-womb or embryo) doctrine by stating: 'By the merit I have acquired through [writing] this [treatise], may all living beings come to perceive the Lord Amitabha endowed with infinite light.' Such

references attest to the influence wielded by Pure Land thought in the devotional lives of the commentators."
Tana: 12
III. *NOTE:*
"In the sutra *Rebirth According to One's Vows*, Buddha Sakyamuni was asked by a Bodhisattva, 'Honored One! There are pure lands in all ten directions. Why do you especially extol the Western Pure Land and urge sentient beings to focus continuously on Amitabha Buddha, seeking rebirth in His Land?' The Buddha replied, 'Sentient beings in this Saha World generally have polluted, scattered minds. Therefore, I extol only the Pure Land of the West, focussing their minds on a single realm. If they meditate on all Buddhas, the scope of attention will be too broad, their minds will be lost and scattered and they will find samadhi difficult to attain. Thus, they will fail to achieve rebirth in the Pure Land.' Furthermore, seeking the virtues of *one* Buddha is the same as seeking the virtues of *all* Buddhas -- as all Buddhas have one common Dharma Nature. That is why to focus on Amitabha Buddha is to focus on all Buddhas, to be born

in the Western Pure Land is to be born in all pure lands.'"
P.L. Dia: 15-16
See also Pure Land Buddhism (Summary) for details. #0014

◙ **AMITABHA BUDDHA'S VOWS**
see Dharmakara's Vows

◙ **AMITABHA** *SUTRA*
Syn: Smaller Sukhavati-Vyuha Sutra; Shorter Amitabha sutra; Sutra of Amida.
See also: Three Pure Land Sutras; Longer Amitabha Sutra; Exclusion Clause; Pure Land Buddhism (Summary)

▸"*Amitabha Sutra* or *Shorter Amitabha Sutra*; one of the three sutras that form the doctrinal basis for the Pure Land school in East Asia (China, Japan, Korea, Vietnam etc...). This sutra, also known 'as the short *Sukhavati-vyuha*, describes the simplest form of the practice of this school -- recitation of Buddha Amitabha's name..."
Sham: 6
"Three Chinese translations were made: by Kumarajiva of the later Ch'in dynasty in the year 402; by Gunabhadra of the Liu Sung dynasty in 455; and by Hsuan-tsang of the T'ang dynasty in 650. Of these, Kumarajiva's

and Hsuan-tsang's are still extant. Kumarajiva's version is entitled 'Amitabha Sutra' and consists of one fascicle. [It is the one most commonly used nowadays.] The *Amitabha Sutra* is one of the Three Pure Land Sutras (q.v.), together with the *Longer Amitabha Sutra* and the *Meditation Sutra.*
Sokk: 10-11

I *SUMMARY*

"Written in the form of a discourse by Shakyamuni to Shariputra and others at the Jetavana Monastery, the *Amitabha Sutra* describes the blessings and virtues of Amitabha Buddha and his Pure Land of Perfect Bliss in the western region of the universe. It further teaches that one can attain rebirth in this Pure Land by relying on Amitabha. Subsequently the Buddhas in the Six Directions are described as bearing witness to the truth of Shakyamuni's teaching."
Sokk: 10-11

"The *Amitabha Sutra* is an address delivered by Sakyamuni to Sariputra in the Jeta grove near Sravasti. Like the *Longer Amitabha Sutra,* which it may slightly predate, this sutra deals mainly with a description of the Pure Land -- the gorgeous palaces, parks, and gardens; the gem trees made of gold, silver, crystal, and coral; the fragrant flowers and luscious fruits; the rivers and lotus lakes with their perfumed water that is either hot or cold for bathing as desired; the delightful, soothing sounds of birds and angelic singers. The major difference between the two sutras lies in the fact that the *Shorter Amitabha Sutra* [emphasizes] salvation through faith and the recitation of Amida's name [Buddha Recitation, q.v.], rather than through works."   Okaz: 15

II *BACKGROUND*

"The story of the *Amitabha Sutra* is set in a world of tradition and myth. Time and location, temporal and spatial dimensions, are without question of a special kind--one that we could perhaps call sacral or mythical, for lack of a better word. Extraordinary rules and boundaries also apply to body and action, spirit and matter, the ideal and the real. Access to these special dimensions of reality is possible through a set of assumptions about the world and the beings that inhabit it and through an accompanying belief and confidence in the spiritual realities and processes embodied in the mythology. Among many differences between the world view of the two texts and the world view of contemporary Western secular culture, two stand out as central to understanding the message of the two sutras. *First*, existence after death is a given; but it is not simply an extension of human life. Existence after death means the possibility--or rather, the reality--of many lives, in a variety of realms other than our world, and in a variety of roles or 'incarnations' that include rebirth as an animal, as a hungry ghost, or in one of many paradises, or rebirth in a hell or purgatory, and rebirth in other world systems as well. *Second*, the process of rebirth is for most of us sentient beings an unending cycle of suffering. This cycle would be a desperate, hopeless, and meaningless eternal return if it were not for the possibility of deliverance. The moral and spiritual quality of our lives can have a significant effect on the course of our wandering through the many rounds of rebirth. Human beings who attain moral and spiritual perfection may in fact attain liberation from the cycle of rebirth. Those who attain liberation through their own spiritual effort are the Buddhas of the universe. *In turn, the moral and spiritual quality of Buddhas can also have a significant effect on the course of our journey through the many stations of rebirth*--in other words, the liberation of Buddhas facilitates the liberation of other, less perfect sentient beings. Much of Mahayana Buddhist literature is devoted to these two issues: the manner in which human beings attain the perfection of Buddhas and Bodhisattvas, and the manner in which Buddhas and Bodhisattvas assist other beings in their quest for liberation from suffering."

Gomez/Land: 7-8

III *AMITABHA SUTRA / LOTUS SUTRA*

"The *Lotus Sutra* is the *Amitabha Sutra* preached in detail, and the *Amitabha Sutra* is the *Lotus Sutra* in summary. In contrast to other sutras which expound many terms in connection with the nature and characteristics of things and persuade people to understand the principles and to work on self-cultivation, these two sutras deal only with perception of phenomenal reality by the direct reasoning mind. In the *Amitabha Sutra*, Buddha said, 'If there is a

good man or a good woman who hears someone speak of Buddha Amitabha and holds firmly his name... when this person approaches the hour of death, Buddha Amitabha and his holy company will manifest themselves in front of him. This person, since he is not confused, will be reborn in the most blissful country of Buddha Amitabha.'.. To quote from the 23rd chapter of the *Lotus Sutra*, 'Anyone who hears this Sutra and practices accordingly, when his present life ends, will go to the Western Paradise.' The similarity of these two passages is apparent. Other descriptions in the *Amitabha Sutra* of the grandeur and splendor of the Land, of Buddha's life, of Buddha's radiance and of the protection and care by the Buddhas of the Six Directions, though different in comprehensiveness and language, are, in fact, identical in their content and significance. Therefore, one invocation of Buddha Amitabha's name represents the supreme Dharma and covers unlimited approaches."
Master T'ai Hsu: 20-22
See also: Three Pure Land Sutras. #0020

◙ **AMITAYUS**
see Amitabha Buddha

◙ **AMRAPALI**
See also: Vimalakirti Sutra

▶"A courtesan of Vaisali who gave her garden to the Buddha and his retinue, where they stayed during the events of the *Vimalakirti Sutra*."
Thur/1976: 137
"Not long before the Parinirvana of the Buddha, Amrapali, the famous courtesan of Vaisali, made a formal offering of a mango grove for the Buddha and the brethren. The Buddha accepted the gift from her. She changed her life and became a great devotee of the Lord."
Latika: 90 #0015

◙ **AN SHIH-KAO**

▶"A Persian priest who came to China in 148, which was during the Later Han Dynasty, and translated some thirty Buddhist sutras. He was the crown prince of a country [which lay within the present boundaries of Iran], but renounced the throne to study Buddhism earnestly."
Dait: 10
"An Shih-kao is the first historical figure of Chinese

Buddhism. He initiated the systematic translation of Buddhist texts through so-called 'translation bureaus.' Records concerning the number of works he translated vary between 34 and 176. These works may be divided into two categories: (1) texts on the practice of dhyana (meditation), which also treat preparatory techniques such as counting the breath, mindfulness of body, and so forth; and (2) texts that treat enumerated categories like the five skandhas. An Shih-kao used many Taoistic terms in his translations in an effort to convey specialized Buddhist expressions in Chinese."
Sham: 9 #0025

◙ ANAGAMIN
See also: Arhatship

▶"'Never-returner'; designates those followers of the Theravada who are in the third stage of the supramundane path, [the fourth stage being Arhatship, the goal of Theravada cultivation]."
Sham: 6
"Non-returning. The third of the four levels to be attained by a follower of Theravada. Such a person may be reborn in either the material world or the non-material or spiritual world,

but he never will be reborn in the World of Desire (our world), so his attainment is called 'non-returning.'"
Dait: 8 #0017

◙ ANAGARIKA
See also: Anagarika Dharmapala

▶"Lit. 'Homeless One'; one who enters the homeless (monastic) life without formally being ordained as a monk."
Snel: 261
"Lit. 'homeless wanderer'. A Buddhist layperson who has taken vows including celibacy."
Batc: 380 #0720

◙ ANAGARIKA DHARMAPALA
Syn: Dhammapala
See also: World Parliament of Religions

▶"Name used by D. H. Hewavitarne, the famous Buddhist propagandist. Born in Ceylon in 1865, he joined the Theosophical Society in 1884. Inspired by H. P. Blavatsky he studied Pali, and in 1891 founded the Maha Bodhi Society. He then proclaimed himself as an Anagarika, a homeless wanderer, and worked hard for the main object of the Society, the restoration of Buddha Gaya into

Buddhist hands, which was only achieved in 1949. In 1925 he founded the British Maha Bodhi Society in London. In 1931 he entered the Order as Sri Devamitta Dhammapala, and died in 1933."

Hump: 67 #0494

◙ **ANANDA**
See also: Buddhist Councils; Tripitaka; Sunaksatra

▸"A cousin of the Buddha, the brother of Devadatta (q.v.). One of the ten great disciples of the Buddha. Ananda accompanied the Buddha for more than twenty years and was the Master's favorite disciple. He attained enlightenment after the demise of the Buddha under the guidance of Mahakasyapa. He was famed for his excellent memory and recited the Sutra-Pitaka (the sermons contained in the Tripitaka, *q.v.*) at the First Buddhist Council."

Dait: 8

"Ananda was more than any other an advocate for the cause of women. He gave Dharma discourses in the presence of women, and it was at his intercession that Buddha consented to the founding of an order of nuns. He is said to have attained Arhatship only after the death of the Buddha, immediately before the First Council." (See *Buddhist Councils* for details).

Sham: 7
NOTE:
According to Mahayana teachings, Ananda, like many other disciples of the Buddha was in reality a Bodhisattva who expediently took the form of a monk to assist Sakyamuni Buddha ... Thus, at one time he "defended" the cause of women, at another time he was "lured" by a beautiful prostitute (See the *Surangama Sutra* for example).

Editor: na #0018

◙ **ANATHAPINDIKA**
Syn: Sudatta
See also: Jeta Grove; Golden-Colored King

▸"Another name for Sudatta who lived at Sravasti, India, during the time of Sakyamuni Buddha. He was wealthy and often donated food and clothing to orphans and old people. Hence he was called Anathapindika or 'one who takes care of widows and orphans.' He presented Sakyamuni with the Jetavana-vihara (Jeta grove or garden)."

Dait: 84

"The chief supporter of the

Buddha was Anathapindika, the millionaire. Amongst lay followers he was regarded as the foremost alms-giver. The original name of Anathapindika, which means 'Feeder of the Helpless', was Sudatta. Owing to his unparalleled generosity he was latterly known by his new name. His birthplace was Savatthi (Sravasti). Anathapindika bought the park belonging to Prince Jeta at a price determined by covering, so the story goes, the whole site with gold coins and erected the famous Jetavana Monastery at a great cost. Here the Buddha spent nineteen rainy seasons. This monastery where the Buddha spent the major part of his life was the place where he delivered many of his sermons. (Narada Maha Thera, *The Buddha and His Teachings*)."

Narada: 93

"Sudatta's wife and children also became disciples of the Buddha. Ananda and Sariputra visited Sudatta when he fell ill, and he is said to have been reborn in the Tusita Heaven after his death."

Dait: 333

NOTE:
The name Anathapindika has come to be synonymous with extreme generosity in connection with Buddhist activities.

However, this is not his only claim to fame. An interesting story about Anathapindika goes like this: at the time of the Buddha, the role of lay people was merely to provide material support to monks and nuns. It was not the practice to teach them the higher truths, which were reserved for those who had joined the Order. At Anathapindika's deathbed however, the Elder Sariputra made an exception and conveyed to him the Buddha's teaching on Wisdom. Anathapindika was moved to tears and requested that henceforth, such teachings be shared with lay people also, as some of them could benefit from these ideas. It was as a result of this plea that lay people may now be exposed to the higher teachings of the Buddha.

Editor: na #0019
See also: Jeta Grove

◙ **ANATMAN**
See also: Atman; Cause and effect

▸*Mahayana Buddhism*
"Non-self. Non-ego. Absence of a permanent, unchanging self or soul.

I. Non-existence of the permanent self. The body

consists of the five elements and there is no self.

II. Non-substantiality of elements (dharmas). Elements exist only by means of the union of conditions. There is no eternal and unchangeable substance in them."   Dait: 224 #0021

◉ **ANCESTOR WORSHIP**

See also: Death; Ullambana; Dedication of Merit

▸[In accordance with its practice of 'adapting to conditions but remaining unchanged'], "Buddhism in East Asia promoted ancestor worship by the practice of chanting sutras for the dead and in the popular festival of Departed Spirits (Yu Lan P'en Hui; *Vn/* Vu-Lan) held on the 15th day of the 7th month of the lunar calendar."
Ling: 20-21 #1113

◉ **ANGER**

See also: Ego; Letting go; Afflictions; Cause and Effect; Herbs (Pungent)

▸A major affliction, one of the three poisons in Buddhism.

Buddhism of Wisdom & Faith/ excerpts:
"Among the various afflictions, only anger manifests itself in a very crude manner, destroying the practitioner in a most effective way. Therefore the ancients said: 'When we allow an angry thought to arise, we open the door to millions of obstructions.' For example, while reciting the Buddha's name, a practitioner may suddenly think of a wicked, ungrateful, stern and evil person who has treated him cruelly; or, he may remember close relatives who are troublesome and unreliable and have caused him grief. He therefore becomes sad and angry, fidgety and uneasy. In that state of mind, his mouth recites the Buddha's name while his mind is saddened and full of delusive thoughts. Some practitioners drop their rosaries and stop reciting; lying down, they put their arms on their foreheads and let their minds wander aimlessly. Others are so afflicted and saddened that they forget about eating and sleeping in their desire to confront the culprit and shout at him; or they look for ways to take revenge and get even. The angry mind can harm the practitioner to that extent. To combat and subdue anger and resentment, *we must develop a compassionate mind*. The *Lotus Sutra* teaches: 'We should take the mind of great compassion as

our house, forbearance as our armor, the Truth of Emptiness as our throne.' We should think: we ourselves and all other sentient beings are common mortals drowning in the sea of Birth and Death, all because of karma and afflictions. However, afflictions by their very nature are illusory and unreal. For example, where does an angry thought come from before it arises? Where does it return to when it dissipates? When we are angry and resentful, we are the first to suffer, because we have ignited the fire of afflictions, which will consume us. Anger, moreover, can neither convert nor bring a single benefit to anyone. Is it not then a useless case of delusion? We should think further: those who have harmed us by their wrongful actions have, through delusion, planted evil seeds; they will necessarily suffer retribution. They should therefore be the objects of pity, not anger. This is because, if they were clear-minded and understood the causes of merit and retribution, they would never dare do such things. We are offspring of the Buddhas and should apply their teachings to dissolve our own afflictions -- because the goal of cultivation is to seek liberation

and happiness, not to descend upon the path of suffering. We should feel compassionate and forgiving of injurious actions and practice forbearance, understanding that everything is illusory and void. We should remember the words of the ancient masters: 'The fire of the three poisons, greed, anger and delusion,/ Burns up all the forests of virtue/. Those who would tread the Bodhisattva Path,/ Should be forbearing in mind and body.'"
Tam: 149-150

"Coming at the conclusion of the section devoted to the protection of Bodhicitta (Bodhi-Mind), patience is celebrated as the supreme austerity. It is the antidote to *anger*, regarded in Buddhism as the most destructive and perilous of all mental factors. Anger, defined as the flooding of the mind with violent and aggressive feelings, leading naturally to hostility and conflict, is *outlawed in Buddhism as in no other religious tradition*. Even so-called righteous anger, so often excused as having injustice and abuse as its object, is utterly condemned if this involves the overpowering of the mind in a wave of uncontrollable and destructive passion. Aside from a

purely external and as it were artificial indignation, put on for educational purposes--which has compassion as its motive and is acted out by one whose mind is under control--*anger has absolutely no place in the scheme of spiritual development*. It is totally inimical to mental training and will ruin and annihilate in an instant all progress and merit gained. This being so, the crucial question of how to behave in a hostile environment begins to emerge. Step by step, patriarch Shantideva (q.v.) focuses on the real source of the problem, the basis of anger as of every other defilement. This is the ego, the self, the sense of 'I,' experienced as the center of the universe, and a universe interpreted as friend and enemy in relation to how it is perceived from the egocentric viewpoint. In Buddhism, this is of course the central issue, and it is only in the light of the full teachings on emptiness that it can be satisfactorily discussed."
Shantiveda: 13
NOTE:
As a practical application, if family members constantly "dangle the word Death before their eyes," realizing that it can strike at any time, there will be less friction, less anger, more tolerance of others' shortcomings -- more compassion.
Editor/Zen: 27   #1262

◙ **ANGKOR WAT**
See also: Cambodia (Buddhism)

►"Temple complex in central Cambodia, considered the high point of classical Khmer art and architecture. Built under King Suryavarman II (1113-50), Angkor Wat was initially a holy site consecrated to Vishnu. Following the conversion of the succeeding Khmer kings to Buddhism, Angkor Wat served as a Buddhist holy place. After the destruction of Angkor by the Thais and the flight of the Khmer kings to Phnom Penh in the fifteenth century, Angkor Wat fell into oblivion and was covered by jungle. It was not rediscovered until the nineteenth century."
Sham: 8   #0321

◙ **ANGULIMALA**
See also: Paritta

►"According to the *Angulimala Sutra*, Angulimala originally studied under a teacher of Brahmanism in Shravasti. When he spurned the advances of his teacher's young and beautiful

wife, she slandered Angulimala to her husband. Enraged, the teacher resolved to destroy the young man without dirtying his own hands. He told Angulimala that if he killed a hundred people (some sources say one thousand) and cut off their fingers, he could complete his religious practice. Torn between his own moral sense and belief in his duty to obey his teacher, Angulimala went mad. He had already killed ninety-nine people and was about to kill his mother for the hundredth, when he met the Buddha who instructed him and converted him to Buddhism."
Sokk: 12

"The life story of the Venerable Angulimala is one of the most moving accounts in the Buddhist canon. After killing ninety-nine persons, Angulimala was converted by the Buddha, repented his evil ways and joined the Order: One day as he went on his round for alms he saw a woman in labor. Moved by compassion, he reported this pathetic woman's suffering to the Buddha who then advised him to pronounce the following words of truth, which later became known as the Angulimala Paritta (Mantra) ... 'Sister, since my birth in the Arya clan [i,e., since

my ordination], I know not that I consciously destroyed the life of any living being. By this truth may you be whole and may your child be whole.' He went to the presence of the suffering sister and uttered these words. Instantly, she delivered the child with ease." (Narada Maha Thera, *The Buddha and His Teaching*, p. 124.)" #0022

◉ ANIMAL
See also: Evil Paths; Animal Slaughter

▸"One of the six forms of rebirth and one of the three Evil Paths is rebirth as an animal in the human world. Beings who are reborn as animals suffer at the hands of hunters, trappers, and butchers, and by being forced to work as beasts of burden for farmers and merchants."
Gomez: 282-283 #1697

◉ ANIMAL EXPERIMENTATION
See end of entry "Killing"

◉ ANIMAL SLAUGHTER
See also: Vegetarianism; Killing; Abortion

▸Note the following stanza from an ancient Buddhist poem, linking animal slaughter to bad

karma, particularly insurrection and warfare:

"For hundreds of thousands of years,/ the stew in the pot/ has brewed hatred and resentment/ that is difficult to stop./ If you wish to know why there are disasters/ of armies and weapons in the world,/ listen to the piteous cries/ from the slaughterhouses at midnight."
Erricker: 117

In Mahayana Buddhism, violence and warfare can never be ended as long as animal slaughter and other forms of violence (castration, forced feeding, etc.) against the animal realm continue unabated. To seek world peace while continuing the slaughtering of animals for food is no different from trying to cool a boiling pot by fanning the top, all the while keeping the flame going underneath.
NOTE:
See also the following excerpt about Dr. Temple Grandin, a cattle expert who devoted her life to designing humane slaughtering systems that *would at least* drastically reduce pain and fears for the animals: "When a... humane system was installed in Alabama a few years ago, Dr. Grandin operated the hydrautic gears of the restraining box [where the animal was going to be killed] herself [as a test run], concentrating on easing the animal into the box as gently as possible. 'When I held his head in the yoke, I imagined placing my hands on his forehead and under his chin and *gently* easing him into position,' she wrote in her book. 'Body boundaries seemed to disappear, and I had no awareness of pushing the levers.' She compared it to a state of Zen meditation: 'The more gently I was able to hold the animal with the apparatus, the more peaceful I felt. *As the life force left the animal, I had deep religious feelings*. For the first time in my life logic had been completely overwhelmed by feelings I did not know I had.' A slaughterhouse certainly 'makes you look at your own mortality,' said Dr. Grandin. 'Those animals just walk into the chute and it's all over. *If you see them cut up, they're so fragile inside. People are made of the same stuff.*'"
NY Times: Aug 5 '97 #2009

◙ **ANTHOLOGIES**
See also: Tripitaka

▶"Buddhism seems always to have suffered a surfeit of sutras. Even in the centuries when the

teachings were maintained only in memory, it appears that no one monk was expected to remember everything: we find reference to 'reciters of the middle-length discourses.' With the explosion of Mahayana sutra writing about four centuries after the Buddha's death, the problem of a surplus of sutras was greatly compounded. A remedy was attempted in the form of the anthology. The first of these is attributed to the Indian master, Nagarjuna (second-century C.E.). Entitled *Compendium of Sutras*, it consist of passages from sixty - eight, mostly Mahayana, sutras. The history of anthologies in the West began in 1871 when Samuel Beal, who described himself as 'a Chaplain in Her Majesty's Fleet,' published *A Catena of Buddhist Scriptures from the Chinese*. This book included a wide variety of Buddhist texts -- for the most part Indian works -- that had been translated into Chinese ... The first major attempt at anthologizing occurred as part of the *Sacred Books of the East* series, published in 1894. Ten of the forty-nine volumes of the series were devoted to Buddhism. Reflecting the opinion of the day that Pali texts represented the most accurate record of what the

Buddha taught (an opinion since rejected), seven of these volumes contain translations of Pali works. In 1895, Paul Carus (q.v.) published *The Gospel of Buddha According to Old Records*. The work was arranged like the Bible, with numbered chapters and verses, and was intended to point up the many agreements between Buddhism and Christianity, thereby bringing out 'that nobler Christianity which aspires to be the cosmic religion of universal truth.' Carus drew from the Buddhist sources that were available to him in English, French, and German. He was free in his manipulation of his s o u r c e s , p a r a p h r a s i n g , abbreviating, and rearranging the translations ... One year later, the Harvard Pali scholar Henry Clarke Warren published what was to be one of the most widely read anthologies of Buddhist texts, *Buddhism in Translations*. Drawn entirely from Pali sources, it contained a much wider range of materials than had been available. These works provided much of the material for future anthologies, which were often made up entirely of extracts (often no more than snippets), with the bulk of the materials drawn from the Pali.

There were, however, some important exceptions. Dwight Goddard's popular 1938 collection, *A Buddhist Bible*, was organized by language of origin and contained works that had not previously been translated into English. Going against the trend to excerpt 'key' passages, Goddard included full translations of these texts. A *Buddhist Bible* is not, however, without its eccentricities. Goddard rearranged the *Diamond Sutra* into a more 'sensible' order, including the *Tao Te Ching* ... Another exception to the 'recycling' trend was Edward Conze's *Buddhist Texts through the Ages* (1954), which brought together some of the leading scholars of the day to translate works never before rendered into English, including tantric texts. More recently, Stephan Beyer's *The Buddhist Experience: Sources and Interpretations* (1974) includes a rich range of works from Pali, Sanskrit, Tibetan, Chinese, and Japanese, all translated by Beyer. It has been replaced in the same series by John Strong's excellent new anthology, *The Experience of Buddhism: Sources and Interpretations* (1995). This long and venerable tradition loomed before me as I set out to make a new anthology... entitled *Buddhism in Practice*". (Donald S. Lopez, Jr./ 1996)
Tric/Winter/96: 92-93 #2268

◉ ANURUDDHA

▸"One of the great disciples of the Buddha. Anuruddha was a cousin of the Buddha. Having often fallen asleep in the presence of the Buddha, he vowed one day that he would never sleep again. He eventually lost his eyesight, but acquired 'the miraculous eye,' one of the six supernormal powers, which enabled him to see intuitively."
Dait: 8-9 #0023

◉ ANUTTARA-SAMYAK-SAMBODHI
see Supreme, Perfect Enlightenment

◉ APHRODISIACS
see Herbs (Pungent --)

◉ APPEARANCE OF A BUDDHA
see Voice of a Buddha

◉ ARANYA

▸A small Buddhist temple or retreat place usually located in a forest or on a mountain.

◙ ARHAT

See also: Arhatship (Four Stages); Buddhist Councils; Sravaka; Bodhisattva

----

▸"A Buddhist saint; one who has attained enlightenment and is no longer subject to death and rebirth."
Stro: 357

Arhatship is the highest rank attained by Sravakas (senior disciples of the Buddha). An Arhat is a Buddhist saint who has attained liberation from the cycle of Birth and Death, generally through living a monastic life in accordance with the Buddha's teachings. This is the goal of Theravadin practice, as contrasted with Bodhisattvahood in Mahayana practice.
Editor/Tam: 142

"One of the ten appellations of the Buddha. In early Buddhism, the Buddha was called Arhat, but after the rise of Mahayana, the word Arhat was limited to the saints of Theravada Buddhism."
Dait: 11

Background

"In the passage of Buddhism to China, the conception of the Arhat underwent a particular development and became one of the most important elements in Chinese Buddhism, even of the Mahayana schools. The prime vehicle for the veneration of Arhats was the Ch'an (Zen) school. Because of its emphasis on the human side of things and its aversion to any worship of deities, it saw in these saints, who had attained liberation through their own effort, beings corresponding to the mind of Ch'an (Zen). Magical abilities were attributed to the Arhats as the fruit of their wisdom. In East Asian monasteries, groups of 500 Lohan [Arhat] images are found, arranged in special halls, and also groups, originally of sixteen, later mostly of eighteen, located left and right on the short walls of the halls of the monasteries. Each individual Arhat has unique features that are characteristic of him and that are highly expressive. The depictions of 500 Lohans derives from the canonical descriptions of the first Buddhist Council, at which 500 Arhats were present. Also the council of Kashmir is said to have been attended by 500 Arhats." (*See also:* Buddhist Councils).
Sham: 127-128

"Evidence of the contrast between the Bodhisattva and the Arhat is plentiful in the Mahayana scriptures, but for a

really vivid impression you have only to look at the Buddhist paintings and sculptures produced in India and China, and now preserved in temples and museums throughout the World. The Bodhisattva is usually depicted as a beautiful young man (or woman) sitting on a delicate lotus flower. He has a graceful figure, long flowing locks, and many fine ornaments. The Arhat, on the other hand, is usually an old man with a bald head and bushy eyebrows. Clad in a shabby monastic robe, he leans wearily on a knotted staff. No lotus seat for him--he is usually standing on solid rock, or sometimes, for a change, floating on the ocean. The Bodhisattva represents the ideal in all its perfection and purity, the abstract ideal not stained or touched by anything of the world, but lifted above it. The Arhat, by contrast, represents the realization of the ideal under the conditions and limitations of space and time, the stress of history. No wonder the Arhat has a weather-beaten, worn look."
Sangha/Drama: 10 #0027

◉ **ARHATSHIP (FOUR STAGES)**
See also: Arhat; Beyond learning stage; Anagamin

▶Refers to four levels of Enlightenment, culminating in Arhatship. Arhats are no longer subject to rebirth in Samsara, i.e., in the cycle of Birth and Death.
Editor: na
"These are the four stages of enlightenment on the Theravada path, namely, the stage of *Stream-enterer* (Srotapanna), the *Once-returner*, the *Non-returner* (Anagamin), and the *Arhat*."
Chan: 489 #0608

◉ **ARISING**

▶"This word appears frequently in Mahayana texts, often in the negative form. It denotes the appearance, production, or coming into being of a thing or event. According to the emptiness (sunyata) view, that which arises from dependent generation is by nature empty; hence all arising things are illusory (maya)."
Chan: 470 #0495

◉ **ARNOLD, SIR EDWIN (1832-1904)**
See also: Light of Asia

▶"Nineteenth-century author whose book, *The Light of Asia*, published in 1879, popularized

Buddhism. Born in England, he went to King's College in London, eventually winning a scholarship to University College, Oxford. He later became Principal of Deccan College in Poona, India. He published his first book of verse in 1853, translated texts from Sanskrit, and even compiled a Turkish grammar in 1877. *The Light of Asia* became immediately popular upon publication in 1879. The book inspired many other authors, and was seen as an antidote to a number of mid-century writers and scholars (such as Eugene Burnouf, Barthélemy Saint-Hilaire, and others) who saw Buddhism as a wholly nihilistic religion. Although he never publicly avowed a personal commitment to the Buddhist religion, many observers felt that Arnold was a Buddhist at heart. To this end he worked diligently for the restoration of Buddhist sites, especially Bodhgaya (q.v)."
Preb: 52-53　#0998

◙ **ART (BUDDHIST)**
See also: Buddha Images; Icons; Ajanta; Tun-Huang

►"Much of the art of Buddhist countries has been directly inspired by Buddhist ideas and practices, although very little has been the work of Buddhist monks. The production of works of art has been primarily done by Buddhist laymen. Sculpture, painting and architecture are the major fields; music is not encouraged in Buddhist devotional contexts and is not used by monks, whose corporate chanting of sutras in devotional services bears some slight similarity to European plain-chant but is basically a reciting aloud.

In the field of sculpture, however, Buddhism has a rich record, particularly in the development of the rupa, or Buddha-statue, from early beginnings in N.W. India to its modern forms in S.E. Asian countries (Taiwan, Thailand, Vietnam, etc...). The painting of murals on walls of monasteries and temples has also had a long development and has produced many different styles; the principal subjects have been, and still are, scenes from the life of the Buddha, and from Jataka stories. In the field of architecture, the stupa has provided ample scope for rich development."
Ling: 26　#1114

◎ **ARYASIMHA**
See also: Twenty Eight Indian Patriarchs

▸"Twenty-fourth Indian patriarch of the Zen school. He lived in central India during the sixth century. When Aryasimha was propagating Buddhism in Kashmir in northern India, King Dammira (Sanskrit unknown), an enemy of Buddhism, destroyed many Buddhist temples and stupas and murdered a number of priests. He finally beheaded Aryasimha. It is said that instead of blood, pure white milk gushed from Aryasimha's neck."
Sokk: 16   #0202

◎ **ASAMKHEYA**

▸Innumerable, countless. #1104

◎ **ASANGA (310-390)**

▸"Famous Buddhist who founded the Yogacara (or Mind-Only) school of Buddhism. Born to a Brahman family in North India sometime in the fourth century A.D., Asanga was the eldest of three brothers. He was converted to the Mahisasaka (one of the 20 early) schools of Buddhism and became a monk in this tradition. Apparently he received teaching,

through a vision, directly from the future Buddha Maitreya who provided him with a series of texts. Quickly converting to Mahayana as a result of this interaction, Asanga began composing texts in his own name, founded the Yogacara school of Buddhism, and converted his brother Vasubandhu." (q.v.)
Preb: 56
The famous Chinese patriarch Hsuan-tsang was a follower of Asanga and the Yogacara school.
Editor: na #0999

◎ **ASCETIC PRACTICES**
Syn: Dhuta; Austere practices

▸"Practices or precepts to purify one's body and mind and shake off adherence to clothes, food, and dwelling. There are twelve items of this practice."
Dait: 377
"Twelve such ascetic practices are known: (1) wearing patched robes, (2) wearing a robe made of three pieces (trichivara), (3) eating only begged food, (4) eating only one meal a day, (5) refraining from all further food, (6) taking only one portion, (7) living in a secluded, solitary place, (8) living on a charnel ground, (9) living under a tree, (10) living in the open, (11)

living in whatever place presents itself, (12) sitting only, never lying down." Sham: 56 #0145

◙ **ASITA**

►"A hermit-sage of Kapilavastu, India. According to the scriptures, when Shakyamuni was born, King Shuddhodana asked Asita to examine the newborn child's physiognomy. Asita, perceiving the thirty-two features of a great man, foretold that if the boy remained in the secular world, he would become a wheel-turning (supreme) king by the age of twenty-nine, but if he renounced secular life, which was more probable, he would achieve supreme wisdom and attain Buddhahood. Asita lamented that since he himself was already ninety years old, he would die before the prince attained enlightenment and thus would be unable to hear the Buddha's teaching."
Sokk: 18 #0203

◙ **ASOKA (270-230 B.C.)**
See also: Maurya dynasty

►"India's foremost royal patron of Buddhism and the first monarch to rule over a united India."
Reat: 320

"Emperor of India, founder of the Maurya Dynasty. A great Buddhist ruler, who was converted to Buddhism from Hinduism after a long period of wars of conquest. He abolished wars in his Empire, restricted hunting or killing for food, built hospitals for man and beast, and engraved on rocks and pillars throughout the Empire his famous Edicts, setting forth the moral precepts of Buddhism. He sent his son Mahinda and daughter Sanghamitta to Sri Lanka where they converted the ruler and people to Buddhism."
Hump: 36
"Held the third Buddhist Council at the capital Pajaliputra, India, in the seventeenth year of his reign. He erected stupas and stones pillars all over the country and dispatched missionaries abroad. He launched many philanthropic activities based on the spirit of Buddhism. During his reign Buddhism spread throughout India, Southeast Asia, and into some areas of western Asia."
Dait: 4-5 #0031

◙ **ASTASAHASRIKA**

►"*Astasahasrika-Prajnaparamita-Sutra* or *'The Sutra of Perfect*

Wisdom in 8,000 Lines'. Early (c.100 B.C.) *'Perfection of Wisdom Sutra'*. It became the basis of many later elaborations (into 18,000, 25,000, 100,000, etc., lines)."
Oxf: 102

◙ **ASTROLOGY**
See also: Fortune Telling; Spirit World

▶"The question many people ask is whether Buddhism accepts or rejects astrology. Strictly speaking, the Buddha did not make any direct pronouncement on this subject, because as in many other cases, He stated that discussion on matters such as these do not pertain to spiritual development. Buddhism, unlike some other religions, does not condemm astrology and people are free to use the knowledge they can get from it to make their lives more meaningful. If we study the Buddha's teaching carefully, we will come to accept that a proper and intelligent understanding of astrology can be a useful tool. There is a direct link between the life of an individual human being and the vast workings of the cosmos. Modern science is in accordance with the teachings of Buddhism.

We know for example that there is a close link between the movement of the moon and our own behaviour. This is seen especially among mentally disturbed and abnormally violent people. It is also true that certain sicknesses like asthma and bronchitis are aggravated when the moon waxes. There is, therefore, sufficient basis for us to believe that other 'planets' can also influence our lives. Buddhism accepts that there is an immense cosmic energy which pulsates through every living thing, including plants. This energy interacts with the karmic energy which an individual generates and determines the course that a life will take. The birth of an individual is not the first creation of a life but the continuation of one that had always existed and will continue to exist so long as the karmic energy is not quelled through final liberation in the unconditioned state. Now, for a life to manifest itself in a new existence, certain factors, namely seasons, germinal order and nature, must be fulfilled. These are supported by mental energy and karmic energy and all these elements are in constant interaction and are interdependent with each other, resulting in constant changes to a human being's life. According to astrologers, the time at which a person is born is predetermined by cosmic energy and karmic energy. Hence, it can be concluded that life is not merely accidental: it is the result of the interaction between an individual's karma and the universal energy force. The course of a human life is predetermined, caused partly by a being's own actions in the past and by the energies that activate the cosmos. Once started, a life is controlled by the interaction between these two forces even to the moment at which a birth takes place. A skillful astrologer then, as one who understands cosmic as well as karmic influence, can chart the course of one's life, based on the moment of a person's birth. While we are in one sense at the mercy of these forces, the Buddha has pointed out a way through which we can escape their influence. All karmic energies are stored in the subconscious mind normally described as mental purities and impurities. Since karmic forces influence one's destiny, a person can develop his mind and negate certain evil influences caused by

previous bad karma. A person can also 'purify' his mind and rid himself of all karmic energies and thus prevent rebirth. When there is no rebirth, there is no potential life and there will consequently be no 'future' existence which can be predicated or charted. At such a stage of spiritual and mental development, one will have transcended the need to know about his life because most imperfections and unsatisfactoriness would have been removed. A highly developed human being will have no need for a horoscope."
Dham: 315-317 #1981

◙ **ASURA**

►"Originally in Brahmanism and Hinduism a devil who fights with the gods headed by Indra (or Sakra). Asura was introduced into Buddhism, and came to be regarded as a devil who is fond of fighting by nature. He is sometimes counted as one of the [protectors of Buddhism]."
Dait: 12-13
"A class of contentious demons in Indian mythology who fight continually with the god Indra. They are said to live at the bottom of the ocean surrounding

Mt. Sumeru. In Buddhism they constitute one of the eight kinds of beings (Eight Divisions of Divinities/ q.v.) and represent the world of anger among the Ten Worlds."
Sokk: 19
In popular Buddhism, an inveterately angry person, subject to frequent outbursts of anger, is referred to as an Asura.
Editor: na #0034

◉ **ASVAGHOSA**
Syn: Asvaghosha
See also: Vasubandhu; Nagarjuna

▸"Asvaghosa is one of the four great Indian Buddhist sages who are called the 'four suns that illuminate the world'. Buddhist poet best known for his famous epic poem called the *Buddha-Carita* which represents the first complete biography of the Buddha. Information concerning his life is conflicting, but it appears that Asvaghosa was a contemporary of King Kaniska (second century A.D.)."
Preb: 59
"Indian poet and Mahayana philosopher who lived in the first to second centuries and is considered one of the most important Buddhist authors." Author of the famous work:

Treatise on the Awakening of the Faith ... Asvaghosha was originally a brahman and is said to have been converted to Buddhism by a monk named Parshva. All of his works contain easily graspable instructions and similes concerning the Buddhist teaching."
Sham: 13
NOTE:
"In India, the Pure Land teaching was advocated by Asvaghosha, Nagarjuna and Vasubandhu. It was based upon various sutras such as the two *Amitabha Sutras*."
Dait: 17 #0030

◉ **ASVHAGHOSHA**
see Asvaghosa

◉ **ASVARA**
see Outflows

◉ **ATHEISM**
See also: Agnosticism

▸"Buddhism is atheistic in that it does not recognize an absolute Personal Deity, but it is not philosophically atheistic as it does not deny Ultimate Reality."
Hump: 37 #0476

◉ **ATISA (982 - 1054)**

▸"Famous Indian scholar of

profound learning. Arrived in Tibet in 1038 and stayed till his death. Entirely reformed the prevailing Buddhism, enforcing celibacy in the existing Order and raised the level of morality. Founded the Kahdam-Pa school ('those bound by ordinance'). In the fifteenth century Tsong-kha-pa again reformed this School, renaming it the Gelug-pa."
Hump: 37

"The so-called second spreading of Buddhist teaching in Tibet was initiated in the tenth century by the West-Tibetan royal family. First they sent subjects to India, as for example, the translator Richen Zangpo; later they sought suitable Indian masters and their choice fell on Atisa. In the year 1038 Atisa entered West Tibet. Soon, however he transferred his principal seat to Netang in Central Tibet, whence his teachings spread rapidly." #0035

◉ ATMAN
See also: Anatman

▸Sanskrit for "soul". In Pali, "atta". "When a man clung to his ego, or soul, (*atman* in Sanskrit), and its enjoyment of worldly pleasures, the Buddha revealed the non-existence of ego (*anatman*) to wipe out his

conception of ego. Unfortunately, adherents of the Southern School grasp this word *anatman* in their argument to silence those clinging to ego (*atman*) and interminable discussions have been going on in the West since the introduction there of the term *anatman*. If we examine both words closely, we come to the conclusion that *atman* means the 'existing ego' and *anatman*, the 'non-existent ego'; in other words the two extremes 'is' and 'is not' of a dualism which has no independent nature of its own.

For this reason, in His Mahayana teaching, the Buddha taught His disciples to release their hold of not only 'is' but of 'is not', that is of both *atman* and *anatman*, in order not to be held in bondage by either of them. He said in the *Diamond Sutra*: 'Even the Dharma should be cast aside, how much more so the Not-Dharma?' Thus we come to this:
(1) The worldly man grasps *atman*, or ego, or soul,
(2) The Southern School man grasps *anatman*, or non-existent ego, and
(3) The Mahayana man grasps *n e i t h e r* a t m a n n o r anatman."(Charles Luk, *Ch'an and Zen Teaching*, p. 10.)
Luk: 10

◉ **ATONEMENT**
See also: Dedication of Merit

▶"Early Buddhism (i.e. Theravada) does not stress vicarious atonement; each person must work out his own salvation. We may help each other by thought, word and deed, but cannot bear another's results or take over consequences of another's errors or misdeeds. In Mahayana the stress on compassion has produced the doctrine of Bodhisattvas, who help humanity by renouncing benefit of their accumulated store of 'merit', and 'handing it over' to offset the bad karma of humanity. This has further developed into salvation by grace of Amitabha by calling on his name [thereby developing Concentration and Wisdom]."
Hump: 37-38
NOTE:
Salvation by grace *alone* principally exists in the Jodo-Shinshu (or Shin) school of Japanese Pure Land. All other Pure Land denominations in East Asia (including the Jodo or Pure Land school of Japan) stress a combination of self-help and grace, the self-help aspect being r e p r e s e n t e d   b y Recitation/Visualization of Amitabha's name accompanied by conventional merit-making activities.
Editor: na #0475

◉ **ATTACHMENT**
Syn: Grasping; Clinging
See also: Self; Love-attachment

▶"Attachment, grasping (upadana) or, as sometimes translated, 'clinging', is according to Buddhist thought an intensified form of craving. It is of 4 kinds: (1) sensuous-clinging, i.e., clinging to sensuous desires and pleasures (2) clinging to views (false or mistaken) (3) clinging to rules and rituals, with the idea that one may through them gain salvation (4) clinging to the notion of individual personality. The Anagamin is regarded as entirely free from all these manifestations of grasping or clinging."
Ling: 131
"In the Four Noble Truths, Buddha Shakyamuni taught that attachment to self is the root cause of suffering: 'From craving [attachment] springs grief,/ From craving springs fear;/ For him who is wholly free from craving,/ There is no grief, much less fear.'" (*Dhammapada Sutra*)
Hua: xxx

Specifically for *monks and nuns*, Buddhist cultivation entails ridding themselves ultimately of all attachments, beginning with attachment to their own body and mind (Mark of Self). Once this is achieved, they will be able to transcend attachment to family and friends (Mark of Others), attachment to sentient beings other than family and friends (Mark of Sentient Beings) and finally, attachment to the duration of their life (Mark of Lifespan). The more successful their cultivation is, the more detachment they achieve, the ealmer their mind becomes and the closer they are to the Way (i.e. salvation).

Editor/Tam: 307-308

For the seasoned practitioner, even the Dharma (teachings of the Buddha) must not become an attachment. As an analogy, to clean one's shirt, it is necessary to use soap. However, if the soap is not then rinsed out, the garment will not be truly clean. Similarly, the practitioner's mind will not be fully liberated until he severs attachment to everything, including the Dharma itself.

Editor/Van Hien: 214

Pure Land Buddhism

"*Question: I venture to think that the True Mind has always been equal, clear and even. If there is still revulsion for the Saha World and fondness for the Pure Land, then there is still love and hate, grasping (attachment) and rejection. Are we not still in error?*

Answer: 'You raise this question because you still do not understand the issue in depth. This revulsion and fondness is not the mundane mind of love and hate, but is rather the common method employed by all the Buddhas of the Ten Directions, to transform ordinary beings into sages. If there is no revulsion and rejection, how can c o m m o n   m o r t a l s   b e transformed? If there is no fondness and grasping, how can sagehood be attained? Therefore, in the span of cultivation from ordinary person to sagehood and from sagehood to Equal Enlightenment, everything is within the cycle of grasping and rejection, revulsion and fondness. Only when the practitioner has attained the highest level of Wonderful Enlightenment (the stage immediately before Buddhahood) will he be free of such feelings and enter the state of Equal Thusness [Buddhahood]. For this reason, the ancients have said: *At the beginning, cultivators should have feelings of grasping and rejection, in order to arrive at the point of no grasping and no rejection. When that grasping and rejection have reached the ultimate stage, they will be found to be the same as non-grasping and non-rejection.* Moreover, the Pure Land method was taught by Buddha Sakyamuni and Buddha Amitabha, with Buddha Sakyamuni exhorting people to seek rebirth and Buddha Amitabha playing the role of welcoming and escorting. If the Pure Land cultivator does not have feelings of revulsion and rejection, how can he leave the Saha World? If he does not have feelings of fondness and seeking, how can he be reborn in the Western Pure Land? To achieve rebirth is nothing more than to rely on the auspicious environment of that Land to achieve Buddhahood swiftly. Therefore, such grasping and rejection, revulsion and fondness are of great benefit; how can they possibly be considered liabilities?'"

P.L. DIA: 76

"As stated in the Pure Land classic *Direct Pointing to the Source* (*Kuei Yuan Chih Chih/Qui-Nguyên Trực-Chỉ*): 'If your illness becomes serious, and you are facing the end, your relatives should not weep or wail or utter sounds of lamentation and distress. This may throw your mind into confusion and make you lose correct mindfulness. They should just join together and recite the Buddha-name to help you go to the Pure Land. Only after your breathing has stopped for a long time can they weep and wail. As soon as there is the least bit of longing for the world, it immediately becomes an obstruction, and you will not achieve liberation. If you find people who clearly understand the Pure Land [i.e. good spiritual advisors], let them come frequently to urge you on and encourage you. This would be a great good fortune'" (J.C. Cleary, *Pure Land, Pure Mind*).

NOTE:
Love-attachment is, along with killing, one of the two major impediments to rebirth in the Pure Land.

Editor/Tam: 322 #2023

◙ **ANT (PARABLE)**
See also: Pure Land Buddhism (summary)
▸*Pure Land School.* "The ancients used to say, by way of

comparison: Practicing other methods is as difficult and laborious as an ant climbing a high mountain; reciting the Buddha's name seeking rebirth in the Pure Land is as swift and easy as a boat sailing downstream in the direction of the blowing wind. This observation is very appropriate indeed. Moreover, once reborn there, living in an auspicious and peaceful environment, always in the company of Buddha Amitabha and the Bodhisattvas, the practitioner will swiftly achieve success in whatever Dharma method he chooses. He is like a log rolling down a high mountain, which just keeps going and never stops, even for a moment."   Thich: 236

◙ **AUSPICIOUS KALPA**
Syn: Good Eon; Good Kalpa; Propitious Kalpa
See also: Cosmic Age

▶"A kalpa is the period of time between the creation and recreation of a world or universe. In the Mahayana tradition, the present kalpa is called 'Worthy' because during its span, 1,000 Buddhas will appear to save sentient beings."
Chan: 485 #0174

◙ **AUSPICIOUS MARKS**
see   Eighty Auspicious Marks; Thirty-two Auspicious signs

◙ **AUSTERE PRACTICES**
see   Ascetic Practices

◙ **AVAIVARTIKA (skt)**
see Non-Retrogression

◙ **AVALOKITESVARA**
Syn: Kuan-yin
See also: C h e n r e z i; Mahasthamaprapta; P'u-T'o Mountain; Om Mani
----
▶The Bodhisattva Avalokitesvara (*Chin*/Kuan Yin, *Vn*/Quan-Âm) is one of the Three Pure Land Sages, the others being Buddha Amitabha and the Bodhisattva Mahasthamaprapta (q.v.). Amitabha Buddha is frequently depicted standing between A v a l o k i t e s v a r a a n d Mahasthamaprapta (Ta Shih Chih). The *Meditation Sutra* teaches, *inter alia*, visualization of their features. In some texts, these two Bodhisattvas are referred to in the masculine form. However, feminine forms are commonly used to reflect popular East Asian imagery.
Editor/Tam: 189-190
Also called Kuan Yin, the Bodhisattva of Compassion.

Usually recognizable by the small Buddha adorning Her crown or headdress.

Editor/Tam: 142-143

"Known as the 'Goddess of Mercy' in China and as 'she who hears the cries of the world'. A Bodhisattva linked with the compassion aspect of mind. Attained enlightenment by means of the faculty of hearing. The name means 'sound regarder'. Kuan-yin's bodhimandala is at Pu-to."

Insa: 393

"Chenrezi is the Tibetan form of Avalokiteshvara, the Bodhisattva of compassion. She is considered as the patron and protector of the 'Land of Snow'. Important events and personalities of Tibetan Buddhism are regarded as connected with Chenrezi's action."

Sham: 44

"In the Buddhism of faith, Kuan-Yin is a refuge and protector, who 'suffers vicariously in the hells out of great compassion.' Reflectively, however, Kuan-Yin exemplifies the compassion of one who knows that, 'in some way, all suffering is his own suffering, and all sentient beings the disguises of his own inmost nature.' 'A skylark wounded in the wing, a churub does cease to sing.' The Bodhisattva is sick because his fellow-being is sick. (C.N. Tay, *Kuan-Yin: The Cult of Half Asia.)*"

"The 'Avalokitesvara [twenty-fifth] Chapter' of the *Lotus Sutra* states: If ... living beings much given to carnal passion keep in mind and revere the Bodhisattva 'Regarder of the Cries of the World', they will be set free from their passion. If those much given to irascibility (hatred and anger) keep in mind and revere the Bodhisattva 'Regarder of the Cries of the World,' they will be set free from their irascibility. If those much given to delusion keep in mind and revere the Bodhisattva 'Regarder of the Cries of the World,' they will be set free from their delusion."

Kato: 320

The same is true of reciting the Buddha's name. However, you should concentrate your mind to the utmost and put a stop to 'sundry [distracting] thoughts,' doubts and uncertainties. Whatever you seek will then materialize. As the Bodhisattva Avalokitesvara has great affinities with sentient beings in the Saha World, you should, in addition to your regular Pure Land sessions, recite Her name.

Alternatively, you may also recite the Surangama Mantra or the Great Compassion Mantra" (Patriarch Yin Kuang).

PLZ: 153

I. ILLUSTRATIVE STORY

"During the years 363-366 there flourished the monk Zhu Fayi, who dwelled in the mountains and was fond of study. He lived in the Bao Mountains in Shining (probably in today's Yunnan Province). In his travels he learned many scriptures and especially excelled in the *Lotus Sutra*, and he attracted many disciples -- most of the time more than a hundred studied under him. In 372 he suddenly felt an illness localized in the region of his heart. For a long time he tried various preparations and techniques, but none cured him. After many attempts he gave up trying to heal himself and devoted himself exclusively to taking sincere refuge in Guan-yin (Avalokiteshvara). After several days of devotional acts he fell asleep and saw, in a dream, a monk who came to attend him in his illness. To cure him, this monk cut him open, extracted his stomach and intestines, and washed them. He saw that there had been many impure objects inside him. After thoroughly cleansing them, the monk replaced the organs and told Fayi: 'Your sickness is now expelled.' When Fayi woke up, all his symptoms were gone, and he soon felt like his old self again. It is said in the [Lotus] Sutra that sometimes he (Guan-yin) appears in the form of a monk or brahmacarin (Buddhist ascetic). Perhaps Fayi's dream was an instance of this."

Lopez/96: 90

II. NOTE:

"Next to Amitabha, the most popular deity of the Pure Land school of Mahayana Buddhism throughout East Asia... Numerous legends and stories have arisen in China regarding her origin, life and saving activities. Temples in her honour are to be found all over China and elsewhere in Asia."

Ling: 161 #0172

◎ **AVATAMSAKA** *MANTRA (SYLLABARY)*

See also: Avatamsaka Sutra

►Consists of 42 syllables taken from the Sanskrit alphabet. Since alphabets are the roots of writing and of languages, this mantra (a combination of syllables in one of the most ancient of alphabets) represents knowledge and wisdom.

This Mantra is found in the *Avatamsaka* and *Prajna Paramita Sutras.*

Editor: na #1233

◉ **AVATAMSAKA SAGES/SAINTS**
See also: Three Pure Land Sages

▸The three saints of the *Avatamsaka Sutra* are a) Vairocana Buddha, b) the Bodhisattva Manjusri and c) the Bodhisattva Samantabhadra.

See separate entries.

Editor: na #1202

◉ **AVATAMSAKA *SCHOOL***
See also: Five Teachings; Avatamsaka Sutra; Six Aspects

▸*Chin/* Hua-yen; *Jpn/* Kegon; *Vn/* Hoa Nghiêm.

"Important school of Mahayana Buddhism in which the highly metaphysical doctrines represent the highest development of Mahayana Buddhist thought. The school based its principal teachings on the Hua-yen Ching or the *Avatamsaka Sutra* (The *Flower Ornament Sutra or The Flower Adornment Sutra*). This was accepted as the first discourse of Buddha on his enlightenment, preached to

Bodhisattvas, and is beyond the comprehension of mortals, to whom he proceeded to preach a simpler doctrine. *Tu-shun* (557-640) is reputed to be its first Chinese master, followed by *Chih-yen* (601-68) and *Fa-tsang* (643-712). Fa-tsang, who had been a disciple of Hsuan Tsang, was the greatest exponent of Hua Yen philosophy."

Ling: 139

"The Avatamsaka school distinguishes itself from the other Mahayana schools in an important point. It concentrates on the relationship among phenomena and not on that between phenomena and the absolute. All things are in complete harmony with one another, since they are all manifestations of one principle. They are like individual waves of the same sea. From this point of view everything in the world, whether animate or inanimate, is an expression of the highest principle and is thus one with the Buddha-mind."

Sham: 93

"The Avatamsaka school teaches that since the true nature of all things is non-substantiality from the standpoint of the Buddha's enlightenment, all phenomena are one with each other and

interpenetrate without obstruction; one permeates all and all are contained in one."
Sokk: 223-224
Unlike other Buddhist schools, this school is based on a single book, the *Avatamsaka Sutra*. The sutra is an encyclopedic work with a single theme: enlightenment. Enlightenment is presented as the understanding of emptiness, through which one comes to realize the interpenetration or non-obstruction of all things -- the characteristic doctrine of the Avatamsaka school (A.J. Prince). The Sutra also teaches the doctrine of Dependent Origination (see separate entry). The teaching is expressed in an affirmative way through the figurative language and metaphors which abound in the Sutra. The best example is the metaphor of the 'Brahma Net.' The school reached its apogee under Empress Wu (q.v.) of the Tang dynasty. It declined as a major separate school beginning in the 9th century with its teachings being absorbed into Zen, Esoteric and Pure Land schools. It is interesting to note that chapter 40 (last chapter) of the *Avatamsaka Sutra*, 'The Vows and Practices of Samantabhadra,'

is considered as the fourth Sutra of the Pure Land school.
Editor: na　#0195
See also: next entry Avatamsaka Sutra and Scriptural Studies School

◙ AVATAMSAKA *SUTRA*

Syn: Flower Adornment Sutra; Flower Ornament Sutra; Flower Garland Scripture; Kegon Sutra
See also: Avatamsaka school; Gandavyuha Sutra; Six Aspects

▸*Chin*/ Hua-yen Ching; *Jpn*/ Kegon-kyo; *Vn*/ Hoa-Nghiêm Kinh. The basic text of the Avatamsaka school. It is the second longest sutra in the Buddhist Canon and records the highest teaching of Buddha Shakyamuni after Enlightenment. It is traditionally believed that the sutra was taught to the Bodhisattvas and other high spiritual beings while the Buddha was in samadhi. The sutra is studied by all schools of Mahayana Buddhism, in particular, Pure Land and Zen.
Editor/Tam: 143
This major sutra is revered by all Mahayana schools and has been described by Dr. D. T. Suzuki as the "epitome of Buddhist thought, Buddhist sentiment and Buddhist experience." It was taught by

Buddha Sakyamuni right after Enlightenment (6th century B.C.), under the bodhi tree in India to Bodhisattvas and other enlightened beings. The Sutra was subsequently "lost," only to be rediscovered by Nagarjuna in the 3rd century A.D. Most of the original Sanskrit text is unavailable; however, the entire Sutra can be read in Chinese, having been translated into that language three times between the 5th and 8th centuries A.D. The versions are known as the 40-fascicle, 60-fascicle and 80-fascicle, with the 80-fascicle the most popular today (translator: Patriarch Sikshananda). There are currently at least three translations of the Sutra into English. This Sutra is also known in English as the *Flower Ornament Sutra* or *Flower Garland Scripture* or by its Chinese (Hua-yen) and Japanese (Kegon) names.

Editor: na

I. Background

"Mahayana sutra that constitutes the basis of the teachings of the Chinese Hua-yen (Jap., Kegon) school, which emphasizes above all 'mutually unobstructed interpenetration.' In addition, it teaches that the human mind is the universe itself and is identical with the Buddha, indeed, that Buddha, Mind, and all sentient beings and things are one and the same. This aspect of the Mahayana teaching was specially stressed by the Chinese Ch'an (Jap., Zen) school, whence the frequent citations of the *Avatamsaka Sutra* by this school. The *Avatamsaka Sutra* is one of the Vaipulya (q.v.) sutras and consists of 40 chapters, of which the longest is the *Gandavyuha*; another important part is the *Dashabhumika* or 'Ten Stages' chapter. Only a few chapters of the Sutra are extant in Sanskrit: Chapter 40, *Vows of Samantabha* and Chapter 26, *Dashaburnika*. The oldest Chinese translation is from the 5th century. The teachings presented here are not spoken by Shakyamuni Buddha himself; He is present but remains silent most of the time [or just approves by praising the text at the end, as in the last chapter 'The Practices and Vows of the Bodhisattva Samantabhadra']. They are rather utterances of the Dharmakaya aspect of all the Buddhas."

Sham: 31-32

II. Note:

It is interesting to note that chapter 40 (last chapter) of the

Avatamsaka Sutra, 'The Vows and Practices of Samantabhadra,' is considered as the fourth Sutra of the Pure Land school.
Editor: na   #0038

◙ **AVICI**
Syn: Hell of Uninterrupted Suffering
See also: Hell

▶"The hell of incessant suffering, the worst hell. It is located under the ground of Jambudvipa (our cosmos). Those who are born in this hell suffer from the heat of fire without intermission."
Dait: 1
"The last and deepest of the eight hells, where sinners suffer, die and are instantly reborn to suffer without interruption."
Luk: na
"The worst of the hot hells, in which suffering, death, and painful rebirth are continuous until the retribution for the sufferer's evil karma is exhausted, at which time he or she will be reborn in a higher plane of existence." Chan: 485 #0039

◙ **AWAKENING OF THE FAITH TREATISE**
Syn: Treatise on the Awakening of the Faith
See also: Asvaghosa; Pure Land

Buddhism (Summary); Faith

▶"It was translated into Chinese in 550 by Paramartha who had come from India to China during the Liang dynasty (502-557). The treatise sets forth the fundamental doctrines of Mahayana Buddhism and attempts to awaken people to faith in it. In particular, it takes up the concept of tathata, meaning thusness or suchness, the true aspect of reality. It was widely studied by Mahayanists in India, and there are several Chinese commentaries."
Sokk: 53
"*The Awakening of Faith* is a commentary on Mahayana Buddhism that explains the basic notions of the teaching and is used, particularly in East Asia, as an introduction to the Mahayana. It is one of the few sutras that is also of importance for Zen."
Sham: 136
NOTE:
The Treatise on the Awakening of the Faith specifically recommends Buddha Recitation *for all but the most advanced practitioners*: "Next, suppose there is a man who learns this [Mahayana] teaching for the first time and wishes to seek the correct faith but lacks courage

and strength. Because he lives in this world of suffering, he fears that he will not always be able to meet the Buddhas and honor them personally, and that, faith being difficult to perfect, he will be inclined to fall back. He should know that the Tathagathas have an excellent expedient means by which they can protect his faith: that is, through the strength of wholehearted meditation-recitation on the Buddha, he will in fulfillment of his wishes be able to be born in the Buddha-land beyond, to see the Buddha always, and to be forever separated from the evil states of existence. It is as the sutra says: 'If a man meditates wholly on Amitabha Buddha in the world of the Western Paradise and wishes to be born in that world, directing all the goodness he has cultivated toward that goal, then he will be born there.' Because he will see the Buddha at all times, he will never fall back ... [If a cultivator follows this path], he will be able to be born there in the end because he abides in the correct samadhi.'"

(Y. Hakeda, tr., *The Awakening of the Faith*, p. 102.)
Editor/Zen: 67-68 #0215

◉ AWAKENING VS. ENLIGHTENMENT
See also: Enlightenment

▶*Mahayana Buddhism.* A clear distinction should be made between *Awakening/ Great Awakening* and *Supreme Enlightenment*. To experience a Great Awakening is to achieve (through Zen meditation,Buddha Recitation, etc.) "a level of insight and understanding equal to that of the Buddhas" (Master Yin Kuang). It is to see one's Nature, comprehend the True Nature of things, the Truth. Only after becoming a Buddha can one be said to have truly attained Supreme Enlightenment (Attained the Way). A metaphor appearing in the sutras is that of a glass of water containing sediments. As long as the glass is undisturbed, the sediments remain at the bottom and the water is clear. However, as soon as the glass is shaken, the water becomes turbid. Likewise, when a practitioner experiences a Great Awakening (Awakens to the Way), his afflictions (greed, anger and delusion) are temporarily suppressed but not yet eliminated. To achieve Supreme Enlightenment (i.e., to be rid of *all* afflictions, to discard

all sediments) is the ultimate goal. Only then can he completely trust his mind and actions. Before then, he should adhere to the precepts, keep a close watch on his mind and thoughts, like a cat stalking a mouse, ready to pounce on evil thoughts as soon as they arise. To do otherwise is to court certain failure, as stories upon stories of overconfident monks, roshis and gurus demonstrate.
Editor/Zen: 215-216
NOTE:
The distinction between "Awakening" (Great Awakening) and "Supreme Enlightenment" is very important, because only when a cultivator has attained Supreme Enlightenment can he become a Buddha. There are many degrees of Awakening and Enlightenment. The Enlightenment of the Arhats, Pratyeka Buddhas, Bodhisattvas, etc. is different from Supreme Enlightenment, i.e., Buddhahood. (In practice however, Enlightenment and Supreme Enlightenment are sometimes used interchangeably.) Likewise, there are many levels of Awakenings. The Rinzai (Lin-Chi) school of Zen, for example, distinguishes between "Small Awakening" and "Great Awakening" and teaches that there are an infinite number of Small Awakenings versus eighteen levels of Great Awakenings. Thus, in Zen training, an enlightened teacher is absolutely necessary.
Editor/Zen: 105
On the subject of Awakening, see the following excerpts from *Buddhism of Wisdom and Faith*:
"Furthermore, in the Dharma-Ending Age (i.e., current period), how many cultivators can claim to be Awakened to the Way? Awakening to the Way is not easy. There was once a Zen Master who practiced with all his might for forty years before he succeeded. Another Great Master sat for so long that he wore out more than a dozen meditation cushions before he saw his Original Nature. As far as today's Zen practitioners are concerned (with the exception of a few saints who have taken human form to teach sentient beings), the majority only manage to achieve a temporary calming of the mind and body; at most they may witness a few auspicious realms! Even if they have Awakened to the Way, they can still encounter dangerous obstacles during transmigration.

... The path of Birth and Death, filled with fearful dangers for those who have not attained Supreme Enlightenment, is the same. Therefore, to claim that we should not fear Birth and Death is a superficial point of view."   Thich: 53   #0172

◉ **BACKSLIDING**
see Retrogression

◉ **BAKTI**
see Bhakti

◉ **BALD-HEADED THIEF**
See also: Fault-Finding; Sangha

▸A monk or nun who does not cultivate while receiving offerings from the laity has betrayed the latter's trust and, in effect, stolen the offerings. He has, therefore, incurred immense suffering for the future. The Buddha referred to such monks or nuns as "bald-headed thieves."
Editor/Van Hien: 204   #1669

◉ **BAMBOO GROVE**

▸*Pali*/ Veluvana. "Famous place of retreat near Rajagriha given the Buddha by King Bimbisara of Magadha, India (now Rajgir, Patna district, Bihar)."
Hump: 41   #0472

◉ **BANNERS AND PENNANTS**

▸"Banners and pennants stand for virtues, outward manifestations of qualities or realizations, excellences of character; they also stand for symbolism and representation in general."
Clea/84: 22   #1969

◉ **BARDO**
See also: Death

▸"A Buddhist term meaning the disembodied state between death and rebirth."
Blof: 249   #0322

◉ **BARDO THODOL**

▸"Tib., lit. 'Liberation through Hearing in the In-Between State'; a text known as the *Tibetan Book of the Dead* composed of the group of instructions stemming from Padmasambhava that were elaborated into a systematic teaching in the 14th century."
Sham: 17
"The book purports to describe methods of enabling a dying man to pass through death and rebirth without losing consciousness."
Hum: 199   #0323

◉ **BATHING THE BUDDHA**
See also: Vesak

▸"A ceremony, especially one performed in Asia on the birthday of the historical Buddha Shakyamuni (Vesak), which falls on the fifteenth day of the fourth month. In it a miniature image of Shakyamuni, standing on a lotus throne with right hand pointing toward Heaven and left hand toward Earth, is bathed with water, while flower offerings are made. The entire sangha participates in this ceremony. This custom is based on the tradition that immediately after the Buddha's birth in the Lumbini Grove, nine dragons sprinkled Siddhartha, later the Buddha Shakyamuni, with water."
Sham: 18 #0324

◙ **BEAL, SAMUEL (1825-1889)**
See also: Catena

▸"Professor of Chinese at University College, London, who was instrumental in early translations of Chinese Buddhist texts. Although Beal published *A Catena of Buddhist Scriptures from the Chinese* (in 1871), *The Romantic Legend of Sakya Buddha* (in 1875), and *Dhammapada*, with Accompanying Narratives (1878), he is best known for bringing to light the missionary enterprise of the famous Chinese Buddhist pilgrim Hsuan-tsang who traveled throughout India from 629-645. Hsuan-tsang is famous for bringing back Mahayana texts to China, working on Chinese translations of these classics, and for his work with the Fa-hsiang school of Buddhism (i.e., the Chinese version of Yogacara)."
Preb: 64 #1001

◙ **BEINGS OF THE HIGHEST VIRTUE**
Syn: Superior and Good People
See also: Amitabha Sutra

▸Expression used in the (Shorter) *Amitabha Sutra*. Means Bodhisattvas, Arhats and other spiritually superior beings found in the Pure Land of Amitabha.
Amitabha Sutra:
"Shariputra: the beings who hear this ought to make a vow -- a vow to be born in that land. Why should they? Having succeeded thus, all are then beings of the highest virtue; all are assembled in the same circumstances.'"
Seki: 48 #1412

◙ **BENARES**
Syn: Varanasi; Kashi
See also: Sarnath; Deer Park
▸"The most holy city in India and important in Buddhism (Buddha

having preached his first sermon in Sarnath, on the outskirts); it is also known by the name Kashi. It has immemorially been the centre of pilgrimage, and has been long important for Sanskrit learning. It owes its pre-eminence partly to being situated on the Ganges. It contains a large number of temples, but few are old, because of the repressive policy of Aurangzeb, who built a large mosque now dominating the skyline, beside the stump of a pillar erected by Asoka. The river front is lined with bathing steps or ghats."
Ling: 36-37
NOTE:
Sarnath, the place where the Buddha preached his first sermon, is located just outside Benares, also known by the name of Varanasi or Kashi. See "Sarnath" for further details.
Editor: na #1116

◙ **BEYOND LEARNING STAGE**
See also: Learning and beyond learning

►"The highest stage of Theravada development, that of Arhatship. From the viewpoint of the Theravada school, no more learning or striving for religious

achievement is needed when one reaches this stage."
Chan: 483 #0567

◙ **BHAGAVAT**
see World-honored One

◙ **BHAKTI**

►"Loving devotion to God, recommended as the most effective path to God in most of the religious texts of popular Hinduism. Devotees are drawn into a close personal relationship to God and, in surrender to him, receive grace, however lowly their station."
Larousse: 64
See entry "Faith" for differences between Bhakti and the Buddhist concept of faith.

◙ **BHAISAJYA BUDDHA**
see Medicine Buddha

◙ **BHAISAJYA GURU**
see Medicine Buddha

◙ **BHIKSU / BHIKKU**
Syn: Monk
See also: Bhiksuni; Sangha; Uposattha; Tao-An (Master); Six-fold Respect; Two Hundred and fifty Precepts
►"Monk, male member of the Buddhist sangha who has entered

homelessness and received full ordination. In ancient times the bhikshus formed the nucleus of the Buddhist community, since according to the early Buddhist view, only a person who had renounced the world could reach the supreme goal, Nirvana. The main activities of bhikshus are meditating and presenting the Dharma. They are not allowed to work. Buddhist monks renounce the amenities of the world and lead a life of wandering. The basic principles of the monastic life are poverty, celibacy, and peaceableness. The lifestyle is governed by the rules laid down in the Vinaya pitaka."
Hump: 43
A Bhiksu's life is governed by 250 precepts under the most common monastic code.
Editor: na
"The Three Thousand Awesome Demeanors of monks and nuns are derived from the four deportments: walking, standing, sitting and lying down. It is said, 'Walk like the wind, stand like a pine;/Sit like a bell and lie like a bow.' Walking like the wind does not mean imitating a tornado, nor even the kind of half jog that many people use to get from one place to another. The wind which should serve as a model for walking is the gentle zephyr, which does not even ripple the surface of a still pond. To stand like a pine is to stand up straight, not slumped over as if totally devoid of energy. The head should not hang as if looking only at the ground; the gaze should be regulated and should not dart furtively back and forth like that of a thief. To sit like a bell is to be erect and solid yet quite natural and spontaneous. In lying down, the legs should be drawn up slightly like a bow."
Hua/Earth Store: 42 #0327
"In the beginning all Bhiksus without exception led a life of wandering. During the rainy period, however, they were obliged to spend three months in a monastery (vihara). According to tradition the reason for this was that during the rainy season a wandering monk could cause too much damage to the animal and plant worlds. During this period of repose, leaving the monastery was permitted only under certain conditions, such as visiting...the sick." Sham: 20
Warning
"When a monk lives in the age of the True Law, he should never make discriminations in regard to people. But when a monk lives in this age of the Degenerate

Law, he should fear nothing more than failing to make discriminations in regard to people. The reason is that in this last age of the Law, good and bad elements mingle together. If one does not make a right judgement but chooses the wrong person, if one regards him who is heterodox as orthodox, *if one becomes friendly with him whom he ought to avoid and avoids him whom he ought to be friendly with*, one will surely become the same as one's teacher. Furthermore, in future lives he will always be a companion to Mara (q.v.). Is it then not apparent that one has to be watchful in seeking out a teacher?" (Patriarch Chu Hung) Yu: 177

NOTE

Master Tao-An (China - 4th c. A.D.) was the first priest to call himself Shih (*Jpn*/ Shaku; *Vn*/ Thích), abbreviation of Sakyamuni, denoting a follower of Sakyamuni Buddha.

Dait: 50

See also Two Hundred and Fifty Precepts

◉ **BHIKSUNI / BHIKKHUNI**
Syn: Nun
See also: Bhiksu; Sangha

▸"A full-fledged female member of the Sangha. A female mendicant. A Buddhist nun who has entered into the order of the Buddha and observes the precepts for nuns. The Buddha's aunt, Mahaprajapati, was the first woman permitted to join the order in compliance with the request of Ananda."

Dait: 18

A Bhiksuni's life is governed by 348 or 364 precepts depending on the school. #0088

◉ **BHUMI**
see Ten Stages

◉ **BIASED VIEWS**

▸"The state of clinging to *one* of two extremes in the world of relativity. For instance, clinging to being or to non-being, clinging to permanence or to impermanence and so on..."

NV Hoa: na

◉ **BILLION-WORLD UNIVERSE**
Syn: Cosmos; Three-Thousand-Great-Thousand World
See also: Cosmology; Universe; World system

▸"One of the innumerable systems in Buddhist cosmology, containing a billion worlds or solar systems. Each world has its sun and moon, Mount Sumeru, eight concentric rings of mountains separated by eight concentric rings of oceans, and four inhabited continents. A world reaches up to the first dhyana heaven in the Realm of Form."

Chan: 496

"One World is composed of one Mount Sumeru, one sun, one moon, four great continents; and the various seas and oceans which surround them. One thousand such worlds form a small-thousand-world system. One thousand small-thousand-world systems form a medium-thousand-world system. One thousand medium-thousand-world systems in turn form a great-thousand-world system. This set of worlds is usually referred to as a three-thousand-great-thousand-world-system to indicate that it is composed of smaller sets."

Hua: 232-233

NOTE:

In the Buddhist view, the cosmos is composed of innumerable universes. The expression commonly used in Buddhism is "billions upon billions". Our world is one infinitesimal part of one of those countless universes. Therefore we should see our problems and difficulties within the proper framework and perspective.

Editor: na #0635

◙ **BIMBISARA**

See also: Meditation Sutra; Ajatasatru; Vaidehi

▸"King of Magadha at the time of the Buddha; built the city of Rajagrha (Bihar / India). He converted to Buddhism and presented the Bamboo Grove to the Buddha for the use of the Sangha. He was murdered by his son Ajatasatru."

Thai: 623

Background

"Bimbisara in his past life was also a king. One day, traveling through the Vipula Mountains on a deer hunt, he found himself sadly without a catch. In meeting up with an ascetic, the king decided to chase him on horseback, and in the end he ordered him killed. The ascetic as he was about to die made a malevolent vow, 'I vow to return in my next life and just as you have destroyed me today, I shall mentally and verbally destroy you.'" [The ascetic is said to have been reborn as Ajatasatru, the King's only son and heir to the throne.]   Tana: 136

There is another more poetic version of this story (see Ajatasatru). Both accounts however make the point of Ajatasatru being unjustly killed in his previous incarnation by his present father King Bimbisara. The story of King Bimbisara and Ajatasatru appears at the beginning of the *Meditation Sutra*, a key Pure Land text.

Editor: na #0063

For details, *See also:* Meditation Sutra

◉ BIRTH AND DEATH

See also: Samsara; Four Forms of Birth

▸"The state of transmigration, or Samsara, where beings repeat cycles of birth and death according to the law of karma."

Inag: 393

See the following passage on the need to escape Birth and Death: "But why do we need to escape from the cycle of birth and death? It is because, in the wasteland of birth and death, we truly undergo immense pain and suffering. If students of Buddhism do not sincerely meditate on this Truth of Suffering, they cannot achieve results despite all their scholarship, as they do not experience fear or seek liberation." (*Buddhism of Wisdom and Faith*, sect. 4.)

In the Buddhist world view, the probability of eliminating all Delusions of Views and Thought and escaping Birth and Death *in one lifetime* of cultivation is practically nil. (Apparent exceptions are practitioners in the last lifetime of cultivation or Bodhisattvas who have taken human form to convert sentient beings.) After all, even Buddha Sakyamuni, the founder of Buddhism, underwent eons of rebirth as exemplified in the Jataka Tales. This is also the case with Buddha Amitabha and the Bodhisattva Maitreya -- the Buddha of the future.

Editor/Zen: 120

Illustrative Story

"In India there was once a king who believed in a non-Buddhist religion which taught many kinds of bitter practices ... some spread ashes on their bodies, and some slept on beds of nails. They cultivated all kinds of ascetic practices. Meanwhile, the bhikshus who cultivated the Buddhadharma had it 'easy,' because they didn't cultivate that way. Now, the king of that country said to the Buddha's disciples, 'It's my belief that the ascetic practices which these non-Buddhists cultivate still don't enable them to end their afflictions. How much the less must you bhikshus, who are so casual, be able to sever the affliction of your thoughts of sexual desire.' One of the Dharma Masters answered the king this way: 'Suppose you take a man from jail who had been sentenced to execution, and you say to him 'Take this bowl of oil and carry it in your two hands as you walk down the highway. If you don't spill a single drop, I'll release you when you return.' Then, suppose you send some beautiful women musicians out on the highway to sing and play their instruments where the sentenced man is walking with his bowl of oil. If he should spill any oil, of course, you'll execute him. But if he should come back without spilling a single drop, what do you suppose he will answer if you ask him what he's seen on the road?' The king of country did just that: he took a man destined to be executed and said to him, 'Today you should be executed but I'm going to give you an opportunity to save your life. How? I'll give you a bowl of oil to carry in your two hands as you take a walk on the highway.

If you can do it without spilling a single drop, I'll spare your life. Go try it.' The sentenced man did as he was told. He went out on the highway, and when he returned he had not spilled one drop. Then the king asked him, 'What did you see out on the highway?' The sentenced man said, 'I didn't see a single thing. All I did was watch the oil to keep it from spilling. I didn't see anything else or hear anything at all.' So, the king asked the Dharma Master, 'Well, what is the principle here?' The Dharma Master answered, 'The sentenced man was like the (novice) who has left the home life. Both see the question of Birth and Death as too important to waste time on thoughts of sexual desire, [the most dangerous affliction for ascetics]. Why can't the non-Buddhists sever their afflictions? Because they don't understand Birth and Death. *They don't realize how great the importance of this matter is.*'"
Hua/77: 78-79   #0690

◙ **BIRTH BY TRANSFORMATION**
Syn: Ethereal birth
See also: Four Forms of Birth

►"'Birth by transformation': This refers to metamorphic births,

such as those of devas (gods), asuras, hungry ghosts, and inhabitants of hell, the bardo, and the Pure Lands."
Chan: 475

"When a being is suddenly born with all the sense-organs and limbs of a complete body, without depending on anything such as an egg or a womb, he is said to be born by transformation, or born ethereally. All hell-dwellers, devas, and beings in the Bardo and the Pure Lands; some dragons, garudas, and hungry ghosts; and humans born at the very beginning of a kalpa are born in this manner."
Chan: 471   #0496

◙ **BIRTH CONTROL**
Syn: Contraception
See also: Abortion; Killing

►"According to Buddhist tenets, the life cycle of a sentient being begins when the consciousness enters the womb, and traditionally this has been considered the moment of conception. Therefore, there is no objection to contraception which interferes with conception without damaging sentient life. Termination of pregnancy, on the other hand, necessarily occurs

after conception, so it is not advised."
Tsomo/1995: 101

"*Is birth control allowed in Buddhism?*
Yes, depending on the method. Birth control methods that prevent conception are permitted. However, once conception has taken place and consciousness has entered the fertilized egg, it's a different situation. Thus, morning-after pills and other such methods are discouraged."
Buddhist Union/ Oct. 96: 5

◙ **BIRTH STORIES**
see   Jataka Tales

◙ **BLAVATSKY, HELENA P.**

►"1831-1891, born Russia, co-founder with Colonel Olcott (q.v.) of the Theosophical Society in New York (1875). Declared herself a Buddhist at Galle (Ceylon) in 1880 and, together with Colonel Olcott, inspired a Buddhist revival in Sri Lanka."
Hump: 45   #0470

◙ **BLOFELD, JOHN**

►"Chu Ch'an, (1913-87). English Buddhist. A scholar in Chinese Buddhism, having travelled

widely in China and other Asian countries. Translator for the Buddhist Society of works of Huang Po and Hui Hai."
Hump: 45 #0469

◎ BLOWS
see   Shouts and Blows

◎ BLUE CLIFF RECORD

▶*Chin*: Pi-yen-lu, *Jpn*: Hekigan-roku. "With the Wu-menkuan, one of the most important of the great koan collections of Ch'an (Zen) literature and also the oldest. It was composed in its present form in the first half of the 12th century by the Chinese Ch'an (Zen) master Yuan-wu K'o-ch'in. It is based on a collection of a hundred koans collected approximately a century earlier by the Ch'an master Hsueh-tou Ch'ung-hsien, who provided incidental commentary and 'praise'. Taking Hsueh-tou's text as a basic structure, Yuan-wu added the following components to the text: introductions, which direct the attention of the reader to the essence of a koan; commentaries or incidental remarks on the koans; explanations of every koan; commentaries and explanations

of the 'praise.'" (An English translation is by T. Cleary and J.C. Cleary, 1978.)
Sham: 170-171 #0373

◎ BLUE LOTUS
See also: Lotus Flower

▶Symbolizes being liberated and at peace, and liberating other sentient beings, even while living in this defiled world. The color blue represents intelligence.
Editor: na #1272

◎ BODH-GAYA / BODHGAYA
Syn: Budh-Gaya; Buddha-Gaya
See also: Maha Bodhi Society; Bodhi Tree; Anagarika Dharmapala
----
▶"A place near the bank of the Nairanjana River in Central India (Bihar), where the Buddha attained enlightenment. It came to be regarded as a holy place by Hindus in later days."
Dait: 27
Bodh-gaya is located near the town of Gaya which can be easily reached by overnight express train from Calcutta. The Maha Bodhi temple (located on the very spot where the Buddha achieved enlightenment) and the Bodhi Tree are today under joint Buddhist-Hindu management.

"Rabindranath Tagore when he visited the Maha-bodhi temple at Bodh-Gaya wrote: 'Why was I not born when He, at the touch of whose feet the whole universe was sanctified, personally walked through Gaya; why did I not directly feel the sacred impact of His presence, with my body and soul?' (*Buddha-deva, Rabindra Rachanavali* Vol. II, P. 469.)"
Lahiri: 98
See "Maha Bodhi Society" for further details.

◙ **BODHI**
see Enlightenment; Awakening vs. Enlightenment

◙ **BODHI MIND**
Syn: Great Mind
See also: Bodhisattva

▸*Skt*/Bodhicitta; *Vn*/Bồ-Đề Tâm. The spirit of Enlightenment, the aspiration to achieve it, the Mind set on Enlightenment. It involves two parallel aspects; i) the determination to achieve Buddhahood and ii) the aspiration to rescue all beings. Editor/Tam: 144
The goal of all *Mahayana* practice is to achieve Enlightenment and transcend the cycle of Birth and Death -- that is, to attain Buddhahood. In the Mahayana tradition, the precondition for Buddhahood is the Bodhi Mind (bodhicitta), the aspiration to achieve full and complete Enlightenment for the benefit of all sentient beings, oneself included.
Editor/Zen: 7

Buddhism of Wisdom & Faith/ excerpts:
"The *Avatamsaka Sutra* states: 'To neglect the Bodhi Mind when practicing good deeds is the action of demons.' This teaching is very true indeed. For example, if someone begins walking without knowing the destination or goal of his journey, isn't his trip bound to be circuitous, tiring and useless? It is the same for the cultivator. If he expends a great deal of effort but forgets the goal of attaining Buddhahood to benefit himself and others, all his efforts will merely bring merits in the human and celestial realms. In the end he will still be deluded and revolve in the cycle of Birth and Death, undergoing immense suffering. If this is not the action of demons, what, then, is it? For this reason, developing the supreme Bodhi Mind to benefit oneself and others should be recognized as a crucial step in all Mahayana schools." Tam: 31
Pure Land Buddhism
"The word 'Bodhi' means

'enlightened'. There are three main stages of Enlightenment: the Enlightenment of the Sravakas (Hearers); the Enlightenment of the Pratyeka (Self-Awakened) Buddhas; the Enlightenment of the Buddhas. What Pure Land practitioners who develop the Bodhi Mind are seeking is precisely the Enlightenment of the Buddhas. This stage of Buddhahood is the highest, transcending those of the Sravakas and Pratyeka Buddhas, and is therefore called Supreme Enlightenment or Supreme Bodhi. This *Supreme Bodhi Mind* contains two principal seeds, Compassion and Wisdom, from which emanates the great undertaking of rescuing oneself and all other sentient beings.

To reiterate, the Bodhi Mind I am referring to here is the supreme, perfect Bodhi Mind of the Buddhas, not the Bodhi Mind of the Sravakas or Pratyeka Buddhas.

Tam: 29

"The practitioner should clearly realize the goal of rebirth -- which is to seek escape from suffering for himself and all sentient beings. He should think thus: 'My own strength is limited, I am still bound by karma; moreover, in this evil, defiled life, the circumstances and conditions leading to afflictions are overpowering. That is why other sentient beings and myself are drowning in the river of delusion, wandering along the Evil Paths from time immemorial. The wheel of birth and death is spinning without end; how can I find a way to rescue myself and others in a safe, sure manner? There is but one solution: it is to seek rebirth in the Pure Land, draw close to the Buddhas and Bodhisattvas, and, relying on the supremely auspicious environment of that realm, engage in cultivation and attain the Tolerance of Non-Birth. Only then can I enter the evil world to rescue sentient beings.' The *Treatise on Rebirth* states: 'To develop the Bodhi Mind is precisely to seek Buddhahood; to seek Buddhahood is to develop the mind of rescuing sentient beings; and the mind of rescuing sentient beings is none other than the mind that gathers in all beings and helps them achieve rebirth in the Pure Land.'"

PL/Dia: 33

"Patriarch Tao-ch'o recognized like Tien Tai Patriarch Chih-i that neither the creation of Pure Lands nor their appropriation by

believers was the final goal. The purpose of all sentient beings is the attainment of enlightenment. In fact, *no one can be reborn in the Pure Land until he or she awakens the resolve to attain enlightenment (Bodhi-Mind)*. To support this assertion, Tao-ch'o quoted from the *Wu-liang-shou-ching (Longer Amitabha Sutra)* ... The emphasis that Tao-ch'o placed on the Bodhi-Mind can be seen by the fact that his chapter on the Bodhi-Mind is the longest one in the *An-lo-chi* (Peace and Bliss Collection), occupying more than a quarter of the text."
Saso & Chappell: 44

Illustrative Story

In days of yore, an older master was traveling along a winding country road, followed by a disciple carrying his bags. As they walked, they saw lands being tilled while farmers and oxen were strained to the utmost. Countless worms and insects were maimed or killed in the process, and birds were swooping to eat them. This led the disciple to wonder to himself, "How hard it is to make a living. I will cultivate with all my strength, become a Buddha and rescue all these creatures." *Immediately* the Master, an Arhat able to read

the thoughts of others, turned around and said, "Let me have those heavy bags and I will follow you." The disciple was puzzled but did as instructed, changing places with his teacher and walking in front. As they continued on their way with the hot sun bearing down on them, dust swirling all around them, the road stretching endlessly in front, the disciple grew more and more tired. It wasn't long before he thought to himself, "There are so many sentient beings and there is so much suffering, how can I possibly help them all? Perhaps I should try to help myself first." *Immediately*, the Master behind him said, "Stop. Now you carry the bags and follow me." The puzzled disciple did as told, knowing he was not supposed to ask questions. He took up the bags again and walked behind. This sequence repeated itself several times. The Master walked in front with the disciple carrying the bags, then the disciple in front with the Master carrying the bags, back and forth, until noontime came and they stopped for lunch. Then the disciple gathered his courage and asked the reason why. The Master said, "When you had exalted thoughts of saving all living beings, you

were a Bodhisattva in thought, and I as an Arhat had to follow you. But as soon as you had selfish thoughts of saving yourself only, you were no longer a Bodhisattva, and being junior to me in years and cultivation, you had to carry my bags."
Editor: na
For a detailed explanation on how to develop the Bodhi Mind, see *Buddhism of Wisdom and Faith*, sec. 10. #0497

◎ **BODHI TREE**
Syn: Pippala Tree; Pipal Tree
See also: Bodh-Gaya; Maha Bodhi Society

►"The tree under which the Buddha attained Enlightenment at Bodh-gaya, India (Bodh-gaya is near the town of Gaya in the state of Bihar, in the northern part of India). The Bodhi Tree at Anuradhapura in Sri Lanka, planted by the son of Asoka is the oldest historical tree in the world."
Hump: 47 #0205

◎ **BODHICITTA**
see Bodhi Mind

◎ **BODHIDHARMA**
See also: Hui-K'o; Shao Lin Monastery; Merits and Virtues

►"Deeply learned Indian Buddhist monk who arrived at the Chinese Court in A.D. 520. Known in China as Tamo, and in Japan as Daruma. After his famous interview with Emperor Wu, he meditated for nine years in silence and departed. Bodhidharma was the twenty-eighth Indian and *first Chinese Zen Patriarch*. The father of Zen Buddhism, although it was left to Masters of the eighth century, led by Hui-neng, to consolidate his teaching and technique into a school of Buddhism."
Hump: 46
"After his arrival in what is today the port city of Canton, he traveled at the invitation of the Emperor Wu of the Liang Dynasty (6th C.) to visit him in Nanking. The first example in the *Pi-yen-lu* reports the encounter between Bodhidharma and the emperor. Wu-ti was a follower and fosterer of Buddhism and had many Buddhist monasteries built in his realm. Now he asked the master from India what merit *and* virtues for succeeding lives he had accumulated thereby. Bodhidharma answered curtly, *'no virtues, none'* ... The encounter with Emperor Wu of

Liang showed Bodhidharma that the time was not yet ripe for the reception of his teaching in China. He crossed the Yangtse -- as the legend tells us, on a reed (this is a favorite subject in Zen painting) -- and traveled on to north China, where he finally settled at Shao-lin Monastery (q.v.). It is not certain whether he died there or again left the monastery after he had transmitted the patriarchy to Hui-k'o. The form of meditative practice that Bodhidharma taught still owed a great deal to Indian Buddhism. His instructions were to a great extent based on the traditional sutras of Mahayana Buddhism; he especially emphasized the importance of the *Lankavatara Sutra*. Typical Chinese Zen is a fusion of the Dhyana (meditational) Buddhism represented by Bodhidharma [under a covering of] indigenous Chinese Taoism. It is described as a 'special transmission outside the orthodox teaching.'"
Sham: 23-24

Merits/Virtues

According to the ancient masters, the reason Emperor Wu did not understand Bodhidharma was that he did not grasp the difference between merit and virtue. Merit results from good deeds and therefore brings benefits within the realm of Birth and Death. *Virtues, on the other hand, are the result of actions that the practitioners take to improve themselves and others* (i.e., decrease in greed, anger and ignorance). Thus, the benefits accrued are beyond Birth and Death. Therefore, merits are finite and considered of minor value in comparison to virtues. Had the emperor understood the distinction and realized that Bodhidharma had meant that he (the emperor) only received merits (as he was building temples, etc. with the expectation of receiving blessings, health, and wealth) *not virtues* (i.e., decrease in greed, anger, and stupidity), Bodhidharma would not have left him, the second Zen patriarch Hui K'o (q.v.) would not have had to cut his arms to prove his sincerity and the history of Zen might well have taken a different course!
Editor: na #0155

◙ **BODHIMANDALA**
Syn: Bodhi Seat; Site of Enlightenment

▶"The site or plot or seat where S a k y a m u n i a t t a i n e d Buddhahood." Thai: 527

"The seat is said to be as hard as diamonds. It is believed that the Emperor Asoka made a gift of the polished sand stone-seat, Vajrassana, under the Bodhi-Tree during his pilgrimage to Bodh-Gaya."
Lahiri: 15
By extension, Bodhimandala means the place where *any* Buddha achieves Enlightenment or any temple or place of worship.
Editor: na #0499

◙ **BODHIRUCI (6TH C. A.D.)**
See also: Avatamsaka Sutra

▶"North Indian Buddhist monk who traveled to China in the year 508, where, together with Ratnamati, Buddhasanta, and others, he translated the *Dashabhumika-Sutra* (Ten-Stages chapter of *Avatamsaka Sutra*) into Chinese."
Sham: 24
"He is regarded as one of the patriarchs of the Pure Land school because of his having presented T'an-luan with a copy of the *Meditation Sutra* as well as having translated the *Wu-liang-shou-ching-lun* (*Rebirth Commentary*) of Vasubandhu. His exact dates are unknown."
Dait: 20 #0117

◙ **BODHISATTVA**
See also: Bodhi Mind; Paramita; Four Means of Salvation

▶*Vn*/Bồ-tát. Those who aspire to Supreme Enlightenment and Buddhahood for themselves and all beings. The word Bodhisattva can therefore stand for realized beings such as Avalokitesvara or Samanthabhadra *but also* for anyone who has developed the Bodhi Mind -- the aspiration to save oneself and others.
Editor/Tam: 114
"One who aspires to the attainment of Buddhahood and devotes himself to altruistic deeds, especially deeds that cause others to attain enlightenment."
Chan: 471
Bodhisattvahood has the two aspects of self-perfection and benefitting others.
"Listen, for example, to the following from Asanga: 'If another does harm to the Bodhisattva, the latter endures with patience the worst injuries, with the idea that it is a benefit he has received. To think that the offender does one a service, this is to conduct oneself in accord with the example of the Perfect Ones, i.e., the Buddhas.'" (From Asanga's *Mahayana Sutralamkara*).   Pratt: 219

I. Background

"The notion of the Bodhisattva is already found in Theravada writings, where it refers to the historical Buddha Shakyamuni in his previous existences as they are described in the Jatakas. In Mahayana, the idea of the Bodhisattva is rooted in a belief in future Buddhas, who have long since existed as Bodhisattvas. The Mahayana distinguishes two kinds of Bodhisattvas -- earthly and transcendent. *Earthly Bodhisattvas* are persons (monks, nuns, lay people, etc) who are distinguished from others by their compassion and altruism as well as their striving toward the attainment of enlightenment. *Transcendent Bodhisattvas* have actualized the paramitas and attained Buddhahood but have postponed their entry into complete Nirvana. They are in possession of perfect wisdom and are no longer subject to Samsara. They appear in various forms in order to lead beings on the path to liberation. They are the object of the veneration of believers, who see them as showers of the way and helpers in time of need." Sham: 24-25

"In early Buddhism the term Bodhisattva was used to identify Siddhartha Gautama, the historical Buddha, and it was assumed that only future historical Buddhas would merit this designation prior to their attainment of Buddhahood. *In Mahayana, this term was given a radical, new interpretation,* and used as a designation for anyone aspiring to complete, perfect Enlightenment...to Buddhahood. The entire Mahayana notion of the Bodhisattva was a clear antithesis to the ideal type in early Buddhism, the Arhat, whose effort was found by Mahayanists to be self-centered and ego-based. An enormous literature developed focusing on the Bodhisattva and the Bodhisattva path, including such famous texts as the 'Bodhisattvabhumi-sutra,' 'Dasabhumika-sutra,' and others." Preb: 74-75

"Iconographically the ... Arhats are depicted as elderly shaven-headed monks, clad in yellow robes, and holding a begging-bowl or a staff; they stand stiffly, with compressed lips, and their attitude seems not altogether free from strain. The Bodhisattvas, by way of contrast, are all beautiful young princes. Gem-studded tiaras sparkle on their brows, while their nobly proportioned limbs are clad in light diaphanous garments of coloured silk. They wear gold bracelets and strings of jewels, and round their necks hang garlands of fragrant flowers. Their expression is smiling, their poses graceful and easy. These splendours do not indicate that the Bodhisattvas are laymen; they symbolise their status as heirs of the Buddha, the King of the Dharma, and the untold spiritual riches to which they will one day succeed when, in the final stages of their career, they are themselves consecrated to Buddhahood."

Sangh/67: 168-169

In Mahayana, a number of Celestial Bodhisattvas became extremely important, most notably Avalokitesvara, Manjusri, Mahasthamaprapta, and Samantabhadra. They served as ideal models for their earthly counterparts by exhibiting deep compassion and wisdom (Prebish). The two most popular Bodhisattvas in Mahayana Buddhism are Avalokitesvara and Samantabhadra. Avalokitesvara, the Bodhisattva of compassion and one of the Three Pure Land sages, is represented on the right hand side of Amitabha Buddha (as we look at the Buddha). Samantabhadra is famous for his

Ten Great Vows as described in the *Avatamsaka Sutra*. He is the transcendental first patriarch of the Pure Land school.

II. Illustrative Story

"In a thicket at the foot of the Himalayan Mountains there once lived a parrot together with many other animals and birds. One day a fire started in the thicket from the friction of bamboos in a strong wind and the birds and animals were in frightened confusion. The parrot, feeling compassion for their fright and suffering, and wishing to repay the kindness he had received in the bamboo thicket where he could shelter himself, tried to do all he could to save them. He dipped himself in a pond nearby and flew over the fire and shook off the drops of water to extinguish the fire. He repeated this diligently with a heart of compassion out of gratitude to the thicket. This spirit of kindness and self-sacrifice was noticed by a heavenly god who came down from the sky and said to the parrot: 'You have a gallant mind, but what good do you expect to accomplish by a few drops of water against this great fire?' The parrot answered: 'There is nothing that cannot be

accomplished by the spirit of compassion and self-sacrifice. I will try over and over again and then over in the next life.' The great god was impressed by the parrot's spirit and they together extinguished the fire." (*The Teaching of the Buddha*)
BDK: 139

III. Notes:
A. "Bodhisattvas fear causes, sentient beings fear effects and results. Bodhisattvas, being wary of evil results, eliminate evil causes. Sentient beings all too often vie to create evil causes and then have to endure evil results. When enduring suffering, they do not know enough to practice repentance, but create more evil karma in the hope of escaping retribution. Thus, injustice and retribution follow upon one another continuously, without end. It is so pitiful and frightening to think about it!"
PLZ: 93
B. A Bodhisattva's vow: "With a sincere mind ... the Bodhisattva always compares himself to a handicapped person sitting at the crossroads; although he himself cannot walk, he strives to show others the way, reminding passersby to avoid the dangerous paths and follow the wide, even and peaceful way."
Tam: 94

◉ **BODHISATTVA MAHASATTVA**

▶"Lit. 'Great Bodhisattva'; A Bodhisattva who has reached the a d v a n c e d s t a g e s o f enlightenment."
Chan: 471 #0498

◉ **BODHISATTVA PRECEPTS**
See also: Precepts; Three Bodies of Pure Precepts; Brahma Net Sutra; Four Great Vows
----
▶The Bodhisattva Precepts, 58 in number (10 major, 48 minor), are listed and explained in the *Brahma Net Sutra* (q.v.). However, these precepts all derive from three key precepts called the *Three Bodies of Pure Precepts* (q.v.). The concept that receiving the precepts is not necessarily dependent upon their being administered by the clergy is a high-level teaching of Mahayana Buddhism, which emphasizes the all-encompassing Mind. Any practitioner who wishes to receive the precepts, and sincerely and earnestly accepts them, has in fact received them. This is in line with the teachings of the *Brahma Net Sutra*, though in the case of the

Bodhisattva precepts (the loftiest and most difficult set of precepts), the witnessing of an auspicious sign (light, flowers, the Buddhas coming to rub one's crown, etc.) is additionally necessary.

Editor: na

"The twenty-third minor Bodhisattva precept [taught that] whenever a person with wholesome intention sincerely wishes to receive the Bodhisattva precepts, he should first vow before the Buddhas and Boddhisattvas images, to accept and uphold the precepts and then cultivate repentance and reform for seven days. If during that period he experiences a vision of auspicious signs, he has received the precepts ... It is essential that he experience an auspicious sign, for only then has he received the precepts before the Buddha and Bodhisattva images. If he has not obtained such auspicious signs, though he may have vowed before the Buddha images to accept and uphold the precepts, he has not actually received them." (*The Buddha Speaks the Brahma Net Sutra*, Part II, Commentary by Elder Master Hui Sheng, p. 6.).

NOTE: Auspicious signs attest to the utter sincerity and earnestness of the practitioner. Self-administration of the precepts is recommended only when there are no competent monks or nuns available within a reasonable distance. Otherwise, the practitioner may be guilty of arrogance.

Editor: na   #2025
See also Brahma Net Sutra

◙ **BODHISATTVA STAGES**
See Fifty-two levels of Bodhisattva practice

◙ **BODHISATTVA VOWS**
See Four Great Vows

◙ **BODHISATTVA-IN-PRECEPTS**
See also: Bodhisattva Precepts

►Refers to a monk, nun or layperson who has taken the Bodhisattva Precepts -- usually the 58 major and minor precepts contained in the *Brahma Net Sutra* (q.v.).

◙ **BODY**
See Human body

◙ **BON (RELIGION)**

►"Pronounced Pon. The indigenous, pre-Buddhist religion of Tibet. Little is known of it in detail, but it seems to have much

in common with the Shamanism of Mongolia, a form of nature-worship mixed with psychic and sexual practices."
Hump: 47 #0468

◉ **BORDERLANDS**
See also: Pure Land Buddhism (Summary); Longer Amitabha Sutra

----

▸"In Buddhist doctrine in general, these are places in a world system where there is no opportunity to meet the Dharma because they are isolated, far away from good teachers. In Sanghavarman's translation of the *Longer Amitabha Sutra*, the concept is extended to the Pure Land, so that, as a type of world system, the Pure Land itself has its own borderlands. In this usage, the *borderlands are places in the Pure Lands where living beings who have faltered in their faith will be reborn.*"
Gomez: 286
People who have practiced during their lifetimes with devotion and sincerity and should have earned rebirth in the Pure Land, but who, on their deathbeds, develop feelings of doubt about such rebirth are reborn in the borderlands.
Editor: na #1698

◉ **BOROBUDUR**
See also: Cosmology

▸"Famous Javanese stupa, built around the ninth century. It is probably the most important and extravagant stupa in Buddhist history. Built by rulers of the Sailendra Dynasty, the stupa was constructed as a giant mandala or sacred diagram. It is composed of five terraces, the walls of which are decorated with bas-reliefs. In the first four terraces, the traditional Buddhas of the various directions are represented: Aksobhya (East), Ratnasambhava (South), Amitabha (West), and Amoghasiddhi (North). On the fifth terrace, Vairocana adorns all sides. Circumambulating the stupa reveals scenes from Sakyamuni Buddha's life, Jataka tales, and Mahayana sutras. The ascent to the top of the stupa is a symbolic journey from Samsara to Nirvana (from the world of desire, through the realm of form, to the formless realm). An important pilgrimage site for Buddhists worldwide, it has been (from the nineteenth century onwards) a meaningful site for Buddhist scholarship, particularly that devoted to cosmology."
Preb: 77 #1004

BRAHMA
▸*See also:* Indra

"The god who, in the Hindu view, created the world. When uncapitalized, the word indicates the corresponding god of any particular world, not only the Brahma of this world."
Chan: 472 #0501

◎ BRAHMA NET
see Jewel Net of Indra

◎ BRAHMA NET SUTRA
Syn: Brahmajala Sutra
See also: Three Bodies of Pure Precepts; Bodhisattva Precepts; Bodhisattva

----

▸This is a sutra of major significance in Mahayana Buddhism. In addition to containing the ten major precepts of Mahayana (see below), the sutra also contains forty-eight less important injunctions. *These 58 major and minor precepts constitute the Bodhisattva Precepts, taken by most Mahayana monks and nuns and certain advanced lay practitioners.* It is believed that the current version of the *Brahma Net Sutra* is only a fraction of the original sutra, most of the rest having been lost.   Editor/Tam: 144

"The *Brahma Net Sutra* contains the ten rules of Mahayana, which are obligatory for every follower: avoidance of (1) killing, (2) stealing, (3) unchaste behavior, (4) lying, (5) use of intoxicants, (6) gossip, (7) boasting, (8) envy, (9) resentment and ill will, (10) slander of the three precious ones (Buddha, Dharma and Sangha). Violation of these rules means expulsion from the sangha. The *Brahmajala-Sutra* (*Brahma Net Sutra*) also contains forty-eight less important injunctions. *In this sutra, too, permission is given for self-ordination in cases where the requirements for an official ordination cannot be fulfilled.*"
Sham: 28
NOTE:
"Translated by Kumarajiva of the Later Chin Dynasty in 406, in two fascicles. It is stated in the preface by Seng-chao, the disciple of the translator, that this work is the tenth chapter, 'Bodhisattvahrdayabhumi,' of the *Bodhisattva-Sila Sutra*, consisting of 128 fascicles covering 61 chapters. This work is highly esteemed as the basic canon concerning the precepts of the Bodhisattvas."
Dait: 20-21 #0098
See also Bodhisattva Precepts

◉ **BRAHMAJALA SUTRA**
see Brahma Net Sutra

◉ **BRAHMANISM**
see Hinduism

◉ **BUDDHA**
See also: Sakyamuni Buddha;
Funerary Rites for the Buddha;
Devotion

▶"A Supremely Enlightened One,
or 'Awakened One'. According to
Mahayana tradition, Buddha
Sakyamuni is the present one in
a series of Buddhas, past and
future."
Chan: 472

"Nowadays, the term 'Buddha'
refers to the historical Buddha
Sakyamuni. 'Buddhas' naturally
refers to all enlightened beings."
Yoko: 181

"For many of us, the expressions
'Buddha' or 'the Buddha' refer to
one historical person. This
person is known to us as
Siddharta Gautama, the Buddha
who lived in India more than two
thousand five hundred years ago
and founded the religion of
Buddhism. Another common
name for this historical person,
Shakyamuni ('The Sage of the
Shakya Clan'), may also come to
mind when we speak of 'Buddha.'
But in the mythology of
Mahayana Buddhism,
Shakyamuni is a Buddha,
certainly an important figure, and
yet one of many Buddhas. He
may serve as the mouthpiece, and
the vehicle for revelation, but he
is not unique."
Gomez/96: 9

"The word Buddha means 'one
who has woken up' -- i.e. from
the mental sleep of the untrained
mind -- but Buddhists have often
preferred a traditional
explanation. A Buddha is 'one
who knows' the Dharma or basic
truth of things. So anyone is a
Buddha who has achieved the
goal of the Buddhist path. More
usually the word is used only of
an individual of much greater
cosmic significance: the
Samma-samBuddha, 'one who
has fully awakened in the right
way' or 'one who has fully known
in the right way'. Such a Buddha
is extremely rare in the universe.
Whole eons may pass before one
is born. Buddhist modernists
often lay stress on the human
nature of the Buddha, partly as
an understandable reaction to
pressure from the theistic
missionaries. This can be
misleading. *Buddhahood is
achieved in human circumstances
as the culmination of many lives,
but the penultimate life is always*

divine. It is in fact the result of striving for perfection for countless lives, being reborn in many different forms and conditions of being. Traditional Buddhism understands by the word Buddha neither man nor god, but one who has far transcended the nature of both -- the Teacher of gods and men. From an early date, accounts of the life of the Buddha contained both human and cosmic elements. Modern historical scholarship attempted at first to construct a biography by eliminating all miraculous and marvellous elements as later additions, but there are serious methodological objections to this. Moreover by removing the more poetic and mythic elements of the Buddhist tradition, it creates a false impression of a rather dry intellectual philosophy. *This obscures the devotional aspect of early Buddhism*."
Hinn: 283-285
"The primary object of Buddhist teachings as a whole may be said to be Buddhahood. The term 'Buddha' means enlightened, and as such refers to the fully awake, fully realized, complete human being; what is perhaps more outstanding in the Avatamsaka sutra, however, is the universal or cosmic sense of Buddha. The scripture explicitly states that 'Buddha' is to be seen in all lands, all beings, and all things. This is a basic premise of the scripture's grand descriptions of the scope of Buddhahood; the individual human Buddha may be said to be one who is open to this level of awareness. Buddha is said to have many dimensions of embodiment. The multiplicity of Buddha-bodies at times may refer to all things or beings, or to the potential or realization of full awakening in individual human beings." [TC/FO1, p.17]a #1812

◙ **BUDDHA CARITA**
Syn: Buddhacarita
See also: Asvaghosa

►"Epic poem by Asvaghosa recounting the legendary life of the Buddha."
Reat: 321
"Poetic narrative of the life of the Buddha by Asvagosha -- one of the finest biographies in Buddhist literature" (*Encyclopedia Britannica*).   #2042

◙ **BUDDHA DHARMA**
See Dharma

◙ **BUDDHA FIELDS**
See Buddha Lands

◙ BUDDHA IMAGES
See also: Icons; Art (Buddhist); Kanisha; Gandhara

►"Statues of Buddha or other famous individuals in Buddhism utilized as a symbol of respect and/or an object of devotion for Buddhist disciples. In the earliest tradition, no figures of Buddha were crafted for fear that such a gesture would develop into a cult of personality at best or a deification of Buddha at worst. Such a position is consistent with Buddha's repeated statements that he was just a man. In time, perhaps as early as the reign of King Kanisha (100 A.D.), as Buddha's absence was felt deeply and in similarity with other Indian religious traditions, Buddha-figures gradually began to appear, in both Theravada and Mahayana art. With the development of the Vajrayana tradition, an even greater emphasis developed around various Buddhist images, reflecting the significant role of their symbolism in the Tantric tradition. Within several hundred years, images could be found extensively in cave temples, monasteries, and other sites."
Preb: 145 #1036
NOTE: "Before image-worship came into existence, symbol-worship was very popular in the history of Buddhism. In the beginning of the Christian era, the Bhakti (q.v.) movement started in Buddhism. The Buddha was no longer [simply] a teacher or a superman. He was deified; the image-worship of the Buddha could somewhat satisfy the craving and devotional impulses of the masses. Before the introduction of image-worship, a symbol like the Bodhi tree or the Wheel of Law represented various aspects of the Buddha's life." Lahiri: 59

◙ BUDDHA JAYANTI
see Jayanti celebrations

◙ BUDDHA LANDS
Syn: Buddha fields

►"A Buddha-field (Skt. Buddhakshetra) is a dimension or world manifested through the enlightened aspirations of a Buddha or Bodhisattva *in conjunction* with the meritorious karma of sentient beings. Those born in a Buddha-field are able to progress swiftly to enlightenment."
Shantiveda: 103
"An individual Buddha may assume responsibility for the

spiritual care of a world system, which then becomes the Buddha's field of action, or 'Buddha-field, or Buddha-lands.' Thus, any world system may be called a 'Buddha-field' when it is seen from the point of view of the saving action of the Buddha dedicated to its purification. Buddha-fields can exist in various stages of purification."

Gomez/96: 289　　#1939

◙ **BUDDHA MIND-SEAL**
see　Mind-Seal of the Buddhas

◙ **BUDDHA NATURE**
Syn: Original Nature
See also: Mind

▶The following terms refer to the same thing: Self-Nature, True Nature, Original Nature, Dharma Nature, True Mark, True Mind, True Emptiness, True Thusness, Dharma Body, Original Face, Emptiness, Prajna, Nirvana, T a t h a g a t a W o m b , Tathagata-Garbha, Dharma Realm, Mind, etc. "According to t h e M a h a y a n a v i e w , [Buddha-nature] is the true, immutable, and eternal nature of all beings. Since all beings possess Buddha-nature, it is possible for them to attain enlightenment and become a

Buddha, regardless of what level of existence they occupy ..."

Sham: 31

"According to Mahayana sutras, all sentient beings equally possess the seeds of Buddhahood and therefore have the potential to realize Buddhahood. Illusion prevents these seeds from functioning. But once illusion is destroyed, the seeds will become a c t i v a t e d a n d p e r f e c t enlightenment will ultimately be attained."

Dait: 25

"The internal cause or potential for attaining Buddhahood. Also called the seed of Buddhahood or Matrix of the Tathagata (Skt/tathagatagarbha). Mahayana generally holds that all people possess the Buddha nature inherently, though it may be obscured by illusions and evil karma."

Sokk: 33

"The basic, quintessential nature of sentient beings, which is identical with the nature of B u d d h a , w i t h o u t a n y differentiation whatsoever. Sentient beings wander in Samsara because they do not realize their Buddha-nature. The c o m p l e t e u n f o l d i n g o f Buddha-nature is supreme enlightenment itself. Thus,

Buddha-nature is also the seed of Buddhahood."
Chan: 472
"Defined in the *Maha-Parinirvana Sutra* as being 1) permanent, 2) blissful, 3) True self 4) Pure, the Buddha-nature is also identified with true suchness and universal compassion; it is the 'true self' in Buddhism."
Cleary/Chih-I: 188
NOTE: "The answer to the question whether Buddha-nature is immanent in beings is an essential determining factor for the association of a given school with Therevada or Mahayana, the two great currents within Buddhism. In Theravada this notion is unknown; here the potential to become a Buddha is not ascribed to every being. By contrast, Mahayana sees the attainment of Buddhahood as the highest goal; it can be attained through the inherent Buddha-nature of every being through appropriate spiritual practice."
Sham: 31 #0090

◙ **BUDDHA OF HEALING**
See Medicine Buddha

◙ **BUDDHA RECITATION**
See also: Oral Recitation; Pure Land Buddhism (Summary); Buddhanusmrti; Buddha

Remembrance; Namu Amida Butsu; Amitabha; Prayer; Pure Land School; Koan of Buddha Recitation

----

▸*Chin/* Nien-fo; *Jpn/* Nembutsu; *VN/* Niệm Phật.
The terms *Buddha Remembrance* and *Buddhanusmrti* (q.v.) are sometimes used in the same sense as Buddha Recitation.
I. SUMMARY:
"The term Buddha Recitation has two meanings: 1) Buddhanusmrti. To meditate on the Buddha. This is the so-called Kannen-nembutsu. 2) To invoke the name of the Buddha. This is the so-called shomyo-nembutsu. From the time of T'an-luan (Donran) onward, the term Buddha Recitation has usually referred to the latter, and, in the majority of cases, has referred to the invocation of the name of Amitabha Buddha in order to be reborn in his Pure Land."
Dait: 236
"The 'Buddha Recitation' practice comprises various aspects: hearing and calling the name, and meditating on Amitabha. Each of these actions leads to rebirth if the one condition is fulfilled: *singleminded attentiveness*, which [Patriarch] Shan-Tao in another context

explained as performed from within the three mental dispositions of absolute sincerity, deep faith, and true desire to be reborn in the Pure Land."
[PAS/BTP,p.81]

"In reciting the Buddha-name you use your own mind to be mindful of your own true self: how could this be considered seeking outside yourself? Reciting the Buddha-name proceeds from the mind. The mind remembers Buddha and does not forget. That's why it is called Buddha remembrance, or reciting the Buddha-name mindfully."

Clear: xxx

To recite the Buddha name is to replace deluded thoughts with thoughts about Buddha Amitabha, the Buddha of Infinite Light and Infinite Life (enlightened thoughts). Our Self-Nature True Mind, infinitely Bright and Everlasting, is precisely that Buddha Amitabha. Thus, to recite the Buddha name is to return to our Self-Nature True Mind. As the ancients have said: "if Buddha Recitation is one-pointed, the Six Paramitas are present in full. If Buddha Recitation is one-pointed, our Mind is the Mind of the Buddha."

Editor: na

"To achieve an uninterrupted state of samadhi is not something a person leading a secular life can accomplish. Since it is difficult to achieve samadhi this way, *it is best that you hold fast to the name of the Buddha.* Whenever you have the time, after studying and managing household affairs, you ought to recite it silently. In doing so, you should be careful to articulate each word clearly and to dwell on each utterance with all your heart. If you can continue doing this for a long time without relapsing, your mind will naturally be tamed, and this state is none other than samadhi."

Yu: 95

II. BACKGROUND

"If one were asked to define the single most representative feature of Pure Land practice, nienfo (Buddha Recitation) would probably be one's choice. As used colloquially among Chinese Buddhists today, nienfo can have two different meanings, depending on whether one takes it in its literal sense as 'mindful recollection (nien) of the Buddha (fo)' or its implied sense of 'intonation (nien) of the Buddha's name.' The word nienfo [Buddha Recitation] is originally a Chinese translation of the Sanskrit compound

Buddhanusmrti (q.v.), meaning 'the recollection or the bearing in mind (anusmrti) of the attributes of a Buddha.' The practice of Buddhanusmrti itself has a long history in India, extending back to well before the rise of Mahayana Buddhism...

When the term and its practical lore were introduced to China, they came as a highly developed meditative system, with liaisons to a diversity of Buddhist scriptures and deities. Amitabha and the Pure Land sutras represented but one among many such systems. The major Indian sources and early Chinese treatises on Buddhanusmrti treat it as a complex practice involving several different approaches to contemplation. At its most basic level, Buddha-mindfulness begins with visual recollection of the thirty-two major marks and eighty minor excellencies of the Buddha's glorified 'body of form' (Sanskrit/rupa-kaya). Progressing to successively deeper levels of practice, one may dispense with recollection of the Buddha's physical form and instead contemplate his boundless spiritual powers and omniscience, until one ultimately arrives at the Buddha's formless essence of enlightenment itself -- a practice known as mindful recollection of the Buddha's 'body of truth or reality' (Sanskrit/Dharma-kaya). Thus, although Buddhanusmrti may take a particular Buddha or Bodhisattva (such as Amitabha) as its starting point, it ultimately grounds itself in universal Mahayana truths. This feature plants Buddhanusmrti firmly within the mainstream of Mahayana Buddhist practice, connecting it with the meditations on emptiness that we more often associate with the Perfection of Wisdom and other less devotional traditions of Buddhist scripture."

Lopez/95: 360-361

"The author tells us that some Buddhists find such recitation difficult; that when they begin to recite Buddha their hearts begin to feel very uneasy. 'A thought would pop up suddenly and suddenly fall down -- so restless in this way. The harder I try to keep my heart quiet, the disquieter my heart becomes.' [To such people, the author would reply as follows:] It is indeed not good to recite with the mouth and to think other things. But the mind of an ordinary man is generally disorderly. How can he have a quiet mind when he begins practicing recitation? *You need only to have a sincere heart; slowly and gradually you are sure to have a quiet mind.* Moreover, the disorder in your mind has already been there, and is not due to reciting the Buddha. For instance, we cannot see the dust in the air until the shining of the sun. Before reciting Buddha you are not conscious of your manifold thoughts. Reciting Buddha makes you conscious of them, that's all. When you feel that you have many thoughts, your mind has really improved to a quieter degree. You need only be patient and sincere in your recitation -- you are sure to improve day by day.'"

Pratt: 372

"One invocation to Buddha Amitabha, if uttered properly, will immediately cause the six sense organs to become clean and clear. For instance, now while in the period of [Pure Land] practice, the organ of sight will be clean and pure as we always look at and see the Buddha. The organ of scent will be clean and pure as we inhale the aroma of incense. The tongue will be clean and pure as we recite Buddha's name repeatedly. The body will be clean and pure as we face and worship Buddha all day long in a clean and pure place. The mind will be clean and pure as we contemplate and think of Buddha. When the six sense organs are clean and pure, the three karmas are also cleansed; the physical evils of killing, stealing, and lust will no longer exist, nor the oral evils of hypocritical, harsh, deceitful and suggestive speech. There will be no involvement in the mental evils of greed, hatred, and delusion. The Ten Good Karmas will immediately be practiced. A follower of Buddha finds it most difficult to curb the evil karmas committed by the body, tongue and mind. However, with one invocation of Buddha Amitabha's name, these three evils will be checked."

Amidism: 22

III. BUDDHA RECITATION AND THE PARAMITAS

"Patriarch Chu-hung regarded the method of 'Buddha-invocation with one-pointedness of mind' (i-hsin nien-fo) as the Buddha's greatest gift to man. For if a person can sincerely practice it, he is in fact training himself in the Six Perfections (paramitas) of a Bodhisattva: 'Now if a person practices i-hsin nien-fo [Buddha invocation with one mind], he will naturally stop clinging to external objects; this is the *perfection of giving.* If he practices it, his heart will naturally be soft and pliant; this is the *perfection of patience.* If he practices it, he will never retrogress; this is the *perfection of vigor.* If he practices it, no extraneous thoughts will arise; this is then the *perfection of meditation.* If he practices it, correct thoughts will appear distinctly; this is then the *perfection of wisdom.'* Thus, when Buddha invocation is carried out with one mind, it can lead to Buddhahood."

Yu: 58

We must also recognize that Discipline, Concentration, and Wisdom are equivalent to the Dharma-gate of Buddha Recitation. How so? Discipline [precept-keeping] means preventing wrongdoing. If you can wholeheartedly practice Buddha Recitation, evil will not dare to enter: this is discipline. Concentration means eliminating the scattering characteristic of the ordinary mind. If you wholeheartedly practice Buddha Recitation, mind does not have any other object: this is concentration. Wisdom means clear perception. If you contemplate the sound of the Buddha's name with each syllable distinct, and also contemplate that the one who is mindful and the object of this mindfulness are both unattainable, this is wisdom (Master Chu-Hung, 16th c., China)

Dia: 154-155 #0167

IV. BUDDHA RECITATION -- ESSENCE AND PRACTICE

"There are two aspects to Buddha Recitation -- essence and practice. According to Elder Master Ou-I:

A) *'Buddha Recitation-practice'* means believing that there is a Western Pure Land and a Lord Buddha named Amitabha, but not yet realizing that 'this Mind makes Buddha, this Mind is Buddha.' It consists of resolutely seeking rebirth in the Pure Land and reciting as earnestly as a lost child longing for his mother, never forgetting her for a single moment. 'Buddha Recitation-essence,' on the other hand, means believing and understanding that Lord Amitabha Buddha of the West inherently exists in full within our mind, is created by our mind, and making this sacred name -- inherently existing in full within our mind and created by our mind -- the focus of our recitation, without a moment of neglect. In other words, 'Buddha Recitation-practice' is the method of those who do not understand anything about meaning or essence, who just believe that there is a Land of Ultimate Bliss and a Buddha named Amitabha, and who fervently and earnestly recite the Buddha's name seeking rebirth there.

B) *'Buddha Recitation-essence'* is the method of those who practice in an identical manner, but who also deeply realize that the Pure Land and Lord Amitabha Buddha are all in the True Mind, manifested by the pure virtues of the True Mind. This being so, is there a difference between Buddha Recitation-practice and Buddha Recitation-essence? Of course there is. Those who follow Buddha Recitation-practice see Amitabha Buddha as outside the Mind; therefore, opposing marks of subject-object still exist. Thus, such practice is not yet all-encompassing and complete. Those who practice Buddha Recitation-essence thoroughly understand the True Mind and therefore sever all marks of subject-object -- to recite is Buddha, to recite is Mind, reconciling Mind and Realm."   Tam: 181-182

V. SCATTERED MIND RECITATION

"When the mouth recites Amitabha Buddha's name while the mind is focussed on the Buddha or rests on His name, it is called 'Settled Mind Buddha Recitation.' When we recite the Buddha's name but the mind is not on Amitabha Buddha and is lost in errant thought, it is called 'Scattered Mind Buddha Recitation.' The effectiveness of 'Scattered Mind' is very much weaker than 'Settled Mind' Buddha Recitation. For this reason, since ancient times, good spiritual advisors have all exhorted us to recite with a settled mind, and not let our thoughts wander. Therefore, Buddha Recitation with a scattered mind cannot be held up as an example to be emulated. However, all external activities must reverberate in the Alaya consciousness. If reciting with a scattered mind were entirely ineffective, where would the sacred name of Amitabha come from? The very existence of the sacred name results from two conditions: first, the existing seeds arising from the Alaya consciousness; second, the power of outside action reflecting back inward. Therefore, we cannot say that 'Scattered Mind Buddha Recitation' is entirely without effect, albeit its effectiveness is much more limited than recitation with a settled mind. Thus, while reciting the Buddha's name with a scattered mind has never been advocated, its significance and effectiveness cannot be rejected either. For this reason, the ancients have handed down the following gatha: *The sacred name of Amitabha Buddha is the supreme method,/Why bother and fret over scattered thoughts!/Though clouds thousands of miles thick hide the sun's brightness,/All the world still benefits from its 'amber' light.* Upon reflection, the above verse is quite accurate. This is because once the seeds of Buddha Recitation ripen in the Alaya consciousness, they trigger the sixth consciousness [i.e., the mind], leading to the development of pure thought and pure action. However, when the seeds of Buddha Recitation pass through the sixth consciousness, deep-seated defiled thoughts encroach upon them. Although these seeds ultimately manage to escape, their power has been greatly weakened. They are like the rays of the sun, which, although radiant, are hidden by

many layers of clouds and are seen in the world only as 'amber' light. This residual light, however, comes from the sun. Realizing this, the Pure Land practitioner need not be unduly worried or concerned about sundry thoughts. He should continuously recite, content with whatever number of utterances he manages to produce with right thought. As he recites in such a manner over an extended period of time, the horse-like mind will return to the stable, the monkey-like mind will gradually return to the den. With further recitation, right thought will emerge clearly without any special effort on the practitioner's part. Thus, we should emphasize the continuity of recitation, without worrying whether it is done with a settled mind or not. Like muddy water which, with constant decanting, becomes clear and pure, a person afflicted with many sundry thoughts, through extended recitation, can convert them into right thought. We should know that ancient masters would always recite the Buddha's name, whether walking or standing, asleep or awake, working or resting. If they constantly recited with a settled mind, they would trip and stumble while walking and could not succeed in drafting commentaries or performing other tasks. Therefore, at times they recited with a scattered mind, but they never stopped reciting because even though their minds were scattered, not all benefits were lost."

Tam: 236-238

VI. NOTES:
The strength and pervasiveness of Pure Land are such that its main practice, Buddha Recitation, is found in other schools, including the Tantric and Zen schools. In Pure Land, recitation is practiced for the immediate purpose of achieving rebirth in the Land of Amitabha Buddha. In the Tantric school, the immediate aim is to destroy evil karma and afflictions and generate blessings and wisdom in the current lifetime. In Zen, the koan of Buddha Recitation is meant to sever delusive thought and realize the Self-Nature True Mind. The ultimate goal of all three schools is, of course, the same: to achieve enlightenment and Buddhahood.

Buddha Recitation, like the use of kung an in Zen, is a panacea to destroy the poison of false thinking ... It is like fighting a war to end all wars. According to

the Pure Land school, however, recitation of the Buddha's name contains an additional element: *the practitioner by association absorbs some of the merits and virtues of the Buddha himself.* As the sutras state: "it is like a man walking in the morning mist -- he is not wet, merely refreshed."

Editor: na

"Whether one enters a monastery or prefers to remain in the lay world, there can be no progress in concentration without a *severe reduction in one's involvement in worldly affairs.* Naturally, the external observances of the monastic rule are understood to be peculiarly propitious to the development of mental calm, but in the last analysis, it is inner motive and personal discipline that count. Thus we are counseled at length to be careful about the company we keep, recognizing the simple fact that an unexamined lifestyle, in which we are immersed in the materialistic values and behavior of worldly friends, will get us nowhere. Only frustration and inanity will be the result. Shantideva advises us to [avoid] those whose values are contrary to the Dharma."

Shantideva: 17

For different methods and variants of Buddha Recitation, see "Oral Recitation (Ten Variations)" as well as the following entry "Buddha Recitation (Methods)". #2269

◉ **BUDDHA RECITATION (METHODS --)**
See also: Buddha Recitation; Oral Recitation (Ten Variations); Pure Land Buddhism (Summary); Practice; Ten Recitations Method

----

▶*Note:* Please read entry "Buddha Recitation" before the following excerpts from *Buddhism of Wisdom and Faith*/ Master Thich Thien Tam:
"Buddha Recitation does not consist of oral recitation alone, but also includes *contemplation and meditation.* Therefore, within the Pure Land School, there are, in addition to Oral Recitation, three other methods: Real Mark, Contemplation by Thought and Contemplation of an Image.

I. REAL MARK [SELF-NATURE] BUDDHA RECITATION. This entails penetrating the Mind's foremost meaning -- reciting our own original Buddha Nature. It is to contemplate the Real Mark Dharma Body of the Buddhas,

resulting in attainment of True Thusness Samadhi. This method is really a Zen practice; however; since the realm revealed by the meditational mind is the Pure Land, it also qualifies as a Pure Land practice. This method is not for those of limited or moderate capacities -- if the practitioner is not of the highest capacity, he cannot "become enlightened and enter" into it. For this reason, few Pure Land teachers promote it and the proponents of the method are found chiefly within the Zen tradition. Incidentally, I would venture to say here that while we are still treading the path of Practice, not having reached the stage of Perfect Enlightenment, all Dharma methods are expedient and so is Zen. According to the Three Pure Land sutras, Buddha Sakyamuni provided the expedient teaching of the Western Pure Land, and urged sentient beings to recite Amitabha Buddha's name seeking rebirth there. With this method, they can escape Birth and Death, avail themselves of that wonderful, lofty realm to pursue cultivation, and swiftly attain Buddhahood. Diligent Buddha Recitation also leads to Awakening, as in Zen; however, the *principal goal of the Pure Land School is rebirth in the Land of Ultimate Bliss, while the degree of Awakening achieved is a secondary consideration.* Thus, the goal of Real Mark Buddha Recitation falls within Pure Land teachings. However, from the standpoint of an expedient leading to rebirth in the Land of Ultimate Bliss, it does not truly qualify as a Pure Land method within the meaning of the Three Pure Land sutras taught by Buddha Sakyamuni. This is, perhaps, the reason why Pure Land Patriarchs merely referred to it to broaden the meaning of Buddha Recitation, but did not expound it widely.

II. CONTEMPLATION BY THOUGHT RECITATION.

This entails meditation on the features of Buddha Amitabha and His Land of Ultimate Bliss, in accordance with the *Meditation Sutra.* (The Sutra teaches a total of sixteen contemplations.) If this practice is perfected, the cultivator will always visualize the Pure Land before him. Whether his eyes are open or closed, his mind and thoughts are always coursing through the Pure Land. At the time of death, he is assured of rebirth there. The

virtues obtained through this method are immense and beyond imagination, but since the object of meditation is profound and subtle, few practitioners can achieve it. This is because, in general, the method presents several difficulties: i) without knowing how to use expedients skillfully and flexibly during actual practice, one cannot easily succeed; ii) without the ability to remember images clearly, one cannot easily succeed, iii) with low energy, one cannot easily succeed. Very few can avoid these pitfalls. Thus, upon reflection, this method also belongs to the category of difficult Dharma doors.

III. CONTEMPLATION OF AN IMAGE RECITATION.

In this method, the practitioner faces a statue of Amitabha Buddha and impresses all the features of that statue on his memory -- contemplating to the point where, even in the absence of a statue, and whether his eyes are open or closed, he clearly sees the image of Amitabha Buddha. This method is also difficult, because it requires a great deal of energy, a faithful memory and skillful use of expedients. There are cases of individuals who have practiced it in an inflexible way and have developed headaches difficult to cure. Moreover, upon examination, this method of seeking rebirth in the Pure Land is not mentioned in the sutras. It is merely a technique to assist in the practice of Buddha Recitation, so that the practitioner can harness his mind and achieve right thought. Still, if we practice this method in a pure, devoted frame of mind, we can obtain a response, eradicate our bad karma, develop virtue and wisdom, and, through an "illusory" statue of Amitabha Buddha, awaken to His True Marks and achieve rebirth in the Pure Land.

IV. ORAL RECITATION/ INVOCATION. "In this method, the practitioner recites, aloud or silently, either 'Nam Mo Amitabha Buddha' or 'Amitabha Buddha.' The short form (Amitabha Buddha) has the advantage of easily focussing the cultivator's mind, while the longer version facilitates development of a truly earnest, respectful mind conducive to a response. This method, taught by Sakyamuni Buddha in the *Shorter Amitabha Sutra*, is the dominant form of Pure Land practice at the present time." Tam: 116-119

"The ancients have commented: *Among Dharma methods (Buddhist schools),/ Pure Land is the shortcut for attaining the Way;/ Within Pure Land,/ Oral Invocation is the shortcut.* Nowadays, this method (Oral Invocation) is the most popular form of Buddha Recitation." Tam: 119

See also important entry *Oral Recitation (Ten Variations).* Editor: na #2270

◙ **BUDDHA RECITATION** *SAMADHI*
Syn: Buddha Remembrance Samadhi; One Practice Samadhi; Single Mark Samadhi
See also: Samadhi

▶"The state of concentration in which one visualizes Amitabha; also, a concentrated practice of repeating his name whereby one attains unity with him." Inag: 394

"Also known as the *Samadhi of Mindfulness of the Buddha* or *Door to the Boundless Sea Treasury*. It is the king of all samadhi." Hua: na

"Where does the Buddha that I am contemplating come from? He does not come from somewhere else, and I do not go off to reach him. Whatever feature I turn my attention to thereupon appears. This Buddha is simply mind perceiving mind. Mind is the visualized Buddha that is the object, and likewise mind is the subjective 'I' that sees the Buddha. When it perceives the Buddha, mind is not itself aware of mind, nor does it itself perceive mind. When the mind gives rise to thoughts, then there is delusion. When it is free of thoughts, it is Nirvana...On entering samadhi, the sincere practitioner is able to perceive all the Buddhas of the present age in all the Ten Directions standing directly in front of him. As many stars as a person with keen eyesight can see on a clear night -- that is how many Buddhas he sees!" [DS/TM,p.60-1]ll #1250

◙ BUDDHA REMEMBRANCE

See also: Buddha Recitation; Buddhanusmrti; Pure Land School

►A synonym for Buddha Recitation/Buddhanusmrti in the general sense.
"In what sense is Buddha 'remembered'? 'Buddha' is the name for the one reality that underlies all forms of being, as well as an epithet for those who witness and express this reality. According to Buddhist Teaching, all people possess an inherently enlightened True Nature that is their real identity. By becoming mindful of Buddha, therefore, people are just regaining their own real identity. They are remembering their own Buddha-nature." (J.C. Cleary)
Van Hien: 3 #1660

◙ BUDDHA REMEMBRANCE SAMADHI

see   Buddha Recitation Samadhi

◙ BUDDHA VEHICLE

see   One Vehicle

◙ BUDDHA'S VOICE

see   Voice of a Buddha

◙ BUDDHA-GAYA

see   Bodh-gaya

◙ BUDDHA-YANA

see   One Vehicle

◙ BUDDHABHADRA (359-429)

See also: Avatamsaka Sutra

►"A monk who participated in the translation of Buddhist scriptures into Chinese. He was born in Kapilavastu in northern India. In 408 he came to

Ch'ang-an in China at Chih-yen's invitation and propagated the teachings of meditation. He also assisted Kumarajiva in the translation of Buddhist scriptures. He later went south where he was welcomed by Hui-yuan at Mount Lu, and lectured on the doctrine of meditation at Hui-yuan's request. Later he lived in Chien-k'ang and there translated a number of Buddhist scriptures into Chinese. He translated the sixty-fascicle version of the *Avatamsaka Sutra*. In total, he is said to have translated 13 works in 125 fascicles."
Sokk: 31 #0085

◉ BUDDHACARITA
see Buddha Carita

◉ BUDDHAGHOSA (5TH C. B.C.)
See also: Tripitaka

►"A great Buddhist scholar born in India early fifth century A.D., who translated Sinhalese commentaries into Pali and wrote *Visuddhi Magga* and other works, including commentaries on much of the Pitakas (the Pali Tripitaka)."
Hump: 50
"(Fifth-century) editor of the Pali commentaries on Theravada Buddhism and author of the *Visuddhimagga* (The Path of Purification)."
Reat: 32 #0062

◉ BUDDHAHOOD
See also: Awakening / Enlightenment

►"This is a transcription of Buddhata: 'the state and condition of being awakened,' 'the condition of being a Buddha,' 'the state of being a Buddha.'"
Gomez/96: 289
"The realization of Buddhahood does not mean that anything extra is added. It is simply to make use of the practice of Buddha Recitation or meditation to such an extent that one's self-nature and Buddha nature are totally integrated in the process and all impure thoughts of the mind are totally eradicated. Buddha nature appears whenever the defilements of the mind are completely and permanently removed."
Amidism: 7
NOTE:
Crucial Mahayana teaching: We all have the Buddha nature within us, but it is hidden by delusion. If, through a good a c t i o n (r e c i t i n g t h e

Buddha-name, drawing an image of the Buddha in the sand, etc.) a cultivator has calmed the turbid waters of his mind, he has, in effect, recovered his Buddhahood -- he has achieved Buddhahood for that moment. "Even if little boys in play/ should use a piece of grass or wood or a brush,/ or perhaps a fingernail/ to draw an image of the Buddha,/ such persons as these .../ all have attained the Buddha Way." (Burton Watson, tr., *The Lotus Sutra*, p. 39.) This, of course, does not mean that he has the same spiritual powers as the Buddha, but that his mind is now the mind of a Buddha -- and that is the first step. If he can achieve this, then although he may dwell in the realm of birth and death, he no longer fears birth and death -- birth and death can no longer pollute his mind.

Editor: na #1940

◙ **BUDDHANUSMRTI**
See also: Buddha Recitation; Buddha Remembrance; Pure Land Buddhism (summary)

▸"The word nien-fo [Buddha Recitation] is originally a Chinese translation of the S a n s k r i t   c o m p o u n d Buddhanusmrti, meaning 'the recollection or the bearing in mind (anusmrti) of the attributes of a Buddha.' The practice of Buddhanusmrti itself has a long history in India, extending back to well before the rise of Mahayana Buddhism...

When the term and its practical lore were introduced to China, they came as a highly developed meditative system, with ties to a diversity of Buddhist scriptures and deities. Amitabha and the Pure Land sutras represented but one among many such systems. The major Indian sources and early Chinese treatises on Buddhanusmrti treat it as a complex practice involving several different approaches to contemplation. *At its most basic level, Buddha-mindfulness begins with visual recollection of the thirty-two major marks and eighty minor excellencies of the Buddha's glorified 'body of form'* (Sanskrit/rupa-kaya). Progressing to successively deeper levels of practice, one may dispense with recollection of the Buddha's physical form and instead *contemplate his boundless spiritual powers and omniscience,* until one ultimately arrives at the Buddha's formless essence of enlightenment itself -- a practice known as mindful recollection of

the Buddha's 'body of truth or reality' (Sanskrit/Dharma-kaya). Thus, although Buddhanusmrti may take a particular Buddha or Bodhisattva (such as Amitabha) as its starting point, *it ultimately grounds itself in universal Mahayana truths.* This feature plants Buddhanusmrti firmly within the mainstream of Mahayana Buddhist practice, connecting it with the meditations on emptiness that we more often associate with the *Perfection of Wisdom* and other less devotional traditions of Buddhist scriptures."
Lopez/95: 360-361

"An early form of Buddhanusmrti (Buddha Remembrance or Buddha Recitation) can be found in the Nikayas of the Pali Canon: 'In the Nikayas, the Buddha ...advised his disciples to think of him and his virtues as if they saw his body before his eyes, whereby they would be enabled to accumulate merit and attain Nirvana or be saved from transmigrating in the evil paths.'"
D.T.Suzuki, *The Eastern Buddhist*/Vol 3, No 4 : 317 #2146

◙ **BUDDHAS AND BODHISATTVAS**
See also: "Eight Bodhisattvas"

▶Principal Buddhas and Bodhisattvas of China, Vietnam, Japan and other East Asian Mahayana countries:

Buddhas:

Sanskrit	Chinese	Japanese	Vietnamese
Sakyamuni	Shih-chia Fo	Shakamuni	Thích-Ca-Mâu-Ni
Amitabha	O-mi-to Fo	Amida	A-Di-Đà Phật
Bhaishajya-guru	Yao-shih Fo	Yaku-shi	Dược-Sư Phật
Vairocana	P'i-lo Fo	Dainichi	Tỳ-lô-Giá-Na Phật (Đại Nhật)

Bodhisattvas:

Avalokitesvara	Kuan-yin	Kannon	Quán-Thế-Âm
Ksitigarbha	Ti-tsang	Jizo	Địa-Tạng Bồ-Tát
Manjusri	Wen-shu	Monju	Văn-Thù-Sư-lợi (Mạn-Thù-Sư-Lợi)
Samantabhadra	P'u-hsien	Fugen	Phổ-Hiền Bồ-Tát
Maitreya	Mi-lei	Miroku	Di-lặc Bồ-Tát
Mahasthama-prapta	Ta-Shih-chih	Sei-shi	Đại-Thế-Chí

Pratt: 304   #2123

◎ **BUDDHAYANA**
see   One Vehicle

◎ **BUDDHISM**
See also: Academic Study; Ethics; Hinduism / Buddhism; Politics; Ultimatism; Materialism; Art (Buddhist --); Agnosticism

----

▸"The name given to the Teachings of Gautama Buddha but usually called by his followers the Buddha Dharma. Founded by the Buddha (ca. 560-480 B.C.) and established by him in North-West India, adopted by the Emperor Asoka as the religion of his empire and introduced by him into Sri Lanka and neighboring countries, it spread rapidly all over the East, eventually becoming a major religion in the world."
Murt: 31-32
"The Buddha posited no creator God; no Jehovah, Jesus, or Allah.

His truths are so distinct from the primary concerns of other faiths that some Western observers see Buddhism as a philosophy or even a psychology. By the same logic, employed optimistically by Jewish, Protestant and Catholic Buddhists of the late 20th century, Buddhist practice can be maintained without leaving one's faith of birth."

Time Magazine: Oct 13, 1997

"Buddhism has survived...by adapting and re-inventing itself in different contexts, not by holding on to old ideologies and rituals. In spreading to the broader culture through Hollywood stars, Buddhism is following its age-old pattern of trickling down from prevailing elites. Unlike Christianity, which spread six centuries later by the grass roots, Buddhism traveled from India throughout China, Japan, Korea, Vietnam and Tibet by way of royal courts or the literati." (Kennedy Fraser)

NY Times: Nov. 3/97

I. SALIENT ASPECTS OF BUDDHISM:

"As Buddhism has gained popularity in their countries, Western people have naturally viewed the teachings through the lens of their own cultures and psychology. Among the attractive features are Buddhism's experiential orientation, its pragmatic approach to spirituality, and its variety. The theory of human psychology based on personal responsibility fits well with Western individualism. The teachings on morality, compassion, and selfless service corroborate our own Judeo-Christian cultural heritage. The concept of karma, a law of cause and effect which extends to the mental and personal level, corresponds to the scientific principle of action and reaction in physics. And the common sense approach of Buddhist empiricism finds acceptance in the rational Western mind. At the same time, there are elements that go against the grain of Western cultural conditioning. Whereas the Buddha taught that happiness lies in limiting desires, American culture teaches that happiness can be found in fulfilling desires. While our culture teaches self-assertiveness and the pursuit of self-fulfillment, Buddhism teaches self-denial and other-centeredness. There is a tension between the otherworldliness of Buddhism and the this-worldliness of

contemporary American life. Even within the Buddhist fold there is a tension between the relative values of study and meditation, a tension that has existed in every Buddhist society to date."
Tsomo: 9-10

"It is always the same aspects of the Buddhist religion that attract Westerners: Buddhism is tolerant. There may be a body of teaching but it does not dominate or preach to people. ... People also admire the justice of the Buddhist system, according to which people reap what they sow... The high quality of Buddhist ethics is widely praised. Who would quarrel with the splendid Four Noble Truths and the Eightfold Noble Path?"
Eerd: 242

Buddhism aims at calming the mind, "reining in the wandering, monkey mind," enabling the practitioner to uncover/recover his innate wisdom and achieve Buddhahood. However, the more one reads and studies about Buddhism, the more one engages in discrimination and the more agitated the mind may become. Therefore, studying sutras and commentaries, while desirable, may not be the best method and is not a substitute for practice. (This is why, in Zen, study is not emphasized and is sometimes considered merely a way of exercising the mind, just as sports are a way of exercising the body.) *Note*: One of the main purposes of studying sutras and commentaries from different schools is to prepare oneself to teach the Dharma to as wide an audience as possible. To achieve results in cultivation, on the other hand, one should concentrate on a single method or school.
Editor/PLZ: 54

Important feature of Buddhism expressed in numerous Mahayana scriptures, such as the *Lotus* and *Avatamsaka Sutras*: the true intention of the Buddhas is not simply to rescue sentient beings, who, once saved, play a secondary, subservient role; rather, it is *to help sentient beings attain Enlightenment and Buddhahood*, i.e., to become equal to the Buddhas in all respects. This is a unique and revolutionary feature of Buddhism. Editor/Tam: 307

II. BRANCHES / TRADITIONS:
"The southern branch (Theravada, or school of the Elders) arose in southern India, whence it spread to Ceylon, Burma, Thailand, and Cambodia.

In Theravada Buddhism one strives to become an Arhat, a person who has single-heartedly overcome his passions and ego, thereby gaining liberation for himself. Because of its emphasis on individual self-liberation, Theravada is known in northern Buddhist countries somewhat disparagingly as the Lesser Vehicle. The northern branch (Mahayana, or Great Vehicle) spread from northern India to Tibet, Mongolia, China, Vietnam, Korea, and Japan among other countries. In contrast to Theravada Buddhism, which tended to remain conservative and rigid, the Mahayana adapted itself to the needs of people of diverse racial and cultural backgrounds and varying levels of understanding. Its ideal became the Bodhisattva, one who is ever ready to sacrifice himself in the interest of those lost in ignorance and despair, even at the cost of [delaying] his own supreme enlightenment." Yoko: 182

Since every school or method is an expedient, adapted to a particular target audience, each one is perfect and complete for a given person or group at a given time. *See also:* the following passage from D.T. Suzuki:

"Buddhist theology has a fine comprehensive theory to explain the manifold types of experience in Buddhism, which look so contradictory to each other. In fact the history of Chinese Buddhism is a series of attempts to reconcile the diverse schools ... Various ways of classification and reconciliation were offered, and ... the conclusion was this: Buddhism supplies us with so many gates to enter into the truth because of such a variety of h u m a n c h a r a c t e r s a n d temperaments and environments due to diversities of karma. This is plainly depicted and taught by the Buddha himself when he says that the same water drunk by the cow and the cobra turns in one case into nourishing milk and in the other into deadly poison, and that medicine is to be given according to disease. This is called the doctrine of [skillful] means ..." (*The Eastern Buddhist*, Vol. 4, No. 2, p. 121)

In Buddhism, the *sine qua non* for Enlightenment and Buddhahood is a pure mind, that is, a mind free of greed, anger and delusion. In Pure Land Buddhism, the usual terminology is a mind of utmost reverence and sincerity, leading to one-pointedness of mind. This is because when the cultivator focusses singlemindly on Amitabha Buddha, he cannot harbor thoughts of greed, anger or delusion -- his mind is pure. A pure mind is Enlightenment, is the Pure Land.

Editor/PLZ: 95

III. RECENT DEVELOPMENTS:

"The twentieth century has brought mixed fortunes for Buddhism. Communist rule has meant wholesale destruction, especially to the Sangha, first in the Asian territories of the Soviet Union and in Mongolia, then successively in North Korea, China, Tibet, Vietnam, Laos, and Cambodia. Each of the traditions has suffered [only to see a resurgence in Buddhist devotion toward the latter part of the century, the case of China being the most noteworthy]. The same period has seen a revival of activity and a return to lands long lost. Notably in Indonesia and in India, Buddhism has re-established its presence and won new support. More remarkably, new fields for expansion have emerged. In Europe, Southern Buddhism (Theravada) began to establish itself on a small scale as early as the beginning of the century. Northern Buddhism (Mahayana) in its Zen form started to attract a significant following outside the Asian immigrant communities in the 1950s, especially in North America. The work of Tibetan refugee teachers in the 1960s won support for Tibetan Buddhism. By the early 1980s some hundreds of Buddhist groups and centres were widely scattered across the Western world. Much of this activity is on a fairly small scale, but in many cases is quite well established."

Hinn: 339

NOTE:

"Western images of Buddhism have tended to center on some form of cerebral assimilation of Buddhist ideals. More often than not, Westerners have concerned themselves with a spirituality that is centered on self-cultivation by means of mental training and discipline, or on the theories of monk-scholars. The end result of this self-cultivation is generally described as the attainment, in this life, of a 'direct' spiritual experience. But for millions of Asian Buddhists, this image of Buddhism represents only a fraction of what comes to mind. *There is more to Buddhism than meditation, renunciation, serenity, and mental cultivation, and more than the speculations of philosophers and scholars.* The

other side of Buddhism takes many forms, but if we focus only on the two *Amitabha Sutras*, we may say that throughout their history, they have been valued by Buddhists who believed in a plurality of 'transcendent' or 'celestial' Buddhas and relied on the 'saving grace' of these Buddhas. Thus, among those who consider themselves Buddhists, there are those who turn to the Buddha, or to many Buddhas, as a source of guidance and inspiration, and there are those who base their religious thought and practice on their faith in the saving power of the Buddhas. As one moves towards the latter of these two models, one enters the sphere of a Buddhism of faith and devotion."
Gomez/96: 12 #1892

"In Buddhist tradition, the principles governing human conduct relate the characteristic condition of humanity (suffering, unease, illness, caused by the basic evil of Desire) to the recognized goal of Buddhist endeavour, viz. *complete enlightenment*. Buddhist ethic thus favours those attitudes and kinds of behaviour which help humanity towards the ultimate goal of transcendental enlightenment; as an *intermediate*

criterion, the goal of auspicious and wholesome rebirth [in a Pure Land] is important: whatever is conducive to this end is to be encouraged; whatever detracts is to be discouraged or renounced. The outworking of the Buddhist ethic is seen at the most elementary level in the 5 basic moral precepts (see Five Precepts), binding upon all Buddhists, monastic and lay."
Ling: 113-114 #1127

BUDDHISM *AND* HINDUISM
see Hinduism / Buddhism

◙ BUDDHISM - BURMA
see Myanmar (Buddhism in)

◙ BUDDHISM - CAMBODIA
see Cambodia (Buddhism in)

◙ BUDDHISM - CHINA
see China (Buddhism in)

◙ BUDDHISM - EUROPE
see West (Buddhism in)

◙ BUDDHISM - FINLAND
see Finland (Buddhism in)

◙ BUDDHISM - FRANCE
see France (Buddhism in)

◙ BUDDHISM - GERMANY
see Germany (Buddhism In)

BUDDHISM / HINDUISM
see   Hinduism / Buddhism

◙ **BUDDHISM - INDIA**
see   India (Buddhism in)

◙ **BUDDHISM - INDOCHINA**
see   Indochina (Buddhism in)

◙ **BUDDHISM - INDONESIA**
see   Indonesia (Buddhism in)

◙ **BUDDHISM - JAPAN**
see   Japan (Buddhism in)

◙ **BUDDHISM - KASHMIR**
see   Kashmir (Buddhism in)

◙ **BUDDHISM - KOREA**
see   Korea (Buddhism in)

◙ **BUDDHISM - MONGOLIA**
see   Mongolia (Buddhism in)

◙ **BUDDHISM - NORTH AMERICA**
see North America (Buddhism in); West (Buddhism in)

◙ **BUDDHISM - SRI LANKA**
see   Sri Lanka (Buddhism in)

◙ **BUDDHISM - VIETNAM**
see   Vietnam (Buddhism in)

◙ **BUDDHISM - WEST** see   West (Buddhism in)

◙ **BUDDHIST CANON**
see   Tripitaka

◙ **BUDDHIST CHURCHES OF AMERICA**
See also: Jodo Shinshu School; Shinran; Jodo school

►"The name in western countries of the Japanese Jodo Shinshu ('True Pure Land') tradition. In 1898 two informal missionaries from Hompa Honganji in Kyoto were sent to San Francisco on a fact-finding tour. Their report resulted in the arrival, the following year, of Reverend Shuei Sonoda and Reverend Kakuryo Nishijima who founded the (then called) Buddhist Mission of North America. Their organization ministered to the Japanese community in and around San Francisco. Complicated by the Japanese Immigration Exclusion Act of 1924, and the Second World War, the organization grew only gradually until the late 1940s when, as the renamed Buddhist Churches of America, it began to expand its programs both geographically and financially. It now boasts centers across the United States, has an extensive educational program as well as a study institute in Berkeley,

California, an aggressive publication program, and membership in excess of 100,000 members. It remains one of the most stable organizations in the development of American Buddhism."

Preb: 84

NOTE:

Pure Land Buddhism was introduced to Japan via China and Korea. It eventually developed into the Jodo (Pure Land) school headed by Honen Shonin. Later on, Honen's best known disciple, Shinran Shonin, founded a branch of this school known as Jodo Shinshu or True Pure Land School. The development of this later school in the West has been hampered somewhat by its overwhelming emphasis on faith and grace. Recently, however, there has been a movement within this school to diversify its teaching and membership by nominally including some form of meditational practice and to welcome more non-Japanese members.

Editor: na #1006

◉ **BUDDHIST COUNCILS**

▶"Assemblies of monks held after Shakyamuni's death to compile and confirm the Buddha's teachings in order to preserve and transmit them correctly. It is said that four such councils were held during the four hundred years immediately following the Buddha's death."

Sokk: 37

"The *First Council* was held at Rajagriha (India) immediately after the passing of the Buddha, the Venerable Kasyapa presiding. The Scriptures were recited by all, Ananda leading with the doctrine (sutras) and Upali with the Rules of the Order (precepts). The *Second Council* was held at Vaisali about 100 years later. Its purpose was to resolve a dispute within the Buddhist community over illicit monastic behavior. The *Third Council* was held in the reign of Asoka at Pataliputra (Patna) about 250 B.C. Here the Canon was fixed, though not reduced to writing until the first century B.C. in Ceylon (Theravada canon). *About A.D. 100 a Fourth Council was held in Kashmir under the patronage of King Kanishka, but as the doctrines promulgated were exclusively Mahayana, this council is not recognized by all Buddhists. At that Council, five hundred monks revised the canon and established a definitive Mahayana version.* The *Fifth Council* was held in 1871 at the instance of King Mindon of Burma, when the Theravada Tripitika was carved on 729 marble slabs and preserved at Mandalay. The *Sixth Great Council* was opened in Rangoon at Vesak, 1954, and sat until 1956 when Buddha Jayanti (Observance of the 2,500th year of the Buddha era) opened. Meetings were held in a huge hall built specially near Rangoon in imitation of the Saptaparna Cave: 2,500 Bhikkhus took part in checking the entire Pali Canon."

I. FIRST BUDDHIST COUNCIL:
"The Rajagrha (Rajagriha) council, thought to be the first of its kind in Indian Buddhist history, convened in the year of Buddha's death to establish the Dharma and Vinaya (precepts). Fearful that the community would dissolve through uncertainty over Buddha's teachings, the Sangha decided to hold a council, generally thought to have occurred in 483 B.C., to preclude that possibility. King Bimbisara, one of the Buddha's royal patrons, donated the site in his capital city of Rajagrha, thus accounting for the name of the council. Kasyapa, a senior leading monk of the time who was appointed president of the council, selected 500 Arhat monks to participate in the proceedings. Buddha's disciple Upali recited all of the disciplinary rules, known as the Vinaya Pitaka, fixing that portion of the Buddhist canon. Ananda, Buddha's personal attendant, recited all Buddha's discourses, establishing the Sutra Pitaka. Other business was conducted as well, with the council referring to itself as the 'Chanting of the Vinaya'. Functionally, it marks an important event in the history of the community, for it establishes authority for the group in the absence of its charismatic leader, while at the same time reinforcing communal solidarity."
Preb: 101-102
II. COUNCIL -- MAHAYANA:
"Council held around 100 A.D. under the reign of the Indian King Kaniska. Near the end of the first century when Kaniska assumed the throne of the Kushana (Kusana) Dynasty, he tried to imitate the style of the great Indian ruler Asoka, while supporting the Sarvastivadin school (a precursor of the Mahayana). It was suggested to

Kaniska that invitations be sent to all the learned Buddhists of the era to attend a council to be convened in Gandhara. A great scholar named Vasumitra was made president of the council, consisting of 499 monks, and he was assisted by the learned Asvaghosa. In addition to compiling a new Vinaya, they prepared a commentary called the Mahavibhasa. This work was to become the standard reference work for all Sarvastivadin Abhidharma issues. It can be said that this council fulfilled the same role in Sarvastivadin history that Asoka's council (Third Buddhist Council) did for Theravadin history ... The school possessed a complete canon in Sanskrit, much of which is preserved today in Sanskrit fragments, as well as Chinese and Tibetan translations."
Preb: 98-99;234
III. MOST RECENT BUDDHIST COUNCIL:
"Reckoned to be the sixth Theravada council, held in Rangoon in 1954-1956 to recite and confirm the whole Pali Canon. This council was convened so as to coincide in proximity with the celebration of the 2500th anniversary of Buddha's death. The Prime Minister of Burma, U Nu, delivered the opening address to 2,500 monks in attendance. These monks edited and recited texts for two years, concluding on the anniversary date of Buddha's death according to the Burmese tradition. It was a national festival in Burma, but additionally established solidarity for Theravada Buddhists throughout the world."
Preb: 102 #0459

◙ **BUDDHIST FESTIVALS**
Syn: Festivals
See also: Rains Retreat; Sacerdotal age; Ullambana; Vesak

▶ "Mahayana Buddhist monasteries theoretically celebrate between thirty-five and forty events a year, but most are of minor importance. Apart from festivals common to all Asians, especially the Lunar New Year festival, six are particularly significant for Mahayana Buddhists:

Lunar Calendar:
SECOND MONTH (19th): Festival of the Bodhisattva Avalokitesvara
FOURTH MONTH (15th): Vesak (Birth of Buddha Sakyamuni) [Rains Retreat Begins].

SIXTH MONTH (19th): Festival of the Bodhisattva Avalokitesvara
SEVENTH MONTH (15th): Ullambana ('Festival of Hungry Ghosts'); [Rains Retreat Ends].
NINTH MONTH (19th): Festival of the Bodhisattva Avalokitesvara
ELEVENTH MONTH (17th): Festival of Amitabha Buddha
The 'Rains Retreat' runs from the sixteenth day of the fourth month (one day after Vesak) to the fourteenth of the seventh... it is the festival which terminates the Rains Retreat which is the most important specifically Buddhist festival. The same is the case quite widely in the Buddhist world."   Hinn: 327-328
In addition to the Ullambana festival, a key festival for all Buddhists is *Vesak*. For Theravadins, Vesak commemorates the birth, enlightenment and passing of Sakyamuni Buddha, while for Mahayanists it commemorates His birth only.   #1932

◙ **BUDDHIST, THE**

►"Buddhist monthly periodical published in Colombo. Founded 1888. Organ of the Young Men's Buddhist Association of Colombo, Sri Lanka."
Hump: 51 #0466

◙ **BUDDHIST IMAGES**
see Buddha Images; Icons

◙ **BUDH-GAYA**
see Bodh-gaya

◙ **BUDDHIST TEXTS**
see   Tripitaka; Translation/ Buddhist Texts

◙ **BURMA (BUDDHISM IN)**
see   Myanmar (Buddhism in)

◙ **BURN-OUT**

►*"Question:* How can we [Buddhists] prevent burnout when we are working for others' welfare?
Answer: One way is to keep checking our motivation, continually renewing our compassionate intention. Another is to assess what we're capable of doing and to make realistic commitments. Sometimes we may be so inspired by the Bodhisattva ideal that we agree to participate in every project that comes in our way, even though we may lack the time or ability to complete [a number of these projects]. Then we may push ourselves to the point of exhaustion to fulfill our commitments, or we may begin to resent those who are counting

on our help. It's wise to consider before we commit, and to accept only those responsibilities that we can carry out. In addition, we must remember that difficulties and dissatisfaction are the nature of cyclic existence (Samsara). Preventing nuclear waste, dismantling apartheid, stopping the destruction of rain forests and helping the homeless are noble projects. However, even if all these goals were achieved, it wouldn't solve all the world's ills. *The chief source of suffering lies in the mind*: as long as ignorance, greed and anger are present in people's minds, there will be no lasting peace on the earth. Thus, expecting our social welfare work to go smoothly, becoming attached to the results of our efforts, or thinking, 'if only this would happen, the problem would be solved' leads us to become discouraged. We need to remember that in cyclic existence, there are better and worse states, but all are temporary and none bring ultimate freedom. If we are realistic, we can work in the world without expecting to bring about paradise on earth. And we can also follow our spiritual practice (i.e. keep the precepts and develop Samadhi and

Wisdom) knowing that it will lead to ultimate cessation of problems."
Buddhist Union/ Oct 96: 3

◎ **C.E.**

►Common Era. An alternative for A.D. used in many recent Buddhist books. #2325

◎ **CAKRAVARTIN**

►"In the Indian mythological history of the world, a universal monarch occasionally appears who is supposed to be a most powerful and meritorious king capable of ruling the entire world."
Chan: 485
"Mythological Supreme monarch destined to rule the entire earth."
Reat: 322 #0584

◎ **CAMBODIA (BUDDHISM IN)**
See also: Angkor Wat

►"Ancient seat of Khmer civilization. Buddhism, introduced about fifth century, completely subdued Brahmanism by the twelfth century. Formerly tinged with Mahayanism, now pure Theravada. Capital Phnom-Penh has 'National Institute for Study of Buddhism

of Southern Vehicle', opened in 1930. Has many Buddhist ruins and temples, including famous Angkor Wat."
Hump: 54　#0464

◎ CANDALA

▸"The lowest class in the Indian caste system, beneath even the lowest of the four formal castes. Its members are fishermen, jailers, slaughterers, and so on."
Yoko: 201　#0787

◎ CANOPIES
Syn: Parasols

▸"Canopies or parasols represent protection from afflictions, inclusion in a sphere of activity or enlightenment, compassion, breadth of mind, and universality of knowledge."
Clea/84: 22　#1967

◎ CAPITAL PUNISHMENT
see Death Penalty

CARDINAL SINS
See Five Cardinal Sins

◎ CARUS, PAUL (1852-1919)

▸"Editor, author, and philosopher, born in Ilsenburg, Germany, the son of Dr. Gustav Carus and Laura Krueger Carus. He earned a Ph.D. from Tubingen in 1876. His first professional position was as an educator at the military academy in Dresden, an appointment he soon resigned due to conflicts over his liberal religious views. He then lived briefly in England (1881-1884) before emigrating to the United States, settling in La Salle, Illinois, where he lived for the remainder of his life. At the outset of his literary career in America, Carus published several articles in a new journal called *Open Court*. Shortly thereafter, Carus became editor of *Open Court*, a position he maintained from 1887 until his death in 1919. He also edited *The Monist*, a somewhat more technical quarterly, from 1890-1919. In addition, he was instrumental in founding The Open Court Publishing Company in La Salle, Illinois. It must also be noted that Carus was instrumental in bringing a variety of Asian Buddhists to America, including Dharmapala, Soyen Shaku, and D.T. Suzuki. He was fortunate to meet most of these individuals at the World Parliament of Religions, held in Chicago in 1893 as part of the Columbian Exposition. While living in

Carus' home, D.T. Suzuki began work on his famous *Outlines of Mahayana Buddhism*, his first English language book. Along with his tasks as editor of *Open Court* and *The Monist*, Carus was a prolific author with more than fifty titles to his credit, a number of which continue to be widely read today."   Preb: 87 #1007

◙ **CATENA**
See also: Beal, Samuel

►"A chain. Beal's *Catena of Buddhist Scriptures from the Chinese* is a famous early anthology (1871)."
Hump: 55 #0463

◙ **CAUSAL STAGE(S)**
See also: Jataka Tales

►All the stages before a given level of attainment (Arhatship, Bodhisattvahood, Buddhahood) is reached. The Jataka (rebirth) stories provide good illustrations of Sakyamuni Buddha in the causal stages, that is, as a Bodhisattva, Arhat, human being, even as an animal.
Editor/Zen: 190 #1526

◙ **CAUSE AND EFFECT**
See also: Cause and Conditions; Cause is Result, Result is Cause; Acts of God

►Note the following three related concepts:
I. Cause and Effect
II. Causes and Conditions (q.v.)
III. Dependent Origination (q.v.)
The concept of Cause and Effect is elaborated below. For *Causes and Conditions* and *Dependent Origination*, see separate entries.
"*Cause and effect*: Every action which is a cause will have a result or an effect. Likewise every resultant action has its cause. The law of cause and effect is a fundamental concept within Buddhism governing all situations."
Dait: 141
"*Story of Ch'an master Pai Chang who liberated a wild fox*: One day, after a Ch'an meeting, although all his disciples had retired, the old master Pai Chang noticed an elderly man who remained behind. Pai Chang asked the man what he was doing and he replied: 'I am not a human being but the spirit of a wild fox. In my previous life, I was the head-monk of this place. One day, a monk asked me, "Is an enlightened person still subject to cause and effect?" I replied, "No, He is not subject to causality." For this reply alone, I got involved in retribution and

have now been the spirit of a wild fox for five hundred years, and am still unable to get away from it. Will the master be compassionate enough to enlighten me on all this.' Pai Chang said to the old man: 'Ask me the same question and I will explain it to you.' The man then said to the master: 'I wish to ask the master this: Is an enlightened person still subject to cause and effect?' Pai Chang replied: 'He is not blind to cause and effect.' Thereupon, the old man was greatly awakened; he prostrated himself before the master to thank him and said: 'I am indebted to you for your appropriate reply to the question and am now liberated from the fox's body. I live in a small grotto on the mountain behind and hope you will grant me the usual rites for a dead monk.' The following day, Pai Chang went to a mountain behind his monastery, where in a small grotto he probed the ground with his staff and discovered a dead fox for whom the usual funeral rites for a dead monk were held. Dear friends, after listening to [this story], you will realize that the law of causality is indeed a dreadful thing. Even after His attainment of Buddhahood, the Buddha still suffered a headache in retribution for His former acts. Retribution is infallible and fixed karma is inescapable. So we should always be heedful of all this and should be very careful about creating new causes." (Chan Master Hsu Yun).

Yu: 13-14

True realization of cause and effect can free us from a most pervasive affliction: anger and resentment. Once, it is said, Buddha Sakyamuni was falsely accused of fathering a certain woman's child. When the deceit was discovered, the Buddha's followers wanted to beat the culprit to death. The Buddha calmly stopped them, saying: "Oh, Bhikkus, in a previous lifetime when I was a king, I was once in a grove together with my courtiers. At the sight of an ascetic, the ladies of the party surrounded him, turning their backs on me. Jealous and angry, I exclaimed, How do you know that this ascetic is not a fake? How do you know that he does not spend his nights revelling with women? It is because of that slanderous remark that I have now had to endure that woman's deceit. Oh, monks, release her and let her go in peace." In the Buddhist world view, nothing happens without cause. To escape suffering, we must stop causing further suffering. Acting otherwise is no different than trying to escape one's shadow by running in the blazing sun! (See "Chinchamanavika").

Editor/Thich: 310

Pure Land Buddhism

A question often raised is what happens to the law of cause and effect, the basis of all Buddhist teachings, when a sinner is reborn in the Pure Land thanks to reciting the Buddha's name?

(1) On the level of Mind (noumenon level), since all transgression, worries and fears are born of delusion and ignorance, once we are enlightened (through rebirth in the Pure Land), all these transgressions, worries and fears are gone. This is as if, in the dark, we mistakenly take a rope for a snake. When we switch on the light and realize that it is only a rope, there is no longer worry or fear -- nothing to change or repay, no remaining evil karma.

(2) On the level of everyday life (phenomenal level), good and evil karma do exist, but once we are enlightened and realize that nothing has intrinsic nature, evil karma and retribution no longer

carry the heavy weight they do for ordinary beings. In fact, an enlightened person often uses such karma to help the very person he has wronged. For example, supposing there are two brothers playing a game of chance on the beach. The elder one, in a moment of greed, cheats on the younger one, who becomes angry and upset. Once their father convinces them that the game is only a make-believe, with no real gain or loss, the elder brother is awakened. He can then gladly accept his brother's anger and even turn around to help the younger one understand as well.

(3) Another explanation of how a sinner can be reborn in the Pure Land is the *other-power of Amitabha Buddha*: "A minute grain of sand, dropped on the surface of the water, will sink immediately. On the other hand, a block of stone, however large and heavy, can easily be moved from place to place by boat. The same is true of the Pure Land practitioner. However light his karma may be, if he is not rescued by Amitabha Buddha, he is most likely to revolve in the cycle of birth and death. With the help of the Buddha, his karma, however heavy, will not prevent

his rebirth in the Pure Land" ("Questions of King Milindra", in Thích Thiền Tâm, *Buddhism of Wisdom and Faith*, sect. 68 A).
NOTE:
"Devotional Buddhism does not maintain that rebirth in the Pure Land takes place without a cause, but that the primary factor in its causation is the invocation of the name of Amitabha. Hence this school cannot be regarded as denying the general principle of causality."Sangha/57: 374 #0114

◙ **CAUSE IS RESULT, RESULT IS CAUSE**
Syn: Simultaneity of Cause and Effect
See also: Cause and Effect

▸High level teaching of such Mahayana sutras as the *Avatamsaka Sutra*... "The cause has the result as its cause, while the result has the cause as its result. It is like planting seeds: the seeds produce fruit, the fruit produces seeds."
[TC/FAI, p.37]
"Causes include the sea of results, the result penetrates through to the causal source."
[HH/FAS,39V1, p.61]
This concept from the Avatamsaka and other Mahayana sutras can be understood through

the analogy of apple seeds (causes) leading to the apples of the future (results); the apples, in turn, contain within themselves the seeds of future trees and apples. In the same vein, sentient beings (causes) have the Buddha Nature within themselves, leading to Buddhahood (results); these Buddhas (results), in time, return to the world to rescue sentient beings (causes). Thus, cause and result are inseparable -- cause is result, result is cause. As the sutras put it: "Causes encompass the sea of Results, and the Results extend back through the Causal sources."
Editor/Van Hien: 208-209 #1674

◙ **CAUSES AND CONDITIONS**
See also: Cause and Effect

▸"Also referred to as primary causes and secondary causes or main causes and subsidiary causes. The seed out of which the plant grows is an illustration of the main cause, whereas other elements like labor, the quality of soil, humidity and so on, are considered as subsidiary causes (or conditions)."
NV Hoa: Na

◙ **CELESTIALS**
see   Deva

◙ **CELESTIAL DRUM**
Syn: Drum of the Teaching;
Heavenly Drum

►The *Avatamsaka Sutra* describes how, in the Thirty-Three-Fold Heaven (Heaven of the Thirty-Three), whenever the gods become deluded and caught in the quagmire of the five desires, a Heavenly Drum suddenly appears to warn them that all things are evanescent -- pleasure brings with it the seeds of suffering. Therefore, they should not become lax... This drum symbolizes the result of the gods' good actions accumulated through time immemorial.
Editor: na #1252

◙ **CH'AN**
See Zen School; Patriarchal Zen;
Tathagatha Zen

◙ **CH'ANG-AN**
See also: Lo-yang

►"Major early Chinese Buddhist center in northern China, eventually becoming capital during the Sui and T'ang Dynasties. It was the major *center of Kumarajiva's translation enterprises, and a Pure Land stronghold in the seventh century.*"
Preb: 89

"Ch'ang-an (modern city of Hsi-an in Shensi). Like the ancient capital city of Lo-yang, Ch'ang-an witnessed the rise and fall of many empires. It was the capital city of the Earlier Han, Later Ch'in and Northern Chou Dynasties. Ch'ang-an, the capital of the largest Empire of the world under the T'ang, was the greatest centre of Buddhism in China. The city was teeming with people from all over Asia. The glory of Lo-yang, the ancient stronghold of Buddhism in North China, was overshadowed by Ch'ang-an when it entered into a period of unprecedented development. The population of the capital city during the Dynastic rule of the T'ang rose to over 1.9 million. The city was studded with Buddhist temples, monasteries, pagodas constructed by the devout rulers of the T'ang Dynasty. The great Chinese monk *Hsuan-Tsang* started on his journey to India from Ch'ang-an in 629 A.D. The great Tzu-en monastery was built there in A.D. 648. Here Hsuan-Tsang translated Buddhist scriptures into Chinese after his return from India. The Ta-yen Pagoda was constructed in A.D. 652, designed by the venerable monk Hsuan-Tsang himself to store the

Buddhist scriptures in Ch'ang-an. From the last part of the fourth century, illustrious monks like *Kumarajiva* and Yasa all lived at Ch'ang-an and contributed a great deal to the propagation of Buddha's teachings. In the seventh century there were three Indian astronomical schools in the capital city."
Lahiri: 18-19 #1008

◙ CH'ENG-KUAN (d. 839)
See also: Avatamsaka Sutra

►"The fourth patriarch in the lineage of the Avatamsaka (Hua-yen/ Kegon) school. He lived during the T'ang Dynasty. He is also known as Ta-hsiu, Ch'ing-Liang-Ta-Shih, and Hua-yen-p'u-sa. After studying the various schools of Buddhist teaching, he became ... an eminent follower of the Hua-yen school. He helped Pan-jo-san-tsang translate the forty-fascicle *Hua-yen-ching* (*Avatamsaka Sutra/Kegon-Kyo*) and wrote a commentary on it. It is said that he died in 839 in his one hundred and second year."
Dait: 34 #0089

◙ CHANDAKA

►"A servant of Shakyamuni before He renounced secular life. When Shakyamuni left Kapilavastu to embark on a religious life, Chandaka accompanied him, holding his horse Kanthaka by the bridle. When Shakyamuni had gone some distance to the south, it is said, he cut his hair, handed over his jeweled ornaments to Chandaka and sent him back to Kapilavastu with the message that he would not return until he had fulfilled his objective. After Shakyamuni attained enlightenment, Chandaka became his disciple." Sokk: 41 #0208

◙ CHAO-CHOU (778-897)

►"A famous Chinese Zen master of the T'ang dynasty from whose dialogues many koans were formulated." Kusa: 182
"Buddhist heir of Nan-ch'uan. He is famous for the koan concerning the Buddha-nature known as 'Chao-chou's wu.' In this koan Chao-chou answers with a negative when asked by a monk whether a dog has the Buddha-nature. Later, however, he gives an affirmative reply to another monk who asks the same question. Through these seemingly contradictory answers, Chao-chou expresses the fact that

the Buddha-nature is not to be grasped conceptually."
Yoko: 201 #0788

◙ **CHARITY**
see Dana

◙ **CHENREZI / CHENREZIG**
See also: Avalokitesvara

▶Tibetan for Avalokitesvara. #2320

◙ **CHICAGO COLUMBIAN EXPOSITION (USA)**
See also: World Parliament of Religions

▶"Major event hosting the World Parliament of Religions in 1893. This conference was one of the first occasions in which Asian religions were presented to the American public in an organized fashion. A number of venerable Buddhists were in attendance -- Dharmapala and Soyen Shaku being most notable among them. Virtually all of the major Buddhist schools were represented in the proceedings. During the Parliament, a fortuitous meeting took place between Paul Carus, editor of The *Monist* and *Open Court Press*, and Soyen Shaku that paved the way for D.T. Suzuki to come to the United States. In the aftermath of the Parliament, the American Buddhist movement began its first small steps toward catching the American interest."
Preb: 90-91 #1009

◙ **CHIH-I (538-97)**
See also: T'ien T'ai School; Samatha-Vipasyana

▶"A famous patriarch of the T'ien-t'ai (Tendai) school, who secured its foundation and is regarded as its founder."
Insa: 22
"Also called Chih-che (Jpn./ Chisha), Chih-i was the first in the history of Chinese Buddhism to elaborate a complete, critical, and systematic classification of Buddhist teaching. He did this in order to explain the many apparently contradictory doctrines of Buddhism. As for Buddhist practice, he developed the practice of Chih-Kuan (Samatha-Vipasyana), which is still today one of the most widespread meditation practices in East Asian Buddhism."
Sham: 45
"On the basis of his lectures, the *Three Great Works* were written, *Profound Meanings of the Lotus Sutra, Commentary on the Lotus Sutra* and *Great Concentration*

and Insight [Mo-Ho Chih-Kuan]."
Larousse: 531

NOTE
The last text is among the most widely read works on meditation in China. Part of it was translated recently by T. Cleary as *Stopping and Seeing* (Shambhala, 1997).
Editor: na #0194

◙ **CHIKO**
See also: Pure Land Mandalas; Raigo; Taima Mandala

▸"Name of an eighth-century Japanese monk from Gango-ji (temple). The word is also applied to one of the three Japanese Pure Land mandalas (stylized paintings), which this monk traditionally envisioned."
Okaz: 183 #0636

"*The Chiko Mandala.* Often called 'the first Pure Land mandala' because it is the oldest of the three Jodo mandalas (the Chiko mandala can be traced to a legend from the eigth century). The earliest reference to this mandala as a Chiko mandala seems to be in the description of the Buddhist memorial service held for Fujiwara no Moromichi in 1909, which states that a

paradise mandala --the Chiko Mandala-- was hung as a devotional image. Tradition, however, ascribes it to a much earlier period than this: it is mentioned in the early ninth-century *Nihon ryoiki* (Miraculous Stories from the Japanese Buddhist Tradition) and in the late tenth-century *Nihon ojo gokuraku ki* (Japanese Records of Birth into Paradise). The Chiko mandala also figures in other records and in collections of folk tales and legends, such as the late eleventh-century *Konjaku monogatari* (Stories Ancient and Modern) in which it is related that this mandala was hung in the Paradise Hall of the Gango-ji in Nara -- the traditional residence of the monk Chiko -- whenever there was a gathering to chant the *nembutsu*.

The story of this mandala is as follows. The monks Chiko and Raiko of Gango-ji shared a room in which they had practiced religious austerities from the time of their youth. At one year's end, Raiko ceased speaking, never replying to any of Chiko's questions. Several years later, Raiko died. Worried about Raiko's future existence, Chiko prayed that he might learn what had happened to his friend.

One night in a dream he met Raiko. The setting was an ethereal, splendid place, and when Chiko asked where they were, Raiko replied that it was the Pure Land. He went on to explain that from his earliest days he had studied the sutras and holy scriptures and had longed for birth in Paradise, knowing all the while that this was no easy feat to achieve. He had stopped talking in order to focus his inner vision exclusively on the countenance of Amida and on the magnificence of the Pure Land. As a result, he had finally attained birth in Paradise. But, continued Raiko, Chiko was still disordered in mind and body and his good deeds were few. Since it seemed impossible for him to be born there as well, he should return home straightaway. Chiko began to lament, begging to know how it might be possible for someone like him to achieve birth in the Western Paradise, whereupon Raiko, replying that Chiko should ask that question of the Buddha himself, guided Chiko to Amida. Amida told Chiko that it was necessary to devote one's full attention to an inner visualization of the extraordinary excellences of the Buddha (Amida) and the

sublimity of the Pure Land in order to attain birth there. When Chiko confessed that he could not hold in his mind's eye the mysterious and limitless vision of the Western Paradise-- that this was a feat beyond the capabilities of ordinary men-- Amida held out his right hand and revealed a miniture Paradise in his palm. Immediately upon waking from the dream, Chiko went to an artist and had him paint the vision of the Pure Land as it had appeared in the dream. The monk devoted the rest of his life to a contemplation of this mandala and finally achieved rebirth in the Western Paradise." Okaz: 37

◙ **CHINA (BUDDHISM IN)**
See also: T'ang Dynasty (Buddhism in the); Pure Land Buddhism (Summary); Zen School

----

►"Buddhism was introduced into China in A.D. 67 by two Indian Bhikkhus, *Kasyapa Matango* and *Dharmaraksha*; the White Horse Monastery that was built to accommodate them exists today. It made rapid progress, eventually becoming one of the 'tripod' of religions with Taoism and Confucianism. Many schools of Buddhist thought developed and flourished. The two predominant schools were the Ch'an (Jpn./ Zen) and Pure Land." Hump: 56-57

"When Buddhism spread to China [around the first century A.D.], it evolved, through the teachings of the Patriarchs, into ten schools. Among them are two schools which belong to the Southern (Theravada) tradition, the Satysiddhi School and the Abhidharma School. However, the faculties and temperament of the Chinese people did not correspond to the Southern tradition, and, therefore, within a short period of time it faded away. The other eight schools, are all Mahayana: the T'ien T'ai (Tendai) School, the Avatamsaka School, the Madyamika (Three Treatises) School, the Mind-Only (Yogacara) School, the Vinaya (Discipline) School, the Zen School, the Esoteric School and the Pure Land School. The vehicle for popularizing the Pure Land School is the Buddha Recitation method."
Tam: 32

"The worship of Amitabha was introduced into China at an early period and Chinese tradition credits a Parthian prince, An-Shih-Kao, with having preached the doctrine and translated the *Sukhavativyuha* (*Amitabha Sutra*) about the middle of the first century A.D. It was Hui-yuan (333-418), however, who is generally regarded as having made of the doctrine a separate school. This proved most successful and produced several renowned scholars of whom Shan-tao (Zendo) was the most celebrated. He is regarded in Japan as an incarnation of Amida himself and his works are considered sacred texts. By about the ninth century, the worship of Amitabha had become so popular in China that it ceased to be the tenet of any particular school and became instead an aspect of all schools. The explanation seems to be that the doctrine of salvation by faith was so easy that no [school] could afford to neglect it."
(Encyclopedia of Buddhism, v. I: p.436)

"Buddhism brought to the Chinese a vivid concept of an after-life, and a doctrine of future punishment for sins committed in this life, an idea that present sufferings are the result of past sins. It taught that future retribution for sin could be avoided by accumulation of merit by such means as chanting liturgies, repentance, meritorious actions, asceticism and the like. It introduced a soteriology (doctrine of salvation) by its doctrine of transferred merit. Buddhas and Bodhisattvas had accumulated infinite stores of merit; by appealing to them in penitence and faith, the consequences of sin could be wiped out and a blissful future life guarenteed. These Buddhist ideas exercised a profound influence on Confucians and Taoists alike, and on popular beliefs." Ling: 233

"The great contribution which the Buddhist Order makes to the life of China consists in keeping before the minds and imaginations of the people the fact of religion, the reality of the spiritual life. Doubtless this great function of keeping the lamp of religion alight is [sometimes not well] performed by the Buddhist clergy. But as things actually are in China today, and have been for many a century, the clergy are the torch-bearers of religion, and if they should drop their light, it might well be extinguished in the darkness of worldly, unspiritual preoccupation. It is not without value in the life of the Chinese people that they should be constantly reminded of the fact of Buddhism, reminded of it as at least an unfailing potentiality. It is not without value that an Order of men and women should be consecrated to the lifelong study and service of religion, that buildings of ancient beauty should be devoted to the praises of the highest ideal that China knows, that quiet cloisters should be set aside for meditation of holy men and of all who wish to meditate. It is not without value that the poorest beggar, the busiest politician, the saddest woman, the most guilty sinner should carry ever in the subconscious regions of their minds the thought that, if they will, they may go any morning or any night to a nearby temple, hear the solemn music of gong and drum and chanting monks, watch the smoke of incense ascend before the image of the Blessed One, and catch some intimation of a higher life, a loftier world, a deeper peace than they have known before." Pratt: 350-351

NOTE

"In Japan, the ancient schools of Buddhism (Tendai, Avatamsaka, Zen, Pure Land ...) grew more and more into independent sects

with their own organization and separate lay following. It is important not to read this Japanese development back into the classical Chinese situation. The ancient Chinese schools were much less institutionalized sectarian entities than their successors in Japan. In China there arose a movement towards syncretism which tended to unite the Buddhist sects and in some cases sought to harmonize the teachings of Buddhism with those of Taoism and Confucianism. This led to a much more integrated and united form of Buddhism. Japanese writers tend to view this as degeneration, but it can also be viewed as a successful victory for ecumenism..."
Hinn: 327 #2162

◉ CHINCHAMANAVIKA
See also: Cause and Effect

▸"A Brahman woman who slandered Sakyamuni. According to the Scriptures, Chinchamanavika tied a pot to her belly under her robe and publicly declared that she was pregnant by Shakyamuni. But the god Indra assuming the form of a rat, crept under her robe and gnawed through the string

holding the pot in place. It dropped to the ground, exposing her falsehood. Then the earth split open and Chinchamanavika fell into hell alive."
Sokk: 44 #0209

CHRISTIANITY
see Reincarnation

◉ CHU-HUNG (1535-1615)
See also: Yung-ming; Yin-kuang; Han-shan; Koan of Buddha Recitation; Seven-day Retreat

----

▸Also known as Lien Ch'ih and Yun-ch'i Chu-Hung. "Important Chinese monk of the Ming Dynasty who developed a practical path based on a combination of Zen and Pure Land and initiated a strong Buddhist lay movement. He first entered the monastic order at the age of thirty-two and became a student of noted masters of various schools. He spent most of his life in the neighborhood of Hang-chou, where he built the Yun-chi Temple. In this monastery particular emphasis was laid on strict observance of the rules of the Vinaya. Through this, Chu-hung wished to purify the sangha. His effort to link the practice of the Pure Land school with that of Zen was based on

his conviction that, although externally the followers of each school travel different paths, their inner attitude is the same. The recitation of Buddha's name, which banishes everything from the mind but the name of Amitabha, invokes the same state of mind as meditating on a koan in Zen. Under Chu-hung's influence many lay followers began intensively to practice the recitation of Buddha's name and strictly to observe the rules of discipline without formally entering the monastic order."
Sham: 48

"From as early as the Tang period we hear of the existence of 'Pure Land Cloisters' within larger monastic complexes, where a congregation of self-professed Pure Land mendicants could pursue a collective regimen of Pure Land practice and study. Over the centuries that followed, influential Pure Land masters have periodically sought to organize individual monasteries along Pure Land lines ... The Ming dynasty master Chu Hung (1535-1615) and Republican period master Yin Kuang (1861-1940) represent two such figures who have had a profound impact on the monastic form of Pure Land Buddhism in modern times. Both instituted comprehensive plans for adapting traditional monastic structures and routines to the specific purposes of Pure Land devotion, including the creation of halls for the concentrated recitation of the Buddha's name that were modeled on the traditional Chan meditation hall. At the same time, monks and nuns of the Pure Land school have developed a number of distinctive forms of retreat that are organized along the lines of the seven-day rite of Buddha-mindfulness (Seven-Day Retreat/q.v.) but apply its program to a more intensive monastic setting."
Lopez: 366-367 #0332

◉ **CHUNDA**

►"A blacksmith in Pava Village, India, who offered Shakyamuni the last meal he ate before his death. When Shakyamuni visited Pava Village on the day before he entered Nirvana, Chunda heard him preach the teachings that were later compiled as the *Nirvana Sutra*. Moved and delighted, Chunda invited the Buddha and his monks to his home and had a special meal prepared for them. After leaving Chunda's house, the Buddha

proceeded to Kushinagar (q.v.) where he passed away in a grove of sal trees."
Sokk: 46
"The metal-worker who invited the Buddha to the meal after which he died. The food [served to the Buddha] means truffles, on which pigs feed."
Hump: 57 #0210

◙ **CINTA-MANI**
see Wish-fulfilling jewel

◙ **CIRCLE OF WHITE HAIR**
see Curl of white hair

◙ **CLINGING**
see Attachment

◙ **CLOUD OF VIRTUES BODHISATTVA**
See also: Avatamsaka Sutra; Pure Land Buddhism (Summary); Samantabhadra
----
►Name of a Bodhisattva in the *Avatamsaka Sutra* whose virtues are as immense as the sky and clouds. First of 53 wise advisors the Youth Sudhana (i.e., the Bodhisattva Sudhana) met on his journey to enlightenment. Taught the Youth Sudhana the Dharma door (school) of Pure Land.
Editor: na
In the *Avatamsaka Sutra* the first

wise advisor is *Clouds of Virtues Bodhisattva* and the last is *Samantabhadra Bodhisattva.* Both taught the Youth Sudhana the Pure Land path.
Avatamsaka Sutra:
"'Good man, I have only obtained this Dharma of Recollecting all the Buddhas' States of Wisdom Light and Universal Vision'(i.e. *Dharma of Buddha Recitation*) 'But how could I possibly know the doors of the conduct of all great Bodhisattvas' boundless, Pure Wisdom?'."
Hua/39(II): 11 #1320

◙ **COMBINE THE PROVISIONAL AND THE TRUE**
See also: True Teaching; Provisional Teaching

►Expression meaning the simultaneous practice of the provisional and the true teachings. #1257

◙ **COMMENTARIES**
See Sastra

◙ **COMMENTARY ON THE LONGER AMITABHA SUTRA**
see Rebirth Treatise

◙ **COMMON TEACHING**

►"The teaching of emptiness is

called common because it is common to all vehicles of Buddhism, whether implicitly or explicitly."

Cleary/Chih-I: 189

◉ **COMMUNITY OF MONKS AND NUNS**
see Sangha

◉ **COMPASSION**
Syn: Karuna
See also: Avalokitesvara; Anger; Purna; One is All, All is One

----

►"Compassion, active sympathy. The outstanding quality of all Bodhisattvas and Buddhas. Compassion extends itself without distinction to all sentient beings. It is based on the enlightened experience of the oneness of all beings. *Compassion (Karuna) must be accompanied by wisdom (prajna) in order to have the right effect.* The virtue of compassion is embodied in the Bodhisattva Avalokiteshvara."

Sham: 113

"Sympathy for people who suffer, and the will to end their sufferings. Mahayana Buddhism greatly emphasized compassion, along with wisdom. These two form the outstanding Mahayana virtues, sometimes called the 'two-in-one' (compassion-wisdom). The infinite compassion of the Buddhas and Bodhisattvas is reflected in their constant attempt to succor sentient beings."

Chan: 472

See the following passage on Bodhisattva practice, from the "Practices and Vows of the Bodhisattva Samantabhadra": "Because of living beings, Bodhisattvas bring forth great compassion. From great compassion the Bodhi Mind is born; and because of the Bodhi Mind, they accomplish Supreme, Perfect Enlightenment." (*Avatamsaka Sutra*, ch. 40.)

Editor: na

I. How to develop compassion

"In the Buddha-Dharma, there are many meditation methods for helping to cultivate equanimity and compassion. One method, taught by the Buddha directly is that *every being--whether human, animal, spirit, friend, or enemy-- has been your own mother at some point in the cycle of rebirth.* In our Western society, we don't always have a respectful relationship towards our mother. I don't really know why, but people often harbor a lot of resentment towards their mothers. In Asian cultures,

people understand that without a mother, we wouldn't exist as we do now. Whether she has been angry or loving, hurtful, or helpful, she gave us a human body, which is an incomparable gift. So there is an appreciation for archetypical motherhood and a respect for the dignity of the mother who has given birth to us. When we consider that everybody has been our mother, the concept is immense. It is illuminating when we begin seeing the lady at the bank, our children's preschool teacher, our friends, our workers, our employers, and people in other countries as our mother. *Everyone we see was once the most important person in our existence. Then we realize that all these beings now only want to be happy, yet they don't quite know how to do it*. In fact, most are constantly complicating their conditions--creating worse and worse karmic conditions for themselves by hatred, greed, ignorance, pride, and jealousy. This way we develop compassion and a real aspiration to liberate them from pain and suffering in an ultimate way."
Tsomo/Budd: 111 #0385
"The ideal of the Bodhisattva illustrates the Mahayana Buddhist principle that Ultimate Reality is itself all-embracing, inclusive of every living being and of the nature of compassion. One who truly understands this principle cannot help but feel suffering as long as there is even one individual who suffers, for that unfortunate individual is one's very self."
World Script: 368
"In the psycho-ethical social philosophy of Buddhism, this concept of compassion has two main aspects. *First*, as a desirable quality in human character, it is meant to regulate our attitude to other people. *Secondly*, it has its transcendental aspect known as great or grand compassion (*maha-karuna*) found only in sages like Buddhas, [Bodhisattvas] and Arhats. It is the higher kind and is super-individual in scope and covers all beings in their entirety. It 'seeketh not its own' and hence is the result of coming into contact with spiritual reality. Cleansed of individualised exclusiveness, it becomes unlimited ... If compassion is the desire to relieve the suffering of others, *the best way to do so is to lead them to the freedom of Buddhahood* and hence it is this kind of compassion that makes the concept truly meaningful."

Encyclopedia of Religions.
Malalasekera: Vol. 4, p. 201

II. Illustration

"It is recorded in the *Mahabhinishkramana* that Devadatta, the cousin of Prince Siddhartha, took a bow and arrow and shot down a swan. The creature was grounded but not killed. The future Buddha took the bird upon his knees and comforted it. Devadatta was sent to claim his prize, no doubt intending to kill it, but the Buddha refused to hand over the swan, saying that the bird was his. An exquisite description of the incident is to be found in *The Light of Asia* by Sir Edwin Arnold:

'Then our Lord
      Laid the swan's neck beside his own smooth cheek
      And gravely spake, "Say no! the bird is mine,
      The first of myriad things that shall be mine
      By right of mercy and love's lordliness..."'"

Shantiveda: 209-210

See last para. of "Deer Park"; "Great Compassion Mantra"

◙ COMPRESS ALL EONS
See also: Three Periods of Time; Kalpa

►Expression used in such Mahayana sutras as the Avatamsaka. The advanced practitioner always has his mind under control and dwells only in the present, without thinking of the past or the future. He is said to have compressed all eons (or the three periods of time -- past, present and future).

Ed/Saman: 51,53 #1617

◙ CONCENTRATION AND INSIGHT
see Samatha-Vipasyana

◙ CONDITIONED DHARMAS
Syn: Dharmas-with-Outflows
See also: Unconditioned Dharmas

►Describes the various *phenomena in the world* -- made up of elements "with outflows." That is to say these phenomena are worldly and impure, indeed "leaking", because they are tainted by the three poisons of greed, anger, and ignorance.

Conditioned merits and virtues lead to rebirth within Samsara, whereas *unconditioned* merits and virtues are the causes of liberation from Birth and Death.

Editor/Tam: 146 #0506

◙ CONDITIONS
see Causes and Conditions

◙ **CONFIRMATORY SIGNS OF REBIRTH**
see   Proofs of rebirth in Pure Land

◙ **CONQUERORS**
See also: Jina; Leader

▶An epithet for the Buddhas. "Buddhas are 'conquerors' or 'victors' because they have conquered their own passions and have defeated the forces of fear, confusion, greed, hatred -- in short, they have conquered the armies of Mara, the Buddhist tempter and spirit of evil."
Gomez/96: 290 #1941

◙ **CONSCIOUSNESS SCHOOL**
see   Yogacara school

◙ **CONSCIOUSNESSES**
See also: Alaya Consciousness

▶"The term 'consciousness' (vijnana) refers to the perception or discernment which occurs when our sense organs make contact with their respective objects. They are: i. sight consciouness; ii. hearing consciousness; iii. scent consciousness; iv. taste consciousness; v. touch consciousness; vi. mind consciousness (Mano

consciousness/ *Vn*/ Ý-Thức); vii. klistamano consciousness (defiled mind/ *Vn*/ Ý-Căn) and viii. Alaya consciousness. The first five consciousnesses correspond to the five senses. The sixth consciousness 'integrates the perceptions of the five senses into coherent images and makes judgments about the external world."
Sokk: 314.)
"The seventh consciousness is the active center of reasoning, calculation, and construction or fabrication of individual objects. It is the source of clinging and craving, and thus the origin of the sense of self or ego and the cause of all illusion that arises from assuming the apparent to be real (Sung-peng Hsu)."
Tam: 335-336 #0048

◙ **CONTEMPLATIONS**
see   Visualizations

◙ **CONTRACEPTION**
see   Birth control

◙ **CONZE, EDWARD (1904-1979)**

▶"Ph.D. (Cologne). Born 1904. English Buddhist. Recognized authority on Sanskrit and Tibetan Buddhism. Specialist in the Prajnaparamita philosophy and

literature. Vice-President of the Buddhist Society, London. Author of *Buddhism* (1951)." Hump: 58 #0460

◙ **COSMIC AGE**
See also: Cosmology; Five Corruptions; Auspicious Kalpa

▸"In [Buddhist] cosmology, the world goes through cycles of cosmic ages, usually from a time of generation and harmony to a time of decay and conflict. Cosmic ages at the end of a cycle are usually corrupt and evil times. The time of the Five Corruptions is the last part of one such cycle, sometimes called the evil cosmic age or the evil end of a cosmic age. The cosmic age in which Shakyamuni appeared in this world (our cosmic age) is regarded as evil because many things are corrupted or corrupting: the views held by living beings, the afflictions that oppress them, living beings themselves, and their life-span (see Five Corruptions). Some texts, however, call the present cosmic age the Auspicious Kalpa (Cosmic Age), because a number of Buddhas have appeared or will appear in our world system during this period." Gomez: 291

NOTE:
The references to a cosmic age as both evil *and* auspicious may appear contradictory, but they are not so in reality, because the Buddhas' teaching is audience-specific. For example, a patient with a low temperature will be given a medicine to raise his temperature, but then if a few minutes later his temperature is too high, he will be given another medicine to lower it. Thus, two medicines with diametrically opposite action are administered to the same patient, but each is effective because each is directed toward a different stage of the same disease.
Editor: na #1695
See also next entry.

◙ **COSMOLOGY**
See also: Universe; World Origin; Cosmic Age; Eschatology; Four Kalpas; Adamantine Mountains; Borobudur; Four Continents

----

▸"A number of cosmological schemata are present in Buddhism. Possibly the earliest of these emerges from the Pali Canon, in which the universe is divided into three realms, the 'Realm of Desire,' 'Realm of Forms' and 'Formless Realms.' Hell beings, hungry ghosts, animals, men, anti-gods (Asuras), and six classes of gods dwell in the first Realm (desire). In the second Realm (forms) dwell gods who have practiced certain dhyanas or meditations. In the third realm (formless) dwell those beings who have attained the four stages of formlessness. A variation on this pattern can be found in Vasubandhu's famous Abhidharmakosa. In this framework, the earth sits atop six cold and six hot hells. A huge mountain called Sumeru is located in the center of the earth, circumscribed by four continents. An enormous mountain range surrounds the entire system, thus maintaining the oceans in their integrity. Above the world, gods and other heavenly beings dwell in two categories of heavens: Desire Heavens and Form Heavens.

"According to the Theravada treatise *Abhidharma-kosabhasya*, at the end of the Kalpa (eon) of Destruction, all beings, except those whose root of merits is destroyed, are reborn in the Abhasvara heaven, the second meditation (dhyana) heaven, where they will reside throughout the duration of the kalpa of emptiness. Those beings whose root of merit is destroyed are reborn in the hells of other universes. When the merit of the beings in the Abhasvara heaven is exhausted, they descend to be reborn as men. They still have all the characteristics of the radiant gods of the Abhasvara heaven: they are made of mind, feed on joy, radiate light, traverse the air, and continue in glory. Gradually, the earth appears as a kind of foam on the surface of the primeval waters. It is a savory earth (ti-wei; prthivirasa), which tastes as sweet as honey. One being of greedy disposition smells its fragrance and eats of it; other beings follow suit. With the eating of the savory earth, their bodies become grosser and heavy, and their radiance disappears. Thus are born the sun, moon, and stars. As the savory earth disappears with beings' attachment to it, earth cakes (ti-ping; prthiviparpataka) appear. As beings become attached to their taste, they too begin to disappear, and forest creepers (lin-t'eng, vanalata) appear in their stead. These also disappear with beings' attachment to them, and rice/wheat spontaneously begins to grow. Being a still grosser form of food, when beings eat this grain, some of it remains

undigested and their bodies produce wastes. It is at this juncture in the process of materialization that beings first become differentiated sexually. One being of a lazy nature begins to store up rice for future consumption, and others, fearing that there will not be enough to go around, follow his example, With this, the rice begins to disappear and cultivation becomes necessary. The people then divide the land up into fields, but since some steal rice from others' fields, they elect a ruler to protect the fields. Thus the process of social differentiation begins."
Greg: 286

"Buddhist texts convey immeasurable dimensions of time and space without lapsing into abstract terminology. In the Buddhist view of the universe one thousand solar systems make up what is called one small universe, one thousand small universes comprise one middle universe, and one thousand middle universes make one -- and only one -- large universe. In Buddhist cosmology, time, too, is seen as boundless, but again we are given 'handles,' through vivid and concrete descriptions, by which to grasp in some measure this infinitude. Thus a kalpa, or world cycle of time, is described as the time it would take one to empty a huge bowl of poppy seeds, forty cubic miles in size, by taking out just one poppy seed every three years."
Kapl/80: 273

Pure Land Buddhism:
In the Buddhist cosmology, the human and celestial realms are among the many realms subject to Birth and Death. Above these realms are those of the Arhats, Pratyeka Buddhas, Bodhisattvas and Buddhas. The Pure Lands, the most representative of which is the Land of Bliss of Amitabha Buddha, are expedient realms of the Buddhas and as such are beyond Birth and Death. To be reborn there is therefore to have transcended birth and death.
Editor / Zen: 81 #0831
See also other poetical definitions of the concept of kalpa under *Kalpa; Cosmic Age.*

◉ **COSMOS**
see   Billion-world universe; Dharma Realm; Universe

◉ **COUNTLESS**
see   Inconceivable

◉ **CRAVING**
see   Greed

◙ **CREMATION**
See also: Funerary Rites for the Buddha; Death and Burial; Death

----

▶"Cremation is the usual mode of treating the dead in hot countries, and the Buddha's body was cremated. The ashes were divided into ten parts, and Stupas erected over each of them. It is from surviving stupas that undoubted relics of the Buddha have been recovered."
Hump: 59-60   #0458

◙ **CRITICISM & SLANDER**

▶"When a cultivator is subjected to criticsm and slander, he should think: 'that person is bringing me merit.' Why is this so? It is because, from time immemorial, we have committed obstructive transgressions. If we are the object of one word of scorn and belittlement, our bad karma has been lightened by one part. Are we not then receiving merit and benefit? Those who engage in scornful speech and slander will certainly suffer retribution; through delusion, they bring calamity upon themselves"
Tam: 157
"Listen, for example, to the following from Asanga: 'If another does harm to the

Bodhisattva, the latter endures with patience the worst injuries, with the idea that it is a benefit he has received. To think that the offender does one a service, this is to conduct oneself in accord with the example of the Perfect Ones, i.e., the Buddhas.'" (From A s a n g a ' s   *M a h a y a n a Sutralamkara*).
Pratt: 219 #1332

◙ **CROSSING THE RIVER IN A DREAM**

▶Zen allusion to people who practice the Buddha Dharma without realizing the relative nature of their actions. They are no different than those who cross the Samsara river, not in fact, but only in their dreams. #1234

◙ **CULTIVATION**
see   Practice

◙ **CURL OF WHITE HAIR**
Syn: Circle of white hair
See also: Thirty-two Auspicious Signs

▶"A white-hair mark between the Buddhas' eyebrows which emits great brightness when they are about to proclaim the Dharma. The substance and function of this light represent the Middle

Path, which is without outflows."
[HHFAS39I117] #1296

◉ **CYCLE OF BIRTH AND DEATH**
see Samsara

◉ **ĐẠI-BỬU-TÍCH KINH**
see Maha-Ratnakuta sutra

◉ **DAIBUTSU**

▸"(*Jpn*/ Great Buddha). Name
given to several large images of
Buddhas and Bodhisattvas in
Japan, usually made of bronze, in
a sitting or standing posture. The
three most important Daibutsu
are at Nara, Kyoto and
Kamakura. The Daibutsu at
Kamakura, though smaller than
that at Nara, is the best known of
the three. It is an image of
Amitabha Buddha, 49 ft. 7 in. in
height. Erected in 1252, it marks
the success of the great Pure
Land schools. The temple in
which it was originally housed
was destroyed in 1369, and again
in 1494, and was never rebuilt."
Ling: 88-89 #1118

◉ **DAINICHI**
see Vairocana Buddha

◉ **DALAI LAMA**

▸"The word Dalai, 'great Ocean'
(pronounced to rhyme with
valley) is Mongolian, and was a
title granted to the third Grand
Lama of the Gelugpa School in
1587 by Gusri Khan, a Mongol
prince ... There have been
fourteen Dalai Lamas, of whom
the Fifth (1615-1680), a great
administrator and reformer, was
the first to gain full temporal
power of all Tibet in addition to
being Grand Lama of its leading
School, the Gelugpa... The
current Fourteenth Dalai Lama
was born in Amdo on 6 June
1935, and was enthroned in
1940." Hump: 61-62
The current Dalai Lama is "HH
the XIVth, (Gyalwa Tenzin
Gyatso): Exiled spiritual and
temporal leader of the Tibetan
people. Born 1935 in East Tibet,
of humble origins. Located and
recognized as Dalai Lama
incarnation 2 years later. At age
16 assumed full temporal powers
early because of Chinese
Communist threat. 1954: went to
Peking to hold discussions with
Chinese Communist leaders.
1956: visited India for 2500
Buddha Jayanti celebrations; held
political discussions with Pandit
Nehru and Chou En-lai. 1959:
left Tibet following the Lhasa
Uprising. Made unsuccessful
appeals to United Nations on

behalf of Tibetan people. 1963: promulgated draft democratic constitution for Tibet; since then has conducted a government-in-exile at Dharamsala, North India, in accordance with this. Has also very successfully worked to resettle 100,000 Tibetan refugees and to preserve Tibetan religion and culture."
Snel: 277
HH the current XIVth Dalai Lama was awarded the Nobel Peace Prize in 1989.
Editor: na   #0737

◙ **DANA**
Syn: Alms; Charity
See also: Offerings; Golden-Colored King; Anathapindika

▸"[alms-giving]; hence, often used to refer to an offering, especially of food, to a monastic community."   Sume: 138
When practicing charity, keeping the precepts and performing all kinds of good deeds, Pure Land practitioners should always dedicate the merits gained toward rebirth in the Western Pure Land for themselves and all other sentient beings and vow to return to Samsara for the benefit of all.
Edit/Dia: 36   #2028

◙ **DASABHUMIKA SUTRA**
Syn: Ten Stages Chapter (Avatamsaka Sutra)
See also: Ten Stages; Avatamsaka sutra;   Fifty-two Levels of Bodhisattva Practice
----
▸"Mahayana text, the title of which translates to the 'Sutra on the Ten Stages.' It is [the 26th] chapter of a longer work known as the *Avatamsaka Sutra*, each circulating in its own right as an independent text. It is highly important in Mahayana practice because it clearly and thoroughly establishes the Ten Stages, or the last 10 of a total of 52 levels of cultivation, that the Bodhisattva must traverse on the path to Complete, Perfect Enlightenment (i.e. Buddhahood).
These are: the (1) 'Joyful Stage' (pramudita-bhumi), (2) 'Immaculate Stage' (vimala-bhumi), (3) 'Radiant Stage' (prabhakari-bhumi), (4) 'Blazing Stage' (Arcismati-bhumi), (5) 'Hard-to-Conquer Stage' (sudurjaya-bhumi), (6) 'Face-to-Face Stage' (abhimukhi-bhumi), (7) 'Going-Far-Beyond Stage' (durangama-bhumi), (8) 'Immovable Stage' (acala-bhumi), (9) 'Good-Thought Stage' (sadhumati-bhumi), and (10) 'Cloud-of-Dharma Stage'

(dharmamegha-bhumi). Other Buddhist texts, such as the Mahavastu in Sanskrit and the *P'u-sa-pen-yeh ching* in Chinese, present a tenfold path for Bodhisattva practice also, but none has attained the status and importance of the *Dasabhumika Sutra*."

Preb: 105-106 #1017

◙ **DAVID-NEEL, ALEXANDRA (1868-1969)**

►"Pioneering French mystic, traveler, and author. Born in Saint-Mandé (suburb of Paris). Discovered Eastern religion and philosophy at Musée Guimet in Paris at age 23: 'My vocation was born then and there.' Became a singer with Opera Comique; later turned to journalism. Married briefly in 1894. In East for next 20 years. Met exiled XIIIth Dalai Lama in Darjeeling. In Sikkim met Lama Yongden, her future traveling companion and adopted son. Went into retreat in Himalayan cave-hermitage; met Tibetan teachers who taught her Tibetan language and Buddhist philosophy. Ventured three times into Tibet. Subsequently left for Burma, Sri Lanka, and Japan, accompanied by Yongden; then to Korea, China, and Mongolia.

1925: returned to Europe; subsequently engaged in study and writing at Digne (Haute Provence) until death at age 101. 1964: made Commandeur de la Legion d'Honneur."

Snel: 277 #0738

◙ **DEAD TREE SAMADHI**
See also: Samadhi

►Samadhi and wisdom should always coexist and form a whole. Wisdom without Samadhi is termed "Dried-Up Wisdom". Samadhi not leading to wisdom is called "Dead Tree Samadhi" or deviant Samadhi.

Editor: na #1675

◙ **DEATH**
See also: Death and Burial; Rebirth in the Pure Land; Supportive Recitation; Three Doubts and Four Narrow Passes; Right Thoughts; Honen

----

►"The passage into the next life at the moment of death is a nearly impenetrable mystery for us who have not yet experienced it. There are published accounts of near-death experiences by people who have been resuscitated from clinical death ... the religions of the world are nearly unanimous in describing

[an uncomfortable event]: The individual undergoes a judgment where he must review his life with unsparing honesty. Yet even at that crucial moment *the dying person may, by focusing his mind on [a transcendental being] and accepting the Light that seems to embrace him, leap to a higher realm.*" (*World Scripture*)
Wilson: 240

"According to Buddhism, the death of any living being is inherent in its nature as a compounded entity: it is the dissociation of the constituent elements of a being. 'For the born there is no such thing as not dying'. Death is thus a natural function of the ongoing process of life. For just as a birth leads inevitably to a death, so a death leads inevitably to a birth. Of the five Skandhas, the most important is consciousness. At the death of an individual, these five skandhas contract, so to speak, to a zero-point; the momentum of life itself, however, carries the constituent elements on beyond this zero-point, to open out into new life; thus consciousness becomes associated with another form, another series of feelings, perceptions, etc."
Ling: 90

(I) Rebirth in Pure Land

"In literary and oral Buddhist lore, it is commonly believed that the last thoughts of a dying person have a direct influence on the status of rebirth in the next life. While this may seem a fairly straightforward matter of self-control -- just 'think good thoughts' -- it is complicated by the belief that, with the waning of one's conscious powers, the mind is overwhelmed by subliminal karmic propensities or 'memories' that manifest themselves as visions before the dying person. In this way, the habits and events of one's current and previous existences quite literally draw one towards one's future destiny. As frightful and unpredictable as it might seem, this liminal moment of transition between death and rebirth is considered a time of enormous spiritual potential. For at no other time (except, perhaps, upon attaining the knowledge of former lives that comes to accomplished meditation masters) is a person afforded such a chance to remove the veil between the conscious and unconscious dimensions of self, review directly his or her karmic stock, and refashion one's being. Master Shan Tao's rites for a

dying person, as well as the diverse repertoire of funerary ceremonies that are performed for the deceased over the forty-nine days following death, revolve around a common belief in the potency of this moment. The primary aim of Shan Tao's deathbed procedures is to ensure that the dying person successfully forges what is known as, 'the connection or nexus of conditions that will bring rebirth in the Pure Land' ... The successful forging of this 'connection with the Pure Land' is indicated by the appearance of the desired auspicious signs at the time of the person's death or, as the case may be, during the weeks of funerary observances that follow. Precedents for such a concept can be found in the Pure Land sutras themselves. The *Meditation Sutra*, for example, distinguishes various visionary things that will confirm for the dying person that he or she is destined for the Pure Land. Having set this prognostic tone, the 'ten moments of recollection (10 recitations) of Amitabha' are described as the only effective means for turning the situation around should less desirable omens appear and salvation be in doubt."
Lopez/95: 592

"Compared to the more difficult visualization, oral recitation is more accessible to the faithful. The *Meditation Sutra* offers recitation to spiritually limited beings on their deathbed. For instance, beings in the lowest of the nine grades of birth, who commited the Five Grave Offenses and the Ten Transgressions, cannot be mindful of the Buddha as instructed by even a virtuous teacher. But if they follow their teacher's exhortation to recite [on their deathbed] with sincere mind the name of Buddha Amitabha, they thereby eradicate their karmic retribution and are assured of rebirth. Recitation brings with it the eradication of karmic retribution. The prototype of recitation occurs in early Buddhist scriptures and invariably exemplifies a magical nature that often wards away imminent dangers. In the *Mahavastu*, for example, 500 merchants in a boat were about to be devoured by a giant fish but were saved when collectively they recited aloud with one pointedness of mind: 'We take refuge in the Buddha.'"
Tana: 10-11

"Among some Pure Land practicers, great attention is

given to ways of attending the dying so that the mind will remain focused on Amida and they will be capable of utterance of the nembutsu (Buddha Recitation) to the very end. For example, an image of Amida is often placed before dying people and strings leading from it are attached to their hands. At the same time, nembutsu (Buddha Recitation) practice throughout life is considered useful for maintaining such mindfulness at death. (See Patriarch Honen's death under 'Honen')"
Ueda: 250

"Also several like-minded companions should join together in an agreement so that when the end of life [of one of the companions] approaches, they will take turns until dawn reciting the name of the Buddha Amitabha and wish for the rebirth [of the dying companion] in Sukhavati. Voice follows upon voice until [one pointedness of mind] is accomplished."
Tana: 71 #1122

"Pure Land literature offers many stories presented as real life biographical accounts which corroborate the description of the Pure Land paradise drawn from the scriptures ... The stories often relate people's early experience of Buddhism, and note the various practices they took up and the scriptures they studied. In due time, their faith in Pure Land is awakened, perhaps by meeting an inspirational teacher, perhaps through a dream or vision, perhaps from hearing the Pure Land scriptures ... The climax of a Pure Land biography comes in the subject's death scene, when Buddha-name recitation is rewarded and the Pure Land teachings are confirmed. The believer dies peacefully, even joyously, with mind and body composed, in full confidence of rebirth in paradise, reciting the Buddha's name. (J.C Cleary, *Pure Land, Pure Mind*)"
Van Hien: 8

"There is even a place in the Western Paradise for the worst sinners. The *Meditation Sutra* relates that even if a person has committed the five or ten cardinal sins, if this sinner earnestly recites Amitabha's name ten times on his deathbed, a lotus throne will appear and will bear him to the lowest stage in the Pure Land -- the lowest birth of the lowest degree. Instead of being condemned to eighty million kalpas in hell, the sinner will be born in the Western Paradise in a closed lotus flower; after a period of six kalpas the lotus throne will open and release him. This teaching of the nine possible levels of birth was an extremely effective way to reward good deeds on earth while still offering the promise of salvation to all, regardless of how much merit they had accumulated." (Joji Okazaki, *Pure Land Buddhist Painting*: 52)

Okaz: 52

(II) Dedication of merits to the dead

To be truly effective in dedicating merit to others, the practitioner must be utterly sincere and singleminded in his recitation. Even so, the *Ksitigarbha Sutra* teaches that the deceased can only receive a small part of this merit. Furthermore, since the crucial conditions of sincerity and singlemindedness are seldom achieved in full, most intercessions are, at best, partially effective and can seldom erase a lifetime of bad karma. Thus, it is imperative for the practitioner himself to cultivate during his lifetime and not rely on family members, monks or nuns at the time of death. See "Right Thoughts"

Editor/Tam: 325

(III) Three Doubts / Four Narrow Passes

"Elder Master Tzu Chao once said: *The Pure Land practitioner on the verge of death usually faces Three Points of Doubt and Four Narrow Passes which obstruct his rebirth in the Pure Land. He should be prepared, reflecting on them in advance to eliminate them.*

[A] The Three Points of Doubt are:

1) *Fearing that his past karma* is heavy and his period of cultivation short, and that therefore, he may not achieve rebirth in the Pure Land;

2) *Fearing that he has not* yet fulfilled his vows and obligations or severed greed, anger and delusion, and that therefore, he may not achieve rebirth in the Pure Land;

3) *Fearing that even though* he has recited the Buddha's name, Buddha Amitabha may not come, and that therefore, he may not achieve rebirth in the Pure Land.

[B] The [main] Narrow Passes are:

1) Because of suffering due to illness, he may come to malign the Buddhas as ineffective and unresponsive;

2) Because of love-attachment, he may chain himself to his family, unable to let go.

Once aware of the doctrine of

the Three Doubts and the Four Narrow Passes, the wise can ponder and find a solution. The author shall merely summarize a few points below. Fellow cultivators can expand on them according to their own backgrounds and understanding.

[A] Overcoming the Three Doubts

(1) Previous heavy karma, present perfunctory practice. Amitabha Buddha is renowned for his Eighteenth Vow: not to attain Buddhahood unless sentient beings who sincerely desire to be reborn in the Pure Land, and who singlemindedly recite His name, are reborn there. The Buddhas do not engage in false speech, and therefore the practitioner should believe in them. Ten utterances or thoughts represent a very short cultivation period, yet the practitioner can still achieve rebirth in the Pure Land. We who have recited the Buddha's name many times over should, therefore, eliminate all doubts. Moreover, no matter how heavy the karma of sentient beings is, if they sincerely repent and rely upon Amitabha Buddha, they will all be welcomed and guided back to the Pure Land. Do we not recall that the *Meditation Sutra* teaches: If anyone who has committed the Five Grave Offenses or Ten Evil Deeds sees an evil omen appear as he is on the verge of death, he need only recite the Buddha's name one to ten times *singlemindedly*, and Buddha Amitabha will descend to welcome and escort him back to the Pure Land. In the commentary *Accounts of Rebirth*, there are cases of individuals who throughout their lives were breaking the precepts and engaging in all manner of evil conduct. Nevertheless, on their deathbeds, when the 'marks of hell' appeared and, desperate, they singlemindedly recited the Buddha's name, they immediately saw Amitabha Buddha arriving to welcome them. Why should we, who are not that sinful or deluded, worry about not achieving rebirth in the Pure Land?

(2) Unfulfilled vows; non-severance of greed, anger and delusion. Cultivators' vows can be divided into two categories: religious and mundane. *Religious vows*: Some practitioners have vowed to build a temple, practice charity or recite various sutras or mantras a certain number of times, etc. However, they have not completely fulfilled their vows when it is time for

them to die. These cultivators should think: reciting the Buddha's name *singlemindedly* will earn them rebirth in the Pure Land, where they will have ample opportunity to achieve immeasurable merits and virtues. Their present vows to build temples and recite sutras are merely secondary matters. The fact that they may not have fulfilled them should be of no great concern. *Mundane vows*: These include family obligations such as caring for sick, aging parents or helpless wives and young children, as well as business debts to be paid or certain other commitments to be fulfilled. Faced with these worries, the practioners should think: on our deathbed, there is nothing that can be done, whether we worry or not. It is better to concentrate on Buddha Recitation. Once we are reborn in the Pure Land and Buddhahood is achieved, all vows, wishes and debts can be taken care of, as we will be in a position to rescue everyone, family and foes alike. The *Questions of King Milinda Sutra* contains the following parable: A minute grain of sand, dropped on the surface of the water, will sink immediately. On the other hand, a block of stone, however large and heavy, can easily be moved from place to place by boat. The same is true of the Pure Land practitioner. However light his karma may be, if he is not rescued by Amitabha Buddha, he must revolve in the cycle of Birth and Death. With the help of Amitabha Buddha, his karma, however heavy, will not prevent his rebirth in the Pure Land. We can see from this passage that thanks to 'other-power,' the Pure Land method can benefit the practitioner, however heavy his karma may be. The huge block of stone represents the weight of heavy karma, the boat symbolizes the power of Amitabha Buddha's Vows. Therefore, the cultivator should not think that residual greed, anger and delusion will prevent him from achieving rebirth in the Pure Land. This example should also resolve doubts concerning past heavy karma, as in doubt number one above.

(3) Despite recitation, Amitabha Buddha may not come, after all. At the time of death, the Pure Land practitioner will see, depending on his virtues, Amitabha Buddha, the Bodhisattvas or the Ocean-Wide

Assembly come to welcome him. Sometimes he may not see anything, but, thanks to the power of his vows and the 'gathering in' power of Amitabha Buddha, he will be reborn in the Pure Land all the same. The difference lies in his level of cultivation, whether subtle or gross, transcendental or mundane. What is most important at the time of death is to recite the Buddha's name in all earnestness and not worry about anything else. Any doubts at that time will give rise to obstructions and impediments. In summary, at the time of death, the practitioner should not be concerned about whether or not he witnesses auspicious signs. He should just concentrate on reciting the Buddha's name in all earnestness until the very end.

[B] Overcoming the Narrow Passes
These 'passes' can be described as follows:
- Slandering the Buddhas because of suffering and disease;
- Binding and chaining oneself to family and friends through love-attachment.

1. Sincere practitioners who meet with accidents, disease and disaster should reflect that these are sometimes due to virtues accrued through cultivation.

Either the heavy karma (which he should have endured) has been commuted to light karma (which he is now enduring), or else, future karma has been transformed into current karma, giving him the opportunity to repay karmic debts before achieving rebirth in the Pure Land. Should he doubt this and speak ill of the Dharma, he would lack faith and understanding, display ingratitude toward the Buddhas and bring evil karma upon himself. Among the rebirth stories, we find instances where this 'bunching and compressing of karma' has allowed cultivators to hasten their rebirth in the Pure Land. Therefore, when Pure Land cultivators encounter such instances, they should be aware and understand them thoroughly. Furthermore, this body is illusory and provisional. Depending on his merit or bad karma, the practitioner's life will be long or short, happy or filled with hardship. He should systematically rely on the Buddhas and firmly believe in the law of cause and effect.

When ill or in bad health, the practitioner should direct his thoughts toward Amitabha Buddha exclusively. He should not seek the help of externalist gurus, shamans or healers. Nor should he listen to those who do not yet understand the Dharma and revert to a non-vegetarian diet, drink alcoholic beverages, etc. Our bodies are truly full of filth; the sooner we return to the Pure Land, the better. It is like casting off a smelly, ragged garment and donning a beautiful, fragrant outfit. What is there to worry about?

2. Concerning the danger of love-attachment at the time of death, as indicated earlier, the practitioner should think thus: family members, including parents, brothers, sisters, husbands, wives and children, are temporarily gathered together in this life as a result of previous causes and conditions, such as karmic debts or love and hatred, accumulated from time immemorial. When these causes and conditions come to an end, we all part and go our separate ways. If we truly care for them, we should endeavor to be reborn in the Pure Land, so as to be able to save everyone, friend and foe alike. Although we may have attachments to family and friends, when death approaches, there is nothing we can bring along or do, as even our very

body disintegrates and returns to dust. If we harbor thoughts of attachment and love, not only will we fail to achieve rebirth in the Pure Land, we will not escape the endless cycle of Birth and Death. The practitioner should ponder and clearly recall the Three Doubts and Four Narrow Passes to prepare himself. His mind will then be calm and undisturbed at the time of death."

Tam: 276-281

NOTES:

(1) Buddhism makes a distinction between physical (clinical) death and mental death, with the former preceding the latter by a period of some three to eight hours. Actual death is defined as that moment when the Alaya consciousness leaves the body -- not when the heart has stopped or brain waves can no longer be detected. This is the reason for the waiting period of at least three hours after clinical death before the body is disturbed.

Editor / Tam: 324

(2) "Although *the last state of consciousness of one 'life' is held to be of great importance for the first state of consciousness of the ensuing one*; if it was wholesome, this will produce a 'wholesome' inauguration of a new life.

Similarly, if it was unwholesome, the ensuing new life will be unwholesomely inaugurated. It is not this last state only which determines the character of the new life; the whole previous life has produced a momentum of a wholesome or unwholesome kind, in varying degrees, which will inevitably have effects upon the ongoing course of life."
Ling: 90-91
For details, *See also:* "Seeing Buddha" and "Death and Burial".
#2292

🔘 DEATH AND BURIAL (BETWEEN --)
See also: Death; Supportive Recitation

▸"Tibetans' casual attitude toward corpses is in marked contrast to their attentive behavior at the very hour of death and immediately after it has occurred. This behavior, quite dissimilar to ours in the West, seems to objective eyes far more civilized, for it is the Western practice to remove a body from its deathbed in crude haste, almost before it is cold, in order to embark immediately on whatever is needed to prepare it for public display, or cremation. Dehumanized hospital

regulations permit [little] latitude for any possible 'rites of passage' at this great moment when life is exchanged for death. [Buddhists among them], Tibetans, on the contrary, pay special attention to such rites."
Ross: 128 ﹏
"When a person has just died, the most important thing is not to rush to move him. Even if his body is soiled with excrement and urine, we should not hasten to clean it. We should wait about eight hours -- or a minimum of three hours -- before cleaning the body and changing its clothes. Relatives should not weep and wail immediately before and after the actual death. Doing so is not only useless, it can be harmful, as this can cause the deceased to develop thoughts of attachment, which may prevent him from achieving liberation. To be of true benefit to the patient, we should concentrate on reciting the Buddha's name in all earnestness, without crying until at least eight hours have passed. Why is this necessary? It is because although the patient has left his body, if, during this period, we move the body, clean it, change its clothes, or weep and lament, the deceased may still experience feelings of pain,

sadness, anger or self-pity, and descend upon the Evil Paths. This is a crucial point -- a critical one -- that relatives should note and remember well. The practice of touching the body of the deceased to locate the last warm spot and deduce his place of rebirth is grounded in the sutras and commentaries. However, we should not be inflexible. *If the patient had sincere, earnest faith and vows in normal times and clearly exhibits right thought at the time of death, this is sufficient evidence of rebirth in the Pure Land.* Some persons who are not careful keep 'feeling' the body, touching one spot after another, disturbing the deceased. This can cause great harm. After the patient has expired, the persons who came to recite the Buddha's name should continue doing so for another three hours. After that, the body should be left alone, free of all disturbances, for another five hours (or a total of eight hours), at which time it can be bathed and given a change of clothing. If, during the entire eight-hour period, someone, or a group of persons, can remain near the deceased reciting the Buddha's name, so much the better. Except for recitation, nothing should be done. *A*

reminder and caveat: during this period, the 'deceased' may still have consciousness and feelings. After the eight-hour period, if the limbs have grown stiff and cannot be moved, we should put a towel soaked in hot water around the joints. After a while, the body can be repositioned."
Thich: 288-289
NOTE:
Buddhism makes a distinction between physical (clinical) death and mental death, with the former preceding the latter by a period of some three to eight hours. Actual death is defined as the moment when the Alaya consciousness leaves the body -- not when the heart has stopped or brain waves can no longer be detected. This is the reason for the waiting period of at least three hours after clinical death before the body is disturbed, as taught in Mahayana Buddhism, particularly the Pure Land and Tantric schools. Many hospitals nowadays recognize these beliefs and are prepared to meet the wishes of bereaved families and relatives. Editor/Thich: 323-324

◉ **DEATH (PHYSICAL VS. MENTAL)**

►Buddhism makes a distinction

between physical (clinical) death and mental death, with the former preceding the latter by a period of some three to eight hours. Actual death is defined as the moment when the Alaya consciousness leaves the body -- not when the heart has stopped or brain waves can no longer be detected. This is the reason for the waiting period of at least three hours after clinical death before the body is disturbed, as taught in Mahayana Buddhism, particularly the Pure Land and Tantric schools. Many hospitals nowadays recognize these beliefs and are prepared to meet the wishes of bereaved families and relatives.

Editor/Thich: 323-324　#1377

◉ **DEATH MEDITATION**
see　Meditation on Death

◉ **DEATH PENALTY**
syn: Capital Punishment

▸"*Question*: What is the Buddhist view on the death penalty?
Answer: Life is the most valuable possession any person has, even if that person acts in a criminal manner. Buddhism recommends rehabilitation or imprisonment rather than execution. The proper motivation is needed for imprisoning others, however. That is, imprisonment is to protect a person from harming others and from creating more negative karma that would bring him or her misery later. Seeking revenge or feeling glee at punishing others are opposite to the kind heart that Buddhism encourages us to develop."
Buddhist Union/ Oct. 96: 6-7

◉ **DEATH SIGNS**
see　Proofs of rebirth in Pure Land

◉ **DEDICATION OF MERIT**
Syn:　Merit Transference; Transfer of merit
See also: Other Power; Atonement; Pure Land School

▸The concept of dedication of merit (merit transference) is particularly important in Mahayana Buddhism, and is stressed in the Pure Land School with its teaching of Other Power, the power of the Buddha Amitabha.
Editor: na
"The concept of merit transference, or sharing one's own merits and virtues with others, is reflected in the following passage:
'Some of us may ask whether the

effect of evil karma can be ... changed by repeating the name of Kuan-Yin (Avalokitesvara). This question is tied up with that of rebirth in Sukhavati [the Pure Land] and it may be answered by saying that the invocation of Kuan-Yin's name forms another cause which will right away offset the previous karma. We know, for example, that if there is a dark, heavy cloud above, the chances are that it will rain. But we also know that if a strong wind should blow, the cloud will be carried away somewhere else and we will not feel the rain. Similarly, the addition of one big factor can alter the whole course of karma ... It is only by accepting the idea of life as one whole that both Theravadins and Mahayanists can advocate the practice of transference of merit to others. With the case of Kuan-Yin then, by calling on Her name we identify ourselves with Her and as a result of this identification, Her merits flow over to us. These merits which a r e n o w o u r s, t h e n counterbalance our bad karma and save us from calamity. The Law of Cause and Effect still stands good. All that has happened is that a powerful and immensely good karma has overshadowed the weaker one.' (Lecture on Kuan-Yin by Tech Eng Soon - Penang Buddhist Association, c. 1960. Pamphlet.)"
Tam: 141

"If the Buddha's name or a passage from the Sutras, is properly repeated and if one puts one's mind upon it with deep reverence, one will thereby acquire merit. *The amount of merit thus acquired will depend upon the mental state.* Mere mechanical repetition is (in theory) worthless. On the other hand, the repetition of almost any text may acquire merit if repeated with great reverence. The merit thus acquired is transferable (a good Mahayana doctrine, it will be remembered), though a certain amount of it will be lost in the process. Pious women often transfer the merit they have acquired through vows and penances to the members of their family. Most frequently it is to the dead that merit is transferred."
Pratt: 363

"The conception of vicarious suffering and the transference of merit is on the surface hardly in harmony with what I have called the intellectual aspect of the Buddha's teaching and his emphasis upon self-help. On the

other hand, it is the natural, perhaps even the necessary, outcome of the heart element of Buddhism, of the Founder's devotion and of the devotion of all loving souls. If the great enlightenment is not merely an intellectual achievement but a new experience of sharing our common life, we may perhaps say with Professor D.T Suzuki that the possibility of sharing our merit and others' is the 'logical outcome of enlightenment-consciousness.' 'What made Buddhism great as a universal religion [Suzuki adds] was the discovery of this principle. . . . The law of Karma may be true and should be made to work in our practical and intellectual plane of life, but it is too rigid, too exclusive, too individualistic, and above all, it goes against our religious yearnings. We want to suffer for others and when this is not practicable, we want to send out our thoughts and sympathies to them. If we are at all spiritual beings capable of enlightenment, this thought communication or mystical interpenetration must be possible.'" (D.T. Suzuki, "Development of the Pure Land Doctrine in Buddhism," *Eastern Buddhist*, III, 311-12.)
Pratt: 218

NOTE:
To be truly effective in dedicating merit to others, the practitioner must be utterly sincere and singleminded in his recitation. Even if he is, the *Ksitigarbha Sutra* teaches that the deceased can only receive a small part of this merit. Furthermore, since the crucial conditions of sincerity and singlemindedness are seldom achieved in full, most intercessions are, at best, partially effective and can seldom erase a lifetime of bad karma. Thus, it is imperative for the practitioner himself to cultivate during his lifetime and not rely on family members, monks or nuns at the time of death.
Editor/Tam: 325   #0076

◙ DEER PARK (SARNATH/ INDIA)

See also: Sarnath

▸"The name of a park in Varanasi, India, the site of present-day Sarnath. The Deer Park was also called Rishi-patana or 'the place where hermits gather.' Here Shakyamuni delivered his first sermon. After his enlightenment under the Bodhi tree, the Buddha went to the Deer Park where he expounded the Four Noble

Truths and converted five ascetics including Kaundinya. Hsuan-tsang's *Records of the Western Regions* explains the origin of the name Deer Park: The lord of Varanasi once hunted and killed many deer on this land. The deer king implored him to stop the unnecessary killing and promised that each day he himself would give the lord the number of deer which he required. One day, he was faced with the necessity of sending a pregnant deer. Rather than sacrifice her with her unborn child, the deer king went to the lord to offer his own flesh instead. The lord was so moved by the deer king's compassion that he stopped the daily killing and gave it the land. Hence it was named the Deer Park. Varanasi prospered until the Muslim invasion in the thirteenth century. Many stupas and monasteries were built in this area." Sokk: 59-60 #0313

◉ **DEFILEMENTS**
see Thoughts

◉ **DEFINITIVE MEANING**
Syn: Foremost meaning; Exhaustive meaning
See also: Ultimate Truth

▸"Those teachings of Buddha that are in terms of ultimate reality, as opposed to relative reality. Definitive meaning relates to voidness."
Thur: 132 #1227

◉ **DEGENERATE AGE**
see Dharma-Ending Age

◉ **DELUSION**
Syn: Ignorance
See also: Delusions of Views and Thoughts; Surangama Sutra; Wrong Views
----
▸"Delusion refers to a belief in something that contradicts reality. In Buddhism, delusion is a lack of awareness of the true nature or Buddha-nature of things, or of the true meaning of existence. According to the Buddhist outlook, we are deluded by our senses -- among which intellect (discriminating, discursive thought) is included as a sixth sense. Consciousness, attached to a sense, leads us into error by causing us to take the world of appearances for the world of reality, whereas in fact it is only a limited and fleeting aspect of reality." (*Shambhala Dictionary of Buddhism and Zen.*)
"[Delusion is] the fundamental error which brings about

existence. The word is used in the common sense of the most basic cause in the development of discriminations. It is the initial perception of either existence or non-existence when in reality there is neither one nor the other. This topic is treated at very great length in the *Surangama Sutra*." Hua: 230

Buddhism of Wisdom & Faith/ excerpts:

"Delusion (ignorance) is the source of all afflictions. Greed and anger stem from delusion, as do pride, doubts and 'wrong views'. For example, when we have such thoughts as: 'I have few equals in hard and assiduous cultivation, even among the ranks of monks and nuns' -- this is the affliction of pride and self-love. If, on the other hand, we develop such thoughts as: 'The Land of Ultimate Bliss is so well-adorned, while I have heavy karma and few merits; how do I know I will achieve rebirth there?' -- this is the affliction of doubt. Wrong views consist of seeing and understanding in a wicked and grasping manner. They include five types: Wrong Views of the Body, One-Sided Views, Wrong Views Not Consistent with the Dharma, Wrong Views Caused by Attachment to one's own Erroneous Understanding and Wrong Views (understanding) of the Precepts. For example, during cultivation a thought suddenly arises: 'My health has always been poor, and today I feel tired, worn out; if I continue to recite the Buddha's name, I may fall ill.' This is an example of a *Wrong View of the Body*. Or else, we think: 'Death is like a candle which has gone out; if there was a previous life, how come I cannot remember it? It is better for me to follow Taoism, to prolong my life and avoid death.' This is an instance of a *One-Sided View*. Or else, we wonder why someone who had performed only good deeds had a short life and met a violent death, while others who had committed numerous transgressions lived long lives and died peacefully; thus, cultivation brings no benefit whatsoever! These are instances of *Wrong Views Not Consistent with the Dharma*, and failure to understand that the law of cause and effect spans many lifetimes. Or else, someone might think, 'I used to follow the externalist practice of circulating energy currents, and was achieving results in barely a few months. How is it that I have been

reciting the Buddha's name for a long time, but have not yet seen any change?' This is an instance of *Attachment to one's own Erroneous Understandings.* Or else, we may think: 'In other religions, people who hurt and kill other sentient beings can still be reborn in paradise; therefore, in seeking rebirth in the Pure Land, there is no need to keep the precept against killing.' This is an instance of *Wrong View of the Precepts.* The karma of delusion takes numerous forms. The Pure Land practitioner should, first and foremost, follow the sutras and put his entire faith in them. If he fails to understand certain passages, he should seek out good spiritual advisors for an explanation. Delusion can easily lead the practitioner astray when he is challenged by other teachings and ideologies."
Tam: 161-162
NOTES:
According to Mahayana teaching, there are, in total, 52 levels of ignorance (delusion), in ascending order of subtlety.
Editor / Tam: 146
"The real problem for Buddhist practitioners is... spiritual ignorance, which is not just an intellectual defect but a lack of understanding of reality which can be overcome by meditational insight."
Larousse: 136 #1334
See also: next entry.

◙ **DELUSIONS OF VIEWS AND THOUGHT**
See also: Upside-down living; Wrong Views

▸*Delusions of Views* refer to lust and greed for externals (clothing, food, sleep, etc.), which are viewed as real rather than empty in their true nature.
Delusions of Thought consist in being confused about principles and giving rise to discrimination .. Thought delusions are unclear, muddled thoughts, taking what is wrong as right, and what is right as wrong (Master Hsuan Hua).
Ou-i/3rd ed.: 170
Delusions of Views, simply put, are delusions connected with seeing and grasping at the gross level. *Delusions of Thought* are afflictions at the subtle level.
NOTE:
"In the Buddhist world view, the probability of eliminating all delusions of views and thought and escaping Birth and Death in one lifetime of cultivation is nil. (Apparent exceptions are practitioners in the last lifetime of cultivation or Bodhisattvas

who have taken human form to convert sentient beings.) After all, even Buddha Sakyamuni, the founder of Buddhism, underwent eons of rebirth as exemplified in the Jakata Tales. This is also the case with Buddha Amitabha and the Bodhisattva Maitreya -- the Buddha of the future."

PLZ: 120

Unless a practitioner has succeeded in severing both types of delusions *completely*, he will not be able to escape Birth and Death. This is the rationale for seeking rebirth in the Pure Land, an ideal place to continue cultivation until all such delusions are severed.

Editor: na #2250

◉ DEMONS

Syn: Devil; Hallucinations
See also: Mara; visions; obstacles to cultivation

▶Evil influences which hinder cultivation and impede one's practice and liberation. These can take an infinite number of forms, including evil beings and hallucinations. Disease and death, as well as the three poisons of greed, anger and delusion, are also equated to demons, as they disturb the mind. The *Nirvana Sutra* lists four types

of demons: 1) greed, anger and delusion; ii) the five skandas, or obstructions caused by physical and mental functions, iii) death; iv) the demon of the Sixth Heaven (Realm of Desire).

Editor: na

The Self-Nature has been described in Mahayana sutras as a house full of gold and jewelry. To preserve the riches, i.e., to keep the mind calm, empty and still, we should shut the doors to the three thieves of greed, anger and delusion. Letting the mind wander opens the house to 'demons,' that is, hallucinations and harm. Thus, Zen practitioners are taught that, while in meditation, 'Encountering demons, kill the demons, encountering Buddhas, kill the Buddhas.' Both demons and Buddhas are mind-made, Mind-Only. For a detailed discussion of demons/hallucination, see Master Thích Thiên Tâm, *Buddhism of Wisdom and Faith*, sect. 51.

Editor: na

"There are numerous classes of demons mentioned in the Buddhist scriptures. The personification of evil is usually called Mara or the Demon of the Sixth Heaven."

Hump: 64 #2205

◙ **DEMONS (HOW TO COPE WITH --)**

See also: Mara; Visions

<u>*Buddhism of Wisdom & Faith*/ excerpts:</u>

▸"Ancient masters have said: 'When we see demons yet remain undisturbed, the demons self-destruct; when we see ghosts yet remain undisturbed, the ghosts are vanquished.' This saying means: if we see demons and ghosts but our minds are unmoved and unafraid, holding fast to correct thoughts or singlemindedly reciting the Buddha's name, these demons and ghosts cannot hurt us in any way and will leave of their own accord. Not only should we act in such a manner when seeing demons, but even when we achieve some results or see auspicious marks during cultivation, we should not be moved to astonishment, sadness or joy. It is as if we had lost a diamond at the bottom of the lake and because the water was murky, we were unable to recover it despite our best efforts. However, once the water became still and transparent, we found it. Since the diamond had always belonged to us, why should we have been astonished and happy? If the cultivator's mind is not calm and peaceful and is overly given to sorrowful compassion, he will be harmed by the demon of sorrow and cry all the time. If he is given to too much happiness, he will be harmed by the demon of happiness and laugh all the time, as though insane. Thus, although the Pure Land practitioner may also hope to see transcendental realms and scenes, he should not long for or dream of them too much, because to recite is already to seek. He should be calm and 'seek, but not seek, not seek but seek,' so as to avoid disturbing his mind. He should just earnestly recite the Buddha's name and in time, when the power of his recitation is pure, there will be a response and he will witness auspicious realms. To continuously seek and hope for them is deluded thought which brings harm."

Thich: 204 #1371

◙ **DEPENDENT AND MAIN REWARDS**

See also: Sukhavati

▸In the Pure Land tradition, the "main rewards" are the exalted features of Buddha Amitabha and other superior beings in the Land of Bliss, while the "dependent reward" is the ideal environment of the Land itself. The concept of main and dependent rewards can be found in our everyday life where a person with a good karma usually has noble features (main rewards) and inhabits a safe area free of crime and drugs (dependent rewards).

"Dependent and main rewards are based on past karmic actions. The 'main rewards' refer to living beings, while the 'dependent rewards' refer to the physical environment on which the living beings 'depend,' such as the land, ponds, trees, and so forth."

Tana: 244 #1733

◙ DEPENDENT ORIGINATION

Syn: Interdependent Origination. Dependent causation, dependent origination, conditioned co-arising or co-production.

►(Skt / pratitya-samutpada.)"The central principle that phenomena do not come into existence on their own but as a result of conditions. Nagarjuna identifies inter-dependent origination (pratitya-samutpada) with emptiness (shunyata)."

Cleary/Chih-I: 197

"A fundamental Buddhist doctrine of the interdependence of things. It teaches that all beings and phenomena exist or occur only because of their relationship with other beings or phenomena. Therefore, nothing can exist in absolute independence of other things or arise of its own accord. The doctrine of the Twelve-Linked Chain of causation is a well-known illustration."/Sokk:62

"Since all things in the phenomenal world are brought into being by the combination of various causes and conditions, they are relative and without substantiality or self-entity. From the transcendental viewpoint, this absence of self-entity is called emptiness; from the phenomenal viewpoint, it is called dependent generation, and is the central doctrine of Buddhism that denies the existence of any form of eternal or substantial being. When applied to sentient beings' endless lives in Samsara, it becomes the Twelve Links of Dependent Origination."

Chan: 473

◙ DESCENT (OF AMITABHA)
see Raigo

◙ DEVA
Syn: Gods; Celestial; Heavenly being

▸"A divinity or god; a heavenly being. Devas, including Hindu gods, are believed to inhabit the heavens above the human realm, but are still unenlightened, bound to Samsara and subject to Birth and Death. Many such beings have already been converted to Buddhism and become its protectors."
Inag: 395
"A 'celestial,' one of the inhabitants of the heavens. In the Buddhist conception of the cosmos, celestials and godlings inhabit marvel-filled realms on the summit of Mount Sumeru and beyond. These are utopian places of rest, bliss and peaceful abstraction. Living beings reborn in one of these blissful realms are gods. Any living being can be reborn as one of the gods if that living being has the required merit and virtue."
Gomez: 300   #0692

◉ **DEVA-EAR**
Syn: Divine ear; Supernatural hearing
See also: Spiritual powers

▸"One of six miraculous powers. Supernatural hearing is the ability to hear the sounds of humans and nonhumans, distant and near sounds, and so on. The degree of this power differs according to one's karmic reward or yogic (samadhi) achievement."
Chan: 474   #0512

◉ **DEVADATTA**
See also: Good Spiritual Advisors

▸"A cousin of Sakyamuni Buddha and his most persistent enemy. According to the Pali Canon, he twice tried to kill him, as well as attempting to cause schisms in the Sangha (community of Monks and Nuns)."
Hump: 64
In the Mahayana canon (particularly in the *Lotus Sutra*) Devadatta is considered to be a Bodhisattva in disguise who through his constant "needling" of the Buddha helped the latter perfect his Enlightenment. Thus Devadatta is called an "adverse-practice" Good Spiritual Advisor.
Editor: na   #0056

◉ **DEVANAMPIYA TISSA**
See also: Sri Lanka (Buddhism in)

▸"King who ruled Sri Lanka from 247-207 B.C. and was responsible for the introduction of Buddhism to the island. Although Devanampiya Tissa already knew

about Buddhism from King Asoka, his first real occasion for receiving Buddhist teaching came from Mahinda, Asoka's missionary to Sri Lanka. After meeting, quite possibly in Mihintale, Mahinda and his associates were invited to the capital of Anuradhapura. The king offered Mahameghavana Park to the Sangha, on the site that eventually became the Mahavihara monastery. Within a short period, young men from Sri Lanka were initiated into the Sangha, thus establishing a valid ordination lineage on the island. A branch of the Bodhi Tree was brought from India, the Vinaya was recited, and an order of nuns was established. By the end of Devanampiya Tissa's reign, Buddhism in Sri Lanka was firmly entrenched." Preb: 107
"The order of nuns essentially died out in Sri Lanka in the eleventh century."
Preb: 12   #1018

◙ DEVOTION

See also: Faith; Pure Land Buddhism in Summary; Other Power; Buddha Recitation

----

▸"Sometimes it is suggested that the emphasis on devotion as providing a special kind of

salvation is unnatural in Buddhism and alien to the earlier tradition. Yet even the earliest form of Buddhism known to us taught that faith in the Buddha was able both to bring about a heavenly rebirth and to set one firmly on the path to liberation. The difference is in the Mahayana emphasis on the 'power of resolve' [other power] of a Buddha, which is capable of creating enormously favourable conditions."
Hinn: 324 #1930

◙ DHAMMA (Pali)
see Dharma

◙ DHAMMAPADA SUTRA

▸Exists in 2 versions : Theravada and Mahayana
"The Path or Way of the Buddha's Dhamma or Teaching. The most famous scripture in the Pali Canon."   Hump: 66
(1) "The *Dhammapada* [in its Theravada version] came to be written down in the first century BC. It is one of the fifteen books of the Khuddaka-Nikaya and it is made up of some 423 verses arranged by topic into 26 chapters. These verses are descriptions of the way to live, the life of meditation and the

practice of reason and intelligence. There are many exhortations to cast off craving and orient yourself towards enlightenment. It is not just a book of morality, it seeks to go further than that. Luckily the verses are easy to read and to memorize, and the many translations have given the Dhammapada worldwide popularity, representing for Buddhism what the Bhagavad Gita is for Hinduism and the Tao Te Ching is for Taoism." Bancroft: 4

(2) "In its Mahayana version, a sutra consisting of two sections and divided into thirty-nine chapters. It was translated into Chinese during the Wu dynasty (A.D. 222-80). A collection of moral teachings, it stresses good conduct stabilized by concentration and strengthened by perfect Wisdom."/ Yoko: 202

The *Dhammapada* was translated into Latin in 1855. This is said to have been one of the first Buddhist texts to be introduced to the West.   Sokk: 164

◉ **DHAMMAPALA**
see Anagarika Dharmapala

◉ **DHARANI**
see Mantra

◉ **DHARANI OF THE MOST COMPASSIONATE ONE**
see Great Compassion Mantra

◉ **DHARMA / DHAMMA**
Syn: Buddha Dharma; Dhamma

▸"The word Dharma has several meanings: a) The teachings of the Buddhas (generally capitalized in English); b) law, doctrine; c) things, events, phenomena."   Tam: 147

"In the centuries that followed the Buddha's death, various attempts were made to organize and formulate his teachings. Different systems appeared, basing themselves on the recorded scriptures, each purporting to express the Buddha's intended meaning... That there should be a multiplicity of systems is not in itself surprising. From the time of his enlightenment until his death fifty years later, the Buddha bestowed his teachings for the benefit of many different audiences. The purpose of his doctrine was always the same: to liberate beings from the round of suffering. The expression of this purpose, however, differed according to the capacity of his hearers. It is therefore to be expected that the body of

teachings remaining after his departure from the world should be rich and varied, containing elements that sometimes even contradict each other. The Madhyamika deals with this state of affairs by saying that statements made by the Buddha are of two kinds: *absolute* (nitartha), corresponding to his true meaning, as understood by himself, and *expedient* (neyartha), corresponding to a partial expression of his meaning, geared to the understanding of his hearers, intended to lead them along the path to perfect comprehension and being therefore of provisional validity. Parallel with this division is the doctrine of the two truths: *absolute truth* (paramartha) corresponding to reality, and *relative truth* (samvriti) corresponding to empirical experience. According to Nagarjuna, the Buddha skillfully graduated his teaching according to pedagogical necessity. He affirmed the existence of the *atman*, the self, as against the 'nihilist' (who disbelieves in survival after death), in order to maintain the truth of karma and ethical responsibility. By contrast, he denied the existence of the *atman*, as against the 'eternalist' (who takes the self to be a changeless essence). [In other words,] He said that there is neither self nor no-self."
Shantiveda: 21

Birds, trees preaching the Dharma:
This can be understood as an allegory, similar to the traditional definition of a Pratyeka Buddha: a sage who becomes enlightened by observing the falling leaves and realizing, for example, the impermanence of life. In this sense the falling leaves can be said to preach the Dharma (the Buddha's teachings). The image of inanimate objects, such as the ground, trees, rain, precious stones, etc. expounding the Teachings is found throughout such high-level Mahayana texts as the *Avatamsaka Sutra*: "Buddha's blessings and mystical powers/ Adorn everywhere with precious gemstones;/ The ground and the enlightenment tree/ Alternately emit light and sound expressing the truth./ Precious lamps, infinite, rain from the sky,/ Studded with regal sapphires,/ All emitting subtle sounds speaking truth ..." (T. Cleary, *The Flower Ornament Scripture*, Vol. I, p. 139).
Editor: na

NOTE: The various teachings of the Buddha constitute a totality. While it is said that the Buddha taught 84,000 methods in accordance with the capacity of his listeners, *on another level* we can also say that individuals receive and understand these teachings differently. It is like rain which falls equally on all vegetation. However, the big trees absorb more of the rain water than the smaller trees, while a dead bush cannot benefit at all. The differences between Buddhist schools are similar: they are caused by the different capacities of Buddhist followers and not by the Buddha preaching different teachings to different audiences. (See the *Lotus Sutra*). Editor: na   #0508

◉ **DHARMA BODY**
Syn: Dharma-kaya; Dharmakaya
See also: Three Bodies of the Buddha

▸"In Mahayana Buddhism, the 'truth-body' or Dharma Body of the Buddhas is conceived as a universal metaphysical principle."
Reat: 324
"'Dharma-Body,' third of the three bodies of the Buddha in Mahayana, and used as a synonym for ultimate reality.

Although present in earlier Mahayana thought, later texts like the *Lankavatara Sutra* developed the notion of the three bodies of the Buddha more fully, with the concept coming to maturity in the Yogacara school. There, the historical body of Buddha was referred to as an 'a p p a r i t i o n a l   b o d y' (*Nirmana-kaya*) visible to ordinary, common worldlings as an inspiration to begin the (Mahayana) Buddhist path. Once on the path, as a Bodhisattva, one relates to a Buddha in another form: 'enjoyment body' (*S a m b h o g a - k a y a*), a quasi-physical preacher of Mahayana sutras. Finally, at the completion of the path, one attains the 'Dharma Body' (*Dharma-kaya*), the true nature of Buddhahood, described in a variety of technical terms, all used virtually synonymously: Tathata (Suchness), Tathagata-garbha (Womb of the Tathagata), Buddhata (State of Buddhahood), and so forth. In other words, each of the three bodies of the Buddha speaks to an individual at a different level of spiritual development, with Dharma-kaya representing the true, ultimate reality."
Preb: 111   #0249

◙ **DHARMA DOOR**
Syn: Dharma Gate; School;
Method; Tradition
See also: Door of Liberation

▶"A figurative term [for a
particular school or tradition, for
example, Zen, Pure Land], a
specific doctrine, implying that it
is an entry-way to an
understanding the Dharma."
TC Chen: 477 #1254

◙ **DHARMA DOOR OF
EMPTINESS**
see Existence/Emptiness

◙ **DHARMA DOOR OF
EXISTENCE**
see Existence/Emptiness

◙ **DHARMA ENDING AGE**
see Dharma-Ending Age
(note hyphen!)

◙ **DHARMA EYE**

▶"The eye of truth that perceives
reality. Usually stands for the
perception of Bodhisattvas and
Buddhas." Chen: 166 #0837

◙ **DHARMA GATE**
see Dharma door

◙ **DHARMA KING**
Syn: King of the Dharma

See also: Buddha; Dharma
Prince; Dharma

▶"Refers to a Buddha because he
has realized the Dharma, become
one with it and is capable of
employing it freely."
Inag: 405 #0708

◙ **DHARMA MASTER**

▶In Mahayana Buddhism, an
honorific title for a monk of
maturity and high standing.

◙ **DHARMA NATURE**
See also: Suchness

▶"Dharmata, the absolute nature
underlying all phenomena;
Reality. Often used as a synonym
for Nirvana, Buddha-nature,
suchness, etc." Chen: 166
"The quintessence, or true
nature, of all things. Same as
emptiness, suchness, reality,
Dharma-realm, Buddha-nature."
Chan: 474 #0515

◙ **DHARMA PRINCE**
See also: Dharma King

▶"Refers to a Bodhisattva
because he will become a
Dharma King, i.e. a Buddha;
especially used as the honorific
title for Manjusri." Inag: 396

◎ DHARMA REALM

Syn: Mind; Cosmos; Dharmadhatu; Realm of Reality; Realm of Truth

See also: Avatamsaka Sutra; Universe; Buddha Nature; Four Dharma Realms; Mind

----

▶ "Dharma Realm or Dharmadhatu. Literally, 'the realm of dharmas' or the cosmos, the universe. The reader should bear in mind that the term Dharma Realm can also mean the 'Mind'." Chan: 474

In Buddhist texts, the term Dharma Realm has several meanings: 1. The nature or essence of dharmas; 2. Infinity; 3. The infinite universe *per se*; 4. The mind, our mind, which has a fourfold activity ... In other words, "the universe is fourfold: a World (Realm) of factual, practical reality; a World of principle or theory; a World of principle and facts harmonized; and a World of factual realities interwoven and mutually identified. The last is the harmonious whole taught by the Avatamsaka, while the first three are the particular emphasis of other schools."

[NEB15,286]llVa

Stated in a different way, "these Four Realms are: i) the realm of events (or phenomena), which is the world of ordinary unenlightened perception; ii) the realm or truth ('principle' or noumenon) which is the ultimate non-dual reality, identified with 'mind' or 'emptiness' and which lies behind the illusory manifestation of phenomena; iii) the realm of non-obstruction of truth and phenomena which means that noumenon and phenomena are two aspects of the same thing, and that phenomena, rightly perceived, are noumenon or ultimate reality; iv) the realm of non-obstruction of phenomenon and phenomenon (Dharma Realm of All Phenomena Unobstructed), corresponding to Tu Shun's 'all in all,' and implying that each phenomenon, each spatio-temporal event, simultaneously includes all others."

[TP/HYV, p.149]

Dharma Realm is all things, all time, all places. It is one and we all are it.

NOTE:

"Ordinary people usually consider it difficult to become a Buddha. In fact, it is not so difficult. Both Buddhas and ordinary sentient beings are invariably molded out of perception and contemplation. In one thought, Buddhas pervade the ten Dharma Worlds (Dharma Realms). Likewise, a sentient being also pervades ten Dharma Worlds in one thought. If avarice arises at one thought, he is, indeed, a hungry ghost. If hatred arises at one thought, he is a hell-dweller. If delusion arises at one thought, he is a beast. If doubt and arrogance arise at one thought, he is an asura, a malevolent spirit. If one's thoughts fall on the Five Virtues, as well as the Five Precepts, he will enter the world of humans. If his thoughts touch upon the ten Good Karmas, he will be reborn in heaven. If his ideas are centered on the Four Noble Truths, he equals the Buddha's immediate disciples. If his mind dwells on the doctrine of Twelve Links of Causation, he is a Pratyekabuddha. If his ideas center on the Six Paramitas, he is a Bodhisattva. If his thoughts dwell on altruism and equality, he is indeed a Buddha." (Master T'an Hsu)

Amidism: 23-24 #0514

◙ **DHARMA REALM OF ALL PHENOMENA UNOBSTRUCTED**
Syn: Dharma realm of unobstructed phenomena

See also: Avatamsaka Sutra; Four Dharma Realms

►Avatamsaka school terminology. "Corresponds to Tu Shun's 'all in all,' and implies that each phenomenon, each spatio-temporal event, simultaneously includes all others." (Tony Prince) "Whatever their apparent differences, phenomena are the same in the sense of being dependent and hence void of absolute identity. The noumenal nature, or emptiness, of one phenomenon, being the same as that of all phenomena, is said to at once pervade and contain all phenomena; and as this is true of one, so is it true of all. Furthermore, the interdependence of phenomena means that ultimately one depends on all and all depend on one, whether immediately or remotely; therefore, the existence of all is considered an intrinsic part of the existence of one, and vice versa."

[TC/F01, p.20]a #1267

See also: Dharma Realm

◙ **DHARMA REALM OF UNOBSTRUCTED PHENOMENA**
see Dharma Realm of All Phenomena Unobstructed

◙ DHARMA REALM TREASURY BODY

▸In Pure Land Buddhism, Amitabha Buddha is the Dharma Realm Treasury Body because He is present everywhere in the Dharma Realm, i.e., the cosmos.
Editor/Zen: 48 #1438

◙ DHARMA SEALS

Syn: Three Dharma Seals; Three Marks of Existence
See also: Birth and Death; Impermanence; Suffering

▸Sakyamuni Buddha taught three *basic* Dharma seals, or criteria, to determine the genuineness of Buddhist teachings or truths: Impermanence; Suffering and No-self. In the Mahayana tradition, an additional set of Dharma Seals is often mentioned. The set, as taught in Mahayana sutras, consists of three seals: Emptiness, No-Mark (Marklessness, Signlessness), and No-Wish (Wishlessness).
Editor: na

NOTE:
An interesting corollary of the concept of Dharma seals is that much of the speculation about whether or not this or that sutra is genuine is, in a sense,

pointless. A sutra is a sutra because it contains the words of the Buddhas/ Bodhisattvas or because the ideas expressed in it conform to the Dharma seals. An example of the latter is the *Platform Sutra*, which records the words of the Sixth Patriarch.
Editor/Zen: 27 #1423

◙ DHARMA WHEEL

Syn: Dharmacakra

▸"Symbolizes the preaching of a Buddha. Dharma wheel is likened to a wheel because it crushes all illusions."
Yoko: 187 #0815

◙ DHARMA-ENDING AGE

Syn: Degenerate Age; Last Age; Mappo

▸The present spiritually degenerate era, twenty-six centuries since the demise of Shakyamuni Buddha. The concept of decline, dissension and schism within the Dharma after the passing of the Buddha is a general teaching of Buddhism and a corollary to the Truth of Impermanence. See, for example, the *Diamond Sutra* (sect. 6 in the translation by A.F. Price and Wong Mou-lam). The time following Buddha Shakyamuni's demise has been divided into three periods: i) the Perfect Age of the Dharma, lasting 500 years, when the Buddha's teaching was correctly practiced and Enlightenment often attained; ii) the Dharma Semblance Age, lasting about 1,000 years, when a form of the teaching was practiced but enlightenment seldom attained; iii) the Dharma-Ending Age, lasting some 'ten thousand' years, when a diluted form of the teaching exists and Enlightenment is rarely attained. (See entry, *Ten Thousand*)

Editor/Tam: 148

See also: the following poetic prophecy:

"In the last stages of degeneration (Dharma-Ending Age), all Buddhist texts will disappear, the saffron robes of the monks will turn white (the color of the robes of laymen), and, in the end, all relics of the cremated Buddha -- the teeth, bones, fingernails and hair -- will break free from their reliquaries, the stupas and pagodas, and magically travel to Bodhgaya where they will reassemble beneath the tree where the Buddha achieved enlightenment. There they will be worshiped one last time by the gods before they burst into flames and vanish."

Lopez: 266 #0876

◙ **DHARMA-KAYA** (skt)
see Dharma Body

◙ **DHARMA*CAKRA*** (skt)
see Dharma Wheel

◙ **DHARMADHATU** (skt)
see Dharma Realm

◙ **DHARMAKARA**
See also: Dharmakara's Vows; Amitabha Buddha

▸The Bodhisattva who later became Amitabha Buddha, as related in the *Longer Amitabha Sutra*. The Bodhisattva Dharmakara is famous for forty-eight Vows, particularly the eighteenth, which promises rebirth in the Pure Land to anyone who recites His name with utmost sincerity and faith (i.e., singlemindedly) at the time of death.

Editor/Tam: 148

"Dharmakara -- Amitabha Buddha in his previous life -- pledged to the Buddha preceding him (Lokesvara) that he would fulfill 48 vows in his pursuit of Buddhahood. They appear in the *Larger Sukhavati-vyuha (Longer Amitabha Sutra)*. These vows

were made by Dharmakara in order to establish his own Buddha-World, namely Sukhavati (Pure Land), on the basis of the 21 billion Buddha-worlds which he had seen."
Dait: 305

"In the sacred Buddhist texts of China, the *Longer Amitabha Sutra* concerns Amitabha Buddha and his Pure Land. On a certain occasion, Sakyamuni Buddha (the Buddha of our present age) was on Vulture Peak, surrounded by his disciples. Ananda, the Buddha's personal attendant, noticed the radiant beauty of Buddha and inquired about the cause of the Buddha's joy. Sakyamuni relates the following story: In an infinite time in the past, Bhiksu Dharmakara observed the misery of all sentient beings, and moved by compassion, vowed to establish a pure and perfect land where all could be liberated from their suffering. He then made forty-eight Vows in which he promised to establish this land or else he would not attain enlightenment. The Sutra states that Bhiksu Dharmakara practiced for many eons until he accomplished all his vows. Since he has achieved his aims, he is the Buddha of that land--*The Buddha of Infinite Light and Life.*"
Amidism: preface #0132
See also next entry.

◙ **DHARMAKARA'S VOWS**
See also: Sukhavati; Pure Land School; Longer Amitabha Sutra

▶ **(I) Forty-eight vows**
"The vows which Amitabha Buddha made while still engaged in Bodhisattva practice as Bodhisattva Dharmakara. They are listed in the *Longer Amitabha Sutra*. According to this sutra, Bodhisattva Dharmakara wished to create a splendid Buddha land in which he would live when he attained Buddhahood. Under the guidance of Lokeshvara Buddha, he studied the characteristics of twenty-one billion Buddha lands and then meditated for five aeons, pondering the features which should dignify his own Buddha land. After completing this meditation, Bodhisattva Dharmakara made forty-eight vows ... Among these vows, *the eighteenth -- that all who place their trust in Amitabha Buddha shall obtain rebirth in the Pure Land*, excepting those who commit any of the Five Cardinal Sins or slander the True Law -- is the one most emphasized in Pure Land."   Sokk: 114

(II) How The Vows Work

"Amitabha Buddha is foremost. This is because of the power of his vows. This power is so great that when you *singlemindedly* recite 'Nam Mo Amitabha Buddha,' you can very quickly realize Buddhahood. To become a Buddha, all you need to do is recite the Buddha's name. The Dharma-door of Buddha Recitation works on the same principle as the mother-son relationship. Those who recite the Buddha's name are like the 'sons' and the Buddha is like everyone's 'mother'. Whoever recites Amitabha Buddha's name is like Amitabha Buddha's son. In the *Surangama Sutra*, in the section in which the twenty-five sages explain their ways to enlightenment, the Bodhisattva Great Strength (Mahastamaprapta) says, 'It is like a mother thinking of her son. If the son has gone to roam...' If the son leaves his mother, it is hard for his mother to find him again. But if the son wants to find his mother, all he has to do is return home. If the mother thinks of her son, but the son cares not for his mother, he will run farther and farther away. If the mother thinks of her son and the son is mindful of his mother, then they will always be together. All of us are the sons and daughters of Amitabha Buddha. All we need to do is wish to return home and we can. If we don't want to return home, our father and mother might wait for us, but there is nothing they can do."   Hua/Root Farm: 56

(III) Exclusion Clause

The 18th vow of the Bodhisattva Dharmakara promises rebirth in the Pure Land to anyone who puts his utmost faith in him, except "those who have committed one of the Five Cardinal Sins or slandered the Dharma" (Exclusion Clause).

Editor: na

"Both Patriarchs T'an-luan and Shan-tao discuss the clause, partly to resolve apparent inconsistencies with a similar provision stated in the *Meditation Sutra*. Shan-tao states, however, that its purpose is not to exclude certain beings. Rather, the Buddha, fearing that we would commit these two kinds of faults (Cardinal Sins and slandering the Dharma), seeks to stop us by declaring that we will then not be able to attain birth in the Pure Land... *the clause is intended [as a warning] to make us realize the extreme gravity of the offenses.*"
Veda: 194   #0253

◙ **DHARMAKAYA**
see Dharma body

◙ **DHARMAPALA (1865-1933)**
see Anagarika Dharmapala

◙ **DHUTA**
see Ascetic Practices

◙ **DHYANA**
see Meditation

◙ **DHYANA HEAVENS**
Syn: Heavens
See also: Heaven and Hell

▶"This refers to the four dhyana heavens of the Realm of Form and the four dhyana heavens of the Realm of Formlessness. Each of the first four contains four heavens; so together with the four formless dhyana heavens, they total 20. According to tradition, one who attains certain kinds of meditation will be reborn in the dhyana heavens, but he will not stay there eternally. The dhyana heavens are still in the realms of Samsara." Chan: 475 #0517

◙ **DHYANI BUDDHAS**
see Five Buddhas

◙ **DIAMOND RECITATION**
See also: Buddha Recitation

▶In this method of Buddha Recitation, neither the lips nor the teeth move, while the tongue does not touch the gums but merely moves slightly within the mouth.
Editor/Zen: 119 #1488

◙ **DIAMOND SUTRA**
Syn: Vajracchedika Sutra
See also: Scriptural Recital

▶"The Vajracchedika *Prajna-Paramita Sutra*, 'the Perfection of Wisdom which cuts like a Diamond'. One of the two most famous Scriptures in the vast Perfection of Wisdom (Prajna-paramita) group of the Mahayana Canon. The *Heart Sutra* is a smaller epitome of this 'Wisdom which has gone beyond'."
Hump: 68
"This sutra sets forth the doctrines of sunyata and prajna. It is a very popular scripture, and many commentaries have been written on it. It is highly esteemed as a basic sutra in the Zen Sect. There are six Chinese translations: the most popular being by Kumarajiva of the Later Chin (Shin) Dynasty."
Dait: 200-201
I. Summary
"In an assembly of monks

(bhikkus) numbering 1250, the venerable Subhuti got up and asked the Buddha how they should proceed to attain the p e r f e c t w i s d o m (anuttara-samyak-sambuddhi). He then explained at considerable length six practices (paramitas) -- of charity (dana), of keeping the precepts (shila), of patience (kshanti), of resolution (virya), of meditation (dhyana), and of direct knowledge or wisdom (prajna). Each of these in turn is related to freedom from separate selfhood involved in their respective perfection since the true selfness or suchness (tathata) of all beings and things is a void (shunya/sunya) as far as separate characteristics are concerned. In the detailed explanations of these matters in the *Diamond Sutra*, there is very much food for Zenic meditation. Finally, Subhuti asked by what name this scripture should be known, and Buddha said as the Vajracchedika Prajna Paramita. Vajra means diamond, because it is impregnable." Wood: 35-36
II. Note
"One of its most ardent translators, Professor Edward Conze, remarks in his introductory note to Buddhist Wisdom Books, that the meaning of the text is so difficult to elicit because its particulars are '(1) Buddhist technical terms, (2) in Sanskrit, (3) used by sages, and (4) for the purpose of spiritual emancipation.' The last two points reveal that the text 'discloses itself not to erudition but to meditation.'"
Preb: 113 #0193

◉ **DIAMOND VEHICLE**
see Esoteric school

◉ **DIET**
see Food/Food rules; Macrobiotic Diet

◉ **DIFFERENTIATING KNOWLEDGE**
See also: Discrimination

►For ordinary beings, it is the everyday mind continually making distinctions between self and others, right and wrong, etc. For the Bodhisattvas and Buddhas, it is *provisional wisdom*. Editor: na #1259

◉ **DIFFICULT PATH OF PRACTICE**
Syn: Path of the Sages; Self-Power Path
See also: Easy Path of Practice
►One of the two categories into

which Nagarjuna divides Buddhist practice in the *Dasabhumika* (Ten stages) *Commentary*. The difficult-to-practice way means the exertion of strenuous effort in austere practice for countless aeons in order to attain enlightenment. It means the attainment of enlightenment through one's own power. The expression 'difficult-to-practice way' is used in contrast to the 'easy-to-practice way.' In the Pure Land school, the difficult-to-practice way is interpreted as the practice of any of the sutras other than the three basic sutras of the school."   Sokk: 69
According to Pure Land teachings, the Difficult Path of Practice refers to all conventional Buddhist ways of practice and cultivation (Zen, Theravada, the Vinaya School ...), which emphasize self-power and self-reliance. This is contrasted to the Easy Path of Practice, that is, the Pure Land method, which relies on both self-power and other-power (the power and assistance of the Buddhas and Bodhisattvas).
Editor/Tam: 149 #0251

◎ **DIGHA NIKAYA**

▸"Section of the Pali canon containing the long discourses of the Buddha."
Reat: 325 #2049

◎ **DIPAMKARA BUDDHA**

▸"Dipamkara is traditionally the Buddha who preceded the Buddha of our own era, Siddhartha Gautama, known in the lineage of Buddhas as Sakyamuni."
Sangh/95: 118
"The Buddha who prophesied Sakyamuni's attainment of enlightenment."
Chan: 475 #0518

◎ **DISCIPLES (HEARERS)**

▸*See:* Sravaka

◎ **DISCIPLINE METHOD**
see Vinaya School

◎ **DISCOURAGEMENT**
See also: Obstacles to Cultivation; Perseverance; Afflictions; Drowsiness
----
Buddhism of Wisdom & Faith/ **excerpts:**
▸"Compassionate individuals, or those who have the interests of the Dharma at heart, generally go through three stages: in the first, they are eager and enthusiastic; in the second, they

grow sad and discouraged; in the third and last stage, they achieve the mind of compassion and wisdom, adapted to circumstances. Unfortunately, however, these good and eager individuals usually give up and lose their determination during the second stage; very few reach the third stage. To get past the second stage and reach the third, we must have a mind of great compassion and wisdom, like the mythical dragon which can soar to the blue yonder or hide in the ocean depths. Confucian followers express this idea as follows: 'The true scholar teaches the Way if the world is receptive; if the time is not right, he retreats and lives in seclusion.' Confucius himself, at one point in his career, saw his teachings rejected by the local rulers. At that time, he retreated to write books and teach his disciples, his determination to help the world intact. Those who do not understand this principle of timing and conditions are usually discouraged and stricken with sadness! The fervent resolve that some possess when first developing the Bodhi Mind resembles that of the great Bodhisattvas. However, with time, because of karmic obstructions within and adverse conditions without, they grow lazy and arrogant. Their thoughts are then no different from those of ordinary people. These practitioners, in general, do not yet understand the world of the Five Turbidities; therefore, they easily regress when faced with reality. For this reason, many monks and nuns, witnessing errors within their own ranks or seeing the many afflictions and attachments of the laity, develop retrogressive thoughts. From there, they either abandon the Order and return to lay life, or they lose their altruistic determination, preferring to live in seclusion, practicing by themselves, unwilling to teach and save others. Likewise, many lay Buddhists, discouraged at the number of monks and nuns who commit transgressions, abandon Buddhism and cut off relations with the clergy; or else, they grow scornful and decide to take refuge only in the Buddha and the Dharma, but not in the Sangha. Still others, hearing rumors that their teacher has committed certain transgressions, hastily abandon all practice, without even taking time to investigate the matter. These people have only a shallow grasp of the Dharma, failing to realize that we cultivate for ourselves, not for our teachers and that to abandon practice is detrimental to ourselves alone, not to others. As a general comment, the states of sadness and discouragement described above are all misguided and wrong. This is because, in life, as within the Order, genuine and honest practitioners, while rare, do indeed exist. 'Sugar cane is eaten by worms only in certain spots; a roof leaks only in certain places.' Just because certain individuals transgress, let us not generalize and think that everyone is bad and wrong. Moreover, *human beings are bad and false; the Way is neither bad nor false.* Even if everyone were in the wrong, the Dharma would still be the shining, enlightened Way that leads us to liberation." Tam: 164-166 #2003

◙ **DISCOURSE ON THE GOLDEN LION**
Syn: Treatise on the Golden Lion
▸*Avatamsaka Sutra*:
A famous discourse which Master Fa-Tsang delivered to Empress Wu of China, illustrating a key point of the Avatamsaka philosophy -- the interpenetration of noumenon and phenomena.
Editor: na
When Fa-Tsang expounded the philosophy of Hua-yen to the Royal Court, he used the golden lion in the palace to illustrate the unimpeded mutual interpretation between *li* (noumenon) and *shih* (phenomena). The lion symbolizes *shih*, or appearance, which has no reality without the gold. On the other hand, gold lacks meaningful expression without the form of the lion as its appearance. The existence of each is dependent upon the other. Yet the gold and the lion distinctly exist by themselves. When by mutual interpretation gold is lion and lion is gold, the dichotomy between reality and appearance disappears.
Chang Chung-Yuan: 43
See also: Gold #1264

◙ **DISCRIMINATION**
See also: Ego; Intellect

▸"The fundamental cause of Samsara: the mental function of distinguishing things. In reality, all phenomena are one and empty. The phenomenal world appears to exist as a result of discrimination. Transcendental

wisdom goes beyond discrimination, reaching the realm of equality and non-differentiation."
Chan: 475 #0519

◙ **DIVINE EAR**
see Deva-Ear

◙ **DIVORCE**

▸"Separation or divorce is not prohibited in Buddhism though the necessity would scarcely arise if the Buddha's injunctions were strictly followed. Men and women must have the liberty to separate if they really cannot agree with each other. Separation is preferable to a miserable family life for a long period of time."
Dham: 238 #1975

◙ **DOGEN (1200-1253)**
See also: Shikantaza; Soto Zen School; Politics

▸"Author of the Shobogenzo, and the Japanese Zen master usually credited with introducing the Ts'ao Tung branch of Chinese Chan to Japan, where it came to be known as Soto Zen"
Reat: 325
"The Japanese Founder of Soto Zen, the largest Zen school of Buddhism in Japan (1200-1253). Dogen studied the teaching of the T'sao-tung school in China for four years before bringing it in 1227 to Japan. He stands alone as the Founder of the Japanese school, and is by far its greatest name. He would have no dealings with the Court, but retired to the mountains where he founded Eiheiji temple, near Fukui. There he taught that moral training (*precepts*), *meditation* and *wisdom* are three facets of one process. All is Buddha, and we have but to realize what we are." See "Three Non-Outflow Studies".
Hump: 69
NOTE:
Most ancient masters, including such figures as the Patriarch Dogen, held that only monks and nuns could achieve Enlightenment through Zen. This is because Zen requires a total dedication to cultivation which is beyond the capacity of most people. (See, for example, Kenneth Kraft, *Zen: Tradition and Transition*, p.186.)
Tam: 319 #0052

◙ **DOGMA**
See also: Wisdom

▸"Dogmatic belief ... chokes the

healthy growth of religion. Dogmatic belief and intolerance go hand-in-hand. One is reminded of the Middle Ages with its pitiless inquisitions, cruel murders, violence, infamy, tortures and burning of innocent beings. One is also reminded of the barbaric and ruthless crusades. All these events were stimulated by dogmatic beliefs in religious authority and the intolerance resulting therefrom. Before the development of scientific knowledge, people had many superstitious beliefs. For example a lot of people believed that the eclipse of the sun and moon brought bad luck and pestilence. Today we know that such beliefs are not true. Again some unscrupulous religionists encourage people to believe in superstitions so that they can make use of their followers for their own benefit. When people have truly purified their minds of ignorance, they will see the universe as it really is and they will not suffer from superstition and dogmatism. This is the 'salvation' that Buddhists aspire to."

Dham: 327-328 #1988

◉ **DOKUSAN**
Syn: Interview

▸"Private interview with a Roshi, or Zen teacher, in a Rinzai (Lin Chi) Zen temple."
Hump: 69 #0454

◉ **DOOR OF LIBERATION**
See also: Dharma Door; Samadhi

▸*Avatamsaka school*:
Bodhisattva gate of liberation, i.e. samadhi. Gates are basically within our self-nature, not outside. The gates open through practice, cultivation of the paramitas and holding precepts.

◉ **DOUBTS (ABOUT REBIRTH IN THE PURE LAND)**
see Three Doubts and Four Narrow Passes; Rebirth in the Pure Land

◉ **DROWSINESS/TORPOR**
See also: Obstacles to Cultivation; Practice; Afflictions; Discouragement
----
Buddhism of Wisdom & Faith/ excerpts:
▸"The cultivator at times drifts into a dark, heavy mental state, akin to sleep; this is the delusive obstruction of drowsiness. At other times, while he recites the Buddha's name, his mind wanders and is filled with sundry thoughts. This is the delusive condition of 'mind-scattering.'

Drowsiness and mind-scattering are two very dangerous obstacles because they hinder cultivation and prevent the practitioner from entering samadhi. As the cultivator practices, his delusive thoughts may suddenly be submerged and stilled. He recites the Buddha's name in an even monotone, with calm mind and thought, oblivious even to the weather and insect bites. This state usually lasts from one-half to one hour. Sometimes sweat soaks his clothing without his knowledge, and only when he suddenly awakens does he perceive an uncomfortable sensation of extreme heat. Experiencing this, he should not hasten to rejoice, thinking that his mind has settled, or that his practice is bearing some results. In reality, this is only the state of drowsiness in its subtle, mild form. The ancients have said: *Gently, gently, if drowsiness is not exposed, the demons will have their fill all day*. In this situation, the cultivator should take steps to practice steadfastly, with increased diligence and vigor. As he recites, he should 'turn the light around,' to subdue and destroy drowsiness. In general, according to the author's experience, as drowsiness approaches, it is preceded by delusive, scattered thoughts. There are, of course, times when drowsiness and delusive thoughts arise at the same time. However, this is a gross manifestation, easily detectable. When subtle drowsiness approaches, at first subtle errant thoughts arise. The practitioner feels that a dim spot is climbing from the back of his neck to the top of his head, then descending to the eyes, ending somewhere deep in the Alaya consciousness. Wherever drowsiness goes, that part of the body is affected. If it reaches the head, the head droops slightly; if it reaches the eyes, the eyes close; if it reaches the mind, the mind becomes clouded. The practitioner should possess a very keen, discerning mind to detect this subtle form of torpor."

Tam: 133-134 #2001

◙ DRUM OF THE TEACHING
see Celestial drum

◙ DRY WISDOM
see Wisdom

◙ DUAL BIRTH
See also: Non-Dual Method
►Said of pairs of apparent opposites such as Form and

Emptiness, Birth and Death, Noumenon and Phenomena which are concurrent aspects of the same non-dual reality. Thus these opposites always go together -- they are said to be born simultaneously, to have dual birth. The most famous example is found in the *Heart Sutra*: Form is emptiness, Emptiness is form.

Illustrative Story
"Once a beautiful and well-dressed woman visited a house. The master of the house asked her who she was; and she replied that she was the goddess of wealth. The master of the house was delighted and so greeted her with open arms. Soon after another woman appeared who was ugly looking and poorly dressed. The master asked who she was and the woman replied that she was the goddess of poverty. The master was frightened and tried to drive her out of the house, but the woman refused to depart, saying, 'The goddess of wealth is my sister. There is an agreement between us that we are never to live apart; if you chase me out, she is to go with me.' Sure enough, as soon as the ugly woman went out, the other woman disappeared. Birth goes

with death. Fortune goes with misfortune. Bad things follow good things. Men should realize this. Foolish people dread misfortune and strive after good fortune, but those who seek Enlightenment must transcend both of them and be free of worldy attachments." (*The Teaching of the Buddha*)
BDK: 144-145 #2260

◙ **ĐỨC-NIỆM, THÍCH (*DHARMA MASTER*)**

►Important Vietnamese Buddhist leader and religious academic in the USA. Ordination and advanced religious training in Vietnam. 1978: PH.D. (Taiwan). President, Vietnamese Refugee Relief Association (Taiwan). 1981: Founder and Head of *International Buddhist Monastic Institute* (which includes a Publishing House) -- an institution mainly devoted to the training of monks and nuns as well as to the publication of sutras and commentaries. 1992 -- : head of Leadership Council, Vietnamese-American *Unified Buddhist Congress*, an umbrella organization covering several Vietnamese Buddhist organizations in the USA. In addition to reprinting and

distributing over two hundred titles, Master Đức-Niệm has also written/translated a dozen Dharma books including *A Commentary on Mahayana Pure Land Thought.* #2247

◙ **DUKKHA**
Syn: Suffering
See also: Eight Sufferings

▶"Term used in Buddhist tradition for one of the three characteristic marks of existence (Dharma Seals). Variously translated into English as 'suffering,' 'ill,' 'evil,' 'unsatisfactoriness' and 'unrest,' the term covers all these meanings. The affirmation that all human existence is characterised by dukkha (suffering) is the first of the Buddhist Four Holy Truths."
Ling: 108
"Suffering; a central concept in Buddhism, which lies at the root of the Four Noble Truths. The characteristic of suffering is one of the three Marks of Existence (three Dharma Seals) ... Dukha arises because of desire and craving and can be overcome by the elimination of desire. The means to bring about the extinction of suffering is shown by the Eightfold Path. The nature of suffering is described in the first of the Four Noble Truths as follows: 'Birth is suffering; aging is suffering; sickness is suffering; dying is suffering; care, distress, pain, affliction, and despair are suffering; the non-attainment of what one desires is suffering; in short, the five aggregates [skandhas] connected with attachment are suffering."
Sham: 61 #1124
See also: "Eight Sufferings"

◙ **DUST**
Syn: Worldly dusts; Hairtip; Pore
See also: Dust and Sand

▶*Worldly dusts*: A metaphor for all the mundane things that can cloud our bright self-nature. These include form, sound, scent, taste, touch and dharmas (external opinions and views). These dusts correspond to the five senses and the discriminating, everyday mind (referred to as the sixth sense in Buddhism).
Editor / Zen: 135

NOTE:
Dust, mote of dust, atom. In the sutras, these words denote the smallest quantity in existence. [HH39Ipxxviii]   #1300

◙ DUST AND SAND

►"*I*. Expression meaning uncountable, endless. *II*. Illusions."
Dait: 151 #0037

◙ DYANA
see Meditation

◙ E-MEI MOUNTAIN
See also: Pilgrimage Sites; Four Famous Mountains

►"A renowned mountain in Ssu-ch'uan Province, China. It is believed that Samantabhadra resided there. Along with Wu-t'ai shan (the mountain where Manjushri is thought to live), and Pu-t'o shan (the mountain where Avalokitesvara is considered to abide), E-Mei shan is one of the four famous (or auspicious) mountains of China. There are approximately seventy temples on the mountain."
Dait: 73 #0065

◙ E-MEI SHAN
see E-Mei Mountain

◙ EAGLE PEAK
see Vulture Peak

◙ EARTH STORE BODHISATTVA
see Ksitigarbha

◙ EASTERN BUDDHIST, THE

►"The Journal of the Eastern Buddhist Society, Kyoto. Published irregularly from 1921 to 1939. Founded and edited by Dr D.T. Suzuki and his wife Mrs B.L. Suzuki. A new series was begun in 1965."
Hump: 71 #0453

◙ EASY PATH OF PRACTICE
syn: Easy-to-Practice Way
See also: Easy Practice Chapter; Other Power; Difficult Path of Practice; Pure Land School; Universal Method

----

►"Refers to Pure Land practice. The Easy Path involves reliance on the power of the Buddhas and Bodhisattvas, in particular B u d d h a   A m i t a b h a ('other-power') in addition to o n e ' s   o w n   c u l t i v a t i o n ('self-power'). Usually contrasted with primary reliance on self-power (Difficult Path of Practice), taught in other Buddhist schools. Simultaneous reliance on self-power and other-power distinguishes the Pure Land School from most other schools of Buddhism. The distinction is, however, a matter of emphasis, as all schools of Buddhism rely, to a greater or

lesser extent, on both self-power and other-power."
Editor / Tam: 149

"In the 'Commentary of the Ten Stages' chapter on 'Easy Practice,' Patriarch Nagarjuna discusses the attainment of the non-retrogressive state and then distinguishes two paths. The first follows the 'easy practice' (i-hsing) of devotion, which is likened to riding on a vessel over water. The 'difficult' (nan) path resembles a Bodhisattva walking on land to his destination. Amitabha is one among numerous transcendent Buddhas to whom devotion of easy practice may be directed. *In East Asia, the distinction between the difficult and the easy path served as one of the primary doctrinal bases for the establishment of Pure Land as an independent school*."
Tana: 12

(I) Why The Easy Path?
"There are two paths of cultivation. The Difficult Path refers to the practices of sentient beings in the world of the Five Turbidities, who, through countless Buddha eras, have aspired to reach the stage of Non-Retrogression. The difficulties are truly countless, as numerous as specks of dust or grains of sand, too numerous to imagine. I will summarize the five major ones: a) Externalists are legion, creating confusion with respect to the Bodhisattva Dharma; b) Evil beings destroy the practitioner's good, wholesome virtues; c) Worldly merits and blessings can easily lead the practitioner astray, so that he ceases to engage in virtuous practices; d) It is easy to stray onto the Arhat's path of self-benefit, which obstructs the Mind of great compassion; e) Relying exclusively on self-power, without the aid of the Buddha's power, makes cultivation very difficult and arduous. It is not unlike the case of a feeble, handicapped person, walking alone, who can only go so far each day regardless of how much effort he expends. 'The Easy Path of cultivation means that if sentient beings in this world believe in the Buddha's words, practice Buddha Recitation and vow to be reborn in the Pure Land, they are assisted by the Buddha's vow-power and assured of rebirth. This is analogous to a person who floats downstream in a boat; although the distance may be many thousands of miles, his

destination will be reached in no time.'" (T'ien T'ai Patriarch Chih I)
Dia: 20-21

(II) Pure Land School

"Everyone can appreciate why Pure Land, particularly Oral Recitation (q.v.), is an Easy-to-Practice method. However, the word 'easy' has many meanings, with which not everyone may be familiar. This is because when practicing other methods, for example, Scriptural Studies, we encounter an immense number of sutras and commentaries, infinitely profound in meaning. In the first instance, the practitioner should fully understand the basic teaching and, from there, penetrate the different shades of meaning. After that, he should reconcile all meanings, extracting their kernel and essence, to discover and choose the method of cultivation that he will follow all his life. All this cannot be done unless he is willing to spend several dozen years of hard work. Should he decide to seek liberation through the *Discipline method*, the practitioner must join the Order and become thoroughly conversant with all aspects of the different bodies of precepts. He

should also possess the wisdom to distinguish meaning from words and apply the precepts in a flexible manner, according to the environment, the times and the occasion. Thus, to study the sutras is not necessarily difficult, but to study the precepts to the point of knowing how to adapt them skillfully, neither breaking them nor being rigidly bound by them, is truly difficult. Once having understood the precepts, the practitioner must exercise patience and fortitude and endure discomfort and suffering in order to achieve success. If he decides to enter the Way through *Zen*, he should have previously sown the seeds of wisdom and have suitably high innate capacities. Otherwise, he has no hope of attaining this lofty Dharma and participating in the 'transmission of the lamp' (the enlightenment experience). Therefore, a famous Buddhist scholar once said: Practicing Zen to achieve Buddhahood is the domain of scholars endowed with wisdom. This observation is certainly not incorrect or exaggerated. With Oral Recitation, once the practitioner has developed the mind of Faith and Vows, he can recite the Buddha's name and engage in cultivation regardless of whether his capacities are high, moderate or limited. Moreover, while other methods depend on self-power alone, the Pure Land Dharma Door first relies to the utmost on self-power and then adds the element of 'other-power.' Other-power is precisely the infinitely great and powerful Vow of Amitabha Buddha 'to welcome and escort.' As long as a practitioner sincerely repents and recites the Buddha's name with one-pointedness of mind, even though he is not yet free of delusions and is still afflicted with heavy evil karma, he, too, will be welcomed to the Pure Land.

"The ancients used to say, by way of comparison: Practicing other methods is as difficult and laborious as an ant climbing a high mountain; reciting the Buddha's name seeking rebirth in the Pure Land is as swift and easy as a boat sailing downstream in the direction of the blowing wind. This observation is very appropriate indeed. Moreover, once reborn there, living in an auspicious and peaceful environment, always in the company of Buddha Amitabha and the Bodhisattvas, the practitioner will swiftly achieve success in whatever Dharma method he chooses. He is like a log rolling down a high mountain, which just keeps going and never stops, even for a moment.

"*In summary, Buddha Recitation is easy for three reasons*: easy practice, easy achievement of rebirth in the Pure Land and easy attainment of Buddhahood. Therefore, the results achieved through Buddha Recitation from time immemorial can be compared to the clear and limpid sound of precious stones striking against genuine gold, or the sight of "smiling lotus blossoms with their fresh and fragrant grades of rebirth." Within these levels and grades, the path from sentient being to Buddhahood contains many ranks, yet is also without rank. This is because, once reborn in the Pure Land, the practitioner has transcended Birth and Death -- and to recite the Buddha's name is to become Buddha. This is like the silkworm, the cocoon and the butterfly, which are inseparable; there is very little difference between saying that a butterfly is originally a worm and that the worm *is* the butterfly."

Thich: 233-236 #1372

◎ EASY PRACTICE *CHAPTER*

See also: Easy Path of Practice; Nagarjuna

►Please read *Ten Stages Sutra (Commentary on)* before the following:

"The chapter on easy practice which Nagarjuna wrote as the ninth chapter of his *Commentary on the Ten Stages Sutra* (*Dhasabumika/ Shih-chu-p'i-p'o-sha-lun*). Translated into Chinese by Kumarajiva (Jpn/ Raju). In this chapter, Nagarjuna explains the doctrine of Amitabha as taught by the Buddha, saying that human beings can easily attain enlightenment by chanting the name of Amitabha Buddha. He stresses the salvation of Amitabha Buddha. Honen, the founder of the Japanese Pure Land School, esteemed this text as one of the most important scriptures teaching the doctrine of the Pure Land tradition."
Dait: 137-138 #0103

◎ EATING WHEN HUNGRY

See also: Zen School

►"*Eating when hungry, sleeping when tired*": this Zen statement, which usually baffles non-Buddhists, actually reflects a deep truth. Most people do not eat when hungry, that is, they do not eat what is available or what is good for them, but rather seek special dishes prepared to their taste. Likewise, they do not sleep when tired, but are likely to do other things, such as tossing and turning in bed recalling past wrongs or mulling over future events. ... "*All eagerness for study gone*"; the goal of all Buddhist teaching is to stop the mind from wandering, keeping it empty and still, so that our innate wisdom can surface. In that context, love, hatred and eagerness for study are all attachments that disturb the mind.
Editor/Tam: 316-317 #2252

◎ EGO

See also: Anger; Enemies

►"In Buddhism, ego refers to the notion of oneself as a fixed and discrete entity separate from other selves and from an 'outside world.' Thus a silently stubborn or self-deprecating person may be said to have as strong an ego as one who is, say, proud and domineering. Through awakening, the illusory nature of the ego is seen through."
Kapl/1980: 291 #0781

Question/Answer

"I am aware of how much fear affects my behavior and inhibits me from making contact with other people. Fear seems to affect other people in this way too. Does this explain the emphasis on fearlessness in the list of the things that the Bodhisattva gives?" *Answer*: "The Bodhisattva's giving of fearlessness seems to suggest that people are badly in need of it. Fear is produced by a sense of separateness, or ego for want of a better term. You should not be surprised to experience fear in all sorts of situations. It is just an indication of the fact that you experience yourself as self, as an ego; whenever you experience yourself in that way there is the possibility of fear. Until you have transcended the sense of separateness there will be fear, because you are bound to be afraid of whatever threatens you. The gift of fearlessness is therefore ultimately the gift of insight into egolessness, and this is why it is so important. It could even be called an aspect of the gift of the Dharma, in the sense of some actual experience of insight, not just the words of the Dharma."

Sangha/Drama: 29　#0781

◙ EIGHT ABSTINENCES

Syn: Eight Precepts

▶"The eight precepts which a lay Buddhist should observe on certain retreats: (1) not killing living beings, (2) not stealing, (3) not having sexual intercourse, (4) not telling lies, (5) not drinking intoxicants, (6) not wearing bodily decoration, not using perfumes, not singing and dancing, and not going to see dances or plays, (7) not sleeping in a raised bed, and (8) not eating after noon."

Inag: 396-397

These special retreats are popular among devout lay Buddhists and are considered a good preparation for joining the Order as monks and nuns, either in this life or in future lifetimes.

Editor: na　#0695

◙ EIGHT ADVERSITIES

▶"These are special types of adversity that prevent the practice of the Dharma; they are rebirth in hell, rebirth in the brute-world, rebirth in the ghost-world, rebirth among the long-lived gods, rebirth in an uncivilized country, rebirth with deficient faculties, adherence to false views, and life in a realm

wherein there is no Tathagata."
Thur: 153 #0685

◙ **EIGHT ATTRIBUTES OF NIRVANA**

►"Eternity, tranquility, agelessness, immortality, pureness, harmony, firmness, and happiness."
Dait: 235 #0119

◙ **EIGHT BODHISATTVAS**
See also: Buddhas and Bodhisattvas

►"Eight major archetypical Bodhisattvas, listed variously in different texts, who are Avalokitesvara, Manjushri, Akasagarbha (Kokuzo), Vajrapani, Maitreya, Samantabhadra, Mahasthama-prapta, and Bhaishajyaguru (Medicine Buddha). Their images are used in devotional and meditational exercises."
Chih-I/Cleary: 191

◙ **EIGHT CLASSES OF DIVINITIES**
see Eight Divisions (of Divinities)

◙ **EIGHT DIVISIONS (OF DIVINITIES)**
Syn: Eight Classes of Divinities

►"The eight kinds of gods and demi-gods believed to be protectors of Buddhism: devas, dragons, yaksas, gandharvas, asuras, garudas, kinnaras, and mahoragas."
Inag: 397

"These are various classes of non-human beings that are regarded as protectors of the Buddhist Dharma and often appear as part of the audience attending the Buddha's sermons. Strictly speaking, not all are celestials, but most of them inhabit the celestial or heavenly spheres of a world system. The eight classes, are: (1) gods (deva); (2) asuras; (3) the gandharvas and (4) the kinnaras; local spirits known as (5) yakshas (yaksa), sometimes associated with the Tushita Heaven, but usually located on the human plane; two kinds of mythical serpents, (6) the mahoragas and (7) the nagas; and (8) the celestial eagles known as the garudas. Technically, the nagas and the asuras, perhaps the yakshas, should not be in this class, since their abode is not in the heavens. The nagas are usually placed in the nether world or under the sea. The asuras live on the slopes of

Mount Sumeru, below the lowest heavenly sphere, which is that of the four Guardian Kings. All eight kinds of celestials appear prominently in the sutras, but the classes of celestials and spirits appearing in the sutra literature are not limited to these eight." Gomez: 289-290 #1700

◙ **EIGHT IMPURE THINGS**
See also: Sangha

►"The eight things that monks or nuns are not traditionally allowed to possess: (1) gold, (2) silver, (3) manservant, (4) maidservant, (5) domestic animal, (6) storehouse, (7) business, and (8) grain seeds."   BDK: 21 #1087

◙ **EIGHT LIBERATIONS**
see Eight Samadhis of Emancipation

◙ **EIGHT PRECEPTS**
see   Eight Abstinences

◙ **EIGHT SAMADHIS OF EMANCIPATION**
Syn: Eight Liberations; Eightfold Liberation; Vimoksa

►"The eight types of meditation for removing various attachments to forms and desires: (1) removing passions by meditation on the impurity of one's body, (2) strengthening emancipation from passions by meditating on the impurity of external objects, (3) removing passions by meditating on pure aspects of external objects, (4) removing attachment to material objects by meditating on boundless consciousness, (5) removing attachment to void by meditating on the boundless consciousness, (6) removing attachment to consciousness by meditating on non-existence, (7) removing attachment to non-existence by meditating on the stage of neither thought nor non-thought, and (8) extinguishing all thoughts and perceptions and dwelling in the stage of total extinction." Inag: 397 #0697

◙ **EIGHT SUFFERINGS**
See also: Dukkha

►These sufferings are: Birth, Old Age, Disease, Death, Separation From Loved Ones, Meeting With the Uncongenial, Unfulfilled Wishes and the Suffering Associated with the Five Raging Skandas. (For a detailed exposition of the eight sufferings, see Thich Thien Tam, *Buddhism of Wisdom and Faith*, sect. 5.) Editor: na

To illustrate the point that suffering is an inevitable part of our world, let us consider the example, adapted from the sutras, of worms feeding on rotten apples. The worms are "running" hither and yon among the apples, each worm "elbowing" the others for a better spot, a larger piece of the rotten matter. They all feel their actions necessary and desirable. They all seem very busy and very happy. To us humans, however, theirs is indeed a pitiable lot. The human condition is the same from the viewpoint of celestials, Bodhisattvas and Buddhas -- such a pitiful sight indeed, whether of beggars or presidential hopefuls! Editor/Zen: 5 #1419

◉ **EIGHT TEACHINGS**
see "Five Periods and Eight Teachings"

◉ **EIGHT VIRTUES (WATER Of--)**

▸*Vn*/ Nước Tám Công-Đức. Said *metaphorically* of the characteristics of the water in the lakes and ponds in the Pure Land of Amitabha. "1. Clarity and cleanliness; 2. coolness; 3. sweetness; 4. lightness; 5. moistening power; 6. ability to give comfort; 7. ability to quench thirst; and 8. ability to improve health."   Chang: 493

Smaller Amitabha Sutra:
"Moreover, Shariputra: in the Land of Utmost Bliss there are very many pools of gems brimming with the Water of Eight Virtues. The bottoms of the pools are pure, covered with sand of gold. On the four sides there are stairways of gold, silver, lapis lazuli, and crystal."
Seki: 22   #0686

◉ **EIGHT WINDS**

▸*Vn*/ Bát Phong. "Eight conditions which prevent people from advancing along the right path to enlightenment. They are: prosperity, decline, disgrace, honor, praise, censure, suffering and pleasure. People are often swayed either by their *attachment* to prosperity, honor, praise and pleasure, or by their *aversion* to decline, disgrace, censure and suffering."
Sokk: 82 #0255

◉ **EIGHTEEN UNIQUE QUALITIES OF BUDDHAS**

▸They are: "(1) Impeccability of action, (2) impeccability of speech, (3) impeccability of

mind, (4) having no discriminatory thoughts, (5) unfailing concentration, (6) unfailing discernment and relinquishment, (7) endless volition, (8) endless vigor, (9) endless mindfulness, (10) endless wisdom, (11) endless liberation, (12) endless liberated knowledge and vision, (13) all actions according with knowledge and wisdom, (14) all speech according with knowledge and wisdom, (15) all thoughts according with knowledge and wisdom, (16) unobstructed insight into the past, (17) unobstructed insight into the future, (18) unobstructed insight into the present."
Cleary/Chih-I: 191

◙ **EIGHTEENTH VOW (OF AMITABHA BUDDHA)**
see Original vows

◙ **EIGHTFOLD LIBERATION**
see Eight samadhis of emancipation

◙ **EIGHTFOLD NOBLE PATH**
Syn: Noble Eightfold Path; Eightfold Right Path
See also: Four Noble Truths

▶"The Buddhist scheme of moral and spiritual self-development

leading to Enlightenment."
Hump: 139
"The fundamental teaching of Sakyamuni Buddha; the path to liberation: 1. Right view: understanding the Four Noble Truths and having penetrative insight into reality (emptiness). 2. Right thought: having only thoughts which are unselfish, loving, and non-violent. 3. Right speech: abstention from lying, slander, harsh or abusive language, and idle chatter. 4. Right action: conducting oneself in moral, peaceful, and honorable ways, and keeping the basic precepts. 5. Right livelihoods: living honorably in a profession which is in no way harmful to sentient beings, and avoiding such livelihoods as trading in weapons, intoxicants, or poisons. 6. Right effort: following the four right efforts. 7. Right mindfulness: practicing the four mindfulnesses. 8. Right concentration: developing one's meditation according to the four dhyanas."
Chan: 493
"The eight items of the path may be classified under three headings: the first two under the heading of wisdom and understanding; the next three under ethical conduct; the last

three under mental discipline."
Eerd: 231
NOTE:
The Eightfold Noble Path as a basic Buddhist teaching is emphasized in the Theravada school. The Mahayana tradition puts emphasis on the teaching of the Paramitas.
Editor: na #0492

◙ **EIGHTH CONSCIOUSNESS**
see Alaya Consciousness

◙ **EIGHTY AUSPICIOUS MARKS**
Syn: Eighty Minor Excellencies; Eighty Minor Characteristics; Auspicious Marks
See also: Thirty-two Auspicious Signs

▸"Bodily attributes of a Buddha, more subtle than the thirty-two auspicious signs. Examples: youthful complexion; a soft body; lips colored like a red, bright gourd; face like a full, clear moon; emitting fragrance from the pores and mouth; deportment as awesome as that of a lion; graceful and steady gait."
Chan: 495-496
"The eighty *subordinate* physical characteristics attending the 32 major marks of excellence of the Buddhas."
Inag: 397-398 #0634

◙ **EIGHTY MINOR CHARACTERISTICS**
see Eighty Auspicious Marks

◙ **EIGHTY MINOR EXCELLENCIES**
see Eighty Auspicious Marks

◙ **EIGHTY-FOUR THOUSAND**
See also: Ten Thousand

▸"A traditional expression meaning 'very many.'"
Kusa: 178 #0844

◙ **EKAYANA**
see One Vehicle

◙ **ELIADE, MIRCEA (1907-86)**

▸"Romanian historian and philosopher of comparative religion, born in Bucharest. A student of Indian philosophy and Sanskrit at Calcutta University (1928-31) before becoming a lecturer in the history of religion and metaphysics at Bucharest from 1933 to 1939. He served in the diplomatic service during World War II, and later taught at the Sorbonne (1946-8) and the University of Chicago (1957-85). Author of many books and papers. He was editor-in-chief of *The Encyclopaedia of Religion* (1987)."   Larousse: 157 #2129

◙ **ELIXIR OF LIFE**
see Panacea

◙ **EMEI MOUNTAIN**
see E-Mei Mountain

◙ **EMOTIONS**
See also: Afflictions; Love / Sex

►All feelings and emotions, whether good or bad, wholesome or evil, disturb the peacefulness of the mind, preventing one's innate wisdom from manifesting itself. Therefore, they should all be avoided equally. A person overcome by any kind of emotion is not on an even keel and may not exercise good judgment or do what has to be done. Thus, joy, too, is an affliction!

(Note: The word "joy" used to describe life in the Pure Land of Amitabha Buddha is not the ordinary joy of this world but is rather the joy of "permanence, bliss, self and purity" -- the opposite of the Dharma seals (q.v.) of impermanence, suffering and no-self that characterize the Saha World).
Editor/Zen: 180-181 #1517

◙ **EMPOWERMENT**
See also: Pure Land School

►The Pure Land school is a good example of the simple, pragmatic approach of Buddhism. The accoutrements of practice, while useful as aids, are not essential in themselves and may be adapted to circumstances. There is no absolute need for meditation cushions, mandalas, gurus, etc. Pure Land thus liberates the practitioner, enabling him to concentrate on practice.

For an interesting parallel between Pure Land and the "Zen of the Patriarchs," see the following passage: "While others viewed Zen as purification of the mind ... Bodhidharma equated Zen with Buddhahood -- and Buddhahood with the mind, the everyday, undiscriminating mind ... Bodhidharma's Zen was Mahayana Zen, not Theravada Zen -- the sword of wisdom, not the meditation cushion." (Red Pine, *The Zen Teaching of Bodhidharma*, p. xv.).
Editor/Zen: 181 #1518

◙ **EMPTINESS**
Syn: Sunyata; Void
See also: Existence/Emptiness; Nagarjuna; Subhuti; True Emptiness/Wonderful Existence
----
►*Chin/* Kung; *Jpn/* Ku; *Vn/* Không. "A fundamental Buddhist

concept, variously translated as non-substantiality, emptiness, void, latency, relativity, etc. The concept that entities have no fixed or independent nature. This idea is closely linked to that of dependent origination (Skt./ pratitya-samutpada), which states that because phenomena arise and continue to exist only by virtue of their relationship with other phenomena, they have no fixed substance and have as their true nature emptiness. The concept thus teaches that nothing exists independently. Its practical implications lie in the rejection of attachments to transient phenomena and to the egocentricity of one who envisions himself as being absolute and independent of all other existences. It is an especially important concept in Mahayana Buddhism. On the basis of sutras known as the Wisdom sutras, the concept of emptiness was systematized by Nagarjuna, who explains it as the Middle Way, which here means neither existence nor non-existence.

Broadly speaking, the concept of emptiness or non-substantiality can be divided into two: *non-substantiality of persons and non-substantiality of the dharmas (objects, things, etc.).* Non-substantiality of persons means that a living entity, being no more than a temporary union of the five components, cannot be said to have an absolute self, while non-substantiality of the dharmas means that, because the dharmas or elements of existence arise through dependent origination, they have no unchanging self-nature. The *Tripitaka teaching* [Theravada] progressively analyzed entities or constructs such as the self into their constituent elements or dharmas, until they could be defined neither as existence nor non-existence; this is the analytical view of non-substantiality. On the other hand, the *Connecting Teaching* [early Mahayana] says that because all things arise through dependent origination, their existence is in itself non-substantial. The *Perfect Teaching* (q.v.) reveals that non-substantiality is inseparably united with the truths of temporary existence and the Middle Way, explaining that each of the three truths possesses all three within itself." Sokk: 237-238

As stated in the *Heart Sutra*: "O Sariputra, form does not

differ from the Void, and the Void does not differ from Form. Form is the Void, and Void is Form: the same is true for feelings, conceptions, impulses and consciousness."

Sutra Translation: 45

True emptiness is contrasted with "hollow emptiness," or "stubborn emptiness," which is one-sided and leads to nihilism (the belief that nothing exists after death). Thus, we have the Mahayana expression, "True Emptiness, Wonderful Existence" -- True Emptiness is not empty!

Editor/Tam: 336

On the subject of existence and emptiness, an ancient Zen Master has said: "If we refer to existence, then/ Everything from the smallest mote of dust exists;/ If we refer to emptiness,/ This whole, wide world and everything in it are empty."

Editor: na

See also: related comment below: D.T. Suzuki quotes the Zen Patriarch Fa Yen as follows:

"The sutras preached by the Buddha during his lifetime are said to amount to five thousand and forty-eight fascicles; they include the doctrine of emptiness and the doctrine of being (existence); there are teachings of immediate realization and of

gradual development. Is it not an affirmation?

"But, according to [Zen Master Yung Chia in his *Song of Enlightenment*], 'there are no sentient beings, there are no Buddhas; sages as numerous as the sands of the Ganges are but so many bubbles in the sea; sages and worthies of the past are like flashes of lightning.' Is this not a negation?

"O you, my disciples, if you say there is, you go against Yung Chia; if you say there is not, you contradict our old master Buddha. If he were with us, then how would he pass through the dilemma? ... If you confess your ignorance, I will let you see into the secret. When I say there is not, this does not necessarily mean a negation; when I say there is, this also does not signify an affirmation. Turn eastward and look at the Western Land; face the south and the North Star is pointed out there!"

Suzuki/65: na

"This is a recurring quandary for people who are interested in Buddhist doctrine: If there is no 'I', no 'mine', and all dharmas are utterly empty, how can the law of karma prevail? The answer is: it is precisely because everything is empty and there is

no self or 'I', that everything can exist and the principle of karma can prevail. If things were truly existent, i.e., with a definite, enduring substance or entity, then no change or flow would be possible. Because nothing has self-nature (svabhava), everything is possible. The Buddhist way of thinking is unique in this aspect. To understand this point more clearly, the reader is referred to the Madhyamika and Prajnaparamita literature."
Chang: 411

NOTES:

(I) The Buddha taught countless schools or Dharma methods. Among these methods, Zen, T'ien T'ai, etc. lead to Buddhahood through the *Door of Emptiness*, while Pure Land and the Avatamsaka School enter through the *Door of Existence*. (The *Avatamsaka Sutra* being encyclopedic and expressing the totality of Buddhism, also contains the Dharma of Emptiness of the Zen school.)
Editor: na

(II) Unlike certain other schools of Buddhism (Zen, Tantric, for example), Pure Land does not stress the role of gurus, roshi or mentors. Rather, the emphasis is on recitation of the Buddha's name and the sutras as well as direct contact and communion with Buddha Amitabha -- Buddha Amitabha being understood as an expression of emptiness or ultimate wisdom:
"Kumarajiva [the famous translator of sutras from Indic languages to Chinese] interpreted Amida Buddha as an expression of sunyata [emptiness] and recommended Buddha Recitation as a means of realizing sunyata or ultimate wisdom, prajna." (M. Saso & D. Chappell)
Editor: na

For further details, *See also:* Existence/Emptiness. #0177

◙ **EMPTY EON**
See also: Cosmology (Buddhist)

►"In classical Indian cosmology, every world system moves from an age of emptiness through ages of creation, abiding, destruction, and then another 'empty eon' of nothingness between cycles. 'Before the Empty Eon' in Zen means before this universe came to be, i.e., at the level of mind."
Clea: 171   #0765

◙ **EMPTY STORE BODHISATTVA**
see   Akasagarbha Bodhisattva

◙ ENCYCLOPEDIA OF BUDDHISM

See also: World Fellowship of Buddhists (WFB)

▸"An Encyclopedia sponsored by the Sri Lanka Government in 1956. Editor-in-Chief, the late Dr G.P. Malalasekera (q.v.). National committees set up in many countries."
Hump: 72

Several volumes of the encyclopedia have been published and are available in major libraries. Work on the remaining volumes is in progress.
Editor: na #0452

◙ ENDURANCE (WORLD OF --)
see Saha World

◙ ENEMIES / OPPONENTS
See also: Afflictions; Ego

▸"Viewed objectively, enemies can only be of two kinds. Either they are intrinsically hostile, in which case to resent their behavior is as absurd as to resent fire for being hot; or they are fundamentally well disposed but have momentarily succumbed to a crisis of defilement. Here, too, animosity is out of place: it is as foolish as resenting the sky for

being covered with clouds. Besides, when someone hits me with a stick, I am angry not with the stick but with the one who holds it. By the same token it is illogical to hate my enemy. He may wield the stick, but *he is himself in the grip of his defilements.* It is the emotion of which he is the victim that I should resent. Taking his argument a step further, Patriarch Shantideva points out that in any conflict, the victim and aggressor are both caught up in a situation of mutual dependence. In the case of the physical attack, for example, if pain occurs, it has two equally important sources corresponding to the two terms of the experience.

The fact that suffering happens depends as much on the degree to which the victim's mind clings to his body as on the wound inflicted by the aggressor. Pursuing the argument yet further, Shantideva shows how the enemy should not merely be an object of tolerance; he is to be cherished as an indispensable helper on the Bodhisattva path. Our enemy does for us what no friend or loved one can do. By awakening us to the reality of our own ego-

clinging, the *enemy provides opportunities for patience, purification, the exhaustion of evil karma.*"
Shantiveda: 14

◉ ENERGY CURRENTS

►A practice not accepted in Buddhism. It is referred to nowadays under a variety of names, such as Polarity Therapy, Dr. Randolph Stone's method, Life Energy Healing Arts, Spiritual/Energy Healing, Healing Ministry, Laying on Hands Ministry.
Editor: na
"Buddhism encompasses all methods and dharmas. Not only does it clearly explain the issues of body, mind and life, it does not neglect the small issues of human morality, such as 'filiality, respect for elders, loyalty, faith, propriety, justice, decency and shame." An exception is the practice of 'balancing energy currents,' about which not a single word is said in the Buddha Dharma. Not only that, Buddhism forbids the practice entirely. This is because while Taoism regards the preservation of body and mind as an ideal, Buddhism, on the contrary, teaches that body and mind are

intrinsically false, born of conditions, disappearing also through conditions. They are not the Self-Nature True Mind."
(Patriarch Yin-Kuang)
Zen: 183

Buddhism of Wisdom & Faith/ excerpts:
"There are some who appear to be monks and nuns, residing in temples and pagodas; however they neither study nor understand Buddhism and only follow the practices of other religions. These people are peddling a panoply of other beliefs under the label of Buddhism. They and their followers secretly transmit their beliefs to one another. Many of them, while claiming to practice meditation, in fact specialize in exercises to balance energy currents with little knowledge of what meditation is all about. As far as the Pure Land method is concerned, they teach that one should visualize the Buddha's name 'shooting' from the navel to the back of the body and up the spinal column, and then returning to the navel. This, they say, is 'turning the Dharma wheel.' This is the practice of 'releasing blockages in the energy system,' (i.e., balancing energy currents) according to externalist schools.

Such teaching is not consonant with Buddhism."
Tam: 63 #1519

◙ ENLIGHTENMENT
See also: Awakening vs. Enlightenment

►*Skt*/Bodhi. "The spiritual condition of a Buddha or Bodhisattva. The cause of Bodhi is Prajna or wisdom, and Karuna or compassion. Bodhi is the name given to the highest state of Samadhi in which the mind is awakened and illuminated."
Hump: 46

"W i s d o m,   W a y,   a n d Enlightenment are common translations [of Bodhi]. *I*. The wisdom of the Buddha's enlightenment acquired as the result of cutting off the two hindrances: passions and illusory conceptions. *II*. Nirvana as the state of extinguished passions. The cause of Bodhi is wisdom and compassion."
Dait: 19

"The Buddha originally taught that enlightenment is possible for all beings, both human and non-human. He made it very clear that, within the human realm, women and men have equal capacity for enlightenment. In Theravada countries such as Burma, Sri Lanka, and Thailand, enlightenment means liberation from Samsara, the cycle of birth and rebirth... In the Mahayana countries, enlightenment means achieving Buddhahood. One has to practice for many lifetimes to become a Buddha, but all living beings, can and will."
Tsomo/Budd: 11 #0087

◙ ENTERING THE STREAM
See also: Arhatship; Srotapanna

►"The first step on the Path of enlightenment; a stream-enterer (srotapanna) has only seven more rebirths to suffer before liberation (i.e. Arhatship)."
Stro: 358 #0836

◙ EON
see Kalpa

◙ EONIC FLOOD
see Floods

◙ EQUANIMITY
See also: Four Immeasurable Minds

►Skt/ Upeka. "The state of mental equilibrium in which the mind has no bent or attachment."
Dai: 631

"A detached state of mind, a sustained state of mental calm, a

mental disposition or habit that allows the person to experience opposites without feeling partiality."
Gomez: 296
Equanimity, as a teaching of the Buddha, is one of the Four Immeasurables, along with kindness, compassion and joy.
Editors: na #2278

◉ **ERACLE, JEAN (REV.)**

▸"Swiss Jodo Shinshu leader and translator. Curator and researcher in Ethnographical Museum, Geneva. 1970: President, *Societé Bouddhique Suisse Jodo-Shinshu*, with a temple near Geneva linked to Nishi Hongwan-ji. Publications include the first complete translation of the Pure Land sutras into French. Also *La Doctrine Bouddhique de la Terre Pure; Un Bouddhisme pour Tous*: l'Amidisme."
Snel: 306 #0750

◉ **ESCHATOLOGY**
See also: Ethics; Cosmology (Buddhist); Cosmic Age; Maitreya

▸"Term used to denote beliefs concerning death, judgment, purgatory, heaven and hell. With variations, this eschatological pattern occurs in all religions. Buddhism has no eschatology in the strict sense of term as this is understood in Christianity, since there are no ultimately 'last things' so far as the cosmos as a whole is concerned. So far as individual human existence is concerned, according to Buddhist thought, the consummation of this is in the 'deathless' state of Nirvana. Buddhist cosmology has its heavens and hells, but no one is condemned to eternal existence in these; eventually the inhabitants of both the Buddhist heavens and the hells will return to other levels of existence. The only strictly 'eschatological' moment for the Buddhist is the moment when a man achieves awakening or enlightenment (Bodhi). Buddhism, with its concept of rebirth, and cyclical view of time, envisages great cosmic cycles (kalpas through which the soul proceeds in countless rebirths until its final absorption in Nirvana). Millennialist theories grew up with the worship of Maitreya (Mi Lo Fo), introduced into China in the 4th century AD. According to these theories, several millennia after Buddha Sakyamuni, Buddhism will have reached such

a state of decline that Maitreya will appear and establish his millennial kingdom, and a new cycle of life and hope of redemption for all living creatures. It is thus that Buddhism inculcates hope that at the last hour of a final dispensation (mo-fa), a great saviour and renewer will descend from the Tushita heaven to establish on earth a new era."
Ling: 112-113 #1125

◉ ESOTERIC SCHOOL

Syn: Vajrayana;   Diamond Vehicle; Mantrayana; Tantrism
See also: Tibetan Buddhism; Shingon School

▸"*Esoteric* is a general term for the schools of Buddhism using mantras (q.v.) and mudras (q.v.) as a principal method of cultivation. *These schools exist in the Mahayana tradition of most Asian countries.* However, in practice, the term is often used synonymously with the Tantric School of Tibet (Vajrayana). The esoteric [secret] teachings of Buddhism are found in the Esoteric and Tien Tai schools and refer to those doctrines and rituals, deeply influenced by Hinduism, that developed in India during the seventh and

eighth centuries. These teachings, having magical properties, can only be revealed to those who have been properly initiated. The *exoteric* teachings include all Buddhist teachings other than the above."
Yoko: 203

"According to the doctrines of this school, Vajra-sattva received the teachings directly from Mahavairocana Buddha, compiled them as scripture, and sealed them in an iron tower in south India. This tower was opened eight hundred years after the demise of Sakyamuni, by Nagarjuna, who then revealed the long hidden scriptures. These scriptures were brought to China by Vajrabohi, Subhakaraismha, and Amoghavajra. [The Japanese Esoteric Patriarch] Kukai received them from Hui-kuo (Keika), who was a disciple of Amoghavajra."
Dait: 313

NOTE:
"While the monastic tradition was not abandoned, a highly complex series of initiations, empowerments, and other rituals was integrated into monastic life. The great saints of Vajrayana were called Mahasiddhas, notorious for possessing magical powers and having developed an

extensive oral and written tradition. The Vajrayana tradition [of India] was rather quickly exported, first to Central Asia, and later to Tibet and throughout East Asia. It is most readily seen today in the various schools of Tibetan Buddhism and the Shingon tradition of Japanese Buddhism."
Preb: 272   #0150

◙ **ESSENTIALS OF REBIRTH**
see Ojo Yoshu

◙ **ETERNALISM**
see   Two extreme views

◙ **ETERNITY**
see Kalpa

◙ **ETHEREAL BIRTH**
see   Birth by transformation

◙ **ETHICS**
See also: Eschatology

▶"In Buddhist tradition, the principles governing human conduct relate the characteristic condition of humanity (suffering, unease, illness, caused by the basic evil of Desire) to the recognized goal of Buddhist endeavour, viz. *complete enlightenment*. Buddhist ethic thus favours those attitudes and kinds of behaviour which help humanity towards the ultimate goal of transcendental enlightenment; as an *intermediate criterion*, the goal of auspicious and wholesome rebirth [in a Pure Land] is important: whatever is conducive to this end is to be encouraged; whatever detracts is to be discouraged or renounced. The outworking of the Buddhist ethic is seen at the most elementary level in the 5 basic moral precepts (see Five Precepts), binding upon all Buddhists, monastic and lay."
Ling: 113-114   #1127

◙ **EUROPE (BUDDHISM IN)**
See also: France; Germany; North America (Buddhism In)

▶"Buddhism was born as an object of western knowledge rather late in the Oriental Renaissance (which Schwab dates from 1680 to 1880). The sustained study of Buddhist texts did not really begin in Europe until the delivery of Brian Hodgson's package of Sanskrit manuscripts into the hands of Eugene Burnouf in 1837. [Hodgson was the Assistant Resident for the United Kingdom in Nepal] . By this time Friedrich Schlegel had already proclaimed

that 'everything, yes, everything without exception, has its origin in India.' But Buddhism remained largely excluded from the enthusiasm for Indian wisdom... Burnouf would not publish his *Introduction à l'Histoire du Bouddhisme Indien* until 1844; his translation of the *Lotus Sutra* did not appear until 1852, the year of his death. By the time these and other works gained currency, the wave of enthusiasm for things Indian had largely passed, especially in Britain and France, although it continued in Germany into the present century. The brief period during which India replaced Egypt as the putative source of civilization was over; by the middle of the nineteenth century, both had been demoted in favor of Greece. Buddhist Studies, then, began as a latecomer to Romantic Orientalism, an offshoot of Indology at a time when India was no longer in vogue. Indeed, the portrayals of China and India as abodes of reason and spirit, respectively, which had been popular during the Enlightenment and the Romantic period, had begun to be displaced by 1800, before the Opium War of 1839 and the Indian Mutiny of 1857. India and China were now considered to be corrupt and effete civilizations, precisely at the time the European powers were undertaking their conquest. It was in this milieu that Buddhism was 'created' in Europe."
Lopez: 2

Philip Almond in *The British Discovery of Buddhism*:
[To Westerners], "Buddhism, by 1860, had come to exist, not in the Orient, but in the Oriental libraries and institutes of the West, in its texts and manuscripts, at the desks of the Western savants who interpreted it. It had become a textual object, defined, classified, and interpreted through its own textuality. By the middle of the century, the Buddhism that existed 'out there' was beginning to be judged by a West that alone knew what Buddhism was, is, and ought to be. The essence of Buddhism came to be seen as expressed not 'out there' in the Orient, but in the West through the control of Buddhism's own textual past."
Lopez: 290 #201

◙ EUTHANASIA
See also: Suicide; Killing

►What is the Buddhist attitude on

[this] problem? Like almost all other major religions, Buddhism does not condone any act that results in the deprivation of life of any living being. This is more so with regard to cases involving human beings ... According to Buddhism, the whole [human] existence is suffering, (Dukka/q.v.) of which illness is only one aspect. Death is only a violent break in this continuous process, and brings about only a temporary end to suffering which is bound to recur with the next birth [unless all bad Karma has been extinguished].

(*Encyclopedia of Buddhism*, Volume 5: p. 172)

"My (Roshi P. Kapleau, a well known Zen teacher) own feeling is that the same considerations apply to euthanasia as to other modes of life-taking. If the sufferer intentionally ends his own life, he is committing suicide and must one day face all that entails in terms of karmic retribution. In the same way, someone who enables the sufferer to die, even by request, is culpable, although the mind state in which such an act is performed vitally affects the resulting karma. Nagging questions remain. Is it not selfish to be thinking of one's own karma when someone dear to you, terminally ill and in excruciating pain, implores you to end his or her life? But then, might not a refusal to respond to the patient's entreaties be kinder, karmically speaking, since the sufferer's karma is also involved? In any case, would a sufferer who understood the meaning of pain and its relation to karma -- that is, the grateful acceptance of pain as a means of paying karmic debts -- ask for euthanasia?"
Kapl/1980: 257

"Orthodox Jewry -- out of deep religious belief ... stands in adamant opposition to assisted suicide. So do most Protestants. The Southern Baptist Convention, evangelical Christians and the Lutheran Church-Missouri Synod have been among the most vocal. But it is the Roman Catholic Church--by virtue of its hierarchal structure, sheer numbers and an extensive theology on the sanctity of life -- that commands a dominant role. It is basic to Catholic teaching that human life is formed in the image and likeness of God ... so the value of a human life is not a matter of human choice or convenience."
NY TIMES MAGAZINE:7/21/96,p.22

◙ **EVANS-WENTZ, W.Y. (d. 1965)**

▶"Scholar of Buddhism, most famous for his work on the Tibetan tradition, and particularly on the *Tibetan Book of the Dead.*"
Preb: 122 #1024

◙ **EVERYDAY MIND IS THE WAY**
See also: Chao-Chou

▶"'The everyday mind is the way.' [Nan-chuan's] reply to the question, 'What is the essence of Buddhism?' It means that the everyday activities of an *enlightened* person naturally harmonize with the Buddha-mind [because such a mind is not burdened by discriminations]."
Dait: 113
This famous quote is sometimes attributed to Chao-chou (Nan-ch'uan's disciple) in some Western books. #0069

◙ **EVERYTHING IS MADE FROM MIND**
see   Stanza that destroys Hell

◙ **EVIL**
See also: Afflictions; Dukkha

▶"There is no term in Buddhist usage which exactly corresponds to the term 'evil' in Western religious usage; the nearest is dukkha, variously translated as 'ill,' 'suffering,' 'unsatisfactoriness,' 'evil.' Buddhist thought on the subject of evil does not concern itself with origins; the fact of evil inclinations and attitudes is recognised, the reality of evil is affirmed, and the way to overcoming and negating such evil is proclaimed. In Buddhist thought, evil is most characteristically seen in its three basic roots: greed, hatred and illusion [delusion]. The degree to which these factors are present in the human mind in varying degrees and combinations determines from moment to moment the 'given' situation in which a human individual acts."
Ling: 114

"Buddhism is not dualistic, and, therefore, does not divide phenomena into absolute 'good' or 'evil'. It recognizes 'evil' as 'limitation', and, therefore, purely relative. There is therefore no 'problem of Evil' as in theistic systems of thought. *All evil is traced to desire for self.* The 'basic evil' is the idea of separateness, and the Buddhist goal is the removal of evil by the

eradication of every selfish inclination."
Murt: 40 #1128

◙ **EVIL PATHS**
see Three Evil Paths

◙ **EVIL PLANES OF EXISTENCE**
see Three Evil Paths

◙ **EVIL REALMS**
see Three Evil Paths

◙ **EXCLUSION CLAUSE**
See also: Dharmakara's Vows; Original Vows; Pure Land School

►The 18th vow of the Bodhisattva Dharmakara, the future Amitabha Buddha, promises rebirth in the Pure Land to anyone who puts his utmost faith in him, *except* "those who have committed one of the Five Cardinal Sins or slandered the Dharma" (Exclusion Clause).
Editor: na
"Both patriarchs T'an-luan and Shan-tao discuss the clause, partly to resolve apparent inconsistencies with a similar provision stated in the *Meditation Sutra*. Patriarch Shan-tao states, however, that its purpose is not to exclude certain beings. Rather, the Tathagata (Buddha), fearing

that we would commit these two kinds of faults (Cardinal Sins and slandering the Dharma), seeks to stop us by declaring that we will then not be able to attain birth in the Pure Land... the *clause is intended (as a warning) to make us realize the extreme gravity of the offenses.*"
Veda: 194 #1166

◙ **EXCLUSIVE PRACTICE**
See also: Sundry Practices; Pure Land Buddhism (Summary)

►"Exclusive Practice consists of the body bowing exclusively to Amitabha Buddha, the mouth exclusively repeating the Buddha's name, and the mind focussing exclusively on the Buddha's name. Out of ten thousand cultivators who practice in such a manner, ten thousand are assured of rebirth in the Pure Land. Sundry Practices entail engaging in various methods of cultivation while dedicating the merits accrued toward rebirth in the Western Land. Since the practitioner's mind is not focussed or singleminded, it is difficult to accumulate merits. Thus, only three or four out of hundreds of thousands can hope to achieve rebirth in the Pure

Land. These are true, golden words of advice, immutable throughout the ages. Both of you should follow them for your own benefit and in counselling everyone else. Reciting mantras, too, should be considered an ancillary practice, rather than a principal method along with Buddha Recitation. The merits derived from mantra recitation are indeed inconceivable. However, ordinary people who achieve rebirth in the Pure Land owe it entirely to utterly sincere Faith and Vows, as these correspond to the lofty Vows of Amitabha Buddha" (Patriarch Yin Kuang, in *Pure-Land/Zen, Zen-Pure Land*).
PLZ: 90

◙ **EXCOMMUNICATION**
See also: Heresy; Heretical Views

►"The only kind of excommunication practiced by Buddhists is that which is applied in case of a fully ordained monk/nun who is found guilty of one of the offenses mentioned in the Patimokkha (Pratimoksa), for which the prescribed penalty is permanent expulsion from the Order (Sangha): sexual misconduct, theft, murder and boasting of supernatural powers.

For offenses of a serious nature other than these, the offender may be temporarily suspended, with the prospect of readmission later, if found worthy. It will be noted that *there is no excommunication on grounds of heretical beliefs.*"
Ling: 115 #1129

NOTE:
Heretical beliefs from the Buddhist perspective are considered a form of delusion (ignorance) and as such will disappear once wisdom develops through correct practice.
Editor: na

◙ **EXHAUSTIVE MEANING**
see Definitive meaning

◙ **EXISTENCE** *(OF AMITABHA / PURE LAND)*
See also: Pure Land Buddhism (Summary); Four Propositions

►The existence or non-existence of the Pure Land is a question, the answer to which depends on the practitioner and his level of cultivation. Consider the following exchange between two Zen monks:
Disciple: "Master, does the Pure Land exist?"/
Monk: "Does this world exist?"/

Disciple: "Of course it does, Master."/

Monk: "If this world exists, then the Pure Land exists all the more."

Buddha Sakyamuni taught that we are all living in a big Dream. Within this Birth and Death Dream, everything, ourselves and all dharmas exist. In this sense, the Pure Land also exists. This is not unlike a child who has no chocolate at all dreaming of receiving, for example, ten boxes of chocolates. If upon "awakening," he finds himself with even one box, it can only mean that he is still dreaming. Otherwise, there should be no box of chocolates at all, as everything was just a dream. Likewise, when we still grasp at the self and still see this world as existent, we are still dreaming the big Dream and therefore everything, including the Pure Land, exists. Only those sages and saints who have transcended all notion of self and dharmas can proclaim that there is no Pure Land.

Editor: na

Questions/answers

Zen Master Chu Hung (16th century): I. "Some people say that the Pure Land is nothing but mind, that there is no Pure Land of Ultimate Bliss beyond the trillions of worlds of the cosmos. This talk of mind-only has its source in the words of the sutras, and is true, not false. But those who quote it in this sense are misunderstanding its meaning. Mind equals objects: there are no objects beyond mind. Objects equal mind: there is no mind beyond objects. Since objects are wholly mind, why must we cling to mind and dismiss objects? Those who dismiss objects when they talk of mind have not comprehended mind."

II. "Some people say: 'To see the Buddha is to see the Buddha of the Self-Nature, not the Buddha of the Western Pure Land.' This being the case, at the time of death, is it the Buddha of the Self-Nature who appears, or is it Buddha Amitabha who comes to receive and guide us?

Answer: Seeing the Buddha at the time of death is due to our own Self-Nature, which has elicited a response from Amitabha Buddha. You should not revert everything to the Self-Nature and think that there is no Buddha Amitabha arriving to receive and guide you!" (Master Zhuhong, in J.C. Cleary, tr., *Pure Land, Pure Mind*.)

Zen: 110

NOTE:
"In secular western thought, awareness of psychological projection as a source of supernatural being has served to demythologize demons, goblins, angels and saints and rob them of their power. The Bardo Thodol [Tibetan Book of the Dead], however, speaks of the deities as 'projections' but never as 'mere projections.' The deities are present and must be dealt with religiously ... not just by intellectual insight." (D.G. Dawe in *The Perennial Dictionary of World Religions*, p. 93.)

For further details, see next entry. #1482

◉ EXISTENCE / EMPTINESS

See also: Emptiness; Practice (Buddhist); Truth; Visions; Four Propositions

----

►Please read entry "Emptiness" before the following:

"The True Mind (True Nature) is an immensely broad and extensive state, encompassing an untold number of lands, Buddhas and sentient beings. In that One True State, the aspect of lands and sentient beings, constantly in flux, pertains to the 'Dharma Door (school) of Birth and Death.' The silent and illuminating aspect -- still, wonderful, clear, bright and everlasting -- is called the 'Dharma Door (school) of True Thusness.' The True Mind or True Nature is a Common True State encompassing those two Doors ... The Buddha taught two approaches for returning to that True Nature. Such methods as Zen, T'ien T'ai (Tendai School) and a division of the Esoteric School enter it through the *Dharma Door of Emptiness*. Other schools, such as the Pure Land School, the Avatamsaka School, the Vinaya (Discipline) School, as well as the Diamond Division of the Esoteric School do so through the *Dharma Door of Existence*. Therefore, those who deeply understand the prajna truth of Zen, or the meaning of the Ten Mysterious Gates of the Avatamsaka School, all clearly realize that form is no different from emptiness, emptiness is no different from form, form is emptiness, emptiness is form. On the other hand, those who lack thorough understanding will cling to emptiness unless they cling to existence. However, clinging to existence at least makes the practitioner fear cause and effect, avoid transgressions and perform good deeds, which leads to

auspicious rebirth in human and celestial realms -- or in the Western Pure Land (in the case of diligent practitioners of Buddha Recitation). On the other hand, if he clings to emptiness, he will end up denigrating cause and effect and rejecting the Buddhas and sages. Thus, he will descend, in the future, upon the Three Evil Paths. Therefore, the ancients have cautioned: 'It is better to be attached to existence, though the attachment may be as great as Mount Sumeru, than to be attached to emptiness, though the attachment may be as small as a mustard seed.'" (Thích Thiền Tâm)
Dia: 51-53

D.T. Suzuki quotes the Zen Patriarch Fa Yen as follows:

"The sutras preached by the Buddha during his lifetime are said to amount to five thousand and forty-eight fascicles; they include the doctrine of emptiness and the doctrine of being (existence); there are teachings of immediate realization and of gradual development. Is it not an affirmation?

"But, according to [Zen Master Yung Chia in his Song of Enlightenment], 'there are no sentient beings, there are no Buddhas; sages as numerous as the sands of the Ganges are but so many bubbles in the sea; sages and worthies of the past are like flashes of lightning.' Is this not a negation?

"O you, my disciples, if you say there is, you go against [Yung Chia]; if you say there is not, you contradict our old master Buddha. If he were with us, then how would he pass through the dilemma? ... If you confess your ignorance, I will let you see into the secret. When I say there is not, this does not necessarily mean a negation; when I say there is, this also does not signify an affirmation. Turn eastward and look at the Western Land; face the south and the North Star is pointed out there!"

D.T. Suzuki/65: na

For details, *See also:* Emptiness; Visions (last part) #2317

◙ **EXPEDIENT MEANS**
Syn: Expedients; Skillful means; Skill-in-means; Upaya
See also: Paramita; Practice

►A. "Temporary or provisional teachings as a means to lead sentient beings to the final doctrine.
B. The seventh of the ten Paramitas (q.v.)."
Dait: 118

Refers to strategies, methods, devices targeted to the capacities, circumstances, likes and dislikes of each sentient being, so as to rescue him and lead him to Enlightenment. "All particular formulations of the Teaching are just provisional expedients to communicate the Truth (Dharma) in specific contexts" (J.C. Cleary). "The Buddha's words were medicines for a given sickness at a given time," always infinitely adaptable to the conditions of the audience.
Editor/Van Hien: 221-222

"The practice of skillful means is the Buddhist approach to teaching the Dharma. Each method (Pure Land, Zen ...) 'has its own area of emphasis. Those who advocate a Dharma door direct all expedient teaching toward that method.' (Master Thích Thiền Tâm, *Buddhism of Wisdom and Faith*, Preface.)"

(I) Unfavorable expedients
An expedient which at first sight seems adverse but which in fact serves to awaken the practitioner to the Truth, for example, of Impermanence. See the following passage from a Zen text, the *Vimalakirti Sutra*:
"They [Bodhisattvas] demonstrate the burning of the earth/ In the consuming flames of the world's end,/ In order to demonstrate impermanence/ To living beings with the notion of permanence... They play with illusory manifestations/ In order to develop living beings,/ showing themselves to be old or sick,/ And even manifesting their own deaths." (Robert Thurman, tr.)
Editor/Zen: 190

A severe illness, a sudden death or even loss of a job may sometimes jolt the practitioner out of his usual complacency and remind him of the need to cultivate. *Note*: whether an unfavorable event is good or bad for one's cultivation depends, in the final analysis, on one's own outlook, one's mind. It can be either an expedient, to help one attain the Way or a "demon," hindering cultivation (*See also: Buddhism of Wisdom and Faith*, section 63, para. 4).
Editor/Thich: 307

Feigning shortcomings and weaknesses is a common expedient of leading disciples of Sakyamuni Buddha. For example, Ananda was allegedly "lured" into the house of the most beautiful courtesan of Vaisali, thus providing the setting for the *Surangama Sutra*. In this key Mahayana text, the Buddha warned cultivators of the various temptations and obstructions to be expected on the way to Enlightenment. Following this example, some monks and nuns at times expediently confess to various transgressions they did not actually commit. This is for the express purpose of providing the assembly with an opportunity to learn and grow. These instances, albeit rare, reflect the essence of Bodhisattva practice.

Editor/Zen: 134

(II) One / Many Teachings

See also: the following passage from D.T. Suzuki: "Buddhist theology has a fine comprehensive theory to explain the manifold types of experience in Buddhism, which look so contradictory to each other. In fact the history of Chinese Buddhism is a series of attempts to reconcile the diverse schools ... Various ways of classification and reconciliation were offered, and ... their conclusion was this: Buddhism supplies us with so many gates to enter into the truth because of such a variety of human characters and temperaments and environments due to diversities of karma. This is plainly depicted and taught by the Buddha himself when he says that the same water drunk by the cow and the cobra turns in one case into nourishing milk and in the other into deadly poison, and that medicine is to be given according to disease. This is called the doctrine of [skillful] means ..." (*The Eastern Buddhist*, Vol. 4, No. 2, p. 121.)

Editor: na

A question that arises is how two methods seemingly so opposite as Pure Land and Zen can lead to the same goal of Buddhahood. As an analogy, supposing a patient is admitted to the hospital with a high fever. The physician will, of course, prescribe a medication to lower the fever. However, if later in the day, her temperature has dropped to a dangerously low level, he will attempt to raise it with another prescription. The immediate goal is different in each case, but the ultimate goal in both is the same: to normalize the temperature of the patient. The Buddha, as the master physician, likewise employs 84,000 methods to treat the 84,000 afflictions of sentient beings."

Editor: na

"Studying Zen, Buddha Recitation, even reading and reciting sutras, all are aids in the path toward seeing the Way. They are like the staves that travelers use to aid them in their journeys. (Zen Master Hakuin 1685-1768)"

Dumou/90: 387

Another interpretation is that the teachings themselves are not simplified, but rather the audience was not ready to understand them to the full extent. As an analogy, the rain may fall equally on big trees and small but the larger ones absorb more water.

Editor: na

Even when the Buddhas and Bodhisattvas are depicted as providing material assistance to the believer, this is always viewed as an "expedient means" -- the ultimate goal is to lead the believer to Enlightenment.

Editor: na

(III) Self-Benefit/ Other-Benefit

See the following explanation of the expression "skillful means are the ultimate" as seen by Kukai (774-835), the founder of the Japanese Shingon, or Esoteric, school: "Kukai interpreted this phrase in two ways. One stresses the imperative sense that skillful means should lead to ultimate enlightenment. The other emphasizes the declarative sense that skillful means themselves *are* the ultimate. The former expresses the view of self-benefit in seeking enlightenment, and the latter, the view of enlightenment fulfilled in compassion toward others."

Yama: 105

(IV) Note

The *Treatise on the Awakening of the Faith* specifically recommends Buddha Recitation for all but the most advanced practitioners: "Next, suppose there is a man who learns this [Mahayana] teaching for the first time and wishes to seek the correct faith but lacks courage and strength. Because he lives in this world of suffering, he fears that he will not always be able to meet the Buddhas and honor them personally, and that, faith being difficult to perfect, he will be inclined to fall back. He should know that the Tathagathas have an *excellent expedient* means by which they can protect his faith: that is, through the strength of wholehearted meditation-recitation on the Buddha, he will in fulfillment of his wishes be able to be born in the Buddha-land beyond, to see the Buddha always, and to be forever separated from the evil states of existence... " (Asvaghosha, The *Awakening of the Faith*, p. 102.)

Editor/Zen: 67-68   #0072

◙ **EXPEDIENTS**
see Expedient means

◙ **EXTERNALIST**
See also: Externalist views

►Lit. "non-Buddhists." This term is generally used by Buddhists with reference to followers of other religions.
Editor/PL Mind: 222
An externalist is someone who does not believe in or follow Buddhist teaching, which can be defined as any teaching conforming to the Dharma seals.
Editor/Thich: 310 #1392

◙ **EXTERNALIST VIEWS**
See also: Externalists; Six Heterodox Teachers

►The sutras usually refer to sixty-two such views. They are the externalist (non-buddhist) views prevalent in Buddha Shakyamuni's time.
Editor/Tam: 152 #0898

◙ **EXTINCTION**
See also: Arhatship

►"Where the term 'extinction' occurs in Buddhist tradition, it refers to extinction of feeling and perception in the special state of meditation achieved only by one who has attained mastery of the 8 Dhyanas, and is an Anagamin (non-returner) or an Arhat. It is incorrectly used in connection with the state of Nirvana, if it is applied to one who has achieved Nirvana. The state thus achieved is not one of 'extinction' or 'annihilation' of all existence; *what has suffered total extinction, according to the Buddhist view, are the passions, greed, hatred, and illusion which are the roots of all evil and suffering.*"
Ling: 115 #1130

◙ **EYE-OPENING CEREMONY (Statues, Buddha-Images, Icons)**
see Icon

◙ **FA-HSIANG SCHOOL**
See also: Yogacara School

►Chinese Yogacara school founded by patriarch Hsuan-Tsang (602-664). #2152

◙ **FA-HSIEN**
See also: Hsuan-Tsang

►"A Chinese monk of the Eastern Chin dynasty (4th - 5th c. AD). In 399 he left China for India, finally arriving there after six years of hard travel. After studying Sanskrit and obtaining many Sanskrit texts of the

Tripitaka (Buddhist canon), he returned to China by sea in 414. After his return he not only translated these texts but also wrote a record of his travels. He died when either eighty-two or eighty-six years old."
Yoko: 203 #0790

◉ **FA-TSANG (643-720)**
See also: Avatamsaka School

►"The third [and best known] patriarch of the Avatamsaka (Hua-yen/Kegon) school in China. His family was originally from Central Asia. At the age of seventeen, he entered Mt. T'ai-po as a layman and began to study the Buddhist scriptures. In 695 he assisted Sikshananda with his eighty-fascicle translation of the Avatamsaka. He contributed greatly to the systematization of the Hua-yen doctrine, with many commentaries, and formulated the classification of the Five Teachings (q.v.) and Ten Doctrines. He lectured widely on the *Avatamsaka Sutra* and built Hua-yen temples in Lo-yang, Ch'ang-an and elsewhere."
Sokk: 92 #0256

◉ **FADS IN BUDDHISM**
see   West (Buddhism In), particularly *note*

◉ **FAITH**
See also: Devotion; Pure Land School;   Faith--Vows--Practice; Awakening of the Faith Treatise

----

►"Faith (Pali/ saddha; Skt/ sraddha) has an important place in the Buddhist scheme, both at the entry upon the Buddhist way, and in perseverance in the way. Faith is said to be a factor associated with any karmically wholesome state of consciousness whatsoever, at any stage of the religious life... The centrality of Saving Faith is notably developed in the treatise *Awakening of the Faith in the Mahayana*, which has had an immense influence in East Asian Buddhism. There it is argued that 'fundamental' faith is a   joyous   recollection   of 'Suchness' (chen ju). Such fundamental faith is finally attained *inter alia* through the limitless   merits   of   Buddha, resulting in worshipping and reverencing him..."
Ling: 116-117
"Sakyamuni Buddha is said to have saved himself 'by his own efforts alone', and this streak of spiritual self-help runs right through Buddhism. You will still hear people today saying, 'You have to do it for yourself -- no one else can do it for you', *which*

is correct, but not altogether true. For faith and devotion perennially arise within the human heart, faith signifying belief that an external agency can help the individual spiritually, and devotion a deep gratitude for the source of that help. There have been such elements in Buddhism from the earliest times. To practice within the Buddhist tradition is in fact to display faith (though hopefully not blind faith) in that tradition. To bow before an image of a Buddha or Bodhisattva, a teacher or a monk or nun is to show both faith and devotion. So is to light incense, to copy or recite the scriptures, to carve images, to endow temples and monasteries, to feed the Sangha, and so on. Such practices grew as the religion itself developed, particularly during the Mahayana phase of its development. An important early devotional practice was that of *buddhanusmrti* or 'Recollection of the Buddha'. This is done by bringing the Buddha to mind, reciting his name, and by visualizing his image and/or his Pure Land or field of activity, which might be either a physical or a transcendental 'place' depending upon the sophistication of the individual view. It is also possible to go beyond recollection of the Buddha as a physical being to a more formless kind of recollection. The benefits to be derived from such practices are considerable. One might have a vision of the Buddha, or attain profound meditative states."
Snell/Buddhism: 84

The concept of faith is very important in all Buddhist schools -- Zen, Pure Land and Tantric alike. See the following quote from D.T. Suzuki:

"A thoroughgoing enlightenment is attained only through the most self-sacrificing application of the mind, supported by an inflexible faith in the finality of Zen ... The necessary requirements are faith and personal effort, without which Zen is a mere bubble." (Suzuki, *An Introduction to Zen Buddhism*: 115)   Editor: na

Faith In Pure Land Buddhism

"A tradition in Buddhism beginning with the Pure Land sutras, and developing into formal traditions in virtually all Buddhist cultures in East Asia. Upon the development of the *Larger* and *Smaller Amitabha Sutras* and the *Meditation Sutra*, the notion of putting one's confidence, or more precisely, faith, in the saving grave of Amitabha Buddha became important in Indian Buddhism. This faith is expressed by the Sanskrit formula 'Namo Amitabha Buddha,' literally, 'Homage to Amitabha Buddha.' As the Buddhist tradition moved into China, this practice of placing faith in Amitabha Buddha became even more popular, and the ritual formula became the basis of religious practice in the Chinese Pure Land school (known as Ching-t'u/Tịnh-Độ.)"

Preb: 123-124

The *Avatamsaka Sutra* teaches: "Faith is the basis of the Path, the mother of virtues
Nourishing and growing all good ways... Faith can assure arrival at enlightenment." (T.Cleary, tr. *The Flower Ornament*:I/331.)

"Therefore, Faith is of great importance to the cultivator. If we lose Faith, not only will our base for progress in the Way crumble, but none of our liberating deeds will succeed. This Faith is not blind faith, but is Faith grounded in wisdom, based entirely on the words of the Buddhas, Bodhisattvas and Patriarchs, as taught in the sutras. Why is it that after relying on wisdom, we should still put our complete Faith in the teachings of the sages? It is because the Pure Land method, belonging as it does to the Mahayana tradition, is concerned with many transcendental realms beyond human knowledge or wisdom. Therefore, there are many realities that ordinary sentient beings cannot readily understand. Once, when Buddha Sakyamuni was lecturing on the *Lotus Sutra* at the Vulture Peak Assembly, five thousand great Sravakas (Hearers), many of whom were Arhats, did not believe His words and left the Assembly. Even these venerable Sravakas endowed with transcendental wisdom had doubts about the Dharma preached by Buddha Sakyamuni Himself. We can see, then, that Mahayana teachings are not easy to understand and believe. For this reason, there are many passages in the Mahayana sutras in which Buddha Sakyamuni requested that such and such a teaching not be preached indiscriminately to those without Faith and with too many view-attachments, lest they develop slanderous thoughts and reap evil karma. When the Mahayana doctrine began to spread widely, the ancient sages, too, admonished Buddhist followers to adopt the following approach to studying Mahayana sutras: Understand with your mind those passages that you can. As for those passages which you cannot fully comprehend through reflection, just put your Faith entirely in the words of the Buddhas. That is the only way to avoid the offense of vilifying the great Dharma and losing merits and virtues thereby."

Tam: 59

"According to the sutras and commentaries, the Pure Land practitioner should follow three guidelines to consolidate his faith.

1. *THE GUIDELINE OF REASON.*

This is the reasoning and understanding of human logic. For example, we may reflect: All realms are created from the mind. If there is a world such as ours, where good karma and bad karma are about equal, there must exist other worlds such as the Three Evil Paths, with a preponderance of evil karma, as well as celestial realms, where good karma prevails. It therefore stands to reason that the Western Pure Land exists, as a result of the pure, good Vows of Amitabha Buddha as well as the virtues of the Bodhisattvas and other morally superior beings.

2. *THE GUIDELINE OF THE TEACHINGS OF THE SAGES.*

These are the words of the Buddhas and Bodhisattvas in sutras and commentaries. Buddha Sakyamuni, with his pure vision, clearly saw the auspicious environment and superior beings of the Western Pure Land and described them in the Pure Land sutras. The great Bodhisattvas, such as Manjusri and Samantabhadra, all extolled the Land of Ultimate Bliss and enjoined sentient beings to seek rebirth there. If Buddhists are not guided by the words of the Buddhas and Bodhisattvas, whom then should they believe?

3. *THE GUIDELINE OF ACTUAL SEEING AND UNDERSTANDING.*

This is a method of reasoning based on actual occurrences, verifiable through our eyes and understanding. The commentary, *Biographies of Pure Land Sages and Saints*, has amply documented the stories of individuals who have achieved rebirth in the Land of Ultimate Bliss through Buddha Recitation

... Moreover, those who have practiced Buddha Recitation with a pure mind have been known to witness scenes of the Pure Land during their current lifetimes.

I [Master Thich Thien-Tam] have described above three guidelines that Pure Land practitioners should follow to consolidate their faith. Moreover, according to Elder Master Yin Kuang, Pure Land followers should not seek guidance on Pure Land matters from Zen Masters. This is because the answer of Zen Masters are all directed towards principle and essence, while the Pure Land approach is based on phenomena and marks. This being the case, and considering the different areas of emphasis, beginning Pure Land practitioners who do not yet fully understand essence and marks, noumenon and phenomena, will not only fail to benefit from the answers of Zen Masters, they may develop even greater doubts, perplexity and inconsistent views."   Tam: 162-164

NOTES

(1) "There is even a place in the Western Paradise for the worst sinners. The *Meditation Sutra* relates that even if a person has commited the Five or Ten Cardinal Sins, if this sinner has faith in Amitabha Buddha and earnestly recites His name ten times on his deathbed, a lotus throne will appear and will bear him to the lowest stage in the Pure Land -- the lowest birth of the lowest degree [see Lotus Grades]. Instead of being condemned ..., the sinner will be born in the Western Paradise in a closed lotus flower ... This teaching of the nine possible levels of birth was an extremely effective way to reward good deeds on earth while still offering the promise of salvation to all, regardless of how much merit they had accumulated." (Okazaki, *Pure Land Buddhist Painting*) Okaz: 52

(2) *Utter complete Faith*, or *Utter Sincerity*, or *Singlemindedness*, or *One-Pointedness of Mind*: in practice, these expressions are used interchangeably, as a cultivator cannot have utter complete faith *without* being utterly sincere and singleminded (and vice versa).

The kind of utter, complete, unquestionable faith spoken of in the Pure Land sutras may be illustrated by the famous example of the monk who, to guard against falling asleep, would practice meditation seated at the edge of a high cliff. One moment of inattention would send him tumbling to his death. According to the *Meditation Sutra*, the practioner, on his deathbed must have this *utmost* level of sincerity to ensure his rebirth in the Pure Land.

Editor: na

See also: Faith-Vows Practice; Notorious Men. #1025

◉ **FAITH HEALING**

See also: Spirit World; Mediums

►"The practice of faith-healing is prevalent in many countries. Many people are trying to influence the public through emotional persuasion designated as faith-healing. In order to impress on their patients the efficacy of their healing powers, some faith-healers use the name of a god or a religious object to introduce a religious flavour into their faith-healing methods. The introduction of religion into faith-healing is actually a guise or decoy to beguile the patient into developing more devotion and enhance the confidence or faith of the patient in the faith-healer. This healing act, if performed in public, is intended to bring converts to a particular religious denomination. In actual fact, insofar as faith-healing is concerned, religion is not all that important. There are numerous cases of faith-healers performing their faith healing acts without using religion at all. A case in point is the science of hypnotism, the practice of which involves no religious aspects at all. Those who associate religion with faith-healing are engaging in a subtle form of illusion, trying to attract converts to their particular religion by making use of faith healing and describing certain cures as miraculous acts. The methods employed by faith healers are to condition the minds of patients into having a certain mental attitude with the result that certain favourable psychological and physiological changes invariably take place. This improves the condition of the mind, the heart, the consequent blood circulation and other related organic functions of the body, thus creating a sense of well-being. If sickness is attributed to the condition of the mind, then the mind can certainly be properly conditioned to assist in eradicating whatever illness may occur. In this context, it is to be noted that the constant and regular practice of meditation can help to minimize, if not

completely eradicate, various forms of illnesses. There are many discourses in the Teaching of the Buddha where it is indicated that various forms of sickness were eradicated through the conditioning of the mind. Thus it is worthwhile to practice meditation [and/or Buddha Recitation] in order to attain mental and physical well-being."
Dham: 326-327 #1983

◎ **FAITH--VOWS--PRACTICE**
See also: Devotion; Vows / Rebirth in Pure Land; Pure Land School; Provisions for Pure Land Rebirth
----
▸Three factors, Faith, Vows and Practice, are the cornerstones of Pure Land Buddhism. If they are present, rebirth in the Pure Land is assured.
"*Faith*" means faith in Amitabha Buddha's Vows to rescue all who recite His name, as well as faith in one's own self-nature, which is intrinsically the same as His (to recite the Buddha's name is to recite / remember the Mind).
"*Vows*" are the determination to be reborn in the Pure Land -- in one's pure mind -- so as to be in a position to save oneself and others.
"*Practice*" generally means

reciting the Buddha's name to the point where one's mind and that of Amitabha Buddha are in unison -- i.e., to the point of singlemindedness. Samadhi and wisdom are then achieved. Please note that all Buddhist teachings are expedient means (q.v.), dividing the one and indivisible Truth into many parts. Faith, Vows and Practice, although three, are really one. Thus, it can be said that rebirth in the Pure Land depends on three conditions or two conditions (faith and vows) or even one condition (faith), as the one contains all and all are contained in one. The formula to be used depends on the audience and the times. The aim is to enable sentient beings to achieve rebirth in the Pure Land as a steppingstone toward Buddhahood.
Editor/Van Hien: 205
For heuristic reasons, Dharma Masters explain Faith, Vows and Practice separately, emphasizing the crucial nature of each one. However, these three preconditions for rebirth in the Pure Land are one and indivisible. True Faith naturally leads to Vows and Practice, while correct Practice cannot exist independent of Faith and Vows.

As the Patriarch Yin Kuang once wrote: "The true Pure Land practitioner always fully combines the three criteria of Faith, Vows and Practice during recitation. He is like an infant longing for his mother. When, lonely and crying, he searches for her; he certainly never lacks Faith or the desire (Vow) to see her. Therefore, why do you ask whether 'Vows and Practices come separately or together?'"
Editor/Tam: 313
NOTE:
"Elder Master Ou I, the ninth Pure Land patriarch, has said, 'To be reborn in the Pure Land or not *depends entirely upon Faith and Vows*; the grade of rebirth (high or low) depends on whether one's Practice is deep or shallow.' He further added, 'Without Faith and Vows, you cannot be reborn, even if you recite the Buddha's name to the point where neither the blowing wind nor the falling rain can penetrate and your recitation is as solid as a bronze wall or an iron gate.' Those who practice Buddha Recitation assiduously but lack Faith and Vows will merely obtain the merits and blessings of the human and celestial realms, according to their level of cultivation. When

their blessings are exhausted they are once again subject to birth and death ..." (Master Thích Thiền Tâm, *Buddhism of Wisdom and Faith*, sect 21)
Tam: 96   #1670

◙ **FALSE THINKING**

▸"Erroneous thinking, deluded thought, false notions, false ideas. The mental processes of living beings based on greed, hatred and stupidity."
[Hs/tsob]   #1305

◙ **FAME**
see Obstacles to Cultivation

◙ **FAULT-FINDING**
See also: Obstacles to Cultivation

▸Proclaiming the errors of others, whether true or not, is an offense for two main reasons: i) the mind of the "proclaimer" is no longer empty and still, but tarnished by dislike or scorn, and ii) the "transgressor" and those who hear of the errors may grow discouraged, abandon further cultivation and retrogress -- thus, potential Buddhas are lost.
Editor/Tam: 316
"According to the *Brahma Net* and *Avatamsaka Sutras*, we should ignore appearances and

external forms when seeking a good spiritual advisor. For example, we should disregard such traits as youth, poverty, low status or lack of education, unattractive appearance or incomplete features, but should simply seek someone conversant with the Dharma, who can be of benefit to us. Nor should we find fault with good spiritual advisors for acting in certain ways, as it may be due to a number of reasons, such as pursuing a hidden cultivation practice or following an expedient teaching. Or else, they may act the way they do because while their achievements may be high, their residual bad habits have not been extinguished. If we grasp at forms and look for faults, we will forfeit benefits on the path of cultivation. Thus, when Buddha Sakyamuni was still alive, the Bhikshu Kalodayin was in the habit of moving his jaws like a buffalo; a certain Bhikshuni used to look at herself in the mirror and adorn herself; another Bhikshu liked to climb trees and jump from one branch to another; still another always addressed others in a loud voice, with condescending terms and appellations. In truth, however, all four had reached the stage of Arhatship. It is just that one of them was a buffalo in a previous life, another was a courtesan, another was a monkey, and still another belonged to the Brahman class. They were accustomed to these circumstances throughout many lifetimes, so that even when they had attained the fruits of Arhatship, their residual habits still lingered. We also h0ave the example of the Sixth Patriarch. Realizing that the cultivators of his day were attached to a literal reading of the sutras and did not immediately recognize their Buddha Nature, he took the form of an ignorant and illiterate person selling wood in the marketplace. Therefore, finding a good spiritual advisor is a difficult task indeed! Students of the Dharma should realize this, to decrease the habits of attachment and grasping -- thus avoiding the mistake of maligning monks and nuns."

Tam: 300-302 #1331

◉ **FEAR**
see Ego; Five Fears

◉ **FEELINGS**
see Emotions

◉ **FESTIVALS**
see Buddhist Festivals

◉ **FETTERS**

▸"This term refers to illusions which chain men to the cycle of birth and death."
Dait: 14 #0083

◉ **FIELD OF BLESSINGS**
Syn: Fields of Merits

▸"A figurative term for someone who is worthy of offerings. Just as a field can yield crops, so people will obtain blessed karmic results if they make offerings to one who deserves them. There are many kinds of 'fields of blessings': monks, enlightened beings, parents, the poor, etc., including animals."
Chan: 475
Buddhas, Bodhisattvas, Arhats and all sentient beings, whether friends or foes, are fields of merits for the cultivator because they provide him with an opportunity to cultivate merits and virtues. For example, needy people provide the opportunity for the cultivator to practice charity. Thus, they are fields of merits for him. As the *Avatamsaka Sutra* (chapter 40) states, "Bodhi (Enlightenment) belongs to living beings. Without living beings, no Bodhisattva could achieve Supreme, Perfect Enlightenment."
Editor: na #0522

◉ **FIELDS OF MERITS**
see Field of blessings

◉ **FIFTY-TWO LEVELS OF BODHISATTVA PRACTICE**
Syn: Stages of Bodhisattva Practice; Bodhisattva Stages
See also: Ten Stages; Three Worthy Positions

▸"Progressive levels through which a practitioner is said to advance, from the time of his first resolve until he finally attains Buddhahood. They are enumerated *inter alia* in the *Avatamsaka Sutra* and consist of ten levels of Faith (Ten Faiths), ten levels of Dwellings (Abodes), ten levels of Practices (Conducts), ten levels of Dedication (transferences), ten Stages or Grounds (Bhumi), a level of 'Equal-Enlightenment', 'Wonderful Enlightenment', and 'Supreme Enlightenment (Buddhahood).'"
Sokk: 93 #0257

◉ **FILIALITY**
See also: Ullambana; Death

▸"Both of you still have your parents at home. Therefore, you

should keep explaining the Pure Land Method and the accounts of rebirth to them, so that they may develop the mind of joy, believe in the accounts and follow the examples therein. *If you do not repay your filial debts in this way, even if you are filial in the mundane sense, what good will it do your parents at the end of their lives?* ... You should wake up and hasten to ensure that, at death, your parents will participate in the Lotus Assembly. They will then be close to Amitabha Buddha and achieve the boundless Self-Nature of Light and Life (Patriarch Yin Kuang)."
Zen: 92 #1458
Afterthoughts
"When I behold the sacred *liao wo* grass my thoughts return/ To those who begot me, raised me, and now are tired./ I would repay the bounty they have given me,/ But it is as the sky: it can never be approached."
(H. Smith: *The religions of Man*)
See also last paragraph of "Sangha (Admonition to)"

◉ **FINGER POINTING AT THE MOON**
See also: Moon

►In the Zen expression "finger pointing at the moon", the moon stands for truth and reality, the finger for the Dharma, the teaching of the Buddha. The Dharma is only an expedient, which should not be taken for the truth, the moon.   Editor: na
"A warning by Buddha not to mistake the teaching or the teacher (the pointing finger) for the moon (the goal). In modern terms, if you follow a Zen or other Master, take care to follow the mastery of the master, not merely the outer form or kaya. There is also a classic entitled *Finger Pointing at the Moon*, which contains many stories of the sayings of Zen Masters."
Wood: 43

◉ **FINLAND (BUDDHISM IN --)**
See also: Europe (Buddhism)

►"Buddhism in Finland is inseparable from the work of its founder, Consul Mauno Nordberg (1884-1956), who studied Buddhism while a Consul in Paris and founded the 'Friends of Buddhism' in Helsinki in 1945. Here he built up a Buddhist Library, lectured and broadcast on Buddhism, translated Buddhist works into Finnish and Swedish. Represented Finland at conferences of the *World*

Fellowship of Buddhists.
"Hump: 77 #0451

◙ **FISH GONG**

►A wooden gong used in
Buddhist temples carved in the
shape of a long fish. Like a fish
which never closes its eyes even
in sleep, monks and nuns should
cultivate hard and never let their
guard down.
Editor: na
"In Buddhism, fish, since they
never [close their eyes even in]
sleep, symbolize the resiliency
and wakefulness necessary on the
path to Buddhahood."
Sham: 146 #0106

◙ **FIVE AGGREGATES**
see Skandhas

◙ **FIVE BUDDHAS**
Syn: Dhyani Buddhas

►"In esoteric Buddhism, the four
Buddhas in the four directions
and Mahavairocana (Dainichi),
who occupies the central position
both in the Vajradhatu and the
Garbhadhatu mandalas. In the
Vajradhatu, the five are as
follows: Mahavairocana
(Dainichi), Aksobhya,
Ratnasambhava, Amitabha, and
Amoghasiddhi." Dait: 85 #0067

◙ **FIVE CARDINAL SINS**
Syn: Five Grave Offenses
See also: Exclusion Clause

►Offenses which cause rebirth in
the Avici or Hell of
Uninterrupted Suffering. They
are: killing one's father, one's
mother, or an Arhat, causing
dissension within the Sangha, and
causing the Buddhas to bleed.
Editor/Tam: 337 #0616

◙ **FIVE CORRUPTIONS**
Syn: Five Turbidities; Five
Defilements; Five Depravities

►They are: 1. the defilement of
views, when incorrect, perverse
thoughts and ideas are
predominant; 2. the defilement of
passions, when all kinds of
transgressions are exalted; 3. the
defilement of the human
condition, when people are
usually dissatisfied and unhappy;
4. the defilement of the life-span,
when the human life-span as a
whole decreases; 5. the
defilement of the world-age,
when war and natural disasters
are rife.

These conditions, viewed from a
Buddhist angle, however, can
constitute aids to Enlightenment,
as they may spur practitioners to

more earnest cultivation.
Editor/Ou-i: 150-151 #2154

◉ **FIVE DEFILEMENTS**
see Five Corruptions

◉ **FIVE DEPRAVITIES**
see Five Corruptions

◉ **FIVE DESIRES**
Syn: Five Sensuous Pleasures

▸"Desires connected with the five senses, i.e., form, sound, aroma, taste and touch."
Tam: 150

Buddha Sakyamuni compared sentient beings chasing after the fleeting pleasures of this world to a child licking honey off a sharp knife. There is no way they can avoid hurting themselves.
Editor/Tam: 306 #0890

◉ **FIVE FEARS**
See also: Ten Stages

▸A Bodhisattva at the Stage of Joy (41st of the 52 levels of Bodhisattvahood) has conquered all fear, which can be summarized as follows: "1. fear of not having enough to live on; 2. fear of a bad reputation; 3. fear of death; 4. fear of falling into the Evil Realms; 5. fear of

intimidation by groups."
T. Clear: na #1251

◉ **FIVE GOOD ROOTS**

▸"1. Faith; 2. vigor; 3. mindfulness; 4. concentration; and 5. wisdom. They are called 'roots' because they can give rise to other wholesome dharmas."
Chan: 492 #0618

◉ **FIVE GRAVE OFFENSES**
see Five Cardinal Sins

◉ **FIVE HOUSES OF CHAN**
see Five schools of Zen

◉ **FIVE IMPEDIMENTS**

▸"These are five mental impediments that hinder meditation: desire; malice; depression and sloth; wildness and excitement; and doubt or perplexity."
Thur: 151 #0681

◉ **FIVE KINDS OF EYES**

▸"The human eyes, the deva eye or unlimited vision, the *Wisdom Eye* that sees all things as unreal, the *Dharma Eye* that penetrates all things, to see the truth that releases men from reincarnation, and the *Buddha Eye* of the

Enlightened Ones who see all and are omniscient."
Rosh: 145 #0824

◙ **FIVE MARKS OF DECAY**

►Refers to symptoms of imminent death and rebirth in the Lower Realms, experienced by celestials and deities at the end of their transcendental lives, such as body odor, restlessness, etc. Please note that celestials and deities are still within the realm of Birth and Death -- the Pure Land of Amitabha Buddha, being a Buddha land, is beyond Birth and Death.
Editor/Tam: 337
"The Five Marks of Decay pertain to celestial beings (1) one's robes becoming dirty, (2) one's hair-flowers fading, (3) one's body smelling bad, (4) sweating under one's arms, and (5) not enjoying one's original status."
Yoko: 204 #0792

◙ **FIVE PERIODS AND EIGHT TEACHINGS (T'IEN T'AI)**
See also: Tien T'ai; Five Teachings

►"In the centuries that followed the Buddha's death, various attempts were made to organize and formulate his teachings. Different systems appeared, basing themselves on the recorded scriptures, each purporting to express the Buddha's intended meaning... That there should be a multiplicity of systems is not in itself surprising. From the time of his enlightenment until his death fifty years later, the Buddha bestowed his teachings for the benefit of many different audiences. The purpose of his doctrine was always the same: to liberate beings from the round of suffering. The expression of this purpose, however, differed according to the capacity of his hearers. It is therefore to be expected that the body of teachings remaining after his departure from the world should be rich and varied...
In China, scholars made numerous attempts to organize the vast array of sutras which had been introduced from India into coherent systems.
The T'ien-T'ai system is called the *Five Periods and Eight Teachings* while the Avatamsaka classification is known as the *Five Teachings* (q.v.)."
Sokk: 107-108
Five Periods/ Eight Teachings
All the teachings (Eight

Teachings) of Buddha Sakyamuni during His entire lifetime (Five periods), as categorized by the T'ien-T'ai school (6th C.).

(I) *The Five Periods* are: (1) The period of the *Avatamsaka Sutra*, which according to tradition was the first sutra Sakyamuni taught after attaining his enlightenment. With this teaching, the Buddha awoke his listeners to the greatness of Buddhism, though it was too profound for most of them to grasp. (2) The period of the *Agama sutras*. Perceiving that his disciples were not yet ready for the teachings of the *Avatamsaka Sutra*, Sakyamuni next expounded the Agama sutras as a means to develop it. These teachings reveal the truths of s u f f e r i n g, e m p t i n e s s, impermanence and egolessness which free people from the six paths, and correspond to the Theravada teachings. (3) The Vaipulya period, or period of the introductory Mahayana. In this period Sakyamuni refuted his disciples' attachment to the Lesser Vehicle and directed them toward provisional Mahayana with such teachings as the *Maha-Vairocana* and *Vimalakirti Sutras*. (4) The Prajna period, or period of the *Wisdom Sutras*. In this period Sakyamuni expounded

a higher level of provisional Mahayana and refuted his disciples' attachment to the distinction between Theravada and Mahayana by teaching the doctrine of non-substantiality or Emptiness. (5) The Nirvana period, in which he taught directly from his own enlightenment, fully revealing the truth. The teachings of this period include the *Lotus Sutra* and the *Nirvana Sutra*.

Note: The Avatamsaka period lasted for twenty-one days, the Agama period for twelve years, the Vaipulya period for eight years, the Prajna period for twenty-two years, and the Nirvana period for eight years." Sokk: 107-108

(II) *The Eight Teachings* organized Sakyamuni's teachings according to content and method. It actually consists of two subclassifications -- the four teachings of doctrine and the four teachings of method. The *four teachings of doctrine is a classification by content* and consists of the Tripitaka teaching, the Connecting teaching, the Specific teaching, and the Perfect teaching. The *four teachings of method are a classification by method* of teaching and consist of the Sudden Teaching, the

Gradual Teaching, the Secret Teaching and the Indeterminate Teaching." (For details see *Shambala Dictionary of Buddhism and Zen*, p. 227). Sokk: 107-108   #0247

◉ FIVE PRECEPTS
See also: Precepts; Ethics

►Five basic prohibitions binding on all Buddhists, monks and laymen alike.   "Traditionally, laymen should observe five precepts: (1) not to take life, (2) not to take what is not given to one, (3) not to engage in improper sexual conduct, (4) not to lie, and (5) not to drink intoxicants."
Yoko: 210
Background
"In Buddhist tradition, the principles governing human conduct relate the characteristic condition of humanity (suffering, unease, illness, caused by the basic evil of Desire) to the recognized goal of Buddhist endeavour, viz. complete enlightenment. Buddhist ethics thus favours those attitudes and kinds of behaviour which help humanity towards the ultimate goal of transcendental enlightenment. *As an intermediate criterion, the goal of auspicious and wholesome rebirth [in a Pure Land] is important*: whatever is conducive to this end is to be encouraged; whatever detracts is to be discouraged or renounced. The outworking of the Buddhist ethic is seen at the most elementary level in the 5 basic moral precepts, binding upon all Buddhists, monastic and lay."
Ling: 113-114
NOTE
According to Buddhist teaching, keeping the *Five Precepts* results in rebirth in human form, while keeping the *Ten Precepts* results in rebirth as a deva (deity). Since the human and celestial realms are still subject to birth and death, however, rebirth there is not the goal of Pure Land Buddhists. They seek rebirth in the Land of Amitabha Buddha, a realm transcending birth and death.
Editor: na
Anyone who keeps the five or ten precepts (basic moral prohibitions) reaps the rewards of human and celestial rebirth, respectively. Such a person need not be a Buddhist as these rewards are a corollary of the Law of Cause and Effect which the Buddha did not invent but merely discovered.
Editor: na   #0677

◎ **FIVE SCHOOLS OF ZEN**
Syn: Five Houses of Ch'an

▸"A generic term for the branches of the Southern school of Ch'an (Jpn/ Zen) Buddhism in China. The five are the Lin-chi (Rinzai), Kuei-yang, Ts'ao-tung (Soto), Yun-men and Fa-yen schools. These five plus the Huang-lung and Yang-ch'i schools which eventually broke away from the Lin-chi school are together called the seven schools. All of the Southern Zen schools trace their lineage to Hui-neng (638-713), the sixth of the Chinese Zen patriarchs who received the transmission from Hung-jen, the fifth patriarch. Hui-neng propagated Zen in the Southern part of China; therefore his lineage is called the southern school of Zen.

Another of patriach Hung-jen's disciples, Shen-hsiu (606-706), spread Zen Buddhism in northern China. His lineage, called the Northern school, [soon died out and was replaced by the Hui-neng School which became known as the Ch'an / Zen school.]"
Sokk: 109 #0259

◎ **FIVE SENSUOUS PLEASURES**
see   Five Desires

◎ **FIVE SKANDHAS**
see   Skandhas

◎ **FIVE TEACHINGS (AVATAMSAKA SCHOOL)**
See also: Five Periods and Eight Teachings (Tien Tai school)

▸"A comparative classification of Buddhist sutras set forth by the Avatamsaka (Hua-yen/ Kegon) school.
This classification was established by Fa-tsang (643-712) during the T'ang dynasty, the third patriarch of the Hua-yen school. He categorized the sutras into five groups according to their level of teaching, and the Buddhist schools into ten according to the content of their doctrine.

The *five teachings* are (1) the Theravada, (2) the elementary Mahayana, (3) the final Mahayana, (4) the Sudden teaching and (5) the Perfect teaching. 'The *Theravada teaching*' corresponds to the Agama sutras. These teachings generally hold that the self is without substance, the separate elements (dharmas) are real, and Nirvana is their total annihilation.

'The *elementary Mahayana teaching*' is divided into two. The first is the teaching which analyzes the specific and distinct character of the dharmas, and the second is the teaching that all dharmas are non-substantial (ku). The former is found in the *Yogachara Sutra* and the latter in the *Wisdom Sutras*.

'The *final Mahayana teaching*' maintains the essentially unchanging true nature of all things and the ability of all beings to attain Buddhahood. This teaching is found in the *Lankavatara Sutra* and the *Awakening of the Faith*.

'The *Sudden teaching*' expounds the abrupt realization of the ultimate truth without relying upon verbal explanations or progression through various stages of practice. This teaching is found in the *Vimalakirti Sutra*.

'The *Perfect teaching*' is taught by the *Avatamsaka* and *Lotus Sutras* which expound the One Vehicle (the Buddhas' vehicle)."

Sokk: 110

"The 'perfect teaching' is further divided into two: the One Vehicle (Buddha vehicle) of the Identical Doctrine and the One Vehicle of the Distinct Doctrine. The former teaches the One Vehicle in a method identical or similar to that of the three vehicles (Theravada, preliminary

Mahayana and Sudden). This corresponds to the *Lotus Sutra*. The Distinct Doctrine on the other hand sets forth the One Vehicle as entirely distinct or separate from the other three. This corresponds to the *Avatamsaka Sutra* and is held to be superior the Identical Doctrine. Thus the Avatamsaka school asserts the superiority of the *Avatamsaka* over the *Lotus Sutra*." Sokk: 111

NOTE: Pure Land Buddhism

"Han-shan (q.v.) did not write any commentary on the [two *Amitabha Sutras*], and it is not clear how he placed [them] in the Hua-yen classification scheme. On the one hand, he regards the Western Paradise as the most expedient land in the immumerable Hua-yen pure lands.

On the other hand, he seems to have considered the Pure Land teaching as a special teaching that lies outside the usual scheme of classification."

Hanshan: 149 #0244

◉ **FIVE TURBIDITIES**
see Five Corruptions

◉ **FLAME**

►"[In Mahayana sutras] flames

are used to represent wisdom, the destruction of ignorance and folly."
Clea/84: 22 #1972

◉ **FLOODS**
See also: Cosmic Age; Cosmology

►"Floods are one of the three calamities which occur at the end of a cosmic cycle; *first*, seven suns appear in the sky and burn out the world, *then* the whole world is flooded with water, and *finally*, everything in the world is blown away by strong winds."
Inag: 401 #0700

◉ **FLOWER ADORNMENT SUTRA**
see   Avatamsaka Sutra

◉ **FLOWER AND SMILE**

►*Zen Buddhism*
"To hold a flower and smile faintly. This refers to a story about the Zen special transmission of the Dharma directly derived from the Buddha. Once Indra, King of the gods, visited a congregation of Buddhists on Vulture Peak, and offering a bouquet of flowers to the Buddha, prostrated himself on the ground and reverently asked the Buddha to preach the Dharma. The Buddha held out some flowers before the congregation. No word, however, was uttered. No one could comprehend what he meant except Maha-kasyapa, who smiled. Then the Buddha exclaimed: 'I am the possessor of the eye of the True Dharma which is Nirvana. I now hand it over to Maha-kasyapa.'"
Dait: 236
Maha-kasyapa thus became the first patriarch of the Ch'an / Zen school.
Editor: na #0120

◉ **FLOWER BANK MYSTERIOUS GATES**
see   Ten Mysterious Gates

◉ **FLOWER GARLAND SCRIPTURE**
see   Avatamsaka Sutra

◉ **FLOWER ORNAMENT SUTRA**
see   Avatamsaka Sutra

◉ **FLOWER STORE WORLD**
See also: Avatamsaka School; Cosmos

►The entire cosmos, consisting of worlds upon worlds *ad infinitum*, as described in the *Avatamsaka Sutra*. It is the realm of

Vairocana Buddha, the transcendental aspect of Buddha Sakyamuni and of all Buddhas. The Saha World, the Western Pure Land and, for that matter, all lands and realms are within the Flower Store World.
Editor/Tam: 151 #0893

◉ **FLOWERS AND FRUITS**

▶"*Flowers* may be used to represent the mind or mental factors or states, particularly the development of wholesome qualities and the unfolding of knowledge. Flowers are also used to symbolize practices employed to further spiritual evolution, and *fruits* symbolize the results of those practices."
Clea/84: 22 #1966

◉ **FOOD / FOOD RULES**
See also: Macrobiotic diet; Vegetarianism; Killing; Herbs; Overeating

----

▶"The most important single rule with regard to food, in Buddhist tradition, is especially for the monk, that of restraint in eating, which covers also an obligation [for Theravada monks] not to eat after 12 noon (Fasting). Alcohol of any kind is forbidden 'as tending to cloud the mind'

(Eightfold Path). The vow, incumbent on all Buddhists, monastic and lay, not to take life, causes them to be vegetarian, though with varying degrees of strictness."
Ling: 122-123

"The motivations for performing such acts [setting free captured fish, refusing to eat meat] are rooted not merely in ethical demands, but religious and psychological factors. When a person kills another sentient being, he breaks the hidden bonds among all forms of life. Violence alienates the violator not only from a sense of cosmic harmony but also, ultimately, from himself. For although the act of killing is extreme assertion of the self, the self which is so isolated and delimited, ironically ceases to have any real life or to have any real meaning. Buddhist vegetarianism is significant when viewed in this context. For even though one does not kill the animal himself, every time one eats meat, one denies the existence of any meaningful relationship between oneself and other beings. By objectifying an animal as 'food,' one can become insensitive to its suffering and regard it as a mere thing. On the other hand, each time he releases

a creature from impending death, each time he returns it to freedom, a person reaffirms the original bond among all sentient beings. The act of releasing is a celebration of reunion, during which the selfish human is momentarily obliterated. The person who releases life in fact releases himself from human selfishness."
Yu: 74   #1884
NOTE:
"If you eat less, will you live longer? It is tempting to quip that life would at least seem longer. But the question is serious and has intrigued scientists since the 1930's, when it was discovered that a very low-calorie diet would lengthen rats' maximum life spans from three years to four, an increase of 33 percent.
Over the years, the finding has been confirmed many times in mice and other small animals, and has proved the only reliable means of extending a mammal's life span...
People are already practicing caloric restriction. Many base their diets on books by Dr. Roy Walford, a researcher at the University of California at Los Angeles who recommends cutting back calories and body weight by

about 20 percent. In eight people he has studied on such a plan, Dr. Walford has found beneficial changes in blood pressure, blood sugar and cholesterol. A person who begins 20 percent calorie restriction at age 18 might live to be 140 years old, Dr. Walford has estimated. At 73, he himself eats only 1,800 calories a day, as opposed to the 2,000 to 2,800 normally recommended for a man his age."
NY Times, Oct 7/97.

◙ **FOREIGN DUST AFFLICTIONS**
see   Guest-Dust Afflictions

◙ **FOREMOST MEANING**
see   Definitive Meaning

◙ **FORGIVENESS**
See also: Sin

▶ "Sin is, first of all, an inheritance: "The sins of the fathers shall be visited upon the children unto the third and fourth generation," says the commandment. And that's optimistic. The chain of blindness, of compulsion, continues a lot longer than that, is handed down endlessly, *l'dor vador*, from generation to generation. We inherit our sins, pass them on to our children, and they to theirs; and all of this we do in the most profound ignorance. Our childhoods are contaminated as were those of our parents', and their parents before them, back and back and back. We are involved and participate in this ignorant sin, and the world around us, with its wars, addiction, pollution, exploitation, testifies to this truth. But it is not our intention, there *are no personal villains; but all are victims, receivers and dispensers of the inheritance*, unless, at some point, the chain is broken.

Forgiveness is the weapon that permits us to open our eyes and see through our veil of protective lies. Your sins are forgotten... Take up your pallet, and walk." Bruder: 225-226

◉ **FORTUNE TELLING**

See also: Astrology; Prophecies; Spirit world; Mediums

▶"Elder Pure Land Master Chu Hung had the utmost disdain for some Taoist beliefs which he regarded as especially superstitious. One was the practice of communicating with spirits by the use of a planchette. He gave the following advice to one of his lay disciples, warning

him of its bad effects: 'Spirits called forth by divination are seldom real. They pretend to be such-and-such a spirit, but in truth they are not. If one engages in this practice, one's spirit (shen) and vital breath (ch'i) will be harmed. In the Triple World, only the Buddha is the great teacher. Recite the Buddha's name with one mind, and then all demons will cease of their own accord.'"   Yu: 186

"In Shanghai recently there were many gatherings where revelations and prophecies were proclaimed. Their messages about abandoning evil ways and practicing wholesome deeds, as well as their pronouncements on Birth and Death, Cause and Effect, while superficial and limited, are very useful for everyday morality and the minds of ordinary persons. However the points they made concerning the future and the Buddha Dharma were somewhat vague and not free of error. As disciples of the Buddhas, we should not oppose or reject those pronouncements, because doing so may hinder the good actions of others. At the same time, however, we should not repeat or extol them, lest we be guilty of chimerical statements and conjectures that bring harm and disorder to the Dharma and engender doubts among the people." (Patriarch Yin-Kuang to a disciple).　Zen: 149　#1500

◙ **FORTY-EIGHT VOWS**
see Dharmakara's Vows

◙ **FORTY-NINTH-DAY CEREMONY**
See also: Death; Bardo; Funerals; Pure Land Buddhism (Summary); Seven (Number); Funerals

----

►"A memorial ceremony performed on behalf of a deceased on what is believed by Buddhists to be the final day in the intermediate state between death and rebirth (bardo)."
Kusa: 178　#0845
The 49-day period applies to most people and is derived from the mystic number 7 x 7. For those whose karma is evil, this number does not apply. Therefore, longterm dedication of merit is essential.

◙ **FOUR ATTRACTIONS**
see　Four means of salvation

◙ **FOUR BASES OF MIRACULOUS POWERS**

►"1. Strong aspiration; 2. vigor; 3. intense concentration; 4. intense

contemplation."
Chan: 489　#0601

◙ **FOUR CHOICES**
see　Four Options

◙ **FOUR CONSTITUENTS**
Syn: Four elements

►"The four basic constituents of matter: 1. Earth (solid matter), 2. Water (liquid), 3. Fire (heat), and 4. Air (energy or motion). These constituents are harmonized by the element 'emptiness'." Chan: 489　#0606

◙ **FOUR CONTINENTS**
See also: Cosmology (Buddhist); Sumeru; Uttarakuru

►"The four land areas centered around Mount Sumeru, according to ancient Buddhist cosmology: Jambudvipa in the south, Purvavideha in the east, Aparagodana in the west, and Uttarakuru in the north."
Chan: 489　#0602

◙ **FOUR CURRENTS**

►"1. Desire; 2. Samsaric existence; 3. Wrong views; and 4. Ignorance. These are the defilements that sweep away the wholesome dharmas and cause

sentient beings to drift and drown in the 'torrential stream' of Samsara." Chan: 489 #0603

◎ **FOUR DEMONS**
See also: Demons; Obstacles to Cultivation

►"Demons refer to obstruction of enlightenment. The four demons are the demon of the mind-body clusters (form, sensation, perception, conditioning, and consciousness), the demon of afflictions, the demon of death, and the demon of heaven (which is in the Realm of Desire and thus blocks transmundane goodness)."
Cleary/Chih-I: 194
For details, see "Demons"

◎ **FOUR DHARMA REALMS**
See also: Dharma Realm

►*Avatamsaka Sutra*:
"The four dharma-worlds: I. The phenomenal world; II. The noumenal world; III. The world in which phenomena are identified with the noumena; and IV. The world in which phenomena interpenetrate one another without hindrance."
Dait: 305
Refers to all phenomena, things and events, i.e., to all the constituents of the world.

"Whatever their apparent differences, phenomena are the same in the sense of being dependent and hence void of absolute identity. The noumenal nature, or emptiness, of one phenomenon, being the same as that of all phenomena, is said to at once pervade and contain all phenomena; and as this is true of one, so is it true of all. Furthermore, the interdependence of phenomena means that ultimately one depends on all and all depend on one, whether immediately or remotely; therefore, the existence of all is considered an intrinsic part of the existence of one, and vice versa."
[TC/F01, p.20]a #0131

◎ **FOUR ELEMENTS**
see Four constituents

◎ **FOUR FAMOUS MOUNTAINS**
See also: Pilgrimage sites; P'u T'o Shan; Wu T'ai Shan; E-Mei Mountain

----

►"Four mountains in China that in Buddhism are regarded as the sacred places of the four great Bodhisattvas. According to tradition, they appeared at these mountains to expound the

Buddhist Teaching. They are (1) Wu-t'ai shan (Shansi province), associated with Manjushri; (2) P'u-t'o shan (Chekiang province), considered the sacred mountain of the Bodhisattva Avalokiteshvara; (3) E-mei shan (Szechuan province), the sacred mountain of the Bodhisattva Samantabhadra and (4) Chiu-hua shan (Anhwei province), the sacred place of the Bodhisattva Kshitigarbha."
Sham: 71　#0333

◙ **FOUR FEARLESSNESSES**

▸"For a Buddha: 1. fearlessly realizing all things; 2. fearlessly extinguishing all defilements; 3. fearlessly expounding all obstructions to liberation; and 4. fearlessly asserting the true path to liberation."
Chan: 489　#0607

◙ **FOUR FORMS OF BIRTH**
Syn: Four Modes of Birth
See also: Birth by Transformation

▸"A classification of the ways of coming into existence. They are: (1) birth from the womb, as is the case with mammals; (2) birth from eggs, as is the case with birds; (3) birth from moisture, the way worms were thought to

be generated; and (4) birth by transformation, as in the case of deities and superior beings of the Pure Lands. It is said that such beings, after the end of their previous lifetime, suddenly appear in this fashion due to their karma, without the help of parents or any other intermediary agency."
Sokk: 116　#0238

◙ **FOUR FRUITS**
see　Arhatship (Four stages of)

◙ **FOUR GREAT DEBTS**

▸"The debt to the Triple Jewel (Buddha, Dharma, Sangha); the debt to our parents and teachers, the debt to our spiritual friends, and finally, the debt we owe to all sentient beings."
Tam: 338-339　#0951

◙ **FOUR GREAT OCEANS**
See also: Four Continents; Saha World

▸"The oceans surrounding Mount Sumeru, the axis of a world system."
Inag: 401　#0701

◙ **FOUR GREAT VOWS**
Syn: Bodhisattva vows
See also: Dharmakara's Vows;

Ten Great Vows; Bodhisattva Precepts

►*Vn*/Tứ-Hoằng Thệ-Nguyện.
The Four Great Vows are: "Sentient beings are numberless; I vow to save them all./ Afflictions are inexhaustible; I vow to end them all./ Schools and traditions are manifold, I vow to study them all./ The Buddha-way is supreme; I vow to complete it."
Ross: 48

These are the *common* vows of all Mahayana practitioners, be they lay or monastic, which are recited at the end of each Meditation/ Recitation session. In addition, individual Buddhas and Bodhisattvas have *specific* vows (original, primal vows), such as the Forty-eight Vows of Amitabha Buddha and the Twelve Vows of the Medicine Buddha.

The Four Great Vows should also be distinguished from the *Bodhisattva precepts* detailed in the *Brahma Net Sutra* (q.v.).
Editor: na

◙ **FOUR GUARDIAN KINGS**
see Four Heavenly Kings

◙ **FOUR HEAVENLY KINGS**
Syn: Four Guardian Kings

See also: Cosmology; Four Continents

►"In the Buddhist cosmology, four mythical kings said to live halfway down Mount Sumeru. They protect the eastern, southern, western, and northern continents of traditional Indian geography."
Yoko: 205

"The lords of the Four Quarters who serve Indra as his generals and protect the four continents. They are said to live halfway down the four sides of Mt. Sumeru."
Sokk: 117 #0237

◙ **FOUR HOLY TRUTHS**
see Four Noble Truths

◙ **FOUR IMMEASUREABLE MINDS**
Syn: Four Boundless Minds, Four Immeasurables Minds

►"Cultivated by Bodhisattvas: a mind of infinite loving-kindness, of infinite compassion, of infinite joy, and of infinite equanimity."
Cleary/Chih-I: 194

◙ **FOUR INTEGRATIVE METHODS**
see Four means of salvation

◙ **FOUR INVERTED VIEWS**
Syn: Four Wrong Views
See also: Wrong Views

▸"1. Considering what is really impermanent to be permanent; 2. Considering what is really suffering to be joy; 3. Considering what is not a self to be a self; and 4. Considering what is impure to be pure."
Chan: 491 #0614

◙ **FOUR KALPAS**
See also: Cosmology; Floods

▸"The four periods of time, each consisting of twenty small kalpas, during which worlds go through formation, destruction, and annihilation: (1) the Kalpa of Existence (vivarta-siddha kalpa), during which the sun and moon rise, sexes are differentiated, and social life evolves; (2) the Kalpa of Destruction (samvarta kalpa), during which fire, water, and wind destroy everything except the Fourth Dhyana Heaven; (3) the Kalpa of Annihilation (samvarta-diddha kalpa), during which nothing exists; and (4) the Kalpa of Formation (vivartakalpa), during which worlds and beings on them are formed."
BDK: 353 #1092

◙ **FOUR KINDS OF DEVOTEES**
See also: Four-fold Assembly

▸"The four categories of Buddhist followers; 1. monks (bhiksus); 2. nuns (bhiksunis); 3. laymen (upasakas) and 4. laywomen (upasikas)."
Chan: 490 #0611

◙ **FOUR LANDS**
see Four Pure Lands

◙ **FOUR MEANS OF SALVATION**
Syn: Four Integrative Methods; Four Means of Integration; Four Attractions; Four Dharmas of Attraction
See also: Paramitas

▸"They are: charity, kind speech, beneficial action and cooperation. These are the means by which... Bodhisattvas integrate with society in order to carry out their work."
[TC/FO1, p.17]
"The four methods by which a Bodhisattva attracts people to the Dharma: 1. giving unsparingly; 2. using pleasant words; 3. always helping others; 4. comaradeship and accommodation."
Chan: 490
NOTE:
Along with the ten paramitas, the Four Means of Salvation form

the basic teachings of Bodhisattvahood.
Editor: na #1298

◙ FOUR MEDITATIONS
Syn: Four Mindfulnesses

▶"Four types of Buddhist meditation for eradicating illusions and attaining enlightenment. The first is to contemplate the body as impure. The second is to contemplate all sensation (feelings) as the cause of suffering. The third is to contemplate the mind as impermanent and the fourth is to contemplate all things as being dependent, without self-nature or self-identity." Sokk: 119
"Four Meditations:
1. Mindfulness of the body as impure; 2. mindfulness of feeling as suffering; 3. mindfulness of the mind as impermanent; and 4. mindfulness of dharmas as dependent, without self-entity."
Chan: 490 #0235

◙ FOUR MINDFULNESSES
see Four meditations

◙ FOUR MODES OF BIRTH
see Four forms of birth

◙ FOUR NOBLE TRUTHS
Syn: Four Holy Truths

See also: Four Truths; Eight-Fold Noble Path

▶"A fundamental doctrine of Buddhism which clarifies the cause of suffering and the way to emancipation. Shakyamuni is said to have expounded the Four Noble Truths in the Deer Park in [Sarnath] during his first sermon after attaining Buddhahood."
Sokk: 120
"A basic Buddhist teaching, which explains the cause of suffering and the means of deliverance therefrom. This was one of the first doctrines taught by the Buddha after his enlightenment. The truths are that (1) all existence entails suffering; (2) suffering is caused by ignorance, which gives rise to desire and illusion; (3) there is an end to suffering, and this state of no suffering is so called Nirvana and (4) the way to end suffering is through the practice of the eightfold Noble Path." Yoko: 205
"The first [Truth] is that the universal human experience of suffering, mental and emotional as well as physical, is the effect of past karma. The second is the perception that the cause of such suffering is craving or grasping for the wrong things, or for the right things in the wrong way.

The basic human problem is a misplaced sense of values, assigning to things or persons in the world a value that they cannot sustain...The third is that it is possible for suffering to cease...The fourth is the Noble Eightfold Path, the way to the solution."
Eerd: 231 #0234

◉ **FOUR OPTIONS**
Syn: Four Choices
See also: Yung-ming Yen-shou; Yin-kuang; Chu-hung; Zen / Pure Land

----

►See the following partial translation of these well-known verses of Zen Master Yung Ming, the best known proponent of the harmonization of Zen and Pure Land:
"With both dhyana [Zen] and the Pure Land/ One is like a tiger with horns;/ In the present age a teacher of man,/ In the future a Buddhist Patriarch./ With dhyana but without the Pure Land/ Nine out of ten will take the wrong road;/ Without dhyana and with only the Pure Land,/ If ten thousand practice, ten thousand will go the right way." (Hsuan Hua, *Pure Land & Ch'an Dharma Talks*, p. 23-24).
Zen: 94-95 #1461

Master Yung-ming said: "Those who devote themselves to Ch'an and neglect Pure Land will fail, nine out of ten, to attain Enlightenment; but those who devote themselves to the practice of Pure Land will, without exception, have their awakening. Those who practice Ch'an and Pure Land at the same time ... will be like tigers [with] horns!"
Chang Chung-yuan: 236

◉ **FOUR PROPOSITIONS**
Syn: Four Alternatives

►They are: a) existence; b) non-existence; c) both existence and non-existence; d) neither. The 100 errors are derived from these propositions. Editor: na
"The 'Four Propositions' are ... said to underlie all human conceptions and to have fallacies which make it impossible for any one of them to be unequivocally true. On the other hand, defining existence as relative existence or conditioned existence, and non-existence as emptiness of absolute existence, Buddhist logic shows how all of them can be both true and untrue, summing up the foundations of philosophy therein."   [TC/SBZ, p.84]
Zen School
"The most important dialectical

formula in the House of Lin-chi, 'the Four Alternatives' (Four Propositions) (Chin., ssu-liao-chien), describes four positions regarding the subject-object relationship. Lin-chi is said to have presented the following at one of his evening conferences: 'Sometimes I take away man and do not take away the surroundings; sometimes I take away the surroundings and do not take away man; sometimes I take both man and the surroundings; sometimes I take away neither man nor the surroundings.' *These four alternatives or positions regarding subject and object represent an ascending grasp of reality*. The formula is based on the well-known four propositions of Buddhist logic: being, non-being, both being and non-being, neither being nor non-being. They correspond to the four levels of reality (Skt., Dharmadhatu) in the Avatamsaka school. In the first and second stages, illusion is overcome first by the subject and then by the object. That is to say, all clinging to subjective intellectual perception and to the objective world is repudiated. The third stage negates both subject and object, but differentiation still remains. This posture of negation corresponds to the state of consciousness achieved in extreme concentration. Only in the fourth stage, which affirms the transcendence of the opposition between subject and object, does all confrontation between subject and object cease. Reality is comprehended in its ultimate oneness. In this formula the philosophy of the Middle Way Madhyamika and the metaphysics of the Avatamsaka school flow together."

Dumou: 219 #1790

◉ **FOUR PURE LANDS**
See also: Pure Land School; Sukhavati

▸In the T'ien-t'ai and Pure Land world views, the Pure of Amitabha Buddha (Sukhavati) is composed of four realms. They are: i) *The Land of Common Residence of Beings and Saints* (Land Where Saints and Ordinary Beings Dwell Together), where all beings, from the six lower worlds (hells, hungry ghosts ...) to the Buddhas and Bodhisattvas, live together. This Land of Common Residence is further divided into two, the Common Residence

Pure Land and the Common Residence Impure Land; ii) *The Land of Expediency* (Land of Expedient Liberation), inhabited by Arhats and lesser Bodhisattvas; iii) *The Land of Real Reward*, inhabited by the highest Bodhisattvas; iv) *The Land of Eternally Quiescent Light*, in which the Buddhas dwell. These distinctions are at the phenomenal level. At the noumenon level, there is, of course, no difference among them.   Editor/Mind-Seal: 174

"Four types of land or realm corresponding to the three bodies of Buddha and four levels of spiritual development ... Of the three bodies of the Buddha, the Body of Enjoyment or Recompense (pao-shen) and Dharma-body (fa-shen) correspond respectively to the third and fourth of these lands, while the two Bodies of Manifestation or Response (ying-chen)--one superior, the other inferior--are distinguished in accordance with the first and second of the Four Lands (See Muranaka, p. 350)."
Donner/1993: 161 #0894

◙ FOUR RELIANCES

►"They are: 1. Relying on the true meaning or spirit of a Dharma statement in a sutra, not merely on the words of the statement; 2. relying on the teaching, not on any person; 3. relying on intuitive wisdom, not on intellectual understanding; and 4. relying on sutras that give ultimate teachings, not on those which preach expedient teachings." (See Expedient Means)
Chan: 491

In other words, "to attain higher realizations and final Enlightenment, the Bodhisattva should rely on (1) the meaning (of the teaching) and not on the expression; on (2) the teaching and not on the person (who teaches it); on (3) gnosis (intuitive) wisdom and not on normal consciousness and on (4) discourses of definitive meaning and not on discourses of interpretable meaning."
Thur: 150 #0613

◙ FOUR RIGHT EFFORTS
Syn: Samyakprahana

►"These are (1) effort not to initiate sins not yet arisen; (2) effort to eliminate sins already arisen; (3) effort to initiate virtues not yet arisen and (4) effort to consolidate, increase,

and not deteriorate virtues already arisen."
Thur: 150 #0676

◙ **FOUR STAGES OF ARHATSHIP**
see Arhatship (Four stages of)

◙ **FOUR STAGES OF THERAVADA ENLIGHTENMENT**
See Arhatship (Four Stages of)

◙ **FOUR SUFFERINGS**
See also: Dukkha

▸"The four universal sufferings of birth, old age, sickness and death. Shakyamuni's quest for enlightenment is said to have been motivated by a desire to find a solution to these four sufferings."
Sokk: 124 #0232

◙ **FOUR TRUTHS**

▸Two sets of Four Truths are found in the sutras:
(I)"There is suffering, suffering is caused, suffering has an end, there is a way to its end." (see Four Noble Truths)
Chih-I/Cleary: 196

(II)The characteristics of living beings and their environment, namely, impurity, suffering, impermanence and no-self.

◙ **FOUR VIRTUES (OF NIRVANA)**
See also: Buddha Nature; Parinirvana Sutra

▸Four characteristics of Nirvana or "four noble qualities of the Buddha's life expounded in the *Nirvana Sutra* -- eternity, happiness, true self and purity. Because common mortals possess the Buddha nature, they too can develop the four virtues when they attain Buddhahood by fulfilling the Buddha's teaching."
Sokk: 127 #0231

◙ **FOUR WRONG VIEWS**
see Four Inverted Views

◙ **FOUR-FOLD ASSEMBLY**
See also: Four Kinds of Devotees; Bhiksu; Bhiksuni

▸"The Assembly of monks, nuns, laymen and laywomen."
Tam: 339 #0953

◙ **FOX**
See also: Intellect; Mind

▸"'The wild fox,' skittish, clever, wary, is a symbol of the rationalizing faculty of the human mind that tries to conceptualize wisdom and thereby obscures it."
Clea: 172 #0766

◙ **FRANCE (BUDDHISM IN)**
See also: Europe (Buddhism);
Lounsbery; Huyen Vi, Thich

►"'Les Amis du Bouddhisme' was
a Buddhist society founded in
Paris in 1929 by Ms Constant
Lounsbery. The Society was
established under the inspiration
of the late Master Tai Hsu (q.v.)
of China, while the latter was on
a visit to Europe... Famous
French Buddhist scholars include
Bigandet, Poussin, Sylvain Levi,
Grousset, David-Neel,
Demieville, Guenon, Benoit...
Hunp: 80

"*Les Amis du Bouddhisme*
declined and ceased to function
effectively by the end of the
1960's in spite of the efforts of
Nelly Kauffman and Paul Adam.
Incidentally, Adam is, to the best
of available information, the first
French national to be ordained a
Theravada Bhikkhu. He entered
the Sangha in India in 1953 with
the name Aryadeva, in
association with the Theosophical
Society of France, brought
Hindu, Mahayana and Vajrayana
tendencies into its successor
organization which is now called
*La Societe des Amis du
Bouddhisme*. The tradition of
Lounsbery was maintained by her
student Teisen Perusat Stork,
who embraced Buddhism in 1941
and took an active part in the
propagation of Theravada
through study groups, classes and
publications. In 1908, she was
ordained in Soto Zen tradition
and since 1972 has been
associated with the work of the
World Federation of Buddhists
through the *Centre Francais de
L'Association Mondiale des
Bouddhiques* ... Stork established
the *Temple Bouddhiste Zen* near
Cannes in 1968. Like Teisen
Perusat Stork, several French
Buddhists have moved from one
Buddhist tradition to another. In
the process it was usually
Theravada which first attracted
them to Buddhism through its
intellectual appeal. But
progressively Zen and Vajrayana,
with their emphasis on
meditation and, to some extent,
symbolic ritual, are found to be
more satisfying. Besides, Zen and
Vajrayana traditions have been
propagated in France by
intensely dedicated and capable
Masters whose example and
living testimony have proved to
be most inspiring.
*Asian Buddhist Masters in France:
Zen and Vajaryana*
1. One such Master was Taisen
Deshimaru of Japan who settled
in France in 1967. A prolific

writer, he has several important publications to his credit ... He founded in 1970, L'Association Zen d'Europe, which since 1982, is known as *L'Association Zen Internationale*. It has established Zen centres in many parts of Europe and its Temple Zen de la Gendronniere accommodates up to 350 participants in retreats of long duration. As could be expected, the popularity of Zen resulted in the proliferation of centres among which some rivalry and dissension cannot be entirely ruled out. But the service they render in the promotion of Buddhism in France is indeed substantial. The most significant characteristic is that Zen organisations are headed, staffed and patronized mainly by French nationals, unlike other Buddhist traditions which continue to involve and even depend on immigrants from Buddhist Asia.

2. The introduction of Tibetan Buddhism to France was a major contribution of Paul Arnold, who ... established the first Tibetan Gelugpa meditation centre in France at Forts-les-Bancs in Ain in 1974.

With the increasing arrival of learned and experienced Tibetan Lamas as exiles, Vajrayana centres increased steadily and attracted substantial numbers of French enthusiasts ... In two decades, the numbers both of the monasteries and meditation centres and of the adherents and practitioners of the different traditions of Tibetan Buddhism have increased in France to the extent that practically every region has a minimum of one or two very active centres with significant congregations, and major centres are being planned and established on the most ambitious scale.

Like Zen, Vajrayana , too, has a large following of French nationals and most of them are professionals and intellectuals.

Influx from Buddhist countries of South and South-East Asia.
The escalation of the political upheaval in Indo-China and the eventual rise of Communist regimes after the Vietnam war had a significant impact on Buddhism in France -- the third phase of the *Buddhist Diaspora* which began with the dispersal of Chinese Buddhists in 1949 and Tibetan Buddhists in 1959. The mid-1970's saw an unprecedented influx of refugees from Asia and the majority were Buddhists. Those from Cambodia and Laos professed Theravada while the

Vietnamese Buddhists were for the most part adherents of the Mahayana tradition. Modest temples and monasteries were established in large numbers not only in and around Paris but in most of the major cities of France ...

It is the Vietnamese Buddhist community which has attained a unique level of visibility and influence ... Three organisations which came into existence around the same time in mid-1970 were *Niem-Phat-Duong Khanh-Anh* founded by Thich Minh-Tam; *L'Association Culturelle Bouddhique Linh-Son*, founded and directed by Thich Huyen-Vi and *L'Association Bouddhique Franco-Vietnamienne*. Many more have since arisen. The most impressive is the record of Thich Huyen-Vi, whose movement is world-wide and basic concentration is on higher learning, research and training in the Ch'an and Pure Land traditions. Himself a scholar, he supports several important international Buddhist activities which include the *Buddhist Studies Review* edited by Russell Webb and published from London. His original temple in Joinville-le-pont has grown into a substantial monastery and his current efforts have succeeded in creating a Buddhist College -- *Dhammaville*, near Limoges in central France. Thich Huyen-Vi's early collaborators have established their own monasteries and pagodas in France. Special mention needs to be made of those founded by Thich Thien Đinh in Marseille, by the late Thich Minh Le in Sèvres [near Paris] and by Thich Minh Tam in Bagneux [also near Paris]." (Ananda W. P. Guruge) *Encyclopedia of Religions*, v.5, p. 265.

Mention should also be made of the Vietnamese Master Thích Nhất-Hạnh (q.v.), who has a large following among Vietnamese and French intellectuals.

Editor: na   #0450

◙ **FRIEND (UNSOLICITED --)**
see Unsolicited friend

◙ **FRIENDS OF THE WESTERN BUDDHIST ORDER**

▶"Lay Buddhist organization, emphasizing Mahayana, founded by the Venerable Sangharakshita in 1967. Sangharakshita is a British-born Buddhist who became a monk in 1950. After spending nearly two decades in

India, working for about half of the time with Ambedkar (q.v.) Buddhists, he returned to England and founded Friends of the Western Buddhist Order." Preb: 127 #1026

◉ FRUITS AND FLOWERS
see Flowers and Fruits

◉ FUNERALS
See also: Death; Forty-ninth-Day Ceremony; Pure Land Buddhism (Summary)

►"The evil deeds done by living beings bear corresponding results, yet even if one ought to fall into the Evil Paths, his offenses may be eradicated if his survivors cultivate holy causes for him. During a period of forty-nine days after the death, they should do many good deeds that can cause the dead one to leave the Evil Paths. (*Sutra of the Past Vows of Earth Store Bodhisattva [Ksitigharba Sutra]*, Master Hsuan Hua, tr. Hua: 168

"Funeral arrangements should be kept simple, not accompanied by superfluous ceremonies occasioning unnecessary expenses. *Another caveat*: only vegetarian food should be served. No non-vegetarian food should be provided as offerings or to entertain guests -- for to take life is to sadden the departed with more karmic obstructions and 'heavy baggage,' making his liberation that much more difficult. Even if he has already been reborn in the Pure Land, his grade of rebirth may be lowered as a result." Tam: 289

NOTE:
To be truly effective in dedicating merit to others, the practitioner must be utterly sincere and singleminded in his recitation. Even if he is, the *Ksitigarbha Sutra* teaches that the deceased can only receive a small part of this merit. Furthermore, since the crucial conditions of sincerity and singlemindedness are seldom achieved in full, most intercessions are, at best, partially effective and can seldom erase a lifetime of bad karma. Thus, it is imperative for the practitioner himself to cultivate during his lifetime and not rely on family members, monks or nuns at the time of death. Editor/Tam: 325 #0076

See also Supportive Recitation.

◉ FUNERARY RITES FOR THE BUDDHA
See also: Death and Burial;

Death; Stupa

►"The methods of disposing of the dead practised by Buddhists were inherited from Indian culture. The Buddha was cremated with honours customarily given to a great king, according to the *Maha-Parinibbana Sutta* (sutra). The cremation was carried out by the Malla tribes-people of Kusinagar, where he died. After 7 days of ceremonial homage, the body was wrapped in 500 layers of new cloth, placed in an iron sarcophagus filled with oil, and placed on a funeral pyre, made of many kinds of fragrant wood. They were unable to ignite the pyre, however, until 500 Buddhist monks led by Maha-Kasyapa arrived and reverenced the Buddha's body. After that, the pyre is said to have burst into flames spontaneously. When the fire had died down, only the bones were left: 'the body of the Blessed One burned itself away . . . neither soot nor ash was seen.' For 7 days the closely guarded bones were honoured 'with dance and song and music, and with garlands and perfumes.' King Ajatasattu, hearing of Buddha's death and cremation, proposed to build a stupa over the remains.

The Licchavis, the Sakiyas, the Bulis, the Koliyas, and the Mallas and a brahman of Vethadipa also claimed a right to build a stupa. The remains were, therefore, divided into 8 parts, and 8 stupas were built, by the various claimants in their respective territories. That the Buddha was cremated indicates not that this was universal practice among Buddhists, but rather his status as a great man. "
Ling: 124-125 #1133

◙ **GANDAVYUHA SUTRA**
See also: Avatamsaka Sutra

►A part of the *Avatamsaka Sutra* which also circulates as a separate sutra; consists of the entire chapter 39, the longest chapter of the sutra (1/4 of the entire sutra). In some older western books, the *Gandavyuha Sutra* is sometimes taken to mean the entire *Avatamsaka Sutra*.
Editor: na #0487

◙ **GANDHARA (AFGHANISTAN)**
Syn: Ghandhara

►"Region in the far northwest of India (now southern Afghanistan) notable in connection with the development and evolution of the doctrines of Buddhist Mahayana

and Buddhist art. Famous for its style of sculpture, which was a blend of ancient Indian modified by Graeco-Roman styles of Asia Minor. Its period was A.D. 100-300. Ancient Indian Buddhist art did not depict the figure of the Buddha but symbolized his presence. Gandhara art depicts the Buddha's figure, the whole life history of the Buddha being given. Under Kusana kings (Kaniska) i.e., during approximately the first 3 centuries A.D., this area was one of a flourishing and vigorous Buddhist culture with many monastic centres of learning. During the 2nd century A.D. and after, Gandhara, was an area which nourished Buddhist missionary expansion northwards and eastwards into China. The multi-storied pagoda which Emperor Kaniska built at Peshawar (Pakistan), was regarded as one of the wonders of the world at the time."
Thai: 497-498 #1635

◉ **GANDHARVA**

►"A kind of celestial musician often associated with the court of the celestial monarch Indra."
Gomez: 300
Gandharva cities are dream-like,

non-existent places, mirages in the desert.
Editor: na #1707

◉ **GANGES RIVER**

►"The Ganges River in India symbolizes the profound virtue of the Buddhas and Bodhisattvas which moistens and quenches the thirst of living beings."
[HHFAS39I,221]uu #1208

◉ **GARDEN OF ANATHAPINDIKA**
see Jeta Grove

◉ **GARLIC**
see Herbs (Pungent --)

◉ **GARUDA**
See also: Eight Divisions (of Divinities)

►"A mythical bird with strong, large wings. It feeds on dragons."
Chan: 476
One of the quasi-divinities of the Eight Divisions (q.v.). #0523

◉ **GASSHO**

►(Jpn). "A symbolic gesture of reverence, representing the unity of body and mind, in which the hands are joined at the palms, fingers extended, and placed near

the breast."
Yoko: 184
"'Palms of the hands placed together'; Buddhist expression for the ancient gesture of greeting, request, gratitude, veneration, or supplication common in many cultures (particularly in the East). In this gesture, a state of mind is spontaneously manifested that suggests the unity of the antithetical forces of the phenomenal world."
Sham: 76 #0813

◙ GATE, GATE

See also: Avalokitesvara; Heart Sutra; Wisdom Sutra

►"The first Sanskrit words of a mantra uttered by the Bodhisattwa Avalokiteshvara in the *Heart Sutra*. The whole mantra runs: 'Gate, gate, paragate, parasangate, bodhi, swaha,' and is translated as follows: 'Gone, gone, gone to the other shore; safely passed to that other shore, O Prajnaparamita! So mote it be!'.
Avalokiteshvara's mantra occurs at the end of the *Heart Sutra*. This Sutra is short (only a few pages) and constitutes a very terse summing up of the meaning of Prajna and enlightenment."
Wood: 44-45 #0986

◙ GATHA

►A stanza, a verse.

◙ GAUTAMA

►"Clan name of the Buddha, hence a name of Sakyamuni."
Thai: 651 #1651

◙ GELONG

►"Tibetan for monk."
Snel: 274 #0732

◙ GELUGPA / GELUK

►(Tib). "Lit. 'virtuous tradition'. One of the four schools of Tibetan Buddhism. Founded by Tsongkhapa in the 15th century."
Batc: 381
"Tsong-kha-pa joined the Buddhist Order as a young boy, and had extensive training in both the exoteric and esoteric Buddhist traditions. The school is sometimes referred to as the 'Yellow Hat School' because they rejected the traditional red hat of the prior Buddhist schools in favor of the yellow hat now traditional in their group. They became the most influential of the Tibetan Buddhist Schools, and once the line of the Dalai Lamas was established within this

school, the Gelugpa school was afforded political leadership as well. Like all other surviving Tibetan Buddhist schools, they pursue their activity in exile in the aftermath of the Tibetan Holocaust."

Preb: 108

The current Dalai Lama belongs to the Gelugpa order.

Editor: na #1019

◉ **GENEROSITY**

see Anathapindika; Golden-Colored King

◉ **GENKU**

see Honen

◉ **GENSHIN (942-1017)**

See also: Honen; Pure Land Buddhism (Summary); Raigo

▸"One of the pivotal figures in the Japanese Pure Land tradition was Genshin of the Yokawa Eshin-in on Mount Hiei. Genshin's name is intimately associated with the development of *raigo* imagery: he is said to have painted many famous paintings of the *Descent* (Raigo / q.v.), and although these attributions are open to doubt, the fact that they have been made with such insistence over the centuries indicates how important

Genshin was for the tradition. The monk's undoubted contribution, however, was his monumental essay, the *Essentials of Rebirth* (*Ojo Yoshu*), whose passages inspired numerous artistic works."

Okaz: 98

"Genshin (942-1017), a Tendai monk, emphasized the efficacy of *nembutsu* recitation *without* meditation. His monumental work, the *Ojo yoshu*, a collection of the principles essential for birth in Paradise, exerted a profound influence not only on later Pure Land thinkers and on Pure Land art, but also on Japanese society at large."

Okaz: 19

See also: Pure Land Buddhism (Summary)

◉ **GERMANY (BUDDHISM IN)**

See also: Europe (Buddhism in)

▸"Germany is and has always been the only [western] rival to England in its interest in Buddhism. Apart from its own pioneer Buddhist scholars, such as Neumann and Oldenberg, German scholars have become famous in other lands, as Nyanatiloka and Govinda. In 1903 a Buddhist Mission Society was founded at Leipzig, and held a Buddhist Congress in 1906. As early as 1888 the Bhikshu Subhadra (Zimmermann) published his *Buddhist Catechism*, while *Buddhist Essays* by Dr Paul Dahlke appeared in 1908. George Grimm's Old Buddhist Community was founded at Utting in Bavaria in 1921; the Gemeinde um Buddha worked in Berlin from 1928-33, and by the Second World War there were active centres also in Hamburg, Stuttgart, Munich, Dusseldorf and Cologne, some publishing their own journals. After the war, Guido Auster founded a Buddhist Secretariat in Berlin to reorganize the suppressed Buddhist activities, and in 1955 a pan-German society was founded as the Deutsche Buddhistische Union, with headquarters in Munich (subsequently moved to Hamburg)."

Hump: 83

"Most Buddhists in Germany adhere to the Theravada but there are also followers of the Mahayana, e.g. the active "Arya Maitreya Mandala" of the Vajrayana school (Berlin and other cities 1952) and the "Buddhistische Gemeinschaft Jodo Shinshu" (Berlin 1956). Since about 1964, also Zen Buddhism has been favoured by quite a number of Germans...Today meditation, both *Satipatthana* and *Zazen*, is being practiced under the guidance of resident or visiting meditation masters from Sri Lanka, Thailand, and Japan, mostly in Berlin and Hamburg (Roseburg)."

[NOTE]
"The Dhamma came first to Germany through books, therefore a word should be added on the Buddhist literature now available in the German language. It is immense in quantity and excellent in quality. Of the original scriptures practically the whole *Suttapitaka* has been translated from the Pali into German, and the Suttas have held to this day the main interest of German Buddhists. Foremost among the translators were Karl Eugen Neumann (1865-1915) Nyanatiloka Mahathera (1878-1957), Karl Seidenstucker, Paul Dahlke (1865-1928), Wilhelm Geiger, and Julius Dutoit. Max Walleser should be mentioned as a translator and interpreter of Mahayana scriptures. Buddhological studies have been conducted at most of Germany's universities in the field of

Indology and Comparative Religion. A special chair for Buddhological studies has been created at the University of Hamburg."
(*Encyclopedia of Buddhism*, Volume 5: p. 335) #0449

◙ **GESHE**
See also: Tibetan Buddhism

►"(Tbt). Title corresponding to Doctor of Divinity; used in the Gelugpa school of Tibetan Buddhism." Snel: 274 #0733

◙ **GHEE**

►"A symbol of Buddha-nature, which is inherent in the human mind as ghee (clarified butter) is latent in milk."
Cleary/Chih-I: 196

◙ **GHOSTS**
see   Hungry Ghost; Li Mei; Tree Spirits

◙ **GODS**
see   Deva

◙ **GOHONZON**
See also: Nichiren Shoshu

►"(Jpn). A mandala-like inscription of Nam-myoho-renge-kyo (Homage to the *Lotus Sutra*), used as an object of worship in Nichiren Shoshu (q.v.) Buddhism."
Batc: 381 #1847

◙ **GOLD**
See also: Avatamsaka Sutra; Middle Way Philosophy

►In the *Avatamsaka Sutra*, gold represents the principle ("noumenon") underlying all phenomena. Just as the essence of all gold ornaments is the metal gold, so the essence of all phenomena centers on the truth of the Middle Way.
Editor: na #1303

See also: Discourse on the Golden Lion

◙ **GOLDEN LION**
see   Discourse on the Golden Lion

◙ **GOLDEN LION TREATISE**
see   Discourse on the Golden Lion

◙ **GOLDEN-COLORED KING**
See also: Anathapindikha; True Emptiness/Wonderful Existence

►"The name of Shakyamuni in a previous lifetime. According to the *Sutra of the Golden-colored*

King, the Buddha was once a king who ruled over his people with wisdom and benevolence. However, the nation suffered twelve years of drought and many people were dying of starvation. The king then gathered all the grain to be found in the country and distributed it equally among the people. At that time a Pratyeka Buddha who had dedicated himself to Buddhist practice for forty kalpas appeared and begged for food. The king gave him his last bit of food as an offering. This good deed caused various grains to fall from the skies like rain for seven days. Thereafter, seven kinds of treasures as well as clothes, food and other necessities rained down every seventh day, putting an end to the people's poverty."
Sokk: 144 #0228

◙ **GOOD DESTINIES**
see   Good planes of existence

◙ **GOOD EON**
see   Auspicious Kalpa

◙ **GOOD KALPA**
see   Auspicious Kalpa

◙ **GOOD PLANES OF EXISTENCE**
Syn: Good Destinies

See also: Three Evil Paths; Six Planes of Existence.

▶"The states of gods, asuras, and humans are the three 'good planes of existence.' These beings are not subject to as much suffering as are animals, hungry ghosts, and hell-dwellers. On the three good planes, one has a better opportunity to practice the Dharma; one cannot easily do so in the lower states."
Chan: 476 #0525

◙ **GOOD ROOTS**
Syn: Roots of merit and virtue; Wholesome roots
See also: Five Good Roots

▶"Virtuous deeds accumulated in past or present lives which contribute to one's practice and realization of the Dharma."
Chan: 476
"The 'roots of good,' 'roots of virtue,' or 'roots of merit' (kusalamula) are those acts and states of mind that are good (kusala) by virtue of the good intentions that motivate them and generate merits, virtues and the attainment of Buddhahood. They include acts of self-restraint, mental cultivation, worship, and generous giving, but also faith and benevolent feelings. They are

like roots because, once performed, they remain as the basis for future virtue, and, if properly cultivated, grow, mature, and bear fruit."
Gomez/96: 322 #1949

◉ **GOOD SPIRITUAL ADVISOR**
Syn: Kalyanamitra; Teacher
See also: Guru; Unsolicited Friend; Lama

▸Kalyanamitras, Gurus, virtuous friends, wise persons, Bodhisattvas, Buddhas -- anyone (even an evil being!) who can help the practitioner progress along the path to enlightenment. This notwithstanding, wisdom should be the primary factor in the selection of such an advisor -- the advisor must have wisdom, and both advisor and practitioner must exercise wisdom in selecting one another.
Editor/Tam: 151-152
Each spiritual advisor in the *Avatamsaka Sutra* takes a different form, but they all flow from Bodhisattva Manjusri, the personification of wisdom. Thus, wisdom is of paramount importance in choosing a spiritual advisor.
Editor: na
"In certain other spiritual traditions, as you know, the guru virtually rules his students' lives, even to the extent of telling them whether to marry and have children. His word is law. If his spirituality is deep, there is little danger. If it is not, God help the student! Shun any teacher who says, 'I am enlightened.' Beware of any guru who claims to be an avatar, an incarnation of a god or Buddha. Above all, avoid the 'master' who allows his followers to shout his praises with arms upraised at mass rallies, and to laud him as the holiest of holies. He is the greatest menace."
Kapl/80: 29
"During the period I was living in ashrams and meditation centers in Southeast Asia I heard it said that no matter what superior qualities a guru may possess, if he is obviously seeking name and fame, is after money, or is carrying on with his female students, these impurities will corrupt his teaching; a prospective student would therefore do well to avoid him."
Kapl/80: 33
"When a monk lives in the age of the True Law, he should never make discriminations in regard to people. But when a monk lives in this age of the Degenerate Law, he should fear nothing more than failing to make

discriminations in regard to people. The reason is that in this last age of the Law, good and bad elements mingle together. If one does not make a right judgement but chooses the wrong person, if one regards him who is heterodox as orthodox, *if one becomes friendly with him whom he ought to avoid and avoids him whom he ought to be friendly with*, one will surely become the same as one's teacher. Furthermore, in future lives he will always be a companion to Mara (q.v.). Is it then not apparent that one has to be watchful in seeking out a teacher?" (Elder Master Chu Hung)   Yu: 177 #0847

"According to the *Brahma Net* and *Avatamsaka Sutras*, we should ignore appearances and external forms when seeking a good spiritual advisor. For example, we should disregard such traits as youth, poverty, low status or lack of education, unattractive appearance or incomplete features, but should simply seek someone conversant with the Dharma, who can be of benefit to us. Nor should we find fault with good spiritual advisors for acting in certain ways, as it may be due to a number of reasons, such as pursuing a hidden cultivation practice or following an expedient teaching. Or else, they may act the way they do because while their achievements may be high, their residual bad habits have not been extinguished. If we grasp at forms and look for faults, we will forfeit benefits on the path of cultivation. Thus, when Buddha Sakyamuni was still alive, the Bhikshu Kalodayin was in the habit of moving his jaws like a buffalo; a certain Bhikshuni used to look at herself in the mirror and adorn herself; another Bhikshu liked to climb trees and jump from one branch to another; still another always addressed others in a loud voice, with condescending terms and appellations. In truth, however, all four had reached the stage of Arhatship. It is just that one of them was a buffalo in a previous life, another was a courtesan, another was a monkey, and still another belonged to the Brahman class. They were accustomed to these circumstances throughout many lifetimes, so that even when they had attained the fruits of Arhatship, their residual habits still lingered. We also have the example of the Sixth Patriarch of Zen. Realizing that the cultivators of his day were

attached to a literal reading of the sutras and did not immediately recognize their Buddha Nature, he took the form of an ignorant and illiterate person selling wood in the marketplace. Or else, take the case of a famous Zen Master who, wishing to avoid external conditions and concentrate on his cultivation, took the expedient appearance of a ragged lunatic, raving and ranting. As a result, both distinguished Masters were criticized during their lifetimes. The Sixth Patriarch was faulted for ignorance, while the Zen monk was called insane and berserk. Therefore, finding a good spiritual advisor is a difficult task indeed! Students of the Dharma should realize this, to decrease the habits of attachment and grasping -- thus avoiding the mistake of maligning monks and nuns.
Tam: 300
See also: "Unsolicited Friend"; Hui-yuan

◙ **G O O D W E A L T H BODHISATTVA**
  see Sudhana

◙ **GRADUAL ENLIGHTENMENT**
see   Sudden / Gradual enlightenment

◙ **GRASPING**
see Attachment

◙ **GREAT AWAKENING**
see   Awakening vs. Enlightenment

◙ **GREAT COMPASSION MANTRA**
Syn.: Dharani of the Most Compassionate One
See also: Avalokitesvara

▸The Great Compassion Mantra is very popular among Mahayana Buddhists, both clergy and laymen. It is associated with the Bodhisattva Avalokitesvara. The mantra is part of the daily liturgy recited by most Mahayana Buddhists in Asia. According to Buddhist teachings, anyone reciting this mantra will have his wholesome wishes fulfilled.
Editor: na
"Why is it called the 'Great Compassion Mantra?' Because its compassion can relieve living beings of all their suffering and difficulty. Because it relieves suffering and bestows happiness, it's called the Great Compassion Mantra."
Hua/Dharani Sutra: 135

In the *Sutra of the Great Compassion Heart Dharani*, the

Bodhisattva Avalokitesvara (Kuan Yin) said to the Buddha: "Great Honored Teacher! If any sentient being should assiduously recite the Great Compassion Mantra and still descend upon the Three Evil Paths, I vow not to attain Buddhahood. If any practitioner should assiduously recite the Great Compassion Mantra and fail to be reborn in the lands of the Buddhas, I vow not to attain Buddhahood. If any practitioner should assiduously recite the Great Compassion Mantra and not achieve innumerable samadhis and great eloquence, I vow not to attain Buddhahood. If anyone should recite the Great Compassion Mantra and not have all the wishes and hopes of his present life fulfilled, this dharani cannot be called the Great Compassion Dharani! The only exceptions are wishes which are unwholesome and those made when the Mind is not utterly sincere.
PL/Dia: 63

Illustrative story: "There was once a man who recited the great Compassion Dharani for about twelve years ... every day at least 108 times, and sometimes many more times ... Once, while travelling, he stopped for the night at an inn. The innkeeper was a thief [who] just sat in his inn and waited for rich guests to come by. He would give them a fine room, a strong dose of drugged wine, and then, in the middle of the night ... he would sneak into their rooms to rob them and sometimes even murder them. The man who recited the great Compassion Dharani believed in the Buddha, however, and so he didn't drink the wine ... At about one o'clock in the morning, he heard someone slowly open the door and sneak into his room. Opening his eyes just a crack, he saw the glint of a butcher's shiny blade flash in the moonlight. 'Someone means to kill me,' he thought, paralyzed with fear. At that very moment, there was a knock on the door. The would-be murderer quickly put the blade behind his back and went to the door. 'Who is it?' he whispered. 'My name is Dou Shu Peng,' came the reply. Peeking through the keyhole, the innkeeper saw a large man dressed in a policeman's uniform. 'What do you want?' he asked nervously. 'I have come to visit my friend who is staying in this room. Won't you please tell him to stop by my house tomorrow morning for breakfast?' 'Yes, I'll do that,' said the innkeeper and the policeman left ... The innkeeper decided he had best do no murdering that night. The next morning the innkeeper told the guest, 'A friend of yours named Dou Shu Peng was by last night. He came to invite you to his house for breakfast.' 'Dou Shu Peng? ...' said the guest, and then he remembered that in the Great Compassion Dharani, there is a line 'Dou Shu Peng'. 'Yes!' he exclaimed, 'I do have such a friend. I was just on my way to meet him.'"

Hua/Dharani Sutra: 6

◉ GREAT NIRVANA SUTRA

see   Parinirvana Sutra

◉ GREAT PERFECTION OF WISDOM (TREATISE)

See also: India (Buddhism in)

►*Chin*/Ta Chih Tu Lun; *Vn*/Đại-Trí-Độ Luận

"Treatise on the Sutra of the Perfection of Wisdom. One of Nagarjuna's major works, (ca 200 AD) an exhaustive commentary on the *Prajna Paramita Sutra.* The Sanskrit and Tibetan texts have been lost; only the Chinese version translated by Kumarajiva

is extant. The work explains the concepts of prajna (wisdom) and of non-substantiality (Skt/ sunyata; Jpn/ Ku). From the viewpoint of religious practice, it sets forth the Bodhisattva ideal and the six paramitas."

Sokk: 50 #0213

◉ GREED

Syn: Craving
See also: Three Poisons

►"Also 'desire', one of the major afflictions. The basic worldly instinct of grasping, especially manifested in lust, avarice, and craving."

Chan: 472

"The five desires in their gross forms are easy to detect. The practitioner should, additionally, pay attention to the deep-seated, subtle manifestations of greed. For example, a hundred thousand dollars might not necessarily excite a person's greed, but an amount in the   millions could move his mind; ordinary beauty can easily be resisted but heavenly charm has the power to lure people down the path of transgression. Even monks and nuns can be infatuated with exquisitely carved rosaries, beautiful statues or auspicious, peaceful realms; these too are in the category of defiled greed. We should see them as expedients, illusory causes and conditions, and not develop defiled greed. To shed light on this state of mind, I shall cite a story as example. Once upon a time there was an official who was well-known for his honesty. He would sternly reprimand those who attempted to bribe him with money and gold. One day, however, a rich and powerful person, seeking the resolution of a private matter, offered him the equivalent of a hundred thousand dollars. The official immediately accepted the bribe. Later on, when a friend asked him why, he replied, 'A hundred thousand in cash can sway the gods.' Thus, this official could only be honest with small bribes, but could not resist huge ones. This is a case of deep-seated greed. Another story dates from the Ming dynasty. One day, an Elder Master was conversing with a visiting monk. The guest lamented, 'The majority of today's monks and nuns are defiled by the desire for fame and profit.' The Master replied, 'I notice that you are pure and clean, because you have always rejected fame and profit.' When the visiting monk heard this, his face brightened for a fleeting moment. This monk, while disliking ordinary fame, was attached to a lofty reputation. This is a case of profound subtle greed. There is another story [which forms the basis of a well-known koan]. Once there was a devoted old woman who built a place of retreat for a monk, arranging that he would not lack for anything, so that he could concentrate upon his meditation and practice. One day, after twenty years, she instructed her daughter: 'Today, after serving the Master his meal, take advantage of the situation to embrace him tightly, asking him at the same time, "how does it feel to be hugged these days?" Come back and let me know his answer as faithfully as you can.' The daughter dutifully did as she was told, putting her arms around the Master and asking the question. The Master replied, 'I am not moved in the very least by sexual desire, no different from a dried up tree leaning against a cold mass of rocks in the middle of winter, when not even a drop of warmth can be found.' The young girl repeated the answer to her mother, who said unhappily, 'I have really wasted my time and

effort during the last twenty years. Little did I know that I was only supporting a common mortal!' Having said this, she went out, evicted the monk, lit a fire and burned the meditation hut to the ground. In truth, it is rare enough these days for anyone to cultivate to the level of that monk. As far as the old woman is concerned, she is said to have been a Bodhisattva in disguise. Her action of burning down the hut was to 'enlighten' the Master. Why is this so? It is because, while not moved by sexual desire, he still saw himself as pure and was still attached to the empty and still aspects of samadhi. Thus, he had not attained true and complete Awakening. Although this Master had reached a fairly high level of attainment, he was *still attached to the mark of purity*. This is another instance of subtle greed, which the practitioner should sever. The same is true for the Pure Land practitioner. He should know that all forms and marks are illusory. Even though he may have reached the level of one-pointedness of mind and seen precious lotus blossoms, other auspicious marks, or transformation bodies of Buddhas and Bodhisattvas, he should realize that these are merely instances of good causes leading to auspicious results. He should be calm and still and not greedy for them -- nor should he deny their occurrence. Only then will he understand and be awakened to the principle of Truth-like No-Void of the Mind-ground."
Tam: 146-148 #0507

◙ **GUEST-DUST AFFLICTIONS**
Syn: Foreign Dust Afflictions
See also: Mind

▸"Guest-defilement, so called because, according to Buddhism, the mind is inherently pure, but is covered by *foreign* (guest) defilements. Once these are removed, its pure nature will shine forth."
Dait: 175

"Afflictions are called 'guest dusts.' They are 'guests' because they come and go, unlike our empty and still True Nature. They are 'dusts' because they stick to and defile the True Mind, just like the dust which covers a bright mirror and prevents it from reflecting the objects before it."
PL Patria: 46

◙ **GURU**

Syn: Teacher
See also: Good Spiritual Advisor;
Lama; Unsolicited friend

▸"Sanskrit term most often rendered as 'teacher.' In some Buddhist traditions, the guru represents the spiritual teacher who guides the adept on the Buddhist path. Precisely because of the significance of the role of the guru in helping the student make spiritual progress, the student must place complete confidence in the guru's knowledge, and thus obediently follow the guru's instructions, however unusual or eccentric they may appear.

The trust required in the guru's guidance has raised curious questions, especially in modern Buddhism, about the authenticity of some rather 'colorful' and unorthodox teachers who have appeared on the Buddhist landscape."
Preb: 132-133

"Whether a teacher is female or male, it is very risky to begin teaching, much more adapting techniques, before we have fully mastered fundamental Buddhist teachings and learned to put them into practice. Without sufficient preparation, there are dangers of misinterpreting the Dharma and of misguiding others in their spiritual development. These dangers are magnified in the case of transmitting Dharma in new lands and to fresh minds where there is little background against which to weigh and measure what is being presented. In such a climate, students need to exercise maximum discretion in choosing a teacher. These days there are many concepts, practices, and styles of behavior being marketed under the label 'Dharma' that have little or nothing whatsoever to do with Dharma. Even allowing for human error, there is a code of ethics involved in giving teachings. Likewise, there is a degree of individual responsibility incumbent upon those receiving teachings. Thoughtful people would do well to consider these matters and to be clear about what is involved in their choice of teachers, for their own psychological well-being as well as for positive development of Buddhism in the West. There are times when it is wise and virtuous to suspend judgment and other times when it can be disastrous. It is therefore essential to allow ample opportunity for assessing a path and a teacher. Well-reasoned adaptation of the Buddhist teachings and traditions to Western situations will be of great benefit to Western people, but slipshod importation, gullible acceptance, baseless fabrication, and shoddy conduct can lead to an altogether mistaken amalgam which may do more harm than good ... We should be ever so much more discerning when choosing a spiritual teacher, not judging by superficial matters such as attractive appearance, charisma, eloquence, or language proficiency. Particularly in America these days, anybody can set up shop and teach practically anything. There is no way to certify the person's character, however, and no assurance of where the path may lead. Experimentation may prove harmless, but in the case of spiritual development, dabblers run the risk of creating much inner confusion. At this critical juncture, it is advisable to see beyond nationality and other external criteria, and to rely upon a qualified teacher with a traceable lineage that has been known to produce enlightened beings in the past. Confidence in the path and the guide are as important as confidence in

oneself, and confidence should be based on sound judgment, remembering the fallibility of even that. *Until full enlightenment is reached, we are liable to err in our perceptions of both self and others*. In all Buddhist traditions, perfect morality is the most fundamental of all qualifications for a teacher. It is the basis of all other accomplishments. For example, there are eight specific qualities required for Vinaya instructors, ten qualities enumerated for a Mahayana guru, and ten further qualities for a guru expounding tantra, pure morality being prerequisite in all cases. To refrain from harming, misappropriation, sexual misconduct, untruthfulness, and intoxication are the precepts for ordinary lay Buddhists and are fairly elemental behavioral guidelines for all decent human beings. It goes without saying that those who claim to be spiritual teachers should be above such misbehavior. Since abuses of authority are unfortunately rampant these days, it behooves spiritual seekers to be judicious in their choice of guidance. In the case of the Tantric school, the matter is far more serious, since one is bound by certain commitments once the master/disciple link is formed. Even the receiving of a simple initiation puts one under these commitments, so great care must be taken to assess the qualities of a teacher before attending such ceremonies. One is allowed up to *twelve* years to observe the conduct and examine the qualities of a potential teacher before establishing a master/disciple relationship." (Karma Lekshe Tsomo, ed., *Daughters of the Buddha*/ proceedings of the first International Conference on Buddhist Nuns: 1987 -- H.H. Dalai Lama: Keynote speaker) Tsomo: 323-325

NOTE:

"The Indian spiritual teacher is often seen as the embodiment of the holy, the presence of the divine in human form. Contrary to the assumption of several generations of Western scholars, in the Indian view of a human religious teacher, if he is in the ranks of spiritual masters, he may have many superhuman traits and faculties (such as wonder-working powers, omniscience, mind reading). Moreover, his disciples may believe in the presence of such traits even during the master's lifetime." Gomez/Land: 11

See also: "Unsolicited Friend" #0335

◉ **HAGIOGRAPHIES**

See also: Proofs of Rebirth in the Pure Land

▶*Biography of Dharma Master Shaokang.*

"The dharma master was from the Zhou clan of Jinyun. His mother was of the Luo clan. Once she dreamed that she journeyed to Dinghu Peak, where a jade maiden gave her a blue lotus blossom ... Even at seven years old, Kang did not speak. Prognosticators thought it very strange. Once his mother took him to Lingshan Monastery. Directing him to the Buddha hall, she said, 'When you reverence the Buddha, don't be hasty.' To which he replied, 'Who wouldn't be reverent towards our Lord Buddha Sakyamuni?' [After this episode,] his mother and father looked upon him with even greater respect and awe. Ultimately, they allowed him to leave home as a novice monk. By age fifteen he had perfectly memorized five scriptures, including the *Lotus* and *Surangama Sutras*. Later he set off for Jiaxiang Monastery in Kuaiji to study the Vinaya codes.

After that he went to Shangyuan where he attended lectures on the *Avatamsaka Sutra* and various treatises such as the *Yogacarabhumi*. At the beginning of the Zhenyuan reign of the Tang dynasty [785-805 A.D.] he was residing at White Horse Monastery in Luoyang. There he once saw light radiating from a text stored in the hall. He picked it up and found it to be the venerable Shan-Tao's Treatise on Converting to the Way of the Western Pure Land. Master Shaokang thereupon proclaimed, 'If I have a karmic connection with the Pure Land, may this text again put out radiance.' No sooner did he speak these words than the text again blazed with light. Shaokang said, 'Though stones may grind me for an eon, I will not deviate from my vow.' Subsequently he proceeded to Shan-Tao's mortuary hall at Radiant Light Monastery in Changan. There he set out a great array of offerings. All of a sudden he saw Shan-Tao's commemorative image rise up into the air and address him, saying, 'By relying on my teaching you will widely convert sentient beings. On a select day in the future your meritorious efforts will bear success and you will assuredly be born in the Land of Ease and Succor.' Thereupon Master Shaokang set off southward for Jiangling. On the road he met a monk who told him, 'If you wish to convert people you should go to Yanzhou.' As soon as he finished speaking these words, he disappeared. When the master entered Xinding commandery, no one there knew him. ... After a little more than a month, he had gathered a considerable crowd of children who would come to recite the Buddha's name. The master thereupon said to them, 'To anyone who can do ten recitations of the Buddha's name without interruption I will give one coin.' He continued this for a full year, after which ... the sound of reciting the Buddha's name (nianfo) filled the streets. In the tenth year of Zhenyuan's reign, Shaokang built a Pure Land chapel on Mount Wulong. He constructed an altar of three levels, where he gathered his followers to perform ritual services and circumambulation. Whenever the master ascended the high seat and chanted the Buddha's name out loud, the congregation would see a single buddha issue from his mouth. When he recited ten such recitations, they would see ten buddhas. The master said, 'Those of you who see these buddhas are certain to achieve rebirth in the Pure Land.' At that time the group numbered several thousand. Those among them who failed to see the buddhas wailed and reprimanded themselves, resolving to persevere even more zealously in their practice. On the third day during the tenth month of the twenty-first year [of the Zhenyuan reign], the master called together his lay and monastic followers and charged them saying:

'You should engender a heart that delights in the Pure Land and despises this deluded world of Jambudvipa. If on this occasion you can see my radiant light then you are truly my disciple.' Thereupon, the master put forth various unusual beams of light and passed away (from *Comprehensive Record of the Buddhas and Patriarchs*).
Lopez/95: 596-597 #1766

⊙ **HAIRTIP**
see Dust

⊙ **HALO**
see Mysticism of Light

⊙ **HALUCINATIONS**
see Visions

⊙ **HAN DYNASTY**

►"(206 BCE-220 CE). Chinese dynasty that saw the introduction of Buddhism into China."
Reat: 328

"Period in Chinese history (206 B.C.-220 C.E.) during which Buddhism entered China. In the first century A.D. the Han Dynasty began to extend its sphere of influence into Central Asia, an area that was rife with Buddhist groups from a variety of traditions. Thanks to the Silk Route, merchants moved freely back and forth between areas and cultures, creating an atmosphere in which Buddhism was able to make its first inroads into China. Although there are a variety of accounts of Buddhism's first entry to China in the Han Dynasty, it met with a Chinese environment dominated by Confucian and Taoist culture. Buddhism made gains in Lo-yang where a translation center was organized by foreign monks. The first Chinese converts joined the Buddhist community, and Buddhist ideas were being circulated by the time of the

downfall of the Han Dynasty in 220."
Preb: 134-135 #1030

◎ **HAN-SHAN (1546-1623)**
Syn: Han-Shan Te-Ch'ing
See also: Yung-Ming; Chu-Hung; Yin-Kuang

▶"An illustrious Chinese monk during the Chinese Ming Dynasty. After joining the Buddhist order at the age of eleven, he studied the *Hua-yen-ching* (*Avatamsaka Sutra*) under Wu-chi. He travelled and visited many teachers in order to acquire knowledge. Then he settled down at Pei-t'ai (the Northern Peak, i.e. Han-shan of the Wu-t'ai-shan) and there practiced Ch'an (Zen). Hence his name Han-shan."   Dait: 181
"Elder Zen Master Han-Shan Te-Ch'ing (1546-1623) was one of the three 'dragon-elephants,' or most illustrious monks, during the final years of the Ming dynasty -- 'an age of corruption, internal oppression and external weakness.'"
Sung-peng Hsu: na
Originally trained in the Sutra Studies and Zen schools, he came to excel in other traditions as well, achieving great renown as a

teacher and exponent of the *Avatamsaka Sutra*. He is particularly credited with reviving the Zen school in China. Born to a humble family, he came to mingle with the greatest political figures of China through his acquaintance with the Empress Dowager. This master/disciple relationship aroused the jealousy of the emperor and led to his imprisonment, banishment and forced return to lay life. Only toward the end of his life was he rehabilitated.
Editor/P.L Patria: na
"Han-shan Te-ch'ing composed an autobiography which is a unique document. The autobiography contains interesting details about his spiritual development from childhood, his various activities during each year of his life, and his tragic involvement in the political power struggles that took place in the Imperial court. In reading Han-shan's autobiography, one can easily imagine how a Buddhist monk lived in China at that time. The state of Ming Buddhism was clearly reflected in the personal life of Han-shan Te-ch'ing. ... Te-ch'ing's thought may be called the philosophy of Mind. The

Mind stands for the ultimate reality, even though there are philosophical problems concerning its metaphysical status. In any case, he used the concept 'Mind' to integrate all the aspects of his thought and to explain all questions about reality and salvation. An outstanding feature of Te-ch'ing's philosophy of Mind is universalism. This philosophy affirms the ultimate unity and identity of all beings and of all doctrines. Reflecting the fact that he was living in China, he argued that Taoism, Confucianism, and Buddhism taught about the same ultimate truth of Mind and that they differed only in degree of penetration."

Sung-peng Hsu: na

NOTE:

"Han-shan did not write any commentary on the [two *Amitabha Sutras*], and it is not clear how he placed [them] in the Hua-yen classification scheme. On the one hand, he regards the Western Paradise as the most expedient land in the immumerable Hua-yen pure lands. On the other hand, he seems to have considered the Pure Land teaching as a special teaching that lies outside the usual scheme of classification."

Hsu: 149   #0112

◙ **HEARER VEHICLE**
see Theravada Buddhism

◙ **HEART SUTRA**
See also: Gate, Gate; Emptiness; Prajna Paramita Sutras

►"Famous Mahayana text that is much more readily known by its English title as '*Heart Sutra*' than by its formal Sanskrit name, *Prajnaparamita-hrdaya Sutra*. It is essentially a one page condensation of Mahayana philosophy, especially emphasizing the doctrine of emptiness."   Preb: 135-136

"Shortest of the forty sutras that constitute the Prajnaparamita group of sutras. One of the most important sutras of Mahayana Buddhism, particularly in East Asia, it is recited by monks and nuns of all schools. The sutra is especially emphasized in Zen, since it formulates in a particularly clear and concise way the teaching of shunyata (emptiness), the immediate experience of which is sought by Zen practitioners. The pith sentence of the *Heart Sutra* is, 'Form is no other than emptiness; emptiness is no other than form,' an affirmation that is

frequently referred to in Zen."
Sham: 84
NOTE:
In the Mahayana tradition, the *Heart Sutra* is recited at the end of each service. There have been in total eight translations of the sutra into Chinese; the one in use today was translated by Patriarch Hsuan-tsang.
Editor: na #0336

◙ HEAVEN AND HELL

See also: Dhyana Heavens; Hell; Death

▶"The Buddhist concept of heaven and hell is entirely different from that of other religions. Buddhists do not accept that these places are eternal. It is unreasonable to condemn a man to eternal hell for his weakness but quite reasonsable to give him every chance to develop himself. From the Buddhist point of view, those who go to hell can work themselves upwards by making use of the merit they had acquired previously. There are no locks on the gates of hell. Hell is a temporary place and there is no reason for those beings to suffer there forever. The Buddha's teachings show us that there are heavens and hells not only beyond this world, but in this very world itself... The fire of hell in this world is hotter than that of the hells in the world-beyond. *There is no fire equal to anger, lust, greed or ignorance.* According to the Buddha, we are burning from eleven kinds of physical pain and mental agony: lust, hatred, illusion, sickness, decay, death, worry, lamentation, pain (physical and mental), melancholy and grief. People can burn the entire world with some of these fires of mental discord. From a Buddhist point of view, the easiest way to define hell and heaven is that wherever there is more suffering, either in this world or any other plane, that place is hell to those who suffer. And where there is more pleasure or happiness, either in this world or any other plane of existence, that place is heaven to those who enjoy their worldly life in that particular place. However, as the human realm is a mixture of both pain and happiness, human beings experience both pain and happiness and will be able to realise the real nature of life. But on many other planes of existence, inhabitants have less chance for this realisation. In certain places there is more suffering than pleasure, while in some other places there is more pleasure than suffering. Buddhists believe that after death, rebirth can take place in a number of possible existences. *This future existence is conditioned to a great extent by the last thought-moment a person experiences at the point of death.* This last thought which determines the next existence results from the past actions of a man either in this life or before. If the predominant thought reflects meritorious action, he will find his future existence in a happy state. But that state is temporary and when it is exhausted a new life must begin all over again, determined by another dominating 'karmic' energy.

This repetitious process goes on endlessly unless one [escapes from the cycle of Birth and Death through cultivation]. Heaven is a temporary place where those who have done good deeds experience more sensual pleasures for a longer period. Hell is another temporary place where evil-doers experience physical and mental suffering. It is not justifiable to believe that such places are permanent ... Each and every person experiences according to his good and bad karma." Dham: 303-305

"There is no hell in the sense of a state of endless torture known to Buddhism. The various hells are purgatorial states called apayas. Avichi is the lowest and most severe of the apaya states." Murt: 42 #1979

◙ **HEAVEN OF FREE ENJOYMENT OF OTHERS' EMANATIONS**
Syn: Sixth Heaven
See also: Mara

►"The Sixth and the highest Heaven in the World (Realm) of Desire; Mara (King of the demons or the Devil of the Sixth Heaven) is said to dwell there." Inag: 402 #0702

◙ **HEAVEN OF SATISFACTION**
see   Tusita Heaven

◙ **HEAVEN OF THE FOUR KINGS**
See also: Four Heavenly Kings

►"The heaven of the guardian kings of the four directions surrounding Mount Sumeru." Inag: 403 #0703

◙ **HEAVEN OF THE THIRTY-THREE**
Syn: Trayastimsa; Thirty-Three-Fold Heaven

▸"A heaven in the Realm of Desire, with thirty-two deva kings presided over by Indra, thus totaling thirty-three; located at the summit of Mount Sumeru."
Chan: 476

"Second (counting from the lowest) of the six heavens in the World of Desire; located on the top of Mount Sumeru; each of the four peaks in the four directions is inhabited by eight gods, and the lord of the Heavens, Indra, lives in the palace at the centre."
Inag: 403

"The heavens of the thirty-three devas, the second of the desire-heavens, the heaven of Indra, located at the summit of Mount Sumeru."
Thai: 301 #0527

◙ **HEAVENLY BEING**
see Deva

◙ **HEAVENLY DRUM**
see Celestial drum; Avatamsaka Sutra

◙ **HEAVENS**
see Dhyana heavens; Heaven and Hell

◙ **HEKIGAN-ROKU**
see Blue Cliff Record

◙ **HEKIGANSHU**
see Blue Cliff Record

◙ **HELL**
See also: Avici Hell; Heaven and Hell; Death

▸"There is no hell in the sense of a state of endless torture known to Buddhism. The various hells are purgatorial states called apayas. Avichi is the lowest and most severe of the apaya states."
Murt: 42 #1895

◙ **HELL OF UNINTERRUPTED SUFFERING**
see Avici

◙ **HERBS**
see Herbs (Pungent)

◙ **HERBS (PUNGENT)**
Syn: Pungent Roots; Garlic; Onions; Herbs; Aphrodisiacs

▸"They are: leek, onion, garlic, and a few other such herbs such as Asafoetida, an ingredient common in curries etc. Eaten raw they are believed to incite people to anger and disputes; eaten cooked they increase one's sexual desire. Buddhist adepts are advised to avoid them, as their consumption tends to disturb the peacefulness of the

mind. According to [the sutras], garlic, three kinds of onions, and leeks are the *five forbidden pungent roots.* 'If eaten raw, they are said to cause irritability of temper, and if eaten cooked, to act as an aphrodisiac; moreover, the breath of the eater, if reading the sutras, will drive away the good spirits.'" (See 4th Minor Precept in the *Brahma Net Sutra.*)
Yu: 312 #1745
NOTE:
Much of the publicized health benefits of garlic and other pungent roots may be industry-inspired and/or commercial puffery. Buddhist practitioners, particularly Tantric ones, are advised to avoid them altogether.

◙ **HERESY**
See also: Excommunication; Heretical views

▸"Heresy is primarily a Western religious concept; there is no exact Buddhist equivalent. The nearest approximation is drsti (Sanskrit), literally a view, usually a 'wrong' view, that is due not to reason but to craving or desire. The most serious form of 'heresy' according to Buddhist tradition is to assert the reality and permanence of the individual

human ego, i.e., the assertion of atta or atman. Since the Western concept of heresy implies an orthodoxy capable of denouncing heresy and willing to do so, the approximation of Buddhist drsti to Western heresy here comes to an end, Buddhism having no authoritative hierarchy, and no sacramental sanctions. On the whole, the attitude of Buddhist schools seems to have been that *more prolonged meditation will eventually cause 'heretics' to see the error involved in their view, and its abandonment.*"
Ling: 133-134 #1136

◙ **HERETICAL VIEWS**
See also: Excommunication; Heresy

▸The sutras usually refer to sixty-two such views. They were the externalist (non-Buddhist) views prevalent in Buddha Shakyamuni's time.
Editor/Van Hien: 223 #2206

◙ **HEROIC GATE SUTRA**
See Surangama Sutra

◙ **HIEI, MOUNT**

▸"A high hill to the N.E. of Kyoto, Japan, chosen by Master Dengyo (8th C.), to establish his

Tendai (Chin. T'ien-t'ai) School of Buddhism. Scores of other temples were later built on the mountainside, and the monks in them played a considerable part in the turbulent politics of Kyoto in the fourteenth century."
Hump: 88 #0448

◙ **HINAYANA**
See Theravada Buddhism
Note: The term Hinayana is not generally used in modern texts. (Synonyms: Southern Buddhism, Monastic Buddhism, Hearer Vehicle, Theravada Vehicle.)

◙ **HINDUISM**
Syn: Brahmanism
See also: Hinduism / Buddhism; Brahma

►"The general name given to the social-cultural-religious system of the Indo-Aryans (who migrated into India just before the dawn of history). In its essence, Brahmanism advocates: 1. Maintenance of the four castes (which assures the supremacy of the priestly cast, the brahmana). 2. Appeasement of the gods by means of rituals derived from the sacred Vedas (which have to be performed by brahmana ...) 3. Fidelity to the theory of karma and reincarnation (almost

universal in India), with rebirth in heaven seen as the final goal of earthly life. From Brahmanism also emerged various popular sects, which worship anthropomorphized gods, such as Brahma, Visnu, and Siva."
Dait: 14
See also: next entry #0086

◙ **HINDUISM / BUDDHISM**
See also: Ambedkar; Hinduism; India (Buddhism in--)

►"Buddhism was initially established as a reform movement opposed to vedic authority, brahmanic ritualism and the caste system of Hinduism. However in the ninth century Hinduism launched a counter-attack. Buddhist ideas were deliberately incorporated into Hinduism and the historical Buddha declared an incarnation of the god Visnu. What once had been attractive in Buddhism could now be found [theoretically] in Hinduism as well."
Wolfg: 167
"In Hindu tradition, the main duties assigned to women were childbearing and housework. Consequently, a single life was seen as a wasted life and unmarried women were subject

to scoffs. On the contrary, in Buddhism, married life was viewed as a hindrance to spiritual pursuits. Wherever the Buddhist point of view prevailed, a woman was no longer compelled to marry to achieve self-respect and approval from her family. Once the order of nuns was established, it provided an even better option for women who were spiritually and religiously inclined."

Tsomo: 92 #2137

Despite the ascetic nature of Hinduism at its higher level, the religion contains a strong element of fertility rites and beliefs. The widespread worship of the *lingam* and *yoni* (male and female sex organs) is a typical example. This is in contrast to Buddhism, where chastity and self-restraint in all matters are considered the most effective way to end the cycle of Birth and Death (by eliminating desire, the root cause of suffering).

Editor: na #2262

◙ HOA-NGHIEM KINH
see Avatamsaka Sutra

◙ HOBEN HOSSHIN SON'EI
See also: Jodo Shinshu School

►"Japanese for a highly stylized

representation of Amitabha as a front-facing image standing on a blue lotus, with forty-eight rays of light, signifying his forty-eight vows, emanating from the halo behind his head."

Okaz: 184 #0637

See also: Pure Land Buddhism (Summary)

◙ HOLY PLACES OF BUDDHISM (INDIA)
See also: Pilgimage sites; Four Famous Mountains

►"The four sites visited by Buddhist pilgrims are the birthplace (Lumbini Park, Nepal); Buddha Gaya (India), which is the site of the Enlightenment; Sarnath (India), where the First Sermon was preached, and Kusinagar (India), the scene of the Great Decease."

Hump: 89-90

For details, see Pilgrimage Sites #0446

◙ HONEN
Syn: Genku
See also: Jodo school; Pure Land School; Pure Land Buddhism (Summary)

►"Honen Shonin (1133-1212), also called Genku established in 1175 the Jodo or 'Pure Land'

school in Japan. He was born in Mimasaka Province and at the age of nine became a disciple of Kankaku at Zendai-ji temple. At fifteen, he entered Mt. Hiei and studied the teachings of the Tendai school. At the age of eighteen, he moved to Kurodani on Mt. Hiei where he studied Pure Land teachings. He left Kurodani on one occasion to study the doctrines of the other schools, and on his return he read through the Tripitaka. He is said to have reached an awakening in 1175 on reading Shan-tao's *Meditation Sutra*, and thereafter dedicated himself solely to the chanting of Amida Buddha's name. The founding of the Jodo school is dated from this event."
Sokk: 164-165

"At age forty-three he became concerned that practitioners were not able to achieve enlightenment through the Tendai path, and turned to the Pure Land teachings of Shan-tao and Genshin, convinced that reliance on Amitabha Buddha was the certain path to salvation. Honen's writings on the Pure Land were seized and burned, but he continued to preach his Pure Land message of the repetition of Amida's name in the formula of the Nembutsu to all listeners. In 1206 Honen was exiled by his rivals, returning to Kyoto in 1211, only a year prior to his death."
Preb: 140

"His fundamental tenet was belief in the power and grace of Amitabha, lord of Sukhavati (the Western paradise). He advocated repeated invocation of Amitabha's name, by which anyone, ignorant or wise, high or low, could be saved. His teachings were based on that of master Hui Yuan, the Chinese founder of the Pure Land school."
Ling: 137-138

(I) Honen's Death
See the following passage on the last moments of Honen:

"At the hour of the serpent (10 a.m.), on the day of his death, his disciples brought him an image of Amida, three feet high, and as they put it on the right side of his bed, asked him if he could see it. With his finger pointing to the sky he said, "There is another Buddha here besides this one. Do you not see him?" Then he went on to say, "As a result of the merit of repeating the sacred name, I have, for over ten years past, continually been gazing on the glory of the Pure Land, and the very forms of the Buddhas and Bodhisattvas, but I have kept it secret and said nothing about it. Now, however, as I draw near the end, I disclose it to you." The disciples then took a piece of cord made of five-colored strands, fastened it to the hand of the Buddha's image, and asked Honen to take hold of it." (Rev. Harper Havelock Coates and Rev. Ryugaku Ishizuka, tr., *Honen, the Buddhist Saint: His Life and Teaching*, p.636.)

(II) Honen's Thoughts

"**A.** *Question 1.* Is it possible for a man to enter the Pure Land simply by concentration of mind and the repetition of the *nembutsu*, and doing nothing else, even though his heart undergoes no change? *Answer:*--It is the rule with common men for their hearts to be in a state of confusion and it cannot be helped. The only thing is that if men do concentrate their minds upon Amida, and call upon his name, their sin will be destroyed, and they will attain rebirth in the Pure Land. Even sins more grievous than that of mental confusion disappear, if men practice the *nembutsu*.

B. *Question 2.* Even if we do not fix the number of times for repeating the *nembutsu* as our daily task, is it not all right to do it as often as one can? *Answer:*-- It is better to fix the number, lest you yield to laziness

C. *Question 3.* Ought we to practice the *nembutsu* after eating leeks, onions or meat, while the scent of them still remains in the mouth? *Answer:*--There is nothing whatever in the world that should interfere with the practice of the *nembutsu*. [For need to avoid leeks and onions as much as possible, however, see Herbs (pungent).]

D. *Question 4.* How many repetitions of the sacred name should one regard as a day's work? *Answer:*--Well, the number of *nembutsu* repetitions may begin with ten thousand, and then go on to twenty, thirty, fifty, sixty or even a hundred thousand. Everyone should in his own heart and according to his own will, determine the number within these limits.

E. *Question 5.* Even if one does not see a Buddha, or fasten a cord from one's hand to the Buddha's, or even call upon the sacred name oneself, is it possible to be born into the Pure Land at death merely by listening to others repeating the *nembutsu?* *Answer:*--It is not always necessary to fasten the cord to one's hands, nor to meet the Buddha face to face, but by means of the *nembutsu* alone, one can attain rebirth in the Pure Land. And so long as one has a very *utterly deep faith*, it is enough to listen to other men's repetitions of the *nembutsu*.

F. *Question 6.* Though one may wish to be eternally free from the experience of birth and death, and never to be born again into this Three-Fold World, is it true as some say, that, even after one has been reborn in the Land of Perfect Bliss, *the karma* which has brought one there [ultimately] loses its efficacy, so that one may be reborn again here into the Three-Fold World? Now I have no wish to be so reborn, even though I might be born a king, or born into the so-called heavenly world above. My one wish is to get entirely free from this world, and never return here, and so to this end what should I do? *Answer*:--Such ideas are entirely wrong. If one is once born into the Land of Bliss, one will never return to this world, but every such one will attain Buddhahood. Only in case one wishes to come back to save others, he may indeed do so, but by so doing, he [is not in fact within the cycle] of birth and death. There is nothing better than the practice of the *nembutsu* to get safely out of this Three-Fold World and be born into the Land of Perfect Bliss. So you ought to practice it most diligently.

G. *Question 7.* When one is about to die, is it enough, in order to attain rebirth in the Pure Land, to repeat the *nembutsu* as one ordinarily does, without calling a religious adviser? *Answer*:--Even though no religious adviser comes in, and one is not able to die as painlessly as he desires, he will attain rebirth in the Pure Land if only he repeats the *nembutsu* [with One-Pointedness of Mind].

H. *Question 8.* When evil thoughts will keep arising within the mind, what ought one do? *Answer*:--The only thing to do is to repeat the *nembutsu*.

I. *Question 9.* Is it all right to make up on one day for religious duties that were neglected on another day? And may one store up merit now, so as to be forehanded for the future? *Answer*:--It is all right to make up for past losses. But to be laying up for the future (forgetting the present) would tend to laziness."
Lu: 129 #0094
See also: Special Teaching; Pure

Land Buddhism (Summary)

◉ HONGAN-JI

See also: Jodo Shinshu school

▶"The head temple of the Jodo Shinshu or 'True' Pure Land school of Japan, founded by Shinran's daughter Kakushin the Nun and Shinran's disciples in 1272. In 1602, the elder brother of the twelfth chief priest founded a temple of the same name. From then on, the original temple was called Nishi (West) Hongan-ji, and the new one, Higashi (East) Hongan-ji. Higashi Hongan-ji is the head temple of the Otani branch of the sect, and Nishi Hongan-ji, that of the Hongan-ji branch. Both are located in Kyoto, Japan."

Sokk: 165   #0223

◉ HORIZONTAL ESCAPE

Syn: Horizontal Transcendence
See also: Special Teaching; Universal Method; Vows/ Rebirth in Pure Land

----

▶"Horizontal" and "vertical" are figures of speech, which can readily be understood through the following example. Suppose we have a worm, born inside a stalk of a bamboo. To escape, it can take the hard way and crawl "vertically" all the way to the top of the stalk. Alternatively, it can poke a hole near its current location and escape "horizontally" into the big, wide world. The horizontal escape, for sentient beings, is to seek rebirth in the Pure Land of Amitabha Buddha.
Editor: na

"These days many people like to talk about studying enlightenment and finally transcend birth and death. They do not realize that in this world complete enlightenment is extremely difficult. They think of it as direct, sudden, 'vertical' transcendence of the Triple World of Desire, Form, and Formless states. But even someone who has overcome desire and reached the stage of a 'once-returner' still has to go to his death and come back once more through rebirth: how much the more so, for an ordinary person! Most of the sentient beings in this world will have to *be reborn in the Pure Land first before they can be completely enlightened.* The Pure Land gate to the West is called 'horizontal' transcendence: not one in ten thousand misses it." (Master Chu Hung in *Pure Land Pure Mind*)
See also: Special Teaching #2310

◉ **HORIZONTAL TRANSCENDENCE**
see Horizontal Escape

◉ **HORNER, MS I.B.**

►"M.A. (Cantab.). English Pali scholar. Librarian, Newnham College, Cambridge, 1923-36. Student of Mrs Rhys Davids and succeeded her in 1942 as Hon. Secretary of the Pali Text Society. Succeeded Dr. W. Stede as President in 1960. Vice-President of the Buddhist Society, London."
Hump: 90

◉ **HOSSO SCHOOL**
see Yogacara school

◉ **HOUSE, ROBE, SEAT OF THE BUDDHA**
see Lotus Sutra

◉ **HOUSEHOLDER**
See also: Layman

►"Part of a list of lay supporters of Buddhism... The title, however, primarily refers to married property owners, that is 'householders' in both senses of the word: head of a family, and the person holding the title to a house or homestead."
Gomez: 303 #1709

◉ **HRDAYA**
See also: Heart Sutra

►(Skt.) Heart, core or mind. #1629

◉ **HSU YUN (CH'AN MASTER) (1840-1959)**

►"Universally regarded as the most outstanding Buddhist of the Chinese Order in the modern era." (Richard Hunn)
"Dharma successor of all five Ch'an schools; main reformer in the Chinese Buddhist Revival (1900-50). Born Chuan Chou, Fukien province. Left home at 19. At 20 took precepts with master Miao Lien and received Dharma name Ku Yen. In 56th year achieved final awakening at Kao Min Ssu in Yang Chou. Thereafter began revival and teaching work. Eventually invited to take charge of the Sixth Patriarch's temple (Ts'ao-Ch'i), then very rundown; restored it along with temples and monasteries; also founded many schools and hospitals. Died in his 120th year. Had also traveled in Malaysia and Thailand, and taught the King of Thailand. Autobiography: *Empty Cloud* (translated by Charles Luk)."
Snel: 296 #0742

◉ HSUAN HUA (DHARMA MASTER)

▸(1918-1995) "Abbot of Gold Mountain Dhyana Monastery (California) and Chairman of Sino-American Buddhist Association. At age 19 mother died; took sramamera ordination. After WWII, traveled to Nan Hua monastery in Canton province to visit Venerable Hsu Yun (q.v.). Received bhikshu ordination at Mt. P'u T'o during journey.

Set up residence in USA in 1962. In summer 1968 conducted a *Surangama Sutra* Assembly lasting 96 days. Has delivered lectures on other sutras; 1971: established the Gold Mountain Monastery; subsequently also set up the Buddhist Text Translation Society, International Institute for the Translation of Buddhist Texts, and City of 10,000 Buddhas Monastery (Talmage, Ca, USA). Has delivered extensive commentaries to canonical texts."
Snel: 297 #0743

◉ HSUAN-CHUANG (PATRIARCH)
see Hsuan-tsang (596-664)

◉ HSUAN-TSANG (596-664)
Syn: Hsuan-chuang
See also: Fa-Hsien; Beal, Samuel

▸*Vn*/Huyèn-Trang. "Famous Chinese pilgrim who travelled throughout India from 629-645, returning with many texts and teachings. ... Hsuan-tsang was so venerated in China that upon his death in 664, the emperor canceled his audiences for three days."
Preb: 141

"In 645 Hsuan-tsang returned to China with Buddhist images and more than 650 Buddhist texts. His description of his seventeen-year journey through India and Central Asia (*Records of the Western Regions*) is the most comprehensive account of its kind ever written in the Orient. He also translated seventy-five Buddhist scriptures in 1,335 fascicles into Chinese, including the 600-fascicle *Wisdom (Prajna-paramita) Sutra. He started a new epoch in the history of the translation of sutras, and his translations are called the 'new translations,'* in contrast to the 'old translations,' or those done before him. Hsuan-tsang himself belonged to the Consciousness-Only (Yogacara) school and is often regarded as

the founder of the Fa-hsiang (Chinese Yogacara) school."
Sokk: 171 #0222

◙ **HUA-T'OU**
see Wato

◙ **HUA-YEN / HUA-YEN CHING**
see Avatamsaka Sutra

◙ **HUA-YEN SCHOOL**
see Avatamsaka School

◙ **HUI-K'O (487-593)**
See also: Hui-neng; Boddhidharma

►"Jpn: Eka. The Second Chinese Zen Patriarch, who received his enlightenment from Bodhidharma. A famous figure in Chinese art for his dramatic gesture in cutting off his arm as he stood outside in the snow, to impress Bodhidharma with his determination to be admitted and given Zen." Hump: 92 #0055

◙ **HUI-NENG (638-713)**

►"The Sixth Patriarch of Chan/Zen Buddhism in China. His words are preserved in a work called the *Platform Sutra*."
Sokk: 173
"Known in Japan as Eno and in Vietnam as Huệ-Năng, he was the sixth and last patriarch of Ch'an Buddhism in China (the first being Bodhidharma). As leader of the Southern branch of Ch'an school, he taught the doctrine of Spontaneous Realization or Sudden Enlightenment, through meditation in which thought, objectivity and all attachment are elimitated. He was the protagonist (central figure) of the only sacred Chinese Buddhist writing which has been honoured with the title Ching or Sutra, the famous *Platform Sutra of Hui Neng.*"
Ling: 140

Hui-Neng / Vegetarianism
In the *Platform Sutra*, the Chinese patriarch Hui Neng relates that after inheriting the Dharma from the Fifth Patriarch, he spent years in seclusion with a group of hunters. At mealtimes, 'he tells us, 'they cooked meat in the same pot with the vegetables. If I was asked to share, I replied, 'I will just pick the vegetables out of the meat. Was he, then, attached to vegetarianism? And if refraining from eating flesh foods is itself an 'attachment,' does it follow that refusing to give up flesh foods shows non-attachment?
Kjolh/Tric/Winter/94

NOTE:

"[Hui-Neng] was the key figure in determining the main historical development of Chan/Zen in East Asia."
Larousse: 228 #0922

◉ **HUI-YUAN (334-416)**
See also: Lu-Shan; Pure Land School (Summary); Sukhavati; White Lotus Society

----

►(Also Lu-Shan Hui-Yuan; *Vn*/Huệ-Viễn.) "Founder of the Pure Land school in China in the Chin Dynasty (4th-5th c.) Student of Tao-an (312-385), inspiration of the White Lotus Society. A native of Lou-fan, in Yen-men, Shansi. His early years were spent in the study of Confucianism and Taoism. In his 21st year, he was converted to Buddhism and became the most brilliant disciple of Tao An (312-385). His fame as a Buddhist master and expositor of Buddhist teachings spread far and wide. He founded the Tung-lin monastery on Lu Shan in Central China, to which he retired, and this became the most famous centre of Buddhism in South China. He drew his inspiration largely from the *Longer* and *Shorter Sukhavati-Vyuha Sutras* [the two *Amitabha Sutras*], with

their vivid descriptions of the 'Pure Land' and the infinite compassion of Amitabha Buddha. In 402 he founded the *White Lotus Society* (Pai-Lien Chiao), when he assembled the monks and laymen of his community before an image of Amitabha, stressing the importance of worship, the use of icons in meditation and devotion to Amitabha. In later times, this event was taken to mark the beginning of the Pure Land school, of which Hui Yuan is reckoned the founder."
Ling: 140

"In 402, Hui-yuan and his group ... made a collective vow to be reborn together in Sukhavati. But because of individual differences in karmic maturity, they realized that some participants would gain rebirth before others. Thus, they vowed that the early arrivals in Sukhavati would exert themselves to share their salvation with those lagging behind. If they could adhere to this pact, they would in the end all be reborn and together 'miraculously behold the great appearance of Amitabha and open their hearts to his pure brightness ...'He fostered translation activities and also composed the influential treatise *Sha-men pu-ching wang-*

che lun (Monks Do Not Pay Homage to the Ruler), which defended the autonomy of the Buddhist clergy. Moreover, his devotional groups exemplify his most enduring influence on Chinese Buddhism."

Tana: 15

"The Tung-lin-ssu (Monastery of the Eastern Grove), finished in ca.386 and located at Kiangsi, China was to serve as Yuan's home for the rest of his life. The location was a perfect setting for a monastery, for the buildings were put up amidst caves, waterfalls, rock formations, mountain springs, and floating clouds. After his quarters were finished, it was said that Yuan did not leave the mountains for thirty years. His biography recorded that 'his shadow never left the mountain, his footprints never entered the secular world. When he bade farewell to his guests, he went only as far as the Tiger Creek.' His fame, however, was truly far-reaching, for monks, laymen, and famous literary figures converged on Lu-shan from all directions. When Huan Hsuan (the local ruler) wanted to purge the monastic community of undesirable elements, he specifically exempted Lu-shan from the scope of the purge,

saying that the community at Lu-shan was a model of religious discipline. It was also Yuan who was able to dissuade the ruler from requiring monks to render obeisance to him."

Chen: 104-105 #1749

NOTE:

"In Theravada Buddhist thought immortality or the deathless state is Nirvana (Nibbana). One of the adjectives applied to Nirvana from earliest days is amata, i.e. deathless (e.g. *Sutta Nipata* 960). The deathless realm is considered to be gained not at the end of one individual's span of existence, but as a result of spiritual refinement which may be continued throughout many generations; it is held to be the outcome of a process of moral and spiritual refinement initiated and pursued by free choice, once the possibility of such a goal has been heard of, through the Buddha-Dhamma.

A modification of this view occurs in the Pure Land Buddhism of East Asia, where an intermediate goal is introduced, attainable without the long preparation through many existences necessary for Nirvana. *This short-term religious goal is rebirth in the heaven of Amitabha Buddha*, known as the Pure Land

or Sukhavati. Such rebirth is made possible by the compassion and spiritual power of the Buddha, faith of the believer and Buddha Recitation. Strictly, however, this is not immortality, in that even such blissful rebirth must be followed up by further cultivation before the ultimate goal, i.e., Buddhahood, is reached."
Ling: 142-143 #1140

◙ HUMAN BODY
Syn: Skin-bag; Body
See also: Illness; Meditation on Death

▶Note the words of Bodhidharma, the first Zen Patriarch in China: "To dwell in the Three Realms is to dwell in a burning house. To have a body is to suffer. Does anyone with a body know peace?" (Red Pine, tr., *The Zen Teaching of Bodhidharma*, p. 5.)
Zen: 193
"The human body is likened to a skin-bag full of excrements which obstructs our realization of the truth."   Xu-yun/1988: 218
"What the Buddha said is that the human body is just a skin-bag full of filth. What does it have inside? What else but excrement and urine? It's all stored in there. What could possibly be good

about that? ... No matter how perfect a person may be on the surface, inside there are just masses of filth. Urine and excrement collect inside, and the Nine Orifices (q.v.) constantly flow with impurities. Matter comes out from the eyes, wax from the ears, mucus from the nose, and saliva from the mouth. Then there is urination and defecation. Now, which of these is pure and clean?"
Hua/77: 53-54
"Therefore, Buddhist practitioners should constantly visualize this body as a mass of flesh and bones, blood and pus, a skinbag containing phlegm, pus, urine, feces and other foul-smelling substances. The *Parinirvana Sutra* states: 'This fortress of a body -- only evil, deluded people could tolerate living in it. Who with any wisdom would ever cling to or delight in such a skin-bag!' Another scripture states: 'This body is the confluence of all kinds of suffering; it is a jail, a prison, a mass of ulcers; everything is impure. In truth, it is not worth clinging to -- even the celestial bodies of deities are no different.' Therefore, whether walking, standing, sitting or reclining, whether asleep or

awake, cultivators should always visualize this body as nothing but a source of suffering, without any pleasure, and develop a deep sense of disgust ... [thus gradually becoming free from lustful thoughts]. Moreover, the cultivator should also engage in the Seven Types of Meditation on Impurity (e.g., as a fetus, in the impure, dirty area of the womb, drinking the mother's blood, emerging from the womb with pus and blood gushing forth and foul odors in profusion ... after death, the body swelling up and rotting away, with flesh and bones in disarray...). Our own bodies being thus, the bodies of others are likewise. If we constantly meditate on these seven impurities, we will develop disgust toward those male and female forms which ordinary people judge handsome and beautiful. The flames of lust will thus gradually diminish. If, in addition, we can practice the meditations on the Nine Kinds of Foulness, (e.g., meditation on the fresh corpse, the bloated corpse, the bleeding and oozing corpse, the skeleton ... and other progressive stages of decay of the human body after death), so much the better."
Dia: 31-33

NOTE:
It should be clear that although the Buddhas taught that the human body is a skin-bag filled with excrements, theirs is not a pessimistic view of life, but a realistic one. The Buddhas recognized the need to use the body as a means to Enlightenment. Thus, one important injunction to monks and laymen is never to entertain the thought of suicide.
Editor / Zen: 28-29

◙ **HUMAN LIFE / HUMAN REBIRTH**
See also: Six Planes of Existence

▸To illustrate the extreme difficulty of rebirth in the human realm (as opposed to the lower realms of hell, hungry ghosts or animality), Sakyamuni Buddha compared it to the likelihood that a blind sea turtle, surfacing from the depths of the ocean only once every century, would encounter a tree trunk with a hole suitable for nesting.
Skeptics beware: millions of humans may be born each year in this world, but how many more million of viruses come into being each moment on a tiny mound of earth?
PLZ: 147

Samyutta Nikaya v. 455

"Sooner, do I declare, would a one-eyed turtle, if he were to pop up to the surface of the sea only once at the end of every hundred years, chance to push his neck through a yoke with one hole than would a fool, who has once gone to the Downfall, be reborn as a man."

NOTE:

"Of special importance is the teaching that the human state -- once lost is hard to regain. Unless careful preparation for death has been made, the consciousness will be reincarnated in non-human forms many, many times -- perhaps for aeons -- before the dual endowment of birth as a human being in a land where the Dharma is preached is obtained once more."

Blof: 190 #1199

◙ **HUMAN NATURE**

See also: Rebirth in Pure Land; Stale Rice; Human Life

▶"To assume that in their present life more than a few advanced seekers are able to conquer craving and ignorance would be to overrate man. Most men will need a long time, a whole series of rebirths, in which by good deeds they gradually work themselves upwards to better forms of existence.

Finally, however, everyone will obtain an embodiment of such great ethical possibilities that he can destroy craving and ignorance in himself and escape the compulsion for further rebirth. It is regarded as certain that all who strive for emancipation will gain it sometime or other."

Wolfg: 67 #1800

◙ **HUMAN WORLD**

see Jambudvipa

◙ **HUMPHREYS, CHRISTMAS (1901-1983)**

▶"Q.C., M.A., LL.B.(Cantab), J.P. English Buddhist. Adopted Buddhism as a way of life in 1918. Attended Buddhist lectures by Francis Payne in 1923. On 19 November 1924 founded, with Miss Aileen Faulkner, later Mrs. Christmas Humphreys, the Buddhist Lodge of the Theosophical Society, which in 1926 became the Buddhist Society. Publisher of the journal *The Middle Way*. Vice president of the World Fellowship of Buddhists."

Hump: 93 #0053

◉ **HUNDRED-FOOT POLE**
See also: Awakening/
Enlightenment

▸"An analogy often used in Zen
to describe one of the final
stages in meditation before an
awakening is reached."
Kusa: 181
"The instant one perceives only
stillness and experiences
liveliness; it is called in Zen
parlance 'reaching the top of a
hundred-foot pole'. All Masters
advise their disciples not to abide
in this state, which is not real."
Xu-Yun 1988: 191
"From the hundred-foot pole, as
the Chinese say, at the top of
which is the height of thought, we
must take the existential leap to
direct awareness, and this
super-thinking is, in particular,
the springboard of the Chinese
'Ch'an' which became in Japan
'Zen' Buddhism."
Hump/90: 152
Title of a well-known Zen koan.
#0848

◉ **HUNGRY GHOST**
Syn: Ghost
See also: Li Mei; Tree Spirits;
Spirit World

▸"A denizen of one of the
miserable planes of existence.
Some hungry ghosts have huge
stomachs which always burn with
hunger, but tiny throats through
which food cannot pass. One may
be reborn in this state if he has
extreme greed or avarice."
Chan: 476
"In Buddhism, unhappy spirits of
the departed, who are unable to
find rebirth in an embodied
form, are referred to by the
ancient Indian term 'preta'
(*hungry ghosts*). Their wretched
existence is regarded as enduring
until their evil karma is
exhausted, when they will achieve
further, possibly more happy,
rebirth. They inhabit the region
immediately below the surface of
the earth; sometimes they are
found on the surface in a
situation somewhat superior to
that of inhabitants of the various
hells in the bowels of the earth."
Ling: 90
"A condition in the cycle of
rebirth reserved for those who
perish in a state of deep
dissatisfaction, usually as a
consequence of their greed.
Hungry ghosts wander in a
limbo-like state in which they can
find no satisfaction for their
desires, especially, but not
exclusively, their hunger and
thirst."
Gomez: 303 #1710

◙ HUYỀN-VI, THÍCH *(DHARMA MASTER)*

►"Important Vietnamese Buddhist leader in the West, propagator and writer. 1970 PhD -- Magadha University (Patna, India) for 'A Critical Study of the Life & Works of Sariputta Thera.' Directs Monastère Bouddhique Linh-Sơn in Paris, France, which is the center of a worldwide network of temples, including many in the US and Canada. Publications include 'The Four Abhidhammic Realms', 'La Vie de Bouddha Sakyamuni' and 'Dharma Talks' [among many others]."
Snel: 313
In keeping with his vows to expand Buddhism in the West, Dharma Master Huyền-Vi established (as of mid 1997) a record 46 temples worldwide. Thirty-two are in North America and Europe, while others are located in such far-flung places as Nepal and Congo (Zaire).
Editor: na #0756
See also: France (Buddhism in)

◙ HWAOM SCHOOL

►"Korean counterpart of the Chinese Hua Yen (Avatamsaka) school."   Reat: 328 #2053

◙ ICCHANTIKA

►"According to early Buddhism, a sentient being who, being inherently unreceptive to the teachings of the Buddha, will never attain enlightenment. Later Mahayana tended to regard an icchantika as one who would ultimately attain Buddhahood, although his path would be difficult."
Dait: 145

"'Unbeliever'; designates a person who has cut all the wholesome roots (kushala) in himself and has no wish to attain Buddhahood."
Sham: 97 #0156

◙ ICHINEN-MANNEN

►"Jpn., lit. 'one moment of consciousness [nen], ten thousand years'; this expression of Mahayana Buddhism, in which the number ten thousand simply means a limitlessly large number, refers to the experience common to mystics and saints of all cultures that in the world of enlightenment there is no time [or space] in the everyday sense.

Thus from the point of view of enlightened consciousness, 'one moment of consciousness is eternity, eternity is the same as a moment of consciousness.'"

Sham: 98 #0388

See also Ten Thousand

◎ **ICONS**

See also: Buddha Images

▶"Before an icon can perform its role in Buddhist ceremonies, it must undergo certain preparations. For a consecration rite, it must be imbued with religious energy. The ways of achieving this differ according to the various schools of Buddhism... A quasi-magical ceremony designed to bring a sculptured icon 'to life' is the *Eye-Opening Rite* which can be traced back to practices in India. The act of dotting in the pupils with ink invested an image with religious power. An undated Edo-period manuscript with commentaries on the *Hizoki*, an early Shingon text often attributed to Kukai (774-835), gives a clear explanation of this ceremony's effect on an icon:

'*As long as the Eye-Opening Ceremony* has not yet been performed on an icon carved of wood or stone, or in painted form, it should be regarded in the same way as inanimate plants or wooden substances. But after the main priest has consecrated the image by dotting in its eyes, and has bestowed upon it the force of grace by means of mudra, mantras, and meditative vision, the now dignified wooden substance or plain woven material [of the painting] has merged inseparably with the original substance of the depicted deity, although the priest has in no way effected a change in the basic material of the wood, clay, or stone. . . . After the Blessing of the Three Mysteries has been performed, the original substance of the deity and its shadow image have become unified into an inseparable whole, and the characteristics of the shadow image will manifest themselves instantly...'

Another common method of investing an image with religious power was the insertion of sacred objects into its hollow interior. This custom can probably be traced back to the deposition of relics in pagodas. Sculptures became the repositories not only for actual relics (q.v.) of deceased holy persons, but also for objects such as mirrors, coins, woodblock prints, books with sutra texts, and hand-written documents giving the reason for the dedication as well as names of the persons involved...

Another possible method for bringing a sculpture 'to life' was the custom of providing real clothing for it, a practice which probably originated in India and which has been observed in China and Japan..."
Wash: 73

◙ **IGNORANCE**
see Delusion

◙ **ILLNESS**
See also: Practice; Human Body

►"In Buddhist teachings ... a person who is not enlightened is -- by definition -- 'ill'. The healing process is the conversion of suffering into the aspiration to attain enlightenment." (R. Birnbaum, *The Healing Buddha*.)
Birn: xiv
"[In the *Vimalakirti Sutra*], the sage Vimalakirti discussed the experience of illness at great length .. With many visitors assembled to inquire after his health, the infirm sage took the opportunity to speak out against the human body and its limitations:
'O, virtuous ones, the wise do not rely upon the body. It is like a mass of froth which cannot be grasped, like a bubble which bursts in an instant. The body is like a flame arising from the thirst of love ... like a shadow, appearing as a result of karma. It is like an echo, responding to causes and conditions ... The body does not act of itself; but it is spun around by the forces of the winds of passion.'
His own face gaunt and creased by illness, vividly impressing upon visitors the transitory nature of earthly existence, Vimalakirti then urged them to seek the Buddha-body." (R. Birnbaum, *The Healing Buddha*)
Birn: 13
NOTE:
"Similar to Vimilakirti's concept and to Sakyamuni's fundamental teachings, an illness when properly dealt with can serve as a major event that propels one onwards towards higher spiritual attainment. In the case of healings by the Medicine Buddha (Bhaishajya-guru), the sincere act of faith by the ill person results in healings granted. During the healing process, insight arises that causes the person to reform the patterns of his deeds, words and thoughts, so that they accord with the quest for Enlightenment. (Raoul Birnbaum, *The Healing Buddha*, p. 69.)" #1426

◙ **ILLUSION**
See also: Emptiness

►"One of the key concepts in Buddhism. Things in the phenomenal world are not real or substantial, as ordinary people regard them to be. They are transient, momentary, indefinite, insubstantial, and subject to constant alteration. In reality they are like phantoms or hallucinations."
Chan: 476

"Phenomenal 'existence,' as commonly perceived by the senses, is illusory; it is not real inasmuch as, though it exists, its existence is not permanent or absolute. Nothing belonging to it has an enduring entity or 'nature' of its own; everything is dependent upon a combination of fluctuating conditions and factors for its seeming 'existence' at any given moment.' Thus we have the expression, 'illusory but not non-existent.'"
Editor: na #0530

◙ **ILLUSORY BUT NOT NON-EXISTENT**
see Illusion; Emptiness

◙ **IMAGES (BUDDHA)**
see Buddha Images

◙ **IMMOLATION**
See also: Vietnam (Buddhism in);

►"Fire was often the theme of the Buddha's sermons. In one sermon, he spoke of the world aflame, of all men on fire with passion, hatred, infatuation, birth, old age, sorrow, grief and despair. He explained that all are blinded by these flames and that when men understand the holy way the fire will be extinguished within them; that they will no longer be blinded by the attractions of the flame and will be free of the fires of passion and desire. In a parable the Buddha told a story of the affection between an old man and a hare. When the old man was starving, the hare threw himself into the flames that his body might supply food for his friend. Transformed, he became a vision of the Buddha; the old man then realized that within the small body of the hare lived the unselfish spirit of the Buddha."
B.Smith/Japan: 58
"Bodhisattvas who gave their life altruistically for other beings were regarded as noble and blameless; one such was the Bodhisattva Vessantara, who sacrificed himself for a hungry tigress and her newborn cubs.

This is recorded in the Vessantara Jataka. There is another form of religious suicide, known as self-immolation. The burning of their own bodies by Buddhist monks in Vietnam as a protest against the regime arguably falls into this category. The important point in these events is, of course, not the act itself, but the question of its motive or intention, and the state of mind in which it was carried out."

Erricker: 123 #1158

"The practice of self-immolation is explicitly countenanced in the *Lotus Sutra*: The story is related of a Bodhisattva who bathed himself in perfumed oil and set fire to himself in an act of self-offering to the Buddha. Although the sutra goes on to say that realisation of the truth of the Dharma is more meritorious than such acts, nevertheless the practice of self-immolation seems to have developed among Chinese Mahayana Buddhists among whom this sutra (translated into Chinese in early 3rd century AD) was very popular."

Ling: 231-232

◙ **IMMORTALITY**
See also: Amitabha Buddha; Pure Land Buddhism (Summary)

►"In Theravada Buddhist thought immortality or the deathless state is Nirvana (Nibbana). One of the adjectives applied to Nirvana from earliest days is amata, i.e. deathless (e.g. *Sutta Nipata* 960). The deathless realm is considered to be gained not at the end of one individual's span of existence, but as a result of spiritual refinement which may be continued throughout many generations; it is held to be the outcome of a process of moral and spiritual refinement initiated and pursued by free choice, once the possibility of such a goal has been heard of, through the Buddha-Dhamma.

A modification of this view occurs in the Pure Land Buddhism of East Asia, where an intermediate goal is introduced, attainable without the long preparation through many existences necessary for Nirvana. *This short-term religious goal is rebirth in the heaven of Amitabha Buddha*, known as the Pure Land or Sukhavati. Such rebirth is made possible by the compassion and spiritual power of the Buddha, faith of the believer and Buddha Recitation. Strictly, however, this is not immortality, in that even such blissful rebirth must be followed up by further cultivation before the ultimate goal, i.e., Buddhahood, is reached."

Ling: 142-143 #1140

◉ IMPERMANENCE

See also: Death; Meditation on Death; Dharma Seals; Kisagotami; Sudhodana; Birth and Death

----

►One of the most basic truths taught by the Buddha. "Everything in the world arises, changes and perishes; nothing remains constant for even a single moment."

Dait: 225

When the practitioner sees the signs of impermanence (e.g., parched skin, gray hair) he should redouble his efforts at cultivation, so as to escape Birth and Death. This is, of course, the opposite of common, everyday behavior, which consists in hiding the truth -- coloring one's hair, for example.

Editor / Tam: 315

Quotes / Unquotes

"Students in this age of the decay of the Dharma are superficial in their learning. They do not understand the real truth. Thus, in their study of Buddhist scriptures, they cling to famous sayings and fail to comprehend the ultimate truth. They increase their (relative) knowledge and become boastful of their achievements. They produce increased karmas leading to a continuation of the cycle of life and death precisely by means of the Buddhist teachings. This is because they did not start with the question of life and death when they began to search for the Mind. ... The first principle of Ch'an [Zen] practice is to empty one's mind. One must first paste the two words "life-death" on the forehead, and regard them as seriously as if one owed a debt of a million taels." (Zen Master Han-Shan Te- Ch'ing, in Sung-peng Hsu, *A Buddhist Leader in Ming China*.)

Hsu: 126; 130

"Dear friends, the murderous demon of impermanence is constantly looking for our lives and will never agree to conclude peace with us! Let us hastily develop a long enduring mind to get out of birth and death.' Master Yuan Miao of Kao Feng said: 'If one sets a time limit for success in the Ch'an [Zen] training, one should act like a man who has fallen to the bottom of a pit one thousand chang [about two miles] deep.

His thousand and ten-thousand thoughts are reduced to a single idea on how to escape from the pit. He keeps it up from morning to evening and from evening to the following morning, and has no other thought. If he trains in this way and does not realize the truth in three, five or seven days, I shall be guilty of a verbal sin for which I shall fall into the hell where tongues are pulled out.'" (*The Ch'an Training* by Master Hsu Yun, p. 42.)

Zen: 103

A Life Story

"You have breast cancer," the surgeon said, a serious look on his face. I just laughed and said, "No, I don't. The lump is nothing. You said so yourself." "You have breast cancer," he repeated. All I could do was look into his eyes and say, "It has to be a joke. I'm only twenty-seven..." I had thought that breast cancer was a disease of my mother's generation or of women who have a family history of the disease. But on February 24, six weeks after my twenty-seventh birthday, I started a war with my body.

My doctor was ashen when he broke the news to me. I stared for what seemed like hours at the picture of his daughter, who looked like me -- young, black hair, brown eyes. A lawyer, I was told. It could have been her; she could have been me. But it wasn't her. I had the disease for which there is no cure -- just treatments that might or might not work. No promises, no guarantees. At twenty-seven, I had thought I had a lifetime in front of me. The day before my biopsy, I wanted a family, kids, a house, a car. Now, three hours after the biopsy, I wanted someone to tell me how I was going to tell my friends that I might not live out the year.

I had recently attended my fifth reunion, where I caught up on what people were doing with their careers and lives. For many of us at the reunion, the fifth year after graduation, seemed to mark a transition time. We were making choices about the direction of our lives -- starting, finishing, or otherwise thinking about going to graduate school, getting married, moving... I never expected that less than a year later, I would be making decisions about how I was simply going to survive."

Barnard: Fall 97

NOTE:

As a practical application, if family members constantly

"dangle the word Death before their eyes," realizing that it can strike at any time, there will be less friction, less anger, more tolerance of others' shortcomings -- more compassion.
Editor/Zen: 27 #0123

◙ **IMPURE LAND**
See also: Pure Lands (Realms)

►"A Buddha-field that has yet to be purified, or a world system in which a Buddha has yet to appear. The world in which we live is an impure field, and Shakyamuni is the Buddha who has initiated its purification."
Gomez: 303 #1711

◙ **INAGAKI, HISAO (PROF.)**

►"Executive Secretary of International Association of Shin Buddhist Studies (founded 1984). Currently Professor of English at Ryukoku University. 1970s: lecture at SOAS (London U); the (British) Pure Land Buddhist Fellowship was initiated in his house at that time.
Editor of the magazine *Pure Land*. Publications include *A Dictionary of Japanese Buddhist Terms* and a *Glossary of the Sukhavativyuhu Sutras*."
Snel: 307 #0751

◙ **INCALCULABLE**
see Inconceivable

◙ **INCONCEIVABLE**
Syn: Incalculable; Countless

►"That which is beyond human understanding. Referring to events in the Pure Land, the commentarial tradition often sees this term as implying that the Pure Land and its marvels are all events outside the realm of karma and human effort. When referring to numerals, inconceivable is synonymous with 'incalculable' or 'countless.'"
Gomez: 304 #1712

◙ **INDETERMINATE TEACHING**

►"The teaching of the Buddha from which his listeners each knowingly received a different benefit."
Sokk: 82 #0315

◙ **INDIA (BUDDHISM IN)**
See also: Hinduism / Buddhism; Pure Land Buddhism (Summary) Pilgrimage sites
----
►"The immediate context of the emergence of Buddhism in India in the fifth century B.C. is the sramana movement, in which independent ascetics freed

themselves from Vedic authority, brahmanic ritualism, and conservative social tradition and established communities for the purpose of exploring new paths to spiritual liberation. The fatalist Ajivakas, the naturalist Lokayatas, the Agnostic school, the Jains, and the Buddhists were the foremost of these groups. The teaching (Dharma) of the Buddhist group is closely associated with the life of its founder Sakyamuni, acclaimed as Buddha, or awakened one."
Yosh: 3

"With the passing of Candrakirti, the Madhyamika master, and Silabhadra, the Yogacara master, both of whom lived during the seventh century, Buddhism in India was slowly beginning to be engulfed by the relentless tide of Hinduism. As a matter of fact, this process of the absorption of Buddhism into Hinduism had already started before the seventh century. During the Gupta period (fourth to sixth centuries), Mahayana Buddhism began to incorporate many of the Hindu deities into its pantheon ... This process of Hinduizing Buddhism meant the slow, inexorable death of Buddhism in India during the eighth and ninth centuries. By that time the line of demarcation between Buddhism and Hinduism was practically obliterated. The final blow was administered by the Moslem invasion. The initial invasion overran northwest India in 1001, with the Moslems carrying out wholesale destruction of Buddhist institutions, including their valuable libraries, manuscripts, and iconography. A few years after the invasion, the Arab scholar Alberuni traveled over northwest India, and in a book which he wrote, he put together considerable information concerning Indian religions, science, and philosophy. There was hardly any mention of Buddhism, however. In 1193 the Moslems attacked and conquered Magadha, the heartland of Buddhism, and with the destruction of the Buddhist monasteries in that area Buddhism was wiped out. With the disappearance of Buddhism as a vital religious and intellectual force in India, the flow of Indian missionaries to China and Chinese pilgrims to India practically came to a standstill."
Chen: 399-400

"Indian Buddhism received its death-blow from Islam. As Gautama's doctrine relies on

monarchism and monasteries, it was unable to survive the forcible destruction of its Indian viharas with their libraries and the slaughter of thousands of defenseless monks between 712 and 1250. Its fate was sealed with the end of the Pala dynasty of Bengal when Buddhism lost its last royal patronage. Among the millions of inhabitants of India, there are today as few as four million followers of the Buddha's doctrine -- mainly former Harijans who in the Indian states of Maharashtra and Madhya Pradesh were won over to Buddhism by the social reformer Dr. B. R. Ambedkar (1893-1956) and the movement founded by him. The remainder are the adherents of the Mahayana and the Tantrayana in the Indian Himalaya regions which are under the influence of Tibetan culture."
Wolfg: 167

"In ancient India, and later in East Asia, one transcendental world dominated the faith and captured the imagination of millions. This is the land of the Buddha Amitabha, the Buddha-field called the 'Land of Bliss' or Sukhavati. This is indeed a world very different from other worlds. Not only is it a land of pure bliss, it is also a land of great marvels. Everything there happens as if by magic; rivers and forests are filled with precious jewels; birds sing expositions of the Buddha's teachings. In this land there is no evil or danger. One will not even find there the storms and inclement weather, nor even the rugged mountains and impassable forests, that made life in ancient India so harsh."
Gomez/96: 9

"Very few treatises on Pure Land have been found in India. In fact the only extant work devoted exclusively to Amitabha Pure Land Buddhism is the fifth-century work attributed to Vasubandhu (*Vn*/ Thế Thân) that survives only in its Chinese translation, the *Rebirth Treatise*. There are, however, a few older writings that comment on aspects of Pure Land doctrine. Among these, the earliest documents are attributed to Nagarjuna (hence, dated around 200 C.E.), the Ta Chih Tu Lun *(Great Perfection of Wisdom Treatise*; Vn/ Đại- Trí- Độ Luận) and the *Commentary on the Dasabhumika-Sutra*."
Tana: 11

NOTE:
"Buddhism was initially established as a reform

movement opposed to vedic authority, brahmanic ritualism and the caste system of Hinduism. However in the ninth century Hinduism launched a counter-attack. *Buddhist ideas were deliberately incorporated into Hinduism and the historical Buddha was declared an incarnation of the god Visnu.* What once had been attractive in Buddhism could now be found [theoretically] in Hinduism as well."

Wolfg: 167　#2350

◎ **INDOCHINA (BUDDHISM IN)**
See also: Vietnam (Buddhism in)

▶"Continental South East Asia, the peninsula formerly known as Indo-China, has a predominantly Buddhist culture. There were two underlying foreign cultural influences prior to that of the West: that of India in the western part of peninsula; and that of China in the eastern part. The area of Indian cultural influence is Burma, Thailand, Cambodia and Laos. The area of Chinese cultural influence is thus considerably smaller, and is confined to Vietnam. Along with these two cultural sub-divisions goes differentiation in the types of Buddhism: in the western part the predominant tradition is that of Theravada, *while in Vietnam it is that of Mahayana.*" (T.O. Ling, *A Dictionary of Buddhism*)

Ling: 144

Theravada Buddhism is also practiced in the southern part of Vietnam, near Cambodia. Thus, Vietnam is the only country where the two forms of Buddhism are substantially represented, although Mahayana is by far the dominant form.

Editor: na　#1141

◎ **INDONESIA (BUDDHISM IN)**

▶"Indonesia boasts the largest Buddhist monument in Southeast Asia: the massive stupatemple of Borobodur on Java. There is also other evidence that various forms of Buddhism were transmitted to the region in the past but were eclipsed by the coming of Islam in the fifteenth century. Today, however, modest efforts are being made to revive both Theravada and Mahayana Buddhism there." Snell/Budd:27

◎ **INDRA**
Syn: Sakra

▶"The god who controls the thunder, lightning, wind, and rain. He is constantly in conflict

with the Asuras. In Buddhism he is identified with Sakra the lord of the Tusita Heaven."
Dait: 140
"The chief god of the Heaven of the Thirty-Three. A protector of Buddhism. When uncapitalized, 'sakra' (Indra) indicates the equivalent god of any world, not Sakra of the Saha World. In a billion-worlds universe there are one billion Heavens-of-the-Thirty-Three and one billion sakras."
Chan: 482 #0118

◉ **INDRA'S NET**
see   Jewel Net of Indra

◉ **INSIGHT INTO THE NON-ARISING OF DHARMAS**
see   Tolerance of non-birth

◉ **INSIGHT INTO THE NON-ORIGINATION OF DHARMAS**
see   Tolerance of non-birth

◉ **INSIGHT MEDITATION**
See also: Samatha-Vipasyana

►"In Vipasyana or Insight Meditation, the calmness and concentrative ability forged in Samatha are used to inquire penetratively into the true nature of things. Intense observation and analysis of phenomena encountered will, according to the classic texts, reveal that all are subject to duhkha (suffering), anitya (impermanence) and anatman (no self), and are inherently painful or unsatisfactory, impermanent and devoid of atman or self -- or put simply: 'everything that arises passes away and is not self.' That is not mere head-knowledge but a deep existential understanding that is at once purifying and liberating. More positively, it is said to also give access to the Unconditioned: to Nirvana."
Snell/Buddhism: 61

◉ **INTELLECT**
Syn: Mind of discrimination
See also: Mind; Fox; Truth; Two Truths; Ego

►A mind of discrimination (intellect) is the ordinary mind subject to thoughts of right/wrong, correct/ incorrect, etc. The truth being one and indivisible in Buddhist teaching, a "discriminating" mind can never grasp the whole truth. Thus, such an approach is bound to result in an imperfect understanding of the world as it really is. This is best expressed by the parable of several blind men trying to

describe an elephant, each touching a different part of the animal, with no one having the total picture.

Editor/Thich: 308

In Buddhism, the higher levels of truth cannot be grasped through mere intellectual understanding or reasoning. In fact, at that level, all reasoning, based on our limited senses and faculties, is a hindrance. The Buddhist analogy is that of a person attempting to lift a chair while seated upon it!

Editor/Van Hien: 210

Core principle of Buddhism: The teachings of the Buddhas have one supreme purpose -- to enable people to calm and purify the wandering, monkey mind. Once the mind is calm and pure, that is, free from the winds of greed, anger and delusion, it becomes a candle sheltered from the wind, radiating brightly (wisdom).

Editor/Zen: 166

"Although we do not necessarily need to know how and why something works in order for it to have an effect, the spirit of enquiry is generally healthy and helpful in one's spiritual life. We are likely to be more committed to spiritual practices and to make more effective use of them if we understand something of their meaning and function. Nonetheless, like many positive mental attitudes, the desire to know all about what we are getting into has a 'near enemy', and one to which Westerners are often prone. The 'near enemy' is that attitude which holds that *we can fully penetrate the significance of things through the intellect alone*, that once we have thoroughly conceptualized something, we know all there is to know about it. A Buddhist, avowedly striving towards a direct knowledge of reality which goes beyond all concepts, should of course not fall into this way of thinking."

Sangh/95: 8

Pure Land Buddhism

"An ancient master once said: Only two types of people can benefit from the Pure Land method. First are those completely ignorant and deluded but truthful and sincere individuals who, upon hearing the teaching, wholeheartedly believe, accept and begin to practice it. Second are those persons with deep wisdom and good roots in the Pure Land method who clearly understand noumenon and phenomena and the virtues achieved through Buddha Recitation and who

therefore resolve to believe and practice it. On the other hand, those with ordinary intelligence can neither understand profoundly, nor do they have the simple belief of the completely deluded. Therefore, it is difficult for them to receive benefits."(From *Buddhism of Wisdom and Faith*.)
Tam: 103-104 #1388

◉ **INTERPENETRATION**
See also: Avatamsaka Sutra

▸Basic teaching of the *Avatamsaka Sutra* which reveals the interpenetration of all dharmas -- the smallest dharma contains (i.e., has the essence of) the largest and vice versa. This teaching is clearly expressed in chapter 26 of the sutra, which describes the last phases of practice of a Bodhisattva before final Buddhahood. In that chapter, it is taught that at each and every stage, *the actions of the Bodhisattva "never go beyond Buddha Recitation*."
Unimpeded Interpenetration
"In one speck of dust are lands as numerous as specks of dust;/ In each land are incalculable numbers of Buddhas./ Each and every Buddha dwells in an assembly, Endlessly proclaiming

all the practices of Bodhi./"
"In Ten Directions throughout the sea of lands,/ Every hairtip encompasses past, present and future./ So, too, there is a sea of Buddhas, a sea of Buddha lands;/ Pervading them all, I cultivate for seas of endless time."
These stanzas express a key concept in the *Avatamsaka Sutra* -- *unimpeded interpenetration of phenomena* (one mote of dust "contains" a multitude of worlds) and *unimpeded interpenetration of space and time* (one hairtip "contains" the past, present and future).
Editor/Saman: 51 #1616

◉ **INTERVIEW**
see Dokusan

◉ **INVERTED VIEWS**
see Four Inverted Views; Wrong Views; Upside-down Living

◉ **IPPEN**
See also: Ji School; Pure Land Buddhism (Summary)

▸"(1239-89). Known in Japan as the itinerant sage, because of his method of propagating Buddhism. An outstanding preacher and missionary of faith in Amitabha Buddha, his missionary journeys covered

nearly the whole of Japan. Ippen combined relief work with his preaching; he propagated the practice of repeating the Buddha name, with which he linked the idea that the believer is thus prepared for death at any moment. His followers formed a school, called Jishu (Time doctrine), which inculcated pious thoughts at every moment, and a religious service six times a day." Ling: 146-147 #1142

◙ **JAMBUDVIPA**
See also: Saha World

▸"Means the *human world*. The world in which we are living. Also ancient name of India."
Thai: 622

Jambudvipa is a small part of the Saha World, the realm of the Sakyamuni Buddha.
Editor: na

"The 'Continent of the Jambu Tree', so called because this continent is overlooked by a gigantic Jambu tree growing on the summit of Mount Sumeru. Jambudvipa is the southermost of the four continents, supposedly the world in which we humans live. It is said to be wide in the north and narrow in the south, shaped almost like an inverted triangle." Chan: 477 #0116

◙ **JAPAN (BUDDHISM IN)**
See also: Jodo School; Temples; Ji School

▸"Buddhism entered Japan (ca. 550) from Korea. The Empress Suiko became a convert, and the Prince Regent, known as Shotoku Taishi, did his best to encourage it. He drew up Japan's first Constitution, proclaiming the 'Three Treasures of Buddha, Dharma and Sangha' as the basis of the national life. From this time on, Japan took over and made her own the fruits of Chinese culture. In the *ninth century*, Dengyo Daishi, the founder of the Tendai school, and Kobo Daishi, the founder of the Shingon Sect, harmonized Buddhism with Shinto, producing the Ryobu Shinto, a fusion which lasted for a thousand years. In the *twelfth century* Honen brought the Jodo School to Japan, from which developed the Jodo Shin-Shu, founded by Shinran. *About the same time*, Nichiren founded his school which is based on the *Lotus Sutra*, and the two branches of Zen, Rinzai and Soto, were re-founded [after the Chinese schools of the same name]. In 1868, at the Meiji restoration, Buddhism was [partly] dis-established. The

largest schools today are Zen and Pure Land."
Hump: 97-98

(I) Pure Land School

"In Japan Amida worship was known from the time of the introduction of Buddhism in the sixth century. Records indicate that the *Meditation Sutra* was recited at the imperial court in 640 and that images of Amida and his two chief attendants, A v a l o k i t e s v a r a   a n d Mahasthamaprapta, were brought from Korea in 689. Some seventh-century images of Amida and Kannon bear inscriptions indicating that they were votive offerings made on behalf of parents. These findings substantiate the contention that early Amida worship occurred primarily... in Buddhist memorial services. Gyogi (670-749) and other seventh and eighth-century monks, though not followers of the Pure Land School exclusively, preached Amida's promise of salvation through faith, and the emperor Uda (866-931) is said to have died invoking Amida's name."

The Pure Land school as presented in this book originated in India and is currently practiced in this form throughout Asia. In Japan, the school is divided into two major branches, the Jodo (Pure Land) school and the Jodo Shinshu (True Pure Land) school. While the teachings of the Jodo school are substantially the same as those described here, in the case of Jodo Shinshu (also known outside Japan as the Buddhist Churches of America), overwhelming emphasis is placed on Faith in Amitabha Buddha and His Original Vow to save all sentient beings.
Editor: na
Okaz: 17-18

(II) Zen School

"In Japan, Zen was established in the early days of the Kamakura period (1185-1335) when Eisai went to Sung China and brought back the teachings of the Lin-chi school. Subsequently Dogen also went to Sung China and brought back the Ts'ao-tung school's teachings. During the Kamakura and the Muromachi periods (1336-1573), Zen teachings became connected with bushido or the way of the samurai and greatly prospered. In 1654, Ingen (Chin Yin-yuan) came from Ming China to Japan and later founded the Obaku school, [which combines Zen and Pure

Land practices]." Sokk: 516-518
(III) Note
"In Japan, the ancient schools of
Buddhism (Tendai, Avatamsaka,
Zen, Pure Land ...) grew more
and more into independent sects
with their own organization and
separate lay following. It is
important not to read this
Japanese development back into
the classical Chinese situation.
The ancient Chinese schools
were much less institutionalized
sectarian entities than their
successors in Japan. In China
there arose a movement towards
syncretism which tended to unite
the Buddhist sects and in some
cases sought to harmonize the
teachings of Buddhism with those
of Taoism and Confucianism.
This led to a much more
integrated and united form of
Buddhism. Japanese writers tend
to view this as degeneration, but
it can also be viewed as a
s u c c e s s f u l   v i c t o r y   f o r
ecumenism..."
Hinn: 327 #0444
See also: "Temples"

◉ **JAPANESE PURE LAND
SCHOOL**
see   Jodo school

◉ **JATAKA TALES**
Syn: Birth Stories

►"'Birth Stories.' Stories of the
previous lives of Shakyamuni
Buddha... These stories depict the
series of good acts by which
Shakyamuni was able to be
reborn as the Buddha in India.
A Jataka story is traditionally
divided into three parts. The first
introduces an incident in the life
of Shakyamuni Buddha in India.
The second relates an incident in
one of his past existences. The
third demonstrates the causal
relationship between the incident
in the past and the one in the
present, and identifies the
persons involved in the past
incident with those living in the
present."
Sokk: 187 #0220

◉ **JAYANTI CELEBRATIONS**
Syn: Buddha Jayanti

►"The year 1956-7 was observed
with great celebrations in the
Buddhist world as the 2,500th of
the Buddhist era, and the
celebrations were named Buddha
Jayanti, from jaya, a victory,
hence a banner, hence
celebration."
Hump: 50 #2116

◉ **JETA GROVE / MONASTERY**
Syn: Jetavana; Garden of Jeta
and Anathapindika

▶"A monastery near Sravasti presented to the Buddha by Anathapindika."
Thai: 461

Background:
"At the time of the Buddha's ministry, there was a wealthy merchant named Sudatta living in the kingdom of Sravasti. Because of his concern and generosity towards the less fortunate, he was given the epithet 'Anathapindika' or 'provider for widows and orphans'. It once happened that having invited the Buddha to preach in Sravasti, Anathapindika set about trying to find a suitable place for the World-honored One and his company of 1,250 monks. Determining that the estate of Prince Jeta, son of King Prasenajit, with its grassy fields and leafy trees, would be ideal, he approached the prince and offered to buy it. The prince, startled, said in jest, 'I am prepared to sell you as much land as you can cover with gold.' Anathapindika remained silent for a moment, at which point the Prince laughed, 'That seems to be too much for you, does it not?' 'Why, no,' replied the merchant, 'I was simply considering which of my storehouses to take the gold from ...' Later in the day, as the prince watched in amazement, bullock cart after bullock cart arrived at his estate, and the workers laid a carpet of gold upon the land, stretching in all directions. The only patches of ground which could not be covered were those where the trees stood. Prince Jeta, realizing that the Buddha must be an exceptional man, then decided to donate these patches of land. In honor of the two benefactors, the estate was henceforth known as the Garden of Jeta and Anathapindika.
"Here the Buddha spent nineteen rainy seasons. This monastery where the Buddha spent the major part of his life was the place where he delivered many of his sermons."
In Buddhist literature, the name of Anathapindika has become synonymous with selfless, extreme generosity in the cause of the Dharma (building temples, printing sutras and commentaries, etc.)
Editor/Mind Seal:153-54 #1753

◙ **JETAVANA**
see   Jeta Grove

◙ **JEWEL NET OF INDRA**
Syn: Brahma Net; Indra's Net; Net of Indra

►A famous metaphor found in the *Avatamsaka Sutra.* It illustrates the concept of unity and universal interdependence, the infinite mutual interrelationships among all things, the realm of non-interference between noumenon and phenomena and non-interference among phenomena.
Editor: na

"Far away in the heavenly abode of the great god Indra, there is a wonderful net which has been hung by some cunning artificer in such a manner that it stretches out infinitely in all directions. In accordance with the extravagant tastes of deities, the artificer has hung a single glittering jewel in each 'eye' of the net, and since the net itself is infinite in dimension, the jewels are infinite in number. There hang the jewels, glittering like stars of the first magnitude, a wonderful sight to behold.

If we now arbitrarily select one of these jewels for inspection and look closely at it, we will discover that in its polished surface there are reflected all the other jewels in the net, infinite in number. Not only that, but each of the jewels reflected in this one jewel is also reflecting all the other jewels, so that there is an infinite reflecting process occurring.

The Hua-Yen [Avatamsaka] school has been fond of this image, mentioned many times in its literature, because it symbolizes a cosmos in which there is an infinitely repeated interrelationship among all the members of the cosmos. This relationship is said to be one of simultaneous mutual identity and mutual intercausality." (Francis H. Cook, *Hua-Yen Buddhism*)
#0099

◉ **JEWEL-HEAP SUTRA**

see Ratnakuta Sutra

◉ **JEWELS AND GEMS**

►"Jewels and precious substances symbolize enlightened teachings; their variety represents the multitude of doctrines expounded by Bodhisattvas and Buddhas in adapting to different situations and audiences."
Clea/84: 22 #1964

◉ **JI SCHOOL**
See also: Ippen; Pure Land Buddhism (Summary)

▸"One of the schools of Pure Land teaching in Japan, founded by Ippen in the Kamakura period (1185-1333). Its head temple is Shojoko-ji in Fujisawa, Kanagawa Prefecture. Ji, the name of this sect, means 'time' or 'hour.' It mirrors the tenet of the sect that now is the last moment and one should therefore chant the the name of Amitabha Buddha in all sincerity. Among the Three Pure Land Sutras (q.v.), the school places special emphasis on the *Amitabha Sutra*. Early adherents disseminated the teaching of Buddha Recitation while traveling throughout the country."
Sokk: 190-191 #0236
See also: Pure Land Buddhism

◙ **JINA** (*Skt*)
See Conquerors

◙ **JIRIKI**
see Self-power

◙ **JIVA**
see Jivaka

◙ **JIVAKA**
Syn: Jiva
See also: Meditation Sutra; Ajatasatru

▸"A skilled physician of Magadha in ancient India and a devout Buddhist. He treated King Bimbisara and Shakyamuni himself and thus won renown.

As told in the *Meditation Sutra*, when Ajatashatru starved his father Bimbisara, and was about to behead his mother Vaidehi, Jivaka dissuaded him. [She was instead confined to her quarters where she eventually died.] Later, when King Ajatashatru broke out in malignant sores all over his body, Jivaka succeded in persuading him to reflect on his past conduct and to seek the Buddha's teaching."
Sokk: 192 #0219

◙ **JIVANJIVA**
See also: Amitabha Sutra

▸"A two-headed bird, the heads representing mind and perception (possibly a kind of pheasant)."
Seki: xxx #2313

◙ **JIZO**
see Ksitigarbha

◙ **JODO SCHOOL**
Syn: Japanese Pure Land School
See also: Honen; Jodo Shinshu School; Namu Amida Butsu; Pure Land Buddhism (Summary); Genshin

▸"'Pure Land school' of Japanese Buddhism. Headed by patriarch Honen (1133-1212). Although originally a Tendai monk, Honen embraced the Pure Land ideal primarily through the teachings of Shan-tao after having become convinced that the Tendai path was becoming increasingly unworkable as a means for attaining salvation. Of course Pure Land teachings had been in Japan at least since the time of Ennin (794-864), who had studied it and other traditions while in China, but Honen is regarded as the founder.

The textual basis of the school was the *Larger* and *Smaller Sukhavativyuha Sutras*, as well as the *Meditation Sutra*, and the religious practice focused on the recitation of the Buddha's name, thus identifying it as an 'other-power' or 'easy path' (q.v.) approach to salvation. For Honen the formula 'Namu Amida Butsu' was a means of strengthening one's faith in Amitabha, not merely an expression of trust, and was considered by him an appropriate religious practice in a period of Dharma decline (Dharma-Ending Age). Unlike its later offshoot, Jodo Shinshu, Honen's school continued the Buddhist monastic tradition.

Honen's school was both threatening and alienating to the more formal and established Buddhist schools of the time, resulting in Honen's five-year exile, terminated only one year prior to his death."
Preb: 149-150

(I) Background

"Having a deep desire to obtain salvation and with faith in the teaching of the various scriptures, I practiced many forms of self-discipline ... But the fact is I do not keep even the precepts, nor do I succeed in any one of the many forms of meditation ... Unless one gets free from evil conduct and evil passion how shall he obtain deliverance from the bondage of birth and death? Alas! alas! What shall I do? What shall I do? The like of us are incompetent to practice the three disciplines of the Precepts, Samadhi, and Wisdom. And so I inquired of a great many learned men and priests whether there is any other way to salvation than these disciplines, but no one could either teach me the way or even suggest it. At last I went into the library where all the Scriptures were, all by myself, and with a heavy heart read them all through. I hit upon a passage in Zendo's Commentary, which runs as follows: '*Only repeat the name of Amitabha with all your heart, whether walking or standing, whether sitting or lying*: never cease the practice of it for a moment. This is the very work which unfailingly issues in salvation; for it is in accordance with the Original Vow of Amida Buddha.'" (Coates and Ishizuka, *Honen*. pp. 185-187.) Prat: 480

(II) Note

Pure Land Buddhism, based on the three elements of Faith, Vows and Practice, is currently practiced throughout East Asia -- in China, Vietnam, Korea and other countries. In the case of Japan, Pure Land is mainly divided into two branches, the Jodo (Pure Land) School and the Jodo Shinshu (True Pure Land) School. The teachings of the Jodo School (founded by Honen, 1133-1212) are substantially the same as the teachings of traditional Pure Land. In the case of Jodo Shinshu (founded by Honen's best known disciple, Shinran, 1173-1262, and represented in the United States by the Buddhist Churches of America), overwhelming emphasis is placed on Faith.

Editor: na

See also: Pure Land Buddhism (Summary) #1037

◙ JODO SHINSHU SCHOOL

Syn: Shin Buddhism; Shin School
See also: Buddhist Churches of America; Shinran; Hongan-ji; Jodo School; Hoben Hosshin Son'ei; Pure Land Buddhism (Summary)

▸"Japanese for 'True Pure Land school.' A school of Pure Land founded by Shinran (Honen's best known disciple), based on the belief that [exclusive] reliance on the power of Amida, rather than one's own power, is the determining factor in achieving salvation. Jodo Shin rejects the monastic rules of traditional Jodo, permitting its priests to eat meat, live as laymen, marry, etc. Shinran stressed *faith* in Buddha Recitation, holding that too much emphasis on repeated recitation implies a tendency to rely on one's own power, rather than Amitabha's grace. He held that even the practitioner's longing for salvation is given by Amitabha, as opposed to Honen's Jodo (q.v.) school which teaches that a believing mind is, strictly speaking, a part of one's own effort.

Shinran propagated his teachings in Kyoto and in the Kanto area, but the school gained little influence during his lifetime.

After his death, a mausoleum was built in Higashiyama (Eastern Hills) in Kyoto by his daughter Kakushin the Nun and his disciples. This later became Nishi (West) Hongan-ji, the head temple of the school. In the fifteenth century, the Jodo Shin school spread widely because of the efforts of Rennyo, the eighth chief priest of Hongan-ji."

Sokk: 196

(I) Background

While the Jodo (Pure Land) school in Japan is identical to the Pure Land School in China, Vietnam, and other Asian countries, Jodo Shinshu (or Shin) is an exclusively Japanese school. It differs from Jodo in several ways, to wit: (1) The clergy is allowed to marry. (2) The position of supreme head of the Church is hereditary, passed on from father to son. (3) Jodo Shinshu emphasizes faith to the exclusion of everything else. For example, the rosary worn on the wrist of Jodo Shin devotees is not used to count recitation but is a symbol of gratitude for the grace of the Buddha Amitabha.

"The nembutsu [recitation of the Buddha's name] then becomes an expression of gratitude to Amida for the gift of faith that leads to birth in the Pure Land, rather than a meritorious act that can affect rebirth." (J. Okazaki, *Pure Land Buddhist Painting*, p. 23.)

Editor: na

(II) Note

"As many writers have pointed out, Shinran was the Martin Luther of Japan, both in leading the way out of the monastic life and in preaching salvation through faith alone."

Pratt: 486　#0216

See also: Pure Land Buddhism (Summary)

◙ **KALALA**

See also: Abortion

▶"The embryo immediately after conception; the human embryo during the first seven days."

Thai: 606　#1640

◙ **KALAVINKA**

▶"A bird [mentioned in the Amitabha Sutra] whose singing is very melodious and which is first heard while still in the shell."

Seki: xxx　#2312

"The Indian cuckoo, a bird of fairyland, whose sweet songs charm all the inhabitants of the forest."

Thai: 623

"A kalavinka bird is a bird

described as having a melodious voice, and is found in the valleys of the Himalayas. It is said to sing in the shell before hatching."
Chan: 98 #1643

◉ KALAYASAS (5TH C.)
See also: Meditation Sutra

►"A monk from Central Asia; went to China in the early Yuan-chia era (424-453) and translated, *inter alia*, the *Meditation Sutra*, one of the Three Pure Land Sutras (q.v.). Died in 442 at the age of 60."
Inag: 404 #0707

◉ KALPA
Syn: Eternity; Eon; Empty Eon
See also: Cosmology (Buddhist)

►"The nearest approach to the conception of eternity in Buddhist thought is the kalpa (Sanskrit), which is an *inconceivably long period of time*. The kalpa is divided into four p a r t s : p e r i o d o f world-dissolution; period of chaos; period of world-formation; period of world-continuation. A simile, used in a discourse of Buddha, is as follows: 'Suppose, O monks, there was a huge rock of one solid mass, one mile long, one mile wide, one mile high,

without split or flaw. And at the end of every 100 years a man should come and rub against it with a silken cloth. Then that huge rock would wear off and disappear quicker than a Kalpa.' Of such world-periods, according to Buddha, there have been many hundred thousands. In the Buddhist view of things, there is no limitation to the process of world-dissolution, chaos, w o r l d - f o r m a t i o n a n d world-continuation, nor to the number of Buddhas who will appear in the course of this process."
Ling: 113

"The period required for a celestial woman to wear away a stone of ten cubic miles if she touched it with her garments once every three years. Of the three kinds of kalpa, that period is a small kalpa; Twenty small kalpas make a medium kalpa, and four medium kalpas make a large kalpa."
Dait: 194-195

"In Buddhism, a kalpa generally indicates the length of time between the creation and recreation of a world or universe, spanning the period of a world's formation, existence, destruction, and non-existence. There are different interpretations of

measurement of a kalpa in Buddhism. It often simply denotes a very long period of time, similar to an aeon. There are small, medium, great, and incalculable kalpas."
Chan: 477

NOTE:
"According to conventional reckoning, a small kalpa would be equivalent to 16.8 million years and a large or great kalpa 1,347 million."
T.Minh Châu: 349 #1126

◙ **KALYANAMITRA**
see   Good spiritual advisor

◙ **KAMAKURA**

▸"Important period of Japanese history (1185-1335) when the rise of the Shoguns (military dictators) made Kamakura, a city on the sea to the south of Tokyo, a second capital which drew teachers and artists from the seat of the Emperor in Kyoto. Here Buddhist Schools from China, notably Rinzai Zen, found a new home. Here was the birthplace of the Samurai cult and the rise in importance of Judo and Kendo. Engakuji (a famous Rinzai Temple) was founded here in 1282, and the Daibutsu (or great

Amitabha statue) was erected in 1252."
Hump: 103 #0443

◙ **KAMI**

▸*(Jpn).* "In Shinto a deity or spirit, but also an impersonal, supernatural force thought to inhabit certain objects, natural phenomena, and people."
Reat: 330 #2054

◙ **KAMMU**

▸"(r. 781-806.) Japanese emperor responsible for moving the capital to Kyoto: a patron of Tendai [Tien T'ai] Buddhism."
Reat: 330 #2055

◙ **KANISHA (100 A.D.)**
Syn: Kaniskha
See also: Buddhist Councils; Images (Buddhist); Kashmir (Buddhism in)

▸"Buddhist ruler of the Kushan empire, which lay to the northwest of India. His accession is dated sometime around 100 A.D. A Buddhist council, reckoned by Mahayana Buddhists as the 4th, was held in his reign, in Kashmir. Kanisha is represented as desirous of settling disputes among various

schools of Buddhist thought, and has a place in the estimation of Mahayana Buddhists similar to that given to Ashoka by Theravadins."
Ling: 154 #1864

◉ **KANISKHA**
see Kanisha (100 A.D.)

◉ **KAPILAVASTU**
See also: Lumbini

►"The capital of the country of the same name, located in Central India. The Buddha was born at Lumbini on the outskirts of this city. His father, Suddhodana, was the king of the country. Present Tilonakot in Nepal."
Dait: 171

"The Buddha frequently visited his home city even after Enlightenment and presented several discourses there. As a result, his father Suddhodana attained the level of stream-entry (shrota-panna). The Buddha's son Rahula was accepted into the monastic order as a novice (shramanera) there."
Sham: 112 #0151

◉ **KAPLEAU, PHILIP (ROSHI)**

►"American Zen teacher and founder of the Zen Center of Rochester, New York, one of the major Buddhist centers in the United States. He was born in 1912, studied law, and became a court reporter. In this role, he worked at both the military tribunal in Nuremberg, and the War Crimes Trials in Tokyo in 1946. At the beginning of the 1950s, Kapleau attended D.T. Suzuki's lectures in Buddhist philosophy at Columbia University, finally deciding in 1953 to travel to Japan in pursuit of genuine Buddhist training. Prior to Kapleau's return to America in 1966, Yasutani Roshi authorized him as a teacher. In August, 1966, the Zen Center was founded in Rochester. In addition to publishing a number of important and influential books such as *The Three Pillars of Zen; Zen: Dawn in the West* and *To Cherish All Life* (a book promoting a vegetarian diet), Kapleau has been a leader in promoting Zen as a American religious practice."
Preb: 154-155 #1038

◉ **KARMA**
See also: No Good Deed Goes Unpunished

►Action leading to future

retribution or reward, in current or future lifetimes.

Common karma: the difference between personal and common karma can be seen in the following example: Suppose a country goes to war to gain certain economic advantages and in the process, numerous soldiers and civilians are killed or maimed. If a particular citizen volunteers for military service and actually participates in the carnage, he commits a personal karma of killing. Other citizens, however, even if opposed to the war, may benefit directly or indirectly (e.g., through economic gain). They are thus said to share in the common karma of killing of their country.

Editor: na

Fixed karma: in principle, all karma is subject to change. Fixed karma, however, is karma which can only be changed in extraordinary circumstances, because it derives from an evil act commited simultaneously with mind, speech, and body. An example of fixed karma would be a premeditated crime (versus a crime of passion).

Editor/Tam: 340

"The doctrine of karma is subtle and exceedingly intricate. Reduced to its most elementary meaning, karma is action; it refers also to the fruits of action. It may be seen as the law of causation on a personal level, a combination of primary and secondary causes. In the case of a plant, for example, the seed is the primary cause, and rain, wind, sunlight, etc., are the secondary causes. Similarly, every thought, utterance, and deed is a seed that ripens over time until, under suitable conditions, it comes to fruition as an event or circumstance. It is, moreover, a continuous process, for the way in which one responds to these circumstances determines the quality of his present life as well as future ones. Thus the doctrine of karma repudiates any notion of 'fate' or 'fixed destiny,' inasmuch as these circumstances and our response to them are constantly changing. Clearly, then, everyone has the potential at each moment to alter the course of his future karma. Within the period of a single lifetime, however, every being has in addition to his mutable karma a particular 'fixed karma,' as for example the species, race, and sex into which he is born. These karmic traits, though set for life, are then recast at the next rebirth in accordance with the individual's ever-ripening past actions. Although we often speak of 'good' and 'bad' (painful) karma, the term is generally used in reference to the latter, as when selfish actions, for instance, are called 'karma-producing.' Karma means that everything that happens to us, without exception, we ourselves directly or indirectly, partly or entirely, set in motion at some time in the past. The Buddha said, 'If you want to know the past [cause], look at your present [effect]. If you want to know the future [effect], look at your present [cause].' The answer to the familiar refrain, 'What have I done to deserve this?' is always 'plenty!' Yet suffering can also follow from the collective karma, in which each member of a group reaps what the group as a whole has sown. And when the conditioning causes of one's karma, whether that karma is of hardship and disgrace or fortune and honor, are exhausted, it will disappear."

Kapl: 293-294.

Poverty and want, for example, are the results of miserly thoughts and actions in past lives. For a destitute person to cheat and steal in order to escape poverty and become wealthy is a classic case of creating more evil karma in the hope of escaping retribution.

Editor: na

Pure Land Buddhism

All evil karma results, ultimately, from delusion, the antithesis of enlightenment. Such practice as Buddha Recitation leads ultimately to enlightenment and thus dissolves away evil karma. It is as though a house were boarded up for ten thousand years. As soon as a window is opened, eons of darkness disappear in a split second. The dissolution of evil karma through Buddha Recitation can be explained in another way:

"A non-individualistic interpretation of the law of karma is provided by the doctrine of parinamana or 'turning over' of merits. According to this doctrine, the merits which one person has acquired by the performance of good actions, can, if he so wishes, be transferred to another ... By sincerely invoking Amitabha Buddha's name, which is in reality identical with Amitabha himself, we identify ourselves with Amitabha. As a result of this identification, a portion of his merits is transferred to us.

These merits, which are now ours, are sufficient not only to counterbalance the effects of our evil actions but also to ensure our rebirth in the Pure Land. The law of karma has not been suspended for our benefit. All that has happened is that a more powerful karma has cancelled out one that was weaker." (as quoted by Sangharakshita)
Editor/Van Hien: 201-202
NOTE:
"Devotional Buddhism does not maintain that rebirth in the Pure Land takes place without a cause, but that the *primary factor in its causation is the invocation of the name of Amitabha.* Hence this school cannot be regarded as denying the general principle of causality."
Sangha/57: 374-375 #0782

◙ KARMIC RESULT

►"The natural reward or retribution for a deed, brought about by the law of karma."
Chan: 477 #0532

◙ KARUNA (Skt)
see Compassion

◙ KASAYA

►A red or yellow monk's robe.

◙ KASHMIR

►"An ancient state northwest of India (covering roughly what is now offically known as Jammu and Kashmir) in which Buddhism was prominent from Asokan times."
Reat: 331 #2056
See also: next entry

◙ KASHMIR (BUDDHISM IN)
Syn: Buddhism - Kashmir
See also: Kanisha; Buddhist Councils

►"Buddhism was early known in Kashmir which Asoka added to his empire. A later Buddhist patron was the Kushan King Kaniskha (Kanisha), who held a Buddhist Council in the capital, Srinagar, which Asoka had founded.　　Hump: 106
"Kashmir was one of the most important centers of Buddhist Sanskrit learning and the center of the most powerful Buddhist school -- Sarvastivadin [a precursor of Mahayana Buddhism]. Kashmir played an important role in the transmission of Buddhism to China. The Chinese traveller Ou-K'ang or Wu-K'ong, while visiting Kashmir, (A.D. 759-763) saw about three hundred

monasteries."
Lahiri: 27
The Buddhist art of Kashmir, of high degree of workmanship, showed Greek influence."
Hump: 106 #0442

◙ **KASYAPA**
Syn: Maha-kasyapa
See also: Zen School; Flower and Smile

▸"A Brahmin of Magadha who became a close disciple of the Buddha, and was at the time of his death the senior member of his Order. He therefore presided over the first Buddhist Council, held immediately after the passing. The Zen School regards him as their First Patriarch from the story of the 'transmission' of the 'Mind-seal' when the Buddha held up a golden flower and Maha-kasyapa smiled."
Hump: 107
"One of the ten major Arhat [vs. Bodhisattva] disciples of the Buddha. He was born in a brahman family and named Pippalayana. The name Kasyapa indicates his clan. He became a disciple of the Buddha about three years after the latter attained enlightenment. Kasyapa is said to have become an Arhat after being with the Buddha for only eight days. He devoted himself to the practice of ascetic practices, and was regarded as chief of the Order. After the demise of the Buddha, Kasyapa presided over the First Buddhist Council. Before his death he is reputed to have entrusted Ananda with leadership of the Order." Dait: 215 #0176

◙ **KATYAYANA**
Syn: Maha-Katyayana

▸"Also known as Mahakatyayana. One of Shakyamuni's ten major disciples, respected as the foremost in debate. He was a native of Avanti in western India. A Brahman by birth, he held a position as religious advisor to the local king. He was converted at Shravasti, where he had been sent by the ruler of Avanti, who had heard reports of Shakyamuni's teachings. After becoming Shakyamuni's disciple, he returned to Avanti, where he converted the king and many others." Sokk: 222 #0201

◙ **KAUDINYA**
Syn: Kondanna; Maha-Kaundinya

▸"Name of the first disciple of Sakyamuni. He was the son of a

very wealthy Brahman family near Kapilavastu and was born before the Buddha."
Thai: 608 #1641

◙ KAUSTHILA

Syn: Maha-Kausthila

►"An eminent disciple of Sakyamuni, ranked foremost among masters of logical analysis."
Thai: 403 #1631

◙ KEGON SCHOOL

See also: Avatamsaka School

►"Japanese counterpart of the Chinese Hua Yen or Avatamsaka school, founded in Japan by a Chinese missionary known to the Japanese as Dosen (720-60)"
Reat: 331 #2057

◙ KEGON SUTRA

see Avatamsaka Sutra

◙ KENSHO

See also: Awakening/ Enlightenment; Satori

►"Semantically kensho has the same meaning as satori and the two terms are often used synonymously. Nevertheless it is customary to use the word satori when speaking of the enlightenment of the Buddha or the Zen patriarchs and to use the word kensho when speaking of an initial awakening experience that still requires to be deepened."
Sham: 115 #2272

◙ KHEMA

►(5th c.)"The perfect or model Buddhist bhikhsuni according to the Buddha. She was a queen of Bimbisara (ca. 5th B.C.), of great beauty; but through the Buddha's teaching, she realized the transience of the body and achieved the condition of the Arhat. She became a wise teacher herself, giving answers to questions posed by king Pasenadi which turned out to be identical to the Buddha's own answers when he was asked the same questions."
Oxf: 545

◙ KHOTAN

►"A city-state on the Silk Road. It is in Turkestan, the principal centre of Central Asian Buddhism until the Moslem invasion. Buddhism was introduced there about 200 B.C. or earlier. It was the centre from which is credited the spread of Mahayanism." Thai: 279 #1620

◙ **KILLING**
See also: Vegetarianism;
Abortion; Euthanesia; Food /
Food Rules; Birth Control;
Precepts; Bimbisara; Simha;
Suicide; Immolation

▸The first Buddhist precept,
binding upon clergy and laity
alike, is not to kill -- and this
includes not to kill oneself:
"A monk who intentionally
deprives a human being of his
life, or provides the means for
suicide, or praises death, or
incites one to commit suicide,
saying, 'Of what use to you is this
evil, difficult life? Death is better
for you than life,' thus having his
mind set on the other's death and
with the idea that he should die,
praises death in various ways or
incites him to commit suicide,
commits an offense entailing loss
of monkhood." (Vinaya Pitaka, as
quoted in *World Scripture*, p.343).
Editor: na
"Whereas the commandment
'Thou shalt not kill' is ordinarily
interpreted to mean 'Thou shalt
not kill humans,' the Buddhist
perspective includes all forms of
animal life as well. To refrain
from killing means to abstain
from killing any sentient being,
including even cockroaches and
ants. Each living creature is as

attached to its life as any other,
as we can see when they scurry
away. In institutions such as the
Society for Prevention of Cruelty
to Animals and in sayings such
as 'She's so kind, she wouldn't
kill a fly,' we see that the notion
of non-harm often extends to
non-human life forms in Western
culture, too. Thus, Buddhism
reaffirms some of our own
cultural ideals."
Tsomo: 101

(I) Self-Defense
"*Question*: What if someone is
trying to harm me physically or
mentally, and in trying to prevent
this I hurt him or her, do I
violate the first precept against
killing?
Answer: You violate the precept.
In kung fu, even though you may
have lethal power, if you are
attacked, you run away. If you
can't run away, you avoid. You
do this dance so they can't get
you. If you can't avoid, you
disarm; take the weapon away
from them. If you can't disarm,
you maim, to slow them down.

The last resort is to kill, to use
your power in a lethal way. If
you do that to protect yourself,
you violate the precept, because
it is a self-centered action. If you

do that to protect someone else, you uphold the precept."
Loori: 248

(II) Abortion

"In a discussion of the first precept, the subject of abortion is bound to arise. The issue of abortion, as you know, has long been the subject of bitter public debate. At one extreme are those who insist, 'All life is sacred, even a human embryo!' These people rage against the 'murderous mind' of those who would deny 'the right of life' to the unborn child, insisting that 'since only God can give life, only He can take it away.' It may be asked: Are these same individuals just as vociferous in demanding a decent life for those already born who are undernourished and exploited? On the other side are those who insist that a pregnant woman alone has the right to decide whether to bear her fetus. To women who cry, 'This is my body, I can do with it as I please!' I would ask, 'How can you say it is your body when you cannot control the circulation of your blood, of your heartbeat, your thoughts, aging, or death? Clearly your body has its own law, which it obeys independently of your wishes. True, in a limited sense it is your body, for it is the outcome of your karma, of your volitional thoughts and actions in this life and previous ones. But don't forget that your karma also includes your biological inheritance from your parents. Moreover, it is not just by chance, as you may think, that the particular fetus within you was conceived. In the profoundest sense, its conception is the expression of the karmic affinity between you and the fetus: your need to provide it with a body and its need to be reborn through you.' Make no mistake, abortion is a grave matter. Even when the danger of the mother's physical death is remote, as in modern clinics, the spiritual dying that accompanies an abortion can be real and painful. For a spiritually sensitive woman who realizes she is the means through which a particular being can be reborn in human form -- that form which is so hard to obtain -- to acquiesce in the aborting of that incipient life can be a soul-scarring experience, just as bearing a wanted child in happy circumstances can be a source of tremendous joy. Many women, and men too, have asked my advice about abortion. I have

seen and heard the delight of those who, though having contemplated an abortion, decided to have the child, and I have observed sorrow etched in the faces of many who did have an abortion."
Kapl/1980: 247-248

(III) Suicide/Sacrifice

Killing sentient beings, including slaughtering animals for food, is a m o n g t h e h e a v i e s t transgressions in Buddhism. This is not only because such acts create untold suffering but also because they cut short the lives of future Buddhas (as all sentient beings have a common Buddha Nature). The injunction against all forms of killing (including suicide), covering all sentient beings, is unique to Buddhism. Jainism, for example, approves of the penance of death by self-starvation (suicide), while Hindu ceremonies such as the Srauta rites "center on offering into the altar fires oblations of milk, butter, honey .. domestic animals ..." (sacrifice). K. Crim, *Dictionary of Religions*, p. 369 and 790, respectively.
Editor/Tam: 324

(IV) Animal Slaughter

"To intentionally deprive any living being, but especially a human being, of life will produce painful karma. Slaughterers as well as hunters and fishermen -- especially those motivated by sport alone -- inevitably incur a heavy karma. Those who do experimental research on animals, often depriving them of their lives, also risk painful karma. The destruction of animals in such experimentation is justified on the ground that it is the only way by which to gain information vital to the health and welfare of human beings. Unfortunately, much animal experimentation today is undertaken without consideration of alternative, more humane methods. Such an unfeeling attitude may arise from the belief that animals, being less developed than man, suffer less. But who would deny that animals, too, suffer pain acutely and try to avoid it as much as humans? And precisely because their minds are less complex than man's and they are more intuitive, animals are more sensitive to impending violence and pain, which generates in them fear that prolongs their suffering. *Porphyry, a Greek philosopher of the fourth century, wrote that anyone who had heard the scream of an animal being slaughtered could never again eat*

animal flesh."
Kapl/1980: 245　#1187
See also: Euthanasia

◙ **KIMNARA**
see　Kinnara

◙ **KING OF THE DHARMA**
see　Dharma King

◙ **KINNARA**
Syn: Kimnara

►"A kind of mythical celestial musician. It has a horse-like head with one horn, and a body like that of a human. The males sing, and the females dance."
Chan: 477　#0533

◙ **KISAGOTAMI**
See also: Impermanence; Dharma Seals

►"Kisagotami was married to a banker's son of considerable wealth. As a young wife, Kisagotami was mistreated by her in-laws, as new brides who moved into their husbands' home sometimes were. When she gave birth to a son, she finally received an honorable place among her husband's relatives. But her child died while still a toddler, and Kisagotami, who had never seen death before, went

mad. In her state of insanity, Kisagotami took up the dead child and carried him on her hip from house to house, begging for medicine. One kind old man directed her to the Buddha. The Buddha said, 'Go and bring a white mustard seed from a house where no one has died.' Hearing his words, she immediately rushed off in the innocent faith that if she brought a white mustard seed to this enlightened sage, it would be the medicine that could miraculously bring her child back to life. Kisagotami went from house to house, at each house asking, and at each house learning that there too, someone had died. The truth struck home. Her sanity returned. 'Little son,' she said. 'I thought that death had happened to you alone; but it is not to you alone. It is common to all people.' Then, still holding the body of her child in her arms, she carried him gently to the forest and left him there."
Murc: 85　#0484

◙ **KOAN**
Syn: Kung-an
See also: K o a n　o f Buddha-Recitation; Wato

►"Literally, Koan means a public

case... However, it now refers to the statements, including answers, made by Zen masters. These statements are used as subjects for meditation by novices in Zen monasteries. Koan are also used as a test of whether the disciple has really [achieved an Awakening]. Helped by koan study, students of Zen may open their minds to the truth. By this method they may attain the same inner experience as the Zen masters. It is said that there are one thousand seven hundred such koans on record. The term wato [hua-t'ou or topic] is also used in this sense."
Dait: 195
"A word or phrase of non-sensical language which cannot be 'solved' by the intellect but which holds a person's attention while a higher faculty takes over. Used as an exercise for breaking the limitations of thought and developing intuition, thereby allowing one to attain a flash of awareness beyond duality (Kensho / q.v.), and later Satori."
Hump: 109
NOTE:
"Koans are statements used as objects of meditation by novices in Zen monasteries of the Rinzai school (q.v.) as a means of transcending the realm of duality,

such as the subject-object split. In the Soto school (q.v.), however, they are studied only as reference points for one's own practice. In Soto Zen, daily life itself is seen as the ultimate koan, that is, the manifestation of the Truth."
Yoko: 207
See also: Wato #0165

◉ **KOAN OF BUDDHA RECITATION**
Syn: Buddha Recitation Koan
See also: Koan

▸"The koan of Buddha recitation uses the invocation of Amitabha Buddha as a koan. At the very moment the name is uttered, it must be the focal point in respect to which all doubts and delusions are laid aside. At the same time you ask 'Who is this person reciting the Amitabha's name?' When you rely steadily on the koan, all illusions and confused thoughts will be broken down the way knotted threads are cut. When there is no longer any place for them to reappear, it is like the shining sun in the sky. When illusion does not arise and delusions disappear, the mind is all calm and transparent."
Yu: 57
"The business of studying Zen is

the epitome of the mystic device of transcendence. It is not possible for those who take it easy. You must generate great bravery and great energy. You also must stop thoughts, forget entangling objects and gather in your seeing and hearing and turn them back [onto inherent reality]. You must take your everyday views of good and evil, your likes and dislikes, and your sentiments of affirmation and denial and totally sweep them away ... It is like one man battling ten thousand men: there is no time to blink, no time to hesitate in doubt. If you can really generate this kind of adamant, fierce will power, you have the mettle to study Zen. Once you have the mettle to study Zen, take hold of the phrase 'Amitabha Buddha' as if you were resting on the Polar Mountain and cannot be shaken. Concentrate your mind and unify your attention. Recite the Buddha-name a few times, turn the light back and observe yourself, asking: Who is this one reciting the Buddha-name? (J.C. Cleary, tr., *Pure Land, Pure Mind*.)"

Zen: 87-88 #1455
NOTE:
The Koan of Buddha Recitation is basically a Zen practice. For the Pure Land view, see "Pure Land Buddhism (Summary)".

◙ **KOKUZO BODHISATTVA**
see Akasagarbha Bodhisattva

◙ **KONDANNA**
see Kaudinya

◙ **KOREA (BUDDHISM IN)**
Syn: Buddhism - Korea
See also: Nine Mountain School

▸"Korean Buddhism was introduced from China between 350-370, and by about A.D. 500 had become the state religion. Under its influence, Korea attained a high state of prosperity and culture. Confucianism became the state religion under a new dynasty about 1500. A revival of Buddhism started about *the beginning of 20th Century*. The Buddhism of Korea is a blend of several Mahayana Schools, but Rinzai Zen has long predominated.
Hump: 110
NOTE:
Korean Buddhist art is largely Chinese, but a special Korean quality was added to the styles passed on to Japan. Thus, much of Nara Buddhist art is Korean, perhaps wrought by Korean craftsmen. The Buddhist

Association of Korea is hard at work rebuilding temples destroyed in the last war, and the Government of South Korea gives generous assistance."
Hump: 110 #0441
See also: Sonjong

◙ **KOTI**

▸A number defined as 10 million.
#2148

◙ **KSANA**

▸"Instant, as a measure of time. Equal to one seventy-fifth of a second."
Dait: 294
"The shortest measure of time; sixty ksana equal one finger-snap, ninety a thought, 4,500 a minute."
Luk: na #0128

◙ **KSATRIYA**

▸"One of the four Indian castes; the warrior and ruling class." [Sakyamuni Buddha belonged to this class.]
Chan: 477 #0534

◙ **KSITIGARBHA**
Syn: Earth Store Boddhisattva
See also: Boddhisattva

▸"'Earth Repository'; name of a Bodhisattva who saves suffering beings in the hells; especially popular in Japan as the saviour of the souls of dead children, particularly aborted ones."
Inag: 139
Usually represented standing, holding in his right hand a pilgrim's staff, and in his left a pearl.
Editor: na

Background
"Ksitigarbha or 'Earth-Womb' is more popular in the Far East than he ever was in India. From a bare mention in the roll of the Eight Bodhisattvas, he has risen, in Asia, and especially East Asia, to a popularity second only to that of Avalokitesvara. The reasons for this development are obscure. As his name suggests, Ksitigarbha is connected with the depths. Like all Bodhisattvas, he aspires to deliver sentient beings wandering astray in the five (or six) paths of mundane existence; but he specializes in delivering them from hell. This expresses an extremely profound and esoteric aspect of the Bodhisattva's compassionate activity: he takes upon himself the fearful task not merely of plumbing the depths of existence, and bringing relief and consolation to those in torment,

but of personally transforming and uplifting the vast inchoate mass of fear, hatred and despair swarming and pullulating in the pitch darkness of the Abyss. He is that loving 'compassion' of the highest to the lowest which, abandoning its own bright seat, does not shrink from working under conditions the most difficult and appalling -- amidst scenes of horror, madness and desolation -- at the seemingly hopeless task of reclaiming what is 'irrecoverably' lost. Ksitigarbha *is* the principle of spiritual sublimation in its most radical aspect, powerful enough to transform not merely hell into heaven but the foulest dregs of the Samsara, even, into the pure radiance of Nirvana. He is the supreme embodiment of spiritual optimism, the most profound development of Mahayana universalism, which wills that not so much as a grain of dust should be left outside the scheme of salvation."

Sangh/67: 198-199

Famous Quote

"Not until the hells are emptied will I become a Buddha;
Not until all beings are saved will I certify to Bodhi."

(Ksitigarbha Bodhisattva)

#0004

◙ **KUAN-YIN**

see Avalokitesvara

◙ **KUCHA**

See also: Kumarajiva

▸"An ancient kingdom and city in eastern Turkestan. It is recorded as the native place of Kumarajiva."

Thai: 645

"A city-state on the Silk Road"

Reat: 332 #1650

◙ **KUMARAJIVA**

See also: Hsuan-Tsang

▸"(344-413). Famous Indian translator of Indian Buddhist works into Chinese. During his thirteen-year stay in China, hundreds of scholars worked under his direction to produce translations of some 35 works, including the *Amitabha Sutra*, the *Lotus Sutra*, the *Maha Prajnaparamita Sutra* and the *Diamond Sutra*. His outstanding genius as a linguist and scholar was largely responsible for the introduction of Buddhism into China."

Hump: 112

"He is the most distinguished translator before Hsuan-tsang, and is especially famous for the translation of the *Lotus Sutra* and

the *Shorter Amitabha Sutra*."
Dait: 207-208

Illustrative story:
For a glimpse of why we should not blindly borrow the words of the sages or emulate their extraordinary actions, see the following passage concerning Kumarajiva, the renowned T'ang Dynasty monk: "When Kumarajiva went to China in the fourth century of this era, the Chinese Emperor thought that such a wise person ought to have descendents so that his wisdom would carry on. He gave concubines to Kumarajiva, and since they were a royal gift, Kumarajiva had no choice but to accept them. Afterwards, his disciples asked, 'Can we have relations with women too?' Kumarajiva said, 'Sure, but first, let me show you something.' He took a handful of needles and ate them as easily as they were noodles. When he finished, he said, 'If you can do that, then you can have relations with women.'"
(Sheng-yen, *The Sword of Wisdom*, p. 229.)
Editor/Tam: 313
NOTE:
"Kumarajiva interpreted Amida Buddha as an expression of sunyata [emptiness] and

recommended nembutsu [Buddha Recitation] as a means of realizing sunyata or ultimate wisdom, prajna." (Allen A. Andrews, 'Nembutsu in Chinese Pure Land Tradition,' in *The Eastern Buddhist*, Oct '70: 20.)
#0164

◎ **KUMBHANDA**

►"A demon who has huge testicles (resembling a water-pot). He is believed to deprive people of their vitality and to be able to run as swiftly as the wind. He is part of the retinue of Virudhaka, the Four-Quarter King who rules the South. When depicted, he is shown with the body of a man and the head of a horse. He appears in the outermost square of the Garbhadhatu mandala (or Taizodai mandara, one of the two major mandalas of Esoteric Buddhism)."
Dait: 205 #0109

◎ **KUNG-AN**
see Koan

◎ **KUSA**

►Grass, sacrificial grass; grass of good omen for divination.
Thai: 275 #1619

◙ K U S H I N A G A R / KUSHINAGARA

►"The capital of Malla in northern India, which was one of the sixteen major states in the age of Shakyamuni. Shakyamuni entered Nirvana in a grove of sala trees north of Kushinagar."
Sokk: 242 #0199

◙ KYOSAKU
Syn: Wake-up stick

►(*Jpn*). "Lit. 'wake-up stick'; flattened stick, 75 to 100 cm. in length, with which the 'sitters' in Zen monasteries are struck on the shoulders. This teaching method originated with the Zen Chinese Masters during long periods of zazen [sitting] in order to encourage and stimulate novices."
Sham: 123 #0384

◙ LA VALLEE POUSSIN, LOUIS DE (1869-1939)

►"Belgian Buddhologist, known worldwide for his important translations, articles, and studies. La Vallée Poussin studied Oriental languages under Sylvain Levi at the Sorbonne, and eventually went to Leyden to work with Hendrik Kern. While there, he learned Chinese and Tibetan. He became a professor at the University of Ghent in 1895, remaining there over thirty years. He founded the Société Belge d'Etudes Orientales in 1921, and was one of the editors of the journal *Le Muséon*. He is best known for his multi-volume French translation of Vasubandhu's *Abhidharmakosa*, published between 1923 and 1931. Largely through La Vallée Poussin's work, the Franco-Belgian School of Buddhist Studies solidified, giving rise to a generation of Buddhist scholarship."
Preb: 168-169 #1041

◙ LADAKH

►"A largely Buddhist district of the Indian state of Jammu and Kashmir."
Reat: 332 #2060

◙ LALITA-VISTARA

►"An early Mahayana scripture dealing with the life of the Buddha."
Reat: 332
"Some Mahayana scriptures speak the language of images almost entirely. There's the *Lalita-vistara*, for example--the

'Extended Account of Sports or Games'. Now we may be forgiven for wondering what kind of spiritual text this might be. And it may come as a surprise to learn that the sports or games are those of the Buddha, that we have here a sutra which offers us what we may say is the Buddha's playful nature. The *Lalita-vistara* recounts various incidents of the Buddha's career which were to him 'child's play', incidents in which he acted freely, easily, naturally, spontaneously--in other words, in a truly spiritual manner. So this sutra is a kind of biography of the Buddha, but it is not biography as we usually understand the term, because it contains a great deal of what scholars like to call 'legendary material'. But this is not just 'legend': the *Lalita-vistara* speaks the language of images..."
Sangha/Drama: 20-21   #2061

◉ **LAMA**
Syn: Teacher
See also: Good Spiritual Advisor; Guru; Unsolicited Friend

▶"Tibetan for a teacher or spiritual master. Equivalent to the Sanskrit term 'guru.'"
Tsomo: 166
"Tib., lit. 'none above'; in Tibetan Buddhism a religious master, or guru, venerated by his students since he is an embodiment of Buddhist teachings. Today, 'lama' is often used as a polite form of address for any Tibetan monk, regardless of the level of his spiritual development."
Sham: 124
"A term which should be reserved for senior members of the Tibetan Order, who by rank or spiritual achievement deserve this title. A mere monk is a Gelong. Certain of the Lamas are recognized as Tulkus and as such are entitled to be called Rimpoche. The three senior Lamas are the Dalai Lama, the Panchen Lama and the Bogdo Lama of Urga, the head of Buddhism in Mongolia."
Hump: 115   #0383

◉ **LAMAISM**
see   Tibetan Buddhism

◉ **LAMOTTE, ETIENNE**

▶"(1903-1983). Belgian Buddhologist, chief disciple of Louis de la Vallée Poussin, and renowned especially for his work on Indian Buddhism. For forty-five years (1932-1977), Lamotte was a professor at the

Catholic University of Louvain. He was a member of the Académie Royale de Belgique and the Institut de France. He was also an Honorary Fellow of the International Association of Buddhist Studies. He will most likely be remembered for his monumental volume *Histoire du Bouddhisme Indien*, published in 1958 and translated into English by Sara Webb-Boin in 1988. Additionally however, Lamotte brought out editions and/or translations of a number of other extremely important Buddhist texts, including the *Vimalakirti Sutra* (1962), and the introductory chapter of Nagarjuna's *Maha-Prajnaparamita-sastra* (1944-1980)."
Preb: 166-167　#1039

◙ **LAMP**
see Transmission of the Lamp; Parable: Lamp of the old woman

◙ **LAMPS AND TORCHES**

►"Lamps and torches are associated with light and flames, representing awareness, knowledge, and wisdom."
Clea/84: 22　#1973

◙ **LAND OF BLISS**
see Sukhavati

◙ **LAND OF ULTIMATE BLISS**
see Sukhavati

◙ **LANKAVATARA SUTRA**
See also: Nagarjuna

►"A sutra which expounds the doctrines of the eight consciousnesses and Tathagatha-matrix (womb). This is one of the sutras upon which *the Zen and Yogacara schools are based*. There are three extant Chinese versions."
Dait: 269
"A scripture of the Yogacara School of Mahayana Buddhism, written in Sanskrit in India (ca. 350 AD). Contains an epitome of nearly all Mahayana teaching. Teaches subjective idealism based on the Buddha's Enlightenment, and the doctrines of Sunyata and Mind-Only. Said to have been given by Bodhidharma to his disciple, the Second Patriarch, Hui-K'o, as containing the Buddha's teaching. For translation into English see Suzuki, *The Lankavatara Sutra* (1932), and for commentary see his companion volume, *Studies in the Lankavatara Sutra* (1930)."
Hump: 115.
Pure Land Buddhism
In the *Lankavatara Sutra*, Buddha Sakyamuni predicted: "In the

future, in southern India, there will be an Elder Master of high repute and virtue named Nagarjuna ... He will attain the first Bodhisattva stage of Extreme Joy and be reborn in the Western Pure Land." (See D.T. Suzuki, tr., *The Lankavatara Sutra*, Sagathakam Chap., p. 239-240.) #0163

◉ **LARGER AMITABHA SUTRA**
see   Longer Amitabha Sutra

◉ **LAST AGE**
see   Dharma-Ending Age

◉ **LAST DISCIPLE OF BUDDHA**
see   Subhadra

◉ **LAW OF CAUSE AND EFFECT**
see   Cause and effect

◉ **LAYMAN**
Syn: Upasaka
See also: Householder

▶"Buddhist lay adherent who through the Threefold Refuge (in the Buddha, the Dharma and the Sangha) identifies himself as such and vows to observe the five shilas (precepts).   In the Mahayana tradition, lay followers are of great importance, since the possibility of their attaining liberation is not discounted. The ideal figure of the Mahayana, the Bodhisattva, is a layperson. In China, formal ordination of lay adherents, usually as part of a ceremony for ordaining monks, is common. Lay ordination consists of taking the 'Three Refuges' and of vowing to observe all or some of the Five Shilas (Five Precepts). Advance lay adherents sometimes go on to take the Bodhisattva Precepts (q.v.) after lay ordination."   Sham: 238-239

Pure Land Buddhism
"Only two types of laymen can benefit from the Pure Land method. *First* are those completely ignorant and deluded but truthful and sincere individuals who upon hearing the teaching, wholeheartedly believe, accept and begin to practice it. *Second* are those persons with deep wisdom and good roots in the Pure Land method who clearly understand noumenon and phenomena and the virtues achieved through Buddha Recitation and who therefore resolve to believe and practice it. *Those with ordinary intelligence can neither understand profoundly, nor do they have the simple belief of the completely deluded. Therefore, it is difficult for them to receive benefits*."
Thich: 103-104   #0491

◙ **LAYWOMAN**
Syn: Upasika

▶"A female lay-devotee. A laywoman who puts her faith in the Three Treasures, and observes some or all of the Five Precepts."
Dait: 359 #0140

◙ **LE DYNASTY**

▶"(981-1009), the third Vietnamese dynasty, during which the first complete Chinese Tripitaka was imported, establishing the scriptural basis of Vietnamese Buddhism."
Reat: 333 #2063

◙ **LEADER**
Syn: Guide
See also: Conquerors

▶"'Leader' or 'Guide' is an epithet of Buddhas, and less often of Bodhisattvas."
Gomez: 306 #1713

◙ **LEARNING AND BEYOND LEARNING STAGE**
See also: Beyond Learning Stage; Arhatship

▶"'Learning' refers to the stage in which one must still undergo religious exercises to reach the

level of Arhat, while 'Beyond Learning' refers to the stage of Arhatship in which one no longer need undergo any religious exercises."
Dait: 75 #0066

◙ **LEAVING HOME**
See also: Bhiksu; Bhiksuni; Sangha

▶"'Staying at home' signifies the life of a layman, while 'leaving home' denotes a person who has left his home and family in order to join the Buddhist community, that is, enter the monkhood."
Yoko: 188 #0817

◙ **LENG-YEN CHING**
see Surangama Sutra

◙ **LESSER VEHICLE**
see Theravada Buddhism

◙ **LETTING GO**
See also: Maitreya; Practice

▶A basic teaching of the Buddha on how to calm and rein in the "monkey" mind.
"Letting Go. This is not such a foreign experience ... It happens every time someone falls asleep. We lie down in a quiet place, put the lights out and let go of our minds and bodies. Try practicing

this same technique by letting go of your judgmental thoughts while awake."
Kabat-Zinn: 31

Illustrative Story

A story about the Bodhisattva Maitreya illustrates the Buddhist concept of "letting go". In a time long past, Maitreya was in his incarnation as a laughing, big-bellied monk with a sack perpetually on his back. He used to travel about the countryside seeking alms and sharing them with whomever happened to be nearby. He would customarily sit under a tree, surrounded by urchins, to whom he would tell stories to illustrate Buddhist teachings. Seeing this, an elder monk of the time became annoyed at what he perceived as untoward conduct on the part of Maitreya. One day, he cornered Maitreya and tried to test him with the following question: "Old monk, pray tell me, just what do you think is the essence of the Buddha's teachings?" Maitreya stopped for a moment, looked him in the eye, and just let his sack fall to the ground. As the puzzled monk wondered what to make of this singular action, Maitreya bent down, picked up his sack and walked away. Dropping the sack, "letting go",

forgive and forget -- that is the teaching of Maitreya, the future Buddha.
Editors: na #2337

◙ **LI MEI**
Syn: Spirits; Ghosts
See also: Tree Spirits; Spirit World

►"A broad category covering manifold nature-spirits, which are formed from the emanations of trees, rocks, mountains, and so forth. They are malevolent and have potent spiritual powers. They correspond to such beings as trolls, bogies, and the little people in their more unpleasant and tricky moments. Such beings often grant wishes and answer petitions with such efficacy that they deceive humans into supplying them with offerings."
Hua: 230 #0771

◙ **LIBERATION IN ONE LIFETIME**
See also: Rebirth in the Pure Land

►"In this Dharma-Ending Age, if we practice other methods without following Pure Land at the same time, it is difficult to attain emancipation in this very lifetime. If emancipation is not achieved in this lifetime, deluded as we are on the path of Birth and Death, all of our crucial vows will become empty thoughts. This is a cardinal point which the cultivator should keep in mind. Those practitioners who follow other schools, stressing only self-help and a firm, never-changing mind, believe that we should just pursue our cultivation life after life. Even if we do not achieve emancipation in this life, we shall certainly do so in a future lifetime. However, there is one thing we should consider: Do we have any firm assurances that in the next lifetime, we will continue cultivating? For, if we have not yet attained Enlightenment, we are bound to be deluded upon rebirth, easily forgetting the vow to cultivate which we made in our previous lifetimes. Moreover, in this world, conditions favoring progress in the Way are few, while the opportunities for retrogression are many. How many monks and nuns have failed to pursue their cultivation upon rebirth...? The sutras state: 'Even Bodhisattvas are deluded in the bardo stage, even Sravakas are deluded at birth.' ... In the interval between the end of this current life and the beginning of the next life, even Bodhisattvas are subject to delusion, if they have not yet attained [a high degree of] Enlightenment. Another passage in the sutras states: 'Common mortals are confused and deluded when they enter the womb, reside in the womb, and exit from the womb. Celestial kings, thanks to their merits, are awake upon entering the womb, but are confused and deluded when residing in or exiting from the womb. Sravakas are awake when they enter and reside in the womb; however, they are confused and deluded when they exit from the womb. Only those Bodhisattvas who have attained the Tolerance of Non-Birth are always awake -- entering, residing in, and exiting from the womb.' In a few instances, ordinary people, because of special karmic conditions, are able to remember their previous lives, but these are very rare occurrences. Or else, they could be Bodhisattvas who took human form in order to demonstrate the existence of transmigration to sentient beings. Otherwise, all sentient beings are deluded when they pass from one life to another. When they are in such a state, all their knowledge of the

Dharma and their great vows from previous lives are hidden by delusion and often forgotten. This author recalls the story of a Dharma colleague. In his youth, each time he happened to be dreaming, he would see himself floating freely, high up in the air, travelling everywhere. As he grew older, he could only float lower and lower, until he could no longer float at all. In the commentary *Guide to Buddhism*, there is the story of a layman who, at the age of four or five, could see everything by night as clearly as in the daytime. As the years went by, this faculty diminished. From the age of ten onward, he could no longer see in the dark, except that from time to time, if he happened to wake up in the middle of the night, he might see clearly for a few seconds. After his seventeenth birthday, he could experience this special faculty only once every two or three years; however, his special sight would be merely a flash before dying out. Such persons had cultivated in their previous lives. However, when they were reborn on this earth they became deluded, and then, as their attachments grew deeper, their special faculties diminished.

There are similar cases of persons who can see everything clearly for a few dozen miles around them. Others can see things underground, through walls, or in people's pockets. However, if they do not pursue cultivation, their special faculties diminish with time and, in the end, they become just like everyone else. Some persons, having read a book once, can close it and recite every line without a single mistake. Others have a special gift for poetry, so that whatever they say or write turns poetic. However, if they do not pursue cultivation, they sometimes end by rejecting the Dharma. An eminent Master once commented that such persons had practiced meditation in their previous lives to a rather high level and reached a certain degree of attainment. However, following the Zen tradition, they sought only immediate awakening to the True Nature, severing attachment to the concepts of Buddha and Dharma (i.e., letting the mind be empty, recognizing no Buddha and no Dharma). Therefore, those who failed to attain *Enlightenment* were bound to undergo rebirth in the Triple Realm, whereupon, relying on

their mundane intelligence, they sometimes became critical of Buddhism. Even true cultivators in the past were thus; how would today's practitioners fare compared to them? As Buddha Sakyamuni predicted, 'In the Dharma-Ending Age, cultivators are numerous, but those who can achieve Supreme Enlightenment are few.' And, not having achieved it, even with bad karma as light as a fine silk thread, they are subject to Birth and Death. Although there may be a few cultivators who have awakened to the Way, being awakened is different from attaining Supreme Enlightenment. During rebirth, they are bound to be deluded and unfree. In subsequent lifetimes, there may be few conditions for progress and many opportunities for retrogression, making it difficult to preserve the vow of liberation intact."
Tam: 49-52

◎ LICCHAVI

See also: Vimalakirti Sutra

▸"Name of the tribe and republican city-state in India whose capital was Vaisali where the sage Vimalakirti lived, and the main events of the Vimalakirti sutra took place."
Thur: 140 #0654

◎ LIFE EXTENSION
see Food/ Food Rules

◎ LIFE PROVISIONS
see Provisions For Pure Land Rebirth

◎ LIFETIME PROVISIONS
see Provisions For Pure Land Rebirth

◎ LIGHT
See also: Mysticism of Light

▸"A sign of sacred presence, royal majesty, or celestial bliss and power, *light is also the characteristic attribute of Amitabha and his Land of Bliss.*"
Gomez: 307

"Light symbolizes knowledge or awareness; variegated light represents differentiating knowledge, different kinds of knowledge, or knowledge of different spheres. Lights, particularly jewel lights, also can represent the experience of a certain kind of meditation in which the attention is focused only on colors, not on things as usually conceived; the colors seen in this kind of concentration are called jewel lights." Clea/84: 22

◙ **LIGHT OF ASIA, THE**
See also: Arnold, Sir Edwin

▸"Famous work by Sir Edwin Arnold, first published in 1879, on the Life and Teaching of the Buddha (in verse). Based on a bibliography of works on the Buddha by the Mahasanghika school."
Hump: 116 #0440

◙ **LIGHT OF THE FUTURE**
see All-knowing

◙ **LIGHT OF THE WORLDS**
see All-knowing

◙ **LIN-CHI**
See also: Ma-Tsu; Shouts and Blows; Soto Zen School; Four Options
----
▸"(*Jap*/Rinzai, *VN*/Lâm-Tế), d. 866/67; Famous Chinese Ch'an (Zen) master, a student of Hung-Po. At the time of the great persecution of Buddhists in China from 842 to 845, he founded the school named after him, the Lin-chi school (Jap., Rinzai school) of Ch'an (Zen). During the next centuries, this was to be not only the most influential school of Ch'an but also the most vital school of Buddhism in China. With the Soto school, it is one of the two schools of Zen. In the tradition of Ma-tsu Tao-i, his 'grandfather in Zen,' Lin-chi made use of such supportive means as the sudden shout and unexpected blows with a stick as well as with a flywhisk. Of these he was best-known for his use of the shout. The single new element in methodology that entered Zen after Lin-chi was the koan."
Sham: 126

"One of two important schools of Chan/Zen. The Lin-Chi (Rinzai) school stresses the importance of Sudden Enlightenment and advocates unusual means of achieving it, such as shouts, slaps, and the use of koans. Lin-Chi (Rinzai) uses collections of koans systematically in its temples and downplays the reading of scriptures (sutras) and the veneration of Buddha images in favor of seeking the Buddha Nature directly through the use of koans and practical living."
Larousse: 441

For details, *See also:* entry "Shouts and Blows" #0337

◙ **LION**
see Discourse on the Golden Lion

◙ **LION AMONG MEN**
See also: All-knowing

◙ **LION ROAR**

▸"A figurative expression to denote the preaching of the Buddhas or advanced Bodhisattvas. Such preaching can overcome all erroneous doctrines, just as a lion's roar can subdue all the beasts of the jungle."
Chan: 478

"The utterances of the Buddha, who, among ordinary men, is comparable to a lion among animals."
Kusa: 179

"Symbolic of Buddha's teaching, especially the teaching of emptiness, which refutes all deluded views, as illustrated in the saying 'The roar of the lion bursts the brains of the jackals.'"
Cleary/Chih-I: 198   #0535

◙ **LIONS AMONG MEN**
see   Lion Among Men

▸"Lights of the Worlds," "Lights of the Future": metaphors for the Buddhas.
Saman: 51   #1614

◙ **LO-YANG**
See also: Ch'ang An

"The city of Lo-yang in Ho-nan witnessed the rise and fall of various Imperial Dynasties throughout the historical epoch of China. Lo-yang was a great centre of Buddhist culture. According to the Chinese tradition, the first Buddhist temple (in China), known as White Horse Pagoda (Pai-ma-Ssu), was built in Lo-yang by the Emperor Ming of the Eastern Han Dynasty in A.D. 65-67, in honor of the two Indian monks Kasyapa Matanga and Dharmaranaya. The greatest Imperial patrons of the new religion (Buddhism) were the Northern-Wei rulers (A.D. 336-534). The Buddhist cave-temples at Lung-men near Lo-yang contain some of the finest artistic remains of early Chinese Buddhism. Under the Emperor Hsuan-wu, three famous temples were constructed in Lo-yang: the Yung-Ming, the Ching-Ming and Yao-kuang. It is said that in Lo-yang there were 1367 Buddhist temples (ca. 6th century)."
Lahiri: 12

◙ **LOKESVARA**
See also: Longer Amitabha Sutra

▸"'World-sovereign-king'. In the *Longer Amitabha Sutra*, name of the Buddha under whom Dharmakara, the future Amitabha Buddha, made Vows and began his career as a Bodhisattva." Inag: 406 #0710

◙ **LONG AND BROAD TONGUE**
See also: Amitabha Sutra

▸"One of the auspicious physical characteristics of the Buddhas. Indicates that a Buddha never indulges in false speech or tells lies. As described in the *Amitabha Sutra*, numerous Buddhas in the ten directions recommend the teaching of this sutra, each extending his tongue and covering the whole universe with it. Such metaphors are often found in the sutras."
Inag: 406 #0711

◙ **LONGER AMITABHA SUTRA**
Syn: Larger Amitabha Sutra; Longer Sukhavativyuha Sutra; Sutra of Infinite Life
See also: Amitabha Sutra; Three Pure Land Sutras; Dharmakara; Lokesvara; Dharmakara's Vows
----
▸"One of the Three Pure Land Sutras (q.v.) or core texts of Pure Land Buddhism, the others being the *Amitabha Sutra* and the *Meditation Sutra*. A Mahayana text important as one of the

foundational bases of the Pure Land School of Buddhism.
"Translated into Chinese in 252 by Samghavarman during the Wei Dynasty, in two fascicles. There were twelve Chinese translations of this sutra, only five now being extant. Its Sanskrit text was published by Max Mueller (19th c.) and others, but none of the five Chinese translations agrees entirely with the extant Sanskrit text. The following points, however, remain unchanged throughout the Chinese translations, viz., the scene of the dialogue is placed at Rajagrha, India, and the Buddha, Ananda, and Maitreya are introduced as the principal speakers -- the subject being the description of the Pure Land, together with the history of Amitabha Buddha from his early stage as a bhiksu under the name Dharmakara. Also this sutra explains the cause and effect through which human beings attain Buddahahood in the Pure Land by invoking the name Amitabha."
Dait: 227

(I) Synopsis / Summary
"The *Longer Amitabha Sutra* ... which was in existence before A.D. 200, describes a discourse offered by the Buddha Sakyamuni

... in response to questions of his disciple Ananda. Sakyamuni tells the story of the Bodhisattva Dharmakara, who had for eons past been deeply moved by the suffering of sentient beings and who had determined to establish a Land of Bliss where all beings could experience emancipation from their pain ... In the presence of the eighty-first Buddha of the past, Lokesvararaja, Dharmakara made forty-eight vows relating to this Paradise, and promised that he would not accept enlightenment if he could not achieve his goals ... When, after countless ages, Dharmakara achieved enlightenment and became a Buddha, the conditions of his [18th] vow were fulfilled: he became the Lord of Sukhavati, the Western Paradise, where the faithful will be reborn in bliss, there to progress through stages of increasing awareness until they finally achieve enlightenment." (Elizabeth ten Grotenhuis, in Joji Okazaki, *Pure Land Buddhist Painting*, p. 14-15.) Okaz: 14

The text of the sutra begins with Buddha on Vulture's Peak surrounded by a huge retinue of sravakas (i.e., hearers, disciples) and Bodhisattvas. Using the premise of instructing Ananda, Buddha tells the story of a monk Dharmakara who made a series of forty-eight vows under a prior Buddha known as Lokesvara. Dharmakara begins pursuit of the Bodhisattva path, focusing all his vows in one Buddha-Land. Eventually, Dharmakara is able to actualize his vows, becoming the Buddha Amitabha residing in the Pure Land of Sukhavati (the Western Paradise). Rebirth in Sukhavati is available to those who (1) make a vow to be reborn there and (2) meditate on Amitabha, or recite his name [with utmost faith and sincerity]. The sutra ends with a vision of Amitabha." Preb: 168

(II) Note

"We should know that Amitabha Buddha has great affinities (causes and conditions) with this world. As the *Longer Amitabha Sutra* states: "In the Dharma-Ending Age, when all other sutras have disappeared, only this sutra will remain for another hundred years to rescue sentient beings and lead them to the Western Pure Land." Dia: 18   #1022

◙ **LONGER SUKHAVATIVYUHA SUTRA**
see Longer Amitabha Sutra

◙ **LONGEVITY**
see Food/ Food Rules

◙ **LOTUS FLOWER**
See also: Cause and Effect; Blue Lotus

▸The Lotus Flower is a symbol of Buddhism. Three characteristics of the flower are: "(1) The petals are made to bear the fruit. In the same manner, expedient teachings are expounded in order to reveal the true teaching. (2) When the lotus-flower opens, the fruit is seen therein. In the same manner, we find the true teaching latent in the expedient teachings. (3) When the fruit is ripened, the flower falls. In the same manner, when the true teaching is established, the expedient teachings are no longer neccessary."
Dait: 287

The lotus flower grows out of the mud but is not sullied by mud (the Buddha although originally a sentient being, is undefiled by the Saha World. Also: Buddhism has its roots in the Truth of suffering but transcends suffering). The lotus is moreover the only plant in which flower and fruit co-exist simultaneously (Cause and Effect exist simultaneously in all phenomena, according to Buddhist teachings).
Editor: na

NOTE:
"The lotus or sea-rose is of almost unique importance in Chinese folklore and symbolism thanks largely, it would seem, to Buddhist influence: the lotus comes out of the mud but is not itself sullied; it is inwardly empty, outwardly upright; it has no branches but it smells sweet; it is the symbol of purity, and one of the eight Buddhist precious things."
Eberhard: 168   #0149

◙ **LOTUS GRADES**
See also: Meditation Sutra; Pure Land Buddhism (Summary); Three Pure Land Sutras; Raigo

----

▸The levels of rebirth in the Western Pure Land as described in the *Meditation Sutra*, a key Pure Land text. According to this sutra, there are nine grades, divided into three sets of three grades each. The more merits and *virtues* the practitioner accumulates, the higher the grade. However, according to the commentaries, the grades can also be considered as infinite in number, corresponding to the infinite levels of karma of those who are reborn in the Pure Land. Editor: na

Rebirth Mudras
In Pure Land iconography, the grade of rebirth of a practitioner is indicated by the mudras adopted by Amitabha Buddha as He appears at the believer's death-bed (Raigo). The following text describes the mudras corresponding to the six lower grades of rebirth -- the levels most commonly attained by earnest practitioners.
Editor: na

"(1) *Middle Class: Lower Life* is represented by the two hands held in front of the breast, each one forming the *an-i-in* (Mudra of Peace and Good Will), while the ring fingers and thumbs touch to form mystic circles. *Middle Class: Middle Life* is represented by the same disposition of the hands but with the middle fingers and the thumbs joined. *Middle Class: Upper Life* shows also the same disposition of the hand, the *an-i-in* being formed by the indexes (forefingers) and the thumbs.
(2) *Lower Class: Lower Life* is represented by the right hand raised to shoulder level the left hand reposing on the left knee,

palm upward. Each hand makes the *an-i-in* with the ring finger and the thumb. *Lower Class: Middle Life* shows the same disposition of the hands, while the an-i-in is formed by the middle fingers and the thumbs. The same disposition of the hands is indicated for *Lower Class: Upper Life* but here the an-i-in is formed by the indexes (forefingers) and the thumbs. This mudra signifies the descent of Amida on the earth to seek the souls of the dead, and is one of the most frequently represented forms of Amida Buddha."
Dale/Mudra: 74 #0904
See also "Pure Land Buddhism (Summary)" as well as last Appendix of this book for pictures of the rebirth mudras just described.

◉ **LOTUS SUTRA / SCHOOL**
Syn: Saddharma Pundarika Sutra
See also: Miracles; Parable

▸A major Buddhist text and one of the most widely read sutras in the present day. One of the earliest and most richly descriptive of the Mahayana sutras of Indian origin. It became important for the shaping of the Buddhist tradition in East Asia, in particular because of its teaching of the One Vehicle under which are subsumed the usual Theravada and Mahayana divisions. It is the main text of the Tendai (T'ien T'ai) school. Okaz: na

Famous Quote

"The house of Buddha is compassion, the robe of Buddha is tolerance, and the seat of Buddha is the emptiness of all phenomena."

(I) Historical/Transcendent Buddha

In the *Lotus Sutra* the Buddha is not presented as a historical person, but rather as a manifestation of the Dharmakaya, which exists eternally. Every being participates in this transcendental nature of the Buddha and can thus become a Buddha."
Sham: 129-130

The Sutra teaches the identification of the historical Buddha with the transcendental Buddha, his appearance in the phenomenal world being only a skillful device (upaya) adopted to preach the Dharma to mankind.

(II) Faith

"The *Lotus Sutra* stresses the importance of faith on the path to liberation, as a result of which the Buddhas and Bodhisattvas can offer their help. *A separate chapter is devoted to the Bodhisattva Avalokiteshvara in which the notion of help from the Bodhisattvas is clearly expressed.*
Sham: 129

"The *Lotus Sutra* praises the wonderful assistance given to sentient beings in all kinds of distress by the Bodhisattva Avalokitesvara, who, in the Pure Land sutras, is one of the two principal assistants of Amitabha."
Yosh: 255

"Salvation is attained by the grace of the Buddhas and Bodhisattvas, the Theravada method of salvation being regarded as inadequate."
Hump: 161.

(III) Tien-t'ai and Pure Land

This school has a historically close relationship with the Pure Land School. Thus, Master T'ai Hsu (q.v.) taught that the *Lotus Sutra* and the *Amitabha Sutra* were closely connected, differing only in length.
Editor / Tam: 154

"*The Lotus Sutra is the Amitabha Sutra preached in detail, and the Amitabha Sutra is the Lotus Sutra in summary.* In contrast to other sutras which expound many terms in connection with the nature and characteristics of things and persuade people to understand the principles and to work on self-cultivation, these two sutras deal only with perception of phenomenal reality by the direct reasoning mind.

In the *Amitabha Sutra*, Buddha said, 'If there is a good man or a good woman who hears someone speak of Buddha Amitabha and holds firmly His name and title for one day, or two days, or three days, or four days, or five days, or six days, or seven days, *whole-heartedly and without distraction*, when this person approaches the hour of death, Buddha Amitabha and his holy company will manifest themselves in front of him. This person, since he is not confused, will be reborn in the most blissful country of Buddha Amitabha.'.. To quote from the 23rd chapter of the *Lotus Sutra*, 'Anyone who hears this Sutra and practices accordingly, when his present life ends, will go to the Western Paradise.' The similarity of these two passages is apparent. Other descriptions in the *Amitabha Sutra* of the grandeur and splendor of the Land, of Buddha's life, of Buddha's radiance and of the protection and care by the Buddhas of the six directions, though different in comprehensiveness and language,

are, in fact, *identical in their content and significance.* Therefore, one invocation of Buddha Amitabha's name represents the supreme Dharma and covers unlimited approaches."

Master T'ai Hsu: 20-22 #0170

◙ **LOTUS TREASURY WORLD**
See also: Ocean of Worlds

▸"The universe as purified by the vows and deeds of Vairocana Buddha, the cosmic aspect of Buddha Sakyamuni. By extension, the Lotus Treasury World represents our True Mind, or Buddha Nature, which encompasses the whole world, yet, like the lotus flower, is untouched by mud or defilements."

[NS/BTC, p.247]

Lotus Treasury World:

"(1) In the *Avatamsaka Sutra*, the pure land of Vairochana Buddha, which was created through the fulfillment of his Bodhisattva vows and practices. At the base of this world is a windy circle, above which is a perfumed sea. Blooming in this sea is a great lotus, and inside the lotus blossom is the Lotus Treasury World. It consists of 20 central worlds surrounded by 111 peripheral worlds. Each of these worlds is ornamented with treasures and inhabited by a Buddha and a great many living beings.

(2) A similar world described in the *Brahma Net Sutra*. The world in the *Brahma Net Sutra* is the thousand-petaled lotus. Each of the thousand petals is a world in itself, consisting of ten billion smaller worlds, each with a sun, a moon, a Mt. Sumeru and four continents. Vairochana Buddha sits in the center of the Lotus. In each of the thousand petals dwells a Shakyamuni Buddha who is regarded as a transformation of Vairochana Buddha."

Sokk: 247-248 #0262

◙ **LOUNSBERY, MS. G. CONSTANT**

See also: France (Buddhism in)

▸"American Buddhist, resident in France, who in 1929 founded *Les Amis du Bouddhisme* in Paris, and for many years financed its activities. Brought to Europe Bikkhus from Ceylon and elsewhere. Procured publication in French of many works on Buddhism. Ran yearly Buddhist Summer School at home in La Tourballe, Brittany. Author of *Buddhist Meditation in the Southern School* (1935)."

Hump: 118 #0439

◙ **LOVE-ATTACHMENT**

See also: Sex; Afflictions; Death; Meditation on Death; Herbs (Pungent); Surangama Sutra

----

▸The basic goal of Buddhist cultivation or practice is to keep the mind empty and still so that our innate wisdom can manifest itself (a Buddha is all wisdom at all times). Thus, Buddhism fosters practices and habits that subdue passions and simplify life, freeing the cultivator for spiritual pursuits. It is in this context that sexual desire, excessive rest and sleep, etc. are considered afflictions.

Editor/Tam: 315

Love is considered an affliction in Buddhism because, like all emotions, it disturbs the peacefulness of the mind-- particularly at the crucial time of death.   Editor: na

Buddhism of Wisdom & Faith/ excerpts:

"Concerning the danger of love-attachment at the time of death, as indicated earlier, the practitioner should think thus: family members, including parents, brothers, sisters, husbands, wives and children, are temporarily gathered together in this life as a result of previous causes and conditions, such as karmic debts or love and hatred, accumulated from time immemorial. When these causes and conditions come to an end, we all part and go our separate ways. If we truly care for them, we should endeavor to be reborn in the Pure Land, so as to be able to save everyone, friend and foe alike. Although we may have attachments to family and friends, when death approaches, there is nothing we can bring along or do, as even our very body disintegrates and returns to dust. If we harbor thoughts of attachment and love, not only will we fail to achieve rebirth in the Pure Land, we will not escape the endless cycle of Birth and Death. The practitioner should ponder and clearly recall the 'Three Doubts and Four Narrow Passes' (q.v) to prepare himself. *His mind will then be calm and undisturbed at the time of death."*

Thich: 281; 306

NOTES

i. According to Buddhist teachings, if there were another obstruction or force as strong as love-attachment, no cultivator could ever hope to attain Enlightenment and Buddhahood: "The Buddha said: ... There is nothing greater than love and desire. Fortunately, it is one of a kind. If there were something else like it, no one in the entire world would be able to cultivate the Way." (*Sutra in Forty-two Sections*, Master Hsuan Hua, tr.)

ii. "The Buddha frequently cautioned monks to be on their guard when dealing with women lest they be overcome by lust and craving.
The following interchange, taken from the *Maha-Parinibbana Sutra*, between the Buddha and Ananda, his attendant, may be taken as typical in this respect.
'-Lord, how should we conduct ourselves with regard to women?
-Don't *see* them, Ananda.
-But if we should see them?
-Don't *talk* to them.
-But if they should talk to us?
-Keep *wide awake*, Ananda.'"
Oxf:1044   #1382
For details, *See also:* Sex

◙ **LU K'UAN YU**
see   Luk, Charles (1898-1978)

◙ **LU-SHAN**
Syn: Mount Lu
See also: Hui-Yuan; White Lotus Society; Pure Land School

▶"Lit. 'Mount Lu'; center of Buddhism in the present-day province of Kiang-si that flourished since 380. Among the renowned monks who lived on Lu-shan were Masters Hui-yuan and Tao-sheng. On Lu-shan, Master Hui-yuan founded the White Lotus Society (q.v) and provided the initial impetus for the Amitabha tradition."
Sham: 131 #0338

◎ **LUK, CHARLES (1898-1978)**
Syn: Lu K'uan Yu

▶"Translator and writer on Ch'an. Born Canton (China). Studied with Tulku of Singkang and master Hsu Yun, who urged him to translate Chinese Buddhist texts into English. Dedicated the last 20 years of his life (from 1958) to this cause. Lived in Hong Kong, maintaining a world-wide correspondence."
Snel: 299 #0745

◎ **LUMBINI**
See also: Kapilavastu

▶"Shakyamuni's birthplace. Buddhist scriptures often refer to it as the Lumbini Gardens. It was located near Kapilavastu in what is now southern Nepal. Pillar edicts erected by King Ashoka discovered here identify the area as the place of Shakyamuni Buddha's birth."
Sokk: 248

"In Lumbini there is a stone column that king Ashoka had erected there on the occasion of his pilgrimage in the year 249 B.C. The inscription reads, 'Twenty years after his coronation, King Devanapiya Piyadasi [i.e., Ashoka] came here and commemorated his veneration, because the Buddha, the sage of the Shakya clan, was born here. He had a stone relief and a stone column set up to show that here a venerable one was born. He exempted the village of Lumbini from taxes and reduced its tribute in kind (from the usual quarter) to an eighth.'"
Sham: 130 #0261

◎ **LUNG-MEN**
See also: Pilgrimage Sites (China)

▶"Series of Chinese caves, near Lo-yang (q.v.), carved into Buddhist shrines c. 500 A.D. Grousset calls the style of many of the images Romanesque. The largest is the colossal image of the Buddha carved in 675 at the

order of the reigning Empress."
Hump: 118 #0438

◙ **MA-TSU TAO-I (709-788)**
See also: Lin-Chi; Shouts and Blows

►"Ma-Tsu Tao-I. Third generation leader of the Ch'an school of Hui-neng. Along with Shih-t'ou Hsi-ch'ien (700-790), he is regarded an originator of one of the two main lineages of the 'Southern School' of Ch'an. Ma-tsu was regarded as the foremost master 'west of the river' or in the provinces of Chiang-shi, while Shih-t'ou was master 'south of the lake' or around Hunan. Ma-tsu was the only Ch'an master in the period after Hui-neng to be called a patriarch."
Yu: 48
"More than any other Ch'an master after Hui-neng, Ma-tsu exercised a shaping influence on the development of Ch'an (Zen) in China. He made use of training methods such as the sudden shout, wordless gestures and unexpected blows with a stick. He knocked his students to the ground, pinched their noses, and shot sudden questions and paradoxical answers at them in order to shake them out of the routine of 'every-man's consciousness.'"
Sham: 141
"Although Ma-tsu had many Dharma heirs, his most famous was Pai-chang Huai-hai (720-814), best known as the proponent of a series of rules used to regulate daily life and conduct in Chinese Buddhist monasteries... The Pure Rules of Pai-chang stipulate that the ritual performed during a monk's cremation ceremony must include the recitation of the Amitabha's name."
Yu: 48 #0379

◙ **MACROBIOTIC DIET**
See also: Food / Food Rules

►"A diet based essentially on the belief that health is best maintained through eating natural, unprocessed foods in a certain balance of yang (alkaline-producing) to yin (acid-producing). It has no connection with Zen Buddhism."
Kapl: 298
The Macrobiotic Diet is related to Taoist ideas about achieving long life.
Editor: na #0783

◙ **MADHYAMIKA**
see   Middle Way Philosophy

◙ **MADHYAMIKA SCHOOL**
Syn: Middle Way school
See also: Middle Way Philosophy;
San Lun School; Nalanda
Monastery
"The 'Middle Way' School of
Buddhism, founded by Nagarjuna
and his followers in the 2nd
century. Its tenets are mainly
based upon the *Prajnaparamita
Sutra* group, stressing the
teaching of emptiness (sunyata)."
Chan: 478
"A Mahayana school based
chiefly on Nagarjuna's Chu Ron.
It was one of the two major
Mahayana schools in India,
together with the Yogachara
school. Nagarjuna is regarded as
the founder."
Sokk: 248
"The Middle Doctrine School of
Mahayana Buddhism founded to
harmonize rival doctrines on the
nature of Reality. Recognizes
two forms of Truth, a relative
(Samvriti) and an absolute
Voidness of all things or
particulars, of which nothing can
be said. Later teachers included
Aryadeva (third century) and
Santideva (seventh century)."
Hump: 119
Background
"In the centuries that followed
the Buddha's death, various
attempts were made to organize

and formulate his teachings.
Different systems appeared,
basing themselves on the
recorded scriptures, each
purporting to express the
Buddha's intended meaning.
Four, or rather three, great
syntheses emerged: that of the
Vaibhashika and Sautrantika
(which for practical purposes
may be taken together), that of
the *Madhyamika*, and that of the
Vijnanavada (also referred to as
Yogachara, the 'mind-only'
school). That there should be a
multiplicity of systems is not in
itself surprising. From the time
of his enlightenment until his
death fifty years later, the
Buddha bestowed his teachings
for the benefit of many different
audiences. The purpose of his
doctrine was always the same: to
liberate beings from the round of
suffering. The expression of this
purpose, however, differed
according to the capacity of his
hearers. It is therefore to be
expected that the body of
teachings remaining after his
departure from the world should
be rich and varied, containing
elements that sometimes even
contradict each other. The
Madhyamika deals with this state
of affairs by saying that
statements made by the Buddha

are of two kinds: *absolute* (nitartha), corresponding to his true meaning, as understood by himself, and *expedient* (neyartha), corresponding to a partial expression of his meaning, geared to the understanding of his hearers, intended to lead them along the path to perfect comprehension and being therefore of provisional validity. Parallel with this division is the doctrine of the two truths: *absolute truth* (paramartha) corresponding to reality, and *relative truth* (samvriti) corresponding to empirical experience. According to Nagarjuna, the Buddha skillfully graduated his teaching according to pedagogical necessity. He affirmed the existence of the atman, the self, as against the 'nihilist' (who disbelieves in survival after death), in order to maintain the truth of karma and ethical responsibility. By contrast, he denied the existence of the atman, as against the 'eternalist' (who takes the self to be a changeless essence). He also said that there is neither self nor no-self."   Shantiveda: 21   #0190

◉ **MAGADHA**

▸"The most powerful kingdom in India in Shakyamuni's time. Rajagriha, Eagle Peak and the Bamboo Grove Monastery were located here. Magadha was ruled in the Buddha's lifetime by Bimbisara and then by his son Ajatashatru. King Ashoka of the Maurya dynasty also ruled this area in the third century B.C." Sokk: 249   #0265

◉ **MAHA (Skt)**

▸Great, eminent, excellent.

◉ **MAHA-BODHI TEMPLE / MAIN TEMPLE**
See Bodh-Gaya;   Maha-bodhi Society

◉ **MAHA-BODHI SOCIETY**

▸"Founded in Sri Lanka in May 1891 by Anagarika Dharmapala, primarily to recover Buddha Gaya into Buddhist hands. The M.B.S. has formed branches in Sri Lanka and many cities in India. It controls the site at Sarnath. Its monthly Journal is [among] the largest Buddhist periodicals in print." Hump: 120
"Buddhist society founded in Sri Lanka in 1891 by Ceylonese monk, the Venerable Anagarika Dharmapala. The primary aims

of the Mahabodhi Society were, *first*, restoration of the Maha Bodhi temple at Buddha-Gaya, in North India (scene of the Buddha's enlightenment); *second*, the revival of the Buddha-Dharma in the land of its birth. At that time, Buddha-Gaya (or Bodh-Gaya) was in the province of Bengal, then part of British-ruled India. The temple was the property of a landowner, and was in seriously neglected condition. The Mahabodhi Society called a conference at Bodh-Gaya in October 1891 to enlist support of Buddhists in various other countries; in the following year publication of the journals *The Maha Bodhi* and *The United Buddhist World* began, which from then on played a not unimportant part in winning sympathy and support from English-speaking people in India and elsewhere. Opposition from both Hindu landowners and British authorities, however, was such that a lengthy process of legal action became necessary, which ended only with India's independence from British rule and the passing by the new Government of Bihar of the Buddha-Gaya Temple Act in 1949, under terms of which a temple management committee,

(consisting of 4 Buddhist and 4 Hindu members [with the District Magistrate of Gaya, a Hindu, as ex-officio chairman]), was entrusted with the care and control of the temple. By this time the Mahabodhi Society had gained considerable support in India and elsewhere. Its journal published in English, *The Maha Bodhi*, circulates throughout the world."

Ling: 171-172 #0436

New Development

A movement to free the Temple Management Committee from non-Buddhist influence by amending the Buddha-Gaya Temple Act has been gathering momentum for a number of years. It appears to have achieved a modicum of success recently under the leadership of an Indian monk of Japanese descent who received his religious training in Thailand. The aim is to have temple affairs invested mainly in Buddhist hands, albeit for the benefit of Buddhists and non-Buddhists alike.

Editor: na #2351

◙ MAHA-KASYAPA
see Kasyapa

◙ MAHA-KATYAYANA
see Katyayana

◙ **MAHA-KAUNDINYA**
see Kaudinya

◙ **MAHA-KAUSTHILA**
see Kausthila

◙ **MAHA-PARINIRVANA**
see Parinirvana

◙ **MAHA-PARINIRVANA SUTRA**
see Parinirvana Sutra

◙ **MAHA-PRAJAPATI**
Syn: Gotami; Prajapati

►"The sister of Queen Maya, the aunt of Sakyamuni. She brought up Sakyamuni after Maya died. The mother of Nanda. She was the first bhiksuni in Buddhism. She is said to have died three months before Sakyamuni."
Dait: 215 #0107

◙ **MAHA-PRAJNA PARAMITA SUTRAS**
see Wisdom Sutras

◙ **MAHA-RATNAKUTA SUTRA**
see Ratnakuta sutra

◙ **MAHA-THERA**

►"A Bhikkhu of 20 years' standing. Mahatheras generally just call themselves 'thera.' The prefixed title 'Maha' when used

in Thailand also denotes having passed a certain examination in Pali."
Snel: 261 #0721

◙ **MAHA-VAIROCANA**
see Vairocana Buddha

◙ **MAHASANGHIKA**
See also: Buddhist Councils

►(*Skt*/The Great Assembly; *Vn*/Đại-Chúng-Bộ). "A body which broke away from the Elder (Theravada) tradition of Buddhism after the Council of Pataliputra in 350 BCE. According to tradition, the assembly gave rise to seven subschools, and it *may be regarded as the forerunner of the Mahayana movement in later centuries*. The Mahasamghikas distinguished themselves from the Sthaviras doctrinally in their conception of the Buddha as supra-mundane, and socially by their acceptance of popular religious beliefs and practices, allowing a greater role to the laity."
Oxf: 601

"According to the Buddhist canonical tradition, a sharp difference broke out among the monks regarding the observance of certain Vinaya rules, just a hundred years after the 'Great Demise'. Two different groups placed their demands for clarification before the second Council at Vaisali. A section of the orthodox monks regarded the Vinaya rules as the very foundation, the rockbed of the monastic life. The rules must be entirely preserved and followed. Some liberal monks opposed this view. According to the Ceylonese Chronicles, this dispute was not solved in the Council; instead, it was followed by the 'Great Schism' (Mahabheda) which split the order into the Theravada and the Mahasanghika schools. 'The Mahasanghika became the *starting point of the development of the Mahayana* by their more liberal attitude and by some of their special theories' (Edward Conze, *Buddhism: Its Essence and Development*, Oxford, 1951.)

◙ MAHASATTVA

"A 'great being,' or Bodhisattva, of the highest ranks."
Chih-I/Cleary: 198

◙ MAHASTHAMAPRAPTA

Syn: Shih-chih; Seishi
See also: Three Pure Land Sages; Avalokitesvara; Surangama Sutra

----

▸Vn/ Đại-Thế-Chí. One of the three key Bodhisattvas in Pure Land Buddhism, recognizable by the water jar (jewelled pitcher) adorning Her crown. Usually represented in East Asian iconography as a female Bodhisattva bearing a lotus bud to escort the elect to the Pure Land. Amitabha Buddha is frequently depicted standing between the Bodhisattvas A v a l o k i t e s v a r a   a n d M a h a s t h a m a p r a p t a   (o n Amitabha's left as one faces the Buddha).   Editor: na

Surangama Sutra:

"Mahasthama, a son of the [Buddha], was the head of a group of fifty-two Bodhisattvas, rose from his seat, prostrated himself with his head at the feet of the Buddha and declared: 'I still remember that in the remotest of aeons countless as the sands in the Ganges, there was a "Buddha called Amitabha who was succeeded by eleven other Tathagatas in that kalpa. The last one was called the Buddha Whose Light Surpassed that of the Sun and Moon"; he taught me how to realize the state of Samadhi by thinking exclusively of Amitabha Buddha. By way of illustration, if a man concentrates his mind on someone else while the latter always forgets him, both may meet and see, but without recognizing, each other. However, if both are keen on thinking of each other, their keenness will grow from one incarnation to another until they become inseparable like a body and its shadow. The Tathagatas in the Ten Directions have compassion for all living beings and always think of them, like a mother who never ceases thinking of her son. If the son runs away, her thoughts of him will not help. But if he also thinks of her with the same keenness, they will not be separated in spite of the passing of transmigrations. If a living being remembers and thinks of the Buddha, he is bound to behold Him in his present or future incarnation. He will not be far from the Buddha and thus without the aid of any other expedient, his mind will be opened. He is like a man whose body, perfumed by incense, gives out fragrance; hence his name "One Glorified by (Buddha's) Fragrance and Light." From my fundamental cause-ground and with all my thoughts concentrated on the Buddha, I achieved the patient endurance of the uncreate [Tolerance of Non-Birth, q.v.].

(This is why) I help all living beings of this world to control their thoughts *by repeating the Buddha's name so that they can reach the Pure Land.* As Buddha now asks about the best means of perfection, I hold that nothing can surpass the perfect control of the six senses with continuous pure thoughts [of Amitabha] in order to realize Samadhi.'"
C.Luk/Suran: 134-135 #0906

◉ **MAHAVASTU**

▸"Mahayana scripture relating the legendary life of the Buddha."
Reat: 334 #2065

◉ **MAHAYANA**
See also: Mahayana / Theravada; Mahayana (A Parable)

▸Mahayana is one of the two main traditions of Buddhism, the other being Theravada (Tantric Buddhism or Vajrayana is a branch of Mahayana).
Editor: na
"The Mahayana branch of Buddhism expounds *Bodhisattva practice* as the means towards enlightenment of both oneself and others, in contrast to Theravada Buddhism, or the teaching of the Agama period."
Sokk: 251

(I) Main Characteristics

"Three main tendencies can be identified: the *full adoption of a heroic ideal*, a *new cosmology* closely related to visualization practices and a *new philosophical orientation* based upon the experience of 'emptiness'... (i) The heroic ideal of the Bodhisattva path was not new. What was new was the claim, explicit or implicit, that this should be adopted by all. Immediate personal enlightenment (Arhatship) was now to be seen as an inferior goal. Greater stress was laid on altruistic action based upon 'skill in means' and compassion. This too was not new, but was now emphasized more than ever before. (ii) The background world picture of early Buddhism was that of an Indian religion in general but modified to fit the Buddhist meditational 'map'. Meditation practices included recollection of the qualities of the Buddha (Buddha Recitation) and various kinds of visualization exercises. The Mahayana took these earlier cosmological and meditational elements and combined them. The result was much more specifically Buddhist in form. Such earlier Indian deities as Brahma and Indra were overshadowed by new figures -- Buddhas and advanced Bodhisattvas. Their names and much of their nature derive from earlier devotional responses to the Buddha. They could and did become much more closely associated with the most spiritual and uniquely Buddhist teachings. (iii) The philosophy of emptiness developed from earlier 'insight meditation' and the related Abhidhamma thought. The aim of both is to dissolve rigid views (ditthi) and bring about a fresher perception of the world. Apparent entities such as the mind are merely changing collections of evanescent events." Hinn: 290, 294

(II) Background

"After Shakyamuni's death, the Buddhist Order experienced several schisms, and eventually eighteen or twenty schools formed, each of which developed its own doctrinal interpretation of the sutras. As time passed, the monks of these schools tended to withdraw more and more from the lay community and sequester themselves in their monasteries, where they devoted themselves to the practice of doctrinal exegeses. Around the end of the first century B.C. [i.e., the beginning of the Common Era], a new

group of Buddhists emerged who were dissatisfied with what they saw as the self-complacency and monastic elitism of the earlier schools and who aimed at the salvation of all people. They called their Buddhism Mahayana (great vehicle), meaning the teaching which can lead all people to enlightenment. They criticized the earlier, traditional schools for seeking only personal enlightenment, contemptuously calling them the Lesser Vehicle. Mahayana seems to have arisen at least in part as a reform movement, seeking to restore the original spirit of Buddhism, and has involved lay believers as well as clergy. Where Theravada teaches the elimination of earthly desires, Mahayana takes a more positive view of earthly desires and aims at redirecting them."
Sokk: 251-252 #0267
See also: next entry.

◙ **MAHAYANA / THERAVADA**
See also: Mahayana Buddhism; Theravada Buddhism; Mahayana/Theravada (parable)

▶**(I) Different Emphasis**
"There are two main forms of Buddhism. The *Theravada* tradition-- meaning the Teachings of the Elders --

adheres to a strict understanding of the teachings of the historical Buddha. It teaches personal individual struggle to find the Path to enlightenment. This is hard, not often achieved and always takes years and many lives, to achieve. The other form of Buddhism is called *Mahayana*, the Great Vehicle tradition. This tradition holds that the individualism and difficulty of the Theravada tradition are unnecessary. It presents a vision of the Buddha and of Buddhism which is accessible to all, religious and lay person alike. It offers the possibility of release from the cycle of suffering and death and rebirth. This comes through personal devotion and reliance upon the salvationary activities of various intermediaries known as Bodhisattvas. Through countless lives of perfection, Bodhisattvas have acquired great merit which they use to free those who suffer. Mahayana Buddhism is called the Great Vehicle because its teachings are like a vast wagon capable of carrying many to release from rebirth."
Palmer: 3
"The devaluation of the empirical world as illusory is also of consequence for the devotional

Ways of the Mahayana ... Rebirth determined by deeds -- in Theravada regarded as an iron law of nature -- softens in Mahayana and this makes it possible to assume that *Bodhisattvas and Buddhas can give the liberation-seeker assistance from outside.* The recognition of such transcendent beings is the most obvious characteristic which distinguishes between Mahayana and Theravada."
Wolfg: 174

(II) Summary Table
(Theravada/Mahayana)
Man as an individual / Man as
  involved with others
Man on his own in the universe
  (emancipation by self-effort) /
  Man not alone (salvation by
  grace and works)
Key virtue: wisdom / Key virtue:
  Karuna, compassion
Religion a full-time job
  (primarily for monks) / Religion
  relevant to life in the world (for
  laymen and monks)
Ideal: the Arhat / Ideal: the
  Bodhisattva
Buddha a saint / Buddha a savior
Eschews metaphysics /
  Elaborates metaphysics
Eschews rituals / Includes rituals
Confines prayer to meditation /
  Includes petitionary prayer

Conservative / Liberal.
H.Smith: 186
(III) Parable:
"As the Theravada and the Mahayana are both stages in the development of Buddhism, both are addressed to all individuals, so we can't distinguish between them in this respect. At the same time, there is a difference, which will perhaps become clear with the help of a parable. Let's suppose that there is famine somewhere, a terrible famine of the kind that still happens in Africa. People are gaunt and emaciated, and there is terrible suffering. In a certain town in the country which has been struck by this famine there live two men, one old, one young who each have an enormous quantity of grain, easily enough to feed all the people. The old man puts outside his front door a notice which reads: 'Whoever comes will be given food.' But after that statement there follows a long list of conditions and rules. If people want food they must come at a certain time, on the very minute. They must bring with them receptacles of a certain shape and size. And holding these receptacles in a certain way, they must ask the old man for food in certain set phrases

which are to be spoken in an archaic language. Not many people see the notice, for the old man lives in an out-of-the-way street; and of those who do see it, a few come for food and receive it, but others are put off by the long list of rules... When the old man is asked why he imposes so many rules, he says 'That's how it was in my grandfather's time whenever there was a famine. What was good enough for him is certainly good enough for me. Who am I to change things?' He adds that if people really want food they will observe any number of rules to get it. If they won't observe the rules they can't really be hungry. Meanwhile the young man takes a great sack of grain on his back and goes from door to door giving it out. As soon as one sack is empty, he rushes home for another one. In this way he gives out a great deal of grain all over the town. He gives it to anyone who asks. He's so keen to feed the people that he doesn't mind going into the poorest, darkest and dirtiest of hovels. He doesn't mind going to places where respectable people don't usually venture. The only thought in his head is that nobody should be allowed to starve. Some people

say that he's a busybody, others that he takes too much on himself. Some people go so far as to say that he's interfering with the law of karma. Others complain that a lot of grain is being wasted, because people take more than they really need. The young man doesn't care about any of this. He says it's better that some grain is wasted than that anyone should starve to death. One day the young man happens to pass by the old man's house. The old man is sitting outside peacefully smoking his pipe, because it isn't yet time to hand out grain. He says to the young man as he hurries past, 'You look tired. Why don't you take it easy?' The young man replies, rather breathlessly, 'I can't. There are still lots of people who haven't been fed.' The old man shakes his head wonderingly. 'Let them come to you! why should you go dashing off to them?' But the young man, impatient to be on his way, says 'They're too weak to come to me. They can't even walk. If I don't go to them they'll die.' 'That's too bad,' says the old man. 'They should have come earlier, when they were stronger. If they didn't think ahead that's their fault. 'But by this time the young man is out of earshot, already on his way home for another sack. The old man rises and pins another notice beside the first one. The notice reads: 'Rules for reading the rules.'

No doubt you've already guessed the meaning of the parable. The old man is the Arhat, representing Southern Buddhism, and the young man is the Bodhisattva, representing the Mahayana. The famine is the human predicament, the people of the town are all living beings, and the grain is the Dharma, the teaching. Just as in principle both the old and the young man are willing to give out grain to everybody, so in principle both the Theravada and the Mahayana are universal, meant for all. *But in practice we find that the Theravada imposes certain conditions. To practice Buddhism within the Theravada tradition, even today, if you're taking it all seriously, you must leave home and become a monk or nun.* You must live exactly as the monks and nuns lived in India in the Buddha's time. And you mustn't change anything. *The Mahayana doesn't impose any such conditions. It makes the Dharma available to people as they are and where they are, because it is concerned solely with essentials.* It's concerned with getting the grain to the people, not with any particular manner in which this is to be done. The Theravada expects people to come to it, so to speak, but the Mahayana goes out to them. This difference between the Theravada and the Mahayana goes back to the early days of Buddhist history. About a hundred years after the Buddha's death, his disciples disagreed about certain issues so strongly that the spiritual community was split in two. Indeed, they disagreed about the very nature of Buddhism itself. One group of disciples held that Buddhism was simply what the Buddha had said. The Four Noble Truths, the Noble Eightfold Path, the Twelve Links or chain of conditioned co-production, the Four Foundations of Mindfulness -- this was Buddhism. But the other group responded that this was not enough. Yes, all of these teachings did form part of Buddhism, but the example of the Buddha's life could not be ignored. *The Buddha's teaching revealed his wisdom, but his life revealed his compassion, and both together made up Buddhism."*

Sangha/Drama:15 #2348 & 1799

NB: The differences between the

two branches of Buddhism, Mahayana and Theravada, are deliberately emphasized in the above passages for the sake of clarity. In actual practice, these differences are less'clear-cut, and depend mainly on the state of mind of the individual practitioner rather than on his affiliation.
Editor: na

(IV) Notes
Unlike Mahayana schools, the Theravada tradition makes no mention of Amitabha Buddha, the Bodhisattva Avalokitesvara, etc. or the Pure Land. Theravadins believe mainly in Sakyamuni Buddha and the Bodhisattva Maitreya, but not in the numerous transhistorical Buddhas and Bodhisattvas of the Mahayana tradition. This is because Theravada stresses the historical Buddha and His early teachings, applying the term Bodhisattva mainly to the previous incarnations of Buddha Sakyamuni.
Editor/Zen: 65
The various teachings of the Buddha constitute a totality. While it is said that the Buddha taught 84,000 methods in accordance with the capacity of his listeners, *on another level* we can also say that individuals

receive and understand these teachings differently. It is like rain which falls equally on all vegetation. However, the big trees absorb more of the rain water than the smaller trees, while a dead bush cannot benefit at all. The differences between the different Buddhist schools are similar: they are caused by the different capacities of Buddhist followers and not by the Buddha preaching different teachings to different audiences. (See the *Lotus Sutra*).
Editor: na

◙ **MAHINDA**
See also: Sri Lanka (Buddhism In)

▶"Asoka's son; Buddhist monk and head of the first Buddhist mission to Sri Lanka in ca. 250 B.C."
Reat: 334
"Son of the Indian King Asoka and leader of a Buddhist missionary enterprise to Sri Lanka. Sometime around 250 B.C., Asoka sought to expand Buddhism from the region around Magadha into a 'world' religion. As such, he sent his son Mahinda to Sri Lanka in hopes of establishing the Dharma on the island. Mahinda converted

the king, Devanampiya Tissa, and received a site on the island to build a monastery. This site eventually developed into the Mahavihara or 'Great Monastery.' A branch of the Bodhi Tree was brought from Bodhgaya and planted in Sri Lanka as well. In a short time, a valid ordination lineage for monks was established, and the religion began to grow on the island, remaining today as a stronghold of Theravada Buddhism."
Preb: 182-183 #1044

◎ **MAHORAGA**

►"A class of demons shaped like a boa or great snake; part of the retinue of Sakyamuni Buddha."
Thai: 584 #1637

◎ **MAITREYA**
Syn: Ajita
See also: Eschatology

►*Jpn*/Miroku; *Vn*/Di-Lặc.
"Translated as Unconquerable, and 'He who is free of the three poisons of greed, anger and stupidity.'"
Dait: 5
"A Bodhisattva predicted to succeed Shakyamuni as a future Buddha. Also called Ajita,

meaning 'invincible.' Some accounts view him as a historical personage who preceded the Buddha in death. He is said to have been reborn in the Tushita Heaven where he is now expounding the [Dharma] to the heavenly beings in the inner palace. It is said that he will reappear in this world [several billion years] after Shakyamuni's death, attain Buddhahood, and save the people in Shakyamuni's stead. For this reason he is also sometimes called Miroku Buddha. In the fourth century, a monk named Maitreya (c. 270-350) became famous as a scholar of the Consciousness-Only (Yogacara) school, and was later indentified with this Bodhisattva."
Sokk: 266-267
Very popular in Buddhist art. Well known in East Asia as a laughing figure with a fat belly.
NOTE:
"As the one destined to become the next human Buddha, *Maitreya enjoys the unique distinction of being the only Bodhisattva recognised throughout the entire Buddhist world*, in Theravadin as well as in Mahayana lands... Though his name occurs only once in the Nikaya sutras, when the Buddha prophesies his advent, he is frequently alluded

to in Pali exegetical literature: Buddhaghosa concludes the Visuddhimagga with a fervent poetical aspiration to attain Arhatship in his presence. He is also mentioned in earlier Sanskrit and Mixed Sanskrit works such as the Lalitavistara, the Divyavadana and the Mahavastu. In the *Saddharma-pundarika [Lotus Sutra]* he plays a prominent part, but is subordinate to Manjusri, who acts as his instructor."
Sangh/67: 196 #0179
See also "Letting Go"

◉ MAITREYA SOCIETY
See also: White Cloud Society; White Lotus Society

▸"A Chinese lay Buddhist group that looks to the coming of Maitreya (the future Buddha)."
Reat: 334 #2067

◉ MAITREYA TOWER
See also: Avatamsaka Sutra

▸A figure of speech to indicate the Mind. In the *Avatamsaka Sutra*, the youth Sudhana, after seeking instruction from some 50 different teachers, met with the Boddhisattva Maitreya, who ushered him into his "tower"-- Sudhana's own Mind. Editor: na

◉ MAKARA

▸"A sea monster, either in the form of a great fish, e.g. a whale, or a great turtle."
Thai: 597 #1638

◉ MALA
A rosary

◉ MALALASEKERA, DR G.P. (1899-1973)
See also: Sri Lanka (Buddhism in)

▸"PH.D (London). Distinguished Sinhalese Buddhist. Dean of the Faculty of Oriental Studies, and Professor of Pali and Buddhist Civilization, University of Ceylon. 1950, Founding President of the World Fellowship of Buddhists. Retired in 1958. 1957 appointed Ambassador for Ceylon to the U.S.S.R. General Editor of the *Encyclopaedia of Buddhism*. Editor in Chief for many years of *The Buddhist*. Author of *A Dictionary of Pali Proper Names*."
Hump: 123
The *Encyclopedia of Buddhism* is a multi-volume reference work still in progress which is available in major libraries throughout the world.
Editor: na #0435

◙ **MANAS**

▸"Mind, the (active) mind."
Thai: 286 #1623

◙ **MANDALA**
See also: Pure Land Mandalas;
Mantra; Mudra

▸"(Skt: meaning 'circle'). Usually means formal, geometric representations that show divinities or the relationship among divinities as they exist in their own spheres of energy within the Buddhist cosmos. May also depict the abodes of deities in Paradise and in sanctuaries on earth."
Okaz: 185
"A ritual or magic circle. In Tibet, a diagram used in invocations, meditation and temple services. Usually seen on Thangkas but also formed in sand and other media. Also found in the Shingon School (q.v.) of Japanese Buddhism as well as other esoteric schools."
Hump: 124
For details, see Pure Land Mandalas. #0341

◙ **MANDARA FLOWER**

▸"A flower that blooms in heaven, according to Indian tradition. It emits a beautiful fragrance and delights those who see it."
Sokk: 256
"The flowers of these Mandara trees shower their petals on the world whenever an auspicious or epoch-making event occurs."
Gomez: 308 #0269

◙ **MANI**
see Wish-fulfilling jewel

◙ **MANJUSRI**

▸*Jpn*/Monju;*Vn*/Văn-Thù-Sư-Lợi.
"Manjusri, who embodies the wisdom of all Buddhas, is sometimes shown as being of more benefit to sentient beings than is the Buddha. The reason for this seeming overstatement is to stress the fact that only the transcendental wisdom of Prajnaparamita, which Manjusri embodies, can conquer demons, and not magical formulas, spells, or other thaumaturgical techniques."
G.C. Chan: xxx
"The Buddha once said, 'I owe it to Manjusri (i.e., transcendental wisdom) that I now become a Buddha. Innumerable Buddhas in the past had been Manjusri's disciples, and those who will become Buddhas in the future

also owe their enlightenment to his awesome power. Just as children in the world have their own parents, so Manjusri assumes parenthood on the Buddha-path.'"

Chang: 71 #0538

Manjusri is portrayed in Buddhist art with the sword of wisdom in one hand and a book (scroll) in the other. He embodies wisdom at the *Buddha/Bodhisattva level*, as opposed to Sariputra, the embodiment of the wisdom of the Arhats.

Editor: na

◙ MANTRA

Syn: Dharani
See also: Paritta; Mudra

►"Incantation, mental command, mnemonic spell, concentration formula. Sanskrit word meaning 'uniting and holding,' that is, uniting all dharmas and holding all meanings."

[ccc/btt, p.256]

"A formula said to protect one who recites it and to benefit him by virtue of its mystic power. The word literally means to preserve and uphold the Buddha's teachings in one's heart. Dharanis are recited in Sanskrit and sometimes have no literal meaning. They are especially valued in esoteric Buddhism."

Sokk: 64

"The practice is based on the scientific knowledge of the occult power of sound. The most famous Mantra is 'On Mani Padme Hum.'"

Hump: 124

"A Dharani is usually *longer* than a Mantra, which can even consist of one word."

Britannica: na

SPIRITUAL POWERS

"Reciting mantras and sutras for the purpose of sowing merits and wisdom and eliminating evil karma and transgressions is all to the good. However, to be deluded and seek spiritual powers is to abandon the roots for the branches -- an error in judgement. If, furthermore, your mind is grasping, your understanding of the Dharma nebulous, your precept-keeping lax, your Bodhi Mind undeveloped and your discriminatory, win-lose mind raging unchecked, you will be exposed one day to demons that may drive you insane! If you want to obtain spiritual powers, you should first attain Enlightenment and Buddhahood. Once Buddhahood is attained, you will naturally have full spiritual powers. If you do not

strive for the Way but merely seek spiritual powers, let us not even speak about whether anything can be gained. If you should obtain anything, it would become an impediment to the Way. For this reason, the Buddhas and Patriarchs have strictly prohibited this erroneous form of cultivation [i.e. seeking spiritual powers]."
PLZ: 91-92

Pure Land Buddhism

"In Pure Land, reciting mantras should be considered an ancillary practice, rather than a principal method along with Buddha Recitation. The merits derived from mantra recitation are indeed inconceivable. However, ordinary people who achieve rebirth in the Pure Land owe it entirely to utterly sincere Faith and Vows, as these correspond to the lofty Vows of Amitabha Buddha. If you are not clear about this truth, thinking that all Dharmas are unfathomable and therefore it does not matter which method you cultivate, you will end up practicing neither the Esoteric nor Pure Land teachings. This will lead to eons of wandering in the wasteland of Birth and Death -- whom, then, could you rely on for help?"
PLZ: 91-92

Question / Answer

"*As for Hsu Chun, he has said that 'according to the Tantric method, wherever the power of mantras goes, be it on a wisp of air or a grain of dust, sentient beings there will all be liberated. Does the Pure Land method bring such benefits?'* **Answer:** You should know that while reciting mantras brings limitless blessings and virtue, reciting the Buddha's name also has unimaginable power! Do you not recall this passage from the *Meditation Sutra*: Even those who have committed the Five Grave Offenses or the Ten Evil Acts, may, on the verge of death, when the marks of the hells appear, recite the Buddha's name with utmost faith and sincerity (i.e. singlemindedly) a few times, and be reborn immediately in the Pure Land."
PLZ: 158 #0191

◉ **MANTRAYANA**
see Esoteric school

◉ **MAPPO**
see Dharma-Ending Age

◉ **MARA**
See also: Demons; Heaven of Free Enjoyment of Others' Emanations

▸"Lit. 'murder, destruction', the Devil of the Sixth Heaven (q.v.). Although the embodiment of death, Mara symbolizes in Buddhism the passions that overwhelm human beings as well as everything that hinders the development of wholesome roots and progress on the path of enlightenment."
Sham: 140

"Lit. death. The tempter. The personification of evil in Buddhist mythology."
Hump: 125

"Many devils appear in Indian and Buddhist scriptures, the most formidable and powerful of which is Mara, the Devil of the Sixth Heaven. This is the highest heaven in the World of Desire, and its ruler delights in manipulating others to do his will. The Devil of the Sixth Heaven is regarded as a symbol of lust for power. Especially in Buddhism, devils are interpreted to mean functions which work to block or hinder people in their Buddhist practice."
Sokk: 258 #0270
See also: World of Desire

◙ **MARGA**
see Path

◙ **MARKS**
see Nature and Marks

◙ **MARPA**
See also: Milarepa

▸"Founder of the Kargyut-pa School of Tibetan Buddhism in the eleventh century. Milarepa was his most famous pupil."
Hump: 125 #0434

◙ **MARRIAGE**
See also: Meiji Restoration; Birth and Death; Overeating

▸**(I) Laymen**
"The Buddhist views on marriage are very liberal: in Buddhism, marriage is regarded entirely as a personal and individual concern, and not as a religious duty. There are no religious laws in Buddhism compelling a lay person to be married, to remain as a bachelor or lead a life of total chastity. It is not laid down anywhere that Buddhists must produce children or regulate the number of children that they produce. Buddhism allows each individual the freedom to decide for himself all the issues pertaining to marriage.
Dham: 238
"In Hindu tradition, the main duties assigned to women were

childbearing and housework. Consequently, a single life was seen as a wasted life and unmarried women were subject to scoffs. On the contrary, in Buddhism, *married life has always been viewed as a hindrance to spiritual pursuits.* Wherever the Buddhist point of view prevailed, a woman was no longer compelled to marry to achieve self-respect and approval from her family. Once the order of nuns was established, it provided an even better option for women who were spiritually and religiously inclined. Sumana, the youngest daughter of Anathapindika remained single and joined the Buddhist Order at an advanced age. There are other instances recorded in the Therigatha."
Tsomo: 92

(II) Clergy

Celibacy of monks and nuns is traditionally a strict requirement in all schools of Buddhism. The only exception appears to be the Japanese clergy, particularly after the Meiji restoration (19th century). Tibetan Lamas, who are not necessarily monks, can be either celibate or married. The single most important reason for monks and nuns to be celibate is to break all attachments and ultimately the cycle of Birth and Death.
Editor: na

"Although Japanese monks often marry and have children, the tradition of celibacy is maintained among the nuns."
Tsomo: 124

Surangama Sutra:

"You should teach worldly men who practice Samadhi to cut off their lustful minds at the very start. This is called the Buddha's profound teaching of the first decisive deed. Therefore, Ananda, if carnality is not wiped out, the practice of dhyana (meditation) is like cooking gravel to make rice; even if it is boiled for hundreds and thousands of eons, it will be only gravel. Why? Because instead of rice grains it contains only stones... You should cut off both sensual body and mind until even the very thought of doing so ceases; only then can you hope to seek the Buddha's Enlightenment. This teaching of mine is that of the Buddhas whereas any other is that of evil demons."
Luk/Surangama: 152   #1974

◉ **MATANGA**
see Matangi

◙ **MATANGI**

Syn: Matanga

►"Name of a low-caste woman who lured Ananda into her home. [This story appears as a backdrop to the *Surangama Sutra*, the meditator's indispensable text.]"

Thai: 601 #1639

◙ **MATERIALISM**

See also: Buddhism

►"The Buddha appears to have made a conscious attempt to avoid the dogmatism of competing religious systems. He aimed to teach only what was essential for spiritual development and carefully excluded from his system everything not directly relevant to that purpose. The result is radically unusual. *The Buddha set out a middle way, based mainly upon pragmatic considerations.* One-sided viewpoints and aims were rejected. Materialistic views of life and spiritually oriented beliefs in personal immortality were considered equally misleading. Mistaken too were extreme goals, seeking either self-satisfaction through indulgence in pleasure or self-purification through ascetic discipline. Traditional religious beliefs, rites and customs were re-evaluated, not so much on the basis of 'reason' as of what might be called 'spiritual common sense'. Extreme forms of superstition and ritualism were opposed, but so was a naive materialism which sought to deny the real experiences of the spiritual path."

Hinn: 282 #1920

◙ **MAUDGALYAYANA**

See also: Ullambana

►"One of Shakyamuni Buddha's ten major disciples, known as the *foremost in spiritual powers.* He was born to a Brahman family in the suburbs of Rajagriha in the kingdom of Magadha. He was a close friend of Shariputra's from childhood. Together with Shariputra, Maudgalyayana was at first a disciple of Sanjaya Belatthiputta, one of six famous non-Buddhist teachers. Later the two became followers of Shakyamuni and entered the Buddhist Order, taking all of Sanjaya's 250 disciples with them. Maudgalyayana died before Shakyamuni, killed by a hostile Brahman while on an alms round in Rajagriha."

Sokk: 260

Maudgalyayana is best known for his association with the Ullambana festival (q.v.). #0180

◙ **MAURYA DYNASTY**

▶"(270-185 BC.) The Indian dynasty to which Emperor Asoka belonged."   Reat: 335 #2068

◙ **MAYA**

▶"Skt., lit. 'deception, illusion, appearance.' (1) Name of the mother of the future Sakyamuni Buddha; (2) the continually changing, impermanent phenomenal world of appearances and forms, of illusion or deception, which an unenlightened mind takes as the only reality. The concept of maya is used in opposition to that of the immutable, essential absolute, which is symbolized by the Dharmakaya."
Sham: 141-142 #0400

◙ **MEAT EATING**
see Animal Slaughter; Vegetarianism

◙ **MEDICINE BUDDHA**

Syn: Bhaisajya Buddha; Bhaisajya-guru; Buddha of Healing

▶"Buddha who heals the ills of body and spirit including that of ignorance; popular figure in early Mahayana Buddhism; reigns over the Pure Lapis Lazuli Paradise in the East."
Okaz: 187
"Iconographically, he is usually depicted with a healing fruit in his right hand and his left in the gesture of protecting or resting in his lap. He often appears as part of a triad with Shakyamuni and Amitabha, in which he is on the left, and Amitabha on the right.
In a sutra dedicated to him, only extant in Tibetan and Chinese, twelve vows are mentioned that Bhaishajya-guru (Medicine Buddha or Healing Buddha) made in a previous life and in the fulfillment of which he is aided by a great number of helpers, including Buddhas, Bodhisattvas, and the yaksas (q.v.). He is of great importance in Mahayana countries, particularly China, Tibet, Vietnam, and Japan."
Sham: 19

Background
"Exponents of Tibetan tantric practice and of the Chinese/Japanese forms of Pure Land practices will recognize

close affinities between what they have learned and what is advocated in the Healing Buddha sutras. Those familiar with works about Kuan Yin (Avalokitesvara/ Chenrezig) will find that the powers attributed to the Healing Buddha, and the reasons for those powers, are very similar in character to those attributed to that Bodhisattva. People who wrongly suppose that Pure Land Buddhism represents a turning away from the methods and values cherished by other schools such as Ch'an (Zen) will discover that this is far from being the case, since it can be confidently asserted that similiar methods and values pertaining to the Healing Buddha are accepted by the vast majority of Mahayana Buddhists, no matter to which school they belong." (John Blofeld in Raoul Birnbaum, *The Healing Buddha*, p. x)
Birn: 159 #0326

◉ **MEDITATION**
Syn: Dhyana
See also: Zen School; Samadhi; Samatha-Vipasyana; Three Non-Outflow Studies; Dogen; Chih-I

▸"*Meditation* is one of the 3 major components of the Buddhist way, the other two being *morality*, (or precept-keeping which precedes and must always accompany the activity of meditation), and *wisdom*, which is reached as a result of meditation. The Western reader is liable to misunderstand what the Buddhist means by meditation, and to imagine that it implies a 'relaxed' or 'inactive' state. But in the Buddhist view, meditation is an activity in which one is engaged in subduing discursive thought, destroying or discouraging unwholesome mental states, and initiating or nourishing wholesome mental states. It is a discipline that has to be learned from a master. Without such personal supervision, it cannot be properly undertaken. Herein is one of the principal reasons for the existence of the Buddhist monastery; it is a school of meditation, where younger monks learn from older, more advanced monks."
Ling: 181-182

"There are two basic kinds of meditative practice. The first is the development of concentration, where we give the mind a single object and rest there (*Samatha*). The second kind

is the development of mindful awareness, in which we use the tranquility that arises from concentration in order to see the impermanent, changing nature of all our experience (*Vipasyana*)."
Goldstein: xxx

Cultivators should exercise wisdom in receiving the teachings, carefully distinguishing the true from the false and the deviant. See the following passage by the late founder of the Buddhist Lodge and Buddhist Society (London), on the true goal of all Buddhist practice: "In the West, the need for some guidance in mind-development was made acute ... by a sudden spate of books which were, whatever the motive of their authors, dangerous in the extreme. No word was said in them of the *sole right motive for mind-development, the enlightenment of the meditator for the benefit of all mankind*, and the reader was led to believe that it was quite legitimate to study and practice mindfulness, and the higher stages which ensue, for the benefit of business efficiency and the advancement of personal prestige. In these circumstances, *Concentration and Meditation* ... was compiled and published by the [British]

Buddhist Society, with constant stress on the importance of right motive, and ample warning of the dangers, from a headache to insanity, which lie in wait for those who trifle with the greatest force on earth, the human mind." (Christmas Humphreys, *The Buddhist Way of Life*, p. 100.)
Tam: 319

"We could use a parable to describe the process of teaching meditation. When people first come along to learn to meditate, they quite often ask 'What is the goal of meditation?' You wouldn't usually reply, straight off, 'Well, the goal of meditation is to become like a Buddha', because that's the last thing most people want to be. They're not interested in anything religious or spiritual; they just want peace of mind in the midst of their everyday life and work. And it's perfectly true to say that meditation gives you peace of mind. But when they've been through meditation, then they might ask 'Well, is this all, or is there something more to meditation?' That would be the right time to say 'Yes, there is something more. Peace of mind in the ordinary psychological sense is not the final goal of meditation, but only an

intermediate stage. Beyond it there's a spiritual goal-- *Supreme Enlightenment* or *Buddhahood*.' Here 'peace of mind' is the magic city in which the traveller is nourished and allowed to rest for the long journey to Enlightenment."
Sangha/Drama: 45

Caveat:

Surangama Sutra: "You should teach worldly men who practice Samadhi to cut off their lustful minds at the very start. This is called the Buddha's profound teaching of the first decisive deed. Therefore, Ananda, if carnality is not wiped out, the practice of dhyana (meditation) is like cooking gravel to make rice; even if it is boiled for hundreds and thousands of eons, it will be only gravel. Why? Because instead of rice grains it contains only stones... You should cut off both sensual body and mind until even the very thought of doing so ceases; only then can you hope to seek the Buddha's Enlightenment. This teaching of mine is that of the Buddhas whereas any other is that of evil demons."
Luk/Surangama: 152

NOTES

i. "[Professor Robert Thurman of Columbia University in New York City] is only slightly less disdainful of *Vipassana* seminars that de-emphasize the supernatural side of the faith for the mechanics of meditation, or who, as Thurman puts it, 'teach laypeople to rationalize their own departures from the traditional view. I did so for 15 years myself.' For Thurman, 'Euro-American Buddhism doesn't exist yet, 'nor can it do so until it can furnish the true motors of devotion and keepers of the flame, 'ordained monks and nuns, supported in vows of celibacy and poverty, divorced from everyday life and supported by a community of lay members.'"
Time Magazine: Oct 13, 1997

ii. Most ancient masters, including such figures as the Patriarch Dogen, the founder of the Japanese school of Soto Zen, held that only those who could devote their full efforts to cultivation (monks and nuns) could achieve Enlightenment through meditation. To practice sporadically, during week-ends, for example, is helpful but cannot lead to enlightenment in one lifetime. The sutras compare such practitioners to those who rub two pieces of wood together but stop to rest before a fire is

lit. (For details, see, for example, Kenneth Kraft, *Zen: Tradition and Transition*, p.186.)
Editor: na #1150

◙ **MEDITATION ON CORPSES**
see Meditation on Death

◙ **MEDITATION ON DEATH**
Syn: Death Meditation; Meditation on Corpses
See also: Impermanence; Love-Attachment

►"In Buddhism, one of several meditations; the recollection of death consists in a monk's frequent calling to mind, every evening and every dawn, the many risks which surround human life, and thus how easily death may come upon him. He must then consider unsubdued evil states within him, which could lead to prolonged future suffering should he die thus. 'If he understands that this is the case, he should use his utmost resolution, energy, effort, endeavour, steadfastness, attentiveness and clear-mindedness in order to overcome these evil unwholesome things.'"
Ling: 90
"The nine types of *meditation on corpses* to free people from

attachment to the human body are: I. vyadhmataka-samjna, in which one perceives a bloated corpse, II. vinilaka-s., in which one perceives a corpse changing color, III. vipadumaka-s., in which one perceives a decaying corpse, IV. vilohitaka-s. in which one perceives blood on the ground that has leaked out from a corpse, V. vipuyaka-s., in which one perceives a corpse covered with pus, VI. vikhaditaka-s., in which one perceives a corpse torn apart by wild birds and animals, VII. viksiptaka-s., in which one perceives the scattered limbs of a corpse, VIII asthi-s., in which one perceives only white bones, and IX. vidagdhaka-s., in which one perceives the bones being reduced to ashes."
Dait: 210 #1121

◙ **MEDITATION SUTRA**
See also: Ajatasatru; Pure Land Buddhism (Summary); Three Pure Land Sutras; Vaidehi; Visualizations

----

►One of the three core sutras of the Pure Land school. This sutra stresses the element of meditation/visualization in Pure Land.
Editor/Tam: 155
"The teachings of the Sixteen

Meditations (q.v.) or contemplations and the nine possible degrees of rebirth (Lotus Grades/ q.v.) are found in this sutra. This sutra no longer exists in Sanskrit."

Okaz: 185

"The *Meditation Sutra* takes the doctrine of salvation through Amitabha (or Amitayus) much further [than the *Amitabha Sutra*].. Its special teaching is contained in a series of sixteen meditations. These are various kinds of visualisations which are elaborated at great length. The last three meditations are to help the devotee to perceive the [nine] grades to Buddhahood into which beings are born in Sukhavati [the Pure Land]. Even those guilty of the most heinous sins will be born there, though in the lowest grade, if they would single-mindedly and with utter faith and sincerity recite ... ten times before death the name of *Amitabha Buddha*. It must be mentioned, however, that earlier in the sutra those who wish to practice these meditations are told that they should cultivate a threefold goodness. *Firstly*, they should support their parents; serve and respect their teachers and elders; be of compassionate mind, abstaining from doing any

injury and perform the ten virtuous actions. *Secondly*, they should take refuge in the Buddha, the Dharma and the Sangha, fulfill all moral precepts and not lower their dignity or neglect any ceremonial observance. *Thirdly*, they should give their whole mind to the attainment of enlightenment, deeply believe in the law of cause and effect, study and recite the Mahayana doctrine and encourage others to do the same. Paradoxically enough, it was the school of the Madhyamikas (an advocate of the supremacy of wisdom) which is also historically associated with upholding the supremacy of simple faith in a whole-hearted devotion to the person of the Buddha. Nagarjuna, the founder of the Madhyamika school, recognised, in the *Dasabhumika Sutra*, two paths to Nirvana, the difficult one of personal effort and self-reliance and the easier one of dependence on the compassion of the Tathagatas. The easier path was further described as simply being the worship of the Buddhas, Amitabha and Maitreya. Vasubandhu, in his commentary on Nagarjuna's work, proposed another division -- which was later also adopted by Tao-ch'o of

China (c. 645) -- that is the way of self-power and the way of another's power."
(Encyclopedia of Buddhism, v. I: p.436)

(I) Background:

"The *Meditation Sutra* begins with a prologue to the story of King Ajatasatru and his parents, former King Bimbisara and Lady Vaidehi. Upon [ascending the throne] Ajatasatru imprisoned Bimbisara with the intent to starve him to death. The Queen mother, Lady Vaidehi, however, succeeded in keeping Bimbisara alive by secretly feeding him during her visits. When Ajatasatru discovers this, he imprisoned her also out of extreme anger. Deeply distressed by her son's actions and her own circumstances, Vaidehi turned to Sakyamuni Buddha for instruction on gaining rebirth in another realm without any suffering. The Buddha then through his transcendental powers illuminated the countless realms in the ten quarters of the universe. Vaidehi selected Amitabha's Sukhavati as the realm of her choice.

The Buddha proceeded to expound the required practices for aspirants' rebirth. They include the 'Three Purified Acts"

that are ethical in nature, to wit, the caring for one's parents and teachers, the adherence to precepts, and the reciting of the Mahayana sutras. The Buddha then led Vaidehi and others to see Amitabha's realm and, in that process, to attain the Insight of Non-arising of dharmas (Tolerance of Non-Birth/ q.v.). Concerned for future beings, who will not have the benefit of Buddha's direct instruction, Vaidehi inquired about the methods for their rebirth. In response, the Buddha instructed her in the sixteen kinds of visualization. *The first thirteen* begin with the visualization of the setting sun in this Saha World, then move on to the physical features of the Sukhavati realm such as the ground, trees and lakes, and conclude with the features of Buddha Amitabha and his attendants, Bodhisattvas A v a l o k i t e s v a a n d Mahasthamaprapata. *The last three visualizations have as their object the people of the nine grades of rebirths, the level of their spiritual attainment, the quality of their death-bed welcome*, and the length of time spent in Sukhavati before hearing the Dharma and attaining complete enlightenment. This

section on the visualizations, which is four times longer than the prologue section, comprises the main body and the primary aim of the sutra. In the epilogue, which is one-third the length of the prologue, Vaidehi attains the Insight of Non-arising, (Tolerance of Non Birth/ q.v.) while the Buddha prophesies that her five hundred female attendants will attain rebirth in the Pure Land."
Tana: 115-116

"This sutra teaches sixteen kinds of meditation as a means for birth in the Pure Land. It concludes by saying that even the most sinful person can attain birth there by invoking singlemindedly and with utmost faith the name of Amitabha. "The *Meditation Sutra* was translated into Chinese by Kalayasas (Ching-liang-yeh-shih) in 424 in one fascicle. There is said to have been another translation in Chinese of this sutra; but it was lost already by 730. Many Chinese commentaries were written on this sutra. The most famous of these is the commentary by Shan-tao (Zendo) which had a great influence on later generations."
Dait: 177

(II) Note:
"There is even a place in the Western Paradise for the worst sinners. The *Meditation Sutra* relates that even if a person has committed the Five Cardinal Sins, if this sinner *on the verge of death singlemindedly* recites Amitabha's name up to ten times, a lotus throne will appear and will bear him to the lowest stage in the Pure Land -- the lowest birth of the lowest degree. Instead of being condemned to eighty million kalpas in hell, the sinner will be born in the Western Paradise in a closed lotus flower ... *This teaching of the nine possible levels of birth has been an extremely effective way to reward good deeds on earth while still offering the promise of salvation to all,* regardless of how much merit they had accumulated." (Joji Okazaki, *Pure Land Buddhist Painting*:52)
See also: Pure Land Buddhism (Summary) #0097

◙ **MEDIUMS**
See also: Fortune-telling; Prophecies; Spirit world

▸"In many countries, people seek the advice and guidance of mediums to overcome their problems in situations which they consider beyond their

comprehension. The medium's help is sought in many ways and for various reasons. In a time of sickness when medical help is apparently ineffective, some people become desperate and turn anywhere to seek solace. At such times, mediums are often consulted. Some people also turn to mediums when they are faced with a complex problem and are unable to find an acceptable solution. Others consult mediums out of greed in order to get rich quickly. Some people believe that when a medium is in a trance, the spirit of a certain god or deity communicates through the medium and offers advice or guidance to those seeking help. Others believe that the trance is the work of the subconscious mind which surfaces and takes over the conscious mind ... The Buddhist attitude towards consulting mediums is one of neutrality. It is difficult to verify whether what the medium conveys is correct or not. The practice of consulting mediums is not a Buddhist practice; it is just a traditional practice. *Consulting mediums is for worldly material gain; the Teaching of the Buddha is for spiritual development.*"

Dham: 320-321

Editor: na

"Mediumship may be positive or negative. The former is rare, for it involves an advanced pupil, highly trained for the purpose, who allows his master to take possession of his lower vehicles or personality while the pupil retains full consciousness. Negative mediumship causes permanent damage to the medium, for as control of the lower principles is loosened by the invasion of some discarnate entity or elemental, it becomes that much easier for evil entities of any kind to take possession, and increasingly hard for the medium to resume responsibility. No evolved being would so use a medium and in such practices there is nothing whatsoever spiritual."

Hump: 127

Caveat: By avidly seeking contact with other worlds, a person may be subject to hallucinations or to manipulation by unscrupulous mediums. #1982

◉ **MEIJI RESTORATION (1868-1912)**

See also: Japan (Buddhism in --); Marriage (clergy)

►"Movement begun in 1868 that marked the end of the military control of Japan by the samurais.

The movement was spurred on by a Shinto nationalistic effort that essentially opposed Buddhism. It brought with it an initial Buddhist persecution that was rather quickly tempered. To some degree Buddhism became more secularized and modern, celibacy became the exception rather than the rule for monks, and lay organizations abounded. Additionally, it set the stage for what eventually became known as the 'new religions' (Sokagakai, Risho Kosekai etc...) in Japan." Preb: 189 #2069

◙ **MENANDER**
see Milinda

◙ **MERIT AND VIRTUE**
Syn: Virtue
See also: Bodhidharma

►"*Merit* is what one establishes by benefitting others... By practicing what is good, (i.e. decreasing greed, anger and ignorance) one improves oneself. This is *virtue*. Ideally both merits and virtues should be cultivated side by side." xxx: na
The two terms (merits and virtues) are sometimes used interchangeably. However, there is a *crucial difference*: merits are the blessings (wealth, intelligence, etc.) of the human and celestial realms; therefore, they are temporary and subject to Birth and Death. *Virtues, on the other hand, transcend Birth and Death and lead to Buddhahood.* An identical action (e.g., charity) can lead either to merit or virtue, depending on the mind of the practitioner, that is, on whether he is seeking mundane rewards (merit) or transcendence by decreasing greed, anger, and delusion (virtue).
Subtle Buddhist teaching: Any good action leads to merit and virtue. The difference is in the level. Good actions performed with sincerity and no *thought of giver, receiver or gift* accrue boundless virtues which lead to rebirth outside the realm of Birth and Death (referred to as "Non-outflow virtues"). Conversely, good actions performed without sincerity, for *gain or fame*, lead to merit "with outflows," i.e., limited and within Samsara. Such tainted merit accumulated within one's current lifetime may lead to rebirth within the human realm, in a position of wealth, power and authority (second lifetime). Since power tends to corrupt, the individual may then create evil karma, resulting in retribution in

the Third Lifetime (q.v.). Therefore, merits and virtues "with outflows" are considered deluded. Thus, the *Pure Land cultivator should not seek mundane merits, for by doing so he would in effect be choosing to remain within Samsara.*
Editor: na #0908
See also Bodhidharma

◙ **MERIT BY ASSOCIATION**

▸"Buddha Recitation, like the use of koan in Zen, is a panacea (a cure-all) to destroy the poison of false thinking ... It is like fighting a war to end all wars. According to The Pure Land school, however, recitation of the Buddha's name contains an *additional element*: the practitioner by association absorbs some of the merit of the Buddha himself. See the following passage, with reference to the Bodhisattva Avalokitesvara (Kuan Yin), one of the Three Pure Land Sages: 'Some of us may ask whether the effect of [evil] karma can be ... changed by repeating the name of Kuan-Yin. This question is tied up with that of rebirth in Sukhavati (the Pure Land) and it may be answered by saying that invocation of Kuan-Yin's name forms another

cause which will right away offset the previous karma. We know, for example, that if there is a dark, heavy cloud above, the chances are that it will rain. But we also know that if a strong wind should blow, the cloud will be carried away somewhere else and we will not feel the rain. Similarly, the addition of one big factor can alter the whole course of karma ... It is only by accepting the idea of life as one whole that both Theravadins and Mahayanists can advocate the practice of transference of merit to others. With the case of Kuan-Yin then, by calling on Her name we identify ourselves with Her and as a result of this identification Her merits flow over to us. These merits which a r e n o w o u r s t h e n counterbalance our bad karma and save us from calamity. The law of cause and effect still stands good. All that has happened is that a powerful and immensely good karma has overshadowed the weaker one ... If we want to go deeper, we may say that this identification with a Bodhisattva also means that a Bodhisattva identifies Himself with us. When this occurs, there is not only the mere transference o f m e r i t , b u t t h e non-discriminate, infinite, unqualifiable compassion of all the Bodhisattvas coming into us, lifting us, as it were, right up into Nirvana.'" (Lecture on Kuan-Yin by Tech Eng Soon - Penang Buddhist Association, c. 1960. Pamphlet.) #1584

◙ **MERIT TRANSFERENCE**
see Dedication of merit

◙ **MERU**
See Sumeru (Mount --)

◙ **METAPHYSICS**
See also: Silence; Universe; *Mahayana/Theravada*

▸*Theravada Buddhism*:
"Buddha preached a religion devoid of speculation. Ample evidence in the record suggests that he could have been one of the world's great metaphysicians if he had put his mind to the task. Instead, he flatly refused to discuss metaphysics. His silence on the subject did not pass unnoticed. 'Whether the world is eternal or not eternal, whether the world is finite or not, whether the soul is the same as the body or whether the soul is one thing and the body another, whether Buddha exists after death or does not exist after death --

these things,' one of his disciples observed, 'the Lord does not explain to me. And that he does not explain them to me does not please me, it does not suit me.' There were many it did not suit. Yet despite incessant needling, he continued his 'noble silence.' His reason was simple. 'Greed for views' on questions of this sort 'tends not to edification.' His practical program was exacting, and he was not going to let his flock be diverted from the hard road of arduous action by the agreeable fields of profitless speculation. His famous parable of the arrow smeared thickly with poison puts the point with precision:
'It is as if a man had been wounded by an arrow thickly smeared with poison, and his friends and kinsmen were to get a surgeon to heal him, and he were to say, "I will not have this arrow pulled out until I know by what man I was wounded, whether he is of the warrior caste, or a brahmin, or of the agricultural, or the lowest caste." Or if he were to say, "I will not have this arrow pulled out until I know of what name of family the man is -- or whether he is tall, or short or of middle height"... Before knowing all this, the man

would die. Similarly, it is not on the view that the world is eternal, that it is finite, that body and soul are distinct, or that the Buddha exists after death that a religious life depends. Whether these views or their opposites are held, there is still rebirth, there is old age, there is death, and grief, lamentation, suffering, sorrow, and despair.... I have not spoken to these views because they do not conduce to an absence of passion, to tranquility, and Nirvana. And what have I explained? Suffering have I explained, the cause of suffering, the destruction of suffering, and the path that leads to the destruction of suffering have I explained. For this is useful.'"
Smith: 142-143 #1888
See also Mahayana/Theravada.

◉ METHOD
see Dharma door

◉ MIDDLE WAY PHILOSOPHY
See also: Madhyamika School; Nagarjuna; Materialism

▶"Generally, a term for the way of the historical Buddha Shakyamuni, which teaches avoidance of all extremes such as indulgence in the pleasures of the senses on one side and self-mortification and asceticism on the other. More specifically, it refers to the Madhyamika (Middle Way) school founded by Nagarjuna, which refrains from choosing between opposing positions, and in relation to the existence or non-existence of all things, treads a middle way."
Sham: 143

"According to Nagarjuna, the Middle Way is the true nature of all things which neither is born nor dies, and which cannot be defined by either of the two extremes, existence or non-existence. This true nature of things is non-substantiality or ku, and is called the Middle Way. In terms of T'ien-t'ai's doctrine of the three truths, the truth of the Middle Way (*Jpn*: chu or chutai) means that the *true nature of all things is neither non-subtantiality (ku) nor temporary existence (ke), but manifests the characteristics of both.*" Sokk: 263 #0104

◉ MIDDLE WAY SCHOOL
see Madhyamika School

◉ MIKKYO
See also: Esoteric School

▶"A Japanese Term for Esoteric Buddhism (q.v.) (as opposed to 'exoteric teaching', i.e., all other

forms of Buddhist teaching). This form of Buddhism came to Japan in the 9th century, with Saicho (founder of Tendai) and Kukai (founder of Shingon). Both established monasteries in Kyoto, which became the main center."
Oxf: 641

◎ **MILAREPA (1025-1135)**
See also: Tibetan Buddhism; Tsong-Kha-pa; Marpa

▸"Tib., roughly 'Mila who wears the cotton cloth of an ascetic'; by far the most famous saint of Tibet."　　Sham: 144　#0378

◎ **MILINDA**
Syn: Menander
See also: Milindapanha; Nagasena

▸"The Greco-Bactrian King Menander or Menandros who reigned over Afghanistan and northern India in the latter half of the second century B.C. He reigned from his capital at Sagala and wielded considerable influence. King Milinda had a series of discussions with the Buddhist monk, Nagasena, concerning Buddhist doctrines, which were compiled into a work entitled Milindapanha. Their dialogue is famous as one of the first encounters between Buddhism and Hellenistic culture. Milinda is said to have eventually become a Buddhist."
Sokk: 265
NOTE:
"The *Questions of King Milinda Sutra* contains the following parable: A minute grain of sand, dropped on the surface of the water, will sink immediately. On the other hand, a block of stone, however large and heavy, can easily be moved from place to place by boat. The same is true of the Pure Land practitioner. However light his karma may be, if he is not rescued by Amitabha Budddha, he must revolve in the cycle of Birth and Death. With the help of Amitabha Buddha, his karma, however heavy, will not prevent his rebirth in the Pure Land."　　Tam: 278
See also: next entry.　#0272

◎ **MILINDAPANHA**
Syn: Questions of King Milinda
See also: Milinda; Nagasena

▸"Lit: 'The Questions of King Milinda.' A record of the dialogues of the Buddhist monk N a g a s e n a a n d t h e Greco-Bactrian king Menander or Menandros (*Pali*/ Milinda), who ruled Afghanistan and

northern India in the latter half of the second century B.C. and was famous for his extensive learning. The questions put by King Menander to the monk Nagasena covered a wide range of subjects such as wisdom and earthly desires, transmigration, karma, the historical existence of the Buddha, the Buddhist Order, the qualification of monks, the respective roles of monks and lay people, and Nirvana. This work is also valued as an account of one of the first major encounters between Hellenistic and Buddhist cultures. According to it, Menander dedicated a monastery to Nagasena and abdicated the throne in favor of his son, entering the Buddhist Order and eventually attaining the state of Arhat."
Sokk: 265

"Important non-canonical Theravada text whose title translates to 'The Questions of King Milinda,' and which contains a running dialogue between the monk Nagasena and the Bactrian King Menander. It is valuable not only because it documents one of the early encounters between Buddhist and Hellenistic cultures, but because it also focuses on a wide variety of issues that were critical for a thorough and accurate understanding of Theravada Buddhism. A number of profoundly important dilemmas are considered in the dialogue, including how rebirth occurs in the absence of an atman or soul, what truth is, why moral people encounter suffering while apparently evil people prosper, why suicide is not a valid antidote to earthly suffering, why philosophical discussion is not profitable, why textual materials appear to present contradictory contents, and a host of others. Often using extremely insightful similes, Nagasena responds to all questions masterfully, resolving the king's concerns one by one."
Preb: 190-191

Pure Land School

"The *Questions of King Milinda Sutra* contains the following parable: A minute grain of sand, dropped on the surface of the water, will sink immediately. On the other hand, a block of stone, however large and heavy, can easily be moved from place to place by boat. The same is true of the Pure Land practitioner. However light his karma may be, if he is not rescued by Amitabha Budddha, he must revolve in the cycle of Birth and Death. With the help of Amitabha Buddha, his karma, however heavy, will not prevent his rebirth in the Pure Land." Tam: 278 #0273

◙ **MILLENNIALISM**
Syn: Millennialism or Millenarianism

▸"In a general sense, millenarian movements are those which envisage a coming age (usually imminent) in which a faithful group will be particularly rewarded on this earth. Such movements are extremely common. Some are derived from Christianity ... but others have no such connection."
Oxf: 642

◙ **MIND**
See also: Intellect; Mind-created; Mind-Ground; Stanza that Destroys Hell; Thoughts
----
▸"Key concept in all Buddhist teaching. Frequent term in Zen, used in two senses: (1) the mind-ground, the One Mind ... the Buddha-mind, the mind of thusness ... (2) false mind, the ordinary mind dominated by conditioning, desire, aversion, ignorance, and a false sense of self, the mind of delusion ..." (J.C. Cleary)
The ordinary, deluded mind

(thought) includes feelings, impressions, conceptions, consciousness, etc. The Self-Nature True Mind is the fundamental nature, the Original Face, reality, the "undiscriminating mind" etc. As an analogy, the Self-Nature True Mind is to mind what water is to waves -- the two cannot be dissociated. *They are the same but they are also different*. To approach the sutras "making discriminations and nurturing attachments" is no different from the Zen allegory of a person attempting to lift a chair while seated on it. If he would only get off the chair, he could raise it easily. Similarly, the practitioner truly understands the Dharma only to the extent that he "suspends the operation of the discriminating intellect, the faculty of the internal dialogue through which people from moment to moment define and perpetuate their customary world of perception."
Editor: na

(I) Mind creating all dharmas
The teaching of the Mind "creating" sentient beings and the environment expressed in many Mahayana sutras such as the *Avatamsaka*, *Surangama* and *Lotus Sutras*, is epitomized in the

following stanza:

"If one wishes to understand fully/ All Buddhas of all time,/ He should contemplate the nature of the Dharma Realm/ Everything is made from Mind alone" (*Avatamsaka Sutra*,ch. 20). "One wholesome thought is the condition/ for the creation of the Buddha-lands;/ One errant thought/ is the very cause of the nine realms of Samsara."

"This does not mean creation in the sense of creating something out of nothing. This doctrine means that, practically speaking, the world only 'exists' as such because of our awareness, and that what we take to be the world in itself is our experience and inference based thereon. The conceptual order which is taken to be characteristic of objective reality is, according to this doctrine, a projection of the mind, a description that filters and shapes experience in accord with mental habits developed throughout the history of the species, the civilization, and the individual" (T. Cleary, The *Flower Ornament Scripture* [the *Avatamsaka Sutra*], Vol. I, p. 23). "The mind ... 'creates' the world in the sense that it invests the phenomenal world with value. The remedy to this situation, according to Buddhism, is to still and calm the mind, to stop it from making discriminations and nurturing attachments toward certain phenomena and feelings of aversion toward others. When this state of calmness of mind is achieved, the darkness of ignorance and passion will be dispelled and the mind can perceive the underlying unity of the absolute. The individual will then have achieved the state of enlightenment and will be freed from the cycle of birth and death, because such a person is now totally above them both." (Burton Watson, *The Zen Teachings of Master Lin-Chi.*)

Tam: 155-156

"In what way can our minds change the environment for the better? Take the case of a person who has performed evil deeds and should be condemned to the sufferings of the hells for untold eons. Suppose that individual suddenly becomes extremely frightened and utterly ashamed, develops the Bodhi Mind, changes his ways, recites sutras and the Buddha's name, cultivates personally and enjoins others to do likewise, seeking rebirth in the Pure Land. Thanks to this change of heart, the previous karma of hell is

dissipated and transmuted into a lesser karma in the current lifetime. Thus, for example, he may be subject to contempt by others, suffer a bout of illness, become destitute or meet with unhappy events. After enduring such minor retribution, that person may escape Birth and Death and enter the 'stream of the sages,' transcending the ordinary world. As the *Diamond Sutra* states: *If there is anyone who receives and keeps this Sutra but is maligned by others, such a person has created evil karma in previous lifetimes and should have descended upon the Evil Paths. As a result of this calumny, however, his past karma is instantly extinguished and he will attain Supreme Enlightenment.* This is precisely the meaning of the mind changing life and the environment for the better."
PLZ: 143-144

"The wind was making the temple flag flutter. There were two monks arguing. One said the flag was moving. One said the wind was moving. They argued back and forth without reaching the truth. The Sixth Patriarch said to them, 'It is not the wind moving, and it is not the flag moving. It is your minds that are moving.' The two monks were startled." (J.C. Cleary, *Meditating with Koans*, p.124.)

"The Buddha said: 'There was once someone who, plagued by ceaseless sexual desire, wished to castrate himself. The Buddha said to him, 'To cut off your sexual organs would not be as good as to 'cut off' your mind. Your mind is like a supervisor: if the supervisor stops, his employees will also quit. If the deviant mind is not stopped, what good does it do to cut off the organs?'"
Hua/77: 62

Illustrative story:

"There was once a Zen monk who practiced in a deserted mountain area. Lonely and isolated, he had a deluded thought, wishing to have some fellow-cultivators practicing along with him to make life more bearable. Immediately, an old woman appeared from nowhere, leading two beautiful young girls by the hand, who, she said, lived in the village down in the valley. They had come, they claimed, to seek guidance in the Way. The monk, unsuspicious, immediately gave a Dharma talk to the group. One day, after many such visits over a period of time, the old woman respectfully requested that the two girls be allowed to become attendants to the monk and relieve him of his daily chores. The monk, hearing this, became suspicious. He reprimanded the old woman severely and refused the offer. The three women left, apparently angry and ashamed.

The monk, intrigued, followed them discreetly until they disappeared around a bend in the road. When he reached the spot, he found it was a dead end with no habitation or anything else around, except for three very old trees, one big tree and two smaller ones. He thought it over and realized that he had been 'tested.' A fleeting thought occurred to him, that he should cut down the trees, start a bonfire, and burn them to the ground. At that moment, the three women reappeared, repentant, begging him to forgive them and spare their lives.

Therefore, the cultivator should remember: when the mind is still, all realms are calm; when delusion arises, demons are born."

Tam: 211

(II) Introspection required

The purpose of the Dharma is not to "feed" the mind but to calm it and rein it in. The monkey mind has to be brought back to its tree for samadhi and, ultimately, wisdom to be achieved. The discriminating, intellectual mind, so prized in everyday life, may assist in the initial understanding of the Dharma but it must be transcended and is certainly no substitute for practice. To approach the sutras with a discriminating mind is no different from the Zen allegory of a person attempting to lift a chair while seated on it.

Editor: na

"Once it is clear, however, that the problem lies in the mind itself, or rather in the emotions that arise there, the simple but difficult task is to become aware of how thoughts emerge and develop. Again we find the same note of practical optimism. Just as the mind is the source of every suffering, likewise it is the wellspring of every joy. And once again, the good news is that the mind can be controlled and trained. *'If, with mindfulness rope,/The elephant of the mind is tethered all around,/Our fears will come to nothing,/Every virtue drop into our hands.'* The essential problem, which a moment's reflection on experience will confirm, is not that defilements occur within our minds, but that nine times out of ten, we are not aware that they are there. Or rather, that by the time they obtrude upon our waking consciousness, they have usually acquired such dimensions and strength that in the ordinary run of things we are powerless to prevent their consequences. The sudden outburst of destructive anger, the lustful impulse, the cruel or arrogant word that can have life-changing consequences, must have had their source, perhaps a long time previously, in a momentary flash of impatience or desire that, had it been addressed to at the time, might easily have been neutralized and dispelled. All very well, but how precisely is one to become so perfectly self-possessed that no impulse of the mind, however slight, is able to pass unnoticed? Alas, there are no magical solutions. The technique prescribed by Shantideva is that of constant, unrelenting vigilance--a continuous advertence to what is happening within the inner forum. He says that we should guard our minds with the same care with which we would protect a broken or wounded arm while moving through an unruly crowd; and here again, the educative

methods of fear and encouragement have their place. Shantideva recommends that as soon as we feel the urge to do anything--to speak or even to walk across the room--we should get into the habit of self-scrutiny. The slightest impulses to negativity should be greeted with a total paralysis of the system: 'It's then that like a log you should remain.' No thought should be allowed to develop unchallenged into action. Given the required degree of self-awareness, it comes as no surprise that Shantideva should refer to the minutiae of everyday behavior--all the little things we habitually overlook, excusing ourselves with the thought that they are too insignificant to bother about. In such a practice, in fact, it is precisely the small, practically subliminal impulses and behavior patterns that require the closest attention."
Shantideva: 11
NOTE:
In the *Sutra in 42 Sections*, the Buddha taught: "Do not trust your mind, only when you have become an Arhat (a sage) can you trust it". Since most of us have not achieved sagehood, the cardinal rule is to keep the mind under constant control and avoid

situations where greed, anger, and delusion may arise.
Editor: na #2352
See also Ten Non-Seeking Practices

◉ **MIND LAMP**

▸"The lamp of the mind; inner light, wisdom."
Luk/ vol I: 239 #0775

◉ **MIND OF DISCRIMINATION**
see Discrimination; Intellect

◉ **MIND, BUDDHA AND SENTIENT BEINGS**
See also: Avatamsaka Sutra

▸"The mind, Buddha and sentient beings: these three entities are not different." The *Avatamsaka Sutra* (Chap. 20) teaches that, if sentient beings are no longer deluded and become enlightened, then their Minds, the Buddhas and other sentient beings are not different, as they all partake of the same basic True Nature.
Editor: na #1286

◉ **MIND-CREATED**
See also: Mind; Mind-Ground; Intellect; "Stanza that Destroys Hell"

▸"Basic doctrine in *Avatamsaka*

and other Mahayana sutras: 'all things are creations of mind.' This does not mean creation in the sense of creating something out of nothing. This doctrine means that, practically speaking, the world only 'exists' as such because of our awareness, and that what we take to be the world in itself is our experience and inferences based thereon. The conceptual order which is taken to be characteristic of objective reality is...a projection of the mind.."
[TC/FO1, p.20] #1214

◉ **MIND-GROUND**
See also: Mind; Mind-Created

▸"A Buddhist term meaning the mind or mental ground from which all things spring."
Luk/1971: 42
"One's mind can include all the myriad things; therefore 'ground' is used as an analogy for the mind. The mind can give birth to all things and can also produce the wisdom of the sages. Likewise, the ground or earth produces myriad things."
[BNS, V, p.26] #1172

◉ **MIND-MIRROR**

▸The sutras commonly compare

the Self-Nature to a mirror. The Mind-mirror of the Buddhas is bright, empty and still; the Mind-mirror of sentient beings is dull and clouded. However, the intrinsic nature of both mirrors (brightness) is the same. If sentient beings can wipe their Mind-mirror completely clean, they will return to their Self-Nature, the nature of the Buddhas -- they will become Buddhas. This is the basis of gradual cultivation, as taught in most Buddhist schools. Editor/Zen: 30　#1428

◙ **MIND-ONLY**
see　Stanza that destroys Hell

◙ **MIND-ONLY PURE LAND**
see　Self-Nature Amitabha

◙ **MIND-ONLY SCHOOL**
see　Yogacara school

◙ **MIND-SEAL OF THE BUDDHAS**
Syn: Buddha mind-seal

▶"The Buddha seal.
I. A sign of the true transmission from a Zen master to his disciple.

II. In Tendai, it indicates the mind in which the Three Truths

are perfectly integrated."
Dait: 25　#0096

◙ **MIND-TO-MIND TRANSMISSION**

▶Literally, special transmission outside the teaching (textual tradition).
"The transmission of the True Law (the Buddhist teaching) from a Zen master to his disciple by personal contact without using the words and letters of the scriptures."
Dait: 143
"A Zen expression for the authentic transmission of Buddha-dharma from master to students and dharma successors within the lineages of transmission of the Zen tradition. This term, which is usually translated 'transmission from heart-mind to heart-mind,' became a central notion of Zen. It comes from the *Platform Sutra* of Hui-neng, the Sixth Patriarch of Ch'an (Zen) in China. He points out that what is preserved in the lineage of the tradition and 'transmitted' is not book knowledge in the form of 'teachings' established in sacred scriptures but rather an immediate insight into the true nature of reality, one's own

immediate experience, to which an enlightened master can lead a student through training in the way of Zen."
Sham: 101 #0036

◙ **MINDFULNESS OF THE BUDDHA**
See also: Buddha Recitation

►Synonymous with Buddha Recitation. #0910

◙ **MING DYNASTY**
See also: White Lotus Society

►"(1368-1644). The so-called 'enlightened' ethnic Chinese dynasty that replaced the Mongol dynasty."
Reat: 335
"A significant development in Buddhism during this period lies in the appearance of three great Buddhist reformers: Yun-ch'i Chu-hung (1535-1615), Tzu-po Chen-k'o (1543-1603), and Han-shan Te-ch'ing (1546-1623). They are sometimes called the three 'dragon-elephants.' Thanks to their efforts, Buddhism was revived, and their lives and teachings have continued to inspire and shape many Buddhists in China. The personalities of the three 'dragon-elephants' differed considerably. A government official of that time once described Chu-hung as a 'gentle grandmother,' Chen-k'o as a 'fierce soldier,' and Te-ch'ing as a 'king of knights.' Han-shan Te-ch'ing's life was indeed colorful and knightly. He was acquainted with Chu-hung and Chen-ko, and after their deaths composed their biographies which provide the best information available about these masters."
Hsu: ix #1877

◙ **MING, EMPEROR**

►"(r. 58-75 AD.) Han dynasty emperor traditionally said to be responsible for the introduction of Buddhism to China."
Reat: 335 #2070

◙ **MIRACLES**
See also: Spiritual Powers

►"What the modern secular imagination would regard as fantastic or extraordinary and what the Western religious imagination would regard as miraculous or supernatural is seen in the two *Amitabha Sutras* as inconceivable, but explainable. Counterintuitive or apparently uncaused events are the natural

consequence of a Buddha's power. This power, rooted in the vows, the merit, and the knowledge of Buddhas, brings about its effects in a manner that is effortless. Although such events may appear to us as being outside the normal chain of causation, they are spontaneous and miraculous only in the sense that they are not the result of our own agency."　　Gomez/96: 289

"Miracles are possible in Buddhism, even though the Buddha discouraged all display of miraculous or parapsychological powers as offering proof of spiritual attainment. He was first and foremost a pragmatist, a patient compassionate pragmatist. A story that is told of his response to a noted ascetic whose path he crossed on one of his journeys nicely illustrates his down-to-earth reaction to any extremes of yogic behavior. Encountering an ascetic practitioner of yoga at a river crossing, he entered into conversation as he often did when traveling, and was told that the yogin had achieved such mastery over his physical body that he could now cross the river walking on the water. The Buddha's comment was to the effect that such a feat, though

remarkable, seemed a rather useless expenditure of physical and psychological energy, since there was a good ferry crossing the river at regular intervals charging less than a penny for the ride."

Ross: 180-181

On how to act in cases of doubtful miracles, see "Fortune Telling" (last para.)　#1704

◙ **MIRACULOUS POWERS**
see Spiritual powers

◙ **MODES OF BIRTH**
see Four forms of birth

◙ **MO-HO CHIH-KUAN**

►"A twenty-section work by Patriarch Chih-i explaining various aspects of meditation from the standpoint of the Chinese T'ien-t'ai school."
Yuho Yokoi/1976: 209　#1182

◙ **MONASTERY**
see Vihara

◙ **MONASTIC BUDDHISM**

►A synonym for Theravada Buddhism (q.v.).

◙ **MONDO**
see Questions and Answers

◉ MONEY

▸"The Dharma is like money. It is up to the individual to use it wisely. To those with money, many courses of action are open. If you can concentrate on cultivating one method, whatever you wish will be fulfilled. Why insist upon reciting this mantra or that sutra to accrue this or that merit, but not other merits? If you follow my instructions in a flexible way, you will naturally 'understand one thing and penetrate one hundred things.' If not, even if I speak at length, your mind will not be focussed and you will not obtain any benefits! (Patriarch Yin-Kuang)" Zen: 210 #1534

◉ MONGOLIA (BUDDHISM IN)
See also: Dalai Lama

▸"The Chinese Emperor Kublai Khan (1259-1294), being converted to Buddhism, encouraged its practice in all countries under his sway, including Mongolia, where he built many monasteries. Before long, however, this wave of interest died down until in the sixteenth century Lama Taranatha revived interest and founded the enormous Kuren monastery at Urga, [Mongolia]. His successors became Grand Lamas of Urga, a rank junior in Tibetan Buddhism only to the Dalai and Panchen Lamas. Under a treaty signed between the Grand Lama of Tibet (later the Dalai Lama) and the Emperor Alten Khan, Mongolia came under the jurisdiction of the Gelug-pa school." Hump: 130 #0429

◉ MONK
see Bhiksu; Sangha

◉ MONKS AND NUNS
see Sangha

◉ MONSOON-SEASON RETREAT
see Rains retreat

◉ MOON
See also: Finger Pointing at the Moon

▸In Mahayana sutras, a metaphor for truth or reality: the moon is reflected in all bodies of water (lakes, ponds, etc.) while its brilliance is undiminished. Editor: na "Many people would like to know the religious significance of the full moon and new moon. To Buddhists, there is a special religious significance especially during a full moon because certain important and outstanding events connected with the life of Lord Buddha took place during a full moon. The Buddha was born on a full moon. His renunciation took place on a full moon. His Enlightenment, the delivery of His first sermon, His passing away into Nibbana and many other important events associated with His life-span of eighty years, occurred on full moons. Buddhists all over the world have a high regard for full moons. They celebrate these days with religious fervour by observing precepts, practising meditation and by keeping away from the sensual worldly life. On such days they direct their attention to spiritual development. Apart from Buddhists, it is understood that other co-religionists also believe that there is some religious significance related to the various phases of the moon. They also observe certain religious disciplines such as fasting and praying during full moon days. ... It is believed that the moon, like the planets, exerts a considerable degree of influence on human beings. It has been observed that people suffering from mental ailments invariably have their passions and emotional feelings affected during full moons. The word 'lunatic' derives from the world 'lunar' (or moon) is most significant and indicates very clearly the influence of the moon on human life. Some people suffering from various forms of illness find their sickness aggravated during such periods. Researchers have found that certain phases of the moon not only affect humans and animals, but also influence plant life and other elements. Low-tides and high-tides are a direct result of the overpowering influence of the moon. ...

In view of the possible influence of the moon, the ancient sages advised people to refrain from various commitments on this particular day and take it easy for the day. They are advised to relax their minds on this particular day and to devote their time to spiritual pursuits. All those who have developed their minds to a certain extent can achieve enlightenment since the brain is in an awakened state. Those who have not trained their minds through religious discipline are liable to be subjected to the strong influence of the moon. The Buddha

attained His Enlightenment on a full moon for He had been developing and attuning it correctly for a long period. In days gone by, full moons and new moons were declared public holidays in many Buddhist countries and people were encouraged to devote their time to spiritual development. It was only during the colonial period in Asia that holidays were switched over to Sundays. In view of this, some Buddhist countries are now trying to re-introduce the former lunar system of holidays. It is advisable to observe full moons as a religious day to concentrate on peace and happiness by calming down the senses. Many Buddhists observe the eight precepts on full moons, to be free from family commitments and to keep away from worldly pleasures in order to have peace of mind for their spiritual development. ... When we consider all those occurences, we can understand why our ancestors and religious teachers have advised us to change our daily routine and to relax physically and mentally on full moons and new moons. The practice of religion is the most appropriate method for people to experience mental peace and physical relaxation. The Buddhists are merely observing the wisdom of the past when they devote more time to activities of a spiritual nature on New Moons and Full Moons."
Dham: 217-221 #1240

◙ **MOUNT GRIDHRAKUTA**
see   Vulture Peak

◙ **MOUNT LU**
see   Lu-shan

◙ **MOUNT SUMERU**
see   Sumeru (Mount --)

◙ **MU**
Syn: Wu

►"Japanese translation of the Chinese term 'Wu'. The word 'Wu' (meaning 'no') can be translated in Buddhism as awakening, cognition, realization, or enlightenment. It is widely used by Zen Buddhists to denote the intuitive realization of the Buddha-nature within one's own mind."
Chan: 485
The koan "Mu" found in the Wu-Men-Kuan (q.v.) is the most famous koan in Zen. #0589

◙ **MUDRA**
See also: Mantra

►Skt., lit. seal, sign. "Ritual gestures of the hands used in symbolic magic, especially in the Esoteric school. They are used in conjunction with Mantras as aids to meditation. Buddha images are found in a variety of Mudra positions."
Hump: 131

"A bodily posture or a symbolic gesture. In Buddhist iconography every Buddha is depicted with a characteristic gesture of the hands. Such gestures correspond to natural gestures (of teaching, protecting, and so on) and also to certain aspects of Buddhist teaching or of the particular Buddha depicted. Mudras acquired special significance in the Mahayana, especially in the esoteric schools. Here mudras accompany the performance of liturgies and the recitation of the Mantras."
Sham: 148 #0401

◙ **MULLER, FRIEDRICH MAX (1823-1900)**

►"German Indologist who, as editor of the *Sacred Books of the East series*, was active in publishing translations of Buddhist texts, and who published some interesting

research of his own on Buddhism.
Following his doctorate from Leipzig in 1843, he studied Sanskrit and philosophy at Berlin, eventually leaving for Paris in 1845. There he met Eugene Burnouf who fueled Muller's interest in Indology. Muller also learned Pali, and set about to conduct research on Theravada Buddhism. Renowned for his work on the history of religions."
Preb: 194-195 #1048

◙ **MUMONKAN**
see Wu-men-kuan

◙ **MUNI**
See also: Sakyamuni Buddha; Buddha

►"In Sanskrit this means a 'seer' or a 'sage'; from the Chinese it translates as 'He who is capable of doing virtuous things'. When used as a proper noun, it refers to Buddha Sakyamuni."
Chan: 479 #0541

◙ **MUSTARD SEED**
see Kisagotami; Sumeru/Mustard Seed

◙ **MUTUAL IDENTITY**
See also: Avatamsaka Sutra;

Mutual Interpenetration

►"A basic concept of Hua Yen (Avatamsaka) Buddhism which reveals that all things are identical on the transcendent (noumenal) plane."
Chan: 257
Hua-yen Buddhism is based on the *Avatamsaka Sutra*, the second longest sutra after the *Prajna Paramita Sutra*. The *Avatamsaka Sutra* is described by D.T. Suzuki as the "epitome of Buddhist thought, Buddhist sentiment and Buddhist experience."
Editor: na #0841

◙ **MUTUAL INTER-PENETRATION**
See also: Avatamsaka Sutra; Ten mirrors

►"One of the two basic concepts of Hua Yen (Avatamsaka) Buddhism, stressing the principle that all things and principles are mutually dependent and interpenetrate one another. It may be called a principle of mutual immanence."
Chan: 257
Hua-yen Buddhism is based on the *Avatamsaka Sutra*, the second longest sutra after the *Prajna Paramita Sutra*. The *Avatamsaka Sutra* is described by D.T. Suzuki

as the "epitome of Buddhist thought, Buddhist sentiment and Buddhist experience."
Editor: na #0840

◙ **MYANMAR (BUDDHISM IN)**
See also: Buddhist Councils

►"Kanishkha introduced Mahayana Buddhism c. A.D. 100, but when Buddhaghosa visited Burma (Myanmar) c. A.D. 450 he established the Theravada as the national religion. Burmese scholars have specialized in the Abhidhamma and the practice of meditation. In 1954-6, the Sixth Buddhist Council was held in a specially built cave near Rangoon designed to reproduce the Saptaparna Cave in which the First Council was held at the Buddha's passing."
Hump: 53
"Various forms of Buddhism were introduced into Burma (Myanmar) and, between the eleventh and thirteenth centuries, a wonderful Buddhist culture bloomed at Pagan. Because of various schisms and dissensions, however, a 'canonically valid monastic succession' was introduced from Sri Lanka in the fifteenth century. Since then Sri Lankan Theravada has been the predominant tradition. During

the British occupation (1885-1948), Buddhism became closely associated with Burmese nationalism."
Snell/Buddhism: 27 #0465

◙ **MYSTICISM OF LIGHT**
See also: Amitabha Buddha; Pure Land Buddhism (Summary)

▶"The light mysticism of Pure Land spirituality is at least as powerful as, if not more than, [similar] examples from Hinduism and Christianity and it has sometimes been asked if it did not enter Buddhism from elsewhere. When this question is answered in the affirmative, Iran, especially its native system of Zoroastrianism, is often indicated as the source of the sun and light symbolism of the sutras on which Pure Land is spirituality based... Hard evidence for the influence of Zoroastrianism on Buddhism is, however, lacking, and in its absence the theory does not seem necessary. *All of the main features of Pure Land Buddhism can be derived from Buddhist sutras and sastras.* The fact that these texts sometimes contain teachings similar to (though of course, not the same as) those of other religions need not be accepted as evidence of

influence. From the Buddhist point of view, the *similarities [should] be taken to show that, where non-Buddhist religions agree with Buddhism, they have correctly understood the nature of reality as it truly is.*"
Yoshi/Corless: 245

◙ **NAGA**
See also: Nagarjuna

▶"Lit. 'serpent'; 'dragon'; a beneficent half-divine being, which in the spring climbs into heaven and in winter lives deep in the Earth. Naga or Maha-naga ('great dragon') is often used as a synonym for the Buddha or for the sages who have matured beyond rebirth.
Naga-rajas ('dragon kings' or 'dragon queens') are water deities who govern springs, rivers, lakes, and seas. In many Buddhist traditions the nagas are water deities who in their sea palaces guard Buddhist scriptures (the *Avatamsaka Sutra* for example) that have been placed in their care because humanity is not yet ripe for their reception."
Sham: 151 #0376

◙ **NAGARJUNA (2ND/3RD C.)**
See also: India (Buddhism in); Madhyamika school

▸"'One of the most important philosophers of Buddhism and the founder of the Madhyamika school. Nagarjuna's major accomplishment was his systematization ... of the teaching presented in the *Prajnaparamita Sutras*. Nagarjuna's methodological approach of rejecting all opposites is the basis of the Middle Way ...'"

Sham: na

"Nagarjuna is revered in all of Mahayana as a great religious figure, in many places as a Bodhisattva. Not only Zen, but also the Tantric branch of Buddhism and the devotional communities of Amitabha Buddha, count Nagarjuna among their patriarchs."(Dumoulin, *Zen Buddhism*)

Dumou: 44

Tradition credits the South Indian Patriarch Nagarjuna with "rediscovering" the *Avatamsaka Sutra* in the 3rd century AD. He is said to have "travelled" to the sea dragon's palace beneath the ocean to retrieve the sutra. Another account has it that he discovered the sutra in an abandoned monastery. Nagarjuna is the patriarch of the Madyamika (Middle Way) school and, interestingly enough, also of the Salvation school (Pure Land).

The latter represents the easy way of salvation, compared to, for example, the arduous path of Zen.   Editor: na

NOTE:

"In the *Lankavatara Sutra*, (Sagakatham: 163-166), the Buddha is asked who will teach the Mahayana after He has passed away. He replies (foretelling the coming of Nagarjuna and Nagarjuna's rebirth in the Pure Land): 'In Vedali, in the southern part, a Bhikshu most illustrious and distinguished will be born; his name will be Nagarjuna, he will be the destroyer of the one-sided views based on being and non-being. He will declare my Vehicle, the unsurpassed Mahayana, to the world; attaining the stage of Joy he will go to the Land of Bliss.' (Suzuki, tr, *The Lankavatara Sutra*, p. 239-40)"

Yosh: 255   #0911

◉ **NAGASENA (2ND C. B.C.)**
See also: Milindapanha

▸"A priest of the second century B.C. According to the *Milidapanha* (the Questions of King Milinda), he was born to a Brahman family but entered the Buddhist Order. He debated on various subjects with the Greek

King Menander, who ruled in northern India and is said to have been converted by Nagasena. This debate is famous as an example of one of the earliest encounters between Greek civilization and Buddhism."
Sokk: 281-282 #0275

◙ **NAGATOMI, MASATOSHI**

►"Buddhist Studies professor at Harvard University's Yenching Institute who is considered to be among the foremost scholars of Buddhism in the United States. Although he has been especially interested in Buddhist logic, he is equally at home working on the disciplinary texts of the monastic tradition as with the texts of Dharmakirti. He has worked closely with the Center for the Study of World Religions at Harvard in developing some of the finest young Buddhologists of the past two decades."
Preb: 196 #1049

◙ **NALANDA MONASTERY / UNIVERSITY**

►"A great Buddhist monastery which was located seven miles to the north of Rajgir, in Bihar, India. As a center of Buddhist study, particularly of Madhyamika philosophy, it prospered from the fifth through twelfth centuries. It was founded in the fifth century by Kumaragupta (r. 414-455), king of the Gupta dynasty, also called Shakraditya. Thereafter, the monastery was enlarged by the kings of the late Gupta period. The Nalanda Monastery was in reality a Buddhist university, where many learned monks came to further their study of Buddhism. Hsuan-tsang and I-ching, Chinese priests who traveled to India in the seventh century, wrote of the imposing structure and prosperity of this monastery. Many outstanding Mahayana Buddhist scholars such as Sharmapala and Shilabhadra studied at the Nalanda Monastery."
Sokk: 282-283
"Buddhist university in India, founded initially as a monastery by Sakraditya, king of Magadha. Harsavardhana of Kanauj (A.D. 606-647), a great patron of Buddhism, donated revenue of a hundred villages for the maintenance of this great establishment. It was a great center of Mahayana thought, noted for its extensive library and its congregation of Madhyamika scholars. Not only was it a home

for famous Buddhist teachers like Dignaga, but it was also a place of learning attractive to visiting pilgrims. Scholars like Hsuan-tsang and I-ching studied there before returning to China with texts and teaching. It eventually became something of a pipeline for exporting Buddhist ideas and scholars to Tibet, an association which dramatically influenced Tibetan Buddhism for centuries. Nalanda was eventually destroyed by Muslim invaders."
Preb: 197-198

"Nalanda lies 7 miles to the north of Rajgir. Nalanda Mahavihara by this time became the premier Buddhist institution not only in India, but its prestige as an educational center of supreme importance became known throughout the Buddhist world. Its fame and honor continued till the end of the twelfth century... During the time of the Pala Rulers (eighth to twelfth century) Nalanda rose to ever greater prosperity and fame. One of the luminaries of the university, Padmasambhava, went to Tibet and founded Tantrism there."
Lahiri: 57 #0276

◙ **NAM-MYOHO-RENGE-KYO**
See also: Nichiren Shoshu

▸"Japanese for 'Homage to the *Lotus Sutra*,' the repeated prayer of Nichiren Buddhists."
Reat: 336 #2072

◙ **NAME (OF BUDDHA / BODHISATTVA)**
See also: Voice of a Buddha; Pure Land Buddhism (Summary)

▸"The name of a Buddha or a Bodhisattva is presumed to embody his virtues and powers. Hence, invocation of the name of the Buddha or Bodhisattva activates those virtues and powers. When the term 'the Name' is used as an epithet in Pure Land discourse, it means Amitabha's name, or more properly, the form used in invoking his name. That form is the Chinese expression Namo-Amito-fo." (*Jpn* / Namu Amida Butsu; *Vn* / Nam-mo A-Di-Da Phat).
Gomez: 311 #1717

See also Voice of a Buddha

◙ **NAMELESS WOMAN**
see "Parable: Woman Who Is Above Worry and Care"

◙ **NAMU AMIDA BUTSU**
Syn: Nembutsu
See also: Buddha Recitation;

Pure Land Buddhism (Summary)

▸"Japanese formula known as the nembutsu (or Buddha Recitation), literally meaning 'Homage to Amida Buddha'.

As Pure Land Buddhism developed in India, China, Japan, Vietnam, and other East Asian countries, faith was placed in the saving grace of Amida (Sanskrit: Amitabha; Chinese A-mi-t'o) Buddha. As the abiding doctrinal tenet of the tradition, this faith was externally expressed in the mantric formula 'Namu Amida Butsu', repeated again and again by adherents of the belief. If properly recited, and with an appropriate mental perspective, it was felt that adepts could be reborn in the Western Paradise of Amida, from which salvation was more readily attainable. In China the practice was called *Nien-Fo*, in Vietnam, *Niệm-Phật*. It was felt that chanting the nembutsu was the most effective Buddhist practice for individuals in a period of Dharma decline (Dharma-Ending Age, q.v.)."

"The nembutsu constitutes the primary religious practice in the Pure Land tradition for individuals hoping to be reborn in the Pure Land of Amida Buddha. Considered by its proponents to be the most effective religious practice in times of Dharma decline, it consists of a repetition of the formula Namu Amida Butsu or 'Homage to Amida Buddha.' It is an expression of tariki or 'other-power', literally, placing one's faith for salvation outside of one's own attainment, a practice which is sometimes contrasted with the notion of jiriki or 'self-power' in Zen."

Preb: 198-199, 200 #1051

◙ NANDA

Syn: Sudarananda

▸"Shakyamuni's disciple and younger half brother, the son of Shuddhodana and Shakyamuni's maternal aunt Mahaprajapati. He had a graceful figure and was known as Sundarananda (Beautiful Nanda). After Shakyamuni renounced the secular world, Nanda took his place as heir to King Shuddhodana. Just as he was about to marry the beautiful Sundari, Shakyamuni returned to Kapilavastu for the first time following his Awakening, and Nanda was persuaded to join the Buddhist Order. It is said that he was for some time tormented by doubts and second thoughts, but

under Shakyamuni's guidance, he was eventually able to fully dedicate himself to Buddhist practice and attained the state of Arhat."
Sokk: 285 #1652

◎ NARA PERIOD

►"(593-784). Period of Japanese history during which the city of Nara was the focus of Japanese civilization, especially the absorption of Buddhism and Chinese culture."
Reat: 336 #2074

◎ NARADA, MAHA THERA (1898-1983)

►"Sinhalese Buddhist, born in Sri Lanka. Pali scholar and a leading exponent of Theravada Buddhism. Travelled throughout the world, lecturing, broadcasting and founding Buddhist organizations. Stimulated Buddhist study in Australia, China, Vietnam, Nepal, the U.S.A. and the U.K. where he opened the London Buddhist Vihara in 1954. Translated the Dhammapada and wrote many books on Theravada Buddhism."
Hump: 134
Publications include *Buddhism in a Nutshell; The Buddha and His Teachings.*"
Snel: 268 #0428

◎ NAROPA

►"(1016-1100). Abbot of Nalanda (some sources say Vikramasila) University in India until 1057, thereafter a member of the founding lineage of the Kagyudpa school of Tibetan Buddhism. A disciple of Tilopa."
Reat: 336 #2075

◎ NATURE AND MARKS

See also: True-Emptiness / Wonderful-Existence; Noumenon/ Phenomena

---

►*Nature*: noumenon, essence. *Marks*: characteristics, forms, physiognomy. Marks are contrasted with nature, in the same way that phenomena are contrasted with noumenon. True Mark stands for the True Form, True Nature, Buddha Nature, always unchanging. The True Mark of all phenomena is like space: always existing but really empty; although empty, really existing. The True Mark of the Triple World is No-Birth/ No-Death, not existent/not non-existent, not like this/not like that. True Mark is also called "Self-Nature," "Dharma Body,"

the "Unconditioned," "True Thusness," "Dharma Realm."
Pure Land
See the following explanation of the *Amitabha Sutra*: "This [*Amitabha*] Sutra is a Mahayana Dharma ... and takes the Real Mark as its substance. The Real Mark is no mark. There is no mark, nothing at all, and yet there is nothing which is not marked. Unmarked, it is *true emptiness*, and with nothing unmarked, it is *wonderful existence* ... True Suchness, the One True Dharma Realm, the Thus Come One's Store Nature, all are different names for the Real Mark" (Master Hsuan Hua, *A General Explanation of the Amitabha Sutra*, p. 23). #0907

◉ **NEMBUTSU**
see Buddha Recitation; Namu Amida Butsu

◉ **NET OF INDRA**
see Jewel Net of Indra

◉ **NHẤT HẠNH, THÍCH (*DHARMA MASTER*)**

►Well-known Vietnamese monk and poet, born 1926. Ordination and advanced religious training in Vietnam. Onetime student at Columbia University. Coined term "Engaged Buddhism" in his book *Vietnam: Lotus in a Sea of Fire*. Other books include *The Miracle of Mindfulness*. Presently lives in France at Plum Village.
Snel / Editor: 300
"What makes Rev. Nhat Hanh distinctive is his extensive arsenal of methods. He recommends meditation, of course, and koan study and breath regulation, but he also puts great stress on Theravada methods (mindfulness and the psychology of the Abhidhamma) and even dips into what sounds like the Tantric-Taoist bag of tricks (the half-smile and the recitation of gathas) ..."
Storm: 2 #0746

◉ **NICHIREN SHOSHU**
See also: Soka-gakkai

►"Modern offshoot of the Nichiren School of Japanese Buddhism. Founded by Tsuneburo Makiguchi informally in 1930 with his disciple Josei Toda, and formally in 1937. This Japanese 'new religion' later changed its name to the present Value Creation Society or Nichiren Shoshu Sokagakkai in 1951 ... Promising material wealth to its constituents, the group emphasizes the practice of

chanting the daimoku (i.e., Nam Myoho Renge Kyo) while contemplating the mandala-like gohonzon. [Current President is Daisaku Ikeda.]"
Preb: 201

"Nichiren was not merely critical of other Buddhist schools; he taught that they would lead their unwitting practitioners to the lowest Buddhist hell. For Soka Gakkai members to define other forms of Buddhism as legitimate, then, would require a break with this centuries-old belief... There is some evidence that such a revision may slowly be taking place."
Natt: 49 #1052

◎ NIỆM PHẬT

►Vietnamese for Buddha Recitation (q.v.).

◎ NIEN-FO

►Chinese for Buddha Recitation

◎ NIHILISM
See also: Two Extreme Views; Middle Way Philosophy

►"The philosophic doctrine that denies a substantial reality to the phenomenal universe. Buddhism takes the middle path between the realists (astika), who maintain the universe to be real, and the non-realists (nastika), who deny all reality. The Buddha condemmed both the astika and the nastika concepts."
Hump: 137 #0426

◎ NINE LOTUS GRADES
see Lotus Grades

◎ NINE MOUNTAIN SCHOOLS
See also: Korea (Buddhism in --)

►"A collective designation for the nine schools of Korean Son (Zen) Buddhism, because of the location of their principal monasteries on nine sacred mountains in Korea."
Reat: 337 #2078

◎ NINE ORIFICES
Syn: Nine Openings

►"The Buddha teaches us that there are nine openings in our body and from each of them there exudes all kinds of excretions all the time (for example phlegm from the throat, sweat from the pores of the skin, etc.). None of the things excreted are pleasant to smell or touch or taste. They are essentially unclean things. Why do we love those unclean things so much?

We love them because 'Worldly beings are inverted' says the Buddha. We do not consider ourselves inverted though, and we can point out that there are some who are more inverted than ourselves."　Cheng Kuan: 42

◎ **NINE REALMS**
See also: Ten Realms

▶"All realms in the cosmos, with the exception of the Buddha realms."
Tam: 343　#0958

◎ **NIRMANAKAYA**
See also: Three Bodies of The Buddha

▶"The transformation Body of Buddha, the Body-of-Form of all Buddhas which is manifested for the sake of men who cannot yet approach the Dharmakaya (the formless True Body of Buddhahood)."
Chan: 257　#0842

◎ **NIRVANA**
See also: Nirvana with Residue; Parinirvana

▶"Originally meant total extinction of desire and suffering. Today it refers to the state of liberation through full enlightenment. In Mahayana, Nirvana is classified into four categories: 1. Nirvana with residue, the state of a person who has realized the nature of Nirvana, but has not yet eliminated the five aggregates; 2. Nirvana without residue, wherein the aggregates have been eliminated; 3. Svabhava Nirvana, the primeval Nirvana which is always present, whether we realize it or not, and 4. Nonabiding Nirvana, in which one abides in neither Samsara nor ultimate quiescence. This is the Nirvana of the Buddhas and the highest Bodhisattvas."
Chan: 479　#0403

"In the West, Nirvana has often been misunderstood as mere annihilation; even in early Buddhism it was not so conceived. In many texts, to explain what is described as Nirvana, the simile of extinguishing a flame is used. The fire that goes out does not pass away, but merely becomes invisible by passing into space. Thus the term Nirvana does not indicate annihilation but rather entry into another mode of existence. The fire comes forth from space and returns back into it; thus Nirvana is a spiritual event that takes place in time but

is also, in an unmanifest and imperishable sphere, always already there. This is the 'abode of immortality,' which is not spatially located, but is rather transcendent, supramundane and only accessible to mystical experience."
Sham: 159

◙ NIRVANA SUTRA
see Parinirvana Sutra

◙ NIRVANA WITH REMAINDER
Syn: Nirvana with Residue

►"Refers to the Nirvana (q.v.) reached by those enlightened beings who have not yet completely rid themselves of their samsaric burdens of skandhas (aggregates)."
Chan: 258 #0843

◙ NIRVANA WITH RESIDUE
see Nirvana with Remainder

◙ NIYUTA

►"A niyuta is an a number variously defined as 100,000; 1,000,000; or 10,000 times 10,000,000." Camp: 318 #1841

◙ NO GOOD DEED GOES UNPUNISHED
See also: Karma; Third Lifetime

►How do we reconcile bad happenings occuring to good people with the law of karma? The general answer is that karma extends over many lifetimes, and therefore our present good deeds may attenuate the bad results of past misdeeds but not necessarily eliminate them completely.
Editor: na

Buddhism of Wisdom & Faith/ excerpts:
"Buddha Sakyamuni once said to his disciple, Ananda, 'Some people perform good deeds all their lives, but at the time of death are reborn in the hells; others create bad karma all their lives, yet at the time of death are reborn in the heavens. Do you know the reason why?' Ananda said, 'Great Master, please teach us the causes.' The Lord Buddha said, 'when those who perform good deeds are reborn in the hells, it is because their good karma in this life has not matured, while their bad karma from time immemorial has come to fruition. Conversely, when those who create bad karma in this lifetime are reborn in the heavens, it is because their bad karma in this life has not reached maturity, while their good karma from past lives has borne fruit. Good and bad karma interact for

many lifetimes before emerging. As with debts, the most important is repaid first. Therefore the cultivator should be diligent in daily life, and not indifferent or lazy.'"

Tam: 178-179

"Cultivators usually face three types of obstacles -- the *Obstacle of Afflictions*, the *Obstacle of Karma* and the *Obstacle of Retribution* -- with the Obstacle of Karma being the most dangerous. Yet, nothing usually happens when the practitioner first begins to cultivate, while the deeper his cultivation, the more obstacles he is bound to encounter. Why is this so? It is because as common people living in the Dharma-Ending Age, most of us, naturally, have heavy obstructing conditions. If not, we would have been reborn in the Dharma Semblance Age or the Perfect Dharma Age (see Dharma-Ending Age). However, it is not cultivation that gives rise to obstacles but rather a phenomenon known as 'Commutation of karma.' *Heavy karma is commuted into light karma, future karma is "reshuffled" into current karma.* Let us suppose that we have ten parts of bad karma but that through cultivation we manage to

eradicate seven parts, so that only three parts remain. Instead of having to repay that karma in the future, thanks to our cultivation we may only have to endure light retribution in this very life, and thus be free to attain liberation swiftly. For example, in one of his previous lives, an Elder Precept Master had been a monarch, who had waged many wars to conquer neighboring kingdoms. Having committed such great karma of killing, he was destined to descend into the hells once his residual merits were exhausted. However, thanks to the Master's earnest cultivation and propagation of the Dharma, his evil karma was commuted into daily bouts of seizures, which made him feel as though many invisible swords were stabbing and slashing his body. This went on for two years before the disease disappeared."

Tam: 244-245   #2271

For details, see also Karma

◙ NO-BIRTH

see Non-Birth

◙ NO-MIND

▸"Phrase used to translate various terms in Zen Buddhism. It describes a state of consciousness before the division into duality created by thought takes place. Wu-hsin (No-Mind) means no-mindness, or no-thoughtness, as the Unconscious behind all conscious activity. Yet this Unconscious is at the same time conscious, a mind unconscious of itself. This is a paradox without meaning save as achieved in direct spiritual experiences. It is the purpose of Zen training to achieve and maintain this state of mind."

Hump: 139 #0425

◉ **NOBLE EIGHTFOLD PATH**
see   Eightfold Noble Path

◉ **NOBLE SILENCE**
see   Silence

◉ **NON-ARISING**

▸"Never coming into being; not truly existing."
Chan: 479 #0542

◉ **NON-BIRTH**
Syn: No-Birth
See also: Tolerance of Non-birth

▸"A term used to describe the nature of Nirvana. In Mahayana Buddhism generally, No-Birth signifies the 'extinction' of the

discursive thinking by which we conceive of things as arising and perishing, forming attachments to them." (Ryukoku University.)
Tam: 157

Pure Land Buddhism: Dialogues (excerpts)
Question:
"I venture to think, is not rebirth in the Pure Land contrary to the Truth of Non-Birth?
Answer:
Elder Master Chih I has said: 'The wise, while earnestly striving for rebirth in the Pure Land, also understand that the nature of rebirth is intrinsically empty. This is true Non-Birth, and also the meaning of "only when the Mind is pure, will the Buddha lands be pure." The dull and ignorant, on the other hand, are caught up in the concept of birth. Upon hearing the term *Birth*, they understand it as actual birth; hearing of *Non-Birth*, they [cling to its literal meaning] and think that there is no rebirth anywhere. Little do they realize that 'Birth is precisely Non-Birth, and Non-Birth does not hinder Birth.' It has also been said by a Zen Master: 'If we understand Birth as meaning real birth, we stray in the direction of Eternalism; if we understand Non-Birth as meaning that there is no actual

birth, we commit the error of Nihilism. Birth and yet no Birth, no Birth and yet Birth, is truly the ultimate meaning.'

Another Zen Master has said: 'Birth is definitely birth, but returning [to the Pure Land] is in fact non-returning.'

The explanations of these three Masters are very clear. I will now give a broader explanation, through the two concepts of 'Nature' and 'Marks.' From the point of view of Nature (noumenon), the True Mind is wonderful and silent; its nature is inherently unborn (no Birth). From the point of view of Marks, whenever there is a congruence of causes and conditions, the various Marks of Birth and Death falsely appear, as in a dream, from the True Mind. Because Nature is usually manifested through Marks, it is said that Non-Birth is Birth. Since Marks appear as a result of Nature, it is said that Birth is Non-Birth. When we truly understand this truth, rebirth in the Pure Land is rebirth in the nature (state) of Mind-Only; between Birth and no Birth, no contradiction in meaning exists!" (Master Tien Ju, 14th c., China.) Dia: 76-77 #0912

◙ NON-DUAL

See also: Non-Dual Method; Paradox

▸The Non-Dual Truth represents No-Self and No-Dharma.

"*No-Self, No Dharma* (Non-dual truth). These two terms refer to 'the concept of emptiness, void, sunyata, i.e., that entities have no fixed or independent nature. In [Theravada], emptiness is only applied to the person; in the Mahayana, on the other hand, all things are regarded as without essence." (*Shambhala Dictionary of Buddhism and Zen.*)

"Non-duality is synonymous with reality, voidness, etc. but it must be remembered that non-duality does not necessarily mean unity, that unity is only one of the pair unity-duality; hence non-duality implies non-unity as well."
(*The Holy Teaching of Vimalakirti*) Thurman: 163
No-Self (emptiness of self) means true understanding that the five skandas, which together represent body and mind, are all born of causes and conditions. When these come apart, body and mind immediately disappear. There is no real 'self' as master. *No-Dharma* (emptiness of all phenomena) means true understanding that the five

skandas are empty [not only because they are aggregates] but by their very nature. Thus, the *Heart Sutra* states: 'The Bodhisattva Avalokitesvara illuminated the five skandas and saw that they were empty.' The truth of Emptiness of all Dharmas is precisely the True Mark, attained through eradication of delusions. Therefore, the *Heart Sutra* continues: 'Thus, the Bodhisattva Avalokitesvara overcame all ills and suffering.' Furthermore, the principle that the Dharma-body -- while being the basis of all marks -- is completely apart from such marks as birth, extinction, impermanence, permanence, existence and emptiness, conforms very much to the Truth. Hence the name 'True Marks.' This True Marks is common to sentient beings and Buddhas, but ordinary humans, as well as followers of the Two Vehicles, deludedly reject it and therefore cannot take advantage of it. It is as though you had a diamond sewn into the hem of your shirt but, unaware of it, must endure poverty and deprivation."

Sham: xxx

NOTE:

According to Patriarch Yin Kuang and others, there is a conceptual difference between Theravada and Mahayana. The Theravada school teaches that the self is a composite, an aggregate of many other elements, and is therefore empty (relative emptiness). In Mahayana Buddhism, all phenomena (including the self) are empty in their very nature (absolute emptiness).

Editor: na #0959

◙ NON-DUAL METHOD

See also: Dual Birth (State of); Ultimatism

***Buddhism of Wisdom & Faith/* excerpts:**

▸"There are many doubts concerning the Pure Land method. This is because most cultivators are still attached to 'duality,' and have not reconciled essence and marks, existence and non-existence, noumenon and phenomena. That is why they embrace essence to reject marks, noumenon to reject phenomena, Emptiness to reject Existence, and vice versa -- thus creating disputes, doubts and perplexity. Little do they suspect that there is mutual identity between noumenon and phenomena -- phenomena are noumenon, noumenon is phenomena. If we divide them and consider them separately, phenomena are not true phenomena, noumenon is not true noumenon. This is true also of essence and marks, existence and non-existence and other dualistic dharmas. For this reason, the *Vimalakirti Sutra* speaks of the non-dual method to destroy this attachment. Non-dual means reconciling all things, penetrating into their very nature; it does not mean 'one.' This is the true realm of 'Mind-Only.' Any other doctrine based on the Dharma Doors (schools) of Existence or Emptiness is merely an expedient for teaching purposes.

The sutras state: 'To tire of and abandon 'conditioned' virtues is the action of demons. Yet, to be greedy and attached to transcendental, unconditioned virtues is also demonic action. 'Ancient sages have also said: 'Conditioned dharmas, while illusory, cannot be abandoned if we are to attain the Way. Although unconditioned dharmas are true, if we become attached to them, our wisdom-nature will not be comprehensive.'

These words clearly show that on the path to Enlightenment, unconditioned and conditioned dharmas, noumenon and phenomena are inseparable.

It is also stated in the *Treatise on the Middle Way*: 'Because common sentient beings grasp at external forms, the sutras destroy this attachment with the truth of Emptiness. If as soon as they are free of the disease of attachment to Existence they fall into the error of grasping at Emptiness, there is no medicine that can help them.' As the Prajna Paramita Truth of Emptiness sounds lofty and miraculous, when worldly, educated people read this literature, they usually get caught up in the error of 'speaking on the level of principle' about everything and look down on those who follow forms and marks in their practice. Thus, they create the karma of arrogance and self-importance. While they expound the Truth of Emptiness, their actions are entirely in the realm of Existence, as exemplified by the following couplet:

'Above, their mouths speak about the totally wonderful,/ Below, their feet do not part with even a mote of dust.'"

Thich: 89-91 #1362

For details, *see also* Ultimatism

◉ **NON-HARMING**
see Ahimsa

◉ **NON-KILLING**
see   Ahimsa

◉ **NON-REGRESSION**
see   Non-Retrogression

◉ **NON-RETROGRESSION**
Syn: Avaivartika; Non-regression
See also: Tolerance of Non-Birth;
Ten Stages; Human Nature

►"One who has reached the realization of emptiness (Tolerance of Non-Birth) will never regress from the Buddha/Bodhisattva-path. Non-regression (non-retrogression) sometimes simply denotes an advanced stage of aspiration and practice from which one will never retreat."
Chan: 479

"Not to turn back. Up to a certain stage in their development, all religious practitioners are subject to backsliding. The Bodhisattva, when he has reached the seventh (in some traditions, the eighth) of the Ten Stages (q.v.) [i.e. the highest ten levels of the fifty-two levels of Bodhisattva practice], cannot backslide."
Hurv/1976: 340

"The state or condition of 'not falling back' is the stage in a Bodhisattva's spiritual career beyond which there is no turning back, sliding back, or retrogression. This condition is presented as one of the blessings bestowed upon (or attained by) those reborn in the Land of Bliss. In the *Amitabha Sutras*, it is not clearly distinguished from the stages or conditions of being only one birth away from Enlightenment."
Gomez: 298

Pure Land Buddhism
Retrogression from the Way is the greatest setback for the cultivator. The core rationale for seeking rebirth in the Pure Land (rather than remaining on earth to pursue cultivation) is that within the Saha World, retrogression is a certainty for all but the most resolute practitioners. Sutras and commentaries abound with tales of retrogression by even the most advanced disciples. (See, for example, the story of Sariputra, a leading Arhat disciple of the Buddha, donating both of his eyes to save a Brahmin's mother as part of his practice of the paramita of charity, but then abandoning that paramita when one of the eyes was crushed and spat upon.)
Editor/Zen: 168

"Another case: it is said that Shariputra was a practitioner of the Mahayana who had progressed far along the path. One day a demon appeared to him and, wishing to put him to the test and if possible contrive his downfall, asked him for his right hand. In reply, Shariputra cut it off and gave it to the demon. But the demon was angry and refused to accept it, complaining that Shariputra had impolitely offered it to him with his left! At this point, it is said that Shariputra lost hope of ever being able to satisfy the desires of beings, and turned from the Mahayana to pursue the path to Arhatship."

Shantiveda: 197

All Buddhist methods lead ultimately to liberation. Most of these methods rely on self-effort. However, human beings are limited in spiritual development and motivation (and burdened with heavy karma accumulated from time immemorial). Thus, they cannot escape Birth and Death in one lifetime, and are in danger of retrogression during transmigration. Pure Land teachings offer an easy method to escape Birth and Death in one lifetime through rebirth in the Pure Land, where practitioners can continue cultivating without fear of retrogression.

Editor: na   #0040
See also Retrogression

◙ **NON-SEEKING PRACTICES**
see   Ten Non-Seeking Practices

◙ **NORTH AMERICA (BUDDHISM IN)**
See also: Buddhism; Chicago Columbian Exposition

▶*NB*: Please read entry "West (Buddhism in the)" before the following:

"Unlike the UK, where Theravada Buddhism has always had a strong presence (see "Europe, Buddhism in"), North America has always been predominantly Mahayana. The Pure Land school arrived early with Chinese and Japanese immigrants, followed at the beginning of the twentieth century by Zen. Proponents of the Meditation or Zen school were Japanese teachers, the most famous being D.T. Suzuki. More recently, other forms of Buddhism, such as Nichiren Shoshu and Tantrism have gained a following among the American public..."

[After identifying the three types of Buddhism which currently co-exist in North America as (1) Elite Buddhism or the Buddhism practiced by the American middle class, (2) Evangelical Buddhism associated with such schools as Nichiren Shoshu, (3) Ethnic Buddhism or the Buddhism of the Asian-American community, professor Jan Nattier of Indiana University continued:] "The import pattern of transmission has resulted in the formation of the Buddhist groups I refer to as Elite Buddhism. These groups attract a clientele well above average in terms of income, education, and status. Almost all are college graduates (with the exception of some artistic and literary dropouts), and a substantial percentage have postgraduate training. Their education is far from ordinary: many have attended Ivy League colleges (or, in their early years, prep schools), and a high percentage have specialized in non-lucrative fields in the arts and humanities. This is a clientele, in sum, for which mere economic survival is seldom viewed as a problem... On the contrary, Elite Buddhists are overwhelmingly affiliated with a small and specific subset of the dozens of brands of Buddhism available on the world market today: namely, Tibetan Buddhism, Vipassana, and Zen.

An important clue as to why these three schools have been selected can be seen at a glance, for the names of two of the three mean 'meditation'... Of the three types of American Buddhism [Elite, Evangelical and Ethnic Buddhism], *it is Elite Buddhism that is likely to bear the least resemblance to Buddhism as practiced in any Asian country...*"
Natt: 44-45

"A fundamental characteristic of Elite Buddhism is its obsession with meditation. Or to put it another way -- for the rhetoric of Zen Patriarch Dogen (q.v.) and his ilk aside. Americans rarely sit in meditation just to sit -- Elite Buddhists are extraordinarily concerned with how to get enlightened. 'But that's what Buddhism is all about!' the reader may be saying. True, no doubt, for the Buddha himself, and for his immediate circle of monastic disciples. True also for a small percentage of monks and nuns down through the centuries in various countries of Buddhist Asia. *But Buddhism has historically consisted of a whole repertoire of ideas, practices, and institutions, and Elite Buddhism in the United Sates is characterized not only by its tremendous emphasis on meditation but also by its 'selecting out' of so many other items.* To choose just two examples: the almost total absence of the central Buddhist institution of monasticism, and a noticeable lack of interest in the ethical precepts. (Note that serious concern with the precepts has generally arisen in Elite Buddhist communities only under duress, most commonly in the wake of a scandal.) Many other elements of Buddhist thought and practice are largely absent from these communities as well. The strong tradition of self-reliance in Elite Buddhist circles is paralleled by a lack of interest in (and even condescension toward) traditional devotional activities involving reliance on various Buddhist divinities, and the emphasis on 'virtuoso' spiritual practices in Max Weber's sense -- e.g., Zen seshins, long Vipassana retreats, and complex Tibetan visualization meditations -- seems to be correlated with a lack of interest in practices (including ethical precepts) that are perceived as elementary..."

Natt: 42-49

"It is among Ethnic Buddhists that we find the most complex and sophisticated picture of Buddhism of any of the groups discussed. For them, Buddhism includes both monastics and laity, both intensive practices and small steps toward a better rebirth. It includes not only the teaching of doctrine but many of the values deeply embedded in specific cultural forms. Ethnic Buddhism, in sum, involves the entire fabric of life, not just of the individual but across generations. From this perspective, the Buddhism of both Elite and Evangelical groups appears quite truncated, since so much has been omitted from their repertoire. Yet this does not mean that Ethnic Buddhists have a panoramic and all-inclusive vision, for many would be surprised to find themselves lumped together with Buddhists they have never heard of before. In fact, the monoethnic character of these communities (at least at the beginning) does not lead to much interaction across ethnic lines. It is quite common for members of a Japanese temple, for example, to be unaware of the existence of a Burmese temple nearby, or for a Chinese group to operate without any knowledge of its Korean neighbors."

Natt: 49

Postscript:

There are a number of reasons for the relative success of Buddhism in the West in recent times. The two most important are its rational approach to the everyday issues of life and its teaching on *compassion* (q.v.). The compassion aspect extends to all creatures, big and small, and has as a corollary the practice of *vegetarianism* (q.v.). Indeed, the teaching of compassion overshadows all other aspects of Buddhism and explains the growing success of Mahayana Buddhism in North America.

Editor: na #2142

◉ **NON-SEEKING PRACTICES**
See Ten Non-Seeking Practices

◉ **NOTORIOUS MEN**
See also: Rebirth in the Pure Land; Pure Land School

▶This refers to two Chinese men, Chang Shan-ho (*Vn.*/ Trương Thiện Hòa) and Chang Chung-k'uei (*Vn.*/ Trương Chung Quì), mentioned repeatedly in Pure Land commentaries. Both made their living slaughtering animals, thus violating the most fundamental Buddhist precept -- not to kill. They achieved rebirth in the Pure Land because at the *time of death*, their minds were pure, i.e., free of greed, anger and delusion. This was accomplished through *singleminded concentration on Amitabha Buddha. It is this purity of mind, not the precise number of recitations, that is the source of liberation.*

Pure Land commentaries add that these cases are extremely rare and are the *result of good karma accumulated in previous lifetimes.* Otherwise, how could such men even meet good spiritual advisors at the time of death, let alone recite with one-pointedness of mind? Therefore the necessity of reciting the Buddha's name until single-mindedness is achieved during one's lifetime.

Editor/Zen: 39-40 #1432

◉ **NOUMENON / PHENOMENA**
See also: Ultimatism

▶**(I) NOUMENON**
"Principle, Inner truth, Inner pattern of things and events."
Clear: 173.

Ultimate truth, principle, the abstract as opposed to the concrete, theory, absolute reality, universals. In the *Avatamsaka Sutra*, noumenon denotes the absolute, the mind. "...Laws that

underline things and events in the phenomenal world."
[CCC/BTT, p.255]

(II) PHENOMENA

Conventional truth, everyday reality, the concrete as opposed to the abstract. "Things, events, particulars..., matter, the concrete, and so forth."
[CCC/BTT, p.256]

Noumenon represents the essence of things in themselves, while phenomena or marks are the forms and characteristics of those things. For example, the phenomenal aspect of the precept not to take life is literally not to kill any sentient beings. The essence, or noumenal aspect of that precept is to foster compassion: it is because of compassion that we refrain from taking life.

Editor/Zen: 31

"*Question.* I have heard some people justify their actions from the so-called absolute perspective (noumenon), by saying that there is no good and no evil. This is used as justification for behaving in a manner that I find disturbing.

Answer. The fact is, there is good and evil. Emptiness, or the absolute, is one side, and the world of phenomena, or the relative, is the other side. The truth is to be found in neither of those. Tweak the nose of the person who says he or she is absolute, beyond good and evil. Ask if it hurts."

Loori: 233

Pure Land Buddhism

"There are two aspects to Buddha Recitation -- essence and practice. According to Elder Master Ou-I:

A) '*BUDDHA RECITATION-PRACTICE*' means believing that there is a Western Pure Land and a Lord Buddha named Amitabha, but not yet realizing that 'this Mind makes Buddha, this Mind is Buddha.' It consists of resolutely seeking rebirth in the Pure Land and reciting as earnestly as a lost child longing for his mother, never forgetting her for a single moment. 'Buddha Recitation-essence,' on the other hand, means believing and understanding that Lord Amitabha Buddha of the West inherently exists in full within our mind, is created by our mind, and making this sacred name -- inherently existing in full within our mind and created by our mind -- the focus of our recitation, without a moment of neglect. *In other words, 'Buddha Recitation-practice' is the method of those who do not understand anything about meaning or essence, who just believe that there is a Land of Ultimate Bliss and a Buddha named Amitabha, and who fervently and earnestly recite the Buddha's name seeking rebirth there.*

B) *'BUDDHA RECITATION-ESSENCE'* is the method of those who practice in an identical manner, but who also deeply realize that the Pure Land and Lord Amitabha Buddha are all in the True Mind, manifested by the pure virtues of the True Mind. This being so, is there a difference between Buddha Recitation-practice and Buddha Recitation-essence? Of course there is. Those who follow Buddha Recitation-practice see Amitabha Buddha as outside the Mind; therefore, opposing marks of subject-object still exist. Thus, such practice is not yet all-encompassing and complete. Those who practice Buddha Recitation-essence thoroughly understand the True Mind and therefore sever all marks of subject-object -- to recite is Buddha, to recite is Mind, reconciling Mind and Realm."
Tam: 181-182

C) *CAVEAT*:
"According to Elder Master Yin Kuang, Pure Land followers should not seek guidance on Pure Land matters from Zen Masters. This is because the answers of Zen Masters are all directed towards principle and essence, while the Pure Land approach is based on phenomena and marks. This being the case, and considering the different areas of emphasis, beginning Pure Land practitioners who do not yet fully understand essence and marks, noumenon and phenomena, will not only fail to benefit from the answers of Zen Masters, they may develop even greater doubts, perplexity and inconsistent views."
Tam: 163

NOTE:
"Prof. Allan A. Andrews has noted that there are two levels of Pure Land practice, which have co-existed in China since the fourth century, beginning with the first two Patriarchs: Hui-yuan used Buddha Recitation to achieve prajna wisdom by his own self-efforts. T'an-luan considered Buddha Recitation the best practice for salvation, that is, for rebirth, because it is the easiest practice through the power of Amida's compassionate vows. ('Nembutsu in the Chinese Pure Land Tradition.' In *The Eastern Buddhist*, Vol. 3, No. 2,

p. 40.)

Please note that understanding the dual nature of the Pure Land, as Mind-Only and as a separate entity, requires meditation and recitation -- not intellectual reasoning.

"In secular western thought, awareness of psychological projection as a source of supernatural being has served to demythologize demons, goblins, angels and saints and rob them of their power. The Bardo Thodol [Tibetan Book of the Dead], however, speaks of the deities as 'projections' but never as 'mere projections.' The deities are present and must be dealt with religiously ... not just by intellectual insight." (D.G. Dawe in *The Perennial Dictionary of World Religions*, p. 93.)
PLZ: 16 #0767

◙ **NOVICE**
see Sramananera / Sramanerika

◙ **NUN**
see Bhiksuni

◙ **NYANATILOKA, MAHA THERA (1878-1957)**

▶"Pioneer European bhikhu and notable Pali scholar. Born as Anton Gueth, in Wiesbaden (Germany). After high school devoted himself to music in Frankfurt and Paris, then journeyed to India, and Ceylon. 1903: samanera ordination in Rangoon; bhikhu ordination the following year (the first non-British Western one). 1910-11: left Sri Lanka and traveled to Europe. 1911: returned to Sri Lanka; thereafter lived at the Island Hermitage in Ratgama Lake, Dodanduwa. Interned during WWI as enemy alien. 1916: traveled to Honolulu and then went to China but was arrested in Chungking and imprisoned in Hankow until 1919. Unable to return to Sri Lanka in 1920, so went on to Japan, became professor at Komazawa University. 1926: finally got back to Sri Lanka. WWII: again interned ... Nyanaponika Thera is one of his best known disciples."
Snel: 269
"Played an important role in the planning of the Sixth Buddhist Council, Rangoon 1954." [Best-known book: *A Buddhist Dictionary*.]
Preb: 204 #0728

◙ **NYINGMA-PA**
See also: Tibetan Buddhism
▶"The Red Hat or Unreformed

school of Tibetan Buddhism. Padma Sambhava is credited with founding it in the eighth century though there is little evidence of the school's existence as such before the twelfth.

The Nyingma-pa is found largely in Nepal, Sikkim and in Kham, to the north-east of Tibet. It is the oldest of the Tibetan schools of Buddhism ... The *Tibetan Book of the Dead* was produced by it." Hump: 140 #0422

◙ **OBAKU ZEN SCHOOL**
See also: Zen/Pure Land; Japan (Buddhism In); Pure Land School; Soto Zen

----

▸"The Obaku (Huang-po) school, the smallest of the three Zen schools of Japan, was introduced by the great Chinese master Yin-yuan (Jpn/Ingen: 1592-1673), who went to Japan in 1654 and subsequently founded Mampuku-ji monastery at Uji, near Kyoto. *His teachings ... emphasized that seated meditation is one with the Pure Land school's practice of nembutsu, the repeated invocation of the Buddha Amitabha in order to be reborn in the Pure Land.*"
Yoko: 21
The teachings of the Obaku

(Huang-po) school follow those of the Great Chinese Master Yin-yuan, who was the teacher of Master Lin-chi, the founder of Rinzai Zen. #0822

◙ **OBON**
see Ullambana

◙ **OBSTACLES TO CULTIVATION**
See also: Practice (Buddhist); Visions; Drownsiness; Discouragement; Fault-finding; Afflictions; Ten Non-seeking Practices

----

▸*Excerpts/ "Buddhism of Wisdom and Faith" (Master T. Thien Tam)*
"The karmic conditions that test and create obstacles for the practitioner have many different manifestations. I will summarize them in six points:
1. *INTERNAL 'TESTING CONDITIONS'*
During cultivation, some people suddenly develop thoughts of greed, anger, lust, jealousy, scorn and doubt. They may also suffer delusion, leading to drowsiness and sleep. These thoughts sometimes arise with great intensity, making the practitioner feel annoyed and upset over, at times, trivial matters. Sometimes auspicious and evil events alternate in his dreams. The

specific details of these events are too numerous to be described. Faced with these occurrences, the practitioner should realize that these karmic marks have appeared as a consequence of his cultivation. He should immediately understand that all karmic occurrences and marks are illusory and dream-like; he should foster right thought and they will disappear one after another. Otherwise, he will certainly be swayed, lose his concentration and retrogress.

The ancients used to say in this respect: Do not fear an early manifestation of evil karma, fear only a late Awakening. Sometimes the practitioner, in the midst of intense cultivation, suddenly becomes confused and weary, which is a state difficult to fight off. At that very moment, he should arise and bow to the Buddhas or circumambulate the altar. Or else, he may take a temporary break, read a few pages of a book or rearrange some flowers, waiting for his mind to calm down before returning to the altar to resume recitation. Otherwise, the more he tries to focus his mind, the more scattered it becomes. This is a case of flexibility in cultivation. It is similar to the situation of a commander-in-chief facing an invading army as powerful as a river overflowing its banks. In such a situation, the general should stay on the defensive, consolidating his position, rather than charging into battle. Some practictioners suddenly feel solitary and isolated when reciting the Buddha's name like a single-note musical piece, and grow melancholy and bored. In such cases, they should not hesitate to add mantra or sutra recitation or visualization to their practice.

2. *EXTERNAL 'TESTING CONDITIONS'*

These are external obstacles creating difficult conditions which can make the practitioner retrogress. These obstacles include heat, noise, dirt and pollution, freezing weather, or an outbreak of insects. When faced with these conditions, the cultivator should be flexible and not become attached to forms and appearances. He should just seek tranquillity and peace of mind. For instance, in sweltering heat, he should not mind donning a light robe to bow to the Buddhas, and then retiring to a shady spot outdoors to recite the Buddha's name. At the end of the session, he can return to the altar to make his vows and transfer the merit. If the practitioner happens to be living in a mosquito-infested area, he can sit inside a net while reciting the Buddha's name. As another example, in northern climes, where the weather can be freezing, monks and nuns must dress carefully in socks, shoes and hats when going to the Buddha hall to recite sutras. Other people, with heavy karmic obstructions, do not experience untoward occurrences as long as they do not cultivate, but as soon as they are ready to bow before the altar, they develop headaches, grow dizzy, and are afflicted with all kinds of ailments. Or else, they may receive sudden visitors or encounter unusual events. Faced with these occurrences, the practitioner should redouble his efforts and find ways to cultivate flexibly. These ways depend on circumstances; they cannot all be described. One point, however, should always be kept in mind: when faced with difficult circumstances, pay attention to the mind, and do not cling to appearances and forms. The evil, turbid Saha World has always been full of suffering and tears. Without perseverance and forbearance, it is very difficult to succeed in cultivation.

3. *TESTING CONDITIONS CAUSED BY ADVERSE CIRCUMSTANCES.*
Practitioners on the path of cultivation are at times impeded by adverse circumstances. Some are prevented from cultivating or frustrated in their practice by parents, brothers and sisters, wives, husbands or children. Others suddenly develop a chronic disease, from which they never completely recover. Still others are continually pursued by opponents and enemies looking for ways to harm them. Others are slandered or meet with misfortunes which land them in prison, subject to torture, or they are sent into exile. Others, again, victims of jealous competition or calumny, lose all peace of mind. This last occurrence is the most frequent. Such cases occur because of the power of evil karma. The ancients had a saying: 'There are instances of sudden praise and unexpected honors which are undeserved, and other instances, not deserving of blame, which create major opportunities for censure and contempt.'

4. *TESTING CONDITIONS CAUSED BY 'FAVORABLE*

CIRCUMSTANCES'.

Some practitioners do not encounter adverse circumstances, but on the contrary, meet with favorable circumstances, such as having their wishes and prayers fulfilled. However, such successes belong to the category of 'binding' conditions, rather than conditions conducive to liberation. Thus, just as some practitioners set their minds to peaceful cultivation, they suddenly encounter opportunities leading to fame and fortune, 'beautiful forms and enchanting sounds.' Or else, family members, relatives and supporters seek to follow and serve them on their retreats. For example, a monk who has made up his mind to cultivate in earnest may suddenly be requested to become the abbot of a large temple complex. Or else, a layman may unexpectedly receive a letter inviting him to become a minister heading such and such a government department, or offering him the chance to participate in a business venture which promises a quick profit. These instances, all of which are advantageous under mundane circumstances, are seductive to the cultivator, and may gradually lead to other complications. Ultimately, he may forget his high aspirations and retrogress. As the saying goes, more lives are lost in a flood than in a fire. Thus, on the path of cultivation, favorable circumstances should be feared more than unfavorable ones. Unfavorable events sometimes awaken the practitioner, making it easier for him to escape thoughts of attachment and redouble his efforts in cultivation. Favorable events, on the other hand, may make him quietly retrogress, without being aware of it. When he suddenly awakens, he may discover that he has slipped far down the slope. The ancients have said: 'Even two or three favorable circumstances may cause one to be deluded until old age.'

This saying is truly a ringing bell to wake cultivators up. Therefore, the challenge of favorable events is very subtle -- practioners need to pay close attention to them.

5. *TESTING CONDITIONS OF A CLEAR, EXPLICIT NATURE.*

These are clear 'testing conditions' which occur right before the practitioner's eyes, without his realizing their implications. For instance, a monk of relatively mediocre talents and virtues becomes the object of adulation, praised for great merit, virtue and talent. He then develops a big ego and looks down on everyone, giving rise to thoughtless action resulting in his downfall. Or else we have the case of a layman with the potential to progress far along the Way. However he is blocked and opposed by others, who advise him, for example, that vegetarianism will make him sick, or that overly diligent mantra and Buddha Recitation will 'unleash his evil karma,' causing him to encounter many untoward events. He then develops a cautious, anxious attitude, retrogressing in his determination to achieve the Way. There are also circumstances in which the practitioner realizes that to advance further is to invite failure and defeat, yet, out of ambition or pride, he continues all the same. Or else, even though the cultivator knows that external circumstances are illusory and dream-like, he cannot let go of them, and thus brings great suffering upon himself. For example, there was once a monk who spent a good deal of effort and money hiring stonecutters, carpenters and masons to build a large temple complex on top of a mountain. As soon as the temple was completed, the monk, by then completely exhausted, became gravely ill. Before passing away, he requested his disciples to carry him around the temple on a hammock, as he touched each and every stone, weeping and lamenting!

6. *SILENT, HIDDEN TESTING CONDITIONS.*

This refers to silent challenges, inconspicuous in nature. If the practitioner is not skillful in taking notice, they are very difficult to recognize and defeat. Some people, who may have recited the Buddha's name diligently in the beginning, grow worried and discouraged by deteriorating family finances or repeated failures in whatever they undertake, and abandon cultivation. Others see their affairs quietly progressing in a favorable way; they then become attached to profit and gain, forgetting all about the Way. Others diligently engage in Buddha and Sutra Recitation at the beginning, but because they fail to examine themselves, the afflictions within their minds increase with each passing day. They then grow lethargic and lazy, to the point where they do not recite a single time for months, or even years. Still others, although their lives are progressing normally, see their living conditions continuously fluctuating with changing external circumstances. With their minds always in confusion and directed toward the outside, they unwittingly neglect recitation or abandon it altogether. All the above are the fluctuating effects of good and bad karma, which have the power to influence the practitioner and retard his cultivation. They are therefore called 'trying, testing conditions.' When first taking up cultivation, every practitioner has a seed of good intentions. However, as they encounter karmic conditions, one after another, both internal and external, ninety-nine cultivators out of a hundred will fail. The ancients had a saying: 'In the first year of cultivation, Buddha Amitabha is right before our eyes; the second year, He has already returned West; by the third year, if someone inquires about Him or requests recitation [at a funeral, for example], payment is required before a few words are spoken or a few verses recited.' This saying reflects the points

just discussed; practitioners should bear them in mind and take heed."
Tam: 247 #2004
For details on how to counter the obstacles to cultivation, *See also:* "Ten Non-Seeking Practices"

◙ **OCCULT WORLD**
see Spirit world

◙ **OCEAN**
Syn: Sea

►"The term 'Ocean' symbolizes i m m e n s i t y , d e p t h , immeasurability, one's self-nature, the Mind. It is our original home and natural state (the source of our own minds: the Buddha's wisdom)."
xxx: na
"Oceans/seas are also used to symbolize immensity, depth, immeasureability. Oceans and clouds represent clusters or groups."
Clea/84: 22 #1221

◙ **OCEAN OF LANDS**
see Ocean of worlds

◙ **OCEAN OF WORLDS**
Syn: Ocean of lands

►The cosmos as seen by the Buddha consisting of worlds upon

worlds *ad infinitum*. #1261

◙ **OCEAN SEAL SAMADHI**

▸A method or state of concentration of the highest level, mentioned in the *Avatamsaka Sutra*. The mind is likened to the ocean, which when calm and without a single wave, can reflect everything throughout the cosmos -- past, present and future.
Editor/Tam: 344

"The 'ocean seal' is the fundamental awareness of true thusness. When delusion ends, the mind is clear and myriad forms simultaneously appear. It is like the ocean: due to the wind there arise waves; if the wind stops, the ocean water is calm and clear, and all images can be reflected. Thus Ocean Seal Samadhi refers to holistic, impartial awareness."
[TC/SHO, p.76] #0961

◙ **OCEAN-WIDE LOTUS ASSEMBLY**

▸The Lotus Assembly represents the gathering of Buddha Amitabha, the Bodhisattvas, the sages and saints and all other superior beings in the Land of Ultimate Bliss. This Assembly is "Ocean-Wide" as the participants are infinite in number -- spreading as far and wide as the multitude of oceans in the Dharma Realm (the cosmos).
The term Ocean-Wide Assembly is generally associated with the *Avatamasaka Sutra*, a text particularly prized by the Pure Land and Zen schools alike.
Editor/Tam: 157 #0913

◙ **OEDIPUS STORY**
see Utpala

◙ **OFFERINGS**
See also: Dana

▸"Buddhist texts often contain ideal, stereotypical, or normative lists of the items to be offered in ritual worship. These lists usually contain most or all of the following: flowers, garlands, instrumental music, ointment, parasols, lamps, incense, cloths (robes), perfumes, and flags and banners."
Gomez: 313-314

Among the various offerings to the Buddhas, the offering of the Dharma is the highest because it enables the audience to transcend Birth and Death and ultimately attain Buddhahood. The offering of the Dharma is generally understood as spreading the Dharma through lectures or the

printing of sutras and
commentaries.
Editor/Saman: 49 #1719

◙ **OJO YOSHU**
See also: Genshin

▸"(Essentials of Rebirth): a
collection of the principles
essential for birth in Amitabha's
Pure Land, written by the
Japanese Tendai monk Genshin
(942-1017)."

"A collection of scriptural
quotations outlining religious
practices that lead to birth in
Pure Land. It was compiled in
985 by the Japanese Buddhist
priest Genshin (942-1017) of the
Tendai school. The primary
practice that he advocated was
the Nembutsu (invoking the
name of the Buddha Amida).

Genshin considered the
Nembutsu best used in
conjunction with meditation on
Amida and his Pure Land, but
for believers untrained in
meditative techniques *he
recommended simple chanting of
the name*. The Ojo Yoshu made
a strong impression on Pure
Land Buddhists because of its
graphic descriptions of the
splendors of Pure Land and the
terrors of hells. It became

popular as a religious handbook
on ways of performing the
Nembutsu, including a deathbed
ceremony involving Nembutsu
chanting and meditation."
Oxf: 712 #0641
NOTE:
See also Lotus sutra and
T'ien-t'ai school for an
explanation of the close
relationship between the
T'ien-t'ai and Pure Land schools.

◙ **OLCOTT, H.S. (*COL.*)**
--- --------------------------------------
▸(1832-1906.) "Founder with H.P.
Blavatsky of the Theosophical
Society in 1875. Organizer of the
Buddhist revival in Sri Lanka.
Author of *Buddhist Catechism*,
and compiler of the *Fourteen
Fundamental Buddhist Beliefs*."
Hump: 140-141
Olcott also designed the
multicolored Buddhist flag used
nowadays throughout the world.
Editor: na #0423

◙ **OM MANI / AUM MANI**
See also: Avalokitesvara; Great
Compassion Mantra

▸"The syllable A U M, usually
spelt OM, is an invocation of
multiple symbolic meaning and
ritual uses. Each constituent
letter has its own meaning of

profound power. It precedes, pronounced as only an initiate knows how, the Tibetan formula Om Mani Padme Hum."
Hump: 38
"Avalokitesvara's outstanding characteristic is the virtue of compassion. In order to rescue beings from suffering, she is said to descend into the deepest hell. She is invoked by calling her name or by the famous mantra 'Om mani padme hum' which refers either to the Absolute that is contained in everything, or to the wish-fulfilling jewel which Avalokitesvara keeps in the hollow of her hands, palms held together, in the form of a lotus bud."
Wolfg: 115
The mantra "Om Mani Padme Hum" is recited by Buddhists of many Mahayana schools; however, its main proponents are found in Tibetan Buddhism.
#0474

◙ **OMENS OF PURE LAND REBIRTH**
see   Proofs of rebirth in Pure Land

◙ **ONCE-RETURNER**
See also: Arhatship

▸"An enlightened being in the second stage of the Theravada path, who has realized the Four Noble Truths and has eradicated a great portion of defilements. He will return to the human world for only one more rebirth before he reaches full realization of Arhatship."
Chan: 480

A sage who has only one rebirth left before reaching Arhatship and escaping birth and death.
Editor/Tam: 157 #0545

◙ **ONE FLAVOR**
see   Same flavor

◙ **ONE HUNDRED AND EIGHT CONCENTRATIONS**

▸"The total number of concentrations spoken of in the major *Prajna-Paramita Sutra* is reckoned to be one hundred and eight."
Chih-I/Cleary: 200

◙ **ONE IN ALL**
see   One is all, All is one

◙ **ONE IN ONE**
see   One is all, All is one

◙ **ONE IS ALL, ALL IS ONE**
Syn: One in One; One in All; All in One

See also: Buddha Recitation Samadhi

▸Key teaching of the *Avatamsaka Sutra* / school. Expresses the essential unity of all things and all phenomena, a major tenet of Mahayana Buddhism.

Editor: na

"Enlightenment, then, sees 'one in one,' 'one in all,' 'all in one,'and 'all in all,' according to the formula of the first [Avatamsaka] Patriarch, Tu Shun (556-640). No viewpoint is rejected, for each one implies all the rest. No being or object is regarded as unimportant, for each embodies the whole of reality, and one's senses (to quote William Blake...) discover 'the infinite in everything.'

This makes possible true *compassion*, which means treating everything, whether animate or inanimate, with respect, because its value is literally infinite; while the task of wisdom is not to become enlightened, but rather to actualize the Enlightenment which all beings already possess in full." (Tony Prince) TP/TSPH6,p.136] #1235

◙ **ONE LIFETIME LIBERATION**
see Liberation in One Lifetime

◙ **ONE PRACTICE SAMADHI**
see Buddha Recitation Samadhi

◙ **ONE VEHICLE**
Syn: Buddha Vehicle; Buddha-Yana; Buddhayana; Ekayana; Tathagata Vehicle
See also: Mahayana Buddhism; Theravada Buddhism

▸"Also called the Buddhayana (Buddha Vehicle), the Mahayana doctrine which contains the final and complete Dharma of the Buddha and not merely a part, or a preliminary stage, as in the Southern Vehicle. It is often identified with the teaching of the *Lotus* and *Avatamsaka Sutras*."
BDK: 352 #1089

"Synonymous with the Buddha-Bodhisattva vehicle and the Mahayana ('Great Vehicle'). 'Bodhisattva vehicle' is used when referring to the cause and practice, while 'Tathagata vehicle' is used when referring to the result." Chan: 484 #0576

◙ **ONE-LIFE BODHISATTVA**
See also: Non-Retrogression

▸A Bodhisattva who is one lifetime away from Buddhahood. The best known example is the Bodhisattva Maitreya.
Editor/Tam: 344 #0962

◙ **ONE-POINTED MIND**
see   One-pointedness of mind

◙ **ONE-POINTEDNESS OF MIND**
Syn: Single-Mindedness;
One-pointed Mind
See also: Pure Land Buddhism
(Summary); Rebirth in the Pure
Land

▸ Single-mindedness or
singleminded concentration. In
Pure Land Buddhism,
achievement of one-pointedness
of mind (or single-mindedness),
is an *absolute necessary condition*
for achieving rebirth in the Pure
Land. (See Rebirth in the Pure
Land)
Editor / Tam: 344
"In this day and age, I have come
across many people who do not
try to concentrate at all, but
recite the Buddha's name with a
scattered mind and languid voice.
As a consequence, we find very
few persons whose efforts have
succeeded during their lifetime,
and occurrences of miraculous
response at the time of death are
[for the most part] weak. For this
reason I have made a special
effort to explain this practice
here. I urge that whenever you
perform recollection of the
Buddha, you do so with
one-pointedness of mind free of

confusion, chanting the Buddha's
name loudly in a steady stream
of invocations. Before long your
efforts will bring success (Master
Zunshi)."
Lopez/95: 370
The concept of one-pointedness
of mind is understood in two
ways. For the Patriarchs Chih-i
and Ou-i and others of the
T'ien-t'ai, Zen and Avatamsaka
traditions, it is equivalent to
concentration and samadhi. For
Pure Land Patriarchs such as
Tao-ch'o and Shan-tao, on the
other hand, it refers to recitation
with utmost faith in Amitabha
Buddha and the Pure Land. The
two concepts are in essence the
same (to recite with utmost faith
necessarily leads to concentration
and samadhi).
Editor: na
*One-pointedness of mind,
Complete faith, or utter sincerity:*
in practice, these expressions are
used interchangeably, as a
cultivator cannot have *complete*
faith without being *utterly sincere*
and singleminded (and vice
versa).
Editor/Tam: 305
Pure Land Buddhism
In the *Meditation Sutra*, the
Buddha taught that if a person,
on the verge of death, can recite
the Buddha's name ten times

singlemindedly, he will be reborn in the Pure Land. The passage raises several questions pertinent to Pure Land teachings that require clarification:

(a) *Singleminded recitation.* On the everyday level, this means focussing on Buddha Amitabha and Buddha Amitabha alone, to the exclusion of all other thoughts while reciting the Buddha's name. At a deeper level, the practitioner always focuses on Buddha Amitabha, be it during reciting sessions or outside of such sessions, when he is engaged in mundane activities -- i.e., at all times.

(b) *Singleminded recitation of the Buddha's name ten times (or from one to seven days).* According to the *Amitabha Sutra*, to achieve rebirth in the Pure Land, it is necessary to recite the Buddha's name from one to seven days to the level of one-pointedness of mind (i.e., singleminded concentration). This, as any practitioner can attest, is an extremely difficult condition -- one which very few cultivators can ever hope to fulfill. Therefore, in the *Meditation Sutra*, the Buddha taught an alternate way: to recite the name of Amitabha Buddha with one-pointedness of mind *ten times at the time of death*. Please note, however, that this is a solution *in-extremis*, as at the time of death we are like turtles being skinned alive! The crucial condition is one-pointedness of mind, which has been rendered variously as "with all one's heart", "without inversion", "with one Mind", "in all sincerity", "with utmost faith", etc. Unless the cultivator fulfills this condition, his mind will not be on the same wave length as that of Buddha Amitabha. Thus, he will not be in a position to take advantage of Amitabha Buddha's vow and achieve rebirth in the Pure Land.

(c) *Scattered Mind Recitation.* Although the aim of Buddha Recitation is one-pointedness of Mind, recitation with a scattered Mind also leads to accumulation of merits, albeit on a much smaller scale. This is because everything has its source in the Mind; thus, all recitation springs, by necessity, from some degree of purity of Mind.

Editor: na   #0963

NOTE:

According to the sutras, "Whether a practitioner focusses on the Buddha constantly throughout his life, or recites assiduously for three months, or forty-nine days, or one to seven days and nights, or recites only ten times each morning, as long as the practitioner holds the Buddha's name with deep faith and fervent vows, like a dragon encountering water or a tiger hidden deep in the mountains, he will be assisted by the Buddha's power and achieve rebirth in the Pure Land." [A dragon outside the ocean or a tiger without the protection of the forest has but one thought in mind: to return to its environment ... Recitation requires the same singleminded intensity.]   PL/Dia: 60

The level of sincerity and devotion required for one-pointedness of mind and rebirth in the Pure land is illustrated by the following story from the *Nirvana Sutra*:

"At that time Sessen Doji [a previous incarnation of Buddha Sakyamuni] had mastered the Brahman and other non-Buddhist teachings but had not yet heard of Buddhism. The god Indra decided to test his resolve. He appeared before Sessein Doji in the form of a hungry demon and recited half a verse from a Buddhist teaching: 'All is changeable, nothing is constant. This is the law of Birth and Death.' Hearing this, Sessen Doji begged the demon to tell him the second half. The demon agreed but demanded his flesh and blood in payment. Sessen Doji gladly consented and the demon taught him the latter half of the verse: 'Extinguishing the cycle of Birth and Death, one enters the joy of Nirvana.' Sessen Doji scrawled this teaching on the rocks and trees for the sake of others who might pass by, and then jumped from a tall tree into the demon's mouth. Just at that moment the Demon changed back into the god Indra and caught him before he fell. He praised Sessen Doji's willingness to give his life for the Dharma and predicted that he would certainly attain Buddhahood."   Sokk: 374

◙ **ONIONS**
see Herbs (Pungent)

◙ **ORAL RECITATION (TEN VARIATIONS)**
See also: Ten Recitations Method

▸*NB.* Please read the entry Buddha Recitation (Methods) before the following excerpts from "*Buddhism of Wisdom and Faith*" (*Master T. Thien Tam*). "Oral Recitation is the most common Pure Land method at the present time. However, this method has many variations to

accommodate the circumstances and capacities of the individual. A few of these variants are summarized below.

1. *REFLECTING THE NAME RECITATION*. With this technique, the ear catches the sound as the mouth recites, examining each individual word and each individual phrase, to make sure they are clear and distinct, phrase after phrase. There are two ways of hearing, with the ears or with the mind. Although the ears 'hear deep inside,' the sounds do not reside anywhere. The practitioner gradually forgets everything inside and out -- even body, mind, realm, time and space -- with only the Buddha's name remaining. This technique of 'reflecting the name,' makes it easy for the cultivator to filter out deluded thoughts and swiftly achieve one-pointedness of mind. The *Surangama Sutra* expresses this very idea when it states, in the words of the Bodhisattva Manjusri: This common method of concentrating the mind on its sense of hearing, turning it inward ... is most feasible and wise. (Wai-tao, tr. The *Surangama Sutra*, in D. Goddard, ed., *Buddhist Bible*, p 260.)

2. *COUNTING ROSARY BEADS RECITATION*. In this method, as the mouth recites, the hand fingers the rosary. At first, thoughts are tied to the rosary beads, but later on they gradually move away from the beads, leading to the state of one-pointedness of mind. This technique increases the power of recitation in the same way that a cane enables a mountain climber with weak legs to ascend higher and higher. With this technique, we should write down the number of recitations per session or per day. This has the advantage of forcing us to keep an exact count, eliminating the affliction of laziness. However, we should take care not to be too ambitious, attempting to achieve too much too soon, or our recitation will not be clear and distinct. The ancients, while reciting the Buddha's name over and over, did so in a clear, distinct manner thanks to two factors: 'correct understanding' and 'correct concentration of mind.'

3. *BREATH-BY-BREATH RECITATION*. This technique consists of reciting silently or softly, with each breath, inhaling or exhaling, accompanied by one recitation of the Buddha's name.

Since life is linked to breath, if we take advantage of breath while practicing Buddha Recitation, we will not be apart from Buddha Amitabha in life, and at the time of death, when breath has stopped, we will be immediately reborn in the Pure Land. The practitioner should remember, however, that once he has mastered this technique, he should recite aloud as well as silently. In this way, the power of recitation will be strengthened and the will to be reborn in the Pure Land more easily developed. Otherwise, his resolve will not be earnest and he might 'stray' into the practice of the 'Five Meditations to calm the mind' of the Theravada tradition.

4. *CONTINUOUSLY LINKED RECITATION.* With this technique, the practitioner recites softly, each word following the one immediately before, each phrase closely following the previous phrase... During this practice, through discretion and patience, there are no empty time frames and therefore 'sundry thoughts' cannot intrude. The cultivator's feelings and thoughts are intense, his mind and words move boldly forward reciting the Buddha's name; the power of right thought embraces everything, temporarily subduing ignorance and delusive thought. Thus, the light of transcendental samadhi breaks through and shines forth. From early times, Pure Land practitioners would avail themselves of this method when their emotions and thoughts wandered or were in a state of confusion.

5. *ENLIGHTENED, ILLUMINATING RECITATION.* With this technique, the practitioner on the one hand recites the Buddha's name and on the other, 'returns the light' and illumines his True Nature. He thus enters into the realm of ultimate transcendental emptiness; what remains is only the consciousness that his body-mind and the True Mind of the Buddha have become one -- all-illuminating and all-encompassing. At that time, meditation rooms, cushions, gongs and all else have disappeared. Even the illusory, 'composite body' is nowhere to be found.

6. *BOWING TO THE BUDDHA RECITATION.* This technique consists of making bows as we recite the Buddha's name. Either we recite once before each bow or we bow as we recite, regardless of the number of

recitations. The bowing should be supple yet deliberate, complementing recitation, bowing and reciting perfectly synchronized. If we add a sincere and earnest mind, body, speech and mind are gathered together. Except for the words Amitabha Buddha, there is not the slightest *deluded* thought. This method has the ability to destroy the karma of drowsiness. Its benefits are very great, because the practitioner engages in recitation with his body, speech and mind. A lay practitioner of old used to follow this method. Each day and night, he would bow and recite an average of one thousand times. However, this practice is the particular domain of those with strong mind-power. Lacking this quality, it is difficult to persevere, because with extended bowing, the body easily grows weary, leading to discouragement. Therefore, this method is normally used in conjunction with other methods and is not practiced in exclusivity.

7. *DECIMAL RECORDING RECITATION.* This is the inscription technique of Buddha Recitation, taking each ten utterances of the Buddha's name as a unit. Individuals with short breath spans can divide the ten utterances into two subunits (five utterances each) or three smaller subunits (two three-utterance units and one four-utterance unit). One rosary bead is fingered after each group of ten utterances is completed. With this practice, the mind must not only recite, it must also remember the number of utterances. In this way, if we are not diligent we must become so; otherwise, it will be impossible to avoid mistakes. This technique, in general, is an excellent expedient forcing the cultivator to concentrate his mind and is very effective with those subject to many errant thoughts. Elder Master Yin Kuang used to recommend it to Pure Land practitioners.

8. *LOTUS BLOSSOM RECITATION.* As he recites, the practitioner contemplates the four colors of the lotus blossom (blue, yellow, red and white), one color after another without interruption. With his first utterance of the Buddha's name, he visualizes a huge, blue lotus blossom before his eyes, emitting a blue light. With the second utterance, he visualizes a yellow lotus blossom, emitting a yellow light. The third and fourth

utterances are accompanied, respectively, by visualization of red and white lotus flowers, each color emitting its own light. He then repeats the visualization in the same sequence. As the flowers appear, he imagines a vague, lingering touch of pure, soft lotus fragrance. Ancient masters devised this method because many practitioners in the T'ien T'ai School, despite using all available techniques, found it difficult to stem their errant thoughts. This method uses various forms and colors to focus mind and thought. These forms and colors take the marks of lotus blossoms in the Seven-Jewel Pond of the Pure Land ('one utterance of the Buddha's name, one jewelled lotus blossom'), because the lotus blossoms appearing in the Pure Land are inseparable from the lotus blossoms created by the virtues of the reciting mind. At the time of death, the mind-consciousness of the practitioner relies on these jewelled lotus blossoms to achieve rebirth in the Western Pure Land. If the Pure Land cultivator should discover that he has an affinity with this technique, he should apply it and quickly enter the Wonderful Lotus Blossom Buddha Recitation Samadhi.

9. *RECITATION AMIDST LIGHT*. This method was specially designed for certain practitioners who, as soon as they close their eyes to recite, suddenly see filthy forms and marks (ugly grimacing faces, for example), or dark forms and colors swirling around. With this technique, the practitioner, while reciting the Buddha's name, visualizes himself seated in the middle of an immense, brilliant zone of light. Within that zone of light, when his mind has quieted down, the practitioner feels bright and refreshed. At that time, not only have deluded thoughts been annihilated, but filthy, evil forms have also disappeared. After that, right thought is reinforced and samadhi is, in time, achieved. Although this is a special expedient to destroy evil deluded marks, even the practitioner who is not in this predicament can apply this method to clear his mind and enter deeply into the Buddha Recitation Samadhi.

10. *'CONTEMPLATION OF THE BUDDHA' RECITATION*. The methods of contemplation taught in the *Meditation Sutra* are very important and lead to immense virtue, but they are not a popular expedient for sentient beings in

the Dharma-Ending Age. Nevertheless, since the ancient masters did not wish to see the special benefits of the meditation method go unused, they selected the easiest of the Sixteen Contemplations (Contemplation of Amitabha Buddha) and combined it with Oral Recitation to form the Contemplation of the Buddha-Oral Recitation technique. (Recitation is predominant, while contemplation is secondary.) Each day, after reciting the Buddha's name, the practitioner reserves a special period of time for concentrating his mind and contemplating the Embellishments and Light of Amitabha Buddha. This method is derived from Contemplation Number Thirteen in the *Meditation Sutra*, in which Buddha Amitabha is visualized as some sixteen feet tall and of golden hue, standing at the edge of the Seven-Jewel Pond. If the practitioner cannot yet visualize the Seven-Jewel Pond, he can picture Amitabha Buddha standing before his eyes in a zone of light, in open space, the left hand held at chest level and forming the auspicious mudra, the right arm extending downward in the position of

'welcoming and guiding.' To be successful in this meditation, it is necessary, at the outset, to visualize the body of Amitabha Buddha in general, then concentrate on the urna (white mark between the eyebrows). This mark is empty and transparent, like a white gem with eight facets ... The urna is the basic mark among the thirty-two auspicious marks of the Buddhas. When this visualization is successful, thanks to the affinity thus created between Amitabha Buddha and the practitioner, other marks will appear clearly, one after another.

However, to ensure success, the practitioner should read through the *Meditation Sutra*, memorizing the thirty-two auspicious marks of Buddha Amitabha before commencing his practice. With this method, Buddha Recitation should be primary, because if the practitioner does not succeed at visualization, he can still fall back on recitation to ensure rebirth in the Pure Land. In truth, however, recitation aids visualization and visualization complements recitation, so that these two aspects work in parallel, leading the practitioner toward the desired goal.

Although this technique is somewhat more difficult than the others, if it can be accomplished successfully, immeasurable benefits are achieved. It is therefore described here at the very end, to foster diligent practice.

As stated earlier, these ten variants of Oral Recitation are also the ten basic techniques to combat the various mental hindrances faced by Buddha Recitation practitioners. Pure Land books discuss several dozen variants. However, they are merely techniques using, *inter alia*, a loud voice or a low voice, at busy moments or at times of leisure. They cannot as such qualify as methods of recitation. For this reason, the author has singled out these ten basic variants of Oral Recitation to combat the obstructions of drowsiness and mind-scattering. They are the methods best suited to the majority of today's practitioners. The cultivator can try them out and select the one that fits his particular case."

Tam: 120-128

For details, *See also* Ten Recitations Method #2000

◉ **ORDER (BUDDHIST)**

see Sangha

◉ **ORDINATION**

See also: Sacerdotal Age; Pratimoksa

►"Ordinations in Buddhism [especially in Theravada] are not considered lifelong commitments. At any time, a monk or nun may voluntarily elect to leave the monastic community and return to lay life."

Preb: 207

"Ordination, in Buddhism, is initiation into the Buddhist Order (Sangha) in the presence of witnesses (i.e., members of Sangha), and self-dedication to monastic life... It is not necessarily life-long or unrepeatable. There are two kinds of Buddhist Ordination: the lower, by which a man becomes a samanera or novice; the higher by which a novice becomes a monk (bhikkhu). The more formal ceremony for admission of a novice who intends to become a monk subsequently consists of a candidate's being brought before a chapter of at least 10 monks, headed by an abbot or senior monk of at least ten years' standing, and taking part in set form for the ordaining of novices and monks. This is held in the sanctuary (vihara). The candidate kneels, and asks for admission as novice, handing to the abbot two yellow robes in which he is to be ordained. The abbot then formally presents to him these robes, reminding him of the frailty and impermanence of the human body which they are to cover. The candidate receives them, and retires to put them on; as he does so he recites a formula reminding himself that his robes are worn as protection against cold and heat and to cover nakedness, and that he wears them in all humility, for use and not for ornament. He then returns, makes obeisance, and asks to have administered to him the Three Refuges and Ten Precepts. Having received them from the abbot, repeating them sentence by sentence, he makes obeisance, seeks forgiveness by his brethren of all faults and declares his wish to share with his brethren any merit he has gained. The samanera spends his time in a monastery learning the life of the Sangha, helping with daily chores, etc. He does not attend recitation, twice monthly, of Pratimoksa (q.v.); this is attended only by bhikkhus. *When a novice subsequently seeks higher ordination (upasampada) as monk*, he first goes through the form for the ordination of a novice again; this is then followed by a further and longer ceremony of ordination in the course of which a candidate must be able to answer satisfactorily a list of questions concerning his status and condition (whether he is free from disease, debt, obligation to serve in the military, is 20 years of age, etc.). He is presented by one of his two tutors. On this occasion, the three robes, including a stole, are presented. These are then ceremonially returned to him by the abbot. An address is then given by the abbot, or president, in which the new bhikkhu is reminded of the glory of the life of a bhikkhu, and of the high moral standards which must now be his, and the chaste, honest, peaceable and humble life he must live. Ordinations are held at any time of the year except the three months of Vesak. The actual date is agreed upon in consultation with the abbot of the monastery where the ordination is to be carried out, which is usually in the man's home village. A favorite time is just before Vesak since it is the Vesak period alone which is reckoned in counting years of service as a monk."

Ling: 200

MAHAYANA BUDDHISM
"In Mahayana, a type of ordination appears, that of the Bodhisattva ordination, on which occasion the ordinand (who can be a lay person or a monastic) takes the formal vow of the Bodhisattva: to gain complete, perfect enlightenment for the sake of all sentient beings." See Bodhisattva Precepts.
Preb: 207
Note: In the Mahayana tradition, there is some stigma attached to a monk or nun leaving the Order, as the departing cleric is seen as a destitute person electing to leave a treasure island empty-handed.
Editor/na #1054

◎ **ORGAN DONATION**
See also: Death (physical vs mental); Death and Burial (Between--)

▸"In general, offering parts of one's body for the benefit of others is virtuous. Nowadays, this is much easier than in the past because a kidney, for example, can frequently be transplanted from one person to another without great complications. However, each case must be regarded separately, depending on one's motivation and the other's condition. Donating one's organs after death is a choice that will vary from person to person, depending on each individual's state of mind and level of spiritual practice. In some cases, removing organs after the heart has stopped but before the consciousness has left could interrupt the death process and be [utterly] detrimental..."
Buddhist Union: 6
"With more than 50,000 Americans on waiting lists for organ transplants... federally supervised organ procurement organizations have become increasingly aggressive about pursuing those whose hearts have stopped. In some cases, hospitals have acted to preserve organs, *possibly causing pain and hastening death*, before family members could be found to give consent. Of 63 federally supervised organ procurement organizations, researchers found that fewer than half had written standards ... The Institute [of Medicine, National Academy of Sciences, USA] recommended in its report [Dec. 97] that these national standards be established: i. Discussion of organ donation with families should take place only after a family has made an

independent decision to withdraw life support; ii. A five-minute wait should be required after life support is withdrawn and before organ recovery begins to insure that a heart would not resume beating on its own; iii. Families should be allowed to attend the death of organ donors ...iv. The doctor who declares death should not be involved with an organ procurement organization."
NY Times: 12/21/97.
On the important question of physical vs. mental death, see Death and Burial (Between--)

◉ ORIGINAL NATURE
see   Buddha nature

◉ ORIGINAL VOWS
Syn: Eighteenth Vow
See also: Dharmakara's Vows; Longer Amitabha Sutra; Exclusion Clause

----
▸"The vows which Bodhisattvas make when they resolve to become Buddhas and save all sentient beings; in the Pure Land sutras they refer to Boddhisattva Dharmakara's 48 Vows."
Inag: 409
Pure Land Buddhism
"The forty-eight (48) vows of Dharmakara are set forth in the *Longer Amitabha Sutra*. In the

eighteenth, Bodhisattva Dharmakara vowed that after he attained Buddhahood, all people who put their hopes of salvation in him would be reborn in the Pure Land, excepting those who had committed any of the five cardinal sins or slandered the Dharma." (See Exclusion Clause)
Sokk: 77-78
"In the *Surangama Sutra*, the Bodhisattva Mahastamaprapta says, 'It is like a mother thinking of her son. If the son has gone to roam...' If the son leaves his mother, it is hard for his mother to find him again. But if the son wants to find his mother, all he has to do is return home."
Hua/Root: 56
NOTE: "The Eighteenth (18th) vow of Dharmakara Bodhisattva -- to effect universal salvation before he sets foot in Nirvana -- is at the heart of Pure Land Buddhism. It represents the highest degree of the Buddha's compassion."*World Scripture*: 457

◉ ORNAMENTS

▸"Personal ornaments such as garlands and jewelry [on images of Buddhas and Bodhisattvas] represent virtues, knowledge, skills, or cultivation of faculties."
Clea/84: 22 #1984

◎ OTHER SHORE
See also: Paramita

►"The other shore of the stream of transmigration, the state of emancipation, i.e., Nirvana, beyond the realm of Samsara."
Inag: 409
"A metaphor for Enlightenment and Buddhahood."
Tam: 344
Returning to the shore: a metaphor for returning to the True Nature, the nature common to sentient beings and Buddhas -- the True Mind.
Editor/Zen: 103 #0714

◎ OTHER-POWER
Syn: Tariki
See also: Self-Power; Dedication of Merit; Other-Worldly

►"The power of the other, i.e., the Buddhas, particularly Amitabha. This term suggests the idea of seeking rebirth in the Pure Land by relying [principally] on the power of Amitabha. Other-power is used in contrast to self-power."
Dait: 349
"Sometimes it is suggested that the emphasis on devotion as providing a special kind of salvation is unnatural in Buddhism and alien to the earlier tradition. Yet even the earliest

form of Buddhism known to us taught that faith in the Buddha was able both to bring about a heavenly rebirth and to set one firmly on the path to liberation. The difference is in the Mahayana emphasis on the 'power of resolve' [other power] of a Buddha, which is capable of creating enormously favourable conditions."
Hinn: 324

(I) Other Power/ Self Power
"*Jiriki* (self-power) is the Wisdom aspect of enlightenment and *tariki* (other-power) is the ... Great Compassion aspect of the same. By wisdom we transcend the principle of individuation, and by Great Compassion we descend into a world of particulars. The one goes upwards while the other comes downwards, but this is our intellectual way of understanding and interpreting enlightenment, in whose movement however there is no such twofold direction discernible." (*The Eastern Buddhist*, Vol. 3. No. 4, p. 314.)
Suzuki: xxx

(II) Amitabha Buddha
"Other-power is a technical term indicating a religious attainment achieved through such activities as placing one's faith in the saving grace of a Buddha or

other religious figures. Other-power is almost always played off against 'Self-power', a term readily utilized in the Zen tradition to indicate a religious attainment achieved [mainly] through one's own striving. 'Other Power' is most often asssociated with the Pure Land tradition, in which rebirth in the Pure Land is obtained by chanting the Buddha's name."
Preb: 256

"As far as the question of 'self-power' vs. 'other-power' is concerned, it is wrong to understand the Pure Land method as exclusive reliance on Buddha Amitabha's power. The Pure Land practitioner should use all his own power to rid himself of afflictions, while reciting to the point where his mind and the Mind of Amitabha Buddha are in unison. At that moment, in this very life, [he will experience an awakening] and at his death, he will be welcomed and guided back to the Pure Land. The 'welcoming and escorting' feature is really the principal manifestation of 'other-power.' As an analogy, for a student to exert his own efforts to the utmost is, of course, a laudable thing. If, in addition, he has the benefit of an excellent

teacher who follows his progress and assists him, his level of achievement will be higher, resulting in assured success in his final examinations. Adding other-power to self-power is similar. Therefore, how can it be considered mistaken to exert all of our own efforts to cultivate and then seek additional help to achieve rapid success?" (from *Buddhism Wisdom and Faith*)
Tam: 74

(III) Medicine Buddha
"Invisible assistance -- provided by the Buddhas and Bodhisattvas of Healing -- can be a potent aid in this process [of elimination of the three poisons of lust, anger and delusion]. This assistance often is described as stemming from the force of their fundamental vows, which they made when they dedicated their lives to spiritual work. The vows to heal all beings and alleviate various sufferings serve as special motivating factors in their spiritual development. Upon fruition of their spiritual work ... they then truly become able to fulfill these vows." (Raoul Birnbaum, *The Healing Buddha*.)
Birn: xv

(IV) Note
The issue of other-power (Buddha's power) is often

misunderstood and glossed over by many Buddhists. However, it must be pointed out that, in Buddhism, other-power is absolutely necessary if a Bodhisattva is to attain Ultimate Enlightenment. The *Avatamsaka Sutra* (described by D.T. Suzuki as the epitome of Buddhist thought) and the *Lankavatara Sutra* (the only sutra recommended by Bodhidharma) are emphatically clear on this point:

"As long as [conversion] is an experience and not mere understanding, it is evident that self-discipline plays an important role in the Buddhist life... but... we must not forget the fact that the Lanka [*Lankavatara Sutra*] also emphasizes the necessity of the Buddha's power being added to the Bodhisattvas' in their upward course of spiritual development and in the accomplishment of their great task of world salvation. If they were not thus so constantly sustained by the miraculous power of the Buddha, they would speedily fall into the group of philosophers and Sravakas, and they would never be able to attain Supreme Enlightenment and preach the doctrine of

universal emancipation." (D.T. Suzuki, tr., the *Lankavatara Sutra*, p. xviii.)
See also: the following quote from the *Avatamsaka Sutra*: "Having purified wisdom and means in the seventh Stage .../ The great sages attain acceptance of non-origination .../ On the basis of their previous resolution,/ The Buddhas further exhort them .../ 'Though you have extinguished the burning of the fire of affliction,/ Having seen the world still afflicted, remember your past vows;/ Having thought of the welfare of the world, work in quest/ Of the cause of knowledge, for the liberation of the world.'" (T. Cleary, tr., *The Flower Ornament Sutra*, Vol II)
Clear: II/86   #0137

◎ OTHER-WORDLY
See also: Other-power; Pure Land Buddhism (Summary)

▶"Among the many varieties of Buddhism, the Pure Land teaching most deserves the epithet 'other-worldly,' often erroneously applied to Buddhism as a whole. Pure Land doctrine teaches that this world is an arena of unavoidable suffering and frustration, and holds out the

vivid prospect of rebirth in another, better world, where sickness, pain and death do not exist. This world is a hopeless trap, from which we can escape only by the power of Amitabha. Unless we attain rebirth in the Pure Land, peace and happiness, to say nothing of enlightenment, are beyond reach ... From a Buddhist perspective, it is the modern 'this-worldly' orientation to life that is a form of unrealistic escapism and unwarranted pessimism about human possibilities. It is unrealistic because it seeks the meaning of life in gratifications that can only be temporary and partial: it seeks escape from mortality in transient pleasures. It is unnecessarily pessimistic because it ignores or denies the transcendental capacity inherent in humankind: 'turning one's back on enlightenment to join with the dusts.'" (J.C. Cleary, *Pure Land, Pure Mind*, Introduction.)

"Here we find an important point of soteriological convergence between Pure Land ritual/meditative manuals and Pure Land hagiographical collections. In certain respects, it requires us to re-evaluate the way in which the long-range goal of rebirth in the Pure Land functions within the lives of Pure Land believers. It is easy, but perhaps ultimately misleading, to think of Pure Land spirituality as having a morbid obsession with death and the afterlife just because its stated aim is rebirth in Sukhavati. This is especially so if we are to take [Masters] Zunshi and Shandao (Shan tao) seriously when they claim that sustained practice of nienfo (Buddha Recitation) will bring a vision of the Buddha in this very life. In effect, such a vision of Amitabha does more than confirm that one is destined for the Pure Land in the near future, for it implies that one already has access to the Buddha now. Thus it becomes a mark of sainthood that is virtually equivalent (in anticipated form) to the irreversibility on the Bodhisattva path that will formally be achieved when one is reborn in the Pure Land itself. In this respect, *it represents a kind of Pure Land 'Enlightenment' experience* that is equally compelling and equally vital to establishing religious identity and authority as the 'seeing into one's original nature' of Chan (Zen)." Lopez/95: 595   #1765

◙ **OUTFLOWS**
See also: Dharma; Unconditioned
Dharmas; Conditioned Dharmas

▸"Sanskrit: asvara. Anything
which serves to divert beings
away from their inherent
Buddha-nature. 'Outflows' are so
called because they are turnings
of energy and attention outward
rather than inward. 'Outflows'
are ended by the practice of the
'Three Non-Outflow Study', i.e.,
morality, samadhi, and wisdom."
Hua: 231
"With outflows: leaking, i.e.,
worldly, mundane or conditioned,
inside the passion-stream.
Without outflows: without
leakage, transcendental or
unconditioned, outside the
passion-stream." Luk/1964: 220
NOTE:
Conditioned merits and virtues
(or Merits and Virtues "with
outflows") lead to rebirth within
Samsara, whereas unconditioned
merits and virtues are the cause
of liberation from Birth and
Death. Single-minded Buddha
Recitation leads to merit
"without outflows".
Editor/Tam: 146 #0870

◙ **OVEREATING**
See also: Vegetarianism; Food /
Food Rules

▸"There is much to be said for a
simple diet. Most people overeat,
and Seneca's observation that
men do not die naturally but kill
themselves with their knives and
forks is as true today as it was in
his time. No one who is troubled
by indigestion, chronic
constipation, and kindred ills
resulting from eating too much
or eating too-rich foods can carry
on Zen practice effectively.
Especially if one has a sedentary
job, exercises little, and
meditates long, to eat little is
better than to eat much.
A sparse diet helps Zen
meditation in yet another way, by
muting sexual desire and the
fantasies that it spawns. In fact,
during the deepest states of
samadhi the body requires little
or no food but seems to extract a
different kind of nourishment
from the atmosphere."
Kapleau: 23 #1168

◙ **P'U T'O MOUNTAIN**
see P'u T'o Shan

◙ **P'U T'O SHAN**
Syn: P'u T'o Mountain
See also: Avalokitesvara;
Potalaka Mountain; Pilgrimage
Sites (China)

▸Mountain in Chekiang Province,

south of Shanghai, China. It is traditionally believed that the Bodhisattva Avalokitesvara attained Nirvana there. This belief is based on the *Avatamsaka Sutra* which refers to a mythical island of Avalokitesvara named Potalaka. Editor/Tam: 77

"One of the mountains in the Chou-shan Islands, located in Che-chiang Province, China. It prospered as a center of Avalokitesvara workship. There are more than 200 temple buildings in the Buddhist complex there. Along with Wu-t'ai-shan and E-mei-shan, it is one of the four famous mountains in China."
Dait: 66

"The island of P'u T'o, known as P'u T'o Shan (P'u T'o Mountain), rises sharply and dramatically out of the East China Sea, one amongst a number of small islands in the Chusan Archipelago, 70 miles from Ningpo. The natural beauty of the island has long been recognized, for its original name was Hsiao Pai Hua Shan, the Small White Flower Mountain... The island has been a holy or sacred place for at least 2,000 years, for it was originally a Taoist sacred mountain, and one

of its other names, lasting throughout most of the T'ang dynasty until the fame of Kuan Yin overcame it, was Mei Tsen Shan, after a 1st century B.C. Taoist Alchemist Mei Fu who retreated to the island to practice his alchemical skills...　T h e significance of P'u T'o Shan is that it is believed to be none other than the mystical island of Kuan Yin, Potalaka, which is described in the *Avatamsaka Sutra*."　Palmer: 30　#2139

◙ **PADMASAMBHAVA**

►"(8th century.) Tantric Saint, instrumental in introducing Buddhism to Tibet. He is regarded by the Nyingmapa order as their founder...The Tibetan King Trisong Detsen (740-98) had invited the scholar Shantarakshita to Tibet, where he disseminated Buddhism and inspired the founding of the first Buddhist monastery at Samye. The king then invited Padmasambhava to exorcise the local demons and gods who resisted the teachings (Dharma). He did so, making them protectors of the Dharma, a story which illustrates how Buddhism incorporated local Tibetan traditions.

The two figures of Shantarakshita and Padmasambhava exemplify two strands of Buddhism in Tibet, the one centred on the celibate, monastic discipline, the other centred on the Tantric traditions of magical power (siddhi) and exorcism."

Larousse: 387

◉ **PAI-CHANG (712-784)**

See also: Pure Rules; Tao An

►*Vn*/ Tổ Bá-Trương. "Famous Chinese Ch'an master, known not only for the importance of his meditational attainment, but also for his rules regulating monastic behavior. Pai-chang was the Dharma heir of Ma-tsu Tao-i and the master of the well known disciple Kuei-shan Ling-yu, founder of one of the 'five houses' of Ch'an Buddhism. Prior to Pai-chang's rules, monks in China followed the Vinaya of the Dharmaguptakas, an Indian Buddhist school. Pai-Chang's system utilized the Vinaya emphasis of both Theravada and Mahayana in structuring a framework uniquely adapted to Chinese monastic life. He is also known for his emphasis on monks establishing their own support through working in the fields. While he maintained the

alms rounds as a form of meditational training, he advocated the notion that 'a day without work is a day without food.'"

Preb: 208-209

"Successor to Ma-zu Dao-Yi (Ma-Tsu Tao-I). Though both Masters are known for their seemingly eccentric behavior quite typical of Chan adepts in the Tang, they were both strict disciplinarians. Their apparently 'uncouth' gestures were [believed] necessary to drive away dualistic views held by their disciples and visitors."

Xu-yun/1988: 199

"Pai Chang was the first to lay out a clearly formulated set of rules for Zen monks ... Drawing on the traditions of ... vinaya (monastic discipline), Pai Chang created a new set of rules adapted to Zen ... The *Pure Rules of Pai Chang* included the basic Buddhist commandments ... as well as additional injunctions against luxury ... Both the lifestyle that Pai-Chang spelled out as well as the architectural form of his monastery became models for later Zen monasteries. The service he rendered the monastic community life of Zen earned him the epithet, 'the patriarch who created the forest.'" (H. Dumoulin, *Zen Buddhism*: 170.)

Pure Land and Zen

"Elder Zen Master Pai Chang of Huai Hai (one of the most famous Zen Masters of all time) was the direct descendant to the great Zen Master Ma Tsu of Chiang Hsi. Zen communities throughout the world are established on his model and have adopted his 'Pure Rules'. Since ancient times, no one has dared to criticize or violate this set of rules.

According to these Rules, prayers for the benefit of seriously ill monks and nuns must include the following passage: 'The fourfold assembly should gather together, and all should recite verses of praise to Amitabha Buddha and chant his name from one hundred to one thousand times. At the end, the following words of transference should be read: 'If conditions have not yet come to an end, let him quickly recover. If the time of death has arrived, we pray that he will be reborn in the Pure Land.' Is this not pointing the way back to the Pure Land? Moreover, the liturgy for sending off deceased monks includes this passage: 'the great assembly should all recite the name of Amitabha Buddha in unison, transferring the merits and making the following vow: "Let his soul be reborn in the Pure Land, his Karma in the world of dust severed; let him be reborn in the upper lotus grade, with a golden body. May he also receive a prediction of Buddhahood in one lifetime.' 'Is this not pointing the way back to the Pure Land? Furthermore, at the time of burial or cremation, the 'Pure Rules' stipulate: The monk in charge of the service should lead the way, striking a small bell, and recite the name of Amitabha Buddha ten times, with the great assembly following in unison. After recitation, the following words of transference should be read: 'We have just intoned the Buddha's name ten times to assist in rebirth ...' Is this not pointing the way back to the Pure Land? *It is for these reasons that this old monk said, 'Zen Masters the world over all set their Minds on the Pure Land*.'"
(Zen Master T'ien Ju in *Pure Land Buddhism: Dialogues with Ancient Masters*)
Zen: 47-48 #1055

◙ **PALA DYNASTY**
See also: India (Buddhism In)

▸"Ruled present-day Bihar and Bengal from about 650 to 950; the last royal patrons of Buddhism in India."
Reat: 338 #2081

◎ **PALI**
See also: Pali Canon

▸"Indian dialect (derived from Sanskrit) in which the canonical texts of the Theravada are composed."
Sham: 167
"The canonical language of Ceylonese Buddhists, believed to be very similar to the colloquial language spoken by Sakyamuni Buddha."
Thur: 142 #0404

◎ **PALI CANON**
See also: Tripitaka

▸"The Scriptures of the Theravada school, part at least written down in Pali in Ceylon in the first century BC. They are divided into three divisions or 'baskets' (Pitaka) (1) the Vinaya or Rules for the Order, (2) the Suttas (Sutras) or Sermons, and (3) the Abhidhamma or Commentaries. The whole was made available in English by the Pali Text Society."
Hump: 143

The Buddhist Canon also exists in a Mahayana version (Mahayana Tripitaka or Mahayana canon) which incorporates virtually all Theravada texts as well as numerous additional sutras and commentaries.
Editor: na
NOTE:
An early form of Buddha Recitation can be found in the Nikayas of the Pali Canon: "In the Nikayas, the Buddha ... advised his disciples to think of him and his virtues as if they saw his body before their eyes, whereby they would be enabled to accumulate merit and attain Nirvana or be saved from transmigrating in the Evil Paths." (D.T. Suzuki, *The Eastern Buddhist*, Vol. 3, No. 4, p.317.) #0420

◎ **PALI TEXT SOCIETY**

▸"Founded in London in 1881 by Professor and Mrs Rhys Davids to publish Pali texts and commentaries in Roman script, and to publish English translations. The whole work is now almost complete. The Canon of the Theravada was in fact available to the English-speaking world in its entirety before the

peoples of Theravada countries could read it in their own language. Miss I.B. Horner succeeded Mrs Rhys Davids as Honorary Secretary in 1942 and became President, on the death of Dr W. Stede in 1960."
Hump: 143-144 #0419

◙ **PANACEA**
see Agada

◙ **PANCHEN LAMA**
See Dalai Lama

▸"The Panchen Lama ranks second only to the Dalai Lama among the Grand Lamas of the Gelugpa School of Tibetan Buddhism. His seat is in the Tashilhumpo monastery at Shigatse. In 1640 the 5th Dalai Lama, having with the aid of the Mongols acquired temporal as well as spiritual control of the whole country, honoured his own tutor with the title of Panchen (from Pandita, learned) Lama, and built the Tashilhumpo Monastery for him. On the death of the title-holder, the new Lama is found in the body of a small child, as in the case of the Dalai Lama, and no new Lama is recognized as such by the people until examined and approved by a Tibetan commission appointed

for the purpose."
Hump: 144 #0418

◙ **PAO-LIN TEMPLE**
See also: Shao Ling Monastery

▸"A temple on Mount Ts'ao-ch'i (China) where Hui-neng, the Sixth Patriarch of Chan / Zen, lived."   Yoko/1976: 210 #1183

◙ **PARABLE: BIRTH AND DEATH**

▸Once the Chinese Emperor Mu Chung of the Tang dynasty, impressed by the level of cultivation of National Master Wu Yeh invited him to come for an audience. To just about any subject, this would have been an overwhelming honor. However, the master kept refusing because he did not want to be disturbed by wordly matters. So the emperor told his envoy, "If you cannot persuade Master Wu Yeh to come, you will have to forfeit your life." The envoy sought out the master and tearfully asked for his cooperation. The monk, unable to refuse the request at this point, said, "All right, I will go." So he gathered the whole assembly and asked his followers, "Who would like to join me for an audience with the emperor?" When a disciple raised his hand, the master asked, "How many miles can you travel in one day?" The disciple answered, "Fifty." The monk said, "That's not good enough". A second disciple was asked the same question and said, "Sixty-five," to which the monk replied again, "That's not good enough." A third disciple said, "Seventy miles," and for the third time, the monk said, "That's not good enough." Then a young monk raised his hand and said, "I will go wherever you go, Master." So the Master did his ablutions, then went back and sat on his elevated seat, entered Samadhi and expired on the spot, in a seated position. The young monk, seeing that, said, "Oh, Master, you have gone. Let me go too." And he expired standing. This anecdote illustrates that truly accomplished monks are free of mundane preoccupations -- beyond the ken of ordinary people, beyond *Birth and Death*. Editor: na

◙ **PARABLE: BODHISATTVA**

►In days of yore, an older master was traveling along a country road, followed by a disciple carrying his bags. As they walked, they saw lands being tilled while farmers and oxen were strained to the utmost. Countless worms and insects were killed in the process, and birds were swooping to eat them. This led the disciple to wonder to himself, "How hard it is to make a living. I will cultivate with all my strength, become a Buddha and save all these creatures." *Immediately* the Master, an Arhat able to read the thoughts of others, turned around and said, "Let me have those heavy bags and I will follow you." The disciple was puzzled but did as instructed and walked in front. As they continued on their way with the hot sun bearing down on them, dust swirling all around them, the road stretching endlessly in front, the disciple grew more and more tired. It wasn't long before he thought to himself, "There are so many sentient beings and there is so much suffering, how can I possibly help them all? Perhaps I should try to help myself first." *Immediately*, the Master behind him said, "Stop. Now you carry the bags and follow me." The puzzled disciple did as told, knowing he was not supposed to ask questions. He took up the bags again and walked behind. This sequence repeated itself several times. The Master walked in front with the disciple carrying the bags, then the disciple in front with the Master carrying the bags, back and forth, until they stopped for lunch. Then the disciple gathered his courage and asked the reason why. The Master said, "When you had exalted thoughts of saving all sentient beings, you had the mind of a Bodhisattva, and I as an Arhat had to follow you. But as soon as you had selfish thoughts, you were no longer a Bodhisattva, and being junior to me in years and cultivation, you had to carry my bags."   Editor: na

◙ PARABLE: BOILING POT

►"An effort to reform society which is not coupled with an equal effort to develop one's spiritual self cannot bring about lasting results. It is like trying to cool a pot of boiling soup by merely stirring it, while ignoring the blazing fuel underneath. One of the simplest yet most subtle methods of cultivation is that of Buddha Recitation, the invocation and/or visualization of Amitabha Buddha."xxx: na #2161

◙ PARABLE: BURNING HOUSE

►*Lotus Sutra*: "A rich man had a very large house. The house had only one entrance, and the timber of which it was made had dried out thoroughly over the years. One day the house caught fire, and the rich man's many children, heedless of the fire, continued to play in the house. Their father called to them from outside that the house was afire and that they would perish in the flames if they did not come out. The children, not knowing the meaning of 'fire' or 'perish,' continued to play as before. The man called out once more, 'Come out children, and I will give you *ox-drawn* carriages, *deer-drawn* carriages, and *goat-drawn* carriages!' Tempted by the desire for new playthings, the children left the burning house, only to find *ox-drawn* carriages (the best vehicle, that of the Bodhisattvas/Buddhas) awaiting them."   Hurv: xi
Just like the children who left the burning house and all received ox-drawn carriages, all Buddhist seekers will receive the ultimate prize: Buddhahood.
Editor: na #1906

◙ PARABLE: CHILD LICKING HONEY

►Buddha Sakyamuni compared

sentient beings chasing after the fleeting pleasures of this world to a child licking honey off a sharp knife. There is no way they can avoid hurting themselves.
Editor/Tam: 306 #2331

◙ **PARABLE: DEMON & VERSE**

▸"The story refers to a well-known story in Chapter Thirteen of the *Parinirvana Sutra*, which recounts that the Buddha in a previous life was told the first two lines of a Buddhist verse by a demon. The demon offered to supply the last two lines if the Buddha would let himself be devoured. The Buddha's search for the truth was so intense that he agreed to the proposal, whereupon the demon revealed himself to be Indra and declared that he had come just to test the Buddha's sincerity. He then taught the remaining two lines of verse."
Dait: 366 #2194

◙ **PARABLE: DUKKHA**
See also: Parable: Suffering

▸The Buddha compares the human condition to that of a traveller on a stormy night. Only from time to time does the dark night give way to a flash of

lightning. Suffering (dukkha) is like the dark night that surrounds the traveller, while the flashes of lightning are those rare occasions of joy that excite the human mind.
Editor: na

◙ **PARABLE: ELEPHANT AND BLIND MEN**

▸"It is said that a group of blind men, each touching a different part of an elephant, argued among themselves as to what its shape was ..."
Yoko: 183

To most people the blind men were indeed wrong; yet in another sense, they were also right because what each felt and described was indeed an aspect of the elephant. On the higher level of noumenon, since "all is one and one is all" (Avatamsaka sutra), each aspect in fact represents the whole and therefore the blind men, although wrong, were also right.
Editor: na #0810

◙ **PARABLE: GEM IN THE ROBE**

▸*Lotus Sutra*:
"A person sewed a jewel into one corner of his friend's garment.

The friend, not aware of this, made no attempt to use the jewel even when in serious straits. Then upon meeting his friend many years later, the man who had sewed it into his garment pointed it out to him and thus enabled him to get out of his difficulties."

Hurv: xiii

The Jewel stands for the omnipresent Buddha-Nature which we all possess as our birthright. Unaware of this, many of us do not seek Buddhahood, but settle for lesser goals.

Editor: na #1909

◉ **PARABLE: GODDESS OF WEALTH AND GODDESS OF POVERTY**

▶"Once a beautiful and well-dressed woman visited a house. The master of the house asked her who she was; and she replied that she was the goddess of wealth. The master of the house was delighted and so greeted her with open arms. Soon after another woman appeared who was ugly looking and poorly dressed. The master asked who she was and the woman replied that she was the goddess of poverty. The master was frightened and tried to drive her out of the house, but the woman refused to depart, saying, 'The goddess of wealth is my sister. There is an agreement between us that we are never to live apart; if you chase me out, she is to go with me.' Sure enough, as soon as the ugly woman went out, the other woman disappeared. Birth goes with death. Fortune goes with misfortune. Bad things follow good things. Men should realize this. Foolish people dread misfortune and strive after good fortune, but those who seek Enlightenment must transcend both of them and be free of worldy attachments." (*The Teaching of the Buddha.*).

BDK: 144-145 #2333

◉ **PARABLE: HUMAN CONDITION**

▶To illustrate the point that suffering is an inevitable part of our world, consider the example, adapted from the sutras, of worms feeding on rotten apples. The worms are 'running' hither and thither among the apples, each worm 'elbowing' the others for a better spot, a larger piece of the rotten matter. They all feel their actions necessary and desirable. They all seem very busy and very happy. To us humans, however, theirs is indeed a pitiable lot. The human condition is the same from the viewpoint of celestials, Bodhisattvas and Buddhas -- such a pitiful sight indeed, whether of beggars or presidential hopefuls!

Editor: na

◙ PARABLE: HUMAN REBIRTH IS DIFFICULT

▸"The story is told in a Buddhist sutra of a lone blind tortoise who dwells in the depths of a vast ocean, coming up for air only once every hundred years. On the surface of the same ocean floats a golden yoke. It is more common for the tortoise to place its head through the yoke when it takes its centennial breath, the sutra says, than it is for a being imprisoned in the cycle of rebirth to be born as a human with the good fortune to encounter the teaching of the Buddha. Human birth in a Buddhist land is compared to a rare jewel, difficult to find and, if found, of great value, because it is in the human body [that one may most easily travel] the path that leads to liberation."

Lopez: 266 #2273

◙ PARABLE: LAMP OF THE OLD WOMAN

▸"King Ajatasatru invited the Buddha to preach and offered as a token of his piety several tens of thousands of lamps. At the time, an old woman (named Nanda) who had been begging, and had only managed to collect two coins, bought some oil with them and offered it all in a small lamp to the Buddha. [With this offering she vowed to eliminate the darkness of the sufferings of all people.] Old and hungry, she later collapsed and died.

By the next morning the many lamps offered by the king had already burned themselves out, but the lamp of the poor old woman was still burning with increasing brilliance. When it proved impossible to extinguish it, the Buddha explained that it was so because of the donor's extremely fervent faith and transcendental vow. 'The light of a Buddha can never be extinguished' said the Lord who then predicted that she would attain Buddhahood."

Dait: 117 #0070

◙ PARABLE: MAN WOUNDED BY AN ARROW

See also: Metaphysics

▶"Parable of the arrow smeared thickly with poison:

It is as if a man had been wounded by an arrow thickly smeared with poison, and his friends and kinsmen were to get a surgeon to heal him, and he were to say, I will not have this arrow pulled out until I know by what man I was wounded, whether he is of the warrior caste, or a brahmin, or of the agricultural, or the lowest caste. Or if he were to say, I will not have this arrow pulled out until I know of what name of family the man is -- or whether he is tall, or short or of middle height ... Before knowing all this, that man would die.

Similarly, it is not on the view that the world is eternal, that it is finite, that body and soul are distinct, or that the Buddha exists after death that a religious life depends. Whether these views or their opposites are held, there is still rebirth, there is old age, there is death, and grief, lamentation, suffering, sorrow, and despair.... I have not spoken to these views because they do not conduce to an absence of passion, to tranquility, and Nirvana. And what have I explained? Suffering have I

explained, the cause of suffering, the destruction of suffering, and the path that leads to the destruction of suffering have I explained. For this is useful."
Smith: 142-143 #2156

◎ PARABLE: MEDICINAL HERBS AND TREES

▶*Lotus Sutra*:
"The parable goes as follows: A cloud envelops the world and sends down life-giving rain equally upon all grasses, flowers, trees and medicinal herbs. Though the rain is the same, the plants, trees, herbs, etc., absorb the moisture differently and grow to varying heights according to their individual nature.

Similarly, the Buddha impartially expounds only the one vehicle of Buddhahood for all people, but they understand and benefit from it differently, according to their respective capacities. The three kinds of medicinal herbs appearing in the parable are lesser medicinal herbs, intermediate medicinal herbs and superior medicinal herbs, and the two kinds of trees are small trees and great trees. On the basis of the description in the text, T'ien-t'ai interprets the lesser medicinal herbs as beings of the worlds of Humanity and Heaven, the intermediate medicinal herbs as persons of the Two Vehicles, and the superior medicinal herbs, small trees and great trees as Bodhisattvas."

Sokk: 339-340 #1914

◙ **PARABLE: MUSTARD SEED/IMPERMANENCE**

see Kisagotami

◙ **PARABLE: PHANTOM CITY**

►*Lotus Sutra*:

"A guide was leading a group of travelers to an island where a treasure lay buried. On the way the travelers wearied, and some spoke of turning back. The guide accordingly conjured up an apparent city and successfully urged his companions to rest and refresh themselves there. When they had done so, they went on and reached the island where the treasure was concealed. Then the guide told them that the city they had seen a while back had been an illusory city, and not a real one, which he had conjured up for the purpose of conquering their discouragement."

Hurv: xii

In this parable the guide is the Buddha and his companions are sentient beings. The treasure

island is the other shore of Buddhahood.

Editor: na #1908

◙ **PARABLE: PHYSICIAN AND HIS CHILDREN**

►*Lotus Sutra*:

"One of the seven parables in the *Saddharma-pundarika-sutra* [*Lotus Sutra*]. It runs as follows: The sons of a physician are suffering from grievous pain because they ingested poison. The father compounds an efficacious antidote for them. However, in their disturbed state of mind, the boys do not appreciate the worth of the remedy, and do not take it. Their very lives are therefore threatened. Determined to save his sons, the father leaves the city and arranges that a messenger shall inform the boys that he is dead. When the sons receive this report, they are shocked. So moved, they throw off their dementia, and at last take the medicine -- which the father, in his love and wisdom, prepared for them. Thereupon they recover from their sufferings. In this parable, the physician-father stands for the Buddha, the sons represent all suffering human beings, and the remedy is the

path of the One Vehicle (Buddhahood)."
Dait: 144 #1910

◙ PARABLE: SKILLFUL MEANS

▸An elderly Zen Master, feeling that his time would soon come, hit upon an expedient to help his chief disciple achieve a Great Awakening. He decided to drive the younger monk out of his complacency through an elaborate plan to "frame" him as a thief in disguise. The disciple was then denounced to one and all throughout the land. The accused monk, once the teacher of a huge congregation, now completely debased and with nowhere to turn, his ego totally shattered, mulled over this flagrant injustice and at times even contemplated suicide. After several weeks of utter desperation, he suddenly experienced a Great Awakening: life is a dream, an illusion, a bubble, a shadow. This is the very teaching he had been trying to impart to the novices for so many years! He then rushed to the Master, who upon seeing him, greeted him warmly and conferred the succession upon him.
Editor/Zen: 146

◙ PARABLE: SPIRITUAL POWERS

▸"Miracles are possible in Buddhism, even though the Buddha discouraged all display of miraculous or parapsychological powers as offering proof of spiritual attainment. He was first and foremost a pragmatist, a patient compassionate pragmatist.
A story that is told of his response to a noted ascetic whose path he crossed on one of his journeys nicely illustrates his down-to-earth reaction to any extremes of yogic behavior. Encountering an ascetic ... at a river crossing, he entered into conversation as he often did when traveling, and was told that the ascetic had achieved such mastery over his physical body that he could now cross the river walking on the water. The Buddha's comment was to the effect that such a feat, though remarkable, seemed a rather useless expenditure of physical and psychological energy, since there was a good ferry crossing the river at regular intervals charging less than a penny for the ride." For another version of this parable, see below."
Ross: 180-181 #2158

Different Version / Same Teaching
During His lifetime, Buddha Sakyamuni discouraged the display of spiritual powers. Once, the story goes, He was waiting at the river's edge for a boat to take him across. An ascetic, passing by, showed off his spiritual powers, crossing the river back and forth by treading over the water. The Buddha had then asked him, "How long did it take you to acquire such powers?" "Thirty years," was the reply. The Buddha then said, "Thirty years of effort? Well, I can cross the river for a five-cent fare." It may be added that for a person still subject to excessive greed, anger, and delusion to have access to unusual powers could be harmful to himself and dangerous to society at large.
Editor/Zen: 96 #2256

◉ **PARABLE: STALE RICE / STALE FARE**

►This is reference to a well-known story about Buddha Sakyamuni's disciple Visakha, who once said: "When a certain Bhikkhu was standing at the door for alms, my father-in-law was eating sweet milk rice-porridge, ignoring him. Thinking to myself that my father-in-law, without performing any good deed in this life, is only consuming the merits of past deeds, I told the Bhikkhu: 'Pass on Venerable Sir, my father-in-law is eating stale fare ...'" (Narada, *The Buddha and His Teachings*, p. 101.) Most people go through life consuming "stale fare," as they enjoy the results of their past merits without thought of creating new ones. For example, a wealthy person (i.e., one who practiced charity in past lives) spending time and money on himself alone, without thoughts of charity, is eating stale fare.
Editor/Zen: 94 #2332

◉ **PARABLE: SUFFERING**
See also: Parable: Dukkha

►The Buddha likens human beings to actors and actresses in the great drama of the universe. Every day they take on a different role with a different set of duties and obligations -- as mothers or fathers, sons or daughters, employees or employers etc. However, in all these roles, the common denominator of change and loss is ever present: loss of loved ones, loss of cherished property, loss of health and youth until the biggest loss of all -- we ourselves are carried to our graves and have to leave everything behind...How do we escape from this vicious cycle? Just walk out of the playhouse, quit acting and return home to our native place where we are always welcomed and loved -- return to our True Nature and Mind. This is the basic teaching of all Buddhist schools.

Question: Life cannot be all suffering. Are there not instances of pleasure and joy?

Yes there are, but these instances are just temporary -- like a mountain climber shifting a burden from one shoulder to another. Moreover, to the sages, these pleasures and joyful moments are illusory and false -- just like the pleasures and joys of a child eating candy. Down the road a visit to the dentist is inevitable!

Editor: na

◉ PARABLE: WEALTHY MAN AND POOR SON

►*Lotus Sutra*:

"A father and son parted company while the son was still a very young man. In the course of time the father became very rich, while the son sank into the

depths of poverty and beggary. One day, during the course of his wanderings, he happened to come to the palatial home of his father. The father, at once recognizing him, had him brought into his presence. This only frightened the poor man, and the father let him go. Then he sent two men to ask the beggar whether he wished to do menial labor on the rich man's estate. The beggar consented, and worked in this way for many years. One day the rich man told the beggar that in view of his many years of honest and conscientious service he would reward him with the charge of all his possessions. After several years more had passed, the rich man gathered his entire household and clan and told them that the beggar was his son, from whom he had been parted many years before, and that he was now reclaiming him and declaring him heir to all his possessions. When the beggar heard this, he was amazed, thinking that he had received something quite unexpected [while in fact it was his all along]. "Hurv: xi-xii #1907

◉ PARABLE: WHITE PATH

"A man on a long journey to the

west suddenly finds, in the middle of a wasteland, that his only way forward is over a narrow *white path* between a river of fire to the south and a river of surging water to the north. Pursued by murderous bandits, he rushes toward the path, but draws back when he sees the surging water and roaring flames. Realizing that whichever way he turns he may die, he decides to try to cross. Just then, he hears a voice from behind (the east) and in front (the west) encouraging him and, despite the cries of the bandits that the way is too perilous, he walks on the path and reaches the other shore in safety. [Patriarch] Shan-tao then explains the parable as follows: 'The east bank is an analogy of this world... The west bank is a symbol of the precious land of highest bliss. The bandits... are an analogy of the six sense organs, the six consciousnesses, the six defilements, the five skandhas, and the four elements. The lonely wasteland is the following of bad companions and not meeting with those who are truly good and wise. The two rivers of fire and water are an analogy of attachment, which is like water, and aversion, which is

like fire. The white path... is analogous to the aspiration for rebirth in the Pure Land which arises in the midst of the passions of attachment and aversion... The man proceeding on the path towards the west is comparable to one who directs all actions and practices towards the Western Pure Land. The hearing of voices from the east bank encouraging and exhorting him to pursue the path straight to the west, is like Sakyamuni Buddha, who has already disappeared from human sight but whose teaching may still be investigated and is therefore like *voices*....Someone calling from the west bank is an analogy of the Vows of Amitabha.' 'And reaching the west bank, of course, is being reborn in Sukhavati.' This parable became very popular in the Pure Land tradition, for its entire spirituality is neatly encapsulated in it."
Yoshi/Corless: 262

◎ **PARABLE: "WOMAN WHO IS ABOVE WORRY AND CARE."**
"A laywoman once approached a well-known Elder Master and asked: 'I have recited the Buddha's name for some time now, but have not seen any sign of progress. Can you explain to

me why this is so?' The abbot said, 'Reciting the Buddha's name is not difficult; the difficulty lies in (1) *perseverance*. Perhaps you have not recited regularly and in a persevering manner.' The laywoman replied, 'You are entirely right. I am usually interrupted in my recitation and have not been persevering, because of family obligations. From now on, I will put aside all distractions and vow to keep reciting exactly as taught.' Some time later, she returned and asked, 'Since receiving your instructions last time, I have put aside all external distractions and recited the Buddha's name regularly, every day. Why is it that I still do not see any results?' The abbot replied, 'Reciting the Buddha's name is not difficult; the difficulty lies in perseverance. Persevering is not difficult; the difficulty lies in (2) being *singleminded*. Although, on the surface, you may have put all distractions aside, in your mind you still worry about possessions and property and are still attached to children and family. You have neither discarded worry nor eliminated the root of love-attachment. How can you achieve one-pointedness of mind

and see Amitabha Buddha?' Hearing this, the woman sighed aloud 'That is so true, Master! Although I have seemingly abandoned all distractions, my mind is still preoccupied with them. From now on, I vow to disregard everything and recite the Buddha's name singlemindedly.' Thereupon she went home and, from that time on, each time her children or anyone else sought her advice or confided in her, she would invariably reply, 'I want peace of mind, and do not wish to be bothered by anything.' For this reason, everyone referred to her as 'the woman who is above all worry and care.' A few years later, she went to bow to the abbot at his temple, saying, 'Thanks to your advice and teaching, I have now achieved one-pointedness of mind and have seen Amitabha Buddha. I have come to pay my respects and take leave of you, Abbot, because I will soon be reborn in the Pure Land.' The laywoman in our story achieved liberation because she was enlightened to two principles: perseverance and singlemindedness. Thus, to be successful, the Pure Land practitioner should consider everything, from personal possessions and property to family and friends, to be illusory and phantom-like, coming together temporarily and then disintegrating. If we care about family and friends, we should ensure our own rebirth and liberation and then rescue them. This is true affection! Therefore, to recite the Buddha's name effectively, we should not only ignore one hundred distractions, we should discard all distractions, be they one thousand or tens of thousands!"

Tam: 229-230

◉ **PARADOX**

See also: Non-Duality; Koan; Truth; Zen School

►"Buddhism regards Truth as Non-duality, and thus beyond the condition of the opposites. Any statement, therefore, is only partially true, its opposite being also partially true. Only in paradox, therefore, taken to its limits, can Truth be, however inadequately, expressed. In Zen teaching it is taught that A is A because A is not A. Or, in the words of a Zen master, 'If you have a staff I will give you one; if you have not, I will take it away'."

Hump: 145

"The sutras preached by the Buddha during his lifetime are said to amount to five thousand and forty-eight fascicles; they include the doctrine of emptiness and the doctrine of being; there are teachings of immediate realization and of gradual development. Is this not an affirmation? But, according to [Zen Master Yung Chia in his *Song of Enlightenment*], 'there are no sentient beings, there are no Buddhas; sages as numerous as the sands of the Ganges are but so many bubbles in the sea; sages and worthies of the past are like flashes of lightning.' Is this not a negation?

"O you, my disciples, if you say there is, you go against [Yung Chia]; if you say there is not, you contradict our old master Buddha. If he were with us, then how would he pass through the dilemma? ... If you confess your ignorance, I will let you see into the secret. When I say there is not, this does not necessarily mean a negation; when I say there is, this also does not signify an affirmation. Turn eastward and look at the Western Land; face the south and the North Star is pointed out there!" (D.T. Suzuki, *Introduction to Zen Buddhism*, p. 65.)

"The critic will be inclined to call Zen absurd, confusing, and beyond the ken of ordinary reasoning. But Zen is inflexible and would protest that the so-called common sense way of looking at things is not final, and that the reason why we cannot attain to a thoroughgoing comprehension of the truth is due to our unreasonable adherence to a 'logical' interpretation of things. If we really want to get to the bottom of life, we must abandon our cherished syllogisms, we must acquire a new way of observation whereby we can escape the tyranny of logic and the onesidedness of our everyday phraseology ... This is because Zen has come to the definite conclusion that the ordinary logical process of reasoning is powerless to give final satisfaction to our deepest spiritual needs." (D.T. Suzuki, *Introduction to Zen Buddhism*, p. 58.) #0417

◎ **PARAMARTHA (499-569)**

►"A monk from western India who went to China in 546 at the invitation of Emperor Wu of the Liang dynasty (502-57). He translated many sutras and other Buddhist works into Chinese."
Yoko: 210

"Name of one of the four great translators in Chinese Buddhism. Paramartha (499-569) was an Indian; he came to China in 546. In that year, the emperor, who wanted to place him at the head of the translation bureau, invited him to the capital (present-day Nanking). However, political turmoil made this plan impractical. Paramartha spent the next years in various places in Southern China. Finally he settled in Canton, where, at the request of the prefect of the city, he translated important works of the Yogachara into Chinese. Among these were the Abhidharmakosha, the Mahayana-samparigraha of Asanga, the Vimshatika of Vasubandhu, and the *Diamond Sutra*. All told, Paramartha translated sixty-four works in 278 fascicles. His translations made possible the development of the Chinese form of Yogachara."
Sham: 169 #0397

◎ **PARAMITA**
Syn: Perfections
See also: Other shore

►Means "the perfection of" or "reaching the other shore"

(Enlightenment) as contrasted with this shore of suffering and mortality. The paramitas are usually six in number (charity, discipline, forbearance, energy, concentration and lastly wisdom) *or* expanded to ten (adding *expedients, vows, power* and *knowledge*). The Mahayana tradition emphasizes the paramita of expedients, or skill-in-means.
Editor/Tam: 158-159
"*Perfections*: The six (or ten) stages of spiritual perfection followed by the Bodhisattva in his progress to Buddhahood. They include the practice and highest possible development of charity, morality, forbearance, zeal, meditation and wisdom. The following four are sometimes added: skillful means of teaching, power over obstacles, spiritual aspiration, and knowledge, these last four being, however, regarded as amplifications of Prajna, or wisdom."
Murt: 52
"*Dana-paramita* (*charity*) consists of beneficence and giving in both the material and spiritual senses. This includes being compassionate and kind and not keeping accumulated merit for oneself but rather dedicating it to the liberation of all beings.

Shila-paramita (*discipline*) includes proper behavior conductive to the eradication of all passions and the securing of a favorable rebirth for the sake of liberating all beings. *Kshanti-paramita* (*forbearance*) refers to the patience and tolerance that arise from the insight that all the problems of beings have causes. *Virya-paramita* (*zeal*) is resolute effort that does not permit itself to be diverted by anything. *Dhyana-paramita* (*concentration*) here means meditation as [a] way of cutting through the illusion of an ego and of not experiencing oneself as separate from other beings. *Prajna-paramita* (*wisdom*) is the realization of supreme wisdom."
Sham: 169-170
Background
"The paramitas constitute an important teaching of the *Prajnaparamita Sutras*, of which the *Diamond* and the *Heart Sutras* are summaries. See the following passage: 'Since that which is real includes nothing worth begrudging, they [Bodhisattvas] give their body, life, and property in charity, without regret, without the vanity of giver, gift or recipient, and without bias or attachment ...

And as with charity, they also practice the other virtues. But while practicing the six virtues [paramitas] to eliminate delusion, they practice nothing at all. This is what's meant by practicing the Dharma.' ('Outline of practice' in Red Pine, tr., *The Zen Teaching of Bodhidharma*, p. 7.)"
Zen: 102

There is no distinction between oneself and other beings, between the savior and the saved because at the supramundane level of the Arhats and above, the ego has been transcended. It is just like one's two hands. Because they belong to the same person, one would automatically clasp the other if hurt and neither would hold a grudge against the other for accidentally striking it (when missing the head of a nail, for example).
Editor/Thich: 308 #0398

◎ PARASOLS
see Canopies

◎ PARENTS
see Filiality; Sangha

◎ PARINIBBANA SUTTA
See also: Parinirvana Sutra

▸"This [Theravada] sutra deals with the last years of life of the

historical Buddha ..., his death as well as with the cremation of his body and the distribution of the relics...It should not be confused with the Mahayana *Maha-parinirvana Sutra* [sometimes called *Nirvana Sutra*.]"
Sham: 134

◎ PARINIRVANA
Syn: Parinibbana; Maha-Parinirvana
See also: Parinirvana Sutra

▸"A more emphatic term for Nirvana, when it is used in reference to the apparent passing away of a physical body of a Buddha." Thur: 142
"Translated as perfect quietude. Although this term originally had the same meaning as Nirvana and referred to the stage in which all illusion had been eliminated, it later was used to indicate Buddha Sakyamuni's entering the state of Nirvana (i.e. death)." Dait: 112 #0093

◎ PARINIRVANA *SUTRA*
Syn: Maha-Parinirvana Sutra; Nirvana Sutra; Great Nirvana Sutra
See also: Funerary Rites for the Buddha; Parinibbana Sutta

▸"The *Maha-Parinirvana Sutra* is

the Sanskrit title of a Mahayana text which translates to 'The Discourse of the Great Parinirvana.' Not to be confused with the Pali text similarly titled [*Parinibbana Sutta*, q.v.], the Mahayana text expounds on the Buddha-nature as equivalent to the Dharma-kaya and being immanent in all sentient beings. Other traditional Mahayana ideas can be found in the text as well. It is an enormously lengthly text, far exceeding its Pali counterpart." Preb: 177

"The *Parinirvana Sutra* refers to Either of the two Chinese versions of the Mahayana *Nirvana Sutra*: the northern version translated by Dharmakshema during the Northern Liang dynasty (AD 423), and the southern translated by Hui-kuan, Hui-yen, and Hsieh Ling-yun

during the Liu Sung dynasty. The latter is a revised version of the former. Both deal with teachings that Sakyamuni is said to have expounded immediately before his death. The [*Parinirvana] Sutra* teaches that the Dharma body of the Buddha is eternal, that all people possess the Buddha nature, and that even those of incorrigible disbelief (Sanskrit: icchantika) can attain Buddhahood. It also contains the stories of Sakyamuni Buddha who as a Boddhisattva offered his body to a demon in exchange for the Dharma, and of Ajatashatru, who put his father to death but later repented and became the Buddha's disciple. The Sanskrit original is not extant."
Sokk: 51-52
NOTE:
"The Chinese Tripitaka contains three translations of the *Maha-Parinibbana* of the Theravada and seven translations of the Mahayana [*Mahaparinirvana Sutra*]."
Lahiri: 36) #0214

◉ **PARITTA**
See also: Angulimala Paritta; Mantra

▸*Pali*, lit. "protection."; a Dharani, a mantra.

"The modern explanation of the meaning of paritta recital [as producing mental well-being] contrasts with the widely held belief among lay people in the efficacy of paritta chant to bring about particular ends, such as curing physical illness. Even in the Pali texts themselves, the Buddha is said to have approved chanting the Karaniya Metta Sutta to ward off evil spirits, and the *Angulimala Paritta* was specifically sanctioned for a difficult childbirth."

Swear: 27

"Such chanting is especially common in the form of 'protection' (parita) discourses. The practice is mentioned only rarely in the Pali Canon and always in contexts of healing and protection. There is a recognized manual of such discourses, selected from the more awe-inspiring and potent contexts. At some point (we do not know when) many new Pali verses and formulae were added in order to create a complex set of recognized forms for ritual purposes. Indeed its strong ritual component has been a major factor in the growth and success of Southern Buddhism. Together with other merit-making activities the chanting of Pali discourses accompanies ceremonial occasions of many kinds, including some of the major events of the individual life-cycle. There are also many traditional ceremonies in which specifically Buddhist ritual plays little part. Chanting paritta comes into its own, however, with events which are in some way dangerous or potentially so: death, illness, possession ... embarking upon some new activity or entering a new house. It may take place on quite a small scale, but often there is an impressive and colourful ceremonial context, involving a great deal of careful preparation, all of which is, of course, also meritorious activity."

Hinn: 310

For an in-depth explanation of Paritta, see entry on *Cause and Effect*, section on Pure Land Buddhism. #1925

◉ PATH

Syn: Marga; Way

▸"The Way; in classical Chinese philosophy, the term for the inherent pattern of reality, which furnishes the proper moral orientation for self and society; used in Buddhist parlance as a synonym for the path of enlightenment." Clea: 171

"A classical Chinese concept best known through its use in Taoism, but also appropriated by the Buddhists to translate the Sanskrit term marga (path). Sometimes used to refer both to the universal principle of One Mind, or Buddha nature, and to the particular path of practice that brings one more and more into harmony with the One Mind."
Kusa: 181 #0764

◙ **PATH OF THE SAGES**
see Difficult path of practice

◙ **PATRIARCH**
See also: Pure Land Patriarchs; Twenty-Eight Indian Patriarchs
----
▸"In [Mahayana] Buddhism, the founder of a school and his successors in the transmission of its teaching."
Sham: 170
"In Buddhism, one of the early leaders of a school or lineage, particularly Chan/ Zen."
Reat: 339 #0399

◙ **PATRIARCHAL ZEN**
Syn: Zen; Southern School of Zen; Zen of the Patriarchs
See also: Tathagata Zen; Twenty-eight Indian Patriarchs; Questions and Answers; Sudden / Gradual Enlightenment; Zen school
----
▸Patriarchal Zen. Known today simply as "Zen", stresses the immediate enlightenment of the practitioner.
"The school deriving from Hui-neng, the sixth patriarch of Chinese Ch'an (Jpn/ Zen). His master was Hung-jen, the fifth patriarch. Hung-jen had another able disciple called Shen-hsiu who spread Zen in northern China and started what came to be called the Northern school of Zen. Although the Northern school soon declined, the Southern was divided into five branches--Ts'ao-tung (Soto), Yun-men (Ummon), Fa-yen (Hogen), Kuei-yang (igyo) and Lin-chi (Rinzai). The Lin-chi school eventually produced two more schools, Huang-ling (Oryu) and Yang-chi (Yogi)."
Sokk: 409
"The Zen School of China and Japan claims a line of twenty-eight Indian Patriarchs beginning with the Buddha himself and passing through many famous names, such as Asvaghosha, Nagarjuna and Vasubandhu to Bodhidharma of India, who was the twenty-eighth Indian and first Chinese Zen

Patriarch. The six ... Patriarchs [in China] were (1) Bodhidharma (Ch./ Tamo, Jpn./ Daruma) who reached China in 520, (2) Hui-k'o (Jpn./ Eka) 486-593, (3) Seng-t'san (Jpn./ Sosan) died 606, (4) Tao-hsin (Jpn./ Doshin) 579-651, (5) Hung-jen (Jpn./ Gunin) 601-675, and (6) Hui-neng (Jpn./ Eno or Yeno) 637-713, who left no successor as Patriarch." Hump: 147

NOTES

i. At the time of the Sixth Patriarch Hui-neng (7th c.), there were two branches of Zen, the Northern (Tathagata) and the Southern (Patriarchal). However, the only remaining branch today is Patriarchal Zen, which has become synonymous with Zen. Editor: na

ii. The two approaches to meditation, the Sudden (Patriarchal Zen, or simply Zen) and the Gradual (Tathagata Zen) represent different facets of the same teaching adapted to different types of people in different locations. To praise one approach while disparaging the other is therefore a form of attachment, a dualistic view of Buddhism not consonant with the Truth.

Editor: na #0168

◙ **PEACE AND BLISS COLLECTION**

See also: Tao-Ch'o; Pure Land School

►*Chin*/ An-lo-chi; *Jpn*/ Anraku chu; *Vn*/ An-Lạc-Tập. "A work by Tao-Ch'o, the second patriarch of the Pure Land school (T'ang dynasty). In this work, based on the *Meditation Sutra*, he divides all of Shakyamuni's teachings into the two categories of Sacred Way teachings and Pure Land teachings. He asserts that the people of the Latter Day of the Law (Dharma-ending age) should embrace only Pure Land teachings and rely upon Amitabha Buddha in order to be reborn in his Pure Land in the western region of the universe. He also makes reference to the difficult-to-practice way and the easy-to-practice way set forth by Nagarjuna. He recommends abandoning the difficult-to-practice way, or the Sacred Way, which teaches the attainment of Buddhahood in this world through one's own power, and embracing the easy-to-practice way, that is, Pure Land teachings which lead one to rebirth in the Pure Land by relying upon Amitabha Buddha. This work formed the basis of

Shan-tao's *Commentary on the Meditation Sutra.*"
Sokk: 14 #0204

◉ **PERFECT SUDDEN TEACHING**
See also: Perfect Teaching; Sudden Teaching; Provisional Teaching; Special Teaching

----

▶"Perfect (i.e. highest) and sudden (immediate). The state of enlightenment aimed at by the T'ien T'ai (Tendai) [and Avatamsaka schools]."
Dait: 60

I. Perfect teaching
Supreme teaching of the Buddhas, as expressed in the *Lotus* and *Avatamsaka Sutras*, among others. Expounds the One-Vehicle or the Vehicle of the Buddhas.
Editor: na

"Sometimes called the round teaching. The supreme teaching of Buddhism. In China, scholars made numerous attempts to organize the vast array of sutras which had been introduced at random from India into coherent systems. In these systems of comparative classification, as they were called, the sutra which was ranked highest was called the perfect teaching. For example, Hui-kuang (468-537) divided Buddhist teachings into three

categories -- gradual, abrupt and perfect -- and designated the *Avatamsaka Sutra* as the perfect teaching. T'ien-t'ai declared the doctrine of the mutually inclusive relationship of ultimate reality of all phenomena to be the perfect teaching."
Sokk: 342-343

II. Sudden Teaching
A teaching which enables one to attain Enlightenment immediately. It is usually associated with the Avatamsaka and/or Zen schools.
Editor: na

"*The Sudden teaching* expounds the abrupt realization of the ultimate truth without relying upon verbal explanations or progression through various stages of practice."
Sokk: 110

III. Pure Land Teaching
"In his commentary on the Pure Land sutras, [Patriarch] Chu-hung classifies Pure Land as a *sudden* (abrupt) doctrine that also shares some aspects of the 'final' doctrine of the *Lotus Sutra* and the *perfect* (round) doctrine of the *Avatamsaka Sutra*. It belongs to the *sudden* doctrine, he says, because the Pure Land devotee 'attains rebirth in the Western Paradise as soon as he relies on the Buddha's name.'

Chu-hung explains that the mind of the devotee of Buddha-recitation, when this is properly done, is a mind without any disturbance and is equivalent to the mind of no-thought spoken of in the Zen school. Like Han-shan, Chu-hung interprets Pure Land teaching in the Zen spirit, but at the same time advocates the more traditional and devotional aspects of the Pure Land faith. For both men, the other-power religion that teaches salvation by faith and Amitabha's grace is wedded to the self-power religion that teaches salvation by self-realization."

Hsu: 150

NOTE:

"These days many people like to talk about studying enlightenment and finally transcend birth and death. They do not realize that in this world complete enlightenment is extremely difficult. They think of it as direct, sudden, 'vertical' transcendence of the Triple World of Desire, Form, and Formless states. But even someone who has overcome desire and reached the stage of a 'once-returner' still has to go to his death and come back once more through rebirth: how much the more so, for an ordinary person! Most of the sentient beings in this world will have to *be reborn in the Pure Land first before they can be completely enlightened*. The Pure Land gate to the West is called 'horizontal' transcendence: not one in ten thousand misses it." (Master Chu Hung in *Pure Land Pure Mind*) #1302

◙ **PERFECT TEACHING**

Syn: Round Doctrine; Round Teaching

See also: Sudden Teaching; Perfect Sudden Teaching; Provisional Teaching; Special Teaching

----

▶Supreme teaching of the Buddhas, as expressed in the *Lotus* and *Avatamsaka Sutras*, among others. Expounds the One-Vehicle or the Vehicle of the Buddhas.

Editor: na

"Sometimes called the round teaching. The supreme teaching of Buddhism. In China, scholars made numerous attempts to organize the vast array of sutras which had been introduced at random from India into coherent systems. In these systems of comparative classification, as they were called, the sutra which was ranked highest was called the perfect teaching. For example, Hui-kuang (468-537) divided Buddhist teachings into three categories -- gradual, abrupt and perfect -- and designated the *Avatamsaka Sutra* as the perfect teaching. T'ien-t'ai declared the doctrine of the mutually inclusive relationship of ultimate reality of all phenomena to be the perfect teaching."

Sokk: 342-343 #0312

◉ **PERFECTION OF WISDOM**
see Prajna paramita

◉ **PERFECTIONS**
see Paramita; Ten paramitas

◉ **PERMANENTLY PRESENT**

►"An attribute related to: 1. The assembly of monks / nuns permanently residing in a monastery, being bound by equal obligations and enjoying equal rights, 2. The everlasting Triple Jewel, i.e. the Buddha, the Dharma, and the Sangha, which together represent Buddhism in general."

NV Hoa: Na

◉ **PERSECUTION OF 845 (CHINA)**
Syn: Suppression of 845
See also: T'ang Wu-Tsung

►"The suppression itself was of short duration. Within a year, in the third month of 846, emperor Wu-tsung died, his health probably affected by the longevity potions which he had been taking, and the imperial scepter was taken up by Hsuan-tsung, who immediately initiated action to call off the anti-Buddhist movement.

To start with, the Taoists, Chao Kuei-chen and Liu Hsuan-ching, along with eleven others, were executed because they had incited the previous emperor to extreme measures. Imperial permission was then given to increase the number of temples in the capital from four to twelve; each prefecture was also permitted to have two, and the regional commandery three, temples. Moreover, monks over fifty who had been defrocked the previous year were permitted to resume their monastic garb."

Chen: 232-233 #1889

◉ **PERSECUTION OF BUDDHISM**
see Persecution of 845; T'ang Wu-tsung

◉ **PERSEVERANCE**

►Perseverance is an especially important quality in Buddhism.

For example, if we were to rub two pieces of wood together but before fire is produced, we stop to do something else, only to resume later, we would never obtain fire. Likewise, a person who cultivates sporadically (e.g., on weekends or during retreats) but neglects daily practice, can seldom achieve lasting results.
Editor/Thich: 308　#1387

◙ PERSONAL PROVISIONS
see Provisions For Pure Land Rebirth

◙ PHENOMENA
see Noumenon / Phenomena

◙ PHƯỚC-HUỆ, THÍCH (*DHARMA MASTER*)

►Important Buddhist leader in Australia and New Zealand (since 1980) and current head of the *Vietnamese Unified Buddhist Congress* (Australia and New Zealand). Also founder of Vietnam Cultural Center in Sydney. Before the end of the Vietnam war in 1975, Master Phuoc-Hue taught for many years at An-Quang Pagoda, the pre-eminent Buddhist center in the southern part of Vietnam. Author and translator of several books including *Forty-Eight Methods of Buddha Recitation* and *Pure Land Lotus Petals* (1996). His chosen field of teaching and cultivation is the Pure Land school.
Editor: na　#2183

◙ PI-YEN-LU
see Blue Cliff Record

◙ PILGRIMAGE SITES
See also: India (Buddhism in); Sacred Mountains

►*(I) Indian sites*
"The ancient tradition of pilgrimage to the Buddhist centers in India associated with the life of the Buddha fell largely into abeyance after the Muslim conquest of North India. It has revived considerably in the last century. Local pilgrimages are widespread. Centers of pilgrimages in India/Nepal include Lumbini (q.v.) [birthplace of the Buddha], Bodh-gaya (q.v.) [Enlightenment site], Sarnath (q.v.) [site of the Buddha's first sermon] and Kushinagar (q.v.) [site of the Buddha's Nirvana]."
Hinn: 313
See also: Ajanta (Caves); Sacred Mountains
(II) Chinese sites
See the following entries: Four

Famous Mountains; E-Mei Shan;
Wu T'ai Shan; P'u T'o Shan;
Lung-men; Tun-Huang #1926

◙ **PIPPALA TREE**
see   Bodhi Tree

◙ **PITAKA**
See also: Tripitaka

▸"A basket, container, receptacle,
thesaurus; hence the Tripitaka
[the Buddhist Canon]."
Thai: 300 #1626

◙ **PITH OF A PLANTAIN**
"A plantain tree has no pith, so
the expression 'the pith of a
plantain' is used to refer to
insubstantiality or absence of
ultimate reality; transient
phenomena are said to be
"pithless as a plantain."
Chih-I/Cleary: 200

◙ **PLANTAIN**
see Pith of a Plantain

◙ **PLATFORM SUTRA**
Syn: Sixth Patriarch Sutra; Sutra
of Hui-neng

▸"The Sutra of the Sixth
Patriarch. This one-fascicle work
is a compilation of lectures given
by the Sixth Patriarch Hui-neng
at the Pao-lin monastery and

recorded by his disciple Fa-hai. It
is divided into ten chapters."
Dait: 118
Key Text, along with the
Diamond and *Lankavatara Sutras*,
for Zen adepts.
Editor: na #0073

◙ **PO CHU-I (772-846)**

▸*VN/* Bạch Cư Dị. A well-known
Chinese official and poet of the
T'ang dynasty (q.v.). Famous for
his socially-conscious Buddhist-
inspired poems which can be
easily understood by all, from the
gentry to the peasants. The
following story illustrates the
need for practice (cultivation) in
Buddhist teaching (vs. study and
scholarship for their own sake).

One day, Po Chu-I, passing along
a road, saw a Zen monk seated
on a tree branch preaching the
Dharma. The following dialogue
ensued:

Po Chu-I: 'Old man, what are you
doing in that tree, in such a
precarious position? One
misstep, and you will fall to your
death!'
Monk: 'I dare say, Your
Lordship, that your own position
is even more precarious. If I
make a misstep, I alone may be

killed; if you make a misstep, it can cost the lives of thousands.'

Po Chu-I: "Not a bad reply. I'll tell you what. If you can explain the essence of Buddhism to me in one sentence, I'll become your disciple. Otherwise, we will go our separate ways, never to meet again.'

Monk: 'What an easy question! Listen! The essence of Buddhism is to do no evil, do what is good, and keep your Mind pure.'

Po Chu-I: 'Is that all there is to it? Even a child of three realizes that!'

Monk: 'True, a child of three may realize it, but it is not sure that a man of eighty can practice it!' Buddhism is Mind, Buddhism is practice -- it is praxis.

Editor: na   #2195

◙ **POLAR MOUNTAIN**
see   Sumeru (Mount)

◙ **POLITICS**
See also: Buddhism

▶"There is an inherent problem in trying to intermingle religion with politics. The basis of religion is morality, purity and faith, while that for politics is power. In the course of history, religion has often been used to give legitimacy to those in power

and their exercise of that power. Religion has been used to justify wars and conquests, persecutions, atrocities, rebellions, and destruction of works of art and culture."

Dham: 229   #1987

◙ **PORES**
Avatamsaka Sutra:
"The realms of non-interference between noumenon and phenomena and non-interference among phenomena are represented symbolically in the *Avatamsaka Sutra* by such images as the Buddha's pores each containing innumerable lands, with each atom in those lands also containing innumerable lands, each land containing innumerable Buddhas, and so on, *ad infinitum*. This illustrates the infinite mutual relation of all things." (Thomas Cleary, tr.)

Clear: I/21

◙ **POSADHA**
see   Uposattha / Upavasatha

◙ **POST MORTEM OMENS**
see   Proofs of rebirth in Pure Land

◙ **POTALA PALACE**

▶"The enormous fortress-palace

built on a high natural hill in the centre of Lhasa, Tibet, in the seventeenth century by the Regent of the fifth Dalai Lama. It is the residence of the Dalai Lama, and contains a complete monastery with its own Temple, the mausolea of previous Dalai Lamas, and enormous treasures, in works of art and specie. Built on the site of an earlier fortress, it is 900 feet long, and the stone walls are painted in various symbolic colours."
Hump: 150 #0414

◙ **POTALAKA MOUNTAIN (INDIA)**
See also: P'u T'o Mountain

►"The name of a mountain located on the southern coast of India. It is believed that Avalokitesvara Bodhisattva manifested herself there." [This belief is based on the *Avatamsaka Sutra* which refers to a mythical island of Avalokitesvara named Potalaka.]
Dait: 65-66
"Potalaka is a mountain where many small white flowers grow; this represents the modesty and compassionate behavior of the Bodhisattva Avalokiteshvara."
Clea/89: 57
NOTE:

The popularity of Kuan-yin is such that two famous mountains with similar names, Potalaka in India and P'u-t'o in China, are dedicated to Her.
Editor: na #0075

◙ **POWER OF KNOWING OTHERS' MINDS**
See also: Spiritual Powers

►"Also rendered as 'power of reading thoughts.' One of the six miraculous powers [which enlightened beings have to a greater or lesser extent depending on their spiritual achievements]."
Chan: 480 #0548

◙ **PRABHUTARATNA BUDDHA**

►"An important image in the *Lotus Sutra*: an ancient monument emerges from the ground, opens up, and reveals an extinct Buddha, named Prabhutaratna, who although extinct is still alive and teaching. This symbolizes the idea that truth is eternal, even though it may sometimes be concealed or forgotten, sometimes revealed or rediscovered."/Cleary/Chih-I:200

◙ **PRACTICE**
Syn: Cultivation

See also: Special Teaching; Buddha Recitation; Expedient means; Existence/ Emptiness; Pure Land Buddhism (Summary); Three Non-Outflow Studies; Sundry Practices; Visions; Visualizations; Obstacles to Cultivation; Seeker; Letting Go

----

▸*Famous quote*:
"For teaching, develop your own school. For self-cultivation, practice Pure Land."
Amidism: 29

Practice/cultivation
"In entering the Buddha Dharma, there are generally three approaches: teaching, interpretation and practice. Teachings are shallow, interpretation is profound, but practice is supreme. (Master Ching-yin Hui-yuan)"
Tana: 23
"A scholar who studies and 'teaches' a sutra with the intent of footnoting and categorizing it, instead of practicing it, is like a starving man who, given food, puts it under a microscope instead of eating it, and who teaches others to starve along with him."
Hua/77: III
In Buddhism, regardless of the school followed, practice (cultivation) is a must. A Buddhist who merely studies or lectures on the Buddha's teaching while failing to put it into practice has been likened to a sick doctor who prescribes medicines for others while refusing to take any himself. According to Buddhist teachings, we all have within us varying degrees of greed, anger and delusion. To practice is to avoid or mitigate the conditions that promote greed, anger and delusion. Thus, for example, whenever anger flares up, one's thoughts should be redirected, as a form of displacement, toward the Buddha through Buddha-remembrance (Buddha Recitation).
Editor/na
The cardinal rule of all Buddhist cultivation, regardless of tradition or school, is *introspection* -- looking at our own mistakes and correcting them. To look at other people's shortcomings and criticize them is bound to disturb the mind and keep us in a perpetual state of anger and frustration.
Editor: na #2347
"In principle, all canonical texts are able to satisfy the spiritual needs of all Buddhists, whether Eastern or Western, but, in practice some texts appeal more

strongly to Buddhists of one kind of temperament, or one kind of spiritual aspiration, than they do to those of another. This is the main reason for the vast extent of the canonical literature, which may be regarded as *one and the same Dharma in varying degrees of expansion and contraction, concentration and dilution*, rather than as a collection of separate teachings. The canonical literature is like a pharmacopoeia. All the different drugs and medicinal preparations which are listed in the pharmacopoeia have one and the same object, the restoration of a sick person to health, but some drugs and medicinal preparations are suited to the cure of one kind of disease and some to the cure of another.

The sick person does not have to swallow the entire contents of the pharmacopoeia. In the same way, it is not necessary for the individual Western Buddhist, any more than for the individual Eastern Buddhist, to study and put into practice the entire contents of the Buddhist canonical literature. What he has to do is find out which canonical text, or which collection or selection of texts, is best suited to his individual spiritual needs,

and then devote himself to the concentrated and intensive practice of the teachings contained in those texts -- of course, without any diminution of his reverence for the canonical literature as a whole." (*The Eternal Legacy*)

Sangha: 277

"In order to demonstrate clearly what true cultivation and the personality of the true cultivator are, I will quote a passage from the No-Mark Stanza of the *Platform Sutra*, by the Sixth Patriarch: *He who treads the Path in earnest/Sees not the mistakes of the world;/If we find fault with others/We ourselves are also in the wrong./When other people are in the wrong,/we should ignore it,/For it is wrong for us to find fault./By getting rid of the habit of fault-finding/We cut off a source of defilement./When neither hatred nor love disturbs our mind/Serenely we sleep.* (Wong Mou-Lam, tr. 'The Sutra of Hui Neng,' p. 34. In *The Diamond Sutra & The Sutra of Hui Neng*.)

Buddhist adherents, whether clergy or laymen, all consider themselves cultivators, concerned with the Way. However, how can we tell the genuine from the sham cultivator? On this issue, the Sixth Patriarch has advanced a simple criterion. He said: *He who treads the Path in earnest sees not the mistakes of the world.* In effect, the genuine cultivator always looks at himself to correct his own mistakes and dwells in empty, still meditation. Having severed the mind of discrimination between himself and others, how can he think about the good and bad points of others? With the sham cultivator, on the other hand, the mind of self and others, right and wrong, jealousy and hate runs rampant; as soon as he opens his mouth, he criticizes others and speaks of the good and bad points of the world. This is very far from the Way. Therefore, when we continue to see the mistakes of others, denigrating and slandering them, we demonstrate that we are the most awkward and wanting of all, because our minds are still deluded, full of discrimination, lacking in wisdom and compassion. We thus bring retribution upon ourselves in the future. Regardless of whether or not others are in the wrong, let us strive not to be in the wrong ourselves. We should learn from great men and let our minds be as clear and bright as a mirror. Without anticipating or hedging about future events, without regretting or dreaming about things of the past, with the mind filled with brightness and equanimity, we will surely receive a wonderful response! If we have distracting thoughts of envy and hate and speak words of scorn and blame, then, internally, our True Nature becomes defiled and externally, we bring rancor and disputes upon ourselves. This results in further errors and transgressions. For this reason, to achieve peace of mind and be free of afflictions, we should not comment on people's shortcomings. The phrase 'by getting rid of the habit of fault-finding' also has the deeper meaning of eliminating the *Four Propositions* and eradicating the *One Hundred Errors*.

'When neither hatred nor love disturbs our mind, serenely we sleep'... describes the state of great liberation, 'all eagerness for study gone, eating when hungry, sleeping when tired'.

True cultivators always have a clear and solid position and viewpoint, and pay no attention to the praise and criticism, likes and dislikes of the outside world. As an example, it once happened that a well-known Zen Master, having awakened to the Way under Elder Master Fu Shan, went to reside in a famous monastery. Although living among the Great Assembly, he did not practice meditation or seek guidance in the Dharma; all he did all day was lay sleeping. Upon hearing this, the abbot arrived at the meditation hall, a big staff in hand. Seeing the guest master reclining with eyes closed, he admonished: 'This place does not have surplus rice to allow you to do nothing but eat and rest!' *Reply*: 'What would you, High Master, advise me to do?' The abbot said: 'Why don't you sit in meditation?' *Answer*: 'Succulent food cannot tempt those who have eaten their fill.' The abbot continued, 'A great many people are unhappy with you.' *Answer*: 'If they were happy, what would I gain?' Hearing these unusual replies, the abbot inquired further, 'Who was your master?' *Answer:* 'I arrived here after having studied under the eminent Master Fu Shan.' The abbot said, 'No wonder you are so headstrong!' They then clasped hands, laughing aloud, and headed toward the abbot's quarters.

One day, many years later, the guest Zen Master, having washed himself, ascended the Dharma seat, bid farewell to the great assembly, wrote a parting stanza, immediately dropped the pen and expired in a seated position. The guest master, as we can see, conducted himself easily and freely, having mastered life and death. Is it not because he had truly internalized the meaning of the passage *'when neither hatred nor love disturbs our mind, serenely we sleep*?'"
Tam: 157-160

Pure Land Buddhism

"The ancients have also commented: *Among Dharma methods (Buddhist schools),/ Pure Land is the shortcut for attaining the Way;/ Within Pure Land,/ Oral Invocation is the shortcut.* Nowadays, this method (Oral Invocation) is the most popular form of Buddha Recitation."
Tam: 119

"The practitioner should singlemindedly put his faith in the Buddha and cultivate with purity throughout his life. Whether seated or reclining, he should face west. Whenever he bows to the Buddha, recites the Buddha's name or makes a vow, he should do so in extreme earnestness, without intruding,

sundry thoughts. *He should act as though he were on the verge of execution, or in prison, or pursued by enemies, or in danger of drowning or being burned alive.* He should singlemindedly seek help, vowing to escape the cycle of danger and swiftly attain Non-Birth, in order to carry on the work of the Triple Jewel, repay the Four Great Debts and rescue sentient beings. With such an earnest Mind, his cultivation will not be in vain. On the other hand, if his deeds do not match his words, his faith is not solid, his recitation is haphazard and he seeks rebirth in this lazy, lethargic manner, it will be difficult for him to encounter good spiritual friends at the time of death. Dragged away by the power of karma, weighed down by pain and suffering, he cannot achieve right thought. Why is this so? It is because present actions are causes, what is received at the time of death are results. Causes should be true for results not to be false, just as an echo which reverberates loud and clear comes from a loud noise, and a straight mirror image requires a straight object."
(Elder Master T'ien Ju, 14th c.)
P.L. DIA: 102
NOTE:

"Whether one enters a monastery or prefers to remain in the lay world, there can be no progress in concentration without a *severe reduction in one's involvement in worldly affairs.* Naturally, the external observances of the monastic rule are understood to be peculiarly propitious to the development of mental calm, but in the last analysis, it is inner motive and personal discipline that count. Thus we are counseled at length to be careful about the company we keep, recognizing the simple fact that an unexamined lifestyle, in which we are immersed in the materialistic values and behavior of worldly friends, will get us nowhere. Only frustration and inanity will be the result. Shantideva advises us to fight shy of those whose values are contrary to the Dharma."
Shantideva: 17

For details on Pure Land practice, see *Buddha Recitation (Methods of).* For a summary of the psychological states of diligent practitioners of various Buddhist methods, see *Visions, Obstacles to Cultivation, Ten Non-Seeking Practices* #2196

◎ **PRACTITIONER**
see Seeker

◙ **PRAJAPATI**
see Maha-prajapati

◙ **PRAJNA**
see Wisdom

◙ **PRAJNA PARAMITA**
Syn: Perfection of Wisdom
See also: Wisdom Sutras

►"The paramita (or perfection) of wisdom. Also refers to an important and voluminous sutra group in which the doctrine of emptiness (sunyata) is taught."
Chan: 480
The *Prajna Paramita Sutra* is the longest of all Buddhist sutras; the second longest is the *Avatamsaka Sutra*.
Editor: na #0549

◙ **PRAJNA PARAMITA SUTRAS**
see Wisdom Sutras

◙ **PRATIMOKSA**
See also: Pratimoksa Sutra; Precepts; Bhiksu; Bhiksuni

►"Moral code of Buddhist monks and nuns, consisting of a list of more than 200 offenses, in descending order of seriousness, recited in an assembly of the whole company of monks in every monastery on Uposattha days. A monk or nun who is guilty of any of these offenses is required to confess the matter and submit to the appropriate penalty (Discipline)."
Ling: 207 #1155

◙ **PRATIMOKSA SUTRA**
See also: Pratimoksa; Precepts

►"Monastic disciplinary text included in the Vinaya, and preserved in separate versions for monks and nuns. The *Pratimoksa Sutra* is an inventory of offenses organized into categories classified according to the gravity of the offense. It is *recited twice monthly*, at the Posadha observance on the new moon and full moon, and is employed as a device for insuring proper monastic discipline. As a ritual liturgy, it includes in addition to the categories of offenses, a series of verses that introduce and conclude the text, an introduction (nidana) used to call the sangha together and initiate the confessional procedure, and an interrogatory formula, recited after each category of offenses, aimed at discovering who was pure and who was not. In the monks' version, the categories of offenses include the (1) Parajika dharmas (offenses requiring expulsion from the community),

(2) Samghavasesa dharmas (offenses involving temporary exclusion from the sangha while undergoing a probationary period), (3) undetermined cases involving sexual matters, (4) offenses requiring expiation and forfeiture, (5) offenses requiring simple expiation, (6) miscellaneous matters which should be confessed, (7) rules concerning matters of etiquette, and (8) legalistic procedures utilized in settling disputes. The nuns' version contains seven categories, the third listed above being excluded. The monks' version ranges from 218 to 263 rules while the nuns' version ranges from 279 to 380 rules. The Posadha observance was not considered concluded until all offenses listed in the *Pratimoksa Sutra* had been confessed and appropriate punishment had been meted out, thus guaranteeing on a fortnightly basis that all members of the sangha were pure in their behavior and worthy of community respect."
Preb: 216-217 #1059

◙ PRATYEKA-BUDDHA

▶"These Buddhas become fully enlightened ... by meditating on the principle of causality. Unlike

the Perfect Buddhas, however, they do not exert themselves to teach others (A. Buzo and T. Prince)."
Prince: 81

"In Buddhism, Pratyekabuddhas generally mean those who live in a time when there is no Buddha but who awaken to the Truth through their own efforts."
Sokk: 344
NOTE:
The vehicles of the Sravakas and Pratyekabuddhas are known as the Theravada or Southern Vehicle of Buddhism.
Editors: na #0277

◙ PRATYUTPANNA *SAMADHI*
See also: Pure Land Buddhism (Summary)

▶(*Vn/* Bát-Chu Tam-Muội) "The essence of this samadhi is that the Buddha is just the mind; the mind creates all Buddhas."
[HH/FAS39II11]

"The Pratyutpanna samadhi is to be performed in isolation. The meditator selects and adorns a hall for pratice, prepares all the necessary accoutrements of offering, and lays out various delicacies, fruit, incense, and flowers. Having washed himself thoroughly, he changes into a new set of robes, which are to be worn at all times in the inner sanctuary where the practice is performed. Whenever he leaves this chamber to tend to necessities, he changes back into an older set. The practice itself lasts for a fixed period of ninety days, over the duration of which the meditator must continuously circumambulate an altar to the Buddha Amitabha. He vows never to entertain worldly thoughts or desires, never to lie down or leave the hall, and, aside from the time when he eats his meals, never to sit down or stop to rest until the three months are completed...The devotional element in this practice...undoubtedly plays a key role; however, as the practitioner becomes more skilled at constructing the mental image of the Buddha, the orientation of the visualization begins to shift radically. Eventually, the eidetic image of Amitabha loses its devotional character altogether and instead *becomes the basis for a simple dialectical investigation into the nature of mind and the noetic act itself*."

[DS/TM,p.58-9]

"When practicing this samadhi, the cultivator has three powers to assist him: the power of Amitabha Buddha, the power of the samadhi and the power of his own virtues. The unit of practice of this samadhi should be ninety days. In that span of time, day and night the practitioner just stands or walks around, visualizing Amitabha Buddha appearing as a body standing on the practitioner's crown, replete with the thirty-two auspicious marks and the eighty beautiful characteristics. He may also recite Amitabha Buddha's name continuously, while constantly visualizing Him. When practice is perfected, the cultivator, in samadhi, can see Amitabha Buddha and the Buddhas of the ten directions standing in front of him, praising and encouraging him. Pratyutpanna is also called the 'Constantly Walking Samadhi.' As the practitioner walks, each step, each word is inseparable from the name of Amitabha Buddha. His body, speech and mind are always practicing Buddha Recitation without interruption, like a continuous flow of water. This method brings very lofty benefits, but only those of high capacity have the endurance to practice it. Those of limited or moderate capacities or lacking in energy cannot pursue this difficult practice."

Tam: 130

NOTE:

"In the *Avatamsaka Sutra*, the first spiritual advisor of the youth Sudhana (q.v.) taught him the 'samadhi of mindfulness of the Buddha' (i.e. Buddha Recitation Samadhi). This was the first Dharma taught to Sudhana, for it appeals to all beings, whether of deep or shallow roots. Specifically, Bhikshu Cloud of Virtue, the first guru, expounded on the Pratyutpanna samadhi (*Avatamsaka Sutra*, ch. 39)."

Huan Hua: na #1278

◙ **PRATYUTPANNA SAMADHI SUTRA**

See also: Pratyutpanna Samadhi

►*Ch*/Pan-Chou San-Mei Ching; *Vn*/Bát-Chu Tam-Muội Kinh. "A sutra that somewhat bridges the gap between distant and immanent Pure Lands. This was first translated into Chinese by Lokaksema in 179 C.E. and can in a sense be regarded as the scriptural foundation for Chinese Pure Land piety. It recommends concentrating the mind on Sukhavati day and night for 90 days after which Sukhavati will appear before one's eyes. The sutra explicitly states that the Pure Land will appear here and now and that one will not have to die and be reborn there. This method, it states, is effective for any Buddha or Buddha-land one wishes to see. Putting it quite straightforwardly, it says 'if you wish to see present Buddhas of the ten directions, you should single-mindedly direct your thought to where they dwell and should not entertain other thoughts. Then you will be able to see them.' This 'is as if a man gets up at night and observes numerous stars.' The reason why the meditation works is simple. We normally 'consider the worldly things as existent and never realize emptiness'; that is, as the *Vimalakirti Sutra* puts it, our world is impure because our minds are impure. But, when we concentrate on reality as it truly is (emptiness or a Pure Land) then, provided that our practice is strong enough, we will begin to see reality truly. The [crucial point], however, is in the proviso. The meditation that results in seeing the Buddhas and their Pure Lands here and now is strenuous and is open only to monastics (with a few rather grudging exceptions) since it requires strict adherence to the

Vinaya as well as long periods of intense meditation. But there is hope for laypeople. 'The Buddha [Sakyamuni said], "Bodhisattvas in this land can *see* Amita Buddha by single-mindedly visualizing him." Now, let it be asked what method of practice they should perform in order to be *born* in the Land. Amita Buddha replies, 'Those who desire to be born should invoke my name unceasingly; then they will attain birth [there].' (*Pratyupanna Samadhi Sutra*) Thus, it appears that the Pan-chou San-Mei ching teaches *invocation of the Name of Amita as a substitute practice for those who are unable to become monks or nuns.* And while invocation will not result in a vision during this life, it will bring rebirth in the Pure Land *after death*, and that, in the end, is just as effective for final liberation. Many practitioners apparently decided that, by and large, this was good enough, and the importance of being a monastic, or having one as a teacher (which this sutra emphasizes) is, in later Pure Land practice, downgraded."
Yoshi/Corless: 254

◙ **PRAYER**
see Dedication of Merit

◙ **PRECEPT AGE**
see Sacerdotal age

◙ **PRECEPT SCHOOL**
see Vinaya School

◙ **PRECEPTS**
See also: Five Precepts; Bhiksu; Bhiksuni; Bodhisattva Precepts
----
▸(*Skt*/Sila) "The rules of conduct and discipline established by the Buddha."
Yoko: 210
Broadly speaking, Buddhist precepts are divided into two categories: the basic precepts common to all traditions, Theravada or Mahayana; and the Bodhisattva Precepts, followed by Mahayana practitioners, both monks and laymen.

(I) *BASIC PRECEPTS*
"Throughout the Buddhist traditions, one of the most important tools for the formation, continuity, and sense of identity of a Buddhist community has been precepts.
a) In addition to taking refuge in the Three Jewels, laypeople took up *Five Precepts*: not to kill, not to steal, not to engage in sexual misconduct, not to lie, and not to use intoxicants. [One who observes these precepts is reborn

as a human being.]

b) Some laypeople would take *Eight Precepts* which they would maintain [on certain special days] each month. These were precepts not to kill; steal; engage in sexual activity; lie; use intoxicants; attend musical performances/ adorn their bodies; sleep on high and wide beds; or eat after noontime.

c) *This same set of precepts, with the addition of two i) not to sing, dance/ perform onstage and ii) not handle gold or silver*, constitutes the ten precepts of novice monks and nuns.

d) Fully ordained monks and nuns held many more precepts; under one of the codes, *monks held 250 precepts, nuns 348.*

All of these precepts, whether lay or monastic, are called *Pratimoksa Precepts*, precepts of liberation. These precepts are regarded as the foundation of the life of a Buddhist. For laypeople, maintaining precepts was a way to accumulate virtuous karma ... For monks and nuns, precepts were regarded as defining monastic identity, a lifestyle designed by the Buddha himself as most conducive to the pursuit of liberation from rebirth.

It was the maintenance of these precepts by monks and nuns that was said to justify the alms they received from the laity. Hence, perhaps, the most important of monastic ceremonies was the Uposadha ceremony, in which the monks of a given monastery or area gathered together to recite the precepts. Prior to the ceremony, monks would gather in small groups of two or three to confess any transgressions of the monastic code to each other. The senior monk would then recite each of the categories of precepts, asking three times at the end of each category whether there were any transgressions to be revealed. Hearing none, because whatever transgressions had occurred would already have been confessed privately, he declared the Sangha to be pure.

(II) *BODHISATTVA PRECEPTS*

With the rise of the various groups that came to be called the Mahayana, we find the development of more precepts, the *Bodhisattva Precepts*.

It seems that in the early Mahayana, persons publicly took the famous Bodhisattva Precepts, promising to achieve Buddhahood in order to liberate all beings from Samsara. In time, a more formal code of conduct was developed, derived from a number of sources, with categories of root infractions and secondary infractions. *The Bodhisattva Precepts, however, could be taken equally by laypeople and monastics, men and women.* Formal ceremonies for doing so are set forth in a number of Mahayana treatises. In addition, there [are] ceremonies for the confession of infractions, modeled on the Uposadha. There is a great deal that could be said about the content of the Bodhisattva Precepts. Some of the precepts have to do with interpersonal relations, prescribing the kind of altruistic behavior that one might expect from a Bodhisattva. Others are more grand. *There is also the suggestion that the Bodhisattva Precepts supersede the Pratimoksa Precepts.*"

Lopez: 504 #2388

The Bodhisattva Precepts include ten major and forty-eight minor precepts. These precepts are derived from the *Three Bodies of Pure Precepts* (q.v.).

(III) *NOTE*

"In Buddhism, there is no cultivation without Discipline (precepts), Concentration and Wisdom, and also there is no Dharma without Discipline, Concentration and Wisdom."

(Hsu Heng Chi, *What's Buddhism?*, p. 39.)

Hsu: 39 #0550

See also Brahma Net Sutra; Bodhisattva Precepts

◎ PRECEPTS SCHOOL

see Vinaya School

◎ PRECEPTS-SAMADHI-WISDOM

see Three Non-Outflow Studies

◎ PREDICTION OF BUDDHAHOOD

Syn: Prophecy of Buddhahood

►"Prophecy of attainment of Buddhahood in a future existence given by a Buddha to some close disciples. In certain cases, the Buddha also reveals the name and type of Buddha-land the disciple will preside over. The *Lotus Sutra* contains many such prophecies."

xxx: na #2168

◎ PRIMAL BUDDHA

see Vairocana Buddha

◎ PROOFS OF REBIRTH IN PURE LAND

Syn: Death signs; Post Mortem Omens; Confirmatory Signs of Rebirth; Rebirth Signs; Omens of Pure Land Rebirth

See also: Testimonials (Pure Land); Visions

▶(I) *PROOFS DURING ONE'S LIFETIME.*

"Pure Land followers should strive earnestly for a response. The lives of sentient beings are ephemeral and easily cut short; the ghost of impermanence waits for no one. Your hair is already streaked with white, your face has grown wrinkled. The marks of decay and old age are very clear, and death is but a short time away. Therefore, *you should strive to cultivate in earnest, to ensure that some auspicious and reliable signs of rebirth appear.* Thus, in ancient China, Elder Master Hui Yuan of Lu Shan saw the Buddha rub his crown three times. Another Elder Master earnestly recited the Buddha's name and immediately saw Amitabha Buddha emit rays of light and display auspicious marks. In the case of still another Elder Master, each time he uttered the Buddha's name, the Great Assembly would see a Buddha flying out of his mouth. This was true for hundreds of thousands of his utterances; hundreds of thousands of Buddhas escaped from his mouth, like so many rosary beads, one

after another. Such responses are countless. If you recite Amitabha Buddha's name in earnest, without interruption, it is very easy to see Him. Otherwise, it is very difficult. If you do not see the Buddha, you do not have affinities with Him. Without affinities, it is certainly difficult to achieve rebirth in the Pure Land. If you are not reborn in the Pure Land, sooner or later you will descend into the Evil Realms. Thus, a single thought of interrupting recitation is precisely the karma of rebirth on the Three Evil Paths. You should bear this in mind and ponder it carefully! (Master Tien Ju)"
Dia: 106-107

"Although death signs are an important and frequent topic of discussion among Pure Land believers, it is essential to realize that *great emphasis is placed on confirmatory signs for the living practitioner as well.* After all, when one has decided to devote a lifetime to Pure Land practice rather than wait until his last breath to turn to Amitabha, it is perfectly natural to expect some confirmation of spiritual progress along the way. Following the cue of such Pure Land scriptures as the *Meditation Sutra,* together with various other buddhanusmrti

sutras popular in China, Pure Land practitioners look to two sorts of visionary phenomena as assurance of their future rebirth in Sukhavati: One is auspicious dreams of Amitabha and the Pure Land; the other, visitations from Amitabha and previous saints or 'spirit journeys' to the Pure Land experienced in a state of samadhi or meditative ecstasy. Both forms of experience are considered valid proof that the 'connection with the pure land' would soon be secured -- provided, of course, that the character and behavior of the individual who claimed the experience fit the profile of a dedicated Pure Land devotee. Nevertheless, in Pure Land hagiography and doctrine, *samadhi is given precedence over dreams.* The biography of nearly every major Pure Land saint -- especially the patriarchal figures -- is marked by the watershed experience of a vision of this sort. Here we find an important point of soteriological convergence "between" the Pure Land ritual and meditative manuals and the Pure Land hagiographical collections. In certain respects, this convergence requires us to reevaluate the way in which the long-range goal of rebirth in the Pure Land actually functions within the lives of Pure Land believers. It is easy, but perhaps ultimately misleading, to think of Pure Land spirituality as having an obsession with death and the afterlife just because its stated aim is rebirth in Sukhavati. This is especially so if we are to take Master Zunshi and Shandao seriously when they taught that sustained practice of nienfo (Buddha-Recitation) will bring a vision of the Buddha in this very life. In effect, such a vision of Amitabha does more than confirm that one is destined for the Pure Land in the near future, for it implies that one already has access to the Buddha now. Thus it becomes a mark of sainthood that is virtually equivalent (in anticipated form) to the irreversibility on the Bodhisattva path that will be formally achieved when one is reborn in the Pure Land itself. In this respect, it represents a kind of Pure Land 'enlightenment' experience that is equally compelling and equally vital to establishing religious identity and authority as the 'seeing into one's original nature' of Chan/Zen."
Lopez/95: 594

(II) *PROOFS AFTER DEATH*
"Among the signs that confirm

rebirth in the Pure Land, deathbed and mortuary anomalies are certainly popular. Some involve the dying person, such as visions of Amitabha and his retinue coming to greet one with a lotus pedestal, as described in the *Meditation Sutra*. An unusually peaceful death (often while seated erect in a meditative posture) or the hearing of marvelous strains of music, the smell of rare fragrances, or the sight of unusual auras on the part of friends and relatives are also common features. Another variety of post-mortem omen centers around the disposition of the corpses or the experience of the mourners over the weeks of mortuary observance that follow. One phenomenon that is a universal sign of sainthood or high spiritual attainment in Chinese Buddhism is the discovery of *auspicious relics* (Skt: sarira) amid the ashes of a cremated corpse, usually in the form of glassine or jadelike beads. If burial is chosen over cremation, natural mummification of individual bodily organs or the corpse itself will be taken as an indication of sanctity. Another frequent occurence, but one which seems to be more peculiar to Pure Land devotees, is the experience of visitations from the deceased to surviving relatives and friends. Usually these occur in dreams and take the form of either a vision of the beatified dead person or a 'spirit-journey' with the dead person to the Pure Land. Upon occasion, however, a layperson or cleric of highly developed religious ability will have a vision of the deceased while in a state of samadhi or meditative transport."
Lopez/95: 594

"After someone dies, the people in the room perceive a magical fragrance and hear celestial music gradually fading away toward the west. A golden lotus might appear on the death bed or on top of the coffin. The dead believer's corpse does not decompose. Auspicious colored clouds hang over the funeral pyre." (J.C. Cleary, tr., *Pure Land Pure Mind*.) #1764

◙ PROPHECIES
see Fortune Telling; Revelations

◙ PROPHECY OF BUDDHAHOOD
see Prediction of Buddhahood

◙ PROPITIOUS KALPA
see Auspicious Kalpa

◙ PROSTRATION

▸"Westerners unused to oriental concepts of politeness sometimes find it embarrassing to prostrate themselves. Asians, however, honor elders and superiors in this way as a matter of course; there is no thought of degradation. [Monks and Nuns] do not exact such homage and would not, I suppose, mind its omission; it is freely given because it is the custom and because it has value. Besides being a salutary check on pride and therefore egoism, it promotes the frame of mind needed for ensuring prompt assent to instructions profoundly affecting the disciple's mental and spiritual welfare."

Blof: 141 #1786

◙ PROVISIONAL TEACHINGS

See also: Perfect, Sudden Teaching

▸"In Mahayana Buddhism it is believed that Buddha Sakyamuni simplified many of his teachings, particularly the earlier ones, in order that people of various capacities could understand them and eventually be led to the final doctrine.

These simplified teachings are thought to have only a provisional nature."

Yoko: 211

NOTE:

Another interpretation is that the teachings themselves are not simplified, but rather the audience was not ready to understand them to the full extent. As an analogy, the rain may fall equally on big trees and small but the larger ones absorb more water. (see *Lotus Sutra*.)

Editor: na #0798

◙ PROVISIONS FOR PURE LAND REBIRTH

Syn: Lifetime Provisions; Life Provisions; Personal Provisions

See also: Rebirth in the Pure Land

▸In Pure Land terminology, provisions stand for Faith, Vows and Practice which are considered the personal provisions that a Pure Land adept needs to have to achieve rebirth in the Pure Land.

Editor: na

"Faith, Vows and Practice are called the 'Three Personal Provisions' of the Pure Land method. Just as travellers embarking on a distant journey must make provisions for medicine, food, clothing and funds sufficient to cover their

needs en route, so, too, Pure Land practitioners require Faith to make firm Vows. However, Faith and Vows are hollow without Practice. Likewise, even if Practice is adequate, without Faith and Vows, that Practice will go astray, lacking criteria and direction. Therefore, Faith, Vows and Practice are the 'provisions' of those returning to the Pure Land from afar" (Thích Thiền Tâm, *Buddhism of Wisdom and Faith*, sect. 21).
Tam: 91 #1292

◙ **PU-TO SHAN**
See P'u T'o Mountain

◙ **PUNGENT ROOTS**
see   Herbs (Pungent --)

◙ **PURE LAND (REALM)**
see   Sukhavati; Pure Lands (As Realms)

◙ **PURE LAND / PURE MIND**
See also: Pure Land School

▶In Buddhism, the *sine qua non* for Enlightenment and Buddhahood is a pure mind, that is, a mind totally free of greed, anger and delusion. In *Pure Land Buddhism, the usual terminology is a mind of utmost reverence and sincerity,* leading to

one-pointedness of mind. This is because when the cultivator focusses singlemindly on the Amitabha Buddha, he cannot harbor thoughts of greed, anger or delusion -- his mind is pure. A pure mind is enlightenment -- is the Pure Land.
Editor/Zen: 95 #1463

◙ **PURE LAND/ ZEN**
see Zen/ Pure Land

◙ **PURE LAND BUDDHISM (SUMMARY)**
See also: Immortality; Universal Method; Special Teaching; Raigo
----
▶*FAMOUS QUOTES:*
#. "Speak one sentence less of chatter;/ Recite once more the Buddha's name./ Recite until your false thoughts die and/ Your Dharma Body will come to life."
#. "Develop the Supreme Bodhi M i n d ; /   A c h i e v e singlemindedness; / The Pure Land is yours."

(I) Dominant school in East Asia
"[Pure Land comprises the schools] of East Asia which emphasize aspects of Mahayana Buddhism stressing faith in Amida, meditation on and recitation of his name, and the religious goal of being reborn in

his 'Pure Land,' or 'Western Paradise.'" (K. Crim, *Perennial Dictionary of World Religions.*) The goal of those devoted to Amitabha and the Pure Land is to be reborn there, and attain enlightenment (Buddhahood)." Larousse: 419

Pure Land Buddhism chiefly consists in hearing and reciting Amitabha Buddha's name with a faithful mind, but it does not exclude meditation (*dhyana*) and insight (*vipasyana*) through which one can visualise the Buddha. Obviously, meditation and insight are mainly practiced by monks, particularly by gifted persons, while hearing and reciting the name with faith are easily practiced even by laymen. Exposition of the higher practices of Amitabha worship first appeared in the *Pratyutpanna Samadhi Sutra*. Later, Vasubandhu propounded the contemplation of Amitabha by *samatha* (concentration) practices. This, however, does not involve the concept of Amitabha as a meditation Buddha. (*Encyclopedia of Buddhism*, v. I: p.452)

"Given its popular appeal, [Pure Land] quickly became the object of the most dominant form of Buddhist devotion in East Asia."

M. Eliade, ed., *Encyclopedia of Religions*, Vol. 12)."

"The Pure Land school is presently the school of Buddhism in China and Japan that has the most followers" (*Shambhala Dictionary of Buddhism and Zen*). Sham: 174

(II) How Pure Land works

The goal espoused by all Buddhist schools is for the practitioner to achieve Buddhahood, i.e., to become an 'Enlightened Being.' Thus, to practice Buddhism is to cultivate enlightenment, to attain Wisdom. Although there are many paths to reach this goal, they all involve severing greed, anger and delusion, thus perfecting the qualities of the Mind (paramitas). Traditionally, Buddhist sutras enumerate six or ten paramitas, but they may be reduced to three: *Discipline*, *Concentration* and *Wisdom* (the second, fifth and sixth paramitas, respectively). Pure Land , symbolized by the Buddha Recitation method, is a Mahayana approach that employs, *inter alia*, the techniques of meditation-visualization (of the Pure Land, Amitabha Buddha) and of oral recitation (q.v.) of the Buddha's name, to realize these paramitas. That is, when a practitioner is busy visualizing the Buddha or reciting the Buddha's name, he cannot commit transgressions or violate the Buddhist precepts. Therefore, he has effectively fulfilled the paramita of *Discipline*. Likewise, reciting the Buddha's name with a completely focussed Mind is nothing less than fulfilling the paramita of *Concentration*. Once Concentration is achieved, the practitioner's Mind becomes empty and still, leading to the emergence of his innate *wisdom* - - the Wisdom of the Buddhas. Thus, a sincere Buddha Recitation practitioner, by dint of his own effort, effectively attains Buddhahood. According to Pure Land doctrine, however, *most practitioners in this Degenerate Age find the 'self-power,' self-help appproach too difficult and arduous*; therefore, in their Pure Land teachings, the Buddhas and Sages compassionately emphasized the additional element of 'other-power.' This *involves reliance on Amitabha Buddha's Vows (q.v.), made countless eons ago, to welcome and escort all sentient beings to his Land of Ultimate Bliss -- an ideal training ground, an ideal environment*. To benefit from these Vows, the cultivator still needs to do his part -- and the easiest practice is Buddha Recitation (q.v.).

Editor: na

"Ultimately, when the practitioner recites to the point of pure, unmixed power, the totality of Mind is Buddha, the totality of Buddha is Mind, Mind and Buddha are as one. I am afraid that this principle and practice are not understood by everyone. It has always been my desire to proclaim them and to disseminate the Original Vows of Amitabha Buddha to rescue all sentient beings." (Patriarch Yin Kuang, 19th c.)

PLZ: 150-151

"Some of our readers may be led to think that the sole object of the Pure Land devotees is to be born in Amida's Land of Bliss and Purity ... But the fact is that the birth itself ... is not the object, but to attain enlightenment in the country of Amida where conditions are such as to ensure a ready realization of the true Buddhist life ... If we can say so, to be born in the Pure Land is the means to the end; for Buddhism in whatever form is a religion of enlightenment and emancipation." (D.T. Suzuki in *The Eastern Buddhist*, v. 3, no. 4)

(III) Why Pure Land?

"The champions of Pure Land Buddhism have always made the case that Pure Land methods are especially valuable because they are particularly effective in meeting the needs of the greatest number of people. When we face facts, most of us have to admit that we see little realistic prospect of achieving salvation through the eons of gradual practice spoken of in the Buddhist scriptures, or the heroic efforts of the Zen masters, or the years of esoteric dedication demanded by the Esoteric Schools. Pure Land practice, on the other hand, is explicitly designed as an easy way, open to all" (J.C.Cleary). Mind-Seal: 3 Traditionally, in Mahayana, it is necessary to go through "fifty-two levels of Bodhisattva practice" (q.v.) to attain Buddhahood. Even in the Sudden School, it is understood that the practitioner has already cultivated in many past lifetimes and reached one of the last levels when he achieves instant Enlightenment. In Pure Land, however, the practitioner seeks rebirth in the Land of Ultimate Bliss, *an ideal environment for cultivation*, where these levels of attainment are *compressed*. Instead of a laborious "vertical" struggle, he achieves a direct "horizontal" escape from the Saha World. ("Horizontal" and "Vertical" are figures of speech, which can readily be understood through the example of a worm born inside a stalk of a bamboo. To escape, it can take the hard way and crawl "vertically" all the way to the top of the stalk. Alternatively, it can poke a hole near its current location and escape "horizontally" into the big, wide world.) Editor: na

NOTE:

"The principal and essential goal of Pure Land practice is to *achieve rebirth in the Pure Land within one lifetime so as to reach the stage of Non-Retrogression (q.v.). This is what sets Pure Land apart from other schools and gives it its name*." (T.T.Tam). To insure success, however, the cultivator needs to fulfill two crucial conditions: develop the *Bodhi Mind* (q.v.) and practice Buddha Recitation to the level of *one-pointedness of mind* (q.v.). Seeking auspicious signs of future rebirth is also recommended. (See entry Proofs of Rebirth in the Pure Land.) Editor: na

◙ PURE LAND MANDALAS

See also: Chiko Mandala; Taima Mandala; Raigo

▸"In the corpus of Jodo painting there is a group of works known as mandalas of the Pure Land. (Here the term 'mandala' has been adapted from its more familiar usage in esoteric Buddhist symbolism.) The three most celebrated Jodo mandalas are the *Chiko mandala* (q.v.), the *Taima mandala* (q.v.), and the *Shokai mandala*. In addition to these, there are a number of other Pure Land designs of this mandala type.

The prototypes for these mandalas were established by the eight century in China. Paradise scenes can be found from as early as the begining of the T'ang dynasty (618-907) at Tun-huang. The Chinese sense of order pervades these formal, geometric depictions of Paradise, and the architectural arrangements reproduce the layout of T'ang monasteries and palaces. The classic paradise scene shows a vast landscape dominated by an architectural complex. There are aerial pavillions constructed on one another at perpendicular angles. Spaced at regular intervals, often in diamond or square-shaped patterns, stand numerous Bodhisattvas and divine attendants. Some deities fly through the air and others descend on clouds, while the elect dance to the sound of instruments played by celestial musicians.

The foreground shows a pond covered with lotus flowers and the famous 'jewel trees' described in the sutras. The Buddha sits on a lotus throne in the center of the composition, behind an altar covered with offerings. Although the pavillions reflect the Chinese style of architecture, all the deities are dressed in Indian costumes."

Okaz: 37

◙ PURE LAND PATRIARCHS

See also: Pure Land School

▸"Devotion to Amitabha Buddha was, prior to the Chinese *Patriarch Hui-yuan* (344-416), an optional practice within Buddhism. Hui-yuan established this practice as an independent activity, and developed a new Buddhist school around it by forming the White Lotus Society in 402. His disciple *T'an-luan* (476-542) organized the school, and is recognized as a patriarch. They emphasize Amitabha's

(shortened to Amita and rendered A-mi-t'o in Chinese) vow to cause all faithful beings to be reborn in his paradise, focusing religious practice on repetition of the phrase known as the Nien-fo: 'Nam-mo A-mi-t'o Fo,' literally meaning 'Homage to Amita Buddha.' Because the school relies on the saving grace of Amitabha Buddha, it is often referred to as the 'easy path' of dependence on outside help (t'zu-li in Chinese; tariki in Japanese). Textually, the school utilizes the *Amitabha Sutras* and the *Meditation Sutra*. The school was passed down through a succession of masters including *Tao-cho* (562-645), *Shan-tao* (613-681), and *Tz'u-min* (680-748). Due to its simplicity of practice, it was better able to survive periods of decline, and thus weathered the Chinese anti-Buddhist persecution of 845 better than virtually all other Buddhist schools. It was founded in Japan as the Jodo school by *Honen* (1133-1212), where [together with a later offshoot, the Jodo-shinshu school], it remains the most popular school." Preb: 92-93

◙ **PURE LAND PHILOSOPHY**
see Special Teaching

◙ **PURE LAND SCHOOL**
See also: Pure Land Buddhism (Summary); Pure Lands (Realms); Rebirth in the Pure Land; Sukhavati; Special Teaching; Zen/Pure Land; Universal Method

----

▸For a summary of this entry, see Pure Land Buddhism (Summary).

(I) *GENERALITIES*
"Pure Land or Amidism: generic term under which are comprehended all schools of East Asian Buddhism that have made Amitabha the central point of their teaching."
Sham: 5
"This is the general name of those doctrines which teach that man can attain Buddhahood by being born in the Pure Land of Amitabha. In India, this teaching was advocated by Asvaghosa, Nagarjuna, and Vasubandhu, and was based upon various sutras such as the two *Sukhavati-vyuhas* [*Amitabha Sutras*]."
Dait: 157
"Historically, the roots of Pure Land go back to Ancient India, albeit the tradition was not emphasized: "Although a school dedicated to Amitabha Buddha worship did arise in India, piety toward this Buddha seems to

have been merely one of many practices of early Mahayana Buddhism." (Joji Okazaki, *Pure Land Buddhist Painting*, p.14.)

(II) *PURE LAND GOAL:*
"The aim of the Pure Land method is the Buddha Recitation Samadhi, achieving, in totality, our Self-Nature Amitabha -- the realm of the 'Ever-Silent Illuminating Pure Land.' However, the *most urgent and immediate aim is rebirth in the Pure Land.* This ensures an end to Birth and Death, and then, through the excellent environment of the Land of Bliss, progress in cultivation and swift attainment of Buddhahood. For this reason, Pure Land cultivators should recite the name of Amitabha Buddha. This is the principal approach of Pure Land; it does not consist of rapidly reaching the realm of No-Thought and becoming enlightened to our Original Nature, as in Zen. However, while working toward that goal, the practitioner should recite until he reaches the state of one-pointedness of mind. Thus, although he does not seek the realm of 'No-Thought,' that realm will nevertheless appear naturally. Moreover, it will

appear that much sooner, thanks to the virtues accumulated through Buddha Recitation, which help to erase bad karma swiftly. Here we can see a new ray of light, a new vista: to achieve 'No-Thought' swiftly, to become enlightened to the Original Nature speedily, we should recite the Buddha's name all the more. Probing deeper, if we have the roots and the temperament of Mahayana followers, we should understand that *the ultimate goal of Buddha Recitation is to achieve Buddhahood.* If we understand that goal to be merely the elimination of deluded thoughts, we have already strayed into the 'Five Meditations to calm the mind' approach of the Theravada tradition. Why is it that the goal of Buddha Recitation is to become a Buddha? It is because as soon as we begin reciting, the past, present and future have lost their distinctions, marks exist but they have been left behind, form is emptiness, thought is the same as No-Thought, the realm of the Original Nature 'apart from thought' of the Tathagata has been penetrated. This state is Buddhahood. What else could it be?" (From *Buddhism of Wisdom and Faith.*) Tam: 78-79

"The immediate goal of Nien-fo [Buddha Recitation] practice is to 'forge the karmic connection or circumstances' that will eventuate in one's rebirth in the Pure Land. Recitation of Amitabha's name and the *earnest wish to be reborn in Sukhavati* are central to this process. However, equally key to their success is the cultivation of 'a *one-pointed and unperturbed mind*' -- a term that admits various interpretations, but which the monastic tradition mainly takes to mean sustained meditative concentration or samadhi. In the eyes of the clerically-centered Pure Land movement, samadhi is both an essential factor in and signature of the successful forging of the karmic conditions for rebirth." Lopez/95: 368

"Some of our readers may be led to think that the sole object of the Pure Land devotees is to be born in Amida's Land of Bliss and Purity ... But the fact is that the birth itself ... is not the object, but to attain enlightenment in the country of Amida where conditions are such as to ensure a ready realization of the true Buddhist life ... If we can say so, to be born in the Pure Land is the means to the end; for Buddhism in whatever form is a religion of enlightenment and emancipation." (D.T. Suzuki in *The Eastern Buddhist*, Vol. 3, No. 4, p.321.) Editor/Zen: 4

(III) *PURE LAND PRACTICE*:
"The practice of the school consists primarily in the *recitation of Amitabha's name (nembutsu) and/or in visualizing Amitabha and his paradise*. The sutras used as the scriptural foundation of the school are the two *Amitabha Sutras* and the *Amitayurdhyana Sutra (Meditation Sutra*). The recitation of Amitabha's name serves to bring the mind under control. The practitioner commits himself to a certain, usually very large, number of repetitions. This recitation can be done out loud or silently, with or without concentration on an image of Amitabha. This is the predominant practice of the school. A less frequent practice consists of visualizations/ meditations -- particularly the sixteenth variant described in the *Meditation Sutra*. The supreme stage of practice is the contemplation of Buddha Amitabha as not separate from

one's own being."
Sham: 174-175
In the Pure Land method, all wholesome practices are valid as long as the merits accrued are dedicated to rebirth in the Pure Land. However, *ideally, the main practice should be Buddha Recitation.* If the practitioner engages indifferently in a variety of practices, his cultivation lacks focus and he may inadvertently forget about the all-important goal of rebirth in the Pure Land. Moreover, the main practice is no longer the main practice because there is, in fact, no main practice at all.
Editor/Zen: 106

Pure Land Retreat

"From as early as the Tang period we hear of the existence of 'Pure Land Cloisters' within larger monastic complexes, where a congregation of self-professed Pure Land mendicants could pursue a collective regimen of Pure Land practice and study. Over the centuries that followed, influential Pure Land masters have periodically sought to organize individual monasteries along Pure Land lines. The Ming dynasty master Chu Hung (1535-1615) and Republican period master Yin Kuang (1861-1940) represent two such

figures who have had a profound impact on the monastic form of Pure Land Buddhism in modern times. Both instituted comprehensive plans for adapting traditional monastic structures and routines to the specific purposes of Pure Land devotion, including the creation of halls for the concentrated recitation of the Buddha's name that were modeled on the traditional Chan meditation hall. At the same time, monks and nuns of the Pure Land school developed a number of distinctive forms of retreat that are organized along the lines of the Seven-Day Retreat for Buddha-mindfulness [Buddha Recitation, q.v.] but apply its program to a more intensive monastic setting."
Lopez: 366-367
See also: Faith-Vows-Practice; Seven-day Retreat
(IV) *SPECIAL FEATURES*:
"The Pure Land or Lotus school of Buddhism is the oldest of the present schools of Buddhism in East Asia. Its influence, I should add, has been very much greater than the number of its recognized members would indicate; for it eventually permeated to a considerable degree all the other schools. Had not Buddhism been presented in

this form, it is unlikely that it ever would have been able to get the strong hold upon [East Asians] in the centuries following [Master] Hui Yuan's (q.v.) time." Pratt: 277

i. "It is like lighting a fire on top of ice. As the fire intensifies, the ice will melt. When the ice melts, then the fire will go out. Those people of a lower grade of rebirth who rely on the power of reciting the Buddha's name ... even though they do not understand the birthlessness of the Dharma Nature, will attain the realm of birthlessness and will see the flame of rebirth spontaneously disappear at that time." (Quoted in D. Chappell, "Chinese Buddhist Interpretations of the Pure Land." *Buddhist & Taoist Studies I*, p.42.

ii. "High-ranking masters of the Buddhist canon have often commented: The Buddha Recitation method encompasses the Zen, Scriptural Studies, Discipline (Vinaya) and Esoteric (Tantric) Schools. Why is it that Buddha Recitation encompasses all four schools? It is because when reciting the Buddha's name, we rid ourselves of all deluded thoughts and attachments, which is Zen. The sacred words 'Amitabha Buddha' contain innumerable sublime meanings, hidden in and springing forth from those words, which is the Scriptural Studies School. Reciting the Buddha's name at the deepest level stills and purifies the three karmas (of the mind, speech and body), which is the Discipline School. The words 'Amitabha Buddha' have the same effect as a mantra, eliminating grievances and wrongs, severing evil karma, granting wishes and subduing demons. This is the Esoteric School." Thich: 72

iii. "Exchanging the virtues of Buddha Recitation for the petty merits and blessings of this world is certainly not consonant with the intentions of the Buddhas. Therefore, practitioners should recite the name of Amitabha Buddha for the purpose of escaping the cycle of Birth and Death. However, if we were to practice Buddha Recitation for the sake of our own salvation alone, we would only fulfill a small part of the Buddhas' intentions. What, then, is the ultimate intention of the Buddhas? *The ultimate intention of the Buddhas is for all sentient beings to escape the cycle of Birth and Death and to become enlightened, as they are.* Thus, those who recite Amitabha Buddha's name should develop the Bodhi Mind (aspiration for Supreme Enlightenment). The word "Bodhi" means "enlightened." There are three main stages of Enlightenment: the Enlightenment of the Sravakas (Hearers); the Enlightenment of the Pratyeka (Self-Awakened) Buddhas; the Enlightenment of the Buddhas. What Pure Land practitioners who develop the Bodhi Mind are seeking is precisely the Enlightenment of the Buddhas. This stage of Buddhahood is the highest, transcending those of the Sravakas and Pratyeka Buddhas, and is therefore called Supreme Enlightenment or Supreme Bodhi. This Supreme Bodhi Mind contains two principal seeds, Compassion and Wisdom, from which emanates the great undertaking of rescuing oneself and all other sentient beings. To reiterate, the Bodhi Mind I am referring to here is the supreme, perfect Bodhi Mind of the Buddhas, not the Bodhi Mind of the Sravakas or Pratyeka Buddhas." Tam: 29

(V) *PURE LAND TEXTS/ BOOKS*
A limited number of books providing an overall, in-depth view of Pure Land Buddhism are available in English. Recent publications include: i) *On Amidism* by Elder Master T'an Hsu (1973 and 1997, Buddhist Association of the US); ii) *Mind-Seal of the Buddhas* (Master Ou-i's commentary on the *Amitabha Sutra*, translated in 1997 by Dr. J.C. Cleary); iii) *Horizontal Escape* by Master Thích Thiền Tâm (1994, Sutra Translation Committee of the US & Canada, Bronx, NY). This same work by Master Thích Thiền Tâm has also appeared as *Buddhism of Wisdom and Faith*, published by three different organizations: the International Buddhist Monastic Institute, (USA), the Corporate Body of the Buddha Educational Foundation (Taiwan) and the Amitabha Buddhist Society (Malaysia). It is also one of six Sutra Translation Committee books on Pure Land reprinted privately in Hong Kong.

(VI) *FAMOUS QUOTES:*
"Speak one sentence less of chatter;/ Recite once more the Buddha's name./ Recite until your false thoughts die and/ Your Dharma Body will come to life."
"Develop the Supreme Bodhi Mind;/ Achieve singlemindedness; / The Pure Land is yours."

(VII) *NOTE*:

"The principal and essential goal of Pure Land practice is to *achieve rebirth in the Pure Land within one lifetime so as to reach the stage of Non-Retrogression (q.v.). This is what sets Pure Land apart from other schools and gives it its name.*" (T.T.Tam). To insure success, however, the cultivator needs to fulfill two crucial conditions: develop the *Bodhi Mind* (q.v.) and practice Buddha Recitation to the level of *one-pointedness of mind* (q.v.). Seeking auspicious signs of future rebirth is also recommended.

Editor: na

See entries: Proofs of Rebirth in the Pure Land; Pure Land School vs. Other Schools; Sincerity and Respect.   #2248

◉ **PURE LAND SCHOOL *VS.* OTHER SCHOOLS**

See also: Pure Land Buddhism (Summary); Other Power; Zen / Pure Land

----

▶"Everyone can appreciate why the Pure Land method, particularly Oral Invocation, is an easy method. However, the word '*easy*' has many meanings, with which not everyone will be familiar. This is because when practicing other methods, for example, *Scriptural Studies* (q.v.) we encounter an immense number of sutras and commentaries, infinitely profound in meaning. In the first instance, the practitioner should fully understand the basic teaching and, from there, penetrate the different shades of meaning. After that, he should reconcile all meanings, extracting their kernel and essence, to discover and choose the method of cultivation that he will follow all his life. All this cannot be done unless he is willing to spend several dozen years of hard work. Should he decide to seek liberation through the *Discipline School* (which teaches the strict application of the precepts), the practitioner must join the Order and become thoroughly conversant with all aspects of the different bodies of precepts. He should also possess the wisdom to distinguish meaning from words and apply the precepts in a flexible manner, according to the environment, the times and the occasion. Thus, to study the sutras is not necessarily difficult, but to study the precepts to the point of knowing how to adapt them skillfully, neither breaking them nor being rigidly bound by them, is truly difficult. Once having understood the precepts, the practitioner must exercise patience and fortitude and endure discomfort and suffering in order to achieve success. If he decides to enter the Way through *Zen*, he should have previously sown the seeds of wisdom and have suitably high innate capacities. Otherwise, he has no hope of attaining this lofty Dharma and participating in the "transmission of the lamp" (q.v.). Therefore, a famous Buddhist scholar once said: Practicing Zen to achieve Buddhahood is the domain of scholars endowed with wisdom. This observation is certainly not incorrect or exaggerated. With the *Pure Land school* particularly Buddha Recitation, once the practitioner has developed the mind of Faith and Vows, he can recite the Buddha's name and engage in cultivation regardless of whether his capacities are high, moderate or limited. Moreover, *while other methods depend on self-power alone, the Pure Land Method first relies to the utmost on self-power and then adds the element of "other-power." Other-power is precisely the infinitely great and powerful Vow of Amitabha Buddha "to welcome and escort."*

As long as a practitioner sincerely repents and recites the Buddha's name with one-pointedness of mind, even though he is not yet free of delusions and is still afflicted with heavy evil karma, he, too, will be welcomed to the Pure Land. The ancients used to say, by way of comparison: *Practicing other methods is as difficult and laborious as an ant climbing a high mountain; reciting the Buddha's name seeking rebirth in the Pure Land is as swift and easy as a boat sailing downstream in the direction of the blowing wind.* This observation is very appropriate indeed. Moreover, once reborn there, living in an auspicious and peaceful environment, always in the company of Buddha Amitabha and the Bodhisattvas, the practitioner will swiftly achieve success in whatever Dharma method he chooses. He is like a log rolling down a high mountain, which just keeps going and never stops, even for a moment. In summary, Buddha Recitation is easy for three reasons: *easy practice, easy achievement of rebirth in the Pure Land, easy attainment of Buddhahood.* Therefore, the results achieved through Buddha

Recitation from time immemorial can be compared to the clear and limpid sound of precious stones striking against genuine gold, or the sight of "smiling lotus blossoms with their fresh and fragrant grades of rebirth." Within these levels and grades, the path from sentient being to Buddhahood contains many ranks, yet is also without rank. This is because, once reborn in the Pure Land, the practitioner has transcended Birth and Death -- and to recite the Buddha's name is to become Buddha. This is like the silkworm, the chrysalis and the butterfly, which are inseparable; there is very little difference between saying that a butterfly is originally a worm or that the worm *is* the butterfly."

Thich: 233-236

"If we were to use Buddha Recitation to discover the Mind-Ground and awaken to our Original Nature, the Pure Land method would be no different from other methods. However, when we rely on Buddha Recitation to seek rebirth in the Pure Land, this method has unique characteristics.

Tam: sec. 27

The strength and pervasiveness of Pure Land are such that its main practice, buddha-remembrance (recitation), is found in other schools, including the Tantric and Zen schools. In Pure Land, recitation is practiced for the immediate purpose of achieving rebirth in the Land of Amitabha Buddha. In the Tantric school, the immediate aim is to destroy evil karma and afflictions and generate blessings and wisdom in the current lifetime. In Zen, the koan of buddha-recitation is meant to sever delusive thought and realize the Self-Nature True Mind. The ultimate goal of all three schools is, of course, the same: to achieve enlightenment and Buddhahood. A question that immediately arises is how two methods seemingly so opposite as Pure Land and Zen can lead to the same goal of Buddhahood. As an analogy, supposing a patient is admitted to the hospital with a high fever. The physician will, of course, prescribe a medication to lower the fever. However, if later in the day, her temperature has dropped to a dangerously low level, he will attempt to raise it with another prescription. The immediate goal is different in each case, but the ultimate goal in both is the same: to normalize the temperature of the patient.

The Buddha, as the master physician, likewise employs 84,000 methods (i.e., an infinite number) to treat the 84,000 afflictions of sentient beings.
Editor: na #2251

◙ **PURE LAND SUTRAS**
see Three Pure Land sutras

◙ **PURE LANDS (AS REALMS)**
See also: Pure Land Buddhism (Summary); Sukhavati

►"In Mahayana Buddhism, Pure Lands are realms created by the compassion of a Bodhisattva or Buddha where beings may aspire to be born in order to complete the path to Enlightenment under more propitious circumstances."
Batc: 382
"In Mahayana cosmology, there are virtually countless Buddhas, and so are there countless 'Pure Lands' where these Buddhas dwell. By their very nature, these Pure Lands are paradises, resplendent with manifold benefits and beauties, and as such, ideal places for rebirth. Nonetheless, existence even in a Pure Land cannot be considered permanent, and must be viewed as only a more favorable location from which to pursue one's on-going path to salvation. It is,

however, an especially important oasis in times of Dharma decline when earthly conditions seem not to favor spiritual development and advancement. A number of Pure Lands became quite important in the development of Mahayana texts. Pursuit of rebirth in Amitabha's Pure Land developed into a formal Buddhist school which gained [the widest] following in East Asian Buddhism."
Preb: 219-220
"The 'pure land' reflects a concept associated with the Mahayana Bodhisattva practice of 'purifying the Buddhaland.' 'Purification' in this context refers to the spiritual process of leading all beings dwelling within the Bodhisattva's realm to enlightenment. This idea finds clear expression in such early Mahayana sutras as the *Prajnaparamita*, *Lotus*, *Dasabhumika* [*Ten Stages*] and *Vimalakirti*."
Tana 205
"There are two kinds of Pure Lands (of Phenomena): (1) those of the heavenly beings (deva), and (2) places such as that of Amitabha's Sukhavati. The difference between the two lies in the nature of the practitioner's intention and the quality of

religious practice involved in attaining rebirth. With regard to the former, the [adepts], who are reborn there, practice pure actions with the intent to attain some form of existence. They are still attached to the idea of rebirth in some higher level of existence. Consequently, they gain rebirth in one of the heavens of the Realm of Desire (kama-dhatu) or Realm of Form (rupa-dhatu). The second subgroup of Pure Lands differs from the first in that its aspirants seek to transcend the Three Realms. Hence, the Pure Lands that they attain, such as Amitabha's Sukhavati and the Realm of Fragrances (*Vimalakirti Sutra*) are not located within the Triple Realm. Beings in those Pure Lands have transcended Birth and Death."

Tana: 104 #1848

◉ **PURE RULES (OF PAI-CHANG)**
See also: Pai-chang

▶"A written work containing the rules for life in a Zen monastery established by the Chinese Ch'an (Zen) master Pai-chang Huai-hai. The regulations recorded in this work are considered authoritative to the present day."   Sham: 166

"Pai-chang Huai-hai stressed monastic discipline and is credited with the writing of the first monastic code for Ch'an monks, the *Pure Rules of Pai-chang*. The Pure Rules stipulate that the ritual performed during a monk's cremation ceremony must include the recitation of Amitabha's name."

Yu: 48 #0375

Excerpts from "Pure Land Buddhism: Dialogues with Ancient Masters."
"Elder Zen Master Pai Chang of Huai Hai [one of the most famous Zen Masters of all time] was the direct successor to the great Zen Master Ma Tsu of Chiang Hsi. Zen communities throughout the world are established on his model and have adopted his *Pure Rules*. Since ancient times, no one has dared to criticize or violate this set of rules.

According to these Rules, prayers for the benefit of seriously ill monks and nuns include the following passage: 'The fourfold assembly should gather together, and all should recite verses of praise to Amitabha Buddha and chant his name from one hundred to one thousand times. At the end, the following words of transference should be read: *If conditions have not yet come to an end, let him quickly recover. If the time of death has arrived, we pray that he will be reborn in the Pure Land.'* Is this not pointing the way back to the Pure Land?

Moreover, the liturgy for sending off deceased monks includes this passage: "the great assembly should all recite the name of Amitabha Buddha in unison, transferring the merits and making the following vow: *Let his soul be reborn in the Pure Land, his karma in the world of dust severed; let him be reborn in the upper lotus grade, with a golden body. May he also receive a prediction of Buddhahood in one lifetime.*" Is this not pointing the way back to the Pure Land?

Furthermore, at the time of burial or cremation, the *Pure Rules* stipulate: "The monk in charge of the service should lead the way, striking the small bell, and recite the name of Amitabha Buddha ten times, with the great assembly following in unison. After recitation, the following words of transference should be read: *We have just intoned the Buddha's name ten times to assist in rebirth ...*" Is this not pointing

the way back to the Pure Land? It is for these reasons that this old monk said, *Zen Masters the world over all set their Minds on the Pure Land.*"
P.L. DIA: 47-48
See also: Zen/ Pure Land

◉ PURNA

▶"One of the ten great disciples of the Buddha. The son of the teacher of Suddhodana, king of Kapilavastu. He was the same age as the Buddha. He is noted as the most eloquent of the disciples of the Buddha."
Dait: 71 #0045

◉ QUEST
see   Spiritual quest

◉ QUESTIONS AND ANSWERS
Syn: Mondo
See also: Koan; Patriarchal Zen

▶"Zen dialogue between masters or between master and student in which one party asks a question concerning Buddhism or some existential problem that has profoundly disquieted him and the other, without recourse in any way to theory or logic, responds in a way that invokes the answer from the deepest layers of his partner's heart-mind.

Many dialogues handed down by tradition later became koans. A famous example of such dialogues is the following: 'A monk asked master Tung-shan 'What is Buddha?' Tung-shan replied, 'Three pounds of flax.'"
Sham: 146 #0377

◙ **QUESTIONS OF KING MILINDA**
see Milindapanha

◙ **RADIANCE**
see Light

◙ **RAFT**

▸"In Mahayana Buddhism, the teaching is likened to a raft; when the goal, the *Other Shore*, is reached, then the raft is left behind. Similarly, according to the 'metaphor of the raft,' the teaching itself is relinquished when its end is attained. This means that the form of the teaching is not final dogma but an expedient method."
Chih-I/Cleary: 201

◙ **RAHULA**

▸"The son of Shakyamuni and Yashodhara. One of the Buddha's ten major disciples, respected as the foremost in inconspicuous practice. He entered the priesthood at the age of fifteen under the guidance of Shariputra and Maudgalyayana, and devoted himself to the inconspicuous observance of the precepts."
Sokk: 352
Note: The name Rahula means bond or hindrance.
#0274

◙ **RAHULA, VEN. WALPOLA**

▸"Sri Lankan scholar-monk. Born 1907, Sri Lanka. Educated privately. At 13 or 14, entered the Sangha. 1936: entered Ceylon University College; gained PhD in 1950; 1930s: well-known preacher criticizing some popular Buddhist practices and publishing pamphlets; took special interest in social and economic matters; entered struggle for political freedom. 1950: to Sorbonne (Paris) on French government fellowship to do research on Mahayana Buddhism (esp. works of Asanga). Worked with Paul Demieville of College de France; met André Bareau *et al* ... worked with Miss I.B. Horner for Pali Text society. Has lectured widely in the USA and Japan. Best known book: *What the Buddha Taught*."
Snel: 269 #0729

◙ RAIGO (*Jpn*)

See also: Pure Land Buddhism (Summary); Pure Land Mandalas

▶"The Raigo--or Welcoming Descent--of Amida, with a few attendants or with a multitude of heavenly deities, represents a new and lyrical artistic conception and was the greatest contribution made by the Japanese to Pure Land painting. Paintings of the Welcoming Descent did appear on the continent, but *the Japanese singled out this theme for special attention and focused on its religious significance to a far greater degree than did the Chinese...*

The textual authority for the concept of the Descent is found in Amida's nineteenth vow in the *Meditation Sutra*: 'If, after my obtaining Buddhahood, all beings in the Ten Quarters awakening their thoughts to enlightenment and practising all deeds of merit should cherish the desire in sincerity to be born in my country and if I should not, surrounded by a large company, appear before them at the time of their death, may I not attain the highest enlightenment.'"
Okaz: 94

◙ RAIN

▶"Rain is used as a metaphor for teaching; showering rains of all manner of jewels and ornaments and other beautiful things refers to the exposition of many principles and teachings."
Clea/84: 22 #1965

◙ RAINS RETREAT

Syn: Monsoon-Season Retreat
See also: Sacerdotal Age; Sangha; Buddhist Festivals

▶*Pali*/ Vassa; *Vn*/ Hạ. "The period of three months, in the monsoon season, during which monks and nuns are expected to reside in one place and devote themselves to their practice. The end of the Rains Retreat coincides with the Ullambana/Obon Festival (Festival of the Hungry Ghosts). It is an auspicious day for monks and nuns, as on that day those who attended the Rains Retreat become one year older in the Order (Sacerdotal Age)."
Stro: 359
"The monsoon-season retreat period. A Bhikkhu's or Bhikkuni's seniority is determined by the number of 'Rains' he/she has spent in the Order."
Sume: 139 #0832

◙ **RAJAGRIHA / RAJAGAHA**
See also: Vulture Peak

▶"An ancient city in central India, near the present-day town of *Rajgir* (Patna District, Bihar). The capital of the ancient kingdom of Magadha ruled by King Bimbisara."
Chan: 481 #0551
Vulture Peak, mentioned in such famous texts as the *Lotus Sutra*, etc. is located on the outskirts of Rajagriha, to the Northeast.

◙ **RAKSASA**

▶"A terrifying ghost or demon with a black body, red hair, and green eyes. Raksasas are reputed to be devourers of humans."
Chan: 481 #0552

◙ **RATNAKUTA SUTRA**
Syn: Maha-Ratnakuta Sutra; Jewel-Heap Sutra

▶*Vn/* Đại-Bửu-Tích Kinh. "Sanskrit for 'Sutra of the Heap of Jewels', 'The *Great Heap Sutra*'; one of the oldest sutras of the Mahayana. It is one of the Vaipulya sutras (q.v.), and is a collection of forty-nine independent sutras. Completely preserved only in Chinese and Tibetan translations. In the *Ratnakuta Sutra*, the thought of the Middle Way is developed, which later became the basis for the Madhyamaka teaching of Nagarjuna. It also contains sutras on transcendental wisdom (*Prajna Paramita Sutra*) and the *Longer Amitabha Sutra*."
Sham: 176
Rendered in part as *A Treasury of Mahayana Sutras* by Garma C. Chang. Among the texts included in the translation is the *Longer Amitabha Sutra*.
Editor: na
NOTE:
"In the *Maharatnakuta*, there are two sutras concerning Buddha's Pure Land... Since the majority of people cannot successfully perform the meditation and intuitive observation practice, nor lead an ascetic monastic life, the alternative path of Pure Land practice is provided. By the power of the original vows of Buddha, such a practitioner is assured rebirth in a Pure Land, which is not considered to be a heaven or celestial paradise, but rather an ideal training ground for furthering one's journey toward enlightenment. According to Buddhist tradition, there are innumerable Buddha's Pure Lands in the infinite universes. Two samples are described in the

Maharatnakuta; one sutra contains a discussion of Buddha Amitabha's Pure Land in the western direction (the *Longer Amitabha Sutra*), and the other that of Buddha Aksobhya in the east."
Chang: xiv #0372

◉ REALITY
See also: Dharma Body; Dharma Realm; Suchness

▸"Can refer to the eternal, unchanging, all-embracing truth, which is no other than Suchness, D h a r m a d h a t u o r t h e Dharma-body. In other contexts it refers to 'reality' in the ordinary sense."
Chan: 481 #0553

◉ REALM OF REALITY
see   Dharma Realm

◉ REALM OF TRUTH
see   Dharma Realm

◉ REBIRTH IN THE PURE LAND
Syn: Pure Land Rebirth
See also: Bodhi Mind; Pure Land Buddhism (Summary); Three Doubts and Four Narrow Passes; Proofs of Rebirth in the Pure Land; Ten Non-Seeking Practices
----
▸"The event of passing away (death, departure) from life in the human realm and being reborn in the Land of Bliss. Although this is a form of rebirth, it is an extraordinary form. For those who have complete faith in the Buddha Amitabha, rebirth is completely miraculous."
Gomez: 320

(I) Ways to attain rebirth
Mahayana sutras teach many ways to attain salvation and rebirth in the Pure Land, i.e., through the power of vows, the power of mantras, the accumulation of good deeds, the recitation of Amitabha's name until one-pointedness of mind is achieved. However, *the main practice for achieving rebirth in the Pure Land is Buddha Recitation -- the singleminded recitation of Amitabha Buddha's name either during one's lifetime or at the time of death.*
Editor: na

(II) How to Ensure Rebirth
A. Normal circumstances: perseverance & singlemindedness.
"A laywoman once approached a well-known Elder Master and asked: 'I have recited the Buddha's name for some time now, but have not seen any sign of progress. Can you explain to me why this is so?' The abbot

said, 'Reciting the Buddha's name is not difficult; the difficulty lies in perseverance. Perhaps you have not recited regularly and in a persevering manner.' The laywoman replied, 'You are entirely right. I am usually interrupted in my recitation and have not been persevering, because of family obligations. From now on, I will put aside all distractions and vow to keep reciting exactly as taught.' Some time later, she returned and asked, 'Since receiving your instructions last time, I have put aside all external distractions and recited the Buddha's name regularly, every day. Why is it that I still do not see any results?' The abbot replied, *'Reciting the Buddha's name is not difficult; the difficulty lies in perseverance. Persevering is not difficult; the difficulty lies in being singleminded.* Although, on the surface, you may have put all distractions aside, in your mind you still worry about possessions and property and are still attached to children and family. You have neither discarded worry nor eliminated the root of love-attachment. How can you achieve one-pointedness of mind and see Amitabha Buddha?'

Hearing this, the woman sighed aloud 'That is so true, Master! Although I have seemingly abandoned all distractions, my mind is still preoccupied with them. From now on, I vow to disregard everything and recite the Buddha's name singlemindedly.' Thereupon she went home and, from that time on, each time her children or anyone else sought her advice or confided in her, she would invariably reply, 'I want peace of mind, and do not wish to be bothered by anything.' For this reason, everyone referred to her as 'the woman who is above all worry and care.' A few years later, she went to bow to the abbot at his temple, saying, 'Thanks to your advice and teaching, I have now achieved one-pointedness of mind and seen Amitabha Buddha. I have come to pay my respects and take leave of you, Abbot, because I will soon be reborn in the Pure Land.' The laywoman in our story achieved liberation because she was enlightened to two principles: perseverance and singlemindedness. Thus, to be successful, the Pure Land practitioner should consider everything, from personal possessions and property to family and friends, to be illusory and phantom-like, coming together temporarily and then disintegrating. If we care about family and friends, we should ensure our own rebirth and liberation and then rescue them. This is true affection! Therefore, to recite the Buddha's name effectively, we should not only ignore one hundred distractions, we should discard all distractions, be they one thousand or tens of thousands!"

Tam: 229-230

B . T i m e   o f   d e a t h : s i n g l e m i n d e d n e s s   a l o n e .
"According to the *Meditation Sutra*, even the most evil person may be reborn in the Pure Land, if at the time of death he or she is able to embrace the Pure Land faith and maintain single-minded and undisturbed recollection of the Buddha Amitabha for 'ten successive moments.' Hence, although Pure Land Buddhism ordinarily encourages that one turn to Amitabha sooner rather than later in life, the ten moments of mindfulness nonetheless provide a last-minute means of assuring one's salvation."

Lopez/95: 365

In the *Meditation Sutra* (q.v.), Sixteenth Meditation, two key phrases are "on the verge of death" and "utmost sincerity and devotion." When a wicked person, on his deathbed, senses evil omens arising from his subconscious and he sees no possible alternative, a mind of utter sincerity and devotion is sometimes possible. Such a frame of mind is extremely difficult to develop in the course of everyday life.

Editor: na

Illustrative story. There was once a Zen monk meditating on a deserted mountain far away from all human habitation. Because of the rigors of the climate and the isolation of the place, he found it difficult to concentrate. His mind constantly wandered toward life in the village down below. One evening, as he was seated lost in errant thought, he had the sensation that he was being watched. He slowly turned his head, and lo and behold, there was a tiger crouched in the bushes behind him! One false move and the tiger would pounce on him. He had no choice but to remain ramrod straight, in singleminded concentration. When dawn broke, the tiger, fearful of the light of day, gave up this cat-and-mouse game and disappeared. The next two evenings, the monk, faithful to his vow, resumed his meditation at the appointed time and place. The tiger returned and the scene repeated itself each evening. When daylight came on the third day, the monk, after three nights of *singleminded concentration*, experienced a Great Awakening, collapsed and died. At his funeral, a tiger was seen watching and wailing in the Editor/Zen: 40

C. Sudden death. "What happens in the case of a Buddhist who dies suddenly without having time to invoke the Buddha's name. Would he achieve rebirth in the Pure Land?"

Answer: "As the Buddha told king Bimbisara, when a man accumulates good acts, at his death he will have no disturbing thoughts. This is like a tree which leans to the west and will necessarily fall in that direction in which it has been bent ..."
Dia: 182 #1304

(III) Seeking an auspicious response
"Pure Land followers should strive earnestly for a response. The lives of sentient beings are ephemeral and easily cut short; the ghost of impermanence waits for no one. Your hair is already streaked with white, your face has grown wrinkled. The marks of decay and old age are very clear, and death is but a short time away. Therefore, you should strive to cultivate in earnest, to ensure that some auspicious and reliable signs of rebirth appear. Thus, in ancient China, Elder Master Hui Yuan of Lu Shan saw the Buddha rub his crown three times. Another Elder Master earnestly recited the Buddha's name and immediately saw Amitabha Buddha emit rays of light and display auspicious marks. In the case of still another Elder Master, each time he uttered the Buddha's name, the Great Assembly would see a Buddha flying out of his mouth. This was true for hundreds of thousands of his utterances; hundreds of thousands of Buddhas escaped from his mouth, like so many rosary beads, one after another. Such responses are countless. If you recite Amitabha Buddha's name in earnest, without interruption, it is very easy to see Him. Otherwise, it is very difficult. If you do not see the Buddha, you do not have affinities with Him. Without affinities, it is certainly difficult to achieve rebirth. If you are not reborn in the Pure Land, sooner or later you will descend

into the evil realms. Thus, a single thought of interrupting recitation is precisely the karma of rebirth on the Three Evil Paths. You should bear this in mind and ponder it carefully!" (Master T'ien Ju, 14th c.)

PL/Dia: 106

(IV) Questions and Answers

A. "*Question*: What is the meaning of the statement: 'birth [in the Pure Land] is certainly birth, but returning [to the Pure Land] is, in fact, not returning?' *Answer*: 'Birth is certainly birth' is from the viewpoint of phenomena; 'Returning is, in fact, not returning' is from the viewpoint of principle or noumenon. However, those who have not yet penetrated the subtle differences between noumenon and phenomena should just follow phenomena and marks, and recite the Buddha's name in an accomplished manner. In this way, they will achieve results. Otherwise, they will make the mistake, common to externalists and demons, of grasping at noumenon and abandoning phenomena."

PLZ: 109-110

B. *Question*: "When practicing Pure Land, we need to attain the Buddha Recitation Samadhi, or at least reach the stage of one-pointedness of mind, in order to achieve rebirth in the Western Land. Those of limited capacities are not necessarily able to practice at such a level. Therefore, how can these sentient beings be reborn in the Land of Ultimate Bliss? And, if such persons cannot achieve rebirth there, how can Buddha Recitation be said to 'gather in' all types of people?

Answer: In truth, the capacities of people being what they are these days, even one-pointedness of mind is extremely difficult to achieve, not to mention the state of Buddha Recitation Samadhi! However, according to the *Meditation Sutra*, if anyone who has committed the 'Five Grave Offenses' or 'Ten Evil Deeds' sees evil omens appear as he is on the verge of death, he need only recite the Buddha's name ten times *with utter faith and sincerity* and Buddha Amitabha will descend to welcome him and guide him back to the Pure Land. Thus, one-pointedness of mind resulting in rebirth in the Pure Land refers to the time of death, not the present time. However, in order to achieve such a state of mind at the time of death, the cultivator should

practice Buddha Recitation in daily life to the point where it becomes second nature. As he constantly recites the Buddha's name in daily life, even though one-pointedness of mind is not yet achieved, the seeds of Buddha Recitation are accumulated and stored away in great quantities. On his deathbed, the practitioner who begins to recite 'activates' those seeds immediately and with great force, resulting in one-pointedness of mind. Those of limited capacities who achieve rebirth in the Pure Land through Buddha Recitation usually fall into this category."
Tam: 76-77 #1354

(V) Supportive recitation
Strongly recommended in Pure Land teaching for all practitioners. See also separate entry.

FAMOUS QUOTES
\# "Speak one sentence less of chatter;/ Recite once more the Buddha's name./ Recite until your false thoughts die/ Your Dharma Body will come to life."
\# "Develop the Supreme Bodhi Mind;/ Achieve singlemindedness; / The Pure Land is yours."
See also Bodhi Mind,

Retrogression, Ten Non-Seeking Practices

◙ **REBIRTH SIGNS**
see Proofs of rebirth in Pure Land

◙ **REBIRTH TREATISE**
Syn: Commentary on the Longer Amitabha Sutra; Treatise on the Pure Land
See also: Bodhiruci; India (Buddhism in); Vasubandu; Exclusion Clause
----
▸*Vn/* Văng-Sanh Luận. "A short treatise on the Longer Amitabha sutra written by Vasubandhu and translated into Chinese by Bodhiruchi in 529. It praises the Pure Land and encourages aspiration for rebirth in the Pure Land. This work is especially valued by the Pure Land school, along with the Three Pure Land Sutras."
Sokk: 194

"In the *Rebirth Treatise*, Patriarch Vasubandu sets forth the five kinds of practices for rebirth, the *Five Contemplative Gates*: worship, praise, aspiration for rebirth, visualization, and the dedication of merit. Significantly, the author places the five practices within traditional

Mahayana categories. He identifies the aspiration for rebirth with concentration (samatha) and visualization with insight (vipasyana). He further correlates the first four Gates with the concept of benefit for oneself and the fifth gate with benefit for others. The treatise also disqualifies Lesser Vehicle adherents, for example, from rebirth in the Pure Land [because rebirth there requires the development of the Bodhi Mind / q.v.]."
Tana: 12 #0218

◙ **REBUTTAL**
see Ten Non-Seeking Practices

◙ **RECITATION**
see   Buddha Recitation; Scriptural recital

◙ **RED AND YELLOW LEAVES**
See also: Expedient Means

▸"The teachings are like red and yellow leaves which a mother calls gold to please her crying child. The crying is *illusion* and *delusion*; red and yellow leaves are the *teachings* to counteract delusion. They are not real gold, for they are only instrumental, not dogma."
[TC/EII, p.219] #1228

◙ **REFUGE (TAKE --)**
see Three Refuges

◙ **REINCARNATION**

▸"The passing away from one body to be reborn in another body. Once a living being (human, celestial being, animal, etc.) dies, this being's destination ('next birth' or 'place of rebirth') is determined by his accumulated merit and demerit (so-called good and bad karma)."
Gomez/96: 320

"Through reincarnation or rebirth all human beings reap the good or evil consequences of their actions. The duality of their deeds of body, their speech and thought in previous lives, determines the circumstances of their rebirth." Eerd: 231
NOTE:
"As a matter of historical fact, the theory of reincarnation was accepted by Christians until the Council of Constantinople held in A.D. 551, and the Bible offers researchers in this subject a number of relevant passages."
Ross: 109 #1873

◙ **RELICS**
Syn: Sarira

▸"The   Buddha's   cremated

remains. Shakyamuni Buddha's ashes are said to have been divided into eight parts, and stupas were built in eight different locations to enshrine them. The *Sutra of the Benefit of Washing the Buddha's Image* mentions two kinds of relics: the Buddha's *physical remains* and the *teachings* which he expounded. The former are called the relics of the physical body, while the latter are called the relics of the Dharma body."
Sokk: 35
(For an interesting discussion on relics/sarira, see *Pure-Land Zen / Zen Pure-Land*, Thích Thiền Tâm, tr., p. 184.) #0206

◉ **RESIDENCES**
see Seats, thrones, and residences

◉ **RESPECT**
see Sincerity and respect

◉ **RETREAT**
see Sesshin; Seven-day Retreat

◉ **RETRIBUTION BODY**

►Our physical body is called the retribution body because we are on this earth, the Saha World or World of Endurance, as a result of a mixture of good and evil karma, with evil karma being the heaviest.
Editor/Zen: 81 #1454

◉ **RETROGRESSION**
See also Non-Retrogression

►Retrogression from the Way is the greatest setback for the cultivator. The core rationale for seeking rebirth in the Pure Land (rather than remaining on earth to pursue cultivation) is that within the Saha World, retrogression is a certainty for all but the most resolute practitioners. Sutras and commentaries abound with tales of retrogression by even the most advanced disciples. (See, for example, the story of Sariputra, a leading Arhat disciple of the Buddha, donating both of his eyes to save a Brahmin's mother as part of his practice of the paramita of charity, but then abandoning that paramita when one the eyes was crushed and spat upon.)
Editor/Zen: 168
Illustrative story
"In T'ang Dynasty China, in a temple called Fragrant Mountain in the district of Loyang, there was a Buddhist monk named Mirror of Emptiness. He came from a destitute family, and,

though diligent in his studies, was a mediocre student in his youth. As an adult, he used to compose poems, few of which are quoted or remembered. He would travel throughout central China seeking support from local leaders, without much result. As soon as he would accumulate some savings he would fall ill, exhausting all his funds by the time he recovered. Once, he travelled to a neighboring district, which at that time was struck by famine. He was thinking of reaching the Temple of the Western Land to eat and regain strength, but on the way, felt too hungry to go further. He decided to rest by a snow-covered spring, reciting verses of self-pity and despondency. Suddenly, an Indian monk appeared and sat down beside him. Smiling, he asked, 'Elder Master, have you already exhausted the sweet dew of distant travel?' He answered, 'I have indeed exhausted the nectar of travel; however, my name is ... and I have never been a high-ranking Buddhist master.' The Indian monk replied, 'Have you forgotten the time you were preaching the *Lotus Sutra* at the Temple of ... ?' -- *Answer*: 'For the last forty-five years, since I was born, I have always been in this vicinity. I have never set foot in the capital and therefore cannot have preached at the temple you mentioned.' The Indian monk answered, 'Perhaps you are starving and have forgotten all about the past.' Thereupon, he took an apple as big as a fist from his bag and gave it to the famished poet, saying, 'This apple comes from my country. Those of high capacities who eat it can see the past and future clearly. Those of limited capacities can also remember events of their past lifetimes.' The poet gratefully accepted the apple, ate it, and proceeded to drink the spring water. Feeling suddenly drowsy, he rested his head on the rocks and began to doze off. In an instant, he awakened and remembered his past life as a high-ranking Buddhist monk, preaching the Dharma along with fellow monks, as clearly as though everything had happened the previous day. He wept and asked, 'Where is the Great Abbot Chan these days?' The Indian monk replied, 'He did not cultivate deeply enough. He has been reborn a monk in Western Szechuan.' The starving poet asked further, 'What has become of the great masters Shen and

Wu?' 'Master Shen is still alive. Master Wu once joked in front of the rock monument at the Fragrant Mountain Temple, "If I cannot attain Enlightenment in this life, may I be reborn as a high-ranking official in the next one." As a result, he has now become a top general. Of the five monks who were close in the past, only I have managed to escape Birth and Death. The three others are as described ... and you, the fourth and last one, are still plagued by hunger in his place.' The starving poet shed a tear of self-pity and said: 'In my previous life, for forty long years I took only one meal a day and wore only one robe, determined to rid myself of all mundane preoccupations. Why is it that I have fallen so low as to go hungry today?' The Indian monk replied: 'In the past, when you occupied the Dharma seat, you used to preach many superstitions, causing the audience to doubt the Dharma. In addition, you were not entirely faultless in keeping the precepts, resulting in today's retribution.' Having finished, the Indian monk took a mirror from his bowl, with flawless reflection on both sides, and said 'I cannot undo what happened in the past. However,

If you want to know your future destiny, whether you will be rich or poor, have a long or short life, even the future ups and downs of the Dharma, just have a look in the mirror and all will be clear.' The poet took the mirror and gazed into it for a long time. Returning it, he said, 'Thanks to your compassionate help, I now know causes and retribution, honor and disgrace.' The Indian monk put the mirror back in his bowl, took the poet by the hand, and started to walk away. After about ten steps, he disappeared. That same night, the poet entered the Order at the Temple of the Divine Seal, and was given the Dharma name Mirror of Emptiness. After receiving the complete precepts of a Bhikshu, he travelled throughout the country practicing the Way, his high conduct and ascetic practices being praised by all. Later on, Zen Master Mirror of Emptiness once met with a certain layman from the Temple of the Western Land. Telling the latter about his past, he said: 'I am now 77 years old, my Dharma age is 32. I have only nine more years to live. After my death, who knows if the Dharma will still exist as it is now?' The layman, puzzled,

tried to inquire further. The Master did not reply. He just requested a pen and began scribbling some lines on the north wall of the tower which housed the Tripitaka (Buddhist canon)...The words represented the prophecy of Zen Master Mirror of Emptiness, the gist of which is as follows: 'The Dharma will experience a decline. There will be ruthless persecution of Buddhism, the period of persecution beginning in the 840's. However, the Dharma will survive; the light of the Dharma will not be extinguished.' This prophecy is consonant with the destruction of Buddhism under the Chinese Emperor T'ang Wu Tsung, who ordered the razing of some 47,000 temples and forcibly returned hundreds of thousands of monks and nuns to the laity."
Tam: 22-25

◙ **REVELATIONS / PROPHECIES**
"In Shanghai recently there were many gatherings where revelations and prophecies were proclaimed. Their messages about abandoning evil ways and practicing wholesome deeds, as well as their pronouncements on Birth and Death, Cause and Effect, while superficial and limited, are very useful for everyday morality and the minds of ordinary persons. However the points they made concerning the future and the Buddha Dharma are somewhat vague and not free of error. As disciples of the Buddhas, we should not oppose or reject those pronouncements, because doing so may hinder the good actions of others. At the same time, however, we should not repeat or extol them, lest we be guilty of chimerical statements and conjectures that bring harm and disorder to the Dharma and engender doubts among the people."
PLZ: 149 #2005

◙ **REVERSE THE LIGHT AND ILLUMINE WITHIN**

►A Zen term for introspection. A basic tenet of Zen and other Mahayana Buddhist teachings.
Hua/76: ii-iii #1310

◙ **RHYS DAVIDS, THOMAS WILLIAM (1843-1922)**

►"Pali scholar, editor, translator. The son of a British Congregational minister, he rejected his early training as a solicitor, entering the University of Breslau (Germany) to study

Sanskrit. After receiving his Ph.D. in 1864, he entered the Ceylon Civil Service. In 1872, he returned to England, and began a legal practice. He was nonetheless more interested in Buddhism, thus beginning a series of translations from the Pali language he had learned in Ceylon. In 1878 his still famous *Manual of Buddhism* appeared. Following his series of Hibbert Lectures in 1881, he founded the *Pali Text Society* and embarked on a career of editing and translating that is still virtually unrivaled in Buddhology. In 1882 he assumed the position of Professor of Pali at University College, London. He also worked tirelessly for the Royal Asiatic Society."

Preb: 223 #1063

◉ RIGHT THOUGHT

See also: Death; Rebirth in the Pure Land

▶In Buddhism, right thoughts are crucial at the time of death as they play a major role in our rebirth. Those who have cultivated throughout life naturally develop right thoughts at the time of death.

Editor/Thich: 321

There are cases where virtuous people develop wrong thoughts at the time of death. This can be due to a number of causes, such as their children fighting over inheritances or too much displacement of the body causing pain and anger to the dying person. These lapses, however, should not be of too much concern to a virtuous person, as he is like a tree which customarily leans to the right. When a storm comes, the tree will naturally fall to the right. *Supportive Buddha Recitation at the time of death is recommended as help of last resort* (the most common occurence).

Editor: na #1404

◉ RINPOCHE

▶"Lit. 'Precious One'; honorific title suffixed to the name of a high lama."

Snel: 274 #0735

◉ RINZAI

see Lin-chi

◉ RISSHO-KOSEIKAI

See also: Soka Gakkai

▶"Modern Japanese Buddhist group, based on the teachings of Nichiren, and founded by Niwano Nikkyo (b. 1906) and Naganuma

Myoko (1889-1957) in 1938. While emphasizing the efficacy of the *Lotus Sutra*, this 'new religion' of Japan also makes Sakyamuni Buddha a figure to be worshipped. The ethical aspects of the Eightfold Path and Bodhisattva path are encouraged, as well as honoring one's ancestors. The organization offers an extensive counseling program based on the teachings of the Four Noble Truths and the *Lotus Sutra*. Has a rigorous publication program. Like many of the new religions of Japan, it is very popular."
Preb: 224 #1064

◙ **ROBINSON, RICHARD HUGH (1926-1970)**

►"Buddhologist and Madhyamika specialist, educated at the University of London, and founder of the Buddhist Studies program at the University of Wisconsin. This University was the first American institution to establish an educational program leading to graduate degrees in Buddhist studies, and it was developed almost exclusively by Richard Robinson. Fluent in all the Buddhist canonical languages, Robinson was primarily interested in the work of

Nagarjuna and the other Madhyamika writers ... Like Louis de La Vallée Poussin and other major scholarly figures of the twentieth century, Robinson trained a large number of scholars before his untimely death in 1970."
Preb: 225 #1065

◙ **ROOTS OF MERIT AND VIRTUE**
see Good Roots

◙ **ROSHI**

►(Jpn) "Quite literally 'elder teacher,' a Zen master who has received the seal of enlightenment from his master."
Preb: 226 #1066

◙ **ROTE RECITATION**
see Scriptural Recital

◙ **ROUND DOCTRINE**
see Perfect teaching

◙ **ROUND TEACHING**
see Perfect teaching

◙ **RUB THE CROWN**
See also: Prediction of Buddhahood

►"The gesture [by a Buddha or Bodhisattva] of rubbing the

crown [of a practitioner] indicates the opening of wisdom. The crown of the head is the summit of all features, the seat of wisdom."
[HH/FAS39II201] #1309

◙ **RULERS OF THE WORLDS**

►*Avatamsaka Sutra*:
Leaders of the various types of beings who appear at the beginning of the Avatamsaka Assembly. Includes such leading Bodhisattvas as Samantabhadra, kings of the different heavens and all kinds of spirits. Also includes the Buddha himself, the ultimate leader.
Editor: na #1276

◙ **SACERDOTAL AGE**
Syn: Age of Monks and Nuns; Precept Age
See also: Rains Retreat; Buddhist Festivals; Ordination; Ullambana
----
►The precedence of monks and nuns in the Order is determined by the number of rains retreats (yearly retreats during the monsoon period) they have attended. This is known as their sacerdotal age or their age in the Order.
Editor: na #2135

◙ **SACRED ART**
see Art (Buddhist)

◙ **SACRED MOUNTAINS**
See also: Pilgrimage Sites
"In India there are five sacred mountains associated with the life of the Buddha. In China there are four mountains considered sacred by the Buddhists."
Lahiri: 119
For details, see Four Famous Mountains; Pilgrimage Sites

◙ **SACRIFICE**
see Killing; Immolation

◙ **SADDHARMA PUNDARIKA SUTRA**
see Lotus Sutra

◙ **SADHANA**

►"A Tantric meditation practice involving rituals, visualization, invocation, and recitation of mantras."
Tsomo: 167 #1994

◙ **SADHU, SADHU**
See also: Avatamsaka Sutra

►*Skt* for "Good Indeed, Good Indeed". This expression uttered by the Buddha at the end of a text expounded by someone other

than Himself (a Bodhisattva for example) has the effect of recognizing the text, giving it authority and turning it into a canonical text -- ie., a Buddhist sutra. This is the case for example of the *Avatamsaka Sutra* which was expounded by different Bodhisattvas and not by the Buddha himself.
Editor: na

◙ **SAGES / SAINTS**
See also: Three Pure Land Sages

►*Four Levels Of Sagehood*:
"Arhats, Pratyeka Buddhas, Bodhisattvas, Buddhas. (The word 'Sage' usually refers to Arhats and Buddhas only). Note the expression 'entering into the flow or the "stream (fellowship) of the sages.'"
D.T. Con: xxx
Although anyone with a body undergoes physical suffering (even Buddha Sakyamuni took ill and died), the difference between sages and ordinary beings is that sages always keep the mind unmoved -- empty and still. See the following passage: "[In the *Vimalakirti Sutra*,] the sage Vimalakirti discussed the experience of illness at great length ... With many visitors assembled to inquire after his health, the infirm sage took the opportunity to speak out against the human body and its limitations. 'O, virtuous ones, the wise do not rely upon the body. It is like a mass of froth which cannot be grasped, like a bubble which bursts in an instant. The body is like a flame arising from the thirst of love ... like a shadow, appearing as a result of karma. It is like an echo, responding to causes and conditions ... The body does not act of itself but is spun around by the force of the winds of passion.'" (Raoul Birnbaum, *The Healing Buddha*, p. 13.) It should be clear that although the Buddhas taught that the human body is a skin-bag filled with excrements, theirs is not a pessimistic view of life, but a realistic one. They recognized the need to use the body as a means to Enlightenment. Thus, one important injunction to monks and laymen is never to entertain the thought of suicide.
Editor/Zen: 28-29 #1217

◙ **SAHA WORLD**
Syn: Endurance (World of)
See also: Jambudvipa; Sumeru; Four Continents

►Sakyamuni's Buddha-Land (q.v.)

or Buddha-Field. Often identified with the galaxy we live in. "The Saha World is said to be a large world system composed of one billion worlds."
Gomez: 323
"This world, which is full of sufferings. The Sanskrit word Saha means endurance. According to the sutras, the Saha World is so called because people in this world [gladly] endure many sufferings stemming from the three poisons of greed, anger and delusion as well as earthly desires."
Sokk: 363
NOTE:
Although "Saha World" and "Jambudvipa" (q.v.) are sometimes used interchangeably to mean *our world* or *galaxy*, Jambudvipa (as the specific human world) is but a small part of the Saha World. #0278

◙ SAICHO

►"The founder of the Tendai school of Buddhism in Japan."
Tsomo: 167 #1995

◙ SAINTS
see Sages/Saints

◙ SAKRA
see Indra

◙ SAKYA TRIBE

►"Name of a tribe dwelling in Northern India in which Gotama, or Sakyamuni Buddha was born as prince Siddhartha."
Thur: 144 #0662

◙ SAKYADHITA

►"The International Association of Buddhist Women founded in Bodhgaya (India) in 1987. Literally, 'Daughters of the Buddha.'"
Tsomo: 167
The Association was founded at a conference opened by the Dalai Lama. #1996

◙ SAKYAMUNI BUDDHA
See also: Buddha; Siddhartha; Funerary Rites for the Buddha

►"Historical founder of Buddhism, Gautama Siddhartha, the Buddha Sakyamuni, who was born circa 581-501 B.C. as the first son of King Suddhodana, whose capital city of Kapilavastu was located in what is now Nepal. At the age of twenty-nine, he left his father's palace and his wife and child in search of the meaning of existence. One morning at the age of thirty-five, he realized enlightenment while

practicing meditation seated beneath the Bodhi tree. Thereafter, He spent the next forty-five years, until his death at the age of eighty, expounding his teachings ... in order that all sentient beings might realize the same enlightenment that he had. Nowadays, the term 'a Buddha' denotes anyone who has realized enlightenment, while 'the Buddha' refers to the historical Buddha, Sakyamuni. 'Buddhas,' naturally refers to all enlightened beings."

Yoko: 181

"The Buddha's active preaching career lasted forty-five years... Recognizing at last that his death was close at hand, he asked that his bed be placed in a clearing in the Sala Grove outside of Kusunagara (Kusinagar). He realized that Nirvana was coming near, and he preached his last sermon, the *Great Nirvana Sutra*. Then, with his head pointing north, his face looking west, lying on his right side, he died. He was eighty years old. After his death, the Malla Tribe, in whose territory he was, moved his body to a temple inside Kusinagar, and held a service for seven days. According to the law of the Wheel-turning King, they cremated his body. Ambassadors from eight great countries of the time arrived to claim his relics. Their conflicting claims were settled by Drona-brahmana, who divided the relics into eight parts. Drona-brahmana obtained for himself the jar in which the relics were put, and gave the ashes to the representative of the Maurya Tribe, who arrived late. Thus there were eight portions in all, and these were placed by the respective owners in eight stupas erected on ground sacred to the Buddha in various areas of India. Four months after the Buddha's death, the First Buddhist Council, chaired by the senior monk, Maha-kasyapa, was held near Rajagrha, the capital of Magadha. This marked the commencement of the effort to institutionalize the sangha and codify the scripture, which has continued to this day."

Dait: 298

In the Theravada tradition, the Birth, Death and Enlightenment of the Buddha are celebrated on the Full Moon of the month of Vesak (April-May). #0115

◙ **SALA / SAL TREE**
Syn: Sala Grove

►"A tree in northern India which grows to be thirty meters tall and

produces light yellow blossoms. Shakyamuni passed away in a grove of sala trees on the outskirts of Kushinagar."
Sokk: 364

"The Sala Grove (Sala translates as 'lofty and far-reaching') is populated by tall and aspiring trees, which symbolize the adornment of the Ten Thousand Conducts."
[HHFAS39I,179] #0189

◙ **SALA GROVE**
see   Sala / sal tree

◙ **SALVATION**
See also: Pure Land School; Horizontal Escape

▸"Buddhism in East Asia offers a satisfactory cosmological explanation of the universe, with an ethical interpretation of the world, thus providing a total solution for human frailties and social ills. It is designed to transform suffering humanity into perfect beings in a Western Paradise (Pure Land of Amitabha Buddha). Its doctrine of universal salvation is readily accepted by East Asians, particularly the Chinese. The history of religions in China reveals that popular imagination was, throughout the centuries,

profoundly stirred by the mythological constructions of Buddhism and Taoism in respect to the after-life, in which the consequences of human frailty and sin are mitigated by the compassionate intervention of gods, Buddhas and Bodhisattvas.
Ling: 223
Question/Answer:
"When practicing Pure Land, we need to attain the Buddha Recitation Samadhi, or at least reach the stage of one-pointedness of mind, in order to achieve rebirth in the Western Land. Those of limited capacities are not necessarily able to practice at such a level. How can these sentient beings be reborn in the Land of Ultimate Bliss? And, if such persons cannot achieve rebirth there, how can Buddha Recitation be said to 'gather in' all types of people?
Answer: In truth, the capacities of people being what they are nowadays, even one-pointedness of mind is extremely difficult to achieve, not to mention the state of Buddha Recitation Samadhi! However, according to the *Meditation Sutra*, if anyone who committed the 'Five Grave Offenses' or 'Ten Evil Deeds' sees evil omens appear as he is on the verge of death, he need

only recite the Buddha's name one to ten times with all his heart (i.e, singlemindedly) and Buddha Amitabha will descend to welcome him and guide him back to the Pure Land. *Thus, one-pointedness of mind resulting in rebirth in the Pure Land refers to the time of death, not the present time.* However, in order to achieve such a state of mind at the time of death, the cultivator should practice Buddha Recitation in daily life to the point where it becomes second nature. As he constantly recites the Buddha's name in daily life, even though one-pointedness of mind is not yet achieved, the seeds of Buddha Recitation are accumulated and stored away in great quantities. *On his deathbed, the practitioner who begins to recite 'activates' those seeds immediately and with great force, resulting in one-pointedness of mind.* Those of limited capacities who achieve rebirth in the Pure Land through Buddha Recitation usually fall into this category."
Thich: 76-77 #1156

◉ **SAMADHI**
See also: Wisdom; Meditation; Buddha Recitation Samadhi; Dead Tree Samadhi; Seeing Buddha (Name of a Samadhi)

▸"Frequently translated as 'concentration,' this word denotes a state in which the mind, free from distraction, is absorbed in intense, 'purposeless' concentration, thereby entering a state of inner serenity. With the mind thus completely absorbed in itself, the essential nature of the Self can be experienced directly."
Yoko: 212

"Meditative absorption. 'Usually denotes the particular final stage of pure concentration.' There are many levels and types of samadhi (Buddha Recitation, Ocean Seal, Pratyutpanna ...)"
Editor: na

Buddha Recitation Samadhi:
"To achieve an uninterrupted state of samadhi is not something a person leading a secular life can accomplish. Since it is difficult to achieve samadhi this way, it is best that you hold fast to the name of the Buddha. Whenever you have the time, after studying and managing household affairs, you ought to recite the Buddha name silently. In doing so, you should be careful to articulate each word clearly and to dwell on each utterance with all your heart. If

you can continue doing this for a long time without relapsing, your mind will naturally be tamed, and this state is none other than samadhi." (Elder Master Chu-Hung)
Hsu: 95 #0280

◙ **SAMANTABHADRA**
See also: Ten Great Vows

►*Jpn*/Fugen; *Vn*/Phổ-Hiền. Also called Universal Worthy. A major Bodhisattva, who personifies the transcendental practices and vows of the Buddhas (as compared to the Bodhisattva Manjusri, who represents transcendental wisdom). Usually depicted seated on an elephant with six tusks (six paramitas). Best known for his Ten Great Vows (q.v.).
Editor: na
Each of the Ten Vows of the Bodhisattva Samantabhadra should be put into practice without interruption, in thought after thought, with body, speech and mind. Thus, the three karmas of body, speech and mind of the practitioner are pure, empty and still. In his lifetime, he has sown the seeds of rebirth in a pure realm. At the time of death, he will naturally be reborn in such a realm, of which the most

representative is the Pure Land of Amitabha Buddha. This is a good illustration of the Pure Land/Zen teaching, "if the mind is pure, the land is pure."
Editor/Saman: 49-51
"In the *Avatamsaka Sutra*, Samantabhadra makes Ten Great Vows concerning his Buddhist practice. In the twenty-eighth chapter of the *Lotus Sutra*, he vows to protect the *Lotus Sutra*, and its devotees. (Samantabhadra is believed to have the power of prolonging life, and esoteric rituals for this purpose are directed toward him.) Worship of Samantabhadra has been popular from ancient times; a number of murals in Central Asia and images in China and Japan remain in existence." Sokk: 128
NOTE:
The Bodhisattva Samantabhadra is considered the transcendental Pure Land Patriarch (Master Hui Yuan was the temporal founder of the school in East Asia).
Editor: na #0092

◙ **SAMATHA-VIPASYANA**
Syn: Concentration and Insight
See also: Meditation

►*Samatha*:
"A meditational technique to calm the mind to a state of

tranquility and concentration. It is practically the equivalent of dhyana."
Chan: 482

Vipasyana: "Insight, clear seeing; intuitive cognition of the three marks of existence, namely, the impermanence, suffering, and egolessness of all physical and mental phenomena. In Mahayana Buddhism, Vipasyana is seen as an analytical examination of the nature of things that leads to insight into the true nature of the world -- emptiness. Such insight prevents the arising of new passions. Vipasyana is one of the two factors essential for the attainment of enlightenment (bodhi). The other is samatha (calming the mind)."
Sham: 245

The name given to the entire system of meditation set forth by the T'ien-t'ai school (q.v.) whose ultimate goal is to perceive 'the region of the unfathomable,' that is, the unification of the Three Truths (q.v.) within one's mind. 'Concentration' (Samatha) means focusing one's mind on one place without any distractions, and 'insight' (Vipasyana) means seeing all things as they are, penetrating to the ultimate reality of all phenomena."
Sokk: 47   #0050

NOTE:
The relationship between samadhi and wisdom (or between samatha and vipasyana) is a crucial point in Buddhism. In the Theravada tradition, the differences between them are emphasized; samadhi and wisdom are considered separate facets of cultivation, to be achieved one after another. In the Mahayana tradition (Zen, Avatamsaka, T'ien-t'ai, Pure Land), however, samadhi and wisdom are indivisible -- true samadhi necessarily includes wisdom and true wisdom is inseparable from samadhi. Moreover, wisdom is not something external to be "obtained" through practice; it is inherent in all sentient beings. It is as though we have lost a pearl at the bottom of a lake. When there is no wind and the water is calm, the pearl naturally becomes visible. To recover the wisdom-pearl, the practitioner need only calm the turbid waters of his mind. Thus, in Mahayana teaching, to cultivate samadhi is to attain wisdom or Enlightenment. This relationship is clearly seen in the expression "three non-outflow (unconditioned) studies," linking precepts, samadhi and wisdom.
Editor: na

◙ **SAMBODHYANGA**
see Seven Limbs of Enlightenment

◙ **SAME FLAVOR**
Syn: One Flavor

▸All of one flavor or taste. Said of the myriad teachings of the Buddha which have one ultimate goal: to help sentient beings achieve liberation from suffering ("that suffering may cease and further suffering may not arise") and lead them to Buddhahood. In practice, that goal means escaping from Samsara, the endless cycle of Birth and Death.

◙ **SAMGHAVARMA**`
see Sanghavarman

◙ **SAMSARA**
Syn: Cycle of Birth and Death
See also: Birth and Death

▸"The endless round of birth, death, and rebirth."
Sangh/95: 118
"The relentless cycle of repeated birth and death in which ordinary, unenlightened sentient beings are deeply entangled. The cause of Samsara is the presence of defilements, particularly greed, hatred, and delusion."
Chan: 482 #0560

◙ **SAMSARA IS NIRVANA**
see Afflictions are Bodhi

◙ **SAN LUN SCHOOL**

▸"School of 'Three Treatises' (*Chin.*/ San Lun), the Chinese Madhyamika school (*Jpn.*/ Sanron), based on works translated by Kumarajiva."
Reat: 342 #2088

◙ **SANGHA**
Syn: Order (Buddhist); Community of Monks and Nuns
See also: Bald-headed thief; Bhiksu; Bhiksuni; Good spiritual advisors; Sangha (admonition to); Sixfold respect
----
▸"Buddhist order or community of at least [four] monks."
Dait: 340

"The third of the Three Jewels of Buddhism (the Buddha, the Teaching, and the Community). Sometimes narrowly defined as the community of mendicants."
Thur: 144

"The monastic order founded by the Buddha, the members of which are called Bhikkhus (males) or Bhikkhunis (females). It is the oldest monastic order in the world. The act of admission to the order is called renouncing the world. The hair of the head and beard is shaved, the yellow robe (consisting of the three garments) is donned, and the Tisarana is recited. The candidate is then a novice. The ordination ceremony takes place before a chapter of senior Bhikkhus and Theras. No oaths are taken, and the Bhikkhu is free to leave the Order at any time if he desires to do so. The Bhikkhu possesses only his robes, alms-bowl, razor, needle and water-strainer."

Hump: 167

"In ancient India the most distinctive feature of the Buddhist Sangha was probably its adoption of a compromise between the settled life-style of many orthodox Brahmans and the wandering characteristic of other traditions. By establishing fixed residences for three months in the rainy season, the Buddha ensured that the life of the bhikkhu would provide both for the establishing of local centres of operation and for the retention of at least something of the simplicity necessitated by the life of the wandering religious mendicant (beggar). Larger settled institutions tended to develop later, but great individual mobility usually remains possible. This kind of inherent compromise is natural to the Buddhist 'middle way' and quite characteristic of the training rules of the Pratimoksa. A similar balance is clearly expected between the demands of discipline and a relaxed approach, as well as between respect for seniority and individual autonomy. Authority is collective rather than hierarchical, but a certain mininum observation is enforced. Only a breach of any one of four rules leads to expulsion (parajika, i.e. 'defeat'): sexual intercourse; taking human life; theft; or a dishonest claim to some spiritual attainment. The majority of the lesser rules are concerned either with ensuring simplicity of life-style or with maintaining a disciplined deportment. The Pratimoksa can be approached fairly laxly and each bhikkhu is in principle free to leave the Sangha if he wishes. Yet taken with a full commitment, it represents a most demanding training, requiring great attention and awareness in every action -- especially for the inexperienced. Such of course is its purpose. It is part of the spiritual training directed

towards the Buddhist goal."
Hinn: 286

"The great contribution which the Buddhist Order makes to the life of [East Asians] consists in keeping before the minds and imaginations of the people the fact of religion, the reality of the spiritual life. Doubtless this great function of keeping the lamp of religion alight is [sometimes not well] performed by the Buddhist clergy. But as things actually are in [East Asia] today, and have been for many a century, the clergy, are the torch-bearers of religion, and if they should drop their light, it might well be extinguished in the darkness of worldly, unspiritual preoccupation. It is not without value in the life of [East Asians] that they should be constantly reminded of the fact of Buddhism, reminded of it as at least an unfailing potentiality. It is not without value that an Order of men and women should be consecrated to the lifelong study and service of religion, that buildings of ancient beauty should be devoted to the praises of the highest ideal that [East Asia] knows, that quiet cloisters should be set aside for meditation of holy men and of all who wish to meditate. It is not without value that the poorest beggar, the busiest politician, the saddest woman, the most guilty sinner should carry ever in the subconscious regions of their minds the thought that, if they will, they may go any morning or any night to a nearby temple, hear the solemn music of gong and drum and the chanting of monks, watch the smoke of incense ascend before the image of the Blessed One, and catch some intimation of a higher life, a loftier world, a deeper peace than they had known before." (J.B. Pratt, *The Pilgrimage of Buddhism*: 1928)

"*A monk's real life is the life of the mind.* However vividly one describes and illustrates the monastic setting -- the architecture, the ceremonial, the externals of preaching and meditation, the daily sights and sounds of the Sangha -- one is still leaving out the most vital ingredient: thought. Perhaps as close as we can come to the essence of Buddhism in a visual image is the face of a monk in meditation [or recitation] ..."
Bech: 116 #0135
See also next entry.

◉ **SANGHA (*ADMONITION TO* --)**
See also: Sangha

►"When the Buddha was in the world, everyone who had left home life was required to recite the following verse: 'watch over the mouth, hold the mind, with the body do no wrong;/Do not, in any way, annoy a single living being;/Keep far away from nonbeneficial ascetic practices;/Cultivation such as this can surely save the world.'"
Hua/Earth Store: 46

From Zen Master T'ien Ju, ca. 14th century China:
"Furthermore, worldly careers and undertakings are like a dream, an illusion, a bubble, an echo, existing for but a moment before returning to the void -- they offer no real benefit to the cultivator on the path of liberation. Even if you have built huge, stately temples and monasteries, achieved great influence and high position, established friendships with numerous important persons of status and wealth, feeling deep pride 'inside,' thinking that you have succeeded on your path of cultivation, little do you realize that you have violated the very admonition of the ancient sages! This is because they have specifically warned: 'Those who have entered the Order should set their Minds and focus on achieving liberation and not be unduly preoccupied with mundane endeavors, as these entail numerous errors. Not only will they fail to see the heavens, the karma of hell has already been created! If the issue of Birth and Death is not resolved, all mundane activities are but the causes of suffering. One day, once their eyes are closed, they will revolve in Samsara according to their karma. At that time, they will discover that their past actions have only added chains to their yoke and firewood and charcoal under the "boiling cauldrons," the Dharma robe no longer covers their bodies, while the paths of various realms keep changing *ad infinitum* throughout the eons!' ...

Repaying one's obligations:
Cultivators have a number of important obligations. Let us put aside temporarily the debts to the Buddhas and our teachers. In your case, as a monk, do you not think that you owe a profound and heavy debt to your parents for giving you life and raising you? Having "left home" and all mundane activities, studying the Dharma far from your birth-place for so many years, you were not aware of the

hardships and sufferings of your parents. You did not know of their old age and illness, and so did not take proper care of them. When they died, you either had no knowledge, or, if you were aware of it, you probably returned home too late. When you were young, in order to provide for you and out of concern for your welfare, your parents, at times, committed numerous transgressions. After death, as they descended upon the path of suffering, they hoped that you would come to their rescue, just as a person might wait for a glass of water to assuage his thirst, or for the pouring of rain to cease. If your cultivation is haphazard, your Pure Land karma will not bring results. Thus, you cannot even save yourself, let alone your parents! In such circumstances, you have not only missed the opportunity to take care of their temporal needs, you are now remiss in your obligations to their souls. You are a most unfilial son indeed! The sutras say: "To be unfilial is to sink into hell." Thus, the Mind of interruption, of failure to cultivate assiduously, is indeed the karma of hell. Moreover, you do not weave, yet you wear clothing; you do not plough, yet you eat your fill. Living quarters, bedding, food, clothing, medicine, etc. are all provided by Buddhist followers. The ancient masters have often admonished: "Buddhist followers, out of respect and veneration for the Triple Jewel, parcel out part of their meager family food budget as a donation to monks and nuns. If the latter are not blameless in their cultivation, even an inch of cloth or a grain of rice will have to be paid back in future lifetimes. To repay the favor of your disciples, you should follow the Pure Land path assiduously, to rescue yourself and others. If you let even a single intrusive thought arise and fail to persevere, you have become enmeshed in Samsara -- endlessly 'borrowing' and 'repaying.' That very intrusive thought is vile karma or the karma of animality. (Master T'ien Ju in *Pure Land Buddhism: Dialogues with Ancient Masters*)" Dia: 91;103;104 #2293

◙ **SANGHARAKSHITA, VEN.**

►"Born D.P.E. Lingwood. Founder of the 'Friends of the Western Buddhist Order'; writer and poet. Born 1925, Stockwell, London. Joined Buddhist Society at 18. 1943: joined Royal Signal Corps; served in India, Ceylon and Singapore during WWII. Left the service in India. 1950: bhikkhu ordination. Founded Young Men's Buddhist Association and established Triyana Vardhana Vihara ('Monastery of the Three Vehicles'). Sat on the education board of Maha Bodhi Journal and founded the journal *Stepping Stones.* 1950s: exodus of lamas from Tibet; received teachings from Dhardo Rinpoche, *et al*; also studied Ch'an. 1957: became active in the Bombay area, working among 'Untouchables'; advised Dr. Ambedkar and 'personally officiated at the conversion of 200,000 people'. 1964: returned to UK, to Hampstead Buddhist Vihara." Snel: 313 #0757

◙ **SANGHAVARMAN**

▶"'Armor of the Sangha'; an Indian monk who went to Lo-yang in 254 and translated sutras at the White Horse Temple. [One of his best known works is a translation into Chinese of the *Longer Amitabha Sutra* considered authoritative to the present day]." Inag: 413 #0715

◙ **SANRON (JPN)**
see   San Lun school

◙ **SARIPUTRA**

▶"One of the ten major disciples of the Buddha. Born in a village to the north of Rajagrha in Magadha, India, he became a follower of [the famous ascetic Master] Samjaya, along with Maudgalyayana. Each had one hundred disciples, and all of the disciples became followers of the Buddha after the conversion of their masters. Sariputra was regarded as the most brilliant of the Buddha's disciples. He died while Buddha was still alive." Dait: 299
Major disciple of Shakyamuni Buddha, foremost in wisdom among His Arhat disciples. (The Bodhisattva Manjusri was foremost in wisdom among the Buddha's Bodhisattva disciples). Editor/Tam: 161 #0129

◙ **SARIRA**
see   Relics

◙ **SARNATH**
See also: Deer Park; Varanasi

▶The place where the Buddha preached his first sermon to his first five disciples and where the

foundation of the Buddhist Order was laid. Located just outside Varanasi (Benares), it can be reached easily by overnight train from Calcutta (India).
Editor: na
"Sarnath (4 miles to the north of Varanasi) is one of the four sacred places for the Buddhists. The Buddha preached his first Sermon or moved the Wheel of Law at Sarnath. This event is known as Dharma-cakra-Pravartana."
Lahiri: 61

◉ SARVASTIVADIN SCHOOL
See also: Buddhist Councils (Council/ Mahayana)

▸ A precursor of Mahayana Buddhism.

◉ SASAKI, SOKEI-AN (1882-1945)

▸"Pioneer teacher of Zen in USA. Born in Japan and trained as a dragon carver. 1931: Buddhist Society of America formed (later First Zen Institute of New York, later still of America). Group slowly grew and in 1938 was joined by Ruth Fuller Everett. Her son-in-law, Alan Watts, studied with Sokei-an for a short time. 1942: internment camp as enemy alien.

1944: married Ruth Everett."
Snel: 302 #0747

◉ SASTRA/ SHASTRA
Syn: Commentaries; Treatises
See also: Abhidharma; Tripitaka

▸"A type of religious, philosophical, or scientific work whose importance lies not in its scriptural authority but in its systematic study of particular problems or techniques. Usually translated as commentary or treatise."
Thur: 144
Buddhist sastras are commentaries and treatises written by Mahayana patriarchs such as Nagarjuna, Asangha, Vasabandhu, etc., while the Abhidharma consists mainly of the commentaries taught by Buddha Sakyamuni and some earlier patriarchs.
Editor: na

Background
"Commentarial literature in Buddhism is that which augments, explains, and expands upon primary texts. In each Buddhist tradition, the primary literature, agreed to be the teaching (or 'speaking') of Buddha, was fixed and closed at a relatively early date in the

history of each tradition. Precisely because the canon was fixed and closed, new ways had to be developed to cope with infusing new meanings and interpretations into Buddha's sermons and disciplinary discourses if Buddhism hoped to remain a vital, meaningful religious tradition.

The vehicle that emerged to meet that need was the creation of an extensive commentarial tradition. By writing new commentaries on old texts, the tradition was able to revitalize itself, to remain current, and to address needs that have become transcultural and transtemporal. In the course of Buddhist history, additional texts appeared in virtually every Buddhist culture and tradition that were clearly not 'the word of Buddha,' identified with individual authors, but nevertheless of critical importance for the understanding and practice of Buddhism. Many of these texts have also generated commentaries, some of them even auto-commentaries, and in the process, kept Buddhism fresh, creative, and facing an increasingly changing definition of modernity."
Preb: 95-96 #1011 & #0664

◙ SATORI (Jpn)
See also: Awakening vs. Enlightenment

◙ SAYADAW

►"Burmese equivalent of 'Maha Thera' (Elder Monk); also given to highly respected Burmese bhikkhus."
Snel: 261
"Name of a 20th c. Burmese master associated with the revival of Insight Meditation."
Hy: xxx #0722

◙ SCHOOL
see Dharma door

◙ SCHOOLS OF EXISTENCE/ EMPTINESS
see Existence/Emptiness

◙ SCRIPTURAL RECITAL
Syn: Sutra Recital
See also: Practice (Buddhist); Pure Land School

►"A traditional practice of single-minded recitation of scriptures...used to effect escalation of consciousness and enhancement of mental powers. [TC/FO3, p.5]
"In the practice of scriptural recital, the focus of concentration works to halt the wandering mind

and take attention off habitual trains of thought, while the structure and imagery of the scripture that then flow into the mind, bypassing the conditioned intellect, are able to set up new patterns of perception..." [TC/FO3, p.6]

Background
(Patriarch Yin-Kuang in "Pure Land Zen, Zen Pure Land"):
"If you wish to be a Dharma master, lecturing on the sutras in public, you should first read the original texts, then study the c o m m e n t a r i e s   a n d subcommentraries. However, should you discover that your intellect is average and your understanding not necessarily above others, you should c o n c e n t r a t e   o n   B u d d h a Recitation rather than wasting time and energy pursuing these non-essential endeavors. If, on the other hand, you would like to engage in *Scriptural Recital* in accordance with your limited capacities for the benefits it confers, you should keep the three karmas of body, speech and mind utterly pure, earnest and sincere, bow to the Buddhas and sit erect, concentrating your mind for a moment or two, before opening the sutra to read aloud or silently. At that time, you should sit up straight as though you were facing the Buddhas, listening to their perfect voices, w i t h o u t   a   s i n g l e   l a z y, discriminating thought. Then, *without trying to find the meaning of the sutra, just recite it in one stretch from beginning to end.* By reciting the sutras in such a manner, if you are of superior capacity, you can awaken to the Non-Dual Truth and reach the Dharma of True Mark. Even if you are dull and of low capacity, you will gain increased merit and wisdom, eradicating karmic obstructions in the process. The Sixth Patriarch once said: 'we can awaken our Mind and see our True Nature just by reciting the *Diamond Sutra.*' This quote refers to the practice of Scriptural Recital as explained above. It is therefore called '*samatha*' (stopping or arresting mental processes). If you follow these steps, reciting any Mahayana sutra can lead to the opening of the Mind, the seeing of your True Nature. This does not apply to the *Diamond Sutra* alone." Zen: 153-154 #1291

▸ **SCRIPTUAL BUDDHISM**
see Scriptual Studies School

◙ **SCRIPTUAL STUDIES SCHOOL**
syn: Teaching School; Sutra studies school; School of Scriptual Studies

----

►A school that combines the teachings of the Avatamsaka, T'ien T'ai and Yogacara philosophies. "These teachings are partially absorbed in the Ch'an and Pure Land schools" (Sung-pen-Hsu)

◙ **SEAS**
see Oceans

◙ **SEATS, THRONES, AND RESIDENCES**

►"Seats, thrones, and residences represent spiritual states, stability, or spheres of awareness and action."
Clea/84: 22 #1968

◙ **SEEING BUDDHA**
see Voice of a Buddha

◙ **SEEING BUDDHA (SAMADHI)**
See also: Death; Honen; Pure Land School

►Name of a light emitted by the Buddha while in a state of samadhi (concentration). It is the source of an ancient practice in northern India (and later China

and Japan) to exhort a dying person to face west, holding onto a thread attached to the finger of an Amitabha Buddha statue (also facing west). The practice is designed to remind dying Buddhists of their vow to be reborn in the Pure Land.

Avatamsaka Sutra:
"It also emits a light called 'seeing Buddha':/ This light can awaken those about to die,/ Causing them to see any Buddha they think of,/ So when their life ends they can be born in that Buddha's pure land./
"To exhort the dying to remembrance of Buddha (Buddha Recitation),/ And show them icons for them to behold,/ Causing them to take refuge in the Buddha,/ Is how this light can be made." (T. Cleary, *Flower Ornament Sutra/Avatamsaka Sutra*, vol. I p. 350)
See also Honen

◙ **SEEKER (BUDDHIST)**
See also: Practice

►"The main problem that besets the modern newcomer [to Buddhism], therefore, is not difficulty in obtaining teachings but the embarrassment of too much choice. At which counters of the spiritual supermarket to shop? Which of the tempting brands to choose? Really, though, we are in a very fortunate position. Because most of the major Buddhist schools and traditions have now been transmitted to the West, we have a clearer view of what is on offer than our former Asian co-religionists. We can therefore allow ourselves a period of shopping around, experimenting with this and that in order to find out what suits us best. Of course, there are some people who just go on shopping around for ever, leaving a particular counter whenever difficulties arise and never really confronting themselves or the demands of Buddhism. So at some point one usually has to make a commitment to a particular course of study and practice, but it is best not to hurry the process. Commitment will generally arise quite naturally of its own accord when a situation feels right, whereas forcing the issue can lead to trouble. Many teachers and groups are moreover eager to recruit and will sometimes subtly (and sometimes not so subtly!) pressure a newcomer to join their party. On the other hand, many newcomers eagerly desire the consolations of belonging and so often make their choices for the wrong reasons. Once committed, guard against running away. When Buddhism really begins to 'work', things often get difficult -- sometimes very difficult. One may, for instance, have to face things in oneself that he has been dodging for years. The ego does not open itself to new growth without a struggle either -- and sometimes an intense one, for every advance demands a kind of death to one's old self. And there are phases when things seem to go dead, like walking through endless, monotonous mud and sleet; or when agonizing doubts or fears arise. Remember the night that the Buddha spent beneath the Bodhi Tree before his Enlightenment. Mara has his ways of trying to deflect us. Try therefore to follow the Buddha's example and not be deterred. On the other hand, do not feel afraid to leave a group or teacher when it is clear that they have ceased to work for you. Again there can be gross or subtle pressure against going: it may be stigmatized as defection, disloyalty or failure. But remember, Shakyamuni Buddha himself was not afraid to leave his teachers when he had absorbed all they had to teach him. Nor was he deterred from discarding practices he had decided were not useful from fear that fellow practitioners would spurn or deride him. Always however, be watchful; delve into your own motivations, check your responses and feelings, and keep a clear eye on what is happening around you, avoiding the extremes of being a destructive critic or a stray-eyed naif. The Buddhist Way is the middle way -- and is all about learning [and practice]. If you do decide to leave a group or teacher, do so if possible in the proper way, with appropriate gratitude. Always be realistic and do not fall prey to illusions, especially collective ones. One illusion that besets many newcomers is that religion is good *per se*, so they expect all the people and institutions they encounter to be thoroughly benign. In fact, with rare exceptions, religious people and institutions are much like worldly ones. They have their dark as well as their light sides. So be watchful on this account, and then perhaps you will not be too disillusioned if, for instance, your teacher, though possessing undeniable virtues and talents, also turns out to have feet of clay. Also do not be bedazzled by charismatic teachers, or ones with mass followings, or great fame, power or worldly wealth. True teachers have perennially kept a low profile, living in seclusion, not seeking crowds or worldly success. What they taught was difficult, for the few rather than for the many. Those who successfully massmarket spiritual teachings often do so by watering them down and adding seductive sweeteners. Be careful too of teachers and groups that pressure you for money or services. The Dharma is said to be beyond price, something that should be freely given. A monk does not ask for *dana* (q.v.); he waits for it silently. It should be left up to you to contribute as and when and to what extent you feel fit. *Try for your part to be generous, however, not least because generosity fosters spiritual growth.*"

Snell/Elements:117-119 #1203

◉ **SEISHI**
see Mahasthamaprapta

◉ **SELF**
See also: Attachment; Evil

▸"Sentient beings consider the Five Aggregates to constitute a unitary self or ego (atman). This wrong idea derives from deep-rooted clinging."
Chan: 482 #0561

◎ **SELF-DEFENSE**
see War

◎ **SELF-HELP BOOKS**
See also: Meditation; Zen school

▸Cultivators should exercise wisdom in receiving teachings, carefully distinguishing the true from the false and the deviant. See the following passage by the late founder of the Buddhist Lodge and Buddhist Society (London), on the true goal of all Buddhist practice: "In the West, the need for some guidance in mind-development was made acute ... by a sudden spate of books which were, whatever the motive of their authors, dangerous in the extreme. No word was said in them of the sole r i g h t   m o t i v e   f o r mind-development, the enlightenment of the meditator for the benefit of all mankind, and the reader was led to believe that it was quite legitimate to study and practice mindfulness and the higher stages which

ensue for the benefit of business efficiency and the advancement of personal prestige. In these circumstances, *Concentration and Meditation* ... was compiled and published by the [British] Buddhist Society, with constant stress on the importance of right motive, and ample warning of the dangers, from a headache to insanity, which lie in wait for those who trifle with the greatest force on earth, the human mind." (Christmas Humphreys, *The Buddhist Way of Life*, p. 100.)
Hump: 100
NOTE
Most ancient masters, including such figures as the Patriarch Dogen, the founder of the Japanese school of Soto Zen, held that only monks and nuns could achieve Enlightenment through Zen. (See, for example, Kenneth Kraft, *Zen: Tradition and Transition*, p.186.)
Editor: na   #2253
See also: Pure Land Buddhism (Summary)

◎ **SELF-NATURE**
See also: Buddha Nature

▸"Things in the phenomenal world are transient, momentary, and without duration; hence they have no self-nature (self-entity)

or individual substantiality.

In some contexts, 'self-nature' is used in an approbatory sense to denote the Buddha-nature within one's mind. This usage is particularly common in Zen literature."

Chan: 483 #0562

◙ **SELF-NATURE AMITABHA**
Syn: Mind-Only Pure Land
See also: Pure Land Buddhism (Summary); Pure Land School

▸The expression "Self-Nature Amitabha, Mind-Only Pure Land" represents the quintessence of Pure Land/Buddha Recitation Practice. At the noumenon level (i.e., at the level of principle), Amitabha, the Buddha of Infinite Light and Infinite Life, is our Self-Nature, always bright and everlasting. To recite the Buddha's name is to return to our Self-Nature -- our Buddha nature... Hence, the expression "Self-Nature Amitabha Buddha, Mind-Only Pure Land" represents the teaching that, if the Mind is pure, the land, the environment is pure as well. This expression is popular in Zen.

Editors: na

Buddhism of Wisdom & Faith/ excerpts:
"Many who like to voice lofty principles frequently reject the Pure Land method in these terms: 'To recite the Buddha's name seeking rebirth in the Pure Land is to grasp at marks, seeking the Dharma outside the Mind, failing to understand that all dharmas are Mind-Only.' These individuals, seeking the subtle and the lofty, are in reality shallow and superficial! This is because they do not understand that if the Saha World is Mind-Only, then the Western Pure Land is also Mind-Only, and nothing can be found outside the True Mind. Thus, to recite Amitabha Buddha's name is to recite the Buddha of our own Nature and Mind; to be reborn in the Pure Land is to return to the realm of our own Mind -- not to an outside realm! Since neither the Saha World nor the Pure Land is outside the Mind, how can remaining in the Saha World, enduring Samsara, scorched and burned by the fire of the Five Turbidities, be compared with returning to the tranquil and blissful Pure Land -- the pure and cool realm of freedom? We should realize that the ones truly in a position to honor the Mind-Only Pure Land are those who have attained the Dharma-Nature Body (i.e., the

Buddhas), and are always free and at ease in all circumstances. At that time, whether in the Saha World or in the Land of Ultimate Bliss, they are in a 'pure land,' in the state of Mind-Only -- in the state of liberation. Otherwise, though they may discourse endlessly on the mystery and loftiness of the Pure Land, they cannot escape bewilderment and delusion in the 'bardo stage,' and, following their karma, revolving in the cycle of Birth and Death!" (Thich Thien Tam, *Buddhism of Wisdom and Faith*, sec. 27)

"As we recite 'Namo Amitabha Buddha,' we each create and adorn our own Land of Ultimate Bliss. We each accomplish our own Land of Ultimate Bliss which is certainly not hundreds of thousands of millions of Buddhalands from here. Although it is far away, it doesn't go beyond one thought. It's not hundreds of thousands of millions of Buddhalands from here; it's right in our hearts. The Land of Ultimate Bliss is the original true heart, the true mind, of every one of us. If you obtain this heart, you will be born in the Land of Ultimate Bliss. If you don't understand your own original true heart, you

will not. The Land of Ultimate Bliss is within our hearts, not outside ... Amitabha Buddha and living beings do not discriminate between this and that, for the Land of Ultimate Bliss is not so far away. In one thought, turn the light within. Know that you are the Buddha, and your original Buddhahood is just the Land of Ultimate Bliss. (Hsuan Hua, *General Explanation of the Buddha Speaks of Amitabha Sutra*, p. 110.)"

QUESTIONS/ANSWERS:
"*Question I*: 'Are the Mind-Only Pure Land and the Self-Nature Amitabha the same as or different from the Western Pure Land and Amitabha in the Pure Land?' *Answer*: 'It is because the Mind-Only Pure Land exists that we are reborn in the Pure Land of the West. If the mind is not pure, it is impossible to achieve rebirth in the Pure Land. Even when those who have committed cardinal transgressions achieve rebirth through ten recitations, such rebirth is due to their reciting the Buddha's name with a pure mind, thus eliciting a response from Amitabha Buddha. Ordinary people generally think that if the Pure Land is Mind-Only, then it does not exist.

This is the understanding of demons and externalists. Such a deluded view, which appears correct but is in reality wrong, affects more than half of all people and causes practitioners to forfeit true benefits. It is precisely because of the Self-Nature Amitabha that the practitioner must recite the name of Buddha Amitabha of the West seeking rebirth in the Pure Land -- so as to achieve the Self-Nature Amitabha through gradual cultivation. If he merely grasps at the Self-Nature Amitabha but does not recite the name of Buddha Amitabha of the West, he cannot achieve immediate escape from Birth and Death -- not even if he is truly awakened, much less if (like most people who ask this question) he is pretentious and just indulges in empty talk without engaging in practice. Thus, the answer to your question [are the Mind-Only Pure Land and the Self-Nature Amitabha the same as, or different from the Western Pure Land and Amitabha in the Pure Land?] is that they are *one yet two* before Buddhahood is attained, *two yet one* after Buddhahood is attained.'"

PLZ: 108-109   #1367

◉ **SELF-ORDINATION**
See Brahma Net Sutra

◉ **SELF-POWER**
Syn: Jiriki
See also: Other Power; Difficult Path of Practice

►"I. One's own power, merit, intelligence, discrimination, etc. II. The term is generally used to indicate the attempt to attain enlightenment through one's own efforts rather than by relying upon the compassion of the Buddhas and Bodhisattvas [in addition to one's own efforts]."
Dait: 153

"'One's own power'; an expression referring to the endeavor to attain enlightenment through one's own efforts (for example, sitting in meditation). Jiriki (Self-Power) is generally used in contradistinction to tariki (Other-Power), which roughly means 'the power of the other.' This refers to the fact that the adherents of some Buddhist schools (Pure Land for example) place their trust in the notion that belief in Buddha (generally, his manifestation as Amitabha) and calling upon his name will bring about rebirth in a Buddha paradise (Pure Land) and thus the liberation of the believer.

This is an approach that places the power of the Buddha principle to liberate human beings in the foreground. In contrast, other schools of Buddhism, such as Zen, place the emphasis on the ability to actualize enlightenment and achieve liberation through one's own efforts, i.e., through meditative training. This is characterized as jiriki. On a deeper level, as is stressed in Mahayana Buddhism, every sentient being and thing from the very beginning is endowed with the Buddha-Nature. From this point of view, the opposition of jiriki and tariki must be regarded as an artificial one [which simply indicates a different emphasis in religious practice]."
Sham: 104 #0147

◙ **SELF-POWER PATH**
see Difficult path of practice

◙ **SELF-SPOKEN SUTRA**
See also: Amitabha Buddha

▶"A Sermon spontaneously expounded by the Buddha without prior request from the assembly.
The *Amitabha Sutra* belongs to the 'self-spoken division' of the Tripitaka (Buddhist canon):

'Because its principles were too profound and wonderful to comprehend, no one requested the Pure Land Dharma-door. Nonetheless, it had to be revealed and so the Buddha spontaneously spoke this very important sutra, doubly important because it will be the last to disappear in the Dharma-Ending Age.'" (Master Hsuan Hua)
The *Brahma Net Sutra* (which contains the full set of the Bodhisattva precepts) and the *Avatamsaka Sutra* (the Mahayana sutra *par excellence*) are other well-known examples of self-spoken sutras.
Editor: na #1693

◙ **SENTIENT BEING**
See also: Tree Spirits

▶"Any living being who has a consciousness." (animals, deities, Buddhas, etc...)"
Chan: 483
"Any discussion of the first precept [not to kill] entails formulating a definition of life and the taking of life. Life, in this connection, has traditionally been defined as 'sentient' life and beings with minds as 'sentient beings.' Since enlightenment is a possibility for all beings with

minds, sentient life is regarded as precious. Sentient beings include hell beings, heavenly beings, ghosts, animals, and humans, but not rocks and plants. Since deities ·and spirits may live in association with plants, plants may react to stimuli, but in the early tradition, they do not have consciousness."

Tsomo: 100-101

Buddha Sakyamuni compared sentient beings chasing after the fleeting pleasures of this world to a child licking honey off a sharp knife. There is no way they can avoid hurting themselves.

Editor/Tam: 306 #0563

◙ **SERENITY**
see Equanimity

◙ **SESSHIN**
Syn: Retreat

▸"Japanese for a period of intensive meditation practice in the Zen tradition."
Tsomo: 168 #1997

◙ **SEVEN (NUMBER)**

▸In Buddhism and some other religions, the number seven has a mystical significance. Thus, the traditional mourning period is forty-nine (seven times seven)

days.
Editor: na

"According to the Esoteric School, the number seven is the ultimate number in the cycle of Birth and Death. Therefore, in the bardo stage, the 'soul' must undergo changes every seven days, and to be efficacious, mantras should be recited at least seven times. Buddhist texts note this with the words 'the Dharma is thus,' i.e., according to the law of nature it has to be that way and cannot be explained, just as it is difficult to explain why fire is hot and ice is cold. Starting with the number seven and multiplying it by three or seven, we have twenty-one or forty-nine. Therefore, the Esoteric School teaches that mantras should be recited [at least] seven times to be effective, twenty-one or forty-nine times if the mind is weak and agitated. Thus, basing themselves on this teaching, practitioners arrange retreat periods of seven, twenty-one or forty-nine days." (*Buddhism of Wisdom and Faith.*)
Tam: 173-174 #1672

◙ **SEVEN BUDDHAS**
▸"Seven Buddhas of antiquity, the seventh being Shakyamuni, or

Gautama Buddha, the historical Buddha. This is an illustration of the perennial nature of the Dharma or Truth realized by Buddhas, discovered and not invented by the historical Buddha."
Chih-I/Cleary: 201

◙ **SEVEN LIMBS OF ENLIGHTENMENT**

▸"The seven limbs (factors) are: 1. Mindfulness; 2. discriminative investigation of the Dharma; 3. vigor; 4. joy; 5. ease of body and mind; 6. concentration; and 7. equanimity."
Chan: 492

In other words, "these are the factors of remembrance, discrimination between teachings, effort, joy, ecstasy, concentration, and equanimity (upeksa). These seven form a part of the Thirty-Seven Limbs of Enlightenment."
Thur: 152-153 #0684

◙ **SEVEN TREASURES**

▸Traditionally listed as: gold, silver, lapis lazuli, crystal, agate, red pearl and carnelian. They represent the seven powers of faith, perseverance, sense of shame, avoidance of wrongdoing,

mindfulness, concentration and wisdom.
Editor/Tam: 161 #0623

◙ **SEVEN-DAY RETREAT**
Syn: Retreat
See also: Chu-Hung; Practice

▸**(I) Background**

"Around the beginning of the Sung dynasty (10th c. China), three hundred years after patriarch Shan Tao (considered to be an incarnation of Amitabha Buddha and whose writings are accepted as scripture in Japan), southeast China witnessed a great resurgence of interest in Pure Land spirituality, especially among T'ien T'ai and Chan masters of the region. Once again, a seven-day ritual retreat for Buddha-mindfulness (Buddha Recitation), known as the 'Amitabha Repentance' or 'Pure Land Repentance,' proved to be an especially popular form of Pure Land practice. Various incarnations of this same basic institution can be traced, intermittently, down through the Ming and Qing periods to the 'Seven Days of Buddha-Recitation' that is widespread among the clergy and laity of Taiwan, Hong Kong, and Vietnam, etc. today. It is difficult to say whether Shan Tao's seven-day rite of Buddha-mindfulness played a direct role in the shaping of Pure Land programs of later periods. Nonetheless, it does describe an institutional and ritual paradigm that has seen repeated incarnations in Pure Land communities over the centuries. As a rule, the laity have been given free access to the seven-day retreats for Buddha-recitation. Nonetheless, such retreats are nearly always held at Buddhist monasteries and are led by the Buddhist clergy. Moreover, their strict codes of ritual and moral purity, as well as their intensive regimen of practice, are more characteristic of monastic life than they are of lay life. In this respect, the seven-day retreat represents a unique and idealized occasion for the Pure Land lay Buddhist -- one in which the ordinary householder is allowed access to an intense world of religious restraint and devotion that is otherwise the domain of the Buddhist professional. Within the world of the monastery itself, the intense devotion characteristic of the seven-day retreat becomes the norm rather than the exception."

Lopez/95: 366

"From as early as the Tang period we hear of the existence of 'Pure Land Cloisters' within larger monastic complexes, where a congregation of self-professed Pure Land mendicants could pursue a collective regimen of Pure Land practice and study. Over the centuries that followed, influential Pure Land masters have periodically sought to organize individual monasteries along Pure Land lines ... The Ming dynasty master Chu Hung (1535-1615) and Republican period master Yin Kuang (1861-1940) represent two such figures who have had a profound impact on the monastic form of Pure Land Buddhism in modern times. Both instituted comprehensive plans for adapting traditional monastic structures and routines to the specific purposes of Pure Land devotion, including the creation of halls for the concentrated recitation of the Buddha's name that were modeled on the traditional Chan meditation hall. At the same time, monks and nuns of the Pure Land school have developed a number of distinctive forms of retreat that are organized along the lines of the seven-day rite of Buddha-mindfulness but apply its program to a more intensive monastic setting."

Lopez: 366-367   #1758

(II) Conducting a Retreat

"If we have not attained Enlightenment, we should recite the Buddha's name seeking rebirth in the Pure Land. To ensure that this occurs, we should recite to the level of one-pointedness of mind. And, in order to practice to that level, we should conduct periodic retreats. To be 'in retreat' is to retire to a small house, meditation hut or small room, cut off all outside activities and conditions and concentrate on reciting the Buddha's name for a period of seven days. Why seven days and not six or eight? The *Amitabha Sutra* states:

'Sariputra: if a good man or a good woman hears Amida Buddha preach and firmly holds the Name wholeheartedly and singlemindedly, be it for one day, two days, three days, four days, five days, six days, or seven days, Amida Buddha, together with all the holy multitudes, will appear before that person as the end of life draws near. When death arrives, that person, with mind undisturbed, at once gains rebirth in Amida Buddha's Land of Utmost Happiness.' (Hozen Seki, *Buddha Tells of the Infinite: the 'Amida Kyo,'* p. 53.) Since the Sutra does not refer to six days only, nor does it speak of eight days, Pure Land practitioners, basing themselves on the words of Buddha Sakyamuni, have traditionally taken the period of retreat as seven days. According to the Esoteric School, the number seven is the ultimate number in the cycle of Birth and Death. Therefore, in the bardo stage, the 'soul' must undergo changes every seven days, and to be efficacious, mantras should be recited at least seven times. Buddhist texts note this with the words 'The Dharma is thus,' i.e., according to the law of nature it has to be that way and cannot be explained, just as it is difficult to explain why fire is hot and ice is cold. Starting with the number seven and multiplying it by three or seven, we have twenty-one or forty-nine. Therefore, the Esoteric School teaches that mantras should be recited [at least] seven times to be effective, twenty-one or forty-nine times if the mind is weak and agitated. Thus, basing themselves on this teaching, practitioners arrange retreat periods of seven, twenty-one or forty-nine days.

In conducting a seven-day retreat,

one can either practice alone, to attain purity more easily, or with many other cultivators. In either case, three types of good spiritual advisors are required.

1. Teaching Spiritual Advisor. This is someone conversant with the Dharma and experienced in cultivation. The retreat members can have him follow their progress, guiding them throughout the retreat, or they can simply seek his guidance before and after the retreat. When several persons hold a retreat together, they should ask a spiritual advisor to lead the retreat and give a daily fifteen-to-thirty-minute inspirational talk.

2. Caretaking Spiritual Advisors. This refers to one or several persons assisting with outside daily chores such as preparing meals or cleaning up, so that those on retreat can cultivate peacefully without distraction. Such persons are called 'retreat assistants.'

3. Common Practice Spiritual Advisors. These are persons who practice the same method as the individual(s) on retreat. They keep an eye on one another, encouraging and urging each other on. These cultivators can either be participants in the same retreat or cultivators living nearby. In addition to keeping an eye out and urging the practitioners on, they can exchange ideas or experiences for the common good.

An Elder Master of great virtue in the Zen tradition once taught: The practitioner should take the Ten Directions as his perfect Enlightenment seat, and not set a limit to the length of retreats. If one year is not sufficient to become enlightened, he should meditate for ten years. If ten years are not enough, then he should meditate for twenty or thirty years, or up to his whole lifetime, always unwavering in his determination. Pure Land followers should do likewise. Attending a seven-day retreat is the best expedient to reach one-pointedness of mind. If one retreat is not sufficient, then he should cultivate during many retreats, never wavering in his determination."

Tam: 173-177

◙ **SEX**

See also: Love-Attachment; Afflictions; Overeating

►"Of all of the desires, sex is the strongest and most difficult one for meditation practitioners to cope with since it encompasses all other desires (form, sound, smell, flavor, and touch), and in sex all of these desires are present in their most poignant form. Also, *we need to be aware that it is just because of sex that we continually return to this world through rebirths.*" See "Marriage (Clergy)".   Cheng Kuan: 65

Illustration

"There is an anecdote concerning a monk who lived in a remote mountain. One day the king of the country, hearing about the accomplishments of the monk, sent his messengers to invite him to the palace as an honored guest. The monk flew to the palace as the king wished and in fact, did it several times. On one of these occasions, the king asked the queen to pay homage to the monk. In doing so, the queen knelt before him and put her hands upon his bare feet to show her highest respect. The queen's hands were very delicate and soft and the practitioner, never having had that kind of experience before, suddenly felt excited and all at once lost all samadhi power. He felt faint and his body became very weak. He had to be carried back to his mountain retreat!"

Cheng Kuan: 61

◙ SHAMAN

►"General term for a person thought to have developed the ability to communicate with and influence the spirit world."
Reat: 342 #2089

◙ SHAN-TAO (613-681)
Syn: Shandao
See also: Pure Land School; Honen

►*Jpn/* Zendo; *Vn/*Thiện-Đạo. "The third patriarch of the Pure Land school in China. He renounced the world at the age of ten and studied the *Lotus, Vimalakirti* and other sutras. Later he studied the *Meditation Sutra* and embraced Pure Land teaching. In 641, at the age of twenty-nine, he visited Tao-ch'o at Hsuan-chung-ssu temple and heard him lecture on the *Meditation Sutra*, which greatly deepened his faith. Thereafter he went to Ch'ang-an where he disseminated the practice of calling upon the name of Amitabha Buddha."
Sokk: 382-383

"The third patriarch of the Pure Land tradition in China whom Honen considered to be an incarnation of Amitabha and whose writings were accepted as scripture in Japan. "Okaz: 187

"He is said to have copied the *Amitabha Sutra* more than 100,000 times and made more than 300 paintings of the Pure Land. He wrote five works in nine fascicles, including commentaries on different sections of the *Meditation Sutra*." Insa: 367-368

NOTE

"The importance of the Shan-tao '*Commentary on the Meditation Sutra*' to the Japanese Pure Land Buddhists can be traced to Honen's personal salvation, which he credits to his reading of a passage from this text. Shinran included Shan-tao as one of the three Chinese patriarchs and quoted extensively from Shan-tao's works." Tana: 202 #0184

◉ **SHANDAO**
see Shan-tao (613-681)

◉ **SHANTIDEVA**

►"Skt.; representative of the Madhyamika school of the Mahayana. Shantideva was a king's son from south India. He flourished in the 7th/8th centuries and was a monk at the monastic university Nalanda. He was the author of two surviving works, the *Collection of Rules* and the *Entering the Path of Enlightenment*. The latter is still used in Tibetan Buddhism as a teaching text." / Sham: 193 #0371

◉ **SHAO-LIN MONASTERY**
See also: Pao Lin Temple

►"Shao-lin monastery is situated on the Sung mountain in Hu-nan Province. This monastery is especially famous for its nine years' association with Bodhidharma (Lo-yang-chia-lan-chi) who first started the Chan/Zen school in China." Lahiri: 87

◉ **SHASTRA**
see Sastra

◉ **SHEN-HSIU (605-706)**
See also: Hui-Neng; Zen School

►"One of the two most famous disciples of Hung-jen, the Fifth Patriarch of Chinese Chan/Zen Buddhism, the other being Hui-neng, the Sixth. The rival Schools founded by the two men, the North and South, became known as the Gradual and the Sudden respectively. Shen-hsiu's school, although patronized by the reigning Emperor, did not last very long, but from the Sudden school of Hui-neng

sprang the present Rinzai and Soto schools of Zen."
Hump: 176
The two schools of Zen, the Gradual and the Sudden, represent different facets of the same teaching adapted to different types of people in different locations. To praise one school while disparaging the other is therefore a form of attachment, a dualistic view of Buddhism not consonant with the Truth.
Editor: na #0412

◙ **SHIH-CHIH**
see Mahasthamaprapta

◙ **SHIKANTAZA**
See also: Dogen; Soto Zen School

▸"Jpn.; lit. 'nothing but (shikan) precisely (ta) sitting (za)'; a form of Zen practice in which there are no more supportive techniques of the type beginners use, such as counting the breath or a koan. According to the *Soto* Zen patriarch Dogen, shikantaza, i.e., resting in a state of brightly alert attention that is free of thoughts, directed to no object, and attached to no particular content, is the highest or purest form of Zen." Sham: 196-197

◙ **SHIKSHANANDA**
see Siksananda (652-710)

◙ **SHILA**
see Precepts

◙ **SHIN BUDDHISM**
see Jodo Shinshu School

◙ **SHINGON SCHOOL**
See also: Mikkyo; Esoteric School; Tibetan Buddhism

▸"One of the esoteric schools of Japanese Buddhism characterized by mystic ritualism and speculative doctrines, introduced by Kukai (774-835). Its monastic center is located on Mount Koya in Wakayama Prefecture."
Okaz: 187 #2151

◙ **SHINRAN (1173-1262)**
See also: Honen; Jodo Shinshu School

▸"Founder of the Jodo-Shin School of Japan. A disciple of Honen (Jodo School), he carried the doctrine of salvation by faith in Amitabha Buddha to the extreme one of recitation of Amitabha's name being sufficient if done with a pure heart.

He advocated marriage of priests, and was himself married.

He popularized congregational worship."
Hump: 177
Except in Japan and, to a certain extent, Korea (as a result of the Japanese occupation), Shinran's reforms (salvation by faith alone, marriage of priests, meat-eating, etc.) are not accepted by the Buddhist traditions of East Asia.
Editor: na #0160
See also: Jodo Shinshu School

◙ SHINTO

►"'Way of the Gods,' the indigenous, pre-Buddhist religion of Japan."
Reat: 343
"Indigenous religion of Japan in which deified ancestors, heroes, and the personified powers of nature are worshiped."
Okaz: 178 #0644

◙ SHOBOGENZO
see Dogen

◙ SHORTER AMITABHA SUTRA
see Amitabha Sutra

◙ SHOUTS AND BLOWS
See also: Zen; Ma-Tsu; Lin-Chi

►"A shout without a single meaning, which is used by Zen masters much in the way a stick is used. It also serves in encounters between masters as a means of expression-transcending words and concepts -- just like a blow of a stick at the right moment can help the Zen student achieve a breakthrough to enlightened vision. According to tradition, such a cry was first used by the great Chinese master Ma-tsu Tao-i, who was known for his thunderous voice. Also famous for his skillful use of the 'stick and shout' was Lin-chi (Jpn./ Rinzai)."
Sham: 114
"It can also be pointed out that by no means did all Ch'an masters of that period display a penchant for unconventional behavior. As Venerable Yin-shun has perceptively noted, the display of such methods as shouts and blows by individual masters is connected to the area of China they come from. It seems that [within the Sudden Zen School of the Sixth Patriarch Hui-Neng], masters from the north (e.g. Lin-chi) tend to be more inclined towards 'crude' behavior in comparison with masters from the south (e.g. Kuei-shan). ... This seems to imply that the iconoclastic elements found among the Ch'an masters of the period are more a reflection of

local cultural patterns than an essential factor in their teaching." See Yin-shun, *Chung-kuo ch'an-tsung shih* (Taipei: Cheng-wen ch'u-pan she, 1983) p. 410-414, as quoted in *Sun-Face Buddha*. #0386

◙ **SICKNESS**
see Illness

◙ **SIDDHARTHA**
See also: Sakyamuni Buddha

▸"Prince Siddhartha was the name of the Buddha before his renunciation of the world. Siddhartha is variously translated as 'he who has accomplished his aim,' 'he whose desire has been fulfilled,' 'he who has been successful in his endeavors,' and so on."
Yoko: 187 #0816

◙ **SIKSANANDA (652-710)**
Syn: Shikshananda

▸"A monk from Khotan famous for his translation of the eighty-fascicle *Avatamsaka Sutra*. He came to China in 695 and brought the original Sanskrit text of the *Avatamsaka Sutra* (Hua-yen-ching/ Kegon-kyo/ Hoa Nghiêm Kinh), which he translated into Chinese with

Bodhiruci. He also translated [twenty] other texts."
Daito: 154-155

"A monk of Khotan in Central Asia. He was versed in Theravada and Mahayana as well as non-Buddhist learning. At the request of Empress Wu of the T'ang dynasty, he brought the Sanskrit text of the *Avatamsaka Sutra* to Lo-yang and began the translation of the sutra there. Bodhiruchi, I-ching and others also joined in the project and finally the eighty-fascicle Chinese translation was completed. Thereafter Shikshananda translated the Lankavatara and other sutras, twenty in all."
Sokk: 387 #0005

◙ **SILA**
see Precepts

◙ **SILENCE**
See also: World-origin

▸"Monastic life is usually either silent or what is called 'noble silence,' speaking only when necessary."
Tsomo: 140

"The truth of non-duality was expressed by means of silence by Vimalakirti in a discussion held at Vaisali, according to the *Vimalakirti-Nirdesa Sutra*. At the

end of the discussion, Manjusri is said to have praised Vimalakirti's silence as the true representation of non-duality. This silence of Vimalakirti is called a silence like thunder."
Dait: 222

"The historical Buddha Shakyamuni refrained from giving a definitive answer to many metaphysical questions of his time. This is often referred to as the silence of the Buddha. Again and again his students asked him if a self exists or not (anatman); if an enlightened one in any way continues to exist after death; if the world is eternal and unending or not. The Buddha explained that he was silent on these questions because answers to them would in no way further progress on the path -- they would not contribute to the overcoming of the passions nor to the attainment of wisdom. He was concerned that preoccupation with these questions would divert people from the path that leads to liberation from suffering."
Sham: 206
NOTE:
"Something which a lot of people notice on meditation retreats during which there are extended periods of silence is that they experience an excess of energy. They feel more alive. This is partly because talking in itself takes effort but perhaps mainly because what we say is often an expression of negative emotions which waste and drain away energy. For this reason silence is an extremely important spiritual discipline, whether in Buddhism, Hinduism, or Christianity. In all these great spiritual traditions, silence is considered important, if not imperative, for the person who seeks to lead a spiritual life. ... So the silent person is very often the wise person, not least because he or she avoids wasting energy on negative verbiage."
Sangh/95: 21 #1992

◙ **SILENCE OF THE BUDDHA**
see Silence

◙ **SILK ROAD**

►The four thousand year-old trade route between India, China and the Mediterranean world. #2091

◙ **SIMA**

►"Skt.; a bounded area, within which official Sangha acts may take place. The main use of sima is for upasampada, the ceremony

of acceptance into the Bhikkhu-Sangha (ordination)."
Sume: 139 #2030

◙ **SIMHA (6TH C. A.D)**
See also: Killing

►"The twenty-fourth Indian patriarch. Born in central India, he propagated Buddhism in the ancient northern Indian country of Kasmira (present day Kashmir). He was executed by the king of that country after having been falsely accused by an influential non-Buddhist."
Yoko: 212

Master Arya Simha lived in Central Asia during the sixth century A.D. While he was preaching Buddhism in Kashmir, King Dammira, an enemy of Buddhism, razed temples and murdered a number of monks. When he finally beheaded Master Arya Simha, it was said that pure white milk gushed from Arya Simha's neck. The Patriarch Arya Simha, like Patriarch Hui K'o and the Elder Maudgalyayana, who also met untimely deaths, are all revered figures in Mahayana Buddhism. Through their violent deaths (a result of their karma of killing in previous lives), sentient beings are

reminded of the crucial importance of adhering to the precept against killing -- a cornerstone of Buddhist ethics.
Editor/Thich: 320-321 #0799

◙ **SIMULTANEITY OF CAUSE AND EFFECT**
see Cause is Result, Result is Cause

◙ **SIN**
See also: Dedication of Merit; Cause and Effect; Forgiveness

►"Buddhism brought to the Chinese a vivid concept of an after-life, and a doctrine of future punishment for sins committed in this life, an idea that present sufferings are the result of past sin. It taught that future retribution for sin could be avoided by accumulation of merit by such means as chanting liturgies, repentance, meritorious actions, asceticism and the like. It introduced a soteriology by its doctrine of [dedication of merit, q.v.]. Buddhas and Bodhisattvas have accumulated infinite stores of merit; by appealing to them in penitence and faith, the consequences of sin can be wiped out and a blissful future life guaranteed. These Buddhist ideas exercised a profound influence

on Confucians and Taoists alike, and on popular beliefs."
Ling: 233

"It is important to grasp that the idea of an eternal damnation as a punishment for sin is foreign to Buddhist understanding. Suffering is a consequence of one's own action, not a retribution inflicted by an external power. Infernal torments, moreover, though they may last for aeons, belong to Samsara and are therefore not exempt from the law of impermanence. And even if the notion of a divine vengeance is regarded as an approximation, in mythological terms, to the concept of karmic consequences, it is perhaps worth suggesting that the impersonal view proposed by Buddhism should have the advantage of exorcising the paralyzing sense of guilt, or revolt, that can so often be the outcome of a too anthropomorphic theism. The doctrine of karma has only one message: the experience of states of being follows upon the perpetration of acts. We are the authors of our own destiny; and being the authors, we are ultimately, perhaps frighteningly, free."
Shantiveda: 6 #1159

◉ **SINCERITY AND RESPECT**
See also: Practice (Buddhist)

▸*Advice from Patriarch Yin-Kuang*
"Ultimately, when the practitioner recites to the point of pure, unmixed power, the totality of Mind is Buddha, the totality of Buddha is Mind, Mind and Buddha are as one. I am afraid that this principle and practice are not understood by everyone. It has always been my desire to proclaim them and to disseminate the Original Vows of Amitabha Buddha to rescue all sentient beings. How would I dare conceal this truth, transmitting it privately to you alone? If there is any secret knowledge to be transmitted privately in a hidden place, it is an externalist teaching, not a Buddhist teaching. Having said so, however, this old monk, in truth, does have a wonderful secret teaching, which only he possesses. Since you have requested it today, I have no qualms about revealing it to all Buddhist followers. What is this wonderful teaching? It is utter sincerity and profound respect. This secret is known to everyone, yet obscure to all! Wishing to eradicate deep-seated karma and repay the kindness of the

Buddhas, I have endeavored, day in and day out, to probe the shining cultivation of the ancients. I have thus discovered that utter sincerity and profound respect constitute a wonderful 'secret' method that lifts human beings to the realms of the saints, enabling them to escape Birth and Death. Time and again I have brought these points to the attention of those who have the right conditions. You should know that sincerity and respect are not reserved exclusively to students of the Dharma, but form the basis of all activities that you want to complete to perfection." Zen: 150-151 #1501

Sincerity and respect are important in all Buddhist practice but they are crucial in Pure Land. Otherwise, the practitioner cannot be in unison with Amitabha Buddha and loses the benefit of the Buddha's Vows.

◙ **SINGLE MARK SAMADHI**
see Buddha Recitation Samadhi

◙ **SINGLEMINDEDNESS**
see One-pointedness of mind

◙ **SITE OF ENLIGHTENMENT**
see Bodhimandala

◙ **SIX ASPECTS**
Syn: Six Forms; Sixfold Nature
See also: Avatamsaka Sutra

▸According to the Avatamsaka teaching, "all the constituents of the world (the dharmas) are interdependent and cannot exist independently .
Each of them possesses a sixfold nature: universality (the whole), speciality (the part), similarity (identity), diversity (difference), integration and differentiation... the ideal is a harmonious totality of things encountered in the perfectly enlightened Buddha -- the Buddha nature is potentially present in all things..."
[NEB15,p.]l1Va

"A doctrine of the... Avatamsaka school which, together with that of the Ten Mysteries, analyzes the phenomenal world from the standpoints of both difference and identity. The six forms are, to the Buddhist's eye, six inseparable aspects inherent in all things. They are: 1) universality -- a whole, which is composed of parts; 2) particularity -- the separate parts which constitute the whole; 3) similarity -- the separate parts are all related to the whole; 4) diversity -- though similar in that

they all help constitute the whole, each part's relationship to the whole is unique; 5) formation -- through the harmonization of the unique parts, the whole is constituted; 6) differentiation -- while uniting to form the whole, each part retains its unique characteristics."
[NS/DBTS,p.401] #1231

◉ SIX CONSCIOUSNESSES
See also: Consciousnesses

►"The consciousnesses associated with the eye, ear, nose, tongue, body, and mind."
Chan: 492 #0620

◉ SIX DIRECTIONS
See also: Ten Directions

►North, South, East, West, above and below i.e., all directions. In the *Avatamsaka Sutra*, they are expanded to include points of the compass in between (Northeast; Northwest; Southeast and Southwest) and are referred to as the Ten Directions.
Editor/Tam: 161 #0919

◉ SIX DUSTS
See Dust

◉ SIX FORMS
see Six Aspects

◉ SIX HETERODOX TEACHERS
See also: Externalist Views

►"These six sought to rival Buddha [Sakyamuni] in his day: Purana Kasyapa, who negated the effects of action, good or evil; Maskarin Gosaliputra, who taught a theory of randomness, negating causality; Samjayin Vairatiputra, who was agnostic in refusing to maintain any opinion about anything; Kakuda Katyayana, who taught a materialism in which there was no such things as killer or killed, but only transformations of elements; Ajita Kesakambala, who taught a more extreme nihilism regarding everything except the four main elements; and Nirgrantha Jnatiputra, otherwise known as Mahavira, the founder of Jainism, who taught the doctrine of indeterminism, considering all things in terms of 'maybe.'"
Thur: 151-152 #0683

◉ SIX KINDS OF MINDFULNESS
Syn: Six Mindfulnesses

►"The six objects of mindfulness practices are: Buddha, Dharma, Sangha, precepts, merits of renunciation and merits of deity."
Tana: 247 #1735

◙ **SIX PATHS**
see   Six Planes of Existence

◙ **SIX PERIODS**

►"The six divisions of a day, three for daytime and three for nighttime: the first, middle, and last parts of the day (morning, midday, and afternoon); and the first, middle, and last parts of the night."
Chan: 492   #0621

◙ **SIX PLANES OF EXISTENCE**
Syn: Six Paths; Six States of Existence
See also: Three Evil Paths; Saha World

►The paths within the realm of Birth and Death. They include the Three Evil Paths (hells, hungry ghosts, animality) and the paths of humans, Asuras and Celestials. These paths can be understood as states of mind.
Editor/Tam: 161

"Representation of the totality of mundane conditional existence: (1) animals (symbolizing ignorance), (2) ghosts (greed), (3) titans/Asuras (aggression), (4) hells (ignorance, greed, and aggression), (5) humanity (social virtue), (6) celestial states

(meditational abstractions)."
Chih-I/Cleary: 202 #0921
All sentient beings in Samsara revolve within these six paths or planes of existence according to their karma. To be liberated is to be freed from destined rebirth in these planes."
Chan: 492.

◙   **SIX   PRINCIPLES   OF HARMONY AND RESPECT**
See Sixfold Respect

◙ **SIX SUPERKNOWLEDGES**
See Spiritual Powers

◙ **SIXFOLD NATURE**
see   Six aspects

◙ **SIXFOLD RESPECT**
Syn: Six Principles of harmony and Respect
See   also: Sangha;   Bhiksu; Bhiksuni

►"Six bases of organization of the Buddhist community: the same acts of devotion, the same recitations, the same faith, the same precepts, the same views, and the same livelihood."
[TC/FO1, p.701] #1230

◙   **SIXTEEN   MEDITATIONS/ CONTEMPLATIONS**
See also: Lotus Grades

▸"The visualizations in the *Meditation Sutra* are distinguished into sixteen kinds [shifting from earthly scenes to Pure Land scenes at Visualization 3]: (1) visualization of the sun, (2) visualization of water, (3) visualization of the ground [in the Pure Land], (4) visualization of the trees, (5) visualization of the lake[s], (6) unified visualization of the [50 billion] storied-pavilions, trees, lakes, and so forth, (7) visualization of the [lotus throne of Amitabha Buddha], (8) visualization of the images of the Buddha Amitabha and Bodhisattvas Avalokitesvara and Mahasthamaprapta, (9) visualization of the [Reward body of Amitabha Buddha, i.e., the form in which He appears in the Pure Land], (10) visualization of Avalokitesvara, (11) visualization of Mahasthamaprapta, (12) visualization of one's own rebirth, (13) [see below], (14) visualization of the rebirth of the highest grades, (15) visualization of the rebirth of the middle grades and (16) visualization of the rebirth of the lowest grades." (K.K. Tanaka, *The Dawn of Chinese Pure Land Doctrine*.)
Tana: 150
The 13th Visualization has been summarized as follows:
"If one cannot visualize the [Reward body of Amitabha Buddha], focus on the small body, which is sixteen cubits high (the traditional height of Sakyamuni while he dwelt on earth); contemplate an intermingling of the [Reward] and small bodies."
Okaz: 52

Visualizations 14-16 refer to the nine Lotus Grades (q.v.), or levels of rebirth in the Pure Land.

◉ **SIXTEENTH MEDITATION**
see Sixteen Meditations/ Contemplations

◉ **SIXTH HEAVEN**
see Heaven of Free Enjoyment of Others' Emanations

◉ **SIXTH PATRIARCH SUTRA**
see Platform Sutra

◉ **SKANDHAS**
Syn: Aggregates; Five Aggregates; Five Skandhas

▸Also translated as "components" or "aggregates." They represent body and mind. The five skandas are form, feeling, conception, impulse and consciousness. For

example, form is the physical body, consciousness is the faculty of awareness. The best known reference to the five skandas is found in the *Heart Sutra*. By realizing that the skandhas are intrinsically empty, the Bodhisattva Avalokitesvara has escaped all suffering. Note the difference between intellectual understanding of this principle and truly internalizing it (a good driver slams on the brakes when another car cuts in front of him, without stopping to think about it). Only by internalizing the Truth of Emptiness, through assiduous cultivation, can suffering be transcended.
Editor/Tam: 338

Background

"All conditioned phenomena are made of aggregates. There are five aggregates, the first being material and representing the substance which constitutes all matter, the remaining four being mental and, therefore, restricted to functions of the mind."
Dait: 361

"In Buddhist philosophy, all physical, mental, and other elements in this phenomenal world are classified into five kinds of aggregates (Skt./ skandhas): (1) rupa-skandha, a generic term for all forms of matter; (2) vedana-skandha, perception; (3) samjna-skandha, mental conceptions and ideas; (4) samskara-skandha, volition; and (5) vijnana-skandha, consciousness or mind. In the case of man, the rupa-skandha is the body, the vijnana-skandha is the totality of the mind, and the other three skandhas are mental functions. Thus the five skandhas comprise the body and mind of all sentient beings in the World of Desire and the World of Form, but those sentient beings in the Formless World of pure spirit have no material element."
Yoko: 203 #0007

◙ **SKILL-IN-MEANS**
see   Expedient means

◙ **SKIN-BAG**
see   Human body

◙   **SMALLER SUKHAVATI-VYUHA SUTRA**
see   Amitabha Sutra

◙ **SMILE**

►"A Buddha's smile is a sign of compassion, and appears when a Buddha contemplates the world or when he is about to make a prediction."
Gomez/96: 326

Zen Buddhism

"It is said that one day Brahma, lord of creation, offered the Buddha a flower and asked him to preach the Dharma. When the Buddha held up the flower, his audience was puzzled, except for Kashyapa, who *smiled*. This is how Zen began. And this is how it was transmitted: with a flower, with a rock wall, with a shout. This approach, once it was made known by Bodhidharma and his successors, revolutionized the understanding and practice of Buddhism in China."

Red Pine: xvi #1950

◉ SNOW MOUNTAINS

►"A name for the Himalayas often used in Buddhist scriptures. Himalaya is a compound of two Sanskrit words hima (snow) and alaya (repository or abode)."

Sokk: 408 #0283

◉ SOKA GAKKAI

See also: North America (Buddhism in); Nichiren Shoshu

►"Lit: Value Creation Society. The Soka Gakkai began in Japan in the 1930s as a lay organization devoted to the support and furtherance of the teachings of the Nichiren Shoshu school. During the postwar period, however, in the volatile atmosphere created by the freedom-of-religion policies imposed by the Allied Occupation, the lay organization experienced tremendous growth. Soon the vast majority of Nichiren Shoshu members were those who had been converted by lay members of the Soka Gakkai, leading to a situation in which the tail (the Soka Gakkai) threatened to wag the dog (the priestly establishment). The Soka Gakkai maintained an alternately supportive and antagonistic relationship with the Nichiren Shoshu priesthood until 1991, when the Soka Gakkai was officially excommunicated from the school. Long before this traumatic event took place, however, the Soka Gakkai had amassed a substantial membership in the United States, and this membership was dramatically different from that drawn by the Elite Buddhist groups [see North America (Buddhism in)]. Advertising higher income, better health, and improved relationships as among the results of Buddhist practice, the Soka Gakkai (first known here as Nichiren Shoshu of

America) attracted a highly diverse following. In contrast to Elite Buddhism, whose members are largely of middle-class background or above ('We call it the Upper-Middle Way,' one western Theravada monk told me with a smile), the Soka Gakkai drew its initial membership from a broad social spectrum. Though it does have a small percentage of highly educated members, only about half attended college, and barely a quarter hold bachelor's degrees. Statistics provided by the organization show a wide range of educational levels and occupations; my own observations suggest a center of gravity in the lower-middle class. But it is not only in its class composition that the Soka Gakkai is unusual, for it has a substantial percentage of African-American, Latino, and Asian-American members, in addition to those of European-American ancestry. According to a 1983 survey, fully 55 percent of its members came from non-European ethnic backgrounds. In sum, in both class and ethnicity, its clientele stands in stark contrast to that of Elite Buddhist groups. A further contrast can be seen in the types of demands made on the

practitioner, for membership in the Soka Gakkai involves no long retreats or training periods. The primary practice -- chanting the mantra 'namu myoho renge kyo'-- can be done in one's own home rather than at a central meeting place and requires only a small commitment of time each day. On the other hand, an integral part of Soka Gakkai practice is spreading the teachings to others, which is seen as a way to change society for the better as well as to improve one's own karmic 'fortune.' Both of these practices can (and indeed should) be performed in the midst of society and not in retreat from it. As a result, working-class and middle-class Buddhists can carry out their religious duties without interrupting the pursuit of conventional occupations. Since these Buddhists view material conditions as the direct manifestation of one's spiritual state, and therefore as amenable to immediate change by the force of religious practice, it is hardly surprising that the Soka Gakkai has a strong appeal to those with significant material needs, including recent immigrants and African-Americans... Small wonder, too, that Buddhists in

this category commonly experience upward economic mobility. For Soka Gakkai members, in other words, there is no sharp break between the material and the spiritual."
Natt: 46-67 #2143

◎ **SON**
See also: Sonjong

►"(Kor.), Korean counterpart of Japanese Zen and Chinese Chan Buddhism"
Reat: 344 #2092

◎ **SONJONG**
See also: Son; Korea (Buddhism In)

►"Korean Zen School. One of two major schools in Korean Buddhism. At the end of the fourteenth century, under the third king in the Yi Dynasty, Buddhism was suppressed, reducing the number of Buddhist schools to seven... The fourth king, Sejong, continued the suppression still further, reducing Buddhism to two schools, the Meditation and the Scriptural studies. The Sonjong, or 'Meditation' school, was a union of the Vinaya, T'ien-t'ai, and Ch'an traditions of Chinese Buddhism; the scriptural school

was a union of the Hua-yen (Avatamsaka), Yogacara and Madhyamika traditions. The two major schools remained as the official divisions of Buddhism until 1935."
Preb: 244 #1068

◎ **SOTAPANNA**
See Srotapanna

◎ **SOTO ZEN SCHOOL**
Syn: Tsao-Tung School
See also: Zen; Lin-chi; Obaku Zen School

►"With the Rinzai school, one of the two most important schools of Zen. It was founded by two great Chinese Ch'an (Zen) masters Tung-shan (807-869) and Ts'ao-Shan (840-901) ... While the goal of training in the two schools of Rinzai and Soto is basically the same, Soto and Rinzai Zen differ in their training methods -- though even here the line differentiating the two schools cannot be sharply drawn."
Sham: 209
"[Rinzai stresses] *sudden enlightenment* and the use of koans (paradoxical questions for jerking the mind out of its normal patterns into a sudden awareness of the truth). Soto

stresses *gradual enlightenment* and a combination of methods including koans, by relying mainly on the silent illumination of seated meditation (zazen), ending in the realization of the individual's oneness with reality."
Larousse: 495-496 #2170

◙ **SOUTH**
See also: Akasagarbha Bodhisattva

▸Represents clarity, detachment, uprightness. In ancient times ruler-kings sometimes sat on their thrones facing south. Also represents the Mind. The youth Sudhana (*Avatamsaka Sutra*) heading south is a metaphor for investigating the deepest recesses of one's own mind.
Editor: na
"South, the direction of Sudhana's pilgrimage in the *Avatamsaka Sutra*, stands for truth, clarity, and openness. When you arrive at open, clear, true knowledge without subjectivity, then everywhere is the South."
Clea/89: 23
"The esoteric tradition considers this the direction from which all treasures come, and South is also associated with the Buddha Hosho [Ratnasambhava], whose name means 'giving birth to treasure.'"
Yama: 185 #1238

◙ **SOUTHERN BUDDHISM**
see   Theravada Buddhism

◙ **SOUTHERN SCHOOL OF ZEN**
see   Patriarchal Zen

◙ **SOUTHERN ZEN**
see   Patriarchal Zen

◙ **SPECIAL TEACHING**
Syn: Vertical Escape
See also: Horizontal Escape; Pure Land School; Universal Method; Sudden Teaching

----

▸See the following passage concerning the illustrious Ming dynasty Zen Master Han-shan (1566-1623): "Han-shan did not write any commentary on the [two *Amitabha Sutras*], and it is not clear how he places [them] in the Hua-Yen (Avatamsaka) classification scheme. On the one hand, he regards the Western Paradise as the most expedient land of the innumerable Hua-yen Pure Lands. On the other hand, he seems to have considered the Pure Land teaching as a special teaching that lies outside the usual scheme of classification." (Sung-peng Hsu, *A Buddhist Leader in Ming China*, p. 149.)

The special teaching of Pure Land is expressed by the metaphor of "horizontal" vs. "vertical" escape. "Vertically" and "horizontally" are figures of speech, which can readily be understood through the following example. Suppose we have a worm, born inside a stalk of bamboo. To escape, it can take the "hard way" and crawl all the way to the top of the stalk. Alternatively, it can look for or poke a hole near its current location and escape "horizontally" into the big, wide world. The horizontal escape, for sentient beings, is to seek rebirth in the Pure Land. Pure Land is considered a special method because its immediate goal is not Enlightenment but rebirth in the Land of Ultimate Bliss. The Pure Land is an ideal environment and training ground for the ultimate achievement of Buddhahood.
Editor/Zen: 137

Pure Land Buddhism: Perfect, sudden method

"Reciting the Buddha's name seeking rebirth in the Pure Land is a 'perfect sudden' method in the Mahayana tradition, because the cultivator takes Enlightenment in the 'effect stage' as his point of departure for awakening the mind in the 'causal stage.' If it were not taught by Buddha Sakyamuni Himself, who would believe that a common mortal of the 'Four Ways of Birth and Six Paths' could reach the stage of non-retrogression, equal to the higher level Bodhisattvas, thanks to Amitabha Buddha's power of 'welcoming and escorting'? After all, cultivators following other methods would have to spend eons in diligent, continuous cultivation to obtain such results. With the Pure Land method, since the cultivator has put his faith in 'other-power' in addition to using all his 'self-power,' every single cultivator will be reborn in the Land of Ultimate Bliss, escape the cycle of Birth and Death and achieve non-retrogression. If we were to use Buddha Recitation to discover the Mind-Ground and awaken to our Original Nature, the Pure Land method would be no different from other methods. However, when we rely on Buddha Recitation to seek rebirth in the Pure Land, this method has unique characteristics. Ancient masters have said:

1. Birth [in the Pure Land] is definitely birth; however, return

[to the Pure Land] is, in truth, no return. This is True Realization of realms, not of beings.

2. Return is definitely return; however, birth is, in truth, No-Birth. This is True Realization of beings, not of realms.

3. Return is, in reality, no return; birth is also, in truth, no birth. This is True Realization of both realms and beings.

4. Return is definitely return; birth is definitely birth. This is not True Realization of realms and beings.

These four statements explain the Four True Realizations of Pure Land teachings. True Realization means thorough comprehension of essence, or noumenon. Since the whole Dharma Realm (cosmos) is only Mind, sentient beings and realms are illusory. If we conceive that there are sentient beings achieving rebirth in the Pure Land and that there are realms to go back to, we are still attached to beings and dharmas and are still making a distinction between here and there. This is not True Realization, i.e., not a complete understanding of essence and noumenon. The reverse is called True Realization. The ancients have summarized the idea in the following stanza: *Recitation is equal to non-recitation, No-Birth is Birth,/ [Having reached that stage] do not bother to move even half a step,/You have arrived at the Enlightened capital city.*

True Realization of beings and realms [No. 3] is the ultimate goal of Pure Land practitioners. Nevertheless, the doctrine taught in the Three Pure Land Sutras and the *Commentary on Rebirth* is No. 4 ('not True Realization of realms and beings'), which is consonant with seeking rebirth in the Pure Land. This is because Buddha Sakyamuni knew that common mortals in this world of the Five Turbidities, especially in this Dharma-Ending Age, would have heavy and deep karmic obstructions; establishing a realm of marks [the Pure Land], enabling them to anchor their minds and cultivate, would be difficult enough -- not to mention abandoning all marks! If common human beings of this Dharma-Ending Age cultivate while grasping at marks (i.e., the Pure Land), their Practice and Vows will be more earnest and the final result of rebirth in the Pure land easier to achieve. Once reborn in the Pure Land, why worry about not attaining the

state of No-Birth and No-Mark?"
Tam: 111-113 #1495

◙ **SPIRIT WORLD**
Syn: Occult World
See also: Tree Spirits; Mediums;
Faith-Healing; Superstitions

►"Buddhism has had little difficulty in accommodating a large number of local beliefs concerning various gods, spirits and the like. Naturally the powers of such entities are circumscribed by the law of kamma (karma) and other laws. The Buddhist perceives the universe as vast enough to encompass many such entities. Numerous cults coexist with Buddhism -- some barely tolerated, some irrelevant and ignored, some incorporated to a greater or lesser degree into the larger scene. Such cultic activities may play a considerable part in the life of the villager. There has been much discussion among scholars as to the precise relationship between Buddhism and such cults. Some see a supernatural hierarchy with the Buddha at the summit. Others contrast the 'great tradition' with the 'little tradition.' The profane or secular level of spirit cults can be set against the superior sacred level of the Buddhist teaching. Many early European observers, followed by some Buddhist modernists, saw the existence of such cults as due to a corruption of the original 'pure' Buddhism. In actual fact Buddhism is not concerned with such matters. They are not rejected. They are simply a different sphere of human activity. Provided there is no direct opposition to Buddhist teaching they can be left to regulate themselves. *There is no inconsistency between believing in the law of kamma and at the same time making offerings to a deity to obtain some desired result. This is no different from asking aid of a king or doctor.* Such aid is itself part of a complex set of relations and subject to various causes and conditions. The help given by a deity is a matter of fact or falsehood. So the striking contrast between the role of spirit cults in Buddhist villages and the tendency of Buddhist modernists to minimize or deny such elements is only superficially a problem. Contact with Western science often leads to the supposition that such spirits or deities do not exist. In that case, they are not a fact and can be discarded. Buddhism is

committed to the notion that various entities and levels of being exist, but not to most particular names. In practice Buddhist traditionalists tend to be committed to at least a part of the local spirit cult."
Hinn: 313-314

"Buddhism does not deny the existence of good and evil spirits. There are visible and invisible beings or spirits in the same way as there are visible and invisible lights. We need special instruments to see the invisible light and we need a special sense to see the invisible beings. One cannot deny the existence of such spirits just because one is unable to see them with the naked eye. These spirits are also subject to birth and death. They are not going to stay permanently in the spirit form. They too exist in the same world where we live. A genuine Buddhist is one who molds his life according to moral causation discovered by the Buddha. He should not be concerned with the worshipping of these gods and spirits. However, this kind of worshipping is of some interest and fascination to the multitude and has naturally brought some Buddhists into contact with these activities. Regarding protection from evil spirits, goodness is a shield against evil. Goodness is a wall through which evil cannot penetrate unless the good person opens the door to an evil influence. Even though a person leads a truly virtuous and holy life and has a good shield of moral and noble living, that person can still lower his shield of protection by believing in the power of evil that would do him harm. The Buddha has never advised His followers to worship such spirits or to be frightened of them. *The Buddhist attitude towards them is to transfer merits and to radiate loving-kindness [and compassion] to them.* Buddhists do not harm them. On the other hand, if a man is religious, virtuous and pure in mind, and if he is also intelligent and possesses strong will-power and understanding capacity, then such a person could be deemed to be much stronger than spirits. The evil spirits would keep away from him, while the good spirits would protect him."
Dham: 306-307 #1927

◉ **SPIRITS**
see   Li Mei; Tree Spirits

◉ **SPIRITUAL POWERS**
Syn: Miraculous Powers;   Six

Superknowledges
See also: Third Lifetime;
Superstitions

▸Also called miraculous power.
Includes, *inter alia*, the ability to
see all forms (deva eye), to hear
all sounds (deva ear), to know
the thoughts of others, to be
anywhere and to do anything at
will.
Editor/Tam: 162
"Extraordinary capacities
developed by Arhats [and other
sages]: (1) clairvoyance, (2)
clairaudience, (3) mental
telepathy, (4) psychic travel, (5)
knowledge of past and future, (6)
ending contamination."
Chih-I/Cleary: 202
"Reciting mantras and sutras for
the purpose of sowing merits and
wisdom and eliminating evil
karma and transgressions is all to
the good. However, to be
deluded and seek spiritual
powers is to abandon the roots
for the branches -- an error in
judgement. If, futhermore, your
mind is grasping, your
understanding of the Dharma
nebulous, your precept-keeping
lax, your Bodhi Mind
undeveloped and your
discriminatory, win-lose mind
raging unchecked, you will be
exposed one day to demons that

may drive you insane! If you
want to obtain spiritual powers,
you should first attain
Enlightenment and Buddhahood.
Once Buddhahood is attained,
you will naturally have full
spiritual powers. If you do not
strive for the Way but merely
seek spiritual powers, let us not
even speak about whether
anything can be gained. If you
should attain anything, it would
become an impediment to the
Way. For this reason, the
Buddhas and Patriarchs have
strictly prohibited this erroneous
form of cultivation."
Zen: 91-92
NOTE:
"The reason why supernormal
powers are not held in high
esteem is that deliberate efforts
to cultivate them would distract
devotees from the infinitely more
rewarding quest for Liberation.
Furthermore, once such powers
are acquired, they can be turned
to profit and people wielding this
means of gaining wealth and
fame might be deflected from the
quest altogether."
Blof: 225
During His lifetime, Buddha
Sakyamuni discouraged the
display of spiritual powers. Once,
the story goes, He was waiting at
the river's edge for a boat to take

him across. An ascetic, passing by, showed off his spiritual powers, crossing the river back and forth by treading over the water. The Buddha then asked him, "How long did it take you to acquire such powers?" "Thirty years," was the reply. The Buddha then said, "Thirty years of effort? Well, I can cross the river for a five-cent fare." It may be added that for a person still subject to excessive greed, anger, and delusion to have access to unusual powers could be harmful to himself and dangerous to society at large. (Note: there are several versions of this story).
Editor/Zen: 96 #0923

◉ **SPIRITUAL QUEST**
Syn: Quest
See also: Dukkha; Expedient Means; Practice

▸"We usually have to be driven out of our complacency to embark on the spiritual quest. A devastating crisis, much suffering, or growing tiredness of going round and round, repeating the same increasingly meaningless patterns: these are the common precipitating factors. (John Snelling, *The Elements of Buddhism*, p. 117.)"
A story illustrates this point. An

elderly Zen Master, feeling that his time would soon come, hit upon an expedient to help his chosen disciple achieve a Great Awakening. He decided to drive the younger monk out of his complacency through an elaborate plan to "frame" him as a thief in disguise. The disciple was then denounced to one and all throughout the land. The accused monk, once the teacher of a huge congregation, now completely debased and with nowhere to turn, his ego totally shattered, mulled over this flagrant injustice and at times even contemplated suicide. After several weeks of utter desperation, he suddenly experienced a Great Awakening: life is a dream, an illusion, a bubble, a shadow. This is the very teaching he had been trying to impart to the novices for so many years! He then rushed to the Master, who upon seeing him, greeted him warmly and conferred the succession upon him.
Editor/Zen: 146 #1497

◉ **S R A M A N E R A /
SRAMANERIKA**
Syn: Novice

▸(Skt.) "A novice who keeps the

Ten Precepts (q.v.) but who has not yet achieved full ordination to the rank of Bhiksu."
Thai: 342

"Novice: term for male or female Buddhist novices who have committed themselves through the lower ordination to observe the ten precepts. Novices are often children. The minimum age for ordination of a shramanera is seven -- that was the age of the historical Buddha's son, Rahula, the patron of shramaneras, when he entered the sangha."
Sham: 202 #1630

◙ SRAVAKA
See also: Arhat

►"Those who follow [Theravada] and eventually become Arhats as a result of listening to the Buddhas and following their teachings."
T. Prince: 81

"Literally 'hearer.' One who has heard the Buddha's teaching. Generally denotes a follower of the Lesser Vehicle path. Sravaka is also translated as 'disciple.'"
Chan: 483
NOTE:
"In Mahayana Buddhism [the term Sravaka] refers to a person in the Theravada school who exerts himself to attain the stage

of Arhat by observing 250 precepts in the case of monks and 348 in the case of nuns. This is a lower stage than that of Bodhisattva."
Yoko: 289 #0819

◙ SRAVASTI
See also: Anathapindika; Jeta Grove

►"A city in ancient India. The Jeta Grove, where Sakyamuni Buddha often preached, is near Sravasti."
Chan: 483 #0566

◙ SRI LANKA
See also: Sri Lanka (Buddhism in)

►"Formerly called Ceylon. Island-nation off the southern tip of India -- the primary homeland of Theravada Buddhism."
Reat: 344 #2093
See also: next entry

◙ SRI LANKA (BUDDHISM IN)
See also: Angarika Dharmapala; Devanampiya Tissa; Maha-Bodhi Society, Olcott, H.S. (Col.)

►"Sri Lanka (formerly Ceylon) was converted to Buddhism by the son and daughter of Asoka (ca. 252 B.C.). Stronghold of

Buddhism for many centuries, but had periods of decline. The teaching became almost extinct on several occasions, being revived by Bhikkhus from Burma [11th c.] and Thailand [18th c.]. Almost exterminated by forced conversions under Portuguese rule, revived under Dutch and British rule, last revival being led by Colonel Olcott (q.v.) in 1880. Always consistently Theravada in doctrine. Present subschools: Siamese; Ramanya (rigid in doctrine and discipline); Amarapura (more liberal in views)."
Hump: 55

"The first successful Buddhist missionary effort was Sri Lanka, and Theravada Buddhism was brought to this gem-like tropical island in the third century. Mahayana and Tantric Buddhism later arrived in Sri Lanka, and their devotees came into contention with those of the orthodox Theravada. However, the matter was settled by a council in 1160, which suppressed all non-Theravada schools. Later, Sri Lanka suffered political upheaval due to European colonization and invasion from south India, and by the mid-eighteenth century its Buddhism

was in such a parlous state that bhikshus (monks) had to be imported from elsewhere to maintain the tradition. Revival got under way during the latter part of the nineteenth century, however, generated both by local Buddhists and by Western sympathizers, such as the pioneer Theosophists H.S. Olcott and H.P. Blavatsky. A relatively healthy, if rather conservative tradition, with a scholarly bias, currently survives in strife-torn Sri Lanka, but there is also a forest tradition of secluded meditator monks and nuns."
Snell/Buddhism: 27 #0462
For details, *See also:* Theravada Buddhism (note).

◙ **SRIMALA SUTRA**

▸*(Vn/* Kinh Thắng-Man) "A sutra translated into Chinese in 436 by Gunabhadra. This sutra takes the form of preaching by Lady Shrimala, the daughter of King Prasenajit of Kosala, [India], with the help of Shakyamuni's power. It expounds the One-Vehicle doctrine and makes clear that the Buddha-Nature is inherent in all sentient beings."
Sokk: 396
"This sutra transmits the teachings of the One Vehicle

(that of the Buddha) and ultimate truth."   Yoko: 213
NOTE:
"Queen Srimala of Ayodhya is the protagonist of a sutra bearing her name on which the great Regent Prince Shotoku (574-622) of Nara, [Japan] wrote a commentary, together with commentaries on the *Lotus* and *Vimalakirti Sutras*, and thus made Buddhism the national religion in Japan."
Hump: 186 #0284

◙ **SROTAPANNA**
See also: Arhatship

►Lit. *stream enterer*. "The first of the four stages toward the realization of liberation [leading to Arhatship]."
Sume: 139 #2031

◙ **STAGES OF BODHISATTVA PRACTICE**
see   Fifty-two levels of Bodhisattva practice

◙ **STALE RICE / STALE FARE**
See also: Cause and Effect

►This is a reference to a well-known story about Buddha Sakyamuni's disciple Visakha, who once said: "When a certain Bhikkhu was standing at the door

for alms, my father-in-law was eating sweet milk rice-porridge, ignoring him. Thinking to myself that my father-in-law, without performing any good deed in this life, is only consuming the merits of past deeds, I told the Bhikkhu: 'Pass on Venerable Sir, my father-in-law is eating stale fare."
(Narada, *The Buddha and His Teachings*, p. 101.)
Most people go through life consuming "stale fare," as they enjoy the results of their past merits without thought of creating new ones. For example, a wealthy person (i.e., one who practiced charity in past lives) spending time and money on himself alone, without thoughts of charity, is eating stale fare. This concept is also related to the idea that merits accrued in the first lifetime are potential enemies of the third lifetime. In the first lifetime, the practitioner engages in wholesome actions which bring blessings (wealth, power, authority, etc.) in the second lifetime. Since wealth and power tend to corrupt, he is likely to create evil karma, resulting in retribution in the third lifetime. Thus the Buddha's injunction against seeking rebirth within Samsara.
Editor/Zen: 94 #1460

◙ "STANZA THAT DESTROYS HELL"
Syn: Mind-Only; Everything is made from Mind

▸(*Vn/* Kệ Phá Địa-Ngục). Name of a verse found in the *Avatamsaka Sutra*, Ch. 20. Expresses one of the key teachings of the sutra:
"If people want to really know/ All Buddhas of all time,/ They should contemplate the nature of the cosmos:/ All is but mental construction (i.e., Everything is made from Mind alone.)"
(T. Cleary, tr., *The Flower Ornament Sutra*, Vol I, p.452)

◙ STEPPING OFF THE HUNDRED-FOOT POLE
see Hundred-foot pole

◙ STICK AND SHOUT
see Shouts and Blows

◙ STILL AND ILLUMINATING

▸"The attribute of the Self-Nature and the functioning of the True-Self, beyond space and time, still and shining, shining and still."
NV Hoa: na

◙ STUPA
See also: Funerary Rites for the Buddha

▸"A Buddhist monument, a relic-shrine. A kind of shrine in India where the relics of Shakyamuni and other saints are housed. Stupas, which originated from burial mounds, are usually dome-shaped or mound-shaped. After Shakyamuni's death, eight stupas were erected to hold his relics, and two more to house, respectively, the vessel used in cremation and the ashes of the fire."
Sokk: 411

"A Buddhist monument, generally of a dome-shaped form, originally erected over sacred relics of the Buddha and at places consecrated as the scenes of his acts. Various materials, such as clay, brick, carved stone, and wood, are used in its construction. In East Asia the stupa developed into the towerlike pagoda, in which are enshrined various objects sacred to Buddhism."
Yoko: 213 #0187

◙ SUBHADRA

▸"A man who became the Buddha's disciple shortly before the latter's death and is therefore known as the Buddha's 'last disciple.' Subhadra realized

Arhathood immediately after hearing the Buddha's last sermon."
Yoko: 213 #0802

◙ **SUBHUTI**
See also: Emptiness

▸"One of the ten great disciples of the Buddha. Of this group, he is thought to have been first in his understanding of sunyata (ku). It is also reported that he was preeminent in compassion, and that he never quarreled with anyone. He is said to have been a son of Sumana, the younger brother of Anathapindika (Sudata), who donated the Jetavana Monastery to the Sangha. In the Prajna-paramita literature, which considers the truth of sunyata, he appears as the person engaged in a dialogue with the Buddha."
Dait: 333 #0133

◙ **SUCHNESS**
Syn: Tathata; Thusness; True Suchness
See also: Dharma Nature; Reality; Tathagata-garbha

▸"Central notion of the Mahayana referring to the absolute, the True Nature of all things. Tathata (suchness) is

generally explained as being immutable, immovable, and beyond all concepts and distinctions. 'Suchness' is the opposite of 'that which is apparent.'"
Equivalent to Buddha Nature, Dharma Body, etc.
Editor/Tam: 353 #0356

◙ **SUDARANANDA**
see Nanda

◙ **SUDATTA**
see Anathapindika

◙ **SUDDEN / GRADUAL ENLIGHTENMENT**
See also: Sudden Teaching; Soto Zen School; Hui Neng

▸"The position that enlightenment comes gradually, as a result of studying the sutras and accumulated practice, was held by the Northern Zen school in China. Eventually only the Southern Zen school [headed by the Sixth Patriarch Hui Neng], which advocated the sudden realization of enlightenment, survived and became known as the Zen school."
Yoko: 214 #0803

◙ **SUDDEN DOCTRINE**
see Sudden Teaching

◉ SUDDEN TEACHING

Syn: Sudden Doctrine
See also: Five Teachings; Special Teaching

►A teaching which enables one to attain Enlightenment immediately. It is usually associated with the Avatamsaka and/or Zen schools.

Editor: na

"*The Sudden teaching* expounds the abrupt realization of the ultimate truth without relying upon verbal explanations or progression through various stages of practice."

Sokk: 110

NOTE:

"In his commentary on the Pure Land sutras, [Patriarch] Chu-hung classifies Pure Land as an *sudden* (abrupt) teaching that also shares some aspects of the 'final' teaching of the *Lotus Sutra* and the *perfect* (round) doctrine of the *Avatamsaka Sutra*. It belongs to the *sudden* doctrine, he says, because the Pure Land devotee 'attains rebirth in the Western Paradise as soon as he relies on the Buddha's name.' Chu-hung explains that the mind of the devotee of Buddha-recitation, when this is properly done, is a mind without any disturbance and is equivalent to the mind of no-thought spoken of in the Zen school. Like Han-shan, Chu-hung interprets Pure Land teaching in the Zen spirit, but at the same time advocates the more traditional and devotional aspects of the Pure Land faith. For both men, the other-power religion that teaches salvation by faith and Amitabha's grace is wedded to the self-power religion that teaches salvation by self-realization."

Hsu: 150 #0969

See also: Perfect Sudden Teaching; Perfect Teaching

◉ SUDHANA

Syn: Good Wealth Bodhisattva
See also: Avatamsaka Sutra; Pure Land Buddhism in Summary

►(*Chin*/Shan-ts'ai; *Vn*/Thiện-tài) The main protagonist in the next-to-last and longest chapter of the *Avatamsaka Sutra*. Seeking Enlightenment, he visited and studied with fifty-three spiritual advisors and became the equal of the Buddhas in one lifetime. Both his first advisor (Meghasri or Cloud of Virtues Bodhisattva/ q.v.) and his last (Samantabhadra) taught him the Pure Land path.

Editor/Tam: 162 #0925

◙ **SUDHODANA**
See also: Sakyamuni Buddha

▸"Father of Gotama [Buddha Sakyamuni]. Suddhodana was a chieftain of the Indian Sakya tribe. His wife was Maya, who died 7 days after giving birth to Gotama. It was predicted of the child Gotama by soothsayers that he would become either a universal monarch or a Buddha. Suddhodana, therefore, sought to protect the boy from any experience of unpleasant aspects of life, such as illness, old age and death, and to surround him with pleasures. In spite of this protection, Gotama is said to have seen in one day a disease-ridden man, an old man, and a corpse, and thus to have been brought to reflection upon the meaning of phenomenal human existence. When news of Gotama's having attained enlightenment reached Suddhodana, he sent messengers inviting the Buddha to come to Kapilavastu. The messengers, however, hearing Buddha preach, were converted and entered the Sangha without delivering their message. This happened repeatedly until the tenth time, when the message reached Buddha. On his visiting Kapilavastu and conversing with Suddhodana, the latter became a soptapanna (a sage). Some years later, when Suddhodana was dying, the Buddha visited him. After hearing the Buddha's discourse, Suddhodana became a lay Arhat, and died soon after." Ling: 236 #1162

◙ **SUFFERING**
see   Dukkha; Eight Sufferings

◙ **SUFISM**
See also: Pure land Buddhism (Summary)

▸"An Islamic mystical movement which represents a move away from the legalistic approach in Islam to a more personal relationship with God. The word comes from suf ('wool'), because the early story-tellers from whom Sufism evolved wore woollen garments. Sufis aim to lose themselves in the ultimate reality of the Divinity by constant repetition of the dhikr or 'repetition of the name of God or of a sacred formula'... Although their main purpose is to increase mystical awareness of God, they also performed an important missionary function, especially on the fringes of the Muslim world in places such as Central Asia,

India, the Sudan and West Africa."

Laro: 504

The Sufis are a mystic Islamic sub-school that seems to resemble Buddhism in several respects. However the basic belief systems are entirely different, Islam being based on an all-powerful God while Buddhism revolves around the Law of Cause and Effect. In the case of Pure Land Buddhism, Amitabha Buddha ultimately is our Self-Nature. To return to the Pure Land is to return to our own Pure Mind (Self-Nature Amitabha, Mind-Only Pure Land).

Editor: na #2130

◙ **SUI DYNASTY**

▸"(581-618), The northern 'barbarian' dynasty responsible for the reunification of China in 589."

Reat: 344 #2095

◙ **SUICIDE**

See also: Immolation; Killing

▸"According to Buddhist doctrine a man cannot avoid suffering by taking his life, nor does he escape from the 'Wheel of Life' by so doing. The destruction of the physical body merely transfers the entity to other spheres of existence, and rebirth into the physical follows. Physical life is considered of great importance, as it is only here that the Way of Liberation can be followed, and Enlightenment attained. *Taking one's life is, therefore, a waste of opportunity.* Voluntary sacrifice of one's life for the welfare of others is considered meritorious, the motive being altruistic."

Hump: 188

According to Buddhist teachings, all suffering derives from past evil karma. To attempt to escape suffering through suicide is no different from a dog trying to free itself by gnawing its leash. Its master will immediately punish the dog and replace the leash with a stronger one. Likewise, the person who commits suicide cannot escape suffering (because he has not altered its cause -- his mind). In fact, he will surely be reborn under worse conditions, as a result of the extreme anger and frustration that led him to suicide in the first place.

Editor/Zen: 81 #0408

◙ **SUKHAVATI**

Syn: Pure Lands (As Realms);

Western Pure Land; Land of Ultimate Bliss; Land of Bliss
See also: Pure Land Buddhism (Summary); Pure Lands (as Realms);Three Pure Land Sutras

----

►"Skt., lit 'the Blissful'; the so-called Western Paradise, the Pure Land of the West, one of the most important of the Buddha-fields to appear in the Mahayana. It is reigned over by Buddha Amitabha, who created it by his karmic merit. Through faithful devotion to Amitabha and through recitation of his name, one can be reborn there and cultivate until entering final Nirvana. Sukhavati is described in detail in the sutras devoted to Amitabha. Sukhavati is set in the west. It is flooded by radiance (light/ q.v.) that emanates from Amitabha ... In this buddha-field all beings cleave to the truth of the teaching until their final entry into Nirvana. Their supreme happiness is hearing the teaching proclaimed by Amitabha, who lives in the center of the land and is accompanied by Avalokitesvara and Mahasthamaprapta."
Sham: 211
"Sukhavati means 'endowed with happiness'; Amitabha's land is so called because those living there are free of afflictions and enjoy the supreme bliss of Nirvana. His land, usually called 'the Pure Land,' is the reward for the long course of practice which he performed when he was a Bodhisattva called 'Dharmakara' (Dharma-store). Although its glorious splendour is described in physical terms in the sutras, this land is above all forms and concepts. It is the sphere of pure spiritual activity; those born there are awakened to the ultimate reality, and compassion spontaneously arises in them. In other words, having become Bodhisattvas, they participate in Amitabha's endless work of delivering beings from delusions and sufferings."
Inag: 405-406
"According to the Pure Land sutras ... Sukhavati lies billions of Buddha lands away from our Saha World-realm. The Buddha Amitabha is the transcendent Buddha who presides over the Sukhavati world-realm... According to the *Larger Sukhavativyuha* [*Longer Amitabha Sutra*], Amitabha established Sukhavati through his compassionate vows in order to lead sentient beings to Buddhahood. He made the vows as a Bodhisattva, named

Dharmakara, and after five Kalpas (eons) of contemplation his vows were consummated. For the past ten Kalpas, Buddha Amitabha has dwelled in Sukhavati and has continuously preached the Dharma..." (Kenneth K. Tanaka, *The Dawn of Chinese Pure Land Buddhism Doctrine.*)

Tana: 1

"Question/ Answer

The Western Pure Land is ten billion Buddha-lands away from here. Common, ordinary people are weak and frail. How can they reach it? ... *Answer*: The Western Pure Land is described as being ten billion Buddha-lands away from here only with respect to the limited concepts of ordinary people with eyes of flesh and blood, mired in Birth and Death. For those who have attained the pure karma of rebirth in the Pure Land, the Mind in samadhi at the time of death is precisely the Mind reborn in the Pure Land. As soon as the thought [of rebirth] arises, rebirth is achieved. Thus, the *Meditation Sutra* states that 'the Land of Amitabha Buddha is not far from here!' Moreover, the power of karma is inconceivable. In the space of one thought, rebirth in the Pure Land is achieved. There is no need to worry about distance. This is analogous to a person asleep and dreaming. Although his body is on the bed, his Mind is travelling all over, to all worlds, as though he were awake. Rebirth in the Pure Land is, generally speaking, similar to this example." (Tien T'ai Patriarch Chih I, *Pure Land Buddhism: Dialogues with Ancient Masters*). Dia: 30-31

For further details, see Pure Land Mandalas; Three Pure Land Sutras. #0364

◉ **SUMERU (MOUNT)**

Syn: Polar Mountain; Mount Sumeru; Meru

▶"The mythical 'world mountain' that rises through the center of a Buddhist universe."

Okaz: 187

"A mountain thought to stand at the center of the world, according to ancient Indian tradition. It is said to measure 84,000 yojana above the surface of the sea and 84,000 yojana below, and to be composed of gold, silver, emerald and crystal, with four sides facing north, south, east and west respectively. The god Indra resides on the summit, while the Four Heavenly Kings live halfway down the four sides. Mt. Sumeru is surrounded by seven concentric mountain ranges made of gold, between which are seven perfumed seas. The seventh gold mountain range is surrounded by a salt ocean, in which are the four continents of Purvavideha, Aparagodaniya, Uttarakura and Jambudvipa, lying respectively to the east, west, north and south. The salt ocean is in turn bounded by a circular range of iron mountains which stands at the rim of the world. A sun and a moon move around Mt. Sumeru." Sokk: 412-413

In Buddhist cosmology, the universe is composed of worlds upon worlds, *ad infinitum*. (Our earth is only an infinitesimal part of one of these countless worlds). The Polar Mountain is the central mountain of each world. Editor/Tam: 159 #0286

◙ **SUMERU / MUSTARD SEED**
See also: Avatamsaka Sutra

▸Mount Sumeru contained in a Mustard Seed, and a Mustard Seed contained in Mount Sumeru: "In the world of relativity, it is out of question that Mount Sumeru is contained in a mustard seed; only the reverse hypothesis is possible. In the world of the 'absolute', the

realm of those who have experienced full enlightenment, however, both hypotheses can be defended as there is no differentiation with regard to time and space."
NV Hoa: Na

◙ **SUNAKSATRA**
See also: Ananda

▸"Name of a monk who acted as personal assistant to the Buddha. Also means an auspicious constellation."
Thai: 662 #1655

◙ **SUNDRY PRACTICES**
See also: Pure Land Buddhism (Summary);Faith-Vows-Practice; Exclusive Practice

----

▸Refers to various apparently unrelated practices which, if properly executed, can lead to rebirth in the Pure Land (for example, practicing charity, building temples, distributing free sutras, keeping precepts etc.). Since the adept's mind is not focused on a single individual practice, it is difficult for him to achieve one-pointedness of mind -- the key condition for rebirth in the Pure Land. Thus, only three or four out of hundreds of thousands who cultivate sundry

practices can hope to be reborn in Sukhavati, the Pure Land of Amitabha Buddha. (Patriarch Yin-kuang)
Editor/Zen: 91 #1213

◉ **SUNIM**

►"The Korean title of address for monks and nuns."
Kusa: 181 #0849

◉ **SUNYATA**
see Emptiness

◉ **SUPERIOR AND GOOD PEOPLE**
see Beings of the Highest Virtue

◉ **SUPERNATURAL HEARING**
see Deva-ear

◉ **SUPERSTITIONS**
See also: Spiritual Powers; Dogma; Wisdom

►"All ailments have cures, but not superstitions. And if for some reason or other any superstition crystallises into a religion, it easily becomes an almost incurable malady. In the performance of certain religious functions, even educated people of today forget their human dignity to accept the most ridiculous superstitious beliefs.

Superstitious beliefs and rituals are adopted to decorate a religion in order to attract the multitude. But after some time, the creeper which is planted to decorate the shrine, as it were, outgrows and outshines the shrine, with the result that religious tenets are relegated to the background and superstitious beliefs and rituals become predominant."
Dham: 327 #1985

◉ **SUPPORTIVE RECITATION**
See also: Death; Buddha Recitation; Pure Land School

►*Vn*/ Hộ-Niệm. Supportive Recitation is recitation performed by one or more Pure Land practitioners alongside a dying person, to assist him in achieving rebirth in the Pure Land. This is important for Pure Land practitioners as at the time of death, one is like a turtle being skinned alive. Filled with pain and fear, without the support of like-minded practitioners, one is likely to forget about Buddha Recitation and Pure Land rebirth.

(I) General Guidelines
"In general, the spiritual advisor, should follow the guidelines set out below.

1. Remind the patient of the sufferings of the Saha World and the joys of the Pure Land, so that he may develop a mind of devotion and attraction to the Pure Land. The good advisor should also enumerate and praise the patient's good deeds, merits and virtues in cultivation. This will make him happy and free of doubts, certain that when the time comes to die, he will, thanks to his good deeds, be reborn in the Pure Land.

2. If the patient has any doubts, the advisor should, depending on the circumstances, explain the *Three Points of Doubts and the Four Narrow Passes*. A critical detail to bear in mind here: the dying person should be reminded to eliminate all regret over wealth and property, as well as attachment to close family and relatives.

3. If the patient has a will, so much the better, but if not, the advisor should counsel against all inquiries in this regard. He should also advise everyone to refrain from useless chitchat that could rekindle the patient's love-attachment to the world, which is detrimental to rebirth in the Pure Land.

4. When relatives and friends come to visit, they should be discouraged from standing before the patient inquiring about his health in a sad, piteous way. If they come out of true concern, they should merely stand on the side, reciting the Buddha's name aloud for a moment. If, lacking understanding of the Dharma, the visitors act conventionally [crying, etc.], they are in effect pushing the dying person into the ocean of suffering -- a most regrettable occurrence indeed!

5. The patient should be counselled to practice charity and give away his personal effects to the needy. Or, better still, in accordance with the *Ksitigarbha (Earth Store Bodhisattva) Sutra*, he should use the proceeds from the sale of his personal possessions to purchase Buddhist images or sutras for free distribution. All this helps the patient increase his stock of merits and eliminate bad karma, thus facilitating rebirth in the Pure Land. The good advisor should keep these general guidelines in mind, but be ready to improvise according to the situation. #2298

(II) Conducting 'Supportive Recitation':

Family members and relatives of a dying patient should remain calm, without weeping or lamenting, from the time he becomes gravely ill until his last moments. Some people, while not crying, still show sorrow and emotion on their faces. This, too, should be avoided, because, at this juncture, the dying person has reached the crossroads which separate the living from the dead, and the mundane from the transcendental. The critical importance and danger of this moment can be compared to standing under a sword -- his fate is determined by a hair's breadth! At this time, the most important thing is to practice supportive recitation. Even though a person may have set his mind on rebirth in the Pure Land, if family members weep and lament, thus arousing deep-seated feelings of love-attachment, he will certainly sink into the cycle of Birth and Death, wasting all his efforts in cultivation! When a patient on the verge of death wishes to bathe, dress in different garments, or change his position or sleeping quarters, we may comply, while exercising caution and acting in a gentle, careful manner at all times. If the patient refuses, or cannot give his consent because he has become mute, we certainly should not go against his wishes. This is because the patient on the verge of death is generally in great physical pain. If he is forced to move, bathe or change clothing, he may experience even greater pain. There are numerous cases of cultivators who had sought rebirth in the Pure Land but failed to achieve this goal because their relatives moved them around, disturbing them and destroying their right thought. This unfortunate development occurs very often ... At the time of death, the cultivator himself should either lie down or sit up, according to what comes naturally, without forcing himself. If he feels weak and can only lie down, forcing himself to sit up, for appearances' sake, is dangerous and should be discouraged. Likewise, even though, according to Pure Land tradition, he should lie on his right side facing west, if, because of pain, he can only lie on his back or on his left side facing east, he should act naturally and not force himself. The patient and his family should understand all this and act accordingly. Supportive recitation by family members or Dharma friends is most necessary when a patient is on the verge of death. This is because, at that time, he is weak in body and mind and no longer master of himself. In such trying circumstances, not only is it difficult for those who have not cultivated in daily life to focus on Amitabha Buddha, even individuals who have regularly recited the Buddha's name may find it difficult to do so in all earnestness -- unless there is supportive recitation. Such recitation should closely follow the guidelines set out below:

1. *Respectfully place a standing* Amitabha Buddha statue in front of the patient, so that he can see it clearly. Place some fresh flowers in a vase and burn light incense with a soft fragrance. This will help the patient develop right thought. A reminder: the incense should not be overpowering, to avoid choking the patient and everyone around.

2. *Those who come to practice supportive* recitation should take turns ... It should be remembered that the patient, in his weakened state, requires a lot of fresh air to breathe. If too many people come and go or participate in the recitation session, the patient may have difficulty breathing and become agitated, resulting in more harm than benefit. Therefore, participants should consult their watches and silently take turns reciting, so that recitation can continue uninterrupted. They should not call to one another aloud. Each session should last about an hour.

3. *According to Elder Master Yin Kuang*, the short recitation form (Amitabha Buddha) should be used, so that the patient can easily register the name in his Alaya consciousness, at a time when both his mind and body are very weak. However, according to another Elder Master, we should ask the patient and use the form he prefers (short or long), to conform to his everyday practice. In this way, the patient can silently recite along with the supportive recitation party. To go counter to his likes and habits may destroy his right thought and create an offense on our part. Furthermore, we should not practice supportive recitation in too loud a voice, as we will expend too much energy and be unable to keep on for very long. On the other hand, neither should we recite in too low a voice, lest the patient, in his weakened state, be unable to register the words. Generally speaking, recitation should not be too loud or too low, too slow or too fast. Each utterance should

be clear and distinct so that it can pass through the ear and penetrate deep into the patient's Alaya consciousness. *One caveat*: if the patient is too weak [or is in a coma], he will not be able to hear "external" recitation. In such a case, we should recite into the patient's ear. This helps the patient keep his mind clear and steady.

4. *With regard to percussion instruments*, it is generally better to use the small hand bell, instead of the wooden fish gong with its bass tone. The hand bell, with its clear, limpid sound, can help the patient develop a pure and calm mind. However, this may not apply in all cases. For instance, an Elder Master once taught, "It is best to recite the Buddha's name by itself without musical accompaniment, but since each person's preferences are different, it is better to ask the patient in advance. If some details do not suit him, we should adapt to the circumstances and not be inflexible. The above are some pointers to keep in mind with regard to supportive recitation." Tam: 283-288 #2305
NOTE:
To be truly effective in dedicating merit to others, the practitioner must be utterly

sincere and singleminded in his recitation. Even if he is, the *Ksitigarbha Sutra* teaches that the deceased can only receive a small part of this merit. Furthermore, since the crucial conditions of sincerity and singlemindedness are seldom achieved in full, most intercessions are, at best, partially effective and can seldom erase a lifetime of bad karma. Thus, it is imperative for the practitioner himself to cultivate during his lifetime and not rely on family members, monks or nuns at the time of death.
Editor/Tam: 325

◙ **SUPPRESSION OF 845**
see   Persecution of 845 (China)

◙   **SUPREME, PERFECT ENLIGHTENMENT**
Syn: Supreme Bodhi; Anuttara-Samyak-Sambodhi *See also:* Buddha
----
▶"Same as supreme Buddhahood. The Sanskrit means 'unexcelled perfect enlightenment'; i.e., the perfect wisdom which comprehends truth that is attained only by a Buddha, in contrast to the different grades of enlightenment attained by Bodhisattvas and saints."
Chan: 484   #0977

◉ SURANGAMA SUTRA

Syn: Heroic Gate Sutra
See also: Mahasthamaprapta

►*Chin/* Leng-Yen Ching; *Vn/* Thủ-Lăng-Nghiêm Kinh

Also called the *Sutra of the Heroic One*; exercised a great influence on the development of Mahayana Buddhism in China [and neighboring countries]. "It emphasized the power of samadhi, through which enlightenment can be attained, and explains the various methods of emptiness meditation through the practice of which everyone can realize enlightenment." (*Shambhala Dictionary of Buddhism and Zen.*)

"This sutra was brought to China by the great Indian monk Paramartha about 717, and translated by him into Chinese with the aid of Wang Yung, formerly a Minister of State. This work took about two years. It angered the Emperor that this had been done without first securing the permission of the Government, so Wang Yung was punished and Paramartha was forced to return with his manuscript to India. No one knows how the Chinese translation of the Sutra was preserved. In the course of time,

however, it came to be tremendously valued by Chinese Buddhists and Taoists as in it Buddha describes the steps to be taken and the meditation to be undertaken to reach the great Enlightenment -- describing the tranquilizing of the mind by exclusion of concepts arising directly and indirectly from sensory experiences, the nature of the Truth realized in the samadhi or deepest contemplation, and the transcendental virtues and powers resulting. Finally, it treats of the highest perfect wisdom, Anuttara-Samyak-Sambodhi."
Wood: 133-134

(I) Zen Buddhism

"The Method of Hearing [expounded by the Bodhisattva Avalokitesvara in the *Surangama Sutra*] is in keeping with the fundamental principle that if one sense-organ is intensely concentrated, all the other five sense-organs would be also held still automatically. This is the most fundamental tenet of the reciting method, as said in the *Surangama Sutra*: "when the six sense-organs [five senses plus mind] are simultaneously held in concentration, there will be every pure thought in succession." (Hsu Heng Chi, *What's Buddhism*: 56.)

(II) Pure Land Buddhism

"The *Surangama Sutra* [in the section describing the method of cultivation of Mahastamaprapta Bodhisattva] states: "Moreover, whoever recites the name of the Amitabha Buddha, whether in the present time, or in future time, will surely see the Buddha Amitabha and never become separated from him. By reason of that association, just as one associating with the maker of perfumes becomes permeated with the same perfumes, so he will become perfumed by Amitabha's compassion, and will become enlightened without any other expedient means." (*A Buddhist Bible*) Goddard: 245 The *Surangama Sutra* is a key text for Ch'an/Zen practitioners, while the section referring to the Pure Land practices of the Bodhisattva Mahasthamaprapta is sometimes classified as the fifth Pure Land text.
Editor: na #0926

◙ SUTRA / SUTTA

See also: Scriptural Recital

▸"Lit. a thread on which jewels are strung. Applied to that part of the Canon containing the dialogues or discourses of the Buddha." Hump: 189

"A preaching of the Buddha as recorded in documents. In the early stages of Buddhist history, sutras were memorized, and only in later times were they written down."
Chan: 484

"The sutras have been preserved in Pali and Sanskrit, as well as in Chinese and Tibetan translations. According to tradition they derive directly from the Buddha.

The sutras are prose texts, each introduced by the words 'Thus have I heard.' These words are ascribed to Ananda, a disciple of the Buddha. He is supposed to have retained the discourses of the Buddha in memory and to have recited them at the first Buddhist council, immediately after the death of the Buddha. After these introductory words, the circumstances that occasioned the Buddha to give the discourse are described, as well as the place, the time of year, etc. Then the actual instruction follows, sometimes in the form of a dialogue.

The style of the sutras is simple, popular, and didactically oriented. They are rich in parables and allegories. In many sutras, songs (gatha) are interpolated. Each sutra constitutes a self-sufficient unit. As for content, two currents of tradition can be recognized in Mahayana sutras: 1. Sutras based on faith, which treat buddhology and Bodhisattva teaching and stress devotion. In these sutras, no bounds are set to the imagination, buddhas and Bodhisattvas performing countless miracles in limitless space and endless time. They are elevated to the level of divine beings, a tendency in the Mahayana that arises from its nature with its doctrines of non-substantiality and emptiness (shunyata), which come to expression in a view that sees the world as illusory (maya). In such a view, all miracles, like the world of appearance itself, are no more than a product of illusion. 2. Philosophically-oriented sutras that have as their theme emptiness, the central notion of the Mahayana. They have been differently interpreted by Mahayana thinkers and this has provided the impetus for the formation of various schools. The most important independent sutras are *Lankavatara sutra, Sukhavati-Vyuha Sutra (Amitabha sutra), Dashabhumika, Brahma Net Sutra, Amitayurdhyana sutra (Meditation Sutra), Vimalakirti sutra, Surangama Sutra.*"

Sham: 212-213

NOTES:

Although most sutras are preached by the Buddhas, there are instances where the words of Bodhisattvas are recorded as sutras. A case in point is the *Avatamsaka Sutra*, chapter 40, where the Buddha merely signifies His approval at the end with the words "Sadhu, sadhu" ("Good indeed, good indeed").

Editor: na

"In some sutras, although the Buddha is present, he stays in the background and one of his disciples speaks, in which case the text ends with the Buddha giving the approval to what the disciple has said, thus making the discourse his own, as it were. Sometimes, especially in Mahayana sutras, it is not even a question of the Buddha giving his approval. A disciple may be doing the actual speaking, but he speaks under the direct inspiration of the Buddha, so that in truth the Buddha is speaking through him. But however it is spoken, it is important to understand that whatever is said in the body of a sutra is not just issuing from the ordinary level of consciousness. It isn't something that has been worked out intellectually. It isn't a proof or an explanation of something in the mundane sense. It is truth, a message, even a revelation, issuing from the depths of the Enlightened consciousness, the depths of the Buddha nature. This is the essential content of any Buddhist scripture, and this is its purpose: to communicate the nature of Enlightenment and show the way leading to its realization."

Sangha/Drama: 36 #2311

◎ SUTRA IN FORTY-TWO SECTIONS

►"The first sutra to be translated i n t o C h i n e s e. T h e *Ssu-Shih-Erh-Chang Ching (Vn/Tú Thập Nhị Chương)* is said to have been brought to the court by emissaries of Emperor Ming-ti who were searching for Buddhist scriptures in ... Central Asia, and to have been translated in the year 67 A.D. by the Indian monks Matanga and Chu-fa-lan.

In this sutra, which was also the first Buddhist written work in the Chinese language, the *essential teachings of the Lesser Vehicle, such as impermanence and desire or craving, are explained*. Many versions of this sutra are extant;

they differ considerably in places."

Sham: 213

"Traditionally the first Buddhist sutra available in China."

Reat: 345 #0363

◎ SUTRA OF AMIDA
see Amitabha Sutra

◎ SUTRA OF HUI-NENG
see Platform Sutra

◎ SUTRA OF INFINITE LIFE
see Longer Amitabha Sutra

◎ SUTRA RECITAL
see Scriptural Recital

◎ SUTRA STUDIES SCHOOL
see Scriptual Studies School

◎ SUZUKI, D.T. (1870-1966)
See also: Pure Land School; Zen School

►"Japanese Buddhist scholar, who, as one of the best known modern interpreters of Zen in the West, did a great deal to arouse interest in Zen [in the U.S]. He was a lay student of Master Shaku Soen (Soyen) from Engaku temple in Kamakura (Japan) and underwent Zen training there. He focused primarily on the intellectual

interpretation of Zen teachings."
Sham: 214

"Japanese philosopher and writer, born 18 October 1870 of a Rinzai Zen family. Studied Zen at Kamakura under the Roshi Imagita Kosen. On the death of the Roshi studied under his successor, Soyen Shaku ... and under him gained his Great Awakening. Went to Chicago in 1897 to help Paul Carus with his Open Court Publishing Co. In 1900 published a translation of the *Awakening of the Faith*, his first major work. In 1908 went to Europe, and again in 1910 where he studied in London and Paris. In 1911, married Beatrice Lane Suzuki, d. 1939. 1936, traveled to London for the World Congress of Faiths. Spent war years at Kamakura in Engakuji, writing. 1949, made Member of the Japanese Academy and decorated by the Emperor with the Cultural Medal. 1950-58, traveled widely in the West; to Honolulu, California, London for three visits, and some years in New York, lecturing. In 1958 retired to Japan to organize the Matsugaoka Library, which he had founded with the library of his wife on her death in 1939. Author of a score of major works in English, more in Japanese, and innumerable articles, nearly all on Zen Buddhism, attempting to explain its nature and importance to the Western world."
Hump: 190

"Books include *Essays in Zen Buddhism* (3 series); *Studies in the Lankavatara Sutra; Introduction to Zen Buddhism; Manual of Zen Buddhism; Japanese Buddhism*. Translations from Sanskrit and/or Japanese include the *Lankavatara Sutra* and the *Awakening of the Faith*."
Snel: 304

NOTE:

"Dr. Suzuki is generally associated with the Zen school, so it is often a matter of surprise to hear that he translated many Pure Land Buddhist texts into English and nourished a belief that Pure Land rather than Zen might be the form of Buddhism most suitable for Westerners." (John Snelling, *The Buddhist Handbook*.)
Snell: 216

"Most Buddhists in the world, by far the vast majority, practice a Faith or devotional form of worship. Dr. D.T. Sukzuki strongly believed that the direction American Buddhism would take was towards Shin Buddhism [Pure Land] and its

practice of Faith. It may turn out at this time that most Westerners, originally seeking personal enlightenment, will find themselves choosing a devotional path." (Ryushin Sarah Grayson in *Butsumon*, Fall 1989.)
Zen: 5 #0362

◉ **SUZUKI, SHUNRYU (1905-71)**

▸"Japanese Zen master of Soto school. In 1958 he came to the United States and founded several Zen centers, among them the Zen Center in San Francisco and the Zen Mountain Center in Tassajara, California -- the first Soto Zen monastery in the West."
Sham: 214 #0361

◉ **SWEET DEW**
see Ambrosia

◉ **T'AI-HSU (1889-1947)**

▸"Famous modern Chinese Buddhist monk. Organized revival of Buddhism in China between the World Wars. Founded Chinese Buddhist Association and the journal *Hai Cha'o Yin* (the Voice of the Tide). Travelled in Europe 1928-9 where he founded *Les Amis du Bouddhisme* in Paris.

Worked hard to improve relations between Buddhists of the East and West. Sole work in English translation, *Lectures in Buddhism*, a booklet published in Paris, 1928."
Hump: 191
"His main doctrinal theme focused on promoting a synthesis of various Chinese Buddhist schools in a harmonious fashion. The reform movement that flourished as a result of the work of T'ai Hsu (and others) was cut short by the takeover of the mainland by the Chinese Communists in 1949."
Preb: 252
"In the summer of 1922, disciples of the famous Chinese monk T'ai Hsu journeyed from Shanghai to Chengtu in Szechuan Province to bring the modernized message of Buddhism as taught by their master. Their coming was the occasion of great rejoicing, and a real revival of Buddhism was the result. They had been heralded for more than a year and their way prepared by a wide circulation of T'ai Hsu's popular magazine *Hai Ch'ao Yin* --'The Voice of the Sea,' or 'The Sound of the Tide.' Very carefully edited articles had prepared the people for the visit of the missionaries, and the new

message found a ready response even before their arrival. It brought a message of peace for the troubled days, and the magazine clearly stated that the new message was destined to lift the sublime teachings of the Mahayana Doctrine for the help of the people tossed about in a sea of modern doubt. The message was essentially spiritual and taught, or stood for, three propositions, (1) a real desire to reform monasticism, (2) a plan to reconstruct Buddhist theology along lines of modern philosophy, and (3) to use the teachings of Buddha to elevate the people and improve social conditions. The missionaries were officially welcomed by the Governor of the Province. Sixteen daily papers all joined in and gave columns to the new teaching, thus supplying a liberal supply of advertising. The opening meetings were attended by large crowds who listened attentively to the new program, and large numbers enrolled for the daily course to be given. In fact, a real program was gotten out, much like a university course, or a summer school curriculum, and fees charged for the course. Then daily the large hall in the Public Garden of the Manchu City was thronged with auditors to hear the public addresses, and the classrooms were filled with eager students. A course in the history of Buddhism was given, what it had done for the world, and how it had become encrusted with many supersitions. Now all was changed. The old simple story of the Enlightened One and how he found the way of salvation was declared. Idolatry was opposed -- in bygone days it was only tolerated as an accommodation to the weakness of ignorant people. Now education was to be stressed. A Buddhist university was to be established. The monks were to be encouraged to be busy as learners and servants of the people. The mercy of Buddha was taught and enjoined so that the wicked might be led to kindness, the selfish to righteousness, and the hungry to find satisfaction in the doctrine. Most emphasized were the daily hours for fasting and meditation. A real revival was effected along the lines, and many of the foremost business and professional men took the vows and followed the course of meditation regularly. Many men who had not been interested in religion came under the sway of the new-found faith, and personally told me of the value of the hours of meditation and how their faith had been strengthened. The course on reading was followed widely. The students burnt incense daily as they read and meditated. At the meetings singing was indulged in, and often tunes quite similar to Christian tunes were used, and one song used with the refrain, 'Take the name of Buddha with you.' They even organized a Young Men's Buddhist Association which is going strong. (A.J. Brace, YMCA secretary in Cheng-Tu, China)." Pratt: 383-384

For the views of Master T'ai-hsu on the close affinities between the T'ien-t'ai and Pure Land schools, see "T'ien-t'ai school". #0360

◙ **T'ANG DYNASTY (BUDDHISM IN THE)**

Syn: Tang Dynasty

►"Also spelled 'Tang'. After the Han, generally regarded the most glorious of Chinese dynasties." Reat: 345

"Period of Chinese history from 618-906, during which time Buddhism in China reached its peak of importance. By the time of the T'ang Dynasty, nearly all of the Buddhist schools were represented on Chinese soil: San-lun, Fa-hsiang, T'ien-t'ai, Hua-yen, Ch'an, and Ching-t'u (Pure Land). During the T'ang Dynasty they took on a fully Chinese character. Buddhism was aggressively supported by a number of T'ang rulers, resulting in the development of monasteries, cave temple projects, and the like. Unfortunately, in about 845, Buddhism was severely persecuted by the Emperor T'ang Wu-tsung. Despite the emperor's death the following year, an enormous number of monks and nuns were laicized, monastic property was seized, images were melted down, and the economic base of the Chinese Buddhist sangha was throughly disrupted. Those Buddhist schools that were either textual, intellectual, or totally monastery-based essentially perished from the landscape, while the traditions that were based on personal, individual practice, especially including the Ch'an and the Pure Land traditions, survived [and thrived to this day]." Preb: 253

"The Dharma was the pride of T'ang Buddhism. From the founding of the dynasty (618) to the An Lu-shun revolt (755), a succession of great minds and the schools they championed laid a philosophical foundation for the future of Mahayana Buddhism. These schools--T'ien-t'ai, Hua-yen, Pure Land, and Ch'an--can also be seen as bringing to maturity different forms of piety, stretching back to Indian origins. It is hard enough to see any unity to Mahayana in India, much less to discern a teleological structure in Sinitic Mahayana. Yet the emergence of these four schools was not a fortuitous event, but accorded with the four optimal poles in Mahayana Buddhology. Buddhas could be either *laukika* or *lokottara* (mundane or transmundane), oriented to either *prajna* or *karuna* (wisdom or compassion)... Early Buddhism knew only the "historic didactic" Sakyamuni Buddha. The idealization of the Buddha began within the Mahasamghika school, which marked the shift from the historical to the transhistorical. It was with Mahayana that [transcendental, salvific Buddhas such as Amitabha] emerged; *compassion* was given equal status with *wisdom* in a host of new salvific Buddhas and Bodhisattvas. A total rehumanization of the Buddha

was accomplished in East Asia." Yoshi/Lai: 331 #1072

◉ **T'ANG WU-TSUNG (814-46)**
Syn: Wu-Tsung
See also: Persecution of 845

►"(r. 840-46). Emperor of the T'ang dynasty responsible for the third [and most severe] Chinese suppression of Buddhism."
Reat: 349
"Chinese emperor of the T'ang Dynasty, who was a fanatical follower of Taoism. At the urging of his Taoist advisors, he promulgated a series of anti-Buddhist decrees. This persecution of Buddhism reached its peak in 845: 260,000 Buddhist monks and nuns were forced to return to worldly life. The art treasures of 4,600 monasteries were confiscated, and even Buddhist families had to surrender their ritual articles to imperial functionaries. This was the most effective persecution of Buddhism [ever, in the history of China]; little by little other 'foreign' religions were to encounter the same treatment."
Sham: 249 #0390

◉ **T'IEN-T'AI MOUNTAIN**

►"The name of a mountain in

China. This is the place where patriarch Chih-i founded the T'ien-T'ai (Tendai) School in 575. There are many temples on this mountain. This is one of the most sacred places of Buddhism in China."

Dait: 351 #0138

◉ T'IEN-T'AI SCHOOL

Syn: Tendai School; Tien-tai School
See also: Five Periods and Eight Teachings; Three Pure Land Sutras

----

▸"A major school of Buddhism founded by the Great Teacher Chih I in China during the Sui dynasty (589-618). The school adopted a system of comparative classification which organized all the Buddhist sutras into *Five Periods and Eight Teachings (q.v.)* to clarify their relative position, and concludes that the true teaching of Buddhism is the unification of the three truths indicated in the *Lotus Sutra.* Enlightenment, the school maintains, is achieved by meditation to 'observe one's mind' or perceive the truth within one's own life."

Sokk: 475

"The school teaches that a phenomenon can be viewed in three different ways within the same instant. First, because a phenomenon is produced by various causes, its essence is devoid of any permanent existence, that is, it is *'empty'.* Second, nevertheless it does have a real, if only temporary, immediate existence (*'false'*). Third, since a phenomenon is thus a blending of both ultimate emptiness and temporary existence, it should be seen as occupying a position midway between the two poles (*'Middle Way'*)."

Yoko: 196

NOTES:

A major school that takes the *Lotus Sutra* as its principal text. Historically, it has had a close relationship with Pure Land. Indeed, acccording to the famous master T'ai-Hsu (q.v.), the *Longer Amitabha Sutra* is a shorter form of the *Lotus Sutra.*

Tam: 165

"'Great Stopping and Seeing' [a major commentary by Patriarch Chih I] is a traditional source-book for Zen and Pure Land Buddhism. Both Zen and Pure Land Buddhism were intimately connected with T'ien-T'ai Buddhism... The T'ien-T'ai patriarch Chih-I appears as a Zen master in Zen literature, as

a Pure Land patriarch in Pure Land literature."
Chih-I/Cleary: viii #0293

◙ **TA CHIH TU LUN**
see Great perfection of Wisdom (treatise)

◙ **TAIMA MANDALA**
See also: Pure Land Mandalas; Chiko Mandala; Raigo

►"A Picture of the Pure Land of Amitabha preserved in Taima-dera in Nara prefecture (Japan). The writing on this picture says that it is made of lotus threads."
Dait: 346

The Taima mandala, the most complex of the three Pure Land mandalas, derives in part from various illustrations based on two sutras, the *Longer Amitabha Sutra* and the *Amitabha Sutra*. Added to these influences, however, is the overwhelming impact of concepts such as the Sixteen Contemplations, taught in the *Meditation Sutra*. For this reason, the Taima mandala ought properly to be called a *Meditation Sutra*. It is popularly called the Taima mandala after the temple, the Taima-dera, where the original mandala, a tapestry of silk thread, is found.

The legend concerning the origin of the original Taima mandala is well known. It is found in various records as well as in the textual portions of the famous thirteenth-century narrative scroll painting the *Legends of the Taima Mandala*, in Komyo-ji in Kanagawa Prefecture (Japan). Although the personages involved and certain details of the legend vary slightly, the story can be summarized as follows.

During the reign of Emperor Junnin (758-64), the daughter of a nobleman named Yokohagi no Otodo lost interest in the mundane world and began to yearn for the Western Paradise of Amida. On the fifteenth day of the sixth month of 763, she cut off her hair to become a nun and for seven days prayed earnestly that she might see a living vision of Amida while in this life. On the twentieth of the same month a nun appeared and ordered the former princess to gather a hundred horseloads of lotus stems. Thanks to an imperial edict, the lotus stems were gathered and sent from Omi Province, and the nun who had appeared spun them into thread. She then miraculously dug a well in which she dyed the thread into five different hues. On the evening of the twenty-third another nun appeared; by the early hours of the following morning, she had finished weaving a beautiful mandala about 4.5 meters square that depicted aspects of the *Meditation Sutra.*

The weaver then disappeared. When asked who the second nun was, the first nun revealed that the weaver was none other than the Bodhisattva Avalokitesvara in human form and that she herself was a human incarnation of Amida. After explaining the significance of the newly woven mandala, the nun departed to the West in the midst of clouds. The former princess spent the next few years as a nun, ceaselessly yearning for the Western Paradise, and at the time of her death on the fourth day of the fourth month, 775, so tradition holds, Amida and his heavenly attendants descended to escort her to the Pure Land..."

Okaz: 44

NOTE:

"The composition of the Taima mandala follows faithfully the exposition in Shantao's commentary on the *Meditation Sutra.* The vertical outer court on the left depicts the story of Prince Ajatasatru as it is related in the *Meditation Sutra.* The vertical outer court on the right shows thirteen of the Sixteen Contemplations. The lower horizontal outer court divides the remaining three contemplations into the nine possible degrees of rebirth in the Western Paradise. The grand interior scene is called the *gengibun:* Amida, attended by Kannon and Seishi and a host of other deities, sits in the midst of the splendor of the Pure Land."

Okaz: 46 #0136

◎ **TAISHO**

see Tripitaka

◎ **TAKAHATSU**

Syn: Almsrounds #1998

◎ **TAKING REFUGE**

see Three Refuges

◎ **TAN**

▸"Thai title roughly equivalent to 'Venerable.'"

Snel: 261 #0723

◎ **TAN T'IEN**

▸(*Skt*/Udana; *Vn*/ Đơn-Điền) "A spot about an inch below the navel where lies the reservoir of vital principle which can be transmuted unto the Elixir of

Immortality according to the Taoists."

Luk: 229 #0759

◙ **TAN-LUAN (476-542)**
See also: Tao-Ch'o

▸"The First Patriarch of the Pure Land school. Next to Hui-Yuan, the founder of the school, Tan-luan is the most important figure in the Chinese Pure Land movement."

Preb: 253

"T'an-luan was not only a believer of the Pure Land path but also the first major Pure Land writer with several works to his credit. His major work, the *T'an-luan Commentary*, is a commentary on the *Rebirth Treatise*. His search for immortality with a Taoist master, his subsequent conversion to Pure Land, and his successes as a healer greatly esteemed by the e m p e r o r   h a v e   b e e n well-chronicled in the Pure Land tradition. T'an-luan's memorial epitaph inspired the conversion of Tao-ch'o to Pure Land teaching. Tao-ch'o in turn served as teacher to Shan-tao."

Tana: 17

See this beautiful account of the meeting between the Pure Land Patriarch T'an Lun (then a Taoist) and the famed translator/monk Bodhiruchi:

"T'an Lun (476-542), seeking immortality, travelled about China obtaining teachings from various noted sages, including the Taoist master T'ao Hung-ching. Eventually (ca. 530) he met with the Indian Buddhist teacher Bodhiruci: T'an Lun opened the conversation by saying 'Is there anything in the Teaching of the Buddha which is superior to the m e t h o d s   f o r   o b t a i n i n g immortality found in this country's scriptures on the immortals?'

Bodhiruci spat on the ground and said, 'What are you saying? There is no comparison! Where on this earth can you find a method for immortality? Suppose that you can obtain youth in your old age, and never die: Even having done that, you would still be rolling around in the Triple World!' So he gave him the *Meditation Sutra* and said, 'these are the recipes of Amitabha Buddha: if you rely on his practices, you will be liberated from Samsara.'" (Raoul Birnbaum, *The Healing Buddha*.)

Birn: 241 #1743

◙ **TANG DYNASTY**
see T'ang Dynasty

◙ TANHA

▸"Pali for craving or thirst or greed; in Buddhism, the cause of suffering."
Ross: 192 #1876

◙ TANTRIC SCHOOL
see Tibetan Buddhism

◙ TAO-AN (312-385)
See also: Hui-Yuan

▸"A Chinese priest in the Eastern Chin (shin) Dynasty. He is popularly called Miten-no-Doan in Japan. After studying Buddhism under Fo-t'u-ch'ang, he actively taught Buddhism to his five hundred disciples, including Patriarch Hui-yuan (q.v.), the founder of Pure Land Buddhism. His influence was so great that the ruless which he formulated were widely observed by all Buddhist priests and nuns. *He was the first priest to call himself Shih (Jpn/ Shaku; Vn/ Thich), an abbreviation of Sakyamuni, denoting a follower of Sakyamuni Buddha.* He wrote commentaries on many sutras."
Dait: 50 #0077
See also: Pai-chang

◙ TAO-CH'O (562-645)
See also: Peace and Bliss Collection; Pure Land School; Tan-luan

----
▸"Important Pure Land master in China, following the tradition of T'an-luan. His main text was the *An-lo-chi (Peace and Bliss collection; Vn/* An Lạc Tập). The main issue confronted by Tao-ch'o involved the proper religious practice for individuals during a period of Dharma decline (mo-fa), resulting in his firm emphasis on Buddha-recitation."
Preb: 255

"The second of the first five Chinese Pure Land masters. He entered the priesthood at 14 and became well-versed in the *Nirvana Sutra*. At 40, when he visited Hsuan-chung-ssu and read an inscription in praise of T'an-luan, he became an aspirant to the Pure Land. He stayed at the temple and practised the recitation of the Buddha's name as many as 70,000 times a day. He lectured on the *Meditation Sutra* more than 200 times, and propagated Pure Land teaching extensively. He wrote a 2-fascicle work, the *Peace and Bliss collection* (q.v.). His greatest disciple was Shan-t'ao (Zendo)."
Insa: 14 #0192

◙ TAOISM

►"Chinese religion founded by Lao Tzu and based on the Tao or 'Way' of nature."
Reat: 324
Taoist practitioners traditionally strive for immortality, which, in Buddhism, is a classic example of deluded attachment to the body.
Editor: na #1523

◙ TARA

►Tibetan for the Bodhisattva Avalokitesvara (q.v.).
Editor: na

◙ TARIKI
see Other-power

◙ TATHAGATA
Syn: Thus-Come One

►"Lit. 'the thus-gone [thus-come, thus-perfected] one'; refers to one who has attained Supreme Enlightenment. It is one of the ten titles of the Buddha, which he himself used when speaking of himself or other Buddhas."
Sham: 220

"Usually translated as 'Thus Come One.' 'He who came as did all Buddhas, who took the absolute way of cause and effect, and attained to perfect wisdom; one of the highest titles of a Buddha'" (Charles Luk).
Luk: xxx

"A title of the Buddha, used by his followers, and also by himself when speaking of himself. Derivation doubtful, but usually derives from tatha-agata (thus come), or tatha-gata (thus gone), and given the meaning 'He who has come and gone as have former Buddhas': i.e. teaching the same truths, and following the same Path to the same goal. The Mahayana Schools prefer: one who has attained full realization of Suchness (Tatha-ta); i.e., become one with the absolute (Dharmakaya), so that he 'neither comes from anywhere, nor goes anywhere.'"
Hump: 195 #0359

◙ TATHAGATA VEHICLE
see One Vehicle

◙ TATHAGATA ZEN
See also: Zen; Patriarchal Zen; Shen-Hsiu

►The opposite of Patriarchal Zen. Tathagata Zen follows the meditation methods and the six Paramitas taught in Mahayana sutras, whereas Patriarchal Zen emphasizes the direct teaching of the patriarchs.

The two schools of Zen, the Gradual and the Sudden, represent different facets of the same teaching adapted to different types of people in different locations. To praise one school while disparaging the other is therefore a form of attachment, a dualistic view of Buddhism not consonant with the Truth.

Editor: na

NOTE:

All schools of Buddhism, whether Patriarchal Zen or Pure Land or Tantrism are merely expedients, "fingers pointing to the moon" -- the True Mind inherent in all sentient beings.

Editor: na #0485

◙ TATHAGATA-GARBHA

Syn: Womb of the Tathagata

▶"1. The innate Buddha-nature (suchness) obscured temporarily by defilements; 2. the 'storehouse' of the Buddha's teaching."

Chan: 484

"[The Tathagata-garbha or] Tathagata-embryo is sometimes translated as the 'womb of the Tathagata' or 'Treasure of the Tathagata'; that is to say, there is

a c o m p l e t e , p e r f e c t Buddha-nature within every sentient being. It cannot manifest itself due to the covering of defilements. When one attains Supreme Enlightenment, the Tathagata-embryo is no more. Then the perfect Buddha-nature within every sentient being manifests itself in full."

Chan: 385 #0575

◙ TATHATA

see Suchness

◙ TEACHER

see Good spiritual advisors; Guru; Lama

◙ TEACHERLESS WISDOM

▶"Autonomous knowledge or inherent knowledge which cannot in itself be taught or learned, but has to be awakened from latency."

[TC/FO1, p.701] #1307

◙ TEACHING SCHOOL

see Scriptual Studies School

◙ TEMPLES

See also: Amida-ji; China (Buddhism); Japan (Buddhism)

▶In East and Southeast Asia, according to most observers,

there is no real division into Zen and Pure Land temples, as the two forms of practice tend to co-exist on the same premises. In Japan, on the other hand, there are distinct Zen and Pure Land temples.
Editor/Dia: 175
NOTE:
Apparently, the synthesis of various Buddhist schools, which took place in China and other parts of East Asia after the golden period of Chinese Buddhism (9th Century), never occured in Japan. Thus, many of the quasi-distinctions and differences that exist among schools and traditions (Zen, Pure Land etc.) in Japan were transfered in toto to America, in spite of the best efforts of D. T. Suzuki and others.
Editor: na #1600

◙ **TEN**

▶The number ten is a symbolic number in the Avatamsaka cosmology, representing infinity. "Because the states of the Sutra are multifaceted, perfectly interfused and mutually non-obstructive, the number ten symbolizes the concept of realm upon realm *ad infinitum.*"
[HHFAS39II10] #1236

◙ **TEN DIRECTIONS**
See also: Six Directions

▶"The eight points of the compass (north, south, east, west, northeast, southeast, northwest, and southwest), plus the zenith and nadir. Ten directions is a figurative term meaning in all directions, 'in all space.'"
Chan: 493 #0628

The expression "Ten Directions" and "Six Directions" are interchangeable and means "everywhere". However, the term Six Directions is found in Theravada and early Mahayana texts, while the expression Ten Directions is used in major Mahayana sutras such as the *Avatamsaka*, in which phenomenal realities are expressed in terms of ten.

◙ **TEN EPITHETS OF A BUDDHA**

▶"Common descriptions of the Buddhas to be found in many sutras: perfect (Tathagata), holy one or saint (Arhat), fully enlightened (Samyak Sambuddha), gifted in knowledge and conduct, well-gone one, knower of the worlds, unsurpassable teacher of men, teacher of gods and men,

awakened one (Buddha), sublime one."

Sham: 221   #0358

◙ **TEN ESOTERIC DOORS**
see   Ten Mysterious Gates

◙ **TEN EVIL ACTS**
see   Ten Evil Deeds

◙ **TEN EVIL DEEDS**
Syn: Ten Evil Acts; Ten Sins
See also: 'Ten Precepts.'

►1. Killing; 2. stealing; 3. sexual misconduct; 4. lying; 5. slander; 6. coarse language; 7. frivolous chatter; 8. covetousness; 9. angry speech; 10. wrong views (q.v.).
Editor/Tam: 163   #0927

◙ **TEN GREAT VOWS**
Syn: Vows of Samantabhadra Bodhisattva; Ten Regal Vows
See also: Samantabhadra; Vows/ Rebirth In Pure Land; Four Great Vows

----

►The famous vows of the Bodhisattva Samantabhadra in the *Avatamsaka Sutra.* These vows represent the quintessence of this sutra and are the basis of all Mahayana practice. Studying the vows and putting them into practice is tantamount to practicing the teachings of the *Avatamsaka Sutra.*   Editor: na

In the *Avatamsaka Sutra,* the Bodhisattva Samantabhadra urges the youth Sudhana ("Good Wealth") and the Ocean-Wide Great Assembly to seek rebirth through the Ten Great Vows.

These Ten Great Vows are: "First, worship and respect all Buddhas./ Second, praise the Thus Come Ones./ Third, make abundant offerings./ Fourth, repent misdeeds and hindrances./ Fifth, rejoice at others' merits and virtues./ Sixth, request the Budddha to turn the Dharma wheel./ Seventh, request the Buddha to remain in the world./ Eighth, follow the teachings of the Buddha at all times./ Ninth, accommodate and benefit all sentient beings./ Tenth, transfer merits and virtues universally."
Each Vow contains the clause: "When the realm of empty space is exhausted, my [Vows] will be exhausted. But because the realm of empty space is inexhaustible, my [Vows] will never end. In the same way, when the realms of living beings, the karma of living beings, and the afflictions of living beings are exhausted, my [Vows] will be exhausted. But the realms of living beings, the karma of living beings, and the

afflictions of living beings are inexhaustible. Therefore, my [Vows] are inexhaustible. They continue in thought after thought without cease. My body, mouth and mind never tire of doing these deeds." (Master Hsuan Hua, tr., *Flower Adornment Sutra*, Ch. 40, p. 48.)

Hua: 48

The practitioner should cultivate these Ten Great Vows with body, mouth and Mind, and without interruption or lethargy. At the time of death, when all family and possessions are left behind and all faculties disintegrate, only these Great Vows will follow close behind, and in an instant, the practitioner will be reborn in the Pure Land.

Editor/Dia: 61-62

Each of the ten Vows of the Bodhisattva Samantabhadra should be put into practice without interruption, in thought after thought, with body, speech and mind. Thus, the three karmas of body, speech and mind of the practitioner are pure, empty and still. In his lifetime, he has sown the seeds of rebirth in a pure realm. At the time of death, he will naturally be reborn in such a realm, of which the most representative is the Pure Land of Amitabha Buddha. This is a good illustration of the Pure Land/Zen teaching, "if the mind is pure, the land is pure". To have faith in the Vows of Samantabhadra is to sow the seeds of Enlightenment. These unconditioned (transcendental) merits and virtues lead to Buddhahood. They are therefore superior to mundane offerings (even gold and jewels), as such offerings can bring only conditioned (temporal) merits and virtues, leading to a favorable rebirth in the human or celestial realms -- not Buddhahood. Anyone who reads, recites, accepts and explains Samantabhadra's vows sows the seeds of Buddhahood and ultimately becomes a Buddha. His rewards are therefore of an unconditioned nature (without outflows) and beyond the Triple Realm -- beyond the knowledge and vision of all, except for the Buddhas.   Editor: na #0928

◎ **TEN GROUNDS**
see   Ten Stages

◎ **TEN MIRRORS**
See also: Mutual Interpenetration

►*Avatamsaka Sutra:*
To illustrate the realm of unobstructed interpenetration of

Vairocana Buddha, the Chinese monk Fa Tsang arranged 10 mirrors to correspond to the Ten Directions of space: one above, one below and another 8 to represent the 4 compass points and the 4 intermediate directions. Then, in the midst of the mirrors, he placed a Buddha image with a lamp before it. At once, the spectators saw the Buddha multiplied to infinity in every direction."
[TPr, p.94]q] #1237

◎ **TEN MYSTERIES**
see Ten Mysterious Gates

◎ **TEN MYSTERIOUS GATES**
Syn: Flower Bank Mysterious Gates; Ten Esoteric Doors; Ten Mysteries; Ten Profound Propositions
----
▶*Avatamsaka Sutra*
"Ten aspects of the interrelationship of all phenomena, as seen from the enlightened point of view. To explain such relationship and harmony, the [Avatamsaka] school advances the Ten Profound Propositions (Ten Mysterious Gates): 1) All things are co-existent, corresponding to one another. 2) The intension and extension of one thing involve those of others without any obstacle. 3) The One and the Many are mutually inclusive. 4) All things are identical with one another. 5) The hidden and the manifested mutually perfect each other. 6) All minute and abstruse things mutually penetrate one another. 7) All things reflect one another. 8) Truth is manifested in facts and facts are the source of Enlightenment. 9) The past, present and future are inter-penetrating. 10) All things are manifestations and transformations of the mind.' (Vergilius Ferm.)"
Editor/Tam: 349 #0971

◎ **TEN NON-SEEKING PRACTICES**
Syn: Non-Seeking Practices
See also: Obstacles to Cultivation

▶*How to Ensure Non-Retrogression of the Mind*:
"A Pure Land treatise on the Buddha Recitation Samadhi has explained the 'ten practices of non-seeking' to eliminate the ten major obstacles encountered by practitioners on the path to Enlightenment. These ten major obstacles encompass all obstructions and impediments. Therefore if we follow the ten non-seeking practices, all

obstacles will disappear. These ten practices are:

1. We should not wish that our bodies be always free of diseases and ailments, because a disease-free body is prone to desire and lust. This leads to p r e c e p t - b r e a k i n g and retrogression.

2. We should not wish that our lives be free of all misfortune and adversity, lest we be prone to pride and arrogance. This leads us to be disdainful and overbearing towards everyone else.

3. We should not wish that our mind cultivation be free of all obstacles because, in such a case, our knowledge would be exceptional. This leads to the transgression of thinking that we have awakened, when in fact we have not.

4. We should not wish that our cultivation be free of demonic obstacles, because our vows would not then be firm and enduring. This leads to the transgression of thinking that we have attained Enlightenment, when in fact we have not.

5. We should not wish that our plans and activities meet with easy success, for we will then be inclined to thoughts of contempt and disrespect. This leads to the transgression of pride and conceit, thinking ourselves to be filled with virtues and talent.

6. We should not wish for gain in our social relations. This leads us to violate moral principles and see only the mistakes of others.

7. We should not wish that everyone, at all times, be on good terms and in harmony with us. This leads to pride and conceit and seeing only our own side of every issue.

8. We should not wish to be repaid for our good deeds, lest we develop a calculating mind. This leads to greed for fame and fortune.

9. We should not wish to share in opportunities for profit, lest the mind of delusion arise. This leads us to lose our good name and reputation for the sake of unwholesome gain.

10. When subject to injustice and wrong, we should not necessarily seek the ability to refute and rebut, as doing so indicates that the mind of self-and-others has not been severed. This will certainly lead to more resentment and hatred ...

Thus, in merit there is misfortune, in misfortune there is merit, in freedom there are obstructions, in obstructions there is freedom. Realizing this,

cultivators in the past have used 'obstacles as conditions for progress.' They have said, 'If others do not bother and disturb us, success in the Way is difficult to achieve.' This is because contempt, slander, calamity, injustice and all other obstacles are the 'yardsticks to measure the practitioner's level of attainment.' Remaining patient and calm in the face of such impediments, the cultivator demonstrates that he has reached a high level of practice. If it were not for these obstacles, how could his level of attainment be measured? In truth, it is not that the practitioner seeks obstacles and impediments, but that he must be ever-vigilant, for the Way is full of dangerous and unforeseen events. He should prepare himself for all eventualities so that when faced with actual obstacles, he can remain calm and unruffled. An Elder Master once said: 'Only those with wisdom and strong determination can apply these ten practices. As long as they meditate, are enlightened and hold steadfastly to these ten practices, even if they enter the realms of the demons, the demons cannot make them retrogress. Even though they may be in the realms of form, sound, fame, fortune, love, hate, right, wrong, prosperity, decline, success, failure ... they will still be calm and at peace.' Thus, if we are deluded, all good and favorable circumstances can become conditions obstructing the Way. If we truly understand that all diseases, suffering and demonic obstacles are inherently empty and false, lacking true substance, they cannot harm us in any way."
Tam: 264-267 #2289

◉ **TEN OX-HERDING PICTURES**
Syn: Ten Oxen Pictures

▸"Representation of the stages of the Zen way or of the different levels of realization of enlightennment shown in ten pictures of an ox (or water buffalo) and his herder. The best-known stems from the Chinese Ch'an (Zen) master K'uo-an Chih-yuan. The stages depicted are (1) seeking the ox; (2) finding the tracks; (3) first glimpse of the ox; (4) catching the ox; (5) taming the ox; (6) riding the ox home; (7) forgetting the ox, self alone; (8) forgetting ox and self; (9) returning to the source; (10) entering the marketplace with helping hands."
Sham: 106

"The ten Ox-herding Pictures, first made known to the West by D.T. Suzuki in his *Manual of Zen Buddhism* (1935), are the work of K'uo-an, a Zen master of China in the Sung Dynasty (10th c.). There are various versions of this symbolic epitome of Zen training, but the point of the Kuo-an ten, as distinct from early shorter versions, is that the empty circle of Sunyata is not the goal. The rider on the now tamed Ox of self returns to the city 'with bliss-bestowing hands.'"
Hump: 142 #0387

◙ **TEN OXEN PICTURES**
see   Ten Ox-herding pictures

◙ **TEN PARAMITAS**
Syn: Perfections
See also: Paramitas

▸"The six paramitas of Charity, Discipline, Forebearance, Zeal, Concentration and Wisdom plus the paramitas of Ingenuity (skill-in-means), Vows, Power, and Knowledge."
Chan: 494 #0630

◙ **TEN POWERS**

▸"The ten powers of the Buddhas, giving them complete knowledge of (1) what is right or wrong; (2) the past, present, and future karmas of all sentient beings; (3) all forms of meditation; (4) the powers and faculties of all sentient beings; (5) the desires, or moral direction, of every being; (6) the different levels of existence; (7) the results of various methods of practice; (8) the transmigratory states of all sentient beings and the courses of karma they follow; (9) the past lives of all sentient beings and Nirvana; and (10) the destruction of all evil passions."
BDK: 355-356

◙ **TEN PRACTICES**
See also: Avatamsaka Sutra

▸Please read "Fifty-Two Levels of Bodhisattva Practices" before the following:
"The ten Bodhisattva Practices are: 1) the practice of giving joy, (2) beneficial practice, (3) the practice of non-oppostion, (4) the practice of indomitability, (5) the practice of nonconfusion, (6) the practice of good manifestation, (7) the practice of nonattachment, (8) the practice of that which is difficult to attain, (9) the practice of good teachings, (10) the practice of truth. For details see *Avatamsaka Sutra*. T. Cleary: 204 #1102

◙ **TEN PRECEPTS**
Syn: Ten Virtues
See also: Five Precepts; Ten Evil Deeds

▸Ten basic prohibitions binding on novice monks and nuns. "The ten precepts for novices are refraining from (1) killing living beings, (2) taking what has not been given, (3) misconduct in sexual matters, (4) telling lies, (5) drinking liquor, (6) wearing adornments and perfume, (7) enjoying singing and dancing, (8) sleeping in large, raised beds, (9) eating after noon, and (10) possessing gold, silver, and other precious metals."
Tana: 244 #0929

◙ **TEN PROFOUND PROPOSITIONS**
see Ten Mysterious Gates

◙ **TEN REALMS**
Syn: Ten Worlds

▸"The Ten Realms of living beings are:
Hells, the worlds of hungry spirits, animals, asuras, men, Heavens, the worlds of sravakas, pratyekabuddhas, Bodhisattvas, and Buddhas."
Dait: 148 #0100

◙ **TEN RECITATIONS METHOD**
See also: Buddha Recitation; Universal Method; Pure Land Buddhism (Summary); Meditation Sutra

----

▸"According to the *Meditation Sutra,* even the most evil person may be reborn in the Pure Land, if at the time of death he or she is able to embrace the Pure Land faith and maintain single-minded and undisturbed recollection of the Buddha Amitabha for 'ten successive moments.' Hence, although Pure Land Buddhism ordinarily encourages that one turn to Amitabha sooner rather than later in life, the ten moments of mindfulness nonetheless provide a last-minute means of assuring one's salvation. The Ten Recitation practice is offered as both a daily meditation and a rehearsal for that fateful moment to come."
Lopez/95: 365

"*'Ten recitations'* refers to the Ten Recitations method taught by a well-known Master, which is based on the lowest grade of rebirth described in the *Meditation Sutra.* It is reserved specifically for those who are busy with mundane activities, so that they, too, can practice Buddha Recitation and achieve rebirth in the Pure Land. The method consists of uttering Amitabha Buddha's name approximately ten times each time one inhales and exhales. The real intent behind this practice is to use the breath to concentrate the mind. Depending on the cultivator's breath span, he may recite more than ten utterances or fewer. After ten inhalations/exhalations (or some fifty to one hundred utterances in total) the cultivator may proceed to recite the Transference of Merit stanza: *'I vow to be reborn in the Western Pure Land,/ The nine lotus grades are my parents./ As the lotus flowers bloom, I will see Buddha Amitabha and reach No-Birth,/ Liberating all sentient beings'*... After reciting the stanza, the practitioner bows to the Buddhas three times before retiring. This practice has its roots in the boundless compassion of Buddha Sakyamuni and the Patriarchs. However busy a practitioner is, he can engage in this method and step into the path of liberation. There is one *caveat* about the Ten Recitations method. While inhaling and exhaling, the practitioner should recite the number of utterances with which he feels most comfortable,

without trying to lengthen or shorten his normal breath span. Otherwise he might develop a respiratory ailment."

Tam: 232

NOTE:

The *Ten Recitations method* is a universal method (q.v.), truly in the spirit of Mahayana Buddhism because it can be of benefit to persons of the lowest spirituality as well as to those of the highest. To those at a low level, it brings moral comfort, rebirth in the Pure Land while to the highly metaphysically inclined, it is a means to concentrate the Mind, achieve samadhi and ultimately Buddhahood.

Editor: na #1757

◙ TEN REGAL VOWS
see   Ten Great Vows

◙ TEN SINS
see   Ten Evil Deeds

◙ TEN STAGES/ BHUMI
Syn: Ten Grounds; Bhumi
See also: Fifty-two Levels of Bodhisattva Practice; Dasabumika Sutra

----

▸"Ten Stages (or Ten Bhumi) through which the practitioner advances in Buddhist practice. In the system of the fifty-two (or fifty-three) levels of Bodhisattva practice, *they are viewed as the forty-first through fiftieth levels.* There are several 'ten stages' of varying content listed in different scriptures. The *Avatamsaka Sutra* divides Buddhist practice into ten Stages, as follows: (1) the stage of joy (Skt./ Paramudita), in which one rejoices at realizing a partial aspect of the truth; (2) the stage of purity (vimala), in which one is free from all defilement; (3) the stage of the emission of light (prabhakari), in which one radiates the light of wisdom; (4) the stage of glowing (archishmati), in which the flame of wisdom burns away earthly desires; (5) the stage of overcoming final illusions (sudurjaya), in which one surmounts the illusions of darkness, or ignorance as the Middle Way; (6) the stage of the sign of supreme wisdom (abhimukhi), in which supreme wisdom begins to appear; (7) the stage of progression (duramgama), in which one rises above the states of the Two Vehicles; (8) the stage of immobility (achala), in which one dwells firmly in the truth of the Middle Way and cannot be perturbed by anything; (9) the stage of the all-penetrating wisdom (sadhumati), in which one preaches the Law freely and without restriction; and (10) the stage of the [Cloud of Teaching] (dharmamegha), in which one benefits all sentient beings with the Law (Dharma), just as a cloud sends down rain impartially on all things."

Sokk: 439

In other words, "the ten Stages of developing Bodhi-wisdom are (1) joy at benefiting oneself and others, (2) freedom from all possible defilement, (3) the emission of the light of Wisdom, (4) glowing Wisdom, (5) overcoming the utmost difficulties, (6) the realization of Wisdom, (7) proceeding far, (8) the attainment of immobility, (9) the attainment of expedient Wisdom, and (10) the ability to spread the teachings over the Dharmadhatu (the whole universe) as clouds overspread the sky."   Yoko: 214-215

Avatamsaka Sutra

Of the Ten Stages of Bodhisattvahood the first stage is the Stage of Extreme Joy, which is described as follows in the *Avatamsaka Sutra*:

"Here, standing on the stage of extreme joy of Bodhisattvas, one is filled with extreme joy, filled with calm, filled with happiness,

filled with ebullience ... One becomes extremely joyful, thinking of the Buddha [Buddha-recitation], of the Buddha's teaching ... Thus thinking, the Bodhisattva gives rise to extreme joy. Why? Because that is what happens to all fears with the Bodhisattva's attainment of the stage of joy -- fears such as fear of not surviving, fear of ill-repute, fear of death, fear of falling into the Evil Realms, fear of intimidation by groups ... thus all fears and terrors are removed." (T. Cleary, tr., *The Flower Ornament Sutra*.)
Clear: II/15
NOTE:
In current Buddhist usage, the word "stage" is sometimes used for any of the fifty-two levels of Bodhisattva practice and not necessarily for one of the ten Bhumis (the 41st through the 50th levels). The reader should therefore keep the distinction in mind when studying Mahayana texts.
Editor: na #0287

◎ **TEN STAGES SUTRA**
see Dasabhumika Sutra

◎ **TEN STAGES SUTRA (COMMENTARY ON THE)**
See also: Dasabhumika Sutra; Easy Path of Practice; Rebirth Treatise

----

▸"Very few treatises on Pure Land have been found in India. In fact the only extant work devoted exclusively to Amitabha Pure Land Buddhism is the fifth-century work attributed to Vasubandhu (Vn/ Thế-Thân) that survives only in its Chinese translation, the *Rebirth Treatise*. There are, however, a few older writings that comment on aspects of Pure Land doctrine. Among these, the earliest documents are attributed to Nagarjuna (hence, dated around 200), the *Ta Chih Tu Lun* (*Great Perfection of Wisdom Treatise*) and the *Commentary on the Ten Stages Sutra*. In the latter text's chapter on 'Easy Practice,' the author discusses the attainment of the non-retrogressive state and then distinguishes two paths. The first follows the 'easy practice' (i-hsing) of devotion, which is likened to riding on a vessel over water. The 'difficult' (nan) path resembles a person walking on land to his destination. Amitabha is one among numerous transcendent Buddhas to whom devotion of easy practice may be directed. In East Asia, the distinction between the difficult

and the easy path served as one of the primary doctrinal bases for the establishment of Pure Land as an independent school."
Tana: 11 #2314
For details, see Easy Practice chapter.

◉ **TEN THOUSAND**
See also: Ichinen Mannen

►In Buddhism, ten thousand generally stands for a limitless number. #1814

◉ **TEN THOUSAND CONDUCTS**

►Metaphor for all the countless beneficial activities and cultivation practices of the Bodhisattvas.
Tam: 350 #0973

◉ **TEN VIRTUES**
see   Ten Precepts

◉ **TEN WORLDS**
see   Ten Realms

◉ **TENDAI SCHOOL**
see   T'ien-t'ai school

◉ **TESTIMONIALS (PURE LAND)**
aee Hagiographies

◉ **THAILAND (*BUDDHISM IN*)**
"Sri Lankan Theravada was established as the predominant tradition in Thailand in the fourteenth century. Today Thai Buddhism is highly hierarchic and organized. It also comes under a degree of state supervision and the king is the Supreme Patriarch. Not surprisingly, therefore, the local 'church' has its radicals and reformers as well as its unbending conservatives. Much of its vitality, however, lies away from the towns and cities in rural forest areas where serious practitioners are ordained and get down to the real business of doing Buddhism. One well-known modern master of the forest tradition is Ajahn Chah, who has trained many Western monks, notably Ajahn Sumedho, the American founder of four new Theravada monasteries in Britain and others elsewhere."
Snell/Buddhism: 27
For details, *See also:* "Theravada Buddhism" (Note)

◉ **THANGKA**
See also: Pure Land Mandalas

►"(Than-ka) roughly 'picture, painting.' In Esoteric and Tibetan Buddhism, a scroll painting framed in silk, which fulfills various religious functions. The themes of

iconography are fixed by tradition and are based on three principles: expression, proportion, detail. Commissioning the painting of thangka and the painting itself are considered highly meritorious actions. The images are painted on linen with vegetable- and mineral-based pigments. In some cases they serve as visual reminders of general Buddhist teachings -- examples are the wheel of life and depictions of the previous existences of the Buddha. In other cases thangkas play an important ritual role -- as, for example, detailed paintings of central personalities of a particular school being used in the Three Refuges Ceremony. However, the most important role of the thangka is connected with the performance of sadhanas (meditations), where the picture functions as a support for memory in the process of visualization. Painted mandalas fulfill the same purpose."
Sham: 223-224　#0352

◉ **THEOSOPHICAL SOCIETY**

▸"Founded in New York in 1875 by Henry Steel Olcott and Madame Blavatsky; an organization dedicated to popularizing Eastern spirituality in the West."
Reat: 346　#2100

◉ **THERAGATHA/ THERIGATHA**
See also: Women

▸*'The Theragatha* consists of a collection of verses (gatha) attributed to some 250 senior (thera) monks, of early Buddhism, renowned for their spiritual attainments and virtue. Similarly the *Therigatha* is a collection of verses attributed to 'senior' (thera) nuns of the same period. The two collections form part of the *Khuddaka-Nikaya*, which is part of the Sutta-Pitaka of the Buddhist Pali canon."
Ling: 243
I - Theragatha:
"The eighth of fifteen collections of texts included in the Khuddaka Nikaya of the Pali Canon. The Theragatha or 'Verses of the Elder Monks,' contains a series of 264 poems attributed to 259 male disciples of the Buddha. They are arranged in twenty-one fascicles, ranging from poems of one verse only up to a final poem of seventy-one verses. The text celebrates the fruits of attainment, including such benefits as freedom from mundane woes and the benefits

of the meditative life."
Preb: 258
II - Therigatha:
Collection of 73 gathas [verses] of elder nuns who became famous through their virtue during the time of Sakyamuni Buddha.

The verses are held by modern scholars to contain authentic compositions of the earliest Buddhist period, although some parts appear to be the work of later redactors on the basis of fragments of reminiscence. The verses are attributed to particular monks or nuns by name. Although such ascriptions may not in every case be entirely correct, in many instances there is sound tradition behind the ascription. Like other early Buddhist literature, they are of value for reconstructing ancient Indian social history. The Theragatha has a total of 1,279 verses; the Therigatha 522. These have been translated into English by C.A.F. Rhys-Davids, the former as *Psalms of the Brethren* (2nd edn. 1937, repr. 1964); the latter as *Psalms of the Sisters* (1909, repr. 1964). [A new translation of part of the Therigatha by Susan Murdock appeared recently as *The First Buddhist Women*]." Ling: 243-244.

A Therigatha story
"Kisagotami was married to a banker's son of considerable wealth. As a young wife, Kisagotami was mistreated by her in-laws ... When she gave birth to a son, she finally received an honorable place among her husband's relatives. But her child died while still a toddler and Kisagotami, who had never seen death before, went mad. In her state of insanity, Kisagotami took up the dead child and carried him on her hip from house to house, begging for medicine. One kind old man directed her to Buddha Sakyamuni. The Buddha said, 'Go and bring a white mustard seed from a house where no one has died.' Hearing his words, she immediately rushed off in the innocent faith that if she brought a white mustard seed to this enlightened sage, it would be the medicine that could miraculously bring her child back to life. Kisagotami went from house to house, at each house asking, and at each house learning that there too, someone had died. The truth struck home. Her sanity returned. 'Little son,' she said. 'I thought that death had happened to you alone; but it is not to you alone. It is common to all people.' ...

She carried him gently to the forest and left him there. (Susan Murdock, *The First Buddhist Women*, p. 85.) #1163

◙ **THERAVADA BUDDHISM**
Syn: Monastic Buddhism; Southern Buddhism; Early Buddhism; Doctrine of the Elders
See also: Mahayana Buddhism; Mahayana / Theravada

▸"One of the two major streams of Buddhism, the other being Mahayana."
Editor: na
"Southern Buddhism. The general name for the early Buddhism propagated after Asoka in the south of India, Sri Lanka, Thailand, Burma, etc. The scriptures preserved in these countries are written in the Pali language and belong to Theravada teachings. Practitioners aim at attaining the state of Arhat."
Dait: 133
"Theravada teaching corresponds to the Agama sutras. These teachings generally hold that the self is without substance, the separate elements (dharmas) are real, and Nirvana is their total annihilation."
Sokk:110

"Southern Buddhism (The early Buddhism). A term coined by Mahayanists to distinguish this school of Buddhism [whose modern descendent is Theravada], from Mahayana. It is distinguished from Mahayana in putting emphasis on one's own liberation, whereas the teaching of Mahayana stresses the attainment of Buddhahood for all sentient beings. Theravada is now prevalent in Southeast Asia, while Mahayana has spread over the northeast area (China, Vietnam, Korea, Japan ...) (G.C.C. Chang)."
Tam: 153
Background
"[Theravada means] the 'Doctrine of the Elders' who formed the 1st Buddhist Council. The sole survivor of the 18 sects into which by the third century B.C. the original primitive School of Buddhism was divided. Until recently this school was known in the West by its generic name of Hinayana, which means smaller or lesser vehicle (of salvation), but this term of reproach, coined by the Mahayanists, has now been dropped in favour of the more accurate and less discourteous name of Theravada, the way of the Elders. As the Theravada school covers Sri

Lanka, Burma, Thailand and Cambodia, it is sometimes called the Southern School, to distinguish it from the Northern or Mahayana School which covers Tibet, Mongolia, China, Korea, Japan and Vietnam, among other countries."
Hump: 197

"After Shakyamuni's death, the Buddhist Order experienced several schisms and eventually split into eighteen or twenty schools. The monks of these schools, in their concern to preserve the Buddha's teachings, tended more and more to seclude themselves in their monasteries, where they devoted themselves to upholding the monastic precepts and writing doctrinal exegeses. Around the end of the first century B.C. or the beginning of the first century A.D., a new group of Buddhists emerged who were dissatisfied with what they perceived as the sterile academicism of the earlier schools. They practiced among the lay people, calling themselves Bodhisattvas, and aimed at the salvation of all people. They called their teachings Mahayana (Great Vehicle), meaning the teaching which can carry many people to enlightenment, and referred to the traditional schools

as the Lesser Vehicle."
Sokk: 157

The dilemma of "Ven. Ajahn Chah [a well know Thai master] reflected a conflict that had beset the Theravada tradition throughout its history in Sri Lanka and Thailand. State support meant that the Buddhist order was guaranteed the material and social security needed to ensure the preservation of the Dharma. But in return the monks were to serve the interests of the State by establishing a moral and spiritual framework whereby the people would live in harmony... This caused the order to fracture into two parts: 'forest monks,' who placed a premium on realizing Nirvana, and 'town monks,' who chose to serve as village priests, administrators in city temples, or scholars and teachers. Once a bhikku's role as a cleric superseded his religious aspirations...the practice of meditation became a luxury for which there was [often] little time and interest."
Tric/Summer/94: 41

NOTES:
Unlike Mahayana schools, the Theravada tradition makes no mention of Amitabha Buddha, the Bodhisattva Avalokitesvara,

etc. or the Pure Land. Theravadins believe mainly in Sakyamuni Buddha and the Bodhisattva Maitreya, but not in the numerous transhistorical Buddhas and Bodhisattvas of the Mahayana tradition. This is because Theravada stresses the historical Buddha and His early teachings, applying the term Bodhisattva mainly to the previous incarnations of Buddha Sakyamuni.   Editor/Zen: 65

Please note that the difference between "meditative forest monks" and "town monks" has been deliberately emphasized to draw home a point. In practice they can be viewed as monks of different specializations, the first group stressing *wisdom* (the result of meditation) and the second *compassion* (serving one's community). As such they are the two indispensable wings of the bird of enlightenment -- of Buddhahood.   Editor: na
For details, *See also:* Mahayana/Theravada. #0169

◙ **THERIGATHA**
see Theragatha/Therigatha

◙ **THIÊN-ÂN, THÍCH (1926-80)**

▸"Late Vietnamese Zen master

and scholar active in the U.S. Trained in the Lin-chi (Rinzai) tradition, but adopted ecumenical approach. 1966: came to USA; lectured at UCLA. 1967: began to teach in Hollywood. Founded International Buddhist Meditation Center and in 1973, College (later University) of Oriental Studies, Los Angeles. 1975: after [the political changeover of 1975], active in helping Vietnamese refugees to U.S." Snel: 305 #0749

◙ **THIEVES**
See also: Consciousnesses

▸"The three poisons (greed, anger and delusion) are present in our six sense organs as six kinds of consciousness, or thieves. They're called thieves because they pass in and out of the gates of the senses, covet limitless possessions, engage in evil, and mask their true identity. And because mortals are misled in body and mind by these poisons or thieves, they become lost in life and death, wander through the six states of existence, and suffer countless afflictions." Pine: 81 #1902

◙ **THIRD LIFETIME**
See also: Karma; No Good Deed

Goes Unpunished

►A general Buddhist Teaching which can be summarized as follows: In the first lifetime, the practitioner engages in mundane good deeds which bring ephemeral worldly blessings (wealth, power, authority, etc.) in the second lifetime. Since power tends to corrupt, he is likely to create evil karma, resulting in retribution in the third lifetime. Thus good deeds in the first lifetime are potential 'enemies' of the third lifetime.

To ensure that mundane good deeds do not become 'enemies,' the practitioner should dedicate all merits to a transcendental goal, i.e., to become Bodhisattvas or Buddhas or, in Pure Land teaching to achieve rebirth in the Pure Land -- a Buddha-land beyond Birth and Death. In the mundane context, these three lifetimes can be conceived of as three generations. Thus, the patriarch of a prominent family, through work and luck, amasses great power, fortune and influence (first lifetime). His children are then able to enjoy a leisurely, and, too often, dissipated life (second lifetime). By the generation of the grandchildren, the family's fortune and good reputation have all but disappeared (third lifetime).

Editor/Tam: 163-164

A Case history
"When you look at the *third generation* of Kennedy men, much of what remains of a once powerful dynasty is good teeth, good hair and the best public relations a trust fund can buy. Some of the boys grew up being spoiled and bratty--belittling the help, once chasing the cook up a tree at Hickory Hill--into full-blown debauchery, driving fast, drinking hard, club hopping like wild men. Most of this got spun up by family retainers into the playful high jinks of a raucous clan. But the escapades got seamier over time when Joe Kennedy II left a young woman paralyzed after an accident on Nantucket. Bobby Jr. was arrested for possession of heroin. David died in a Florida hotel of a cocaine, Demerol and Mellaril overdose..." *Time*: May 12 '97

NOTE:
The concept of the Third Lifetime is the basis of the Pure Land School emphasis on seeking rebirth in the Pure Land in this lifetime, rather than relying on

gradual cultivation, lifetime after lifetime, as in Zen and other schools.
Editor: na   #0930

◉ **THIRTY-SEVEN AIDS TO ENLIGHTENMENT**
see   Thirty-seven Limbs of Enlightenment

◉ **THIRTY-SEVEN LIMBS OF ENLIGHTENMENT**
Syn: Thirty-seven Aids to Enlightenment

▶"These are: (1) the four mindfulnessess; (2) the four right efforts; (3) the four bases of miraculous powers; (4) the five roots; (5) the five powers; (6) the seven factors of enlightenment; and (7) the eightfold noble path."
Chan: 495   #0931

◉ **THIRTY-THREE-FOLD HEAVEN**
see   Heaven of the Thirty-Three

◉ **THIRTY-TWO AUSPICIOUS MARKS**
see   Thirty-two Auspicious signs

◉ **THIRTY-TWO AUSPICIOUS SIGNS**
Syn: Thirty-two Auspicious Marks
See also: Urna;   Eighty

Auspicious Marks

▶"Remarkable physical characteristics possessed by great beings such as Buddhas and wheel-turning kings."
Wats: 339-340
"The major signs adorning the visible body of a Buddha or that of a universal monarch. Some examples are: a protuberance on the crown; a curling, white hair between the eyebrows; a golden complexion; a long, broad tongue; a halo ten feet in radius; an excellent voice."
Chan: 495

Background
"These auspicious marks of great persons originated outside Buddhism and were later adopted as features of the Buddha. Interest in the marks increased in the first century A.D. when the widespread practice of visualization focused on the use of Buddha images with these auspicious marks. These marks include a white hair between the eyebrows, light from between the eyebrows, Buddha's circle of light, a mound of flesh on the head... Several versions of the thirty-two marks are found in Buddhist texts, and those attributes that were not included

among the 32 were eventually grouped together to make up the 80 auspicious marks."
Tana: 241 #1737

◙ **THREE BODIES OF PURE PRECEPTS**
Syn: Three Comprehensive Precepts; Three Kinds of Pure Precepts
See also: Bodhisattva Precepts; Brahma Net Sutra

▸Three goups of precepts which form the basis of all Bodhisattva practice: (1) Do not what is evil, (2) Do what is good and (3) Be of benefit to all sentient beings. All Bodhisattva precepts and vows, *or* for that matter, all precepts derive ultimately from the Three Bodies of Pure Precepts. These precepts may in principle be administered to Buddhists in lieu of the full set of Bodhisattva precepts described in the *Brahma Net Sutra.*
Editor: na
Illustrative Story:
"The *Maha-Maya Sutra* (T 17.585b-586a) recounts the tale of Malika, the wife of King Prasenajit, who lies, seductively adorns her body, entertains, and serves wine to the king. These unlawful things she does in order to mollify the king's anger and keep him from taking the life of a cook who has angered him. Because her motives were wholesome and pure, the Buddha praises her actions. Chan-jan (T 46.205a4-7) notes: 'This [story] tells of breaking the precepts to save beings because of the Bodhisattva's basic desire to benefit others. As such, it is known as 'good in the midst of evil.' . . . Anyone wishing to follow this example must assess his or her motives judiciously. If one is just indulging desire, it is not on the order of observance of the precepts.'"
Donner & Stevenson: 309 #1270

◙ **THREE BODIES OF THE BUDDHA**
Syn: Trikaya
See Dharma body; Nirmanakaya

▸"Three kinds of body which a Buddha may possess. A concept adopted in Mahayana to organize different concepts of the Buddha appearing in the sutras."
Sokk: 448

The three bodies are:
1. *D h a r m a k a y a :* the Dharma-body, or the "body of reality", which is formless, unchanging, transcendental, and inconceivable. Synonymous with

suchness, or emptiness.

2. *Sambhogakaya:* the "body of enjoyment," the celestial body of the Buddha. Personification of eternal perfection in its ultimate sense. It "resides in the Pure Land and never manifests itself in the mundane world, but only in the celestial spheres, accompanied by enlightened Bodhisattvas."

3. *Nirmanakaya:* the "incarnated body" of the Buddha. In order to benefit certain sentient beings, a Buddha incarnates himself into an appropriate visible body, such as that of Sakyamuni Buddha. The incarnated body of the Buddha should not be confused with a magically produced Buddha. The former is a real, tangible human body which has a definite life span. The latter is an illusory Buddha-form which is produced by miraculous powers and can be withdrawn by miraculous powers (G.C.C. Chang).

Tam: 164-165 #0288

◙ **THREE COMPREHENSIVE PRECEPTS**
see Three Bodies of Pure Precepts

◙ **THREE CONCENTRATIONS**
see Three Doors to Liberation

◙ **THREE DHARMA SEALS**
see Dharma Seals

◙ **THREE DIVISIONS OF THE BUDDHA'S TEACHINGS**
see Three vehicles (yana)

◙ **THREE DOORS TO LIBERATION**
Syn: Three Emptinesses, Three Doors to Concentration
See also: Dharma Seals (last section)

►"Liberation is possible only through these three realizations: 1. All things are devoid of a self (emptiness). 2. There are no objects to be perceived by sense-organs (signlessness). 3. No wish of any kind whatsoever remains in the practitioner's mind, for he no longer needs to strive for anything (wishlessness)."

Chan: 488 #0596

◙ **THREE DOUBTS AND FOUR NARROW PASSES**
See also: Rebirth in the Pure Land; Death; Love / Sex

►"Elder Master Tzu Chao once said: The Pure Land practitioner on the verge of death usually faces *Three Points of Doubt and Four Narrow Passes* which

obstruct his rebirth in the Pure Land. He should be prepared, reflecting on them in advance to eliminate them.

The Three Points of Doubt are: 1) Fearing that his past karma is heavy and his period of cultivation short, and that therefore, he may not achieve rebirth in the Pure Land; 2) Fearing that he has not yet fulfilled his vows and obligations or severed greed, anger and delusion, and that therefore, he may not achieve rebirth in the Pure Land. 3) Fearing that even though he has recited the Buddha's name, Buddha Amitabha may not come, and that therefore, he may not achieve rebirth in the Pure Land.

The main Narrow Passes are: 1) Because of suffering due to illness, he may come to malign the Buddhas as ineffective and unresponsive; 2) Because of love-attachment, he may chain himself to his family, unable to let go.

Once aware of the doctrine of the Three Doubts and the Four Narrow Paths, the wise can ponder and find a solution. The author shall merely summarize a few points below. Fellow cultivators can expand on them according to their own backgrounds and understanding.

(I) *Overcoming the Three Doubts*

1. *Previous heavy karma*, present perfunctory practice. Amitabha Buddha is renowned for his Eighteenth Vow: not to attain Buddhahood unless sentient beings who sincerely desire to be reborn in the Pure Land, and who singlemindedly recite His name, are reborn there. The Buddhas do not engage in false speech, and therefore the practitioner should believe in them. Ten utterances or thoughts represent a very short cultivation period, yet the practitioner can still achieve rebirth in the Pure Land. We who have recited the Buddha's name many times over should, therefore, eliminate all doubts. Moreover, no matter how heavy the karma of sentient beings is, if they sincerely repent and rely upon Amitabha Buddha, they will all be welcomed and guided back to the Pure Land. Do we not recall that the *Meditation Sutra* teaches: If anyone who has commited the Five Grave Offenses or Ten Evil Deeds sees an evil omen appear as he is on the verge of death, he need only recite the Buddha's name one to ten times, *singlemindedly*, and Buddha Amitabha will descend to

welcome and escort him back to the Pure Land. In the commentary *Accounts of Rebirth*, there are cases of individuals who throughout their lives were breaking the precepts (particularly the precept against killing) and on their deathbeds, when the 'marks of hell' appeared and, desperate, they singlemindedly recited the Buddha's name, they immediately saw Amitabha Buddha arriving to welcome them. Why should we, who are not that sinful or deluded, worry about not achieving rebirth in the Pure Land?

2. *Unfulfilled vows*; non-severance of greed, anger and delusion. Cultivators' vows can be divided into two categories: religious and mundane. *Religious vows*: Some practitioners have vowed to build a temple, practice charity or recite various sutras or mantras a certain number of times, etc. However, they have not completely fulfilled their vows when it is time for them to die. These cultivators should think: reciting the Buddha's name in all earnestness will earn them rebirth in the Pure Land, where they will have ample opportunity to achieve immeasurable merits and virtues. Their present vows to build temples and recite sutras are merely secondary matters. The fact that they may not have fulfilled them should be of no great concern.

Mundane vows: These include family obligations such as caring for sick, aging parents or helpless wives and young children, as well as business debts to be paid or certain other commitments to be fulfilled. Faced with these worries, the practitioner should think: on our deathbed, there is nothing that can be done, whether we worry or not. It is better to concentrate on Buddha Recitation. Once we are reborn in the Pure Land and Buddhahood is achieved, all vows, wishes and debts can be taken care of, as we will be in a position to rescue everyone, family and foes alike. The *Questions of King Milinda Sutra* contains the following parable: A minute grain of sand, dropped on the surface of the water, will sink immediately. On the other hand, a block of stone, however large and heavy, can easily be moved from place to place by boat. The same is true of the Pure Land practitioner. However light his karma may be, if he is not rescued by Amitabha Budddha, he must revolve in the cycle of Birth and Death. With the help of Amitabha Buddha, his karma, however heavy, will not prevent his rebirth in the Pure Land. We can see from this passage that thanks to 'other-power,' the Pure Land method can benefit the practitioner, however heavy his karma may be. The huge block of stone represents the weight of heavy karma, the boat symbolizes the power of Amitabha Buddha's Vows. Therefore, the cultivator should not think that residual greed, anger and delusion will prevent him from achieving rebirth in the Pure Land. This example should also resolve doubts concerning past heavy karma, as in doubts number one above. 3. Despite recitation, Amitabha Buddha may not come, after all. At the time of death, the Pure Land practitioner will see, depending on his virtues, Amitabha Buddha, the Bodhisattvas or the Ocean-Wide Assembly come to welcome him. Sometimes he may not see anything, but, thanks to the power of his vows and the 'gathering in' power of Amitabha Buddha, he will be reborn in the Pure Land all the same. The difference lies in his level of cultivation, whether subtle or gross, transcendental or mundane. What is most important at the time of death is to recite the Buddha's name singlemindedly and in all earnestness and not worry about anything else. Any doubts at that time will give rise to obstructions and impediments. In summary, at the time of death, the practitioner should not be concerned about whether or not he witnesses auspicious signs. He should just concentrate on reciting the Buddha's name in all earnestness until the very end.

(II) *Overcoming the Narrow Passes* These 'passes' can be summarized as follows:
(1) - Slandering the Buddhas because of suffering and disease and (2) - Binding and chaining oneself to family and friends through love-attachment. Sincere practitioners who meet accidents, disease and disaster should reflect that these are sometimes due to virtues accrued through cultivation. Either the heavy karma (which he should have endured) has been commuted to light karma (which he is now enduring), or else, future karma has been transformed into current karma, giving him the

opportunity to repay karmic debts before achieving rebirth in the Pure Land. Should he doubt this and speak ill of the Dharma, he would lack faith and understanding, display ingratitute toward the Buddhas, and bring evil karma upon himself. Among the rebirth stories, we find instances where this 'bunching and compressing of karma' has allowed cultivators to hasten their rebirth in the Pure Land. Therefore, when Pure Land cultivators encounter such instances, they should be aware and understand them thoroughly. Furthermore, this body is illusory and provisional. Depending on his merit or bad karma, the practitioner's life will be long or short, happy or filled with hardship. He should systematically rely on the Buddhas and firmly believe in the law of cause and effect. When ill or in bad health, the practitioner should direct his thoughts toward Amitabha Buddha exclusively. He should not seek the help of externalist gurus, shamans or healers. Nor should he listen to those who do not yet understand the Dharma and revert to a non-vegetarian diet, drink alcoholic beverages, etc... His mind will then be calm and undisturbed at the time of death."
635

Thich: 276-281 #1415

◉ THREE EMPTINESS
see Three Doors to Liberation

◉ THREE EVIL PATHS
Syn: Evil Planes of Existence; Evil Paths; Evil Realms

►"The three lower states of Samsara: hell-dweller, hungry ghost, and animal. To be born in a miserable state is the result of evil karma committed in a past life. When the retribution for that karma is completed, one will again be born in a higher state."
Chan: 479

The paths of hells, hungry ghosts, animality. These paths can be taken as states of mind; i.e., when someone has a vicious thought of maiming or killing another, he is effectively reborn, *for that moment*, in the hells.
Tam: 221

"According to Buddhist teachings, karmic results follow ineluctably upon the perpetration of acts, irrespective of conscious attitude or moral conscience (although the quality and force of the act may be significantly affected thereby). Thus beings in the lower states, animals for

example, do indeed accumulate karma and must sooner or later experience the consequences of their actions, even though these may be performed under the irresistible influence of instinct. And the Karmic situation is compounded, rather than mitigated, by an unconsciousness of the Dharma. The strength of instinctual habit and the ignorance of what behavior is to be adopted and what behavior is to be abandoned constitutes one of the principal miseries of existence in states other than that of the precious human condition."
Shantideva: 198 #0539

◎ **THREE JEWELS**
see   Three Treasures

◎ **THREE KINDS OF PURE PRECEPTS**
see   Three Bodies of Pure Precepts

◎ **THREE KINGDOMS PERIOD (200-668)**

▸"A period of conflict among three contending dynasties for Korean domination (Koguryo, Paekche and Silla); not to be confused with the Three Kingdoms period of Chinese history (c. 220-80)." Reat: 346

◎ **THREE MARKS OF EXISTENCE**

▸ An expression meaning Three Dharma Seals (q.v.)

◎ **THREE MYSTERIES**
Syn: Three Secrets
See also: Esoteric school

▸"In esoteric Buddhism this term refers to the body, speech, and mind of the Buddha, which are regarded as secret because they are not fully known to ordinary men. An enlightened man can realize the three secrets as a religious ritual by making a mudra with his hand, uttering a mantra, and contemplating an esoteric deity."
Dait: 276

"Also called the Three Secrets. According to the Shingon (q.v.) teaching, since Maha-Vairocana (Dainichi) Buddha is held to be omnipresent, all beings are the mystic body of the Buddha, all sounds the mystic mouth (i.e., voice) of the Buddha, and all thoughts the mystic mind of the Buddha.
However, the Buddha's body, mouth and mind are unimaginably profound and beyond the common mortal's

understanding. Therefore they are called 'mysteries.' Moreover, the body, mouth and mind of common mortals are not essentially different from those of the Buddha, although their Buddha nature is clouded by illusion. In this sense, the body, mouth and mind of the common mortal in their essential aspect are also called the three mysteries. In terms of practice, esoteric teaching defines the mystic body to be the making of mudras with the hands, the mystic mouth to be the uttering of mantras (mystic words), and the mystic mind to be meditation on an esoteric mandala or one of the figures appearing on it. Through the medium of these three practices, the body, mouth and mind of the common mortal are said to be united with those of Vairocana Buddha, enabling the sincere practitioner to attain Buddhahood in his present form." Sokk: 460

Three Mysteries (3 Secrets)

"The *secret of body* finds expression in various hand gestures (mudra), meditation postures, and the use of certain ritual implements, such as vajra or lotus, that are associated with one or another Buddha or Bodhisattva being invoked. The *secret of speech* is related to the recitation of mantras and dharanis; the *secret of mind*, to the 'five wisdoms,' which make the comprehension of reality possible, and to samadhi. Through particular rituals, which are rooted in these three secrets, a connection between the practitioner and a particular Buddha is brought about, through which the state of 'Buddha in me, me in Buddha' can be realized; i.e., Buddhahood [in principle] can be attained in this lifetime." Sham: 198

"For Tantric Buddhists, the elimination of all duality -- the experience of fundamental unity in enlightenment -- is symbolized by the vajra." Sham: 242 #0291

◙ **THREE NON-OUTFLOW STUDIES**

Syn: Three-Fold Training; Three Pillars; Three Practices of N o n - O u t f l o w ; Precepts-Meditation-Wisdom

See also: Dead tree Samadhi

▸"The three inseparable aspects of the practice of Buddhism are (1) Precepts: training in moral discipline, (2) Samadhi: training the mind, and (3) Wisdom: training in wisdom (prajna). These three areas of training cover the entire Buddhist teaching." Sham: 231

"In Buddhism, there is no cultivation without discipline, concentration and wisdom, and also there is no Dharma without discipline, concentration and wisdom." (Hsu Heng Chi, *What's Buddhism?*, p.39.)

"If people want to get rid of anger or greed, they can't do it without wisdom. Greed, anger, and stupidity are called the 'Three Poisons' and are also called 'thieving afflictions.' These thieving afflictions can be arrested through Precepts, Samadhi, and Wisdom. With precepts, you can capture the thief at the source. You will be able to recognize the source of the affliction. With samadhi, you can suppress the thieves. You will be able to keep them in one place so that they won't go wild. But at this point, although you have caught them and bound them, you haven't yet extinguished them. You've got to destroy these thieves so that they will never rise again. Only wisdom can terminate afflictions."

Brahma Net/Commentary: 13

"We must also recognize that this discipline, concentration, and wisdom are equivalent to the Dharma gate of Buddha-Recitation. How so? Discipline [precept-keeping] means preventing wrongdoing. If you can wholeheartedly practice Buddha-remembrance, evil will not dare to enter: this is discipline. Concentration means eliminating the scattering characteristic of ordinary mind. If you wholeheartedly practice Buddha-remembrance, mind does not have any other object: this is concentration. Wisdom means clear perception. If you contemplate the sound of the Buddha's name with each syllable distinct, and also contemplate that the one who is mindful and the object of this mindfulness are both unattainable, this is wisdom." (Master Zhuhong in *Pure Land, Pure Mind*.)

Dia: 154,155 #0405

◙ **THREE PERIODS OF TIME**
Syn: Three Time Periods

▸"The past, the present, and the future. An expression used abstractly to mean 'all time,' or 'for all time.'" Gomez/96: 329

◙ **THREE PERSONAL PROVISIONS**
see Provisions For Pure Land Rebirth

◙ **THREE PILLARS**
see Three Non-Outflow Studies

◙ **THREE POISONS**

▸"Greed, anger, delusion. Sometimes translated as avarice, anger and ignorance. The fundamental evils inherent in life which give rise to human suffering. The three poisons are regarded as the source of all illusions and earthly desires. The three poisons are so called because they pollute people's lives."
Sokk: 464
"The major causes of samsaric suffering:
1. *Desire* (Skt./ kama, raga, or *trsna*): lust or greed. Broadly, to try to 'get hold of' something, and to have more and more of it. In its most specific sense, *trsna* refers to sexual craving. Desire can also mean avarice or any kind of attachment.
2. *Hatred or anger* (Skt./ dvesa): animosity, aversion, rejection of what displeases one or infringes upon one's ego.
3. *Ignorance or delusion* (Skt./ avidya, moha): eradication of ignorance or delusion in Mahayana requires, on the one hand, elimination of wrong views, and on the other, the positive acquisition of all-knowing wisdom."
Chan: 488 #0153

◙ **THREE PRACTICES OF NON-OUTFLOW**
see Three Non-Outflow Studies

◙ **THREE PURE LAND *SAGES***

▸"The three Pure Land divinities, Amitabha Buddha and his two Bodhisattva attendants--Avalokitesvara and Mahastamaprapta. These three divinities are believed to welcome the departed into the Pure Land. In some rare instances Ksitigarbha takes the place of Mahastamaprapta."
Dait: 8 #0082

◙ **THREE PURE LAND *SUTRAS***
See also: Pratyupanna Samadhi; Amitabha Sutra; Longer Amitabha Sutra; Meditation Sutra; Pure Land School

----

▸Pure Land Buddhism is based on three basic sutras:
a) *Amitabha Sutra* (or *Shorter Amitabha Sutra*, or *Smaller Sukhavati-Vyuha*, or the *Sutra of Amida*);
b) *Longer Amitabha Sutra* (or *Longer Sukhavati-Vyuha*, the *Sutra of Infinite Life, Muryoju-kyo*);

c) *Meditation Sutra* (or the *Meditation on the Buddha of Infinite Life*, the *Amitayur Dhyana Sutra, Kammuryoju-kyo*). The last chapter of the *Avatamsaka Sutra* ("The Practices and Vows of the Bodhisattva Samantabhadra") is sometimes considered the fourth basic sutra of the Pure Land tradition. (*Note*: Master T'ai Hsu, the famous Chinese monk who organized the revival of Buddhism in China between the Wars, taught that the *Longer Amitabha Sutra* is a shorter form of the *Lotus Sutra*.) Editor/Tam: 165

"Of the many Mahayana sutras that have at least some mention of the (or a) Pure Land, three are given special prominence in Pure Land Buddhism, as they are wholly concerned with Amitabha's Pure Land. Two sutras, which exist in Sanskrit and have the same title of *Sukhavativyuha*, are commonly referred to as 'larger' and 'smaller' because of their great difference in length. The third sutra exists only in Chinese, and is known by its short title of *Kuan Ching* (*Meditation Sutra*). It is also referred to by the reconstructed Sanskrit title *Amitayur-Dhyana Sutra*." Yoshi/Corless: 250

Background

"Metaphoric interpretations of the Pure Land abound. To some believers, the Land of Bliss, the Pure Land, is an ideal state of being. Some regard Pure Land as the Pure Mind. I read the two *Amitabha Sutras* as stories told for many ends. They entertain and delight, they generate images of wonder and hope, they speak of worlds and ideals of the spirit. But they are also stories about a place, its origin, and its very concrete way of being. Hence, it is difficult, if not impossible, to read the two sutras without envisioning the place. One would like to draw -- in the imagination and on paper -- the layout of purified buddha-fields, trying to depict those features that make them unique, different from those world systems that are easily schematized. Pure Land believers have envisioned such worlds. [The Taima Mandala/ q.v.] is one example of the fruits of this exercise in imagination. It claims to represent the Pure Land of Amitabha as depicted in the *Meditation Sutra*.

Yet, in some ways the two *Amitabha Sutras* challenge the imagination by refusing to close this image of a place, a land, or a world. Unlike the scholastic cosmographies, the sutras do not give dimensions, nor do they give us all the details as to the location of each feature and event in the Land of Bliss. This is as it should be, because this land is a world of many wonders, occuring in different parts, at different times...and the Land is, like the sutras, an ever-changing panorama, a flowing array of marvels.

The two *Amitabha Sutras*, in particular the *Longer Sutra*, present us with images of a buddha-field that coalesce in a single narrative and evoke concrete visions of a paradisiacal land, yet never quite give us a final or closed map of this land. Unlike traditional cosmographies, which seem to have required a closed world with definite dimensions and borders, the geographies of Sukhavati tell us more about the ways in which it is not like a normal world system than they do about how this alternative world is laid out and defined. Traditional representations of the Pure Land seldom depict boundaries, never assume the Pure Land must have a foundation or closure above or around its gardens."

Gomez/Land: 25

"Whatever differences scholars may find between the Three Pure Land Sutras (q.v.), they are regarded as complementary by Pure Land practitioners. The picture (literally, for it appears often in Pure Land Buddhist art) that then emerges is somewhat as follows: Far beyond the setting sun, beyond all the troubles of Samsara, there is an intensely beautiful, sparklingly pure realm called Sukhavati, the Land of Unalloyed Happiness. It is ruled over by an all-wise and all compassionate Buddha whose life and wisdom are immeasurable, and who is therefore called both Amitayus and Amitabha or, for short, just Amitabha ('Immeasurable'). He sits on an immense throne, higher than many cosmic mountains, and although he himself is dressed in the simple robes of a monk, his throne is richly hung with draperies and set with rare jewels. On either side of him are his chief Bodhisattvas, the greatly compassionate Avalokitesvara and the greatly powerful Mahasthamaprapta, and in front of him is a lake covered with lotus buds continually opening to reveal those newly born into Sukhavati. All around him are jeweled palaces, jeweled trees,

and lakes full of jewel-like and perfumed water, and the air is filled with divine music and heavenly incense. All the inhabitants, once they fully emerge from their lotus buds, are great Bodhisattvas only one lifetime away from perfect liberation and they have beautiful, ethereal bodies, as if 'walking in an Air of glory'. The land is flat and even, without boundaries or obstacles, and as limitless as space. If one wishes to be reborn in that marvelous place, one does not have to leave home and become a monk or nun, or meditate far into the night. One merely has to focus one's mind... on Amitabha and Sukhavati, and recite Nam-mo O-mi-t'o fo! at least ten times [singlemindedly at the time of death]. Then because of the wonderfully powerful fruiting of his Bodhisattva Resolve, Amitabha Buddha will ensure that one is reborn in his realm, and one can proceed without delay to one's own enlightenment and then quickly return to Samsara to help other beings, until Samsara is emptied."
Yoshi/Corless: 253
NOTE:
There is a 1996 English language edition of the *Longer* and *Shorter*

Amitabha Sutras entitled the *Land of Bliss*. Each sutra is translated with commentaries and notes from both the Sanskrit and Chinese by Luis O. Gomez (University of Michigan). #0292

◙ **THREE REALMS**
see   Triple Realm

◙ **THREE REFUGES**
Syn: Refuge (Take --); Threefold Refuge; Taking Refuge

▸"The Buddha, the Dharma, and the Sangha are the three refuges in which Buddhists put their trust and reliance."
Chan: 481 #0555

◙ **THREE SECRETS**
see   Three mysteries

◙ **THREE SPHERES OF PURITY**

▸"'Three Spheres Pure,' 'i.e., no giver, no receiver, no gift.' No attachment to giver, receiver or gift. Emptiness of absolute existence of subject, object and medium; usually applied to giving without attachment to the giver, the receiver or the gift."
[TC/ p. 448]n
The expression usually refers to the Paramita or Perfection of Charity (dana-paramita), but

applies to all paramitas as well.
Editor: na   #1269

◙ **THREE TIME PERIODS**
see   Three Periods of Time

◙ **THREE TREASURES**
Syn: Three Jewels; Triple Jewel

►"1. The Buddha--the supremely
enlightened being. 2. The
Dharma--the teaching imparted
by Buddha. 3. The Sangha--the
congregation of monks and nuns,
or of genuine Dharma followers."
Chan: 488   #0597

◙ **THREE TRUTHS (T'IEN-T'AI)**
Syn: Three-Fold Truth
See also: Middle Way Philosophy;
T'ien-T'ai school

►"The T'ien-t'ai school teaches
that a phenomenon can be
viewed in three different ways
within the same instant. First,
because a phenomenon is
produced by various causes, its
essence is devoid of any
permanent existence, that is, it is
'empty.' Second, nevertheless it
does have a real, if only
temporary, immediate existence.
Third, since a phenomenon is
thus a blending of both ultimate
emptiness and temporary
existence, it should be seen as

occupying a position midway
between the two poles."
Yoko: 215-216
The *Three-Fold Truth* (or Three
Truths) refers to emptiness,
conditional existence and the
Middle Way, meaning that things
are not ultimately existent or
non-existent.
Editor: na   #2157

◙ **THREE VEHICLES (YANA)**
Syn: Three   Yanas;   Three
Divisions   of   the   Buddha's
Teachings

►"In Mahayana Buddhism these
are (1) the Sravakayana or
Theravada, in which one rightly
understands   and   practices   the
Four Noble Truths and becomes
a n   A r h a t ;   (2)   t h e
Pratyekabuddhayana, in which
one   rightly   understands   and
practices the Twelve Links of
Causation   and   becomes   a
Pratyekabuddha; and (3) the
Bodhisattvayana or Mahayana, in
which one becomes a Buddha as
a result of religious practice over
innumerable years."
Yoko: 190
NOTE:
The Tantric tradition sometimes
referred   to   as   Vajrayana
(Diamond Vehicle) is part of
Mahayana Buddhism. #0600

◙ **THREE WORTHY POSITIONS**
See also: Fifty-Two Levels of Bodhisattva Practice

▸*Avatamsaka Sutra*
Name for levels 11-40 within the "Fifty-Two levels of Bodhisattva Practice"(q.v.), corresponding to the *Ten Dwellings* (or Abodes), *Ten Practices* (Conducts) and *Ten Dedications* (Transferences). The preliminary levels (or levels 1-10) of Bodhisattvahood (Ten Faiths) while *de facto* included, are not listed explicitly, inasmuch as the concept of Three Worthy Positions refers to advanced Bodhisattvas.
Editor: na   #1268

◙ **THREE YANAS**
see   Three vehicles (yana)

◙ **THREE-FOLD TRAINING**
see   Three Non-Outflow Studies

◙ **THREE-THOUSAND- GREAT-THOUSAND WORLDS**
see   Billion-world universe; World System

◙ **THREEFOLD REFUGE**
see   Three Refuges

◙ **THREEFOLD WORLD**
see   Triple Realm

◙ **THRONES**
see   Seats, thrones, and residences

◙ **THỦ-LĂNG-NGHIÊM KINH**
see   Surangama Sutra

◙ **THURMAN, ROBERT A.**

▸"Upasaka Tenzin Chotrag. Translator and academic. After Harvard and Asian travels (ca. 1963) ... was ordained by the Dalai Lama and spent times at Namgyal monastery. Became fluent in Tibetan and studied Nagarjuna and Tsongkhapa. Later resigned monk status and returned to academic life. 1972: PhD at Harvard with translation of Madyamika text by Tsongkhapa. Currently Jey Tsong Khapa Professor of Indo-Tibetan studies at Columbia University in New York."
Snel: 291
Author of numerous books on Tibet, including *Inside Tibetan Buddhism* and *Essential Tibetan Buddhism*. #0740

◙ **THUS HAVE I HEARD**
See also: Ananda

▸"The words 'Thus have I heard' always precede the exposition of a Buddhist sutra. They are

spoken by Ananda, the Buddha's personal assistant and serve to authenticate the sutras.
Tana: 127
The question is asked, 'Why does Ananda who has realized the status of the Sages still speak of a "self" ... It is as explained by Nagarjuna:

'There are three ways of speaking about the self. The first speaks of a self based on the perverted view of the self ... The second speaks of a self based on pride (mana) ... The third claims an existence of the self in accordance with the ways of the world; this refers to those whose perverted views and pride have been eliminated, but for the purposes of propagation proclaim the self in accordance with the ways of the world.'
Thus, here in this case, when Ananda assembled the teachings of the Buddha, he dwelt in [the saintly stage of] Non-trainers, having eliminated perverted views and pride. Only in order to propagate in accordance with the ways of the world, did he speak of the self."
Tana: 127-128 #1956

◙ **THUS-COME-ONE**
see Tathagata

◙ **THUSNESS**
see Suchness

◙ **TIBET (BUDDHISM IN)**
see Tibetan Buddhism

◙ **TIBETAN BUDDHISM**
Syn: Vajrayana; Tantric School; Tibet (Buddhism in)
See also: Esoteric school

►"Also called Vajrayana, Tantric Buddhism and Lamaism. Type of Esoteric Buddhism found principally in Tibet, also now found in Mongolia, India, and parts of China. It is hierarchical and presided over by the Dalai Lama and the Panchen Lama."
Dait: 257

(I) Historical Developments
"Buddhism was introduced into Tibet about 640 A.D. but made little progress until Padmasambhava arrived in the eighth century when, it seems, that he introduced the Vinaya Rules, some Yogacara doctrines, and something of the Tantras of Bengal. A period of translation followed, but the newly established religion degenerated until in the eleventh century Atisa reformed the existing Buddhism. and founded the Kahdam-pa Order. At about the

same time, Marpa and Milarepa founded the Kargyut-pa school, and the Nyingma-pa appears as an organized school. In the fifteenth century, Tsong-kha-pa carried out sweeping reforms and founded his own Gelugpa Order, the Yellow Hats, to which the Dalai and Panchen Lama of the day belong. Tantric ritual plays a large part in all the Orders or Schools, and all levels of spiritual development are to be found, from the indigenous Bon to the greatest heights of spirituality achieved by man."
Hump: 199

(II) Recent Developments
"The Tibetan diaspora [that followed the occupation of Tibet by China in the 1950's] initiated a new period in the history of the study of Tibetan Buddhism in the west ... Native Tibetan works published by the refugees accumulated in depository libraries across the United States as a result of Public Law 480, under the terms of which the huge debts owed by the government of India to the United States for shipments of American wheat provided for famine relief would be repaid in the form of books. Specifically, a designated number of copies of every book published in India was to be provided to the Library of Congress, which would then distribute them to the depository libraries. In this way, the long mysterious Tibetan archives became as if magically manifest in the stacks of American university libraries. There was constant reference during this period to the present perilous state of how it differed from 'pre-1959 Tibet.' The change was indeed profound. Although Lhasa had been occupied by foreign armies before and the previous Dalai Lama had gone into exile to escape foreign troops, both British and Chinese, this has been the longest exile of a Dalai Lama from Tibet ever, and the damage done to Buddhist institutions in Tibet has been far greater than any before in history. Drastic changes have occurred and yet the reactions they elicited in western students of Tibetan Buddhism are not to be explained simply by taking account of the events of the day; it was not simply the fact of change that brought forth such reactions. The story is told in a Buddhist sutra of a lone blind tortoise who dwells in the depths of a vast ocean, coming up for air once every hundred years [to

represent the difficulty of human rebirth in a land where the Dharma is preached]. Western students of Buddhism imbibed this rhetoric of urgency from the Buddhist texts they studied. This attempt to partake [of the Buddhist teachings before they disappeared with the death of the old masters] marked a new phase in the history of western urgency about Tibet. Here, unlike with Desideri or Waddell, the aim of study is not to defeat Tibetan Buddhism in ideological battle; instead, *Buddhist doctrine is sympathetically regarded as valuable because of its salvific powers for the modern world*, its own myths enlisted in the crusade for its preservation."
Lopez: 265-266 #0396
For details, *See also:* Esoteric School.

◙ TIEN-TAI SCHOOL
see T'ien-t'ai school

◙ TIME AND SPACE
see Cosmology (Buddhist)

◙ TIPITAKA
see Tripitaka

◙ TOLERANCE OF NON-BIRTH
Syn: Insight Into The Non-origination of Dharmas; Insight Into The Non-Arising of Dharmas
See also: Non-Retrogression; Pure Lands (as Realms)

►*Skt*/"Dharmanutpattika-ksanti (*Vn*/Vô-sanh Pháp-Nhẫn.). Insight into the non-substantial nature of all phenomenal existence"
Tana: 249

"Tolerance (insight) that comes from the knowledge that all phenomena are unborn. A Mahayana Buddhist term for the insight into emptiness, the non-origination or birthlessness of things or beings realized by Bodhisattvas who have attained the eighth Stage (Bhumi/Ground) of the path to Buddhahood. When a Bodhisattva realizes this insight, he has attained the stage of Non-Retrogression." (Ryukoku University)
"In the process of practicing the Buddha's teaching, there is a stage where one recognizes, accepts, and complies with the truth that there is no self-substance in any dharma, even though one may not yet have fully realized the *prajna* truth. When one goes a step further and realizes fully this truth of suchness, he is said to have attained the Realization of

the Non-Arising of Dharmas (Tolerance of Non-Birth)."
Chan: 481
"Rest in the imperturbable reality which is beyond birth and death and which requires a patient endurance without which thoughts will arise endlessly. The *Prajna-paramita treatise* defines it as the unflinching faith and imperturbed abiding in the underlying reality of all things, which is beyond creation and destruction. It must be realized before attainment of Buddhahood."
Rosh: 149
NOTE:
The Pure Land school teaches that anyone reborn in the Pure Land attains the Tolerance of Non-Birth and reaches the stage of Non-Retrogression, never to fall back into Samsara. Thus rebirth in the Pure Land is the immediate goal of Pure Land practitioners while Buddhahood is the ultimate goal.
Editor: na #0825
See also Pure Lands (as Realms)

◙ **TORTOISE HAIRS AND RABBIT HORNS**

►"Hairs of tortoises and horns of rabbits. A figurative phrase to show that one sees something

where nothing really exists, e.g., seeing an atman (soul) in a person."
Dait: 193 #0111

◙ **TRADITION/SCHOOL**
see   Dharma door

◙ **TRANSFER OF MERIT**
see   Dedication of merit

◙ **TRANSLATION/ *BUDDHIST TEXTS***

►(I)   *Famous Translators In Mahayana*
See: 1/ An-Shi-Kao; 2/ Bodhiruci; 3/ Kumarajiva; 4/ Hsuan-Tsang
(II) *Problems/ Opportunities*
"For an average person to reach an acceptable proficiency as a translator, some twenty years of intensive study and meditation would constitute a bare minimum."
Doboom: 25
"A Buddhist translator looks at the scriptures as medicine to cure the mental diseases of humans, not as a work of mainly historical and philological interest that has its place in the field of knowledge like every other subject. The Buddha himself compared the Dharma to medecine quite frequently. When such a translator chooses the

texts he likes to work on, he is inclined to take those texts in the first place that are most needed as a foundation for the path to liberation. His decision does not depend on the curriculum of a university or financial considerations."
Doboom: 230

"Professor Griffiths' point about the responsibilities of a Buddhologist is that one should contextualize the text, both within the tradition it comes out of, and within the corpus of writings of the author. I think that he is quite right. We are translating not only into the language of the West but into the culture of the West, and in so doing we are bound by the conventions and expectations of that culture. Western culture (and I use this term with reservation, since it now dominates far more than simply the West) has become an historical one; we see the world in historical terms and we need context. Further, in translating into English, we are bound by the scholarly standards of Western culture. [Buddhists] may not have written their texts with footnotes, with explanations of technical terms and unclear referents, with reference to the Sanskrit of a passage even where

available, but we, in translating into the idiom of our culture, must."
Doboom: 41

"As for concluding procedures [after a translation is completed], generally I try to pass the final manuscript around to a few fellow translators for their appraisal; and then try to have a few literati friends who know little or nothing about... Buddhism read through the material, to see if it works as lite ature in the unreal world of the urban concrete jungle."
Doboom: 218

NOTE:

"The restriction to one tradition and interpretation is sometimes more useful for the spiritual progress of the practitioner than the mixing of various traditions in one work. Furthermore, a translator who is a practicing Buddhist considers his spiritual experience derived from his faithful practice in prayer, meditation and debate as an important condition to complete his understanding of the texts."
Doboom: 231

◙ TRANSMISSION OF THE LAMP

▸"In full, *The Records of the*

Transmission of the Lamp. It was compiled in 1004 A.D. by Tao-yuan. It is the earliest history of Zen still existing. Among other things it records the names of the 28 Indian Meditation School Patriarchs and the gathas (verses) recited at the times of transmission. It is one of the two principal sources of early Zen history in China, the other being *Biographies of the High Priests* which was compiled in 645 by Tao-hsuan."
Wood: 144

"In Chinese, Ch'uan Teng Lu. In Japanese Dento Roku. Collection, compiled about 1004 by Tao-yuan, of stories and sayings of Zen masters. It is the earliest collection extant. It is the source of large numbers of stories quoted by writers on Zen in English, including Dr D.T. Suzuki."
Hump: 202 #0395

◙ **TRAUMA CENTERS**
see Organ Donation

◙ **TREATISES**
see Sastra

◙ **TREATISE ON THE AWAKENING OF THE FAITH**
see Awakening of the Faith Treatise

◙ **TREATISE ON THE PURE LAND**
see Rebirth Treatise

◙ **TREE**
See also: Tree Spirits

►"The word 'tree' is defined by a homonym in Chinese that means upright or perpendicular. Trees represent wisdom. If you are tall, you are said to have wisdom: 'It is like a great regal tree growing in the rocks and sand of a barren wilderness. When the roots get water, the branches, leaves, flowers, and fruits will all flourish. The regal bodhi tree growing in the wilderness of Birth and Death is the same. All living beings are its roots; all Buddhas and Bodhisattvas are its flowers and fruits. By benefitting all beings with the water of Great Compassion, one can realize the flowers and fruits of the Buddhas' and Bodhisattvas' wisdom.'" (*Avatamsaka Sutra*: chap. 40)
Hua: xxx #1347

◙ **TREE SPIRITS**
Syn: Spirits; Ghosts
See also: Li Mei; Spirit World; Tree; Sentient Beings

►"When trees become large and

old they are known to be dwellings for ghosts and spirits who lodge in trees, where they feel a sense of security and comfort. If these spirits are unable to find such a tree they experience a sense of distress. *For this reason bhiksus are not permitted to cut down large trees;* this is specially mentioned in the Dharmagupta Vinaya...

At Nan Hua Monastery a large camphor tree received the precepts from the Venerable Master Hsu Yun, and at Nan Yao, the Dharma seat of the Old Man of Mount Wei, a ginkgo tree also received the precepts." (*Earth Store Bodhisattva Sutra* by Buddhist Text Translation Society and Institute for Advanced Studies of World Religions, New York.) Hua/1974: 61 #2284

◙ **TRIKAYA**
see Three bodies of the Buddha

◙ **TRIPITAKA**
Syn: Buddhist Canon; Tipitaka; Taisho
See also: Translation/ Buddhist Texts; Abhidharma; Sutra; Buddhist Councils; Pali Canon; Twelve Divisions of the Mahayana Canon

▸"The Buddha's teachings form a canon known as the Tripitaka, or 'three baskets,' because they were divided into three categories: the *Sutras* (sermons of the Buddha); the *Vinaya* (precepts and rules of monastic discipline); and the *Abhidharma* (commentarial literature on the Buddha's teachings). There are two major sets of Tripitaka or canon: the Theravada canon written in Pali, and the Mahayana canon written in Sanskrit and preserved in Chinese and Tibetan. The Mahayana canon includes all the texts of the *Theravada canon* in addition to its own sutras and commentaries. The best known edition of the *Mahayana canon* is the Japanese Taisho edition (see below)."

(I) Background
"After the death of Gautama it became necessary to establish his teaching clearly and gather it in a coherent form. So a few months later a council was held in Rajagha (India), and its conclusions were reviewed 100 years later, at the second Buddhist council in Vesali. The crucial meeting, however, was the third, which met in Pataliputta in 253 BC, more than 200 years after Gautama's death, under the

patronage of Emperor Asoka. A thousand monks were occupied for nine months in checking, completing and finally classifying the traditions that had been passed down. At this stage the material was still in spoken form; it was not until the first century BC, on the island of Sri Lanka, that the first Buddhist scriptures were written down. This basic collection of writings is called the Pali canon, after the language in which it was written. It forms the main body of teaching for the conservative Theravada Buddhists; other groups [such as the Mahayanists] have additional writings... (For details, see Buddhist Councils)

"[In addition to the Pali Tripitaka], other Tripitakas were also written by other schools in Sanskrit, containing the same three baskets but a somewhat different set of contents. They now survive mainly in Chinese and Tibetan translations [and are known as the Mahayana Tripitaka]. The Mahayana tradition accepts the Pali Tripitaka, but sees it as a preparation for its own Mahayana sutras which, so to speak, fill the three baskets of the Pali Canon."
Larousse: 532

(II) The Mahayana Canon

"Mahayana Buddhists recognize many more texts as authoritative than do the more traditionalist Theravada Buddhists. Among these are the two *Amitabha Sutras (Sukhavativyuha)*; the *'Lotus Sutra' (Sadharmapundarika)* particularly used by the T'ien T'ai school; the 'Revelation of the Teaching in Lanka' (*Lankavatara*); and, above all, the *'Perfection of Wisdom Sutra' (Prajnaparamita-Sutra)*, a comprehensive explanation of the state of being a Buddha. Some of these writings are geared to practical piety; others are more philosophically oriented. Whole schools of thought gathered around the various manuals or sutras, and then wrote their own teaching books (sastras), to give a thorough grounding in Buddhism." Eerd: 234

(III) Taisho (Taisho Shinshu Daizokyo):

"The Taisho Issaikyo is the name of a Japanese edition in 85 volumes of all Buddhist Scriptures extant in Chinese collected by J. Takakusu in 1924-32. Generally adopted [by Western scholars] as superseding earlier compilations. The Taisho edition is usually quoted as T."
Hump: 191-192

"In the Taisho edition, the division of the Buddhist Canon is as follows:

Vols. 1-21 -- Translations of the discourses (sutras) of the Buddha
Vols. 22-24 -- Translations of the Vinaya (precepts)
Vols. 25-29 -- Translations of the Abhidharma (commentaries)
Vols. 30-31 -- Translations of Madhyamika and Vijnanavada texts
Vol. 32 -- Translations of sastras or treatises
Vols. 33-43 -- Commentaries written by Chinese masters
Vols. 44-48 -- The literature of the various Chinese schools of Buddhism
Vols. 49-52 -- Historical records, such as biographies, annals, travel accounts, Chinese polemical literature
Vols. 53-54 -- Encyclopedias and glossaries
Vol. 55 -- Buddhist catalogues of sutras."
Chen: 378
n.b.: Japanese Buddhism is generally based on the Chinese version of the Tripitaka, which at least until recently could be read by educated Japanese.
Editor: na
NOTE:
"Thirty-one Sanskrit texts and over two hundred Chinese and Tibetan translations refer to Amitabha and/or Sukhavati [in the Mahayana Tripitaka]. For example, the author of the Treatise on the Buddha-womb Theory concludes his highly 'technical' work on the tathagatagarbha (Buddha-womb or embryo) doctrine by stating: 'By the merit I have acquired through [writing] this [treatise], may all living beings come to perceive the Lord Amitabha endowed with infinite light.' Such references attest to the influence wielded by Pure Land thought in the devotional lives of the commentators."
Tana: 12 #0178

For details, *See also:* "Twelve Divisions of the Mahayana Canon"

◙ **TRIPLE JEWEL**
see Three Treasures

◙ **TRIPLE REALM**
Syn: Threefold World; Triple World; Three Realms
See also: World of Desire; World of Form; World of Formlessness
----
▸"The world of desire, the world of form and the world of formlessness (q.v.). The realms inhabited by unenlightened

beings ... (1) The world of desire is so called because its inhabitants are ruled by various desires, representative of which are the desire for food and sex. It comprises the Four Evil Paths (Hell, Hungry Ghosts, Animality and Asura) [and the two Paths of humans and celestials].

(2) Beings in the world of form have material form but are free from desires. This world consists of the four meditation (Skt./ dhyana) heavens, which are further subdivided into eighteen heavens (sixteen or seventeen according to other explanations).

(3) The world of formlessness is free both from desire and from the restrictions of matter. It has four non-substantial realms."
Sokk: 456

"According to Buddhist teaching, if a sentient being is not enlightened and has not escaped Birth and Death, he is revolving within the Three Realms (the Realm of Desire, the Realm of Form, and the Realm of Formlessness). Sentient beings living in the *Realm of Desire* possess lust, hatred, jealousy, infatuation, and other passions. Within this realm there are six different planes of existence: gods, humans, asuras, animals, hungry ghosts, and hell-dwellers. The *Realm of Form* contains sixteen heavens inhabited by various celestial beings who have certain accomplishments in one of the four dhyanas of form. The *Realm of Formlessness* has four heavens, inhabited by those with different accomplishments in one of the four dhyanas of formlessness. The heavens both in the Realm of Form and in that of Formlessness are classified according to the depth of dhyana (meditation) attained in their former lives by the celestial beings who dwell there."
Chan: 488 #0303

◙ **TRIPLE WORLD**
see Triple Realm

◙ **TRÚC LÂM**
See also: Zen / Pure Land

▸"A Vietnamese synthesis of Chan-Pure Land Buddhism with Confucianism and Taoism, initiated by King Trần Nhân Tôn (r. 1258-1308)."
Reat: 347 #2102

◙ **TRUE EMPTINESS**
see True Emptiness / Wonderful Existence; Emptiness

◙ TRUE EMPTINESS / WONDERFUL EXISTENCE

See also: Emptiness; Suchness; Akasagarbha Bodhisattva; Nature and Marks; Golden-Colored King

----

►Lofty and subtle principle of the Mahayana sutras such as the *Avatamsaka*: the perfect fusion and non-obstruction of True Emptiness and Wonderful Existence.

Editor: na

"True emptiness is not empty;/It gives rise to Wonderful Existence./ Wonderful Existence does not exist;/It does not obstruct True Emptiness. /From the void which seemingly contains nothing, /absolutely everything descends." (*Avatamsaka Sutra.*) [HH/FAS39III67]

See also the following quote:

"If we refer to existence, then/ Everything from the smallest mote of dust exists;/ If we refer to emptiness,/ This whole, wide world and everything in it are empty."

Dia: 160

Avatamsaka (chap: 39)

"Since both material and metaphysical generosity are produced by knowledge of emptiness and baselessness, when countless beings came from various lands seeking what they desired from Vidvan [one of Sudhana's spiritual teachers in the *Avatamsaka Sutra*], he looked up to the sky, and all they wanted descended from the sky; and he taught them truths according to their faculties."

[TC/EIR,p.42]xx

Amitabha Sutra

"This [*Amitabha*] *Sutra* is a Mahayana Dharma ... and takes the Real Mark as its substance. The Real Mark is no mark. There is no mark, nothing at all, and yet there is nothing which is not marked. Unmarked, it is *true emptiness*, and with nothing unmarked, it is *wonderful existence* ... True Suchness, the One True Dharma Realm, the Thus Come One's Store Nature, all are different names for the Real Mark" (Master Hsuan Hua, *A General Explanation of the Buddha Speaks of the Amitabha Sutra*, p. 23). #1212

◙ TRUE SUCHNESS

see Suchness

◙ TRUE TEACHINGS

►"[In Mahayana Buddhism] refer primarily to those of the *Lotus* and *Avatamsaka Sutras*. 'Expedient teachings' include all

other teachings."
Yoko: 183 #0811

◙ **TRUTH**
See also: Existence (Amitabha /
Pure Land); Suchness; True
Emptiness / Wonderful
Existence; Two Truths

▸Please read entry "Two Truths"
before the following:
"The word Truth usually denotes
the ultimate, transcendental
truth, or emptiness (sunyata);
also, Buddha-nature, or
suchness." (Ultimate Truth Vs.
mundane truth.)   Chan: 484
The truth being one and
indivisible in Mahayana Buddhist
teaching, the "discriminating"
human mind can never grasp the
whole truth. Thus, such a mind is
bound to result in an imperfect
understanding of the world as it
really is. This is best expressed
by the parable of several blind
men trying to describe an
elephant, each touching a
different part of the animal, with
no one having the total picture.
Editor/Tam: 308
"Relative and absolute,/These the
two truths are declared to
be./The absolute is not within the
reach of intellect,/For intellect is
grounded in the relative."
(Shantiveda)

The meaning of this is that all
statements, all theories, anything
emerging from the operations of
the rational intelligence, have the
nature of relative truth. Theories
may be of practical utility and
may concur with empirical
experience, but as expressions of
the absolute truth, the ultimate
'nature of things,' they are
inadequate. The absolute is
supranational and cannot be
expressed in conceptual terms.
Thus, in the *Majjhima Nikaya*,
the Buddha is recorded as saying
that 'the Tathagata is free from
all theories and again, 'the view
that everything exists is,
Kachchayana, one extreme; that
it does not exist is another. Not
accepting the two extremes, the
Tathagata proclaims the truth
from the middle position.' This
means that any statement
claiming to encapsulate the
ultimate truth, any formulation
that points to 'this' or 'that' as
being ultimately real, is false--
false for the simple reason that it
is a formulation, emanating from
the conceptual intelligence."
Shantideva: 22

D.T. Suzuki quotes the Zen
Patriarch Fa Yen as follows:
"The sutras preached by the
Buddha during his lifetime are

said to amount to five thousand and forty-eight fascicles; they include the doctrine of emptiness and the doctrine of being (existence); there are teachings of immedicate realization and of gradual development. Is this not an affirmation?

"But, according to [Zen Master Yun Chia in his Song of Enlightenment], 'there are no sentient beings, there are no Buddhas; sages as numerous as the sands of the Ganges are but so many bubbles in the sea; sages and worthies of the past are like flashes of lightning.' Is this not a negation?

"O you, my disciples, if you say there is, you go against [Yung Chia]; if you say there is not, you contradict our old master Buddha. If he were with us, then how would he pass through the dilemma? ... If you confess your ignorance, I will let you see into the secret. When I say there is not, this does not necessarily mean a negation; when I say there is, this also does not signify an affirmation. Turn eastward and look at the Western Land; face the south and the North Star is pointed out there!"

D.T. Suzuki/65: na

See also: the following passage which expresses the highest teaching of Buddhism (noumenon level): "According to the Hua-yen [Avatamsaka school] analysis, every belief represents a vision of the truth, as seen from a particular standpoint. Therefore it cannot contradict, or be contradicted by, any other belief -- for that too is a vision of the truth, only seen from a different standpoint. Nor can a given standpoint be right or wrong in itself, since, on the one hand (from the conventional point of view), being partial and limited by definition, it cannot be the whole truth; while on the other hand (from the ultimate point of view), it simultaneously includes all other standpoints, and so cannot be less than the whole truth. Beliefs are mistaken as long as they are supposed to be absolutely true, in contrast to other beliefs which are then considered false. They actually become absolutely true only when their relative nature is fully realized and there is no longer any question of true vs. false." (A.J. Prince, *The World of Hua-yen Buddhism*).

Zen: 112

"What is truth? It is that which helps. And conversely, that which helps has the ring of truth."

Doboom: 221

NOTE:

"Buddha-name recitation is the wondrous gate into the Truth. It merges perfectly with all schools of Buddhism and encompasses all forms of the teaching. Its purity and subtlety are unfathomable, its greatness inexhaustible. Those of dull faculties find it and quickly escape from the world of suffering. Those of keen intellect encounter it and directly pass to the Other Shore..." (Master Chu Hung in *Pure Land Pure Mind*) See also "True Emptiness / onderful Existence".

◎ **TRƯƠNG CHUNG QUÌ**
see Notorious men

◎ **TRƯƠNG THIỆN HÒA**
see Notorious men

◎ **TSAO-TUNG SCHOOL**
see Soto Zen School

◎ **TSONG-KHA-PA (1355-1417)**

▸"'The man from the Land of Onions.' One of the greatest names in Tibetan history, he was born on the site of the present Kum-bum monastery and at an early age dedicated his life to the complete reform of Tibetan Buddhism. He founded the Ganden monastery 26 miles from

Lhasa and called his new Order the Gelug-pa, 'the virtuous ones.' To this day the senior members wear on important occasions a yellow headdress. All others still wearing the red hat which, however, is usually associated with the Red Hat or Nyingma-pa School.

In the New Order, which replaced the Kahdam-pa founded by Atisa, Tsong-kha-pa made no great innovations, but tightened the discipline, abolished alcohol, enforced celibacy, cut down on magic and the proliferation of divinities, and for his students wrote a special set of precepts which are still the Order's basic text-book. Both the Dalai and the Panchen Lama are members of this Order. Other Schools adopted the reforms at least in part, being now referred to as semi-reformed. Others, e.g. the Nyingma-pa, remained unaffected."
Hump: 203 #0061

◎ **TU- SHUN**
see Avatamsaka Sutra

◎ **TULKU**

▸"Tib., lit. 'transformation body'; in Tibetan Buddhism, a term for a person who, after certain tests,

is recognized as the reincarnation of a previously deceased person."
Sham: 234

"A Tibetan term for a person recognized as the present incarnation of an important being (famous monk for example)."
Blof: 251 #0354

◙ TUN-HUANG
See also: Lung-Men; Ajanta

►"Important Chinese political, commercial, and military center in northwest Kansu Province, at the eastern end of the Silk Road, during the first millenium; site of the Thousand Buddhas caves, a superb repository of fourth to fourteenth century Buddhist painting and sculpture."
Okaz: 187

"For over 1,000 years, one of most important Buddhist centers in China. From the Han Dynasty (206 BC--220 AD), an important stage-post at the east end of the 'Silk-Road' to Central Asia, it became a great Buddhist center and place of pilgrimage. In 366 the first of the Buddhist cave temples was begun; the construction of temples and grottoes continued throuogut the next millenium, until the close of Yuan Dynasty (1368). At the

height of its fame, it boasted 1,000 grottoes, of which only some 480 remain, in which have been preserved thousands of sculptures and murals, recording the triumphs of Buddhist art in China. During the Sung Dynasty (960-1279), when flames of war spread to Tun-Huang, the monks of the cave temples, before taking flight, sealed up their scriptures, scrolls and documents in one of the caves. These were accidentally discovered by a Taoist priest in 1900; in 1907 Sir Aurel Stein, and later Paul Pelliot, brought thousands of these scriptures, pictures and scrolls to the West..."
Ling: 258-259

"Oasis town in the province of Kansu in northwestern China, where there are famous caves known by the name of Mo-kao-k'u. It is the largest preserved complex of Buddhist cultic caves in the world. The earliest are from the beginning of the 4th century. Today some 492 caves are still preserved. The complex extends on five levels over a distance of one kilometer. The caves are primarily famed for their frescoes, which cover a surface area of 45,000 square meters. In addition they contain over 2,400 painted statues. In one

of the caves (no. 16), thousands of written scrolls, for the most part sutras, were discovered."
Sham: 236 #0139
NOTE:
The one thousand Buddha caves at Tun-Huang in Northwestern China provide the most fertile source for representations of the Pure Lands.

◎ **TUSITA HEAVEN**
Syn: Heaven of Satisfaction
See also: Maitreya Society

▸"'Heaven of Satisfaction.' The fourth of the six heavens in the World of Desire. It is said that Bodhisattvas are reborn there just before their last rebirth in the human world when they will attain Buddhahood. This heaven consists of an inner court and an outer court. The inner court is said to be the abode of Bodhisattva Maitreya." Sokk:485
"The Heaven in the Realm of Desire from which each Buddha descends to earth. The 'Heaven of Contentment.' The present dwelling-place of Maitreya, the next Buddha of our world."
Chan: 484 #0294

◎ **TWELVE DIVISIONS OF THE MAHAYANA CANON**
See also: Tripitaka

▸*"The 12 kinds of Buddhist scriptures distinguished according to different styles of exposition*: (1) the Buddha's exposition of the Dharma in prose (sutra), (2) verses which repeat the ideas already expressed in prose (geya), (3) verses containing ideas not expressed in prose (gatha), (4) narratives of the past which explain a person's present state (nidana), (5) narratives of past lives of the Buddha's disciples (itivrittaka), (6) narratives of past lives of the Buddha (jataka), (7) accounts of miracles performed by the Buddha or a deva (abdhuta-dharma), (8) an exposition of the Dharma through allegories (avadana), (9) discussions of doctrine (upadesa), (10) an exposition of the Dharma by the Buddha without awaiting questions or requests from his disciples (udana), (11) an extensive exposition of principles of truth (vaipulya), and (12) prophecies by the Buddha regarding his disciples' attainment of Buddhahood (vyakarana)."
Inag: 420-421

"[In other words], *the twelve divisions of the Mahayana Canon are*: (1) sutra, the Buddha's

sermons; (2) geya, metrical pieces; (3) gatha, poems or chants; (4) nidana, sutras written by request or in answer to a query, because certain precepts were violated and because of certain events; (5) itivrittaka, narratives; (6) jataka, stories of former lives of Buddha; (7) adbhuta-dharma, miracles; (8) avadana, parables, metaphors, stories, illustrations; (9) upadesa, discourses and discussions by question and answer; (10) udana, impromptu or unsolicited addresses; (11) vaipulya, expanded sutras; (12) vyakarana, prophecies."
Xu-Yun/1988: 189 #0718

◙ **TWELVE ENTRANCES**
See also: Skandhas

►"The six sense-organs (eye, ear, nose, tongue, body, and mind) and their corresponding objects (forms, sounds, scents, tastes, textures, and mental objects)."
Chan: 495 #0632

◙ **TWENTY-EIGHT INDIAN PATRIARCHS**
See also: Patriarchal Zen; Aryasimha; Zen school

►"According to the Zen sect, men who inherited and passed on that teaching of Shakyamuni which was not expounded in words but transmitted from mind to mind. They are (1) Mahakashyapa, (2) Ananda, (3) Shanavasa, (4) Upagupta, (5) Dhritaka (6) Mikkaka, (7) Vasumitra, (8) Buddhananda, (9) Buddhamitra, (10) Parshva, (11) Punyayashas, (12) Ashvaghosha, (13) Kapimala, (14) Nagarjuna, (15) Aryadeva, (16) Rahulata, (17) Samghanandi, (18) Samgayashas, (19) Kumarata, (20) Jayata, (21) Vasubandhu, (22) Manorhita, (23) Haklena, (24) Aryasimha, (25) Vasiasita, (26) Punyamitra, (27) Prajnatara and (28) Bodhidharma, founder of the Chinese Ch'an (Jpn./ Zen) school."
Sokk: 487
For names of Chinese Patriarchs after Bodhidharma, see "Zen School". #0295

◙ **TWO AMITABHA SUTRAS**
See also: Three Pure Land Sutras

►Stand for the *Shorter Amitabha Sutra (Amitabha Sutra)* and the *Longer Amitabha Sutra.*

◙ **TWO EXTREME VIEWS**
See also: Middle Way Philosophy; Nihilism
►"Two dualistic views expressly

rejected in Buddhism: 1.*Nihilism*: considering that things do not exist in any sense, even the delusory manifestations of the world; also, the tenet that nothing continues after death, i.e., the denial of the doctrine of reincarnation. 2. *Eternalism*: believing that there is true existence of real being in objects, or that there is some entity that exists forever."

Chan: 487 #0594

◙ **TWO HUNDRED AND FIFTY PRECEPTS**

See also: Bhiksu

▶"Rules of discipline to be observed by fully ordained monks. They consist of eight groups:
(1) The four unpardonable offenses (Skt./ parajika) of killing, theft, sexual intercourse and lying, particularly, claiming to have attained insight or understanding that one does not in fact possess. A monk who commits one or another of these offenses is expelled from the Order. (2) Thirteen major prohibitions (Samgha-Avashesha). Monks who violate these are divested of membership in the Order for a certain period. (3) Prohibitions relating to offenses which are committed either in a place where one can be seen or in a place where one cannot. For example, this type of prohibition includes the offense of being alone with a woman, either in a place where one can be seen or in a place where one cannot. This third group comprises two of the two hundred and fifty precepts. These rules are called the indeterminate (aniyata) group because the punishment for going against them varies according to the circumstances.
(4) Thirty standards (naihisargika-prayashchittika), whose violation is said to cause one to fall into the three evil paths. (5) Ninety standards (shuddha-prayashchittika), violation of which requires public confession. (6) Four lesser standards (pratideshaniya), the breaking of which requires confession when one becomes aware of his error. (7) One hundred very minor standards (Shaiksha-dharma), which are easily broken but which should be borne in mind for one's self-development. (8) Seven rules (adhikarana-shamatha) for settling disputes within the Order."

Sokk: 491 #0296

◎ TWO SELVES

▶"Personal self and phenomenal self, which are the ultimately non-existent objects we perceive as the essential core of persons and things."

Thur: 147   #0668

◎ TWO STORES

▶"The stores of merit and of wisdom; all deeds of Bodhisattvas contribute to their accumulation of these two stores, which ultimately culminate in the two bodies of the Buddha, the body of form and the ultimate body."

Thur: 147   #0669

◎ TWO TRUTHS

See also: Truth

▶"The superficial truth and the ultimate truth, or the relative truth and the absolute truth, or the conventional truth and the supreme truth."

Thur: 147

"1) Relative or conventional, everyday truth of the mundane world subject to delusion and dichotomies and 2) the Ultimate Truth, transcending dichotomies, as taught by the Buddhas. According to Buddhism, there are two kinds of truth, the Absolute and the Relative. The Absolute Truth (of the Void) manifests 'illumination but is always still,' and this is absolutely inexplicable. On the other hand, the Relative Truth (of the Unreal) manifests 'stillness but is always illuminating,' which means that it is immanent in everything."

(Hsu Heng Chi/P.H. Wei).

"The Two Truths were generally appealed to as a vehicle for authenticating expedient practices, but eventually they coalesced into an ultimate affirmation of the non-duality of True Reality, of which the Two Truths are but a function."

Saso: 49

NOTE:

Pure Land thinkers, such as the Patriarch Tao Ch'o, accepted "the legitimacy of conventional Truth as an expression of Ultimate Truth and as a vehicle to reach Ultimate Truth. Even though all form is non-form, it is acceptable and necessary to use form within the limits of causality, because its use is an expedient means of saving others out of one's compassion for them and because, even for the unenlightened, the use of form can lead to the revelation of form as non-form" (David Chappell). Thus to reach Buddhahood, which is formless, the cultivator can practice the Pure Land method based on form.

Editor: 167-168 #0670

◉ TWO VEHICLES
See also: Theravada Buddhism; Mahayana/Theravada; Yana

▸*Skt*/yana. The Two Vehicles are those of the Sravakas (q.v.) and Pratyekabuddhas (q.v.). Together they constitute what is called the Theravada Vehicle or Southern Vehicle. The Bodhisattva vehicle which leads to Buddhahood is called the Mahayana vehicle (Third Vehicle).

Editor: na #0595
See also Yana

◉ UDUMBARA FLOWER

▸"An udumbara tree is said usually to bear fruit without flowers. Once in a very long period of time it is said to bloom; hence, the udumbara flower is a symbol of the rare appearance of a Buddha."

Chan: 484

"This flower is said to bloom only once every three thousand years. For this reason it is often used as an illustration of how difficult it is to come in contact with true Buddhist teachings as well as the rarity of encountering a Buddha."

Yoko: 189 #0579

◉ ULLAMBANA
Syn: Obon
See also: Buddhist Festivals; Maudgalyayana; Rains Retreat; Sacerdotal Age; Filiality
----
▸"*Skt*.: festival of the hungry ghosts, celebrated on the fifteenth day of the seventh month (lunar calendar). On this day ceremonies are held in which the sutras are recited in order to soothe the torments of the deceased in the lower realms of existence. The origin of this ceremony is to be found in the story of Maudgalyayana, who thanks to his 'divine eye' saw that his mother had been reborn as a hungry ghost, and he wanted to save her. The Buddha told him that only the combined effort of all Buddhist monks could [help her escape her fate]. From this tradition developed the custom of offering food, clothing, and so on to the [clergy on Ullambana, the date of which coincides with the end of the yearly Rains Retreat].

The combination of the Buddhist world view and the Chinese custom of ancestor veneration explains the tremendous popularity of this festival in East Asia, in which not only Buddhists but also Taoists and Confucians participate."
Sham: 237 #0343

◉ **ULTIMATISM**
See also: Noumenon and Phenomena; Zen school

▸"It seems useful to adopt the term 'ultimatism' to identify the tendency to take what is true from the viewpoint of ultimate truth or at an advanced level of spiritual practice as if it were the whole of Buddhism. In effect 'ultimatism' discards, ignores or even rejects step-by-step discourse in favour of particular teaching. This is a perennial possibility, frequent also in the history of Mahayana Buddhism. In Southern Buddhism today it takes the form of a rejection of much traditional practice and ceremonies as well as many of the outward forms customarily associated with merit-making activities."   Hinn: 315
NOTE:
For a glimpse of why we should not blindly borrow the words of the sages or emulate their extraordinary actions, see the following passage concerning Kumarajiva, the renowned T'ang Dynasty monk (who skillfully translated some thirty-five sutras into Chinese): "When Kumarajiva went to China in the fourth century of this era, the Chinese Emperor thought that such a wise person ought to have descendents so that his wisdom would carry on. He gave concubines to Kumarajiva, and since they were a royal gift, Kumarajiva had no choice but to accept them. Afterwards, his disciples asked, 'Can we have relations with women too?' Kumarajiva said, 'Sure, but first, let me show you something.' He took a handful of needles and ate them as easily as if they were noodles. When he finished, he said, 'If you can do that, then you can have relations with women.' (Sheng-yen, *The Sword of Wisdom*, p. 229.)"
Editor/Tam: 313 #1928
See also: Kumarajiva; Non-Dual Method

◉ **UNCOMPOUNDED**
see   Unconditioned Dharmas

◉ **UNCONDITIONED DHARMAS**
Syn: Uncompounded; Uncreated;

Without Outflows
See also: Conditioned dharmas;
Outflows

▸"Those dharmas which do not arise or cease, and are not transient. Examples: Nirvana, the Dharma-body, and the ancient philosophical concept of space."
Chan: 485
Unconditioned/ Uncompounded: That which exists but is not made up of discrete elements (compounded), nor subject to the law of cause and effect. Uncompounded phenomena include space and Nirvana. By extension, the ultimate truth or emptiness (as the essence of all phenomena).
Editor: na
NOTE:
"The virtues of Buddha Recitation are 'unconditioned' good roots. Ordinary, impure persons who develop the Bodhi Mind, seek rebirth and constantly practice Buddha Recitation can subdue and destroy afflictions, achieve rebirth in the Pure Land and, depending on their level of cultivation, obtain a vision of the rudimentary aspects of the Buddha (the thirty-two marks of greatness, for example). Bodhisattvas, naturally, can achieve rebirth and see the

subtle, loftier aspects of the Buddha (i.e., the Dharma body)." [Tien T'ai Patriarch Chih I]
Dia: 21   #0033

◉ **UNCONVENTIONAL BEHAVIOR IN ZEN**
see   Shouts and Blows

◉ **UNCREATED**
see   Unconditioned Dharmas

◉ **UNEXCELLED VEHICLE**

▸"The highest vehicle of Buddhahood; in many texts, the Mahayana."
Chan: 485   #0582

◉ **UNFIXED CONTEMPLATION**

▸"Meditation exercise that has different effects according to the spirit in which it is practiced; hence it is 'unfixed' in terms of prescription and prognosis."
Chih-I/Cleary: 206

◉ **UNIVERSAL METHOD**
See also: Special Teaching; Salvation; Pure Land Buddhism (Summary)

▸"The Pure Land tradition embraces people of all capacities -- whether limited, moderate or high. Sentient beings of limited and moderate capacities who recite the Buddha's name can rid themselves of afflictions and karmic obstacles and develop merit, virtue and wisdom, leading in time to the state of samadhi. They will then be reborn within the nine 'lotus grades' in the Land of Ultimate Bliss, the exact grade depending on the amount of effort they exert in cultivation. Those of high capacities, on the other hand, enter deeply into the state of samadhi and wisdom as soon as they begin uttering the Buddha's name. Whether walking, standing, lying down or sitting, they are always in the 'Buddha Recitation Samadhi.' After death they will be reborn in the highest lotus grade. Some of the sages of old who entered this realm described it in the following terms: '*Holding the rosary, I am rid of worldly thoughts,/ Suddenly, I already became a Buddha a long time ago.*'

Pure Land embraces people of all levels. For those of high capacities it is a sublime method; for those of limited capacities it turns into a simple method. [It is thus a universal method, a Mahayana method.]"

Thich: 71-72

"This Dharma-Gate (method) of buddha-name recitation does not discriminate between wise and ignorant, or high ranking and lowly, or rich and poor. It does not distinguish between male and female or old and young or monks and nuns and laypeople. It does not matter if you have practiced it for a long time or have just recently started. Everyone can recite the buddha-name. The guidelines for reciting the buddha-name are not rigid. You can recite the buddha-name in a loud voice or a low voice, while doing ablutions or while making prostrations. You can recite the buddha-name while gathering in the mind, while meditating, while contemplating the concept of buddha, while counting beads. You can recite the buddha-name while walking or standing or sitting quietly or lying on your side. You can recite the buddha-name silently or aloud. You can recite the buddha-name a thousand times or ten thousand times. It is all the same mindfulness of buddha. *The only thing that is essential is to have definite faith, and to seek birth in the Pure Land.* If you can actually practice the recitation like this, then there is no need to seek elsewhere for an enlightened teacher." (Zen Master Tsung-pen, 16th c. China)

Tam: 120

Question: "When practicing Pure Land, we need to attain the Buddha Recitation Samadhi, or at least reach the stage of one-pointedness of mind, in order to achieve rebirth in the Western Land. Those of limited capacities are not necessarily able to practice at such a level. Therefore, how can these sentient beings be reborn in the Land of Ultimate Bliss? And, if such persons cannot achieve rebirth there, how can Buddha Recitation be said to 'gather in' all types of people?

Answer: In truth, the capacities of people being what they are these days, even one-pointedness of mind is extremely difficult to achieve, not to mention the state of Buddha Recitation Samadhi! However, according to the *Meditation Sutra*, if anyone who has committed the 'Five Grave Offenses' or 'Ten Evil Deeds' sees evil omens appear as he is on the verge of death, he need only recite the Buddha's name ten times *with utter faith and sincerity* and Buddha Amitabha will descend to welcome him and guide him back to the Pure Land. Thus, one-pointedness of mind resulting in rebirth in the Pure Land refers to the time of death, not the present time. However, in order to achieve such a state of mind at the time of death, the cultivator should practice Buddha Recitation in daily life to the point where it becomes second nature. As he constantly recites the Buddha's name in daily life, even though one-pointedness of mind is not yet achieved, the seeds of Buddha Recitation are accumulated and stored away in great quantities. On his deathbed, the practitioner who begins to recite 'activates' those seeds immediately and with great force, resulting in one-pointedness of mind. Those of limited capacities who achieve rebirth in the Pure Land through Buddha Recitation usually fall into this category."

Tam: 76-77 #1354

"The champions of Pure Land Buddhism have always made the case that Pure Land methods are especially valuable because they are particularly effective in meeting the needs of the greatest number of people. When we face facts, most of us have to admit that we see little realistic prospect of achieving salvation through the eons of gradual practice spoken of in the Buddhist scriptures, or the heroic efforts of the Zen masters, or the years of esoteric dedication demanded by the Esoteric Schools. Pure Land practice, on the other hand, is explicitly designed as an easy way, open to all" (J.C. Cleary).

◙ **UNIVERSE**

Syn: Cosmos
See also: Cosmology (Buddhist); Billion-World Universe; Dharma Realm; World System

----

▸"On certain occasions, the Buddha has commented on the nature and composition of the universe. According to the Buddha, there are a multitude of other forms of life existing in other parts of the universe. As a result of today's rapid scientific progress, we may soon find some living beings on other planets in the remotest parts of our galaxy. Perhaps, we will find them subject to the same laws as ourselves. They might be physically quite different in both appearance, elements and chemical composition, and exist in different dimensions. They might be far superior to us or they might be far inferior. Why should the planet earth be the only planet to contain life forms? Earth is a tiny speck in a huge universe. Sir James Jeans, the distinguished astrophysicist, estimates the whole universe to be about one thousand million times as big as the area of space that is visible through the telescope. In his book, *The Mysterious Universe*, he states that the total number of "universes" is probably something like the total number of grains of sand on all the sea shores of the world. In such a universe, the planet Earth is only one-millionth of a grain of sand. He also informs us that the light from the sun takes probably something like 100,000 million years to travel across the universe! Such is the vastness of the cosmos. When we consider the vastness of the many universes making up what is popularly known as 'outer space,' the hypothesis that other-world systems might exist is scientifically feasible. In the light of modern scientific discoveries, we can appreciate the limitations of the human world. Today, science has demonstrated that our human world exists within the limitations of the vibrational frequencies that can be received by our sense organs. And science has also shown us that there are other vibrational frequencies which are above or below our range of reception. With the discovery of radio waves, X-rays, T.V. waves, and microwaves, we can appreciate the extremely limited perception that is imposed on us by our sense organs. We peep at the universe through a 'crack' allowed by our sense organs, just as a little child peeps out through the crack in a door. This awareness of our limited perception demonstrates to us the possibility that other world systems may exist that are separate from ours or that interpenetrate with ours. As to the nature of the universe, the Buddha said that the beginning and ending of the universe are inconceivable. Buddhists do not believe that the world will suddenly end in complete and utter destruction. There is no such thing as complete destruction of the whole universe at once. When a certain section of the universe disappears, another section remains. When the other section disappears, another section reappears or evolves out of the dispersed matters of the previous universe. This is formed by the accumulation of molecules, basic elements, gas and numerous

energies, a combination supported by cosmic implosion and gravity. Then some other new world systems appear and exist for some time. This is the nature of cosmic energies. This is why the Buddha says that the beginning and the end of the universe are inconceivable. It was only on certain special occasions that the Buddha commented on the nature and composition of the universe. When He spoke, He had to address Himself to the understanding capacity of the enquirer. The Buddha was not interested in the kind of metaphysical speculation that did not lead to a higher spiritual development. Buddhists do not share the view held by some people that the world will be destroyed by god, when there are more non-believers and more corruptions taking place amongst human beings. With regard to this belief people can ask, instead of destroying with his power, why can't this god use the same power to influence people to become believers and to wipe out all immoral practices from men's mind? Whether the god destroys or not, it is natural that one day there will be an end to everything that comes into existence. However, in the language of the

Buddha, the world is nothing more than the combination, existence, disappearance, and recombination of mind and matter. In the final analysis, the Teaching of the Buddha goes beyond the discoveries of modern science however startling or impressive they may be. In science, the knowledge of the universe is to enable man to master it for his material comfort and personal safety. But the Buddha teaches that no amount of factual knowledge will ultimately free man from the pain of existence. He must strive ... diligently until he arrives at a true understanding of his own nature and of the changeable nature of the cosmos. To be truly free a man must seek to tame his mind, to destroy his craving for sensual pleasure. When a man truly understands that the universe he is trying to conquer is impermanent, he will see himself as Don Quixote fighting windmills. With this Right View of himself, he will spend his time and energy conquering his mind and destroying his illusion of self."

Dham: 300-303 #1978

◎ **UNSOLICITED FRIEND**
See also: Good Spiritual Advisors

▸In the *Avatamsaka Sutra*, this term refers to Bodhisattvas who act as friends and benefactors, unbeknownst and unsolicited, to all sentient beings. As the *Avatamsaka Sutra (ch. 21)* states: "The Bodhisattvas also conceive this overwhelming determination: 'If I attain complete perfect enlightenment first without having established all sentient beings on the path of unsurpassed liberation, I would be violating my original vow -- that would never do; so I should first cause all sentient beings to attain Supreme Enlightenment and Nirvana Without Remainder and then after that fulfill Buddhahood. Why? Sentient beings have not asked me to set my mind on Enlightenment. *I, of my own accord, act as an unsolicited friend to sentient beings, wishing to first cause all beings to fully develop their good potential and obtain omniscience.*'" (T. Cleary, tr. *Flower Ornament Sutra*, Vol I/471) #1211

◎ **UNTOUCHABLES**

▸"Members of the lowest castes of Hinduism, whom higher caste Indians must not touch."
Reat: 348 #2103

◙ UPADHYAYA (Skt)
See also: Vinaya School

▶ A teacher, instructor; a master of precepts responsible for the ordination of monks and nuns.

◙ UPALI

▶"One of Shakyamuni's ten major disciples, known as the foremost in observing the precepts. Unlike the other major disciples who came from Brahman families, he was of humble origin, having formerly been a barber at the court of Kapilavastu. He joined the Order at the same time as Aniruddha, Ananda and Devadatta. At the first Buddhist Council held to compile the Buddha's teachings, it is said that Upali recited the vinaya or rules of monastic discipline, while Ananda recited the sutras."
Sokk: 495

"Former royal barber and early disciple of the Buddha, regarded as being the foremost specialist on matters concerning the disciplinary tradition (Vinaya Pitaka). Because he was ordained early in Buddha's ministry, Upali was senior to many of Buddha's best known disciples. He also distinguished himself by learning all of the disciplinary requirements for the monastic community. As such, at the first council, held in Rajagrha during the first rainy season following Buddha's death, Upali recited the entire Vinaya Pitaka or 'Basket of Discipline.' In so doing, he became the first master of Vinaya, beginning a lineage that, according to the Pali tradition, was unbroken at least until Asoka's reign."
Preb: 268   #0297

◙   U P A S A M P A D A / UPASAMPANNA

▶"Higher ordination as a monk, Bhiksu or Bhiksuni."
Thai: 557

◙ UPASAKA
see   Layman

◙ UPASIKA
see   Laywoman

◙ UPAYA
see   Expedient means

◙ UPOSATTHA / UPAVASATHA
Syn: Posadha

▶Literally, "fasting", "a fast", particularly for the purpose of renewing vows.
Thai: 288

"*Uposattha*: On full and new moons, the monastic code (Pratimoksha) is recited before an assembly of monks (or nuns). They are required to attend the ceremony which begins with a public confession or self-criticism."
xxx: na

"Originally a form of meeting. According to the Vinaya, the assembly of monks meets on a full moon and then on a new moon to celebrate the ceremony of reciting the precepts (formerly ordination was also held on this occasion). The ceremony begins with a public confession. The chairman then advises the audience: 'During the past half-month, he who has violated the precepts is invited to confess them and make repentance before the assembly'. This announcement is repeated three times. If there is no answer, he proclaims: 'the Precepts have been cleanly observed by everybody.' Thereupon, follows the ceremony of reciting precepts." NV Hoa: Na #2191

◎ **UPPALAVANNA**
see Utpala

◎ **UPSIDE-DOWN LIVING**
See also: Afflictions; Delusion; Four Inverted Views; Wrong views

----

▸"Sentient beings, lacking wisdom, always live upside down; they mistake the impure for the pure, suffering for happiness, impermanence for permanence, no-self for self. They then develop delusions and become degraded and defiled. Therefore, Buddha Sakyamuni taught sentient beings the Four Truths (q.v.) to sever their delusions.

For example, the human excrement that we consider fetid and dirty is regarded as fragrant, clean and succulent by animals such as insects, dogs and pigs -- because of their deluded karma. They therefore compete and struggle to gobble it up. The defiled desires of this world are considered by humans as lovely and clean. However, the Gods and Immortals see them as foul-smelling, dirty and unclean, not unlike the way human beings regard dogs and pigs eating filthy substances. The various desires of sentient beings, defiled and upside down, are generally thus. The practitioner should strive gradually to destroy them."
Thich: 145
Consider the example, adapted

from the sutras, of worms feeding on rotten apples. The worms are running hither and thither among the apples, each worm "elbowing" the others for a better spot, a larger piece of the rotten matter. They all feel their actions necessary and desirable. They all seem very busy and very happy. To us humans, however, theirs is indeed a pitiable lot. The human condition is the same from the viewpoint of celestials, Bodhisattvas and Buddhas -- such a pitiful sight indeed, whether of beggars or presidential hopefuls!
Editor: na #1328

◉ **URNA**
See also: Thirty-two Auspicious Signs

▸"A white curl between the eyebrows; one of the thirty-two auspicious signs of a Buddha, but also seen on the foreheads of Bodhisattvas and other divinities."
Okaz: 187 #0648

◉ **UTPALA**
Syn: Uppalavanna

▸"A woman renowned for her beauty born to a noble family in the city of Rajagrha in ancient India. When she discovered that her husband had committed adultery with her mother, she left him. Later, after remarrying, she was shocked to find that the mistress of her second husband was her own daughter by her first marriage. The discovery drove her to such despair that she left her second husband and became a prostitute [intent on destroying all men]. Still later, she became a nun under the guidance of Maudgalyayana [whom she had failed to lure away from the Order]."
Yoko/1976: 216 #1184

◉ **UTTARAKURU**
See also: Four Continents

▸"The northern of the four continents of traditional Indian geography. Its inhabitants are said to live a thousand years and to enjoy constant happiness."
Yoko/1976: 216

Because of their happy surroundings, the inhabitants of Uttarakuru do not exert themselves to cultivate the Dharma.

Thus rebirth in such a continent, like rebirth in the borderlands, is considered a potential obstacle to cultivation of the Dharma.
Editor: na #1185

◙ **VAIDEHI**

See also: Meditation Sutra; Bimbisara; Ajatasatru

►The Queen of King Bimbisara of Magadha, India. It was in response to her entreaties that Buddha Shakyamuni preached the *Meditation Sutra*, which teaches a series of sixteen visualizations (of Amitabha Buddha, the Pure Land) leading to rebirth in the Land of Ultimate Bliss.
Editor/Tam: 168
Background
"Wife of Bimbisara, king of Magadha, and the mother of Ajatashatru. She is said to have been the sister of King Prasenajit of Kosala. According to the *Kammuryoju (Meditation) Sutra*, when Ajatashatru imprisoned his father Bimbisara and attempted to starve him to death, Vaidehi regularly covered her body with a mixture of honey and flour and went to visit Bimbisara in prison; thus the king was able to eat and survive. When Ajatashatru discovered this, he was enraged and attempted to kill his mother but was restrained by his ministers Jivaka and Chandra. Instead, Ajatashatru had her confined to the interior of the palace. She faced Eagle (Vulture) Peak where Shakyamuni was preaching and prayed to him. Out of compassion for her, the Buddha interrupted his preaching and appeared in the palace with Ananda and Maudgalyayana. At her request, he taught her how to reach the Pure Land of Amitabha Buddha. On that occasion, Vaidehi asked Shakyamuni why she should be destined to have a son as evil as Ajatashatru, and why Shakyamuni himself should have to be associated with someone as wicked as Devadatta, but these questions are not answered in the *Meditation (Kammuryoju) Sutra*."
Sokk: 498 #0298

◙ **VAIPULYA SUTRA**

See also: Twelve Divisions of the Mahayana Canon

►"A Mahayana form of Scripture. A collection of expanded texts, the converse of a digest or summary."
Hump: 208
"Class name of a category or group of texts generally referred to as 'Extended Sutras.' The Sanskrit term *vaipulya* literally means 'lengthy' or 'extended' and refers to a means by which Buddha taught the Dharma through 'extending' a story or

description. This type of approach is particularly applicable to various Mahayana sutras such as the *Prajna-Paramita* texts, the *Avatamsaka Sutra*, and many others."

Preb: 270-271

"The Vaipulya sutras ... are the most important of all texts. These are *interalia* the *Saddharma-pundarika (Lotus Sutra)*, the *Lankavatara Sutra* and the *Avatamsaka Sutra*."

Lahiri: 106 #0431

◙ VAIROCANA BUDDHA

Syn: Primal Buddha; Maha-Vairocana
See also: Adi-Buddha

▸*Jpn*/Dainichi. "The Dharmakaya of Sakyamuni Buddha; his Sambhogakaya being called Locana and Nirmanakaya, Sakyamuni."

C.Luk/Chan: 244

The main Buddha in the *Avatamsaka Sutra*. Represents the Dharma Body of Buddha Shakyamuni and all Buddhas. His Pure Land is the Flower Store World, i.e., the entire cosmos.

Editor/Tam: 168

"Literally 'Shining Out,' one of the five Celestial Buddhas of Mahayana Buddhism. Although he did not become popular until around the seventh century A.D., in Tantric Buddhism, he is located at the center of the cosmic mandala, surrounded by the other four Celestial Buddhas. His symbol is often represented as the Dharmacakra or 'Wheel of the Teaching,' and is sometimes shown making the 'supreme wisdom' mudra in which the right index finger is held by the fingers of the left hand. He is regularly associated with the Celestial Bodhisattva Samantabhadra. He is also noted, in the Chinese scholastic tradition, to be the Dharma-kaya of Sakyamuni Buddha. Vairocana is regarded in some traditions to be the Adi-Buddha or primoridal Buddha. In iconography, he is depicted as white in color."

Preb: 271

"The 'first Buddha' in the far, far past at the beginning of the present cosmic eon; used to symbolize the buddha-mind beyond space and time, reality prior to anything within our experience."

Clea: 175 #0158

◙ VAISALI

▸'"The name of an ancient country in Central India. One of

the sixteen larger countries in the Buddha's time. The capital, also called Vaisali, was located twenty-seven miles north of Patna, in the northern Indian State of Bihar."
Dait: 19　#0064

◙ VAJRA

▶"The thunderbolt symbol used in art and ritual magic in Tibet."
Hump: 69
"Literally 'a diamond.' Usually a symbol of the indestructible nature of Buddha's wisdom. A weapon to conquer demons and protect Buddhism."
Chan: 485　#0493

◙ VAJRACCHEDIKA SUTRA
see　Diamond Sutra

◙ VAJRAYANA
see　Esoteric school; Tibetan Buddhism

◙ VARANASI
see　Benares

◙ VASSA
see　Rains retreat

◙ VASUBANDHU (420-500)
See also: Asanga; India (Buddhism in); Rebirth Treatise; Gandhara

▶"Famous Indian philosopher and writer. With his brother Asanga founded the Yogacara School of Mahayana Buddhism. His early work, the *Abhidharma-Kosa*, is one of the fullest expositions of Abhidhamma teaching of the Theravada School. Later on, being converted to the Mahayana point of view by his brother, he wrote the *Vijnaptimatra Shastra*, expounding the Mahayana doctrine of Mind-Only."
Hump: 210

"In India, the Pure Land teaching was advocated by Asvaghosa, Nagarjuna, and Vasubandhu, and was based upon various sutras such as the two *Sukhavati-vyuhas* (*Amitabha Sutras*)."
Dait: 157
Author of a famous Pure Land commentary *The Rebirth Treatise* (q.v.).
Editor: na　#00583

◙ VEDAS

▶"The basic scriptures of Brahmanism, not recognized by Buddhists."
Dait: 15　#0080

◙ VEGETARIANISM
See also: Overeating; Killing; Food

▸"Buddhists hold life to be one and therefore sacred. They do not, therefore, kill for sport. For the Mahayana viewpoint, see Suzuki, *Studies in the Lankavatara Sutra*, pp. 368-371."
Hump: 126

"Killing sentient beings, including slaughtering animals for food, is among the heaviest transgressions in Buddhism. This is not only because such acts create untold pain and suffering but also because they cut short the lives of future Buddhas (as all sentient beings have a common Buddha-nature). The injunction against all forms of killing (including suicide), covering all sentient beings, is unique to Buddhism. Jainism, for example, approves of the penance of death by self-starvation (suicide), while Hindu ceremonies such as the Srauta rites 'center on offering into the altar fires, oblations of milk, butter, honey ... domestic animals (sacrifice) ...'" (K. Crim, *Dictionary of Religions*, p.369 and 790, respectively.)
Thich: 324

"Animals have just as much right to life as we on this earth that we share in common, and therefore we have no right to destroy them at our whim. Moreover, since in our ascent and descent on the ladder of innumerable lives (according to causes and conditions) our Buddha-nature assumes many forms -- all of which are aspects of oneself -- to destroy any life form is to destroy a part of oneself."
Kapl/1980: 258

Question/Answer

"*Student:* The *Lankavatara* and *Surangama Sutras* -- both Mahayana scriptures -- are quite eloquent in their condemnation of meat-eating... What reasons do they give?

Master: That there is not one being which in its karmic evolution and devolution through countless rebirths, has not been our mother, our father, husband or wife, sister, brother, son, or daughter -- not one being whose kinship with us, even while living in the animal state, has not continued. How then can any spiritual person who approaches all living things as if they were himself eat the flesh of something that is of the same nature as himself? Seen this way, isn't all flesh-eating a form of cannibalism? How can anyone who seeks liberation from suffering inflict pain directly or indirectly on another creature?

Those who eat the flesh of an animal obviously enjoy it, so in effect they are deriving pleasure from the death of another living being."

Kapl: 232-233

"To intentionally deprive any living being, but especially a human being, of life will produce painful karma. Slaughterers as well as hunters and fishermen -- especially those motivated by sport alone -- inevitably incur a heavy karma. Those who do experimental research on animals, often depriving them of their lives, also risk painful karma. The destruction of animals in such experimentation is justified on the ground that it is the only way by which to gain information vital to the health and welfare of human beings. Unfortunately, much animal experimentation today is undertaken without consideration of alternative, more humane methods. Such an unfeeling attitude may arise from the belief that animals, being less developed than man, suffer less. But who would deny that animals, too, suffer pain acutely and try to avoid it as much as humans? And precisely because their minds are less complex than man's and they are more intuitive, animals are more sensitive to impending violence and pain, which generates in them fear that prolongs their suffering. Porphyry, a Greek philosopher of the fourth century, wrote that anyone who had heard the scream of an animal being slaughtered could never again eat animal flesh."

Kapl/1980: 245 #1192

"For inhabitants of polar regions, vegetarianism would indeed be attachment -- and one that would cost them their lives... But those of us living in modern, industrialized countries in North America, Europe, and Asia are blessed with a vast array of food choices. Most of us are able to obtain an abundance of nonflesh foods that can keep us robustly healthy our whole lives. With such a variety of nonanimal foods available, who would choose to support the slaughter mills and foster the misery involved in factory farming, by continuing to eat flesh? There are those who fear that without meat or fish their health would suffer (the irony!), others who may be unaware of how enormously the meat industry contributes to the misuse and waste of global resources ... Can we maintain a nonmeat diet for reasons of

compassion and still be free of attachment to it? In the *Platform Sutra*, the Chinese patriarch Hui Neng relates that after inheriting the Dharma from the Fifth Patriarch, he spent years in seclusion with a group of hunters. At mealtimes, 'he tells us, 'they cooked meat in the same pot with the vegetables. If I was asked to share, I replied, 'I will just pick the vegetables out of the meat. Was he, then, attached to vegetarianism? And if refraining from eating flesh foods is itself an 'attachment,' does it follow that refusing to give up flesh foods shows non-attachment? It is sad to see how many American Buddhists are managing to find a self-satisfying accommodation to eating meat. Some airily cite the doctrine of Emptiness, insisting that ultimately there is no killing and no sentient beings being killed. Others find cover behind the excuse that taking life is the natural order of things and, after all, 'the life of a carrot and that of a cow are equal.' The truth is, though, that as humans we are endowed with discriminating minds that we can use to educate ourselves to the implications of our volitional acts and to choose those foods that minimize suffering to living beings. Our aspiration in Mahayana Buddhism, inasmuch as we can speak of an aspiration, is to liberate our innate compassion and fulfill the Bodhisattva Vows. In the first of those vows, 'All beings, without number, I vow to liberate,' we commit our compassion to all beings, not just humans. Eschewing meat is one way to express that commitment to the welfare of other creatures. Once we leave habitual preferences behind and forgo nimble rationalizations, the issue of vegetarianism comes down to a question of need. If you need to eat flesh foods to sustain your life or, in extreme cases, your health, do so, and do so with awareness and gratitude. But if you don't, why contribute to unnecessary suffering?"
Kjolh/Tric/Winter/94

On the question of vegetarianism, the magazine *Vegetarian Times* commissioned a survey in 1992 which showed that 12.4 million persons in the United States and Canada considered themselves vegetarian. There were in 1993 some 114 local vegetarian associations in the US and Canada, nearly double the number five years earlier. The largest groups are the Toronto Vegetarian Association in Canada (600 members) and the Vegetarian Society of Colorado, USA (500 members). (From *Vegetarian Times*, May 1993.) Editor/Zen: 211-212

NOTE: "Funeral arrangements should be kept simple, not accompanied by superfluous ceremonies occasioning unnecessary expenses. *Another caveat*: only vegetarian food should be served. No non-vegetarian food should be provided as offerings or to entertain guests -- for to take life is to sadden the departed with more karmic obstructions and 'heavy baggage,' making his liberation that much more difficult. Even if he has already been reborn in the Pure Land, his grade of rebirth may be lowered as a result. ... As stated in the *Ksitigharba Sutra*: The dead one might be due to receive a good retribution and be born among men and gods in his next life or in the future, but because of offenses committed by his family in his name, his good rebirth will be delayed. Everyone must undergo the Evil Paths in accordance with his own deeds; it is even more unbearable when

survivors add to those deeds." Thich: 289;324 #2266

◙ **VEHICLE**
see Yana

◙ **VEILS**

►"Phenomena that obstruct the mind from realization of truth in meditation: lust, anger, sleepiness, excitement, regret, and doubt."
Chih-I/Cleary: 207

◙ **VERTICAL ESCAPE**
see Horizontal Escape

◙ **VESAK**
Syn: Wesak
See also: Bathing the Buddha; Buddhist Festivals

►*Theravada School*
"The month corresponding to April-May, on the Full Moon day of which is celebrated the Birth, Renunciation, Enlightenment and Parinirvana of the Buddha. The festival is called from the name of the month."   Hump: 216
NOTE: Today, all Buddhist schools, Theravada as well as Mahayana, celebrate the Birth of the Buddha on the 15th day of fourth month, but Mahayana s c h o o l s   o b s e r v e   t h e

Renunciation, Enlightenment and Parinirvana on separate dates. Japanese Buddhists observe the same principle, but follow the Western instead of the Lunar calendar (e.g., 15 *April* instead of the 15th day of the fourth month for the Birth of the Buddha).
Editor: na   #0345

◙ **VIETNAM (BUDDHISM IN)**
See also: Immolation

▸"Buddhism may have been introduced to Vietnam by sea as early as the first century. By the second century, Chinese sources record a flourishing Buddhist Community in Tongking (northern Vietnam). [Two monks in particular were active during the 2nd/3rd century, Mâu-Bác (Mou-po) and Khương-Tăng-Hội (K'ang Seng Hui).] The history of Vietnamese Buddhism as such, however, begins in 580, with the arrival of Vinitaruci, an Indian monk who had studied with the third patriarch of Chinese Chan Buddhism, long before its split into northern and southern schools. *This first lineage of Vietnamese Zen masters* ended with the death of its twenty-eighth patriarch in 1216, though the Vinitaruci branch continues to be prominent,

primarily in the north.
The second Zen lineage in Vietnam was initiated by the Chinese monk Wu Yen T'ung (Vô-Ngô-Thông, d. 826), who studied in China with [the famous Zen Master Pai-chang, q.v.]. This lineage of meditation masters also died out in the thirteenth century, though again the school itself survives. Although these first two lineages of Chan Buddhism did not survive as lineages, they did lay the foundations for a thorough integration of Buddhism and Vietnamese nationalism which began in the Đinh dynasty (969-81). King Đinh-Bộ-Lĩnh established a state-sponsored Vietnamese Sangha and initiated the practice of appointing eminent monks to advisory positions at court, offices formerly filled exclusively by Confucian scholars.
In the [earlier] Lê dynasty (981-1009), the first complete Chinese Tripitaka was imported, establishing the scriptural basis of Vietnamese Buddhism.
The Lý dynasty (1010-1225) spanned the golden age of Vietnamese independence and prosperity. Before this period, Vietnam, still confined to Tongking in the north, was

dominated by the Chinese. After this period, Vietnam, though expanding in territory, was harassed by the Mongols, coveted by the Yuan, Ming, and Ch'ing dynasties of China, and finally dominated by France. In 1069 the Lý dynasty's campaign of southward expansion against Champa reached its farthest extent, the seventeenth parallel. In the course of this campaign, a very significant prisoner of war was brought to Tongking from captured Cham territory. This prisoner was the Chinese monk Ts'ao Tang (Thảo-Đường), a proponent of the Chan-Pure Land synthesis, which was prominent at the time in Sung dynasty China. With the avid support of King Lý Thánh Tôn (r. 1054-72), *the Chan-Pure Land synthesis gained a dominant position among the Vietnamese that it maintains to the present day*... As a part of Vietnam's struggle for independence, a movement began in 1932 at the Từ-Đàm Temple in Hue to consolidate Vietnamese Buddhism. This movement resulted first in the foundation of the Central Vietnamese Buddhist Association in 1932, and then, in 1952, the General Association of Buddhism in Vietnam [the precursor of the Vietnamese Unified Buddhist Congress (Giáo-Hội Phật-Giáo Việt-Nam Thống-Nhất), which in 1963 was instrumental in bringing down the regime of President Ngô Đình Diệm. After the fall of the Saigon government in 1975], under the Communist regime, a government-controlled Buddhist Sangha of Vietnam was formed. This last development entailed government regulation of the Sangha ... [a development strenuously opposed by the Vietnamese Unified Buddhist Congress, through its overseas branches]." Reat: 128-131

A major achievement of the Unified Buddhist Congress was the founding of Van Hạnh Buddhist University in Saigon in 1964.

Background

"In ancient times the northern region, Tongking, was for many centuries a province of the Chinese empire. To the south lay the Indianized states of Funan and Champa, which then overflowed beyond the present-day frontiers. The Vietnamese themselves originated in the north, and in time came to dominate the whole land. Independence from China was gained in the tenth century,

but Chinese influences continued to exert a powerful effect and, in the long run, this meant that the standard brand of Sri Lankan Theravada that triumphed elsewhere in Southeast Asia did not do so here; instead, Chinese forms of Mahayana Buddhism, notably a *successful amalgam of Ch'an and Pure Land, prevailed until the country fell to the Communists in 1975*. Since then [the influence of Buddhism has remained strong, although] from time to time we hear reports of active persecution."
Snell: 147
NOTE:
Important feature of Vietnamese Buddhism: "Vietnam is the only country in the world with a national Buddhist association (Giáo-Hội Phật-Giáo Việt-Nam Thống-Nhất) in which both Theravada and Mahayana schools are substantially represented" (Reat). This is noteworthy since the Vietnamese are largely Mahayana, with only a small pocket of Theravada adherents in the region bordering on Cambodia (a Theravada stronghold).
Editor: na #2033

◉ **VIHARA**
Syn: Monastery

See also: Rains Retreat

▸"Literally: 'secluded place'. A Buddhist monastery."
Batc: 384
"In the course of his Ministry, the Buddha was given various places of retreat, or Viharas, where members of the Sangha could spend the rainy period and use as a permanent residence. Such were the Jetavana Park, the Bamboo Grove, the Vulture's Peak and the Deer Park near Benares, now Sarnath."
Hump: 158 #0471

◉ **VIKRAMASILA**
See also: Nalanda

▸"(Sometimes Vikramasika), Buddhist university in ancient India."
Reat: 348 #2105

◉ **VIMALAKIRTI SUTRA**
See also: Amrapali; Licchavi; Ultimatism

▸"The *Vimalakirti Nirdesa Sutra*, in Japanese Yuima Kyo, is a philosophic dramatic discourse written in India about first century A.D., in which basic Mahayana principles are presented in the form of a conversation between famous

Buddhist figures and the humble householder, Vimalakirti. Translated into Chinese by Kumarajiva in 401, it became immensely popular in China."
Hump: 212

"A sutra expounded by the Buddha on Vimalakirti, or 'Spotless Reputation', name of a native of Vaisali, said to be an avatar of 'The Golden Grain Tathagata' appearing in the form of a layman to assist Sakyamuni Buddha in converting people to the Mahayana doctrine."
C.Luk/Chan:244

"[Vimalakirti was] a wealthy man of Vaishali ... who represents the Mahayana lay believer. According to the sutra, he had mastered the profound doctrines of Mahayana and instructed the people by various skillful means. The sutra depicts him as refuting the Theravada views of Shakyamuni's disciples with devastating eloquence and preaching Mahayana doctrines to them on the basis of his understanding of emptiness or non-substantiality."
Sokk: 500-501

"To understand the traditional popularity of the *Vimalakirti Sutra* as a Mahayana text, one need only look to its 'hero,' who is neither the Buddha nor a monk, but a wealthy householder. Vimalakirti was a family man living fully in, but not of, the world, and his spiritual stature is said to have been second only to that of the Buddha. The sutra's profundity, its lively spirit and humor, and its constant emphasis on the non-dual nature of ultimate reality have long endeared it to followers of Mahayana Buddhism ."
Kapl: 288

Mahayana Buddhism emphasizes skill-in-means in conveying the teachings of the Buddha. Thus, when Vimalakirti was shown upbraiding the Arhat disciples, it was for the purpose of exposing the reader to Mahayana principles. Otherwise how could he even meet these Arhat disciples, let alone debate with Manjusri, the Bodhisattva of Wisdom? However, while lay people and the Buddhas may have the same intrinsic wisdom, they are not at the same level in practice. Therefore, the words and deeds of Vimalakirti should not be taken at face value but should be weighed carefully by anyone seeking to emulate them. Note in this regard the story of Kumarajiva (q.v.) and the royal gift of concubines.
Editor: na #0057

For details, see entry "Ultimatism".

◉ **VIMOKSA**
see Eight Samadhis of Emancipation

◉ **VINAYA**
Syn: Vinaya Pitaka
See also: Precepts

►"The precepts for monks and nuns, designed to help them eliminate defilements."
Chan: 485
"*Vinaya Pitaka*: The body of ethical rules and disciplines for Buddhist monks and laypersons prescribed by the Buddha."
Kusa: 181 #0586

◉ **VINAYA**
see Precepts; Tripitaka; Vinaya School

◉ **VINAYA SCHOOL**
syn: Discipline School

►"A school of Buddhism in East Asia that primarily stresses strict observance of the rules laid down in the Vinaya pitaka, the third part of the Tripitaka. Here the life of monks and nuns is regulated in every detail of its moral, ethical, and spiritual aspects. The precise forms for life in a monastery, ordination ceremonies, and so on, are given. In the great Buddhist monasteries of East Asia, which often housed masters of more than one Buddhist denomination, generally a Vinaya master (Skt./ upadhyaya) was responsible for the ordination of the monks."
Sham: 244
"Vinaya is the Sanskrit term denoting the rules of discipline that monks are required to follow. The Vinaya school was so named because it placed particular emphasis on these rules."
Yoko: 190 #0348

◉ **VINITARUCI**
See also: Vietnam (Buddhism in)

►"The history of Vietnamese Buddhism as such began in 580, with the arrival of Vinitaruci, an Indian monk who had studied in China with the third patriarch of Chan (Zen) Buddhism, before it split into northern and southern schools."
Reat: 348 #2106

◉ **VIPARYASA**
see Four Inverted Views

◉ **VIPASYANA**
see Samatha-Vipasyana

◙ **VIRTUE**
See also: Merit and virtue
Note important difference between merits and virtue.

◙ **VIRUDHAKA**

►"The son of the King Prasenajit. When he was the Crown Prince, he was despised by the Sakyas because of his humble birth on his mother's side. After he was enthroned, he attacked Kapilavastu and killed five hundred Sakyas. He died an unnatural death one week after the war ended."
Dait: 18 #0079

◙ **VISIONS**
See also: Demons; Practice (Buddhist)

► Please read entry "Practice" before the following excerpts from *Buddhism of Wisdom and Faith by Master Thich Thien Tam*: "Various realms viewed by earnest practitioners."

I) Internal Realms
If we are not diligent and do not exert efforts along the path of cultivation, nothing usually happens; however, if we are diligent and exert a great deal of effort, we will definitely witness different realms. They either come from within the mind or are caused by outside sources. I will speak first about the realms originating from the mind, called internal realms. Internal realms are also called 'realms of the Self-Mind' because they do not come from outside, but develop from the mind. Those who do not clearly understand the truth that 'the thousand dharmas are created by the mind,' think that all realms come from the outside. This is wrong. When the practitioner reaches the stage of mutual interpenetration [of mind and realms], completely severing external conditions, the seeds of latent dharmas in the Alaya Consciousness suddenly manifest themselves. For the Buddha Recitation or mantra-chanting practitioner, the power of the Buddha's name or the mantra penetrates deep into the mind, eliciting a reaction from the wholesome or evil seeds in the Alaya consciousness. The realms that result are very complex and usually appear in dreams, or even when the practitioner is awake and striving to recite the Buddha's name. In Buddhism, this condition is called 'changing manifestations of the Alaya consciousness.' *Dreaming scenes.*

If the events or scenes result from evil seeds, the practitioner, in his dreams, may see various species of worms crawling out of his body, or witness himself, night after night, removing from his body six or seven loathesome creatures with many limbs, such as scorpions or centipedes. Or else, he may see various species of wild animals and/or spirits or ghosts. Such realms are innumerable and cannot all be described! In general individuals greatly afflicted with greed, who are miserly and wicked, usually see marks of men and women, snakes and serpents and odd species with white features and forms. Those harboring a great deal of anger and resentment usually see tigers and leopards or strange species with red forms and features. Those who are heavily deluded usually see domestic animals, clams, oysters, snails or different species with black forms and features. The above, however, is merely indicative; it does not mean that everything will be exactly as described. If the scenes in his dreams come from good, wholesome seeds, the practitioner sees tall trees and exotic flowers, beautiful scenery, brightly adorned with nets of pearls. Or else, he sees himself eating succulent, fragrant food, wearing ethereal garments, dwelling in palaces of diamonds and other precious substances, or flying high in open space. Thus, in summary, all the seeds of the ten Dharma Realms are found in the minds of sentient beings. If wholesome seeds manifest themselves, practitioners view the realms of Buddhas, Bodhisatvas, human and celestial beings; if evil karma is manifested, they witness scenes from the wretched three Evil Paths. If the cultivator has followed externalist ways in lives past, he usually sees his body emitting electric waves, or his soul leaving the body to roam, meeting demons, ghosts and the like, to discuss politics and the rise and fall of countries and empires. On the other hand, when the practitioner's mind is pure, he will know in his dreams about events that will occur three or four days, or seven or eight months, hence. In general, those who have cultivated in previous lives will immediately see auspicious realms when reciting the Buddha's name. Those with heavy karma, lacking merit and virtue, will usually see evil realms when they begin Buddha Recitation. In time, these evil omens will disappear and gradually be replaced with auspicious omens. *Waking scenes.* If the practitioner's efforts have reached a high enough level, there are times during his waking hours when all deluded feelings suddenly cease for a while, body and mind being at ease and free. At other times, the practitioner may recite for four or five hours but feel that the time was very short, perhaps two or three minutes. Or else, at times during recitation, wholesome omens will appear. At other times, unconsciously, his mind experiences great contentment and bliss. Sometimes, he realizes for a split second that mind and realm are both empty. At other times, just by hearing or seeing something once, he becomes awakened to the truth of suffering, emptiness, impermanence and No-Self, completely severing the marks of self and others. These occurrences are too numerous to be fully described!

II) External Realms

They are realms which are not created by the mind, but come from the outside. For example, some practitioners might see Buddhas and Bodhisattvas appearing before them, preaching the Dharma, exhorting and praising them. Others, while reciting the Buddha's name, suddenly experience an awakening and immediately see the Land of Ultimate Bliss. Some practitioners, in the midst of their pure recitation, see deities and Immortals arrive, join hands and circumambulate them respectfully, or invite them for a leisurely stroll. Still other practitioners see 'wandering souls of the dead' arrive, seeking to 'take refuge' with them. Yet others, having reached a high level in their practice, have to endure challenges and harassment from external demons. For example, there was once a layman of rather dull capacities who constantly worshipped the Bodhisattva Avalokitesvara. During a dream one night, he saw the Bodhisattva urging him to meditate on the following stanza, and in time he would experience a Great Awakening: 'Great wisdom develops from the Mind,/ Where in the Mind can it be found?/ To realize all meanings,/ Is to have neither past nor present.' Another story concerns a nun of the author's acquaintance who was cultivating in the vicinity of Dalat. After her Buddha

Recitation session, as she was seated in meditation, she saw two men of noble countenance, dressed like deities or Immortals, respectfully inviting her to scale the mountains and visit their beautiful grounds. In her samadhi, she asked them, 'How can I go, when the mountains are so high and I am so weak?' One of the men said, 'Do not worry, I have a way.' He then touched her lightly with something similar to a willow branch and requested her to follow him. She suddenly saw her body glide effortlessly over the grass, and, in no time, she was scaling the mountains. There she witnessed ethereal scenes, with gigantic trees and a palace and tower in the distance. At that very moment, a companion in the back room dropped something with a bang. The nun suddenly awakened from meditation. All scenes had disappeared but her thighs were still aching from overexertion."
Tam: 192-195,198-199

Question / Answer

"Some might ask, 'To see Buddhas and lotus blossoms during Buddha Recitation practice -- is it not to see demonic apparitions?' *Answer*: If cause and effect coincide, these are not 'demonic realms.' This is because the Pure Land method belongs to the *Dharma Door of Existence*; when Pure Land practitioners first set out to cultivate, they enter the Way through forms and marks and seek to view the celestial scenes of the Western Pure Land. When they actually witness these auspicious scenes, it is only a matter of effects corresponding to causes. If cause and effect are in accord, how can these be 'demonic realms'? In the Zen School, on the other hand, the practitioner enters the Way through the *Dharma Door of Emptiness*. Right from the beginning of his cultivation he wipes out all marks -- even the marks of the Buddhas or the Dharma are destroyed. The Zen practitioner does not seek to view the Buddhas or the lotus blossoms, yet the marks of the Buddhas or the lotus blossoms appear to him. Therefore, cause and effect do not correspond. For something to appear without a corresponding cause is indeed the realm of the demons. Thus, the Zen practitioner always holds the sword of wisdom aloft. If the demons come, he kills the demons, if the Buddha comes, he kills the Buddha -- to enter the realm of True Emptiness is not

to tolerate a single mark."
Tam: 200 #1341
See also Proofs of Rebirth in the Pure Land.

◙ VISUALIZATIONS
Syn: Contemplations
See also: Meditation Sutra; Sixteen Meditations

▸"The bringing to mind, calling to attention, or imagining in the mind (manasikara) of an idea or visual image."
Gomez: 331

"Meditation. This is essentially supra-mental, in that the mind is illuminated and performs its functions without the process of conscious thought. This is recognized as the highest stage of conscious union with Reality, by both Buddhist and [other] mystics."　　Murt: 33

Pure Land Buddhism

The scriptural basis for visualizations in Pure Land Buddhism can be found in the *Meditation Sutra.*

"Out of concern for future beings who will be without the benefit of the Buddha's revelation, Vaidehi [the Queen to whom the Buddha preached the *Meditation Sutra*] inquires about the way for their rebirth. In response, the Buddha instructs her in the

sixteen kinds of contemplation, beginning with contemplation of the setting sun in this Saha World and moving on to the physical dimensions of Sukhavati, such as the ground, trees, and lakes, and to the features of Buddha Amitabha and the Bodhisattvas Avalokitesvara and Mahasthamaprapta. The last three contemplations have as their object the nine Grades of Rebirth (q.v.) to which people are assigned by virtue of their ability and attainment. The instructions on the contemplations constitute the primary subject of the main body of the sutra." (Kotatsu Fujita, *The Textual Origin of the Kuan Wu-liang-shou Ching.*)
Tana: 150 #0939

◙ VOICE OF A BUDDHA
See also: Name (of Buddha / Boddhisattva)

▸"The presence of a Buddha, his appearance and the vision that his audience has of him are all aspects of a sacred viewing, which in the Indian context implies a transference of power or grace from Buddha to sentient beings. Hearing the voice of the Buddha or hearing his name, seeing his physical body has the power to transform the believer, causing sincere faith, deep concentration of mind and even salvation and rebirth in a purified field."

Gomez: 317, 331

The purpose of seeing the Buddha is to be able to hear his teaching directly, rather than through intermediary sources such as sutras, commentaries, etc. Moreover, if cultivators are reborn in the Pure Land, as is said in the *Surangama Sutra*:

"They will never be far from the Buddha, and their Minds will awaken by themselves, without the aid of expedients. A person who has been near incense will carry a fragrance on his person ."

Editor: na #1721

See also Name (of Buddha / Bodhisattva)

◙ **VOID**
see Emptiness

◙ **VOWS**
See also: Vows/ Rebirth In Pure Land

▶*VOWS AS CRUCIAL ELEMENT*
"Once Sakyamuni Buddha and his disciple Maudgalyayana went with a large gathering of followers to another country to convert living beings. When the citizens saw the Buddha they shut their doors and ignored him. When they saw Maudgalyayana, however, they ran to greet him, and everyone, from the King and ministers to the citizens, all bowed and competed to make offerings to him. The Buddha's disciples thought this most unfair. 'World Honored One,' they said, 'your virtuous conduct is so lofty; why is it that they do not make offerings to you, but instead compete to make offerings to Maudgalyayana?' 'This is because of past affinities,' said the Buddha." I will tell you. Limitless aeons ago, Maudgalyayana and I were fellow-countrymen. He gathered firewood in the mountains and I lived in a hut below. A swarm of bees was bothering me and I decided to smoke them out. But Maudgalyayana refused to help even though they stung him until his hands were swollen and painful. Instead, he made a vow, "It must be miserable to be a bee," he thought. "I vow that when I attain the Way I will try to save these asura-like bees first thing!" Many lifetimes later the bees were reborn as the citizens of this country. The queen bee became the King, the drones became the ministers, and the

workers became the citizens. Because I didn't like the bees, I now have no affinity with these people and therefore no one makes offerings to me. But because of his vow, all the citizens revere Maudgalyayana'".
Huan Hua: na
In *Pure Land Buddhism*, there are two main groups of vows:
i) The vows of Amitabha Buddha, made when He was the Bodhisattva Dharmakara;
ii) The vows made by practitioners to achieve rebirth in Amitabha's Pure Land.
For details, please see the following entries:
i) *Dharmakara's Vows*;
ii) *Vows / Rebirth in the Pure Land.*

◉ VOWS / *REBIRTH IN PURE LAND*
See also: One-pointedness of Mind; Original Vows; Other Power
----
▸Please read "Vows" before this entry.
(I) Vows as Crucial Element
"Making a vow to attain birth in the Pure Land signifies a fundamental reorientation of the believer's motivations and will. No longer is the purpose brute survival, or fulfillment of a social role, or the struggle to wrest some satisfaction from a frustrating, taxing environment. By vowing to be reborn in the Pure Land, believers shift their focus. The joys and sorrows of this world become incidental, inconsequential. The present life takes on value chiefly as an opportunity to concentrate one's awareness on Amitabha, and purify one's mind accordingly." (J.C. Cleary, tr., *Pure Land, Pure Mind.*)

"Elder Master Ou I, a high-ranking Pure Land monk, has said, 'To be reborn in the Pure Land or not depends entirely upon Faith and Vows; the grade of rebirth (high or low) depends on whether one's Practice is deep or shallow.' He further added, 'Without Faith and Vows, you cannot be reborn, even if you recite the Buddha's name to the point where neither the blowing wind nor the falling rain can penetrate and your recitation is as solid as a bronze wall or an iron gate.' Those who practice Buddha Recitation assiduously but lack Faith and Vows will merely obtain the merits and blessings of the human and celestial realms, according to their level of cultivation. When their blessings are exhausted they are once again subject to birth and death." (Thích Thiền Tâm, *Buddhism of Wisdom and Faith*, sec. 21.)

(II) Forms of the Rebirth Vow

Buddhism of Wisdom & Faith/ excerpts:
"In each Buddha Recitation session, after the recitation itself, the practitioner immediately pays respect to Amitabha Buddha, seeking His guidance. He then kneels down and recites verses of repentance, Vows and dedication (transference) of merit. This last part is very important, because it is the time when he concentrates his mind to direct merits and virtues toward the desired goal. This is similar to a boat which moves by human strength or engine power but whose direction is determined by the person at the rudder. The Vow for rebirth is the part of Pure Land cultivation in which the practitioner uses his mind to steer the boat of Buddha Recitation toward the Western Pure Land. As far as the form of the Vow for rebirth is concerned, some cultivators prefer long compositions through which they can develop an earnest mind. Others prefer a shorter version that includes the desire to achieve rebirth in the Pure Land. These ideas are succinctly expressed in the 'Prayer to Amita[bha] Buddha,' as follows: 'Of Buddhas in all places and at all times, Amita[bha] Buddha is the foremost. He delivers sentient beings of all nine grades. His glory and power are unlimited. We now are taking complete refuge in him, and repent our physical, oral and mental sins. If there is any blessing or good action, we sincerely apply it as parinamana [transference of merit]. May we, as fellow Amidists, enjoy miraculous manifestations from time to time. At the end of our lives, the scene of the Western Paradise will manifest itself clearly in front of our eyes. What we see and hear will contribute to our good progress toward rebirth in Paradise. We shall see the Buddha and end further births and deaths, just like Buddhas who deliver all beings. May boundless klesas [afflictions] be severed. May countless approaches be practiced. We vow that we wish to deliver all sentient beings and that all may achieve Buddhahood. Even if the Void is finite, our wish, however, is infinite...'*(The Buddhist Liturgy*, p. 271-273)

"If the cultivator is of limited capacity or failing memory and is unable to recall long involved sentences, he should simply memorize the following short form of the Vow for rebirth in the Pure Land: *On .... (date), this disciple, (name) ... vows that through the virtues just accumulated, he will, at the time of death, be welcomed and guided by Amitabha Buddha to the Land of Ultimate Bliss, so that he may achieve Buddhahood and save sentient beings*. This short Vow, accompanied by its exact date, has the effect of strongly focussing the practitioner's mind at all times on the Pure Land and on rebirth there. This small detail is an expedient that renders the Vow that much more powerful and firm."

Tam: 104

(III) Note

According to the Buddha, as sentient beings, we all have strong attachments -- particularly to our bodies and possessions. At the time of death, as we are about to lose both body and possessions, our consciousness, impelled by these deep-seated attachments, rushes to reincarnate itself in another body. It is at this juncture that vows, particularly the vow for rebirth in the Pure Land, are crucial: instead of just following our karma, good and evil, we may, through the power of these vows, achieve rebirth in the Pure Land.   Editor: na

"When making the Vow for rebirth in the Pure Land, we should do so from the depth of our earnest mind. If we merely recite *pro forma* at our convenience, without earnestness, our practice of Buddha Recitation will not be true and sincere.   Elder Master Yin Kuang has said: *Deep sincerity is a major element that leads to one-pointedness of mind. One part of deep sincerity destroys one part of bad karma and yields one part of merit and wisdom*. Ten parts of deep sincerity destroy ten parts of bad karma and yield ten parts of merit and wisdom. The ancients have also said: *The power of deep sincerity focussed in any direction can explode mountains and melt gold in that direction*."

Tam: 106   #1739

See also "One-pointedness of Mind."

◙ **VOWS OF SAMANTABHADRA**
see   Ten Great Vows

◙ **VULTURE PEAK**
Syn: Mount *Gridhrakuta*; Eagle Peak

See also: Rajagrha

►"A mountain located to the northeast of *Rajagriha*, the capital of Magadha in ancient India, where Shakyamuni is said to have expounded the *Lotus Sutra* and other teachings. Vulture Peak (Eagle Peak) was so called because its summit is shaped like an eagle and because it was inhabited by many eagles. The expression Eagle Peak is also used to symbolize the Buddha-land or the state of Buddhahood."
Sokk: 74

"For strategic reasons Rajagaha, the capital of the old kingdom of Magadha, was built amidst mountains and consequently in the summer was stifling hot and in the monsoon period humid and stuffy. The Buddha, therefore, liked to spend his time on Vulture Peak. Here he preached dozens of sermons. The platform found on top of the [peak] is of later origin. From Vulture Peak the eye wanders back to the now inhabited valley of Rajagaha. The modern town of Rajgir lies outside the valley. The ascent to Vulture Peak begins at the remains of the monastery which Jivaka, the physician to King Bimbisara, presented to the Buddha as a gift. Further up on the path, perhaps on the road section, one passes the place where Devadatta tried in vain to kill the master by hurling down a boulder. After the death of the Buddha (483 B.C.) the first Council took place in a cave in one of the mountains around Rajagaha."
Schumann:. 95-96

"Grdhrakuta mountain (Vulture Peak) was much associated with the life of the Buddha. Grdhrakuta is on the Chhahata hill at Rajagrha (modern Rajgir in the Patna district of Bihar). It was one of the favorite resorts of the Buddha and is one of the five sacred hills surrounding the city of Rajagrha, the capital of the powerful state of Magadha. From the foot of the Grdhrakuta to the top there is a road supposed to have been constructed by King Bimbisara in order to reach the Buddha and listen to his preachings. It was here that Devadatta, a cousin of the Buddha, made an attempt on his life by hurling a rock at him. The hill has many natural caves where the Buddha lived... according to the Record of Hsuan-Tsang."
Lahiri: 15 #0254

◙ **WAKE-UP STICK**
see   Kyosaku

◙ **WAR**

►"*Question*: What can we do in times of war or if someone threatens our loved ones?
Answer: It's best to seek other ways to handle difficult situations without resorting to violence. If we use our intelligence and creativity, we could probably find other solutions. Surely diplomacy is more effective than war. No matter how difficult our situation, we always have a choice of how to act. We can distract or injure someone rather than kill him or her. If there is a war, we can consider carefully what choice to make. We can weigh the advantages and disadvantages of killing in this and in future lives, and the effects of this action on ourselves and others. Then we can decide according to what we consider best (or least harmful!), although there may be no easy solution."
Buddhist Union, Oct. 96: 7
"*Question*: Is self-defense ever justifiable in the light of the Buddhist emphasis on non-violence?
Answer: Self-defense needn't involve violence, and non-

violence doesn't mean becoming a doormat. We can seek ways to protect ourselves from harm without harming others or by inflicting the least amount of harm necessary. When however *much* time is available, we can try to diminish our self-centeredness and reflect on compassion before acting... If we feel we cannot avoid maiming or killing, we can at least try to do it... with regret at having to cause another pain. If our intention to cause harm is weak, the karmic effect of the act will be less."
Buddhist Union/ Oct. 96: 7

◙ **WASTELAND OF BIRTH AND DEATH**
see Samsara

◙ **WAT**

►"Buddhist temple. Wats, often referred to as temple compounds or monasteries, are Buddhist religious centers found in villages and neighborhoods in Thailand, Laos, and Cambodia among other countries. Staffed by Buddhist monks and sponsored by wealthy patrons, wats, also called vats, have traditionally functioned as village centers, often providing lodging for travelers, personal counseling, some form of medical and elderly care, a morgue, a library, gathering places for villagers, sites for fairs and festivals, and a general source of both local gossip and news of the outside world. Central to the wat is a bot, or temple for the monks, many of which are noted for their architectural beauty or for the Buddha images they house. Each *wat* also includes many Buddha images and religious monuments, as well as a separate *wiharn*, or temple for the people, and several *sala*, rooms used for local meetings or to house overnight travelers."   Appiah: 689

◙ WAT PO

►"The largest and oldest temple complex in Bangkok, Wat Po was built during the reign of Rama I (1782-1809). This wat is known for its ... gold leaf and mother-of-pearl statue depicting a reclining Buddha at the moment he is entering Nirvana. Having housed various schools and museums, the Wat Po has also functioned as a general center of Thai culture." Appiah: 689

◙ WAT PAH

►"(Thai), forest monastery, often

a place of dhutanga (austerities) observance."
Sume: 139 #2032

◙ WATER OF EIGHT VIRTUES
see Eight Virtues

◙ WATO
Syn: Hua-t'ou
See also: Koan

►Lit: topic; used nowadays as a synonym for Koan.
"Literally, the source of words (before they are uttered), a method used in the Ch'an school to arouse the doubt sensation. The practitioner meditates on such baffling questions as: 'What is Wu?' 'Where am I?' or 'Who is reciting the Buddha's name?' He does not rely on experience, logic, or reasoning. Often, these phrases are taken from kung-ans, at other times, they are spontaneously generated by the practitioner. The term 'hua-t'ou' is often used interchangeably with 'kung-an.'"
Sheng-yen/Sword: 234 #2263

◙ WAY
see Path

◙ WAYMAN, ALEX

►"Modern American scholar of

Buddhism, best known for his work as a Professor at Columbia University and his prolific publication record on a variety of Buddhist topics. The vast majority of Wayman's scholarly publications are devoted to topics in Tibetan Buddhism."
Preb: 279 #1081

◙ **WEI-T'O**

►"Chin. (Skt./ Veda); image in Buddhist monasteries in China. Wei-t'o, one of the generals of the Guardian of the South, wears full warrior's armor. His head is adorned with a helmet and in his hand he holds either a vajra or a war club, with which he 'annihilates' enemies of Buddhist teaching. Thus he is a guardian of the teaching. Wei-t'o is said to have seen the Buddha face-to - face at the moment when the Buddha charged him with the protection of the Dharma. Thus his statue stands facing an image of the Buddha in the main hall of the monastery.

In most monasteries Wei-t'o is invoked in the course of daily worship. Often the selection of a new abbot of the monastery is symbolically attributed to him."
Sham: 246 #0380

◙ **WESAK**
see Vesak

◙ **WEST (BUDDHISM IN THE)**
See also: Europe (Buddhism in); North America (Buddhism in)

►"A Western interest in Buddhism began during the 19th century as a result of colonial contacts with Buddhist countries and the start of academic studies of the Buddhist tradition ... The visits to the West by Buddhists such as Anagarika Dharmapala, who spoke at the World Parliament of Religions in Chicago in 1893, quickened interest. A small Buddhist movement began in the USA and Europe at the beginning of the 20th century, tending to stress the nontheistic, practical and logical nature of Buddhism in its Theravada rather than Mahayana aspects. After World War II, Zen Buddhism came into vogue due to the work of Daisetz Teitaro Suzuki and Zen practitioners who set up Zen groups in the USA.

Tibetan Buddhism arrived in the West after the flight of the Dalai Lama from Tibet, and Tibetan Buddhist centres which attracted Western followers were set up around the West ... In the last 20

years many more groups have been formed which tend to attract thinking Westerners and to have some sort of allegiance to Theravada, Zen or Tibetan Buddhism. More Westerners tend to be attracted to the Buddhist than to the Hindu or Muslim traditions, and although their numbers are still small their significance is growing."
Larousse: 79
NOTE:
"In the May-July 1994 issue of Gold Drum, the movement's magazine, [the well-known British monk] Sangharakshita wrote of the 'Idols of the Marketplace', three modern views that, especially in the USA, are being increasingly confused with Buddhism: *'democratisation', 'feminization', and 'integration'.* Democratization, however appropriate in society at large, undermines the notion of spiritual hierarchy, [while] the integration of spiritual life into ordinary worldly life overlooks the necessity for renunciation. Sangharakshita is determined that if he is to be respected, it is for what he actually believes and teaches." Subhuti/Budd: 183
For further details, see *Europe (Buddhism in) & North America (Buddhism in).* #2262

◙ **WEST (DIRECTION)**

►Represents compassion. For this reason Amida Buddha and Bodhisattva Avalokitesvara are represented as appearing in the west to help the dead and dying. [TC/EOR, p.57] #1287

◙ **WESTERN PURE LAND**
see Sukhavati

◙ **WHEEL OF LAW**
►"The Buddha delivered his first sermon at Sarnath and this event is known as the first turning of the 'Wheel of Law.'"
Lahiri: 59

◙ **WHITE CLOUD SOCIETY**
see Maitreya Society

◙ **WHITE LOTUS SOCIETY (5TH CENTURY)**
See also: Lu-shan; Hui-yuang; Ming dynasty; Pure Land school

►The White Lotus Society (5th century) and the White Lotus Secret Societies (12th century) have almost the same name and ostensibly the same goal -- edification of members and rebirth in the Pure Land. However, the White Lotus Society had a purely religious goal and therefore was not

opposed by orthodox Buddhists and Confucianists. The White Lotus *Secret* Societies, by contrast, had political goals and were banned by the Chinese government.

Editor: na

Background

I. "*White Lotus Society*,' (Pai-lien She/ Bạch-Liên-Xã - 5th c.) was a group of one hundred and thirty-eight devotees who in the 5th century made a collective vow on Mount Lu to be reborn together in Sukhavati under Master Hui-yuan's leadership, which thereby effected Hui-yuan's fame as a Pure Land devotee."

Tana: xvi

II. "*The White Lotus Secret Societies/ White Lotus Sect* (Pai-Lien P'ai/ Bach Lien Phai - 12th c.) were started during the early years of the Southern Sung Dynasty by an individual named Mao Tzu-yuan, a native of Kiangsu, who had been a disciple of Ching-fan (d. 1128), a T'ien-t'ai master also interested in the Pure Land doctrine... Inspired by the example of Master Hui-yuan in Lushan, he organized a White Lotus Secret Society consisting of monks and laymen devoted to the restraint of the passions and the encouragement of good karma.

The group met regularly to utter invocations and sing praises to the Buddha and to hear confessions from the members... The fact that men and women mixed freely at the meetings of the Societies, [wore white robes and ostensibly practiced magic], aroused the opposition of orthodox Buddhists as well as Confucianists, and the Society was criticized as being a hotbed of debauchery... As a result of these charges, Mao was banished to Chiang-chou (present-day Kiukiang in Kiangsi) and the Society was banned. In spite of this prohibition, however, the Society continued to exist and even to expand. Under the Mongol Dynasty the ban was reaffirmed... "

Chen/64: 429-430

The White Lotus Society (5th c.) headed by Master Hui-yuan should be clearly distinguished from later secret societies of similar name during the 12th century, as the latter had political overtones. Opposed to the Mongol emperors who ruled China, the secret societies galvanized the masses and ultimately succeeded in deposing the Yuan (Mongol dynasty) and establishing the Ming dynasty.

Editor: na   #1953

◙ **WILD-FOX ZEN**

▸"The Zen of persons who, though they possess no genuine Zen realization, pretend to be enlightened and deceive other people by imitating outer forms and mouthing truths concerning which they have no real understanding."
Sham: 250 #0391

◙ **WISDOM**
Syn: Prajna
See also: Three Non-Outflow Studies; Wisdom Sutras; Samadhi; Dogma

----

▸"Fundamental wisdom which is inherent in every man and which can manifest itself only after the veil of ignorance, which screens it, has been transformed by means of self-cultivation as taught by the Buddha. Then the mind is in an internal state of imperturbability, exempt from all external sensation, which is called samadhi."
Luk: vol III 292

Samadhi and wisdom should always coexist and form a whole. Wisdom not accompanied by Samadhi is termed "Dried-Up Wisdom" (Dry Wisdom). Samadhi not accompanied by wisdom is called "Dead Tree Samadhi". Editor: na
Dry wisdom: "Intellectual understanding without mental stabilization; also refers to contemplation of phenomena without realization of noumenon."
Chih-I/Cleary: 190 #0780

See also Three Non-Outflow Studies

◙ **WISDOM MIRROR**

▸Great Perfect Wisdom Mirror. This is a reference to the all-seeing wisdom of the Buddhas, which is likened to an immense, round mirror as large as the universe.
Ou-i's: 138 #1692

◙ **WISDOM SUTRAS**
Syn: Maha-Prajna Paramita Sutras; Prajna Paramita Sutras
See also: Diamond Sutra; Heart Sutra

▸"A generic term for those sutras which deal with the teaching of *Prajna-paramita* or the perfection of wisdom, and expound the concept of non-substantiality (*Jpn*/ ku). Sometimes the term in the singular is used in reference to the 600-fascicle *Wisdom Sutra*

translated by Hsuan-tsang."
Sokk: 151

"[As translated by Hsuan-tsang, the *Wisdom Sutras* consist of] a long sermon, composed of several sutras, expounded by the Buddha in four places at sixteen assemblies; it consists of six hundred rolls (chuan) bound in one hundred and twenty volumes, and is the fundamental work of the Mahayana on wisdom, which is the last of the Six Paramitas."
Luk: Vol III 290

Background

"A corpus of 16 Prajna sutras with anonymous authorship is known as the *Mahaprajna-paramita Sutra*, a group of texts greatly esteemed by the Chinese. All the sutras belonging to the Prajna school were translated into Chinese several times, both in a complete form and in extracts. The first one to be translated was the Mahaprajna-paramita in 600 fasciculi equivalent to 200,000 slokas (karikas). Lokaksema, an Indo-Scythian monk was credited with introducing Mahayana Buddhism in China. His partial translation of the Astasahasrika Prajna-Paramita, based on a manuscript from India started a new epoch in the history of Buddhism in China. Then followed various translations of shorter versions like the *Heart Sutra (Prajna Paramita Hrdaya Sutra)* and the *Diamond Sutra (Vajracchedika Sutra)*... "
Lahiri: 23

NOTE:

This collection forms the longest sutra in the Mahayana canon (followed by the *Avatamsaka Sutra*). The two best known sutras within it are the *Diamond Sutra* and the *Heart Sutra*, the latter being the shortest and representing the epitome of the Wisdom philosophy.

Although the *Wisdom Sutras* are highly esteemed, particularly in the West, according to Buddhist patriarchs, it is in the *Lotus* and *Avatamsaka Sutras* that the highest teachings can be found (see Five Teachings and Five Periods and Eight Teachings).
Editor: na #0778

◙ **WISH-FULFILLING JEWEL**

Syn: Wishfulfilling Gem; Cinta-Mani; Mani

See also: Akasagarbha Bodhisattva

►"A jewel said to possess the power of producing whatever one desires. It symbolizes the greatness and virtue of the Buddha and the Buddhist

scriptures. According to the *Perfection of Wisdom Treatise*, this jewel can be obtained from the head of a dragon king, though another fascicle of the same work defines it as a transmutation of the Buddha's relics."
Sokk: 504-505 #0302

◙ **WISHFULFILLING GEM**
see   Wish-fulfilling jewel

◙ **WITHOUT OUTFLOWS**
see   Unconditioned Dharmas

◙ **WOMAN/ ABOVE WORRY AND CARE**
see   "Parable: Woman Who Is Above Worry and Care"

◙ **W O M B   O F   T H E TATHAGATHA**
see   Tathagata-garbha

◙ **WOMEN**
See also: Theragatha / Therigatha; Ananda

▸"To be born into a woman's body was considered a cause for special suffering on account of menstruation,   childbirth and menopause ..." (Susan Murcott, *The First Buddhist Women*)
PLZ: 78
"On one occasion while the Buddha was conversing with King Kosala of India, a messenger came and informed the King that a daughter was born unto him. Hearing it,   the   King   was displeased.   But   the   Buddha comforted and stimulated him, saying: 'A woman child, O Lord of men, may prove even a better offspring than male.' To women who were placed under various disabilities before the appearance of the Buddha, the establishment of the order of Bhikkhunis was certainly a blessing. In this order queens, princesses, daughters of noble families, widows, bereaved mothers,   helpless   women, courtesans -- all, despite their caste or rank -- met on a common footing, enjoyed perfect consolation   and   peace,   and breathed that free atmosphere which   was   denied   to   those cloistered in cottages and palatial mansions. Many, who otherwise would have fallen into oblivion, distinguished   themselves   in various ways and gained their emancipation by seeking refuge in the order."
Narada: 173
"Buddhism has always aimed at the ideal relationship between men and women. Women played an important part in the spread of early Buddhism, both as lay disciples and Bhikkhuni. Famous

women in early Buddhism were: *Bhadda*, famous for her discourses and for her memories of former lives; *Visakha*, a wealthy patroness of the order; *Ambapali*, a courtesan who became a convert and supported the Sangha; *Dhammadipa*, the great preacher; *Mahaprajapati*, the Buddha's foster-mother, who founded the Sangha for women; *Khema*, the consort of king Bimbisara, renowned for her profound insight and *Yashodhara*, the wife of Gotama, also entered the Sangha. In later times, we have *Sanghamitta*, the daughter of Asoka, who founded the Sangha in Sri Lanka."
Murt: 67

"In Hindu tradition, the main duties assigned to women were childbearing and housework. Consequently, a single life was seen as a wasted life and unmarried women were subject to scoffs. On the contrary, in Buddhism, married life was viewed as a hindrance to spiritual pursuits. Wherever the Buddhist point of view prevailed, a woman was no longer compelled to marry to achieve self respect and approval from her family. From the founding of this order, it has provided an even better option for women who were spiritually and religiously inclined. Sumana, the youngest daughter of Anathapindika did not marry but joined the order at an advanced age. There are other instances recorded in the Therigatha."
Tsomo: 92

NOTE:
"When investigating feminine imagery in Buddhist literature, it is important to keep in mind the social and cultural setting within which the teachings were given. The original texts themselves present a range of variant images, not contradictory in an absolute sense, but speaking to different audiences and to beings of different propensities. One point to be noted, for example, is that many of the discourses in these early texts were aimed at helping celibate males break through attachments to the female form. Had the Buddha been addressing celibate females, the defects of the male form would have been similarly elaborated." (Karma Lekshe Tsomo, *Daughters of the Buddha*)
Tsomo: 22 #1890

◙ **WONDERFUL EXISTENCE**
see Emptiness; True Emptiness/ Wonderful Existence

◙ WORDLESS SUTRA

See also: Avatamsaka Sutra

▶Term found in the *Avatamsaka Sutra*, Ch. 37:

"It is as if there were a great scripture,/ Equal in extent to a universe,/ Existing inside one atom,/ And in all atoms as well;/ Someone with intelligence and wisdom,/ Sees all clearly with pure eyes,/ And breaks the atoms, releasing the scriptures,/ For the benefit of all beings./ Buddha-knowledge, likewise,/ Is in all beings' minds..."
[TC/FO2, p.317]

"The 'great scripture' stands for the wisdom of the Buddhas, measureless and all-pervasive. 'Atoms,' or motes of dust represent sentient beings, all of us. The image has 3 meanings: 1) the false hides the true, 2) the minute encompasses the immense, 3) one is all. The scripture is 'equal in extent to a universe' because the Buddha's wisdom is consonant with the essence of all dharmas. The scripture 'exists in all atoms' because all sentient beings possess in full the wisdom, the mind of the Buddhas.

'This big sutra is wordless, but it also has boundlessly many words. It's just that we do not understand them and we don't know how to read them. Each person is in fact a sutra...The true wordless sutra is just the mind-sutra. What is the mind-sutra? It is the embodiment of the tenet that everything is made from mind alone...'"
[HH/FAS,pref.94]

Buddhism of Wisdom & Faith/ excerpts:

"A king once asked the twenty-seventh Indian Patriarch of Zen, 'Other cultivators all recite the sutras; why is it that you do not?' The Patriarch replied, 'This humble monk, when exhaling, is not in contact with mundane conditions, and when inhaling, does not dwell in the "conditioned world" of the Five Skandas. He has recited that sutra over and over millions of times.' The Patriarch meant that he habitually recited the 'Wordless Sutra of the Mind.' This sutra means, externally, not relying on or clinging to the multitude of conditions and, internally, remaining silent and still, unperturbed by the Five Skandas (Aggregates) and the Eighteen Elements. Even all marks, internal, external and in between, are eliminated forever. This is the meaning of 'mind cultivation.' Nevertheless, we should not be so attached to the above that we reject vegetarianism, charity, repentance, Buddha and sutra recitation. This is because all of these practices, from the standpoint of wisdom, help the practitioner swiftly eliminate karmic obstacles and become enlightened to his Self-Nature; from the standpoint of blessings and merit, they enable him to attain favorable karma and rebirth in auspicious lands or the Western Pure Land, where he may pursue his practice without retrogression. Only when he has perfected both merit and wisdom can he achieve Buddhahood. For this reason, the great Bodhisattvas, completely enlightened as they are to the source of the mind, still practice the ten thousand merits to adorn the pure lands. For example, even though the Bodhisattva Maitreya is in his last rebirth before Buddhahood, he still practices repentance continually to rid himself of subtle obstacles and swiftly achieve Supreme Enlightenment. We should realize that the teaching in the *Sutra in Forty-Two Sections* and the words of the twenty-seventh Zen Patriarch are deliberately one-sided in character, partial examples designed to eliminate attachment to form -- that is, cultivation bereft of the mind. In summary, in addition to reciting the Buddha's name, mantras and sutras and conducting repentance ceremonies, the Pure ` Land cultivator should also devote attention to 'opening up the mind.' For the mind to be awakened so that Buddha Recitation can lead to swift rebirth in the Pure Land, he must rid himself of afflictions. Going deeper, while uttering the Buddha's name is 'form,' it is also 'essence,' because noumenon does not exist outside of phenomena -- to recite is Buddha, to recite is Mind. That is why merit and wisdom are fully encompassed in the sacred words 'Amitabha Buddha,' perfectly fusing noumenon and phenomena, and swiftly leading the practitioner both to the state of Perfectly Enlightened Wondrous Mind and to the pure karma of rebirth in the realm of Amitabha Buddha."   Tam: 140

◙ **WORLD FELLOWSHIP OF BUDDHISTS (WFB)**
See also: Encyclopedia of Buddhism

▸"International association of Buddhists founded in 1950 by the

Singhalese Buddhist scholar Malalasekera. The objective of the World Fellowship of Buddhists is to propagate Buddhist teaching and seek reconciliation among the different currents within Buddhism."
Sham: 247

"The WFB promoted the first World Buddhist Conference at Colombo in 1951, the second in Tokyo in September 1952, the third in Rangoon in 1954, and others every few years since. Headquarters are in Bangkok. Journal: *World Buddhism*."
Hump: 217-218 #0349

◙ **WORLD HONORED ONE**
see World- Honored One

◙ **WORLD OF DESIRE**
See also: Cosmology (Buddhist); Triple Realm

►"The first division of the Threefold World (Triple Realm). It is called the World of Desire because its inhabitants are ruled by various desires, such as the desire for food and sexual gratification. The World of Desire is composed of the four Evil Paths (Hell, Hungry ghosts, Animality and Asuras [and the Paths of humans and celestials.)

The celestials reside in the]... six heavens of the World of Desire. In the sixth or highest of the heavens of the World of Desire lives the Devil [Demon] of the Sixth Heaven, who is said to have a strong desire to control others at his will and prevent them from attaining enlightenment."
Sokk: 506

The human realm is part of the World of Desire, which is subject to Birth and Death. #0304

◙ **WORLD OF FORM**
See also: Cosmology (Buddhist); Triple Realm

►"Sometimes translated as the world of matter. The second division of the Threefold world, located above the world of desire. Beings in this realm have physical bodies and are subject to certain material restrictions, but they have no desire, and feed on light. The world of form consists of the four meditation heavens and is further subdivided into eighteen heavens (sixteen or seventeen according to other explanations). The highest is the Akanishtha Heaven."
Sokk: 506 #0305

◙ **WORLD OF FORMLESSNESS**
See also: Cosmology (Buddhist)

▸"Sometimes translated as the world of spirit. The third division of the Threefold world. It is called the world of formlessness because it has no shape or substance. Being a purely spiritual realm, it cannot strictly be said to be 'above' the world of form, though it is often shown that way on diagrams as a matter of logical sequence. It is said that one can attain the world of formlessness by meditation. This world has four realms, reached through progressively deeper meditation. They are: the realm w h e r e e v e r y t h i n g is non-substantial, the realm where there is only consciousness, the realm where nothing exists and the realm where there is neither thought nor no thought."
Sokk: 506 #0306

◙ **WORLD PARLIAMENT OF RELIGIONS**
See also: Chicago Columbian Exposition

▸"Held in conjunction with the 1893 Chicago World's Fair, the watershed marking the beginning of widespread Western interest in Eastern religions."
Reat: 349

"Major event held at the Chicago Columbian Exposition (USA) in 1893. Dharmapala and Soyen Shaku, well known Asian Buddhists, were in attendance, as well as representatives from a number of other traditions. Also present was Paul Carus, the editor of Open Court Press, who was later to become an important voice for the infant American Buddhist movement. In the aftermath of the Parliament, a growing number of Buddhists, particularly from the Zen school, but also including representatives of other traditions, were to appear on American soil."
Preb: 281

"Although little was achieved by the World Parliament of Religions directly, indirectly a major consequence was the recognition and status which it gave to world religions and their representatives: the spread in the West began of religions other than Christianity and Judaism. A less expected consequence was the impetus it gave to the endeavor among Christians to find common ground in their own missionary endeavor, culminating in the Edinburgh Conference of 1910. A further World Parliament of Religions was held in 1993, to mark the centenary of the first, also in Chicago. Attempts to establish a

World Council of Religions were coolly received. Instead, the possibility of Centers for Interfaith Study were envisaged, which might then form networks of consultation. A Global Ethic was proposed, drawing together the common elements in the ethics of different religions: based on the Golden Rule, it hoped to establish a new human consciousness from which a culture of non-violence would emerge."
Oxf: 1045 #1083

◎ WORLD SYSTEM
See also: Billion-World Universe; Cosmology; Universe

▸"A world consists of a Mount Sumeru, its surrounding seas and mountain ranges, a sun, a moon, and other heavenly bodies, extending upward to the first meditation heaven in the world of form and downward to the circle of wind, which forms the basis of the world. A world is somewhat similar to today's concept of a solar system. One thousand worlds make a minor world system, One thousand minor world systems constitute an intermediate world system, and one thousand intermediate world systems form a major world system. Therefore, one major world system comprises one billion worlds. The Buddha taught there are countless major world systems in the universe."
Sokk: 253-254 #0268

◎ WORLD-HONORED ONE
Syn: Bhagavat

▸"An honorific title of Buddha Sakyamuni, that is, one worthy of being honored because he has destroyed all illusions and rid himself of all defilements."
Yoko: 200 #0784

◎ WORLD-ORIGIN
See also: Cosmology; World System; Universe

▸"There are three schools of thought regarding the origin of the world. The first claims that this world came into existence by nature and that nature is not an intelligent force. However, nature works on its own accord and goes on changing. The second school of thought says that the world was created by an almighty God who is responsible for everything. The third says that the beginning of this world and of life is inconceivable since they have neither beginning nor end. Buddhism is in accordance with this third school of thought. Bertrand Russell supported this school of thought by saying, 'There is no reason to suppose that the world had a beginning at all. The idea that things must have a beginning is really due to the poverty of our thoughts.' Modern science says that some millions of years ago, the newly cooled earth was lifeless and that life originated in the ocean. Buddhism has never claimed that the world, sun, moon, stars, winds, water, days and nights were created by a powerful god or by a Buddha. Buddhists believe that the world was not created once upon a time, but that the world is being created millions of times every second and will continue to do so by itself and will destroy itself. According to Buddhism, world systems always appear and disappear in the universe... The Buddha did not waste His time on this issue. The reason for His silence was that this issue has no religious value for gaining spiritual wisdom. The explanation of the origin of the universe is not the concern of religion. Such theorizing is not necessary for living a righteous way of life and for shaping our future life. However, if one insists on studying this subject, then one must investigate the sciences of astronomy, geology, biology and anthropology. These sciences can offer more reliable and tested information on this subject than can be supplied by any religion. The purpose of a religion is to cultivate the life here in this world and hereafter until liberation is gained. In the eyes of the Buddha, the world is nothing but Samsara -- the cycle of repeated births and deaths. To Him, the beginning of the world and the end of the world are within this Samsara. Since elements and energies are relative and inter-dependent, it is meaningless to single out anything as the beginning. Whatever speculation we make regarding the origin of the world, there is no absolute truth in our notion. One day a man called Malunkyaputta approached the Master and demanded that He explain the origin of the Universe to him. He even threatened to cease to be His follower if the Buddha's answer was not satisfactory. The Buddha calmly retorted that it was of no consequence to Him whether or not Malunkyaputta followed Him, because the Truth did not need anyone's support. Then the

Buddha said that He would not go into a discussion of the origin of the Universe. To Him, gaining knowledge about such matters was a waste of time because a man's task was to liberate himself from the present, not the past or the future. To illustrate this, the Enlightened One related the parable of a man who was shot by a poisoned arrow. This foolish man refused to have the arrow removed until he found out all about the person who shot the arrow. By the time his attendants discovered these unnecessary details, the man was dead. Similarly, our immediate task is to attain Nirvana, i.e., escape Birth and Death, not to worry about our beginnings."
Dham: 297-300 #1977

◙ **WORLDLY DUSTS**
see Dust

◙ **WRONG VIEWS**
See also: Delusion; Upside-down Living; Four Inverted Views

▸"Usually, views belonging *either* to nihilism or eternalism. May also mean wrong ideas about religious teachings."
Chan: 485
Wrong · views are generally understood as views not in

conformity with the Buddha's teachings. #0588
See also: Four Inverted Views

◙ **WU (*Chin*)**
see MU

▸No, Not; also means "Awakening".

◙ **WU EMPEROR**
See also: Bodhidharma; Merit and Virtue

▸"464-549. A Chinese emperor of the Liang dynasty (502-57) and a devout Buddhist, particularly in his later years. Famous for his encounter with Bodhidharma."
Yoko: 217 #0806

◙ **WU-MEN-KUAN**
Syn: Mumonkan (*Jpn*)
See also: Blue Cliff Record; Ma-tsu Tao-i (709-788)

▸"Chin. (Jpn./ Mumonkan), lit. the Gateless Gate; one of the two most important koan collections in Ch'an (Zen) literature, the other is the Pi-Yen-Lu. This collection of Koans compiled in China in the thirteenth century (1184-1260) is second only to the Pi-Yen-lu (Hekigan Roku) in importance."
Hump: 131

"The *Wu-men-kuan* was compiled by the Chinese Ch'an (Zen) master Wu-men Hui-k'ai. It is composed of forty-eight koans, which Wu-men collected and arranged. He provided each koan with a short insightful commentary and with 'praise' and published the collection in 1229. The *Wu-men-kuan* begins with the renowned koan 'Mu' by which master Wu-men himself came to profound enlightenment. It is especially suitable as a koan that can help a practitioner to a first enlightenment experience. It is still given today to many beginners on the Zen path as their first koan. Since the Wu-men-kuan's most famous koan is used with beginners and since from a literary point of view the Wu-men-kuan is much plainer than the Pi-yen-lu, it is often considered less profound than the latter."
Sham: 248

"The text has also attracted a great deal of attention in the West, having been translated into English a number of times by various individuals."
Preb: 282 #0382

◎ **WU-T'AI (MOUNT)**
Syn: Wu-Tai Shan

▸"A mountain located in the Wu-t'ai mountain range in Shan-hsi (Shansi) Province in China. From old, this five-peaked mountain has been identified with Mount Ch'ing-liang where Bodhisattva Manjusri [symbolizing the Buddhas' transcendental wisdom] dwells. It has therefore been revered as sacred. About 100 temples are said to have been built on the flat summit of this mountain.

Today, many Zen temples and lamaseries are located there."
Sokk: 507 #0307

◎ **WU-TAI SHAN**
see Wu-t'ai (Mount)

◎ **WU-TSUNG (Emperor)**
see T'ang Wu-tsung (814-46)

◎ **YAKSA**
See also: Eight Divisions (of Divinities)

▸"A swift, powerful kind of ghost or demon, which is usually harmful, but in some cases acts a protector of the Dharma. Some yaksas, according to Buddhist mythology, live in the air, and some on land."
Chan: 485 #0143

◉ **YAMA**

▸The king of the Yama Heaven (q.v.); also regarded as the ruler of the hells.

"In the post-canonical Buddhist literature, Yama is depicted as the overlord of the purgatory system who assigns to beings the punishments they must undergo in expiation of their karmic misdeeds."
Oxf: 1052 #0173

◉ **YAMA HEAVEN**

▸"One of the heavens in the Realm of Desire, the 'heaven of constant joy' is located above the Heaven of the Thirty-Three."
Chan: 485

"The third of the six heavens in the world of desire. This heaven is always illuminated and its inhabitants enjoy fulfillment of the five desires. It is located eighty thousand yojana above the Trayastrimsha Heaven, which is on the summit of Mount Sumeru. Yama heaven comprises thirty-two realms. The life span of beings in this heaven is said to be two thousand years, each day of which corresponds to two hundred years in the human world. Yama, lord of this heaven, came to be regarded as the judge of the dead and the ruler of the hells."
Sokk: 511-512 #0309

◉ **YANA**
Syn: Vehicle
See also: Path; Three Divisions of the Buddha's Teaching; One Vehicle

----

▸"Vehicle. Metaphor for the Buddha's teaching that carries all living beings to enlightenment and liberation. The so called Two Vehicles are the vehicles of the Sravakas and Pratyekabuddhas (self-enlightened ones). They are said to be expedient soteriological expedients; it is only the One Vehicle (of the Bodhisattvas/Buddhas) that completely discloses the ultimate reality."   Chen: 168 #0839

◉ **YASODHARA**
Syn: Gopa

▸"The wife of the Buddha before he became an ascetic, and mother of Rahula. She became a nun in the fifth year after the enlightenment of the Buddha."
Dait: 366 #0144

◉ **YELLOW HATS**

▸"Members of the Gelug-pa

Order of Tibetan Buddhism. On special occasions members of this Order, founded in the fourteenth century by Tsong-kha-pa, wear yellow hats as distinct from the red hats worn by other sects."
Hump: 219
The Dalai Lama is head of the Gelug-pa order.
Editor: na #0394

◙ **YEN-SHOU**
see Yung-Ming Yen-Shou

◙ **YIDAM**

▸"Tib.; lit. 'firm mind'; in Vajrayana Buddhism, a term for a personal deity, whose nature corresponds to the individual psychological makeup of the practitioner. Yidams are manifestations of the sambhogakaya (see Three Bodies of the Buddha) and are visualized in meditative practice. They can take on either a peaceful or wrathful form and each belongs to a particular Buddha family. Among the most widely invoked yidams are Chenresi and Green Tara (both are manifestations of Avalokitesvara). Other Yidams appear only in strictly secret teachings."
Sham: 253 #0389

◙ **YIN-KUANG (1861-1940)**
See also: Zen / Pure Land; T'ai-Hsu; Yung-Ming; Han-Shan; Chu-Hung; Seven-Day Retreat
----
▸Thirteenth patriarch of the Pure Land School. The life of the Pure Land Patriarch Yin Kuang covers a most eventful period for East Asia and parallels the Sino-Japanese War, the Chinese Revolution of 1911 and two World Wars. "The revolution of 1911 that toppled the Manchu dynasty and established the Republic of China also brought in its wake a number of problems for the Buddhist sangha [clergy]. Following the political revolution, an intellectual climate was ushered in that was unfriendly to the interests of Buddhism ... The attack and criticism against Buddhism resulted in a number of discriminatory measures, such as special taxes and contributions being levied on temples, monasteries being appropriated for use as barracks and police stations, and Buddhist images being destroyed ... [Against this backdrop, two eminent monks rose to lead the resurgence of Buddhism: Master T'ai Hsu, who was instrumental in the revival of the Mind- Only school and

Master Yin Kuang, later to become the Thirteenth Patriarch of Pure Land.] The monk mainly responsible for instilling new life and meaning into [the practice of Buddha Recitation and the chanting of sutras was Master] Yin Kuang who, after his conversion to Pure Land pietism, concentrated on living a pure religious life based on faith, devotion and holiness ... Master Yin Kuang carried on his teachings mainly in the provinces of Kiangsu and Chekiang, where he gained numerous followers and disciples ... These efforts by Master Yin Kuang and his followers brought about an extensive revival of the Pure Land school. Lotus Societies, Nien-fo [Buddha Recitation] Societies, and others of a similar nature sprang up all over China." (Kenneth Ch'en, *Buddhism in China*, p. 455ff.)"
Editor/Zen: xxx

"From as early as the Tang period we hear of the existence of 'Pure Land Cloisters' within larger monastic complexes, where a congregation of self-professed Pure Land mendicants could pursue a collective regimen of Pure Land practice and study. Over the centuries that followed, influential Pure Land masters

have periodically sought to organize individual monasteries along Pure Land lines ... The Ming dynasty master Chu Hung (1535-1615) and Republican period master Yin Kuang (1861-1940) represent two such figures who have had a profound impact on the monastic form of Pure Land Buddhism in modern times. Both instituted comprehensive plans for adapting traditional monastic structures and routines to the specific purposes of Pure Land devotion, including the creation of halls for the concentrated recitation of the Buddha's name that were modeled on the traditional Chan meditation hall. At the same time, monks and nuns of the Pure Land school have developed a number of distinctive forms of retreat that are organized along the lines of the seven-day rite of buddha-mindfulness (see Seven Day Retreat) but apply its program to a more intensive monastic setting."
Lopez: 366-367
NOTE:
Master Yin-kuang's best known work, the *Letters of Master Yin-kuang*, is now available in partial translation in English, French and Spanish from the Sutra Translation Committee of

the United States and Canada, Bronx, NY, USA. (English title: *Pure-Land Zen, Zen-Pure Land.*) Editors: na #1818

◙ **YOGA**
See also: Zen School

►"A form of meditation developed in ancient India aimed at liberating one from the physical limitations of the body, or more broadly, from sufferings, by achieving concentration of mind and fusing with the truth. There are several schools of yoga which employ a variety of disciplines, including breath control, special postures, among others. Today some of the physical yogic disciplines are widely practiced for health and tranquillity of mind, without any particular religious motivation."
Sokk: 513

In contrast to yoga, Buddhist meditation (in Zen, Pure Land, etc.), in its ideal form, centers on the full development of the Bodhi Mind, the aspiration to achieve Enlightenment for the benefit of all sentient beings. For details, see *Hinduism / Buddhism.*
Editor: na #0310

◙ **YOGACARA SCHOOL**
Syn: Mind-Only School;

Consciousness School; Hosso School
See also: Fa-Hsiang School

►"One of the two major Mahayana schools in India, along with the Madhyamika school. Maitreya Boddhisattva is often regarded as the founder of the Yogacara (Consciousness-Only) school. He reportedly inspired a one-hundred-fascicle treatise which explained the Consciousness-Only doctrine. Thereafter, the Consciousness-Only doctrine was further developed by Maitreya's disciples Asanga and Vasubandhu in the first half of the fifth century. This school upholds the concept that all phenomena arise from the vijnana or consciousness and that the basis of all functions of consciousness is the alaya-vijnana or alaya-consciousness. It is said that the Consciousness-Only doctrine constituted the mainstream of Buddhist study in the Nalanda Monastery."
Sokk: 47-48

"The name of a Buddhist school, founded probably in the fourth century by the brothers Asanga and Vasubandhu. It advocates the doctrine of Mind Only (all dharmas are projections of one's own mind); hence everything in the external world is merely an illusion." Chan: 485-486 #0308

◎ YOGIN

▸"A practitioner of yoga; by extension a Buddhist practitioner: someone who gains the knowledge and experience of ultimate reality through meditation."
Hook: 366 #0828

◎ YOJANA

▸"A unit of measurement in ancient India, equal to the distance which the royal army would march in a day. Approximations vary as widely as 9.6, 18 and 24 kilometers."
Sokk: 513 #0311

◎ YOUNG MEN

▸The word "Young men" is used to indicate Bodhisattvas, who either take the appearance of "young men" or are "young" in the sense that their minds and bodies are free from the many defilements that most people accumulate as they go through life (e.g., Manjusri, the Youthful One; Sudhana, the youth Good Wealth). Editor: na #1319

◎ YUNG-CHIA

▸"Ch'an Master Hsuan Chueh of Yung Chia, who attained enlightenment when he called on the Sixth Patriarch. He wrote the Yung Chia collection and composed the *Song of Enlightenment*; died in 712."
Luk: vol II 245
The Song of Enlightenment with commentaries by Master Sheng-yen is available in English. #0777

◎ YUNG-MING YEN-SHOU (904-975)

syn: Yen-shou
See also: Four Options; Yin-Kuang; Chu-Hung; Han-Shan

▸Best known proponent of the harmonization of Zen and Pure Land doctrines. Most famous for his verses on Zen and Pure Land practice, entitled Four Options (q.v.).
Editor: na

"Famous Ch'an master, Dharma successor of state-master Teh Shao. He wrote the extensive collection *The Sect's Mirror* (Tsung Ching Lu) in which he linked all the seemingly contradictory Buddhist doctrines

to one reality. Died in 975 at the age of 72."
Luk: vol I 245
"Ch'an Master Yung-ming's syncretism went so far as to advocate the religious practice of the nembutsu (Buddha Recitation) or invocation of the name of Amitabha Buddha. This was by no means a complete innovation, since three disciples of the Fifth Patriarch of Ch'an -- Fa-chih (635-702) and his disciple Chih-wei (646-722), the fourth and fifth patriarchs of the Ox-head school, as well as Chih-shen (609-702) -- had already practiced the nembutsu in addition to Zen meditation... During the Sung period, sometimes with the support of the masters and sometimes against their opposition, the nembutsu made greater and greater inroads into Zen monasteries. This process of mixing religious practices continued through the Yuan period and came to term during the Ming dynasty. The simultaneous practice of Zen and the nembutsu became a matter of common practice. In trying to judge this whole development, we must not forget the inner affinities of the two practices. The psychological effects of the meditative repetition of the holy name are close to the effects of Zen meditation..." (H. Dumoulin, *Zen Buddhism*: Vol. I, p. 286.).
From Elder Master Yung-ming's fascicle in *Transmission of The Lamp* we learned that the Master recited the *Lotus Sutra* many thousand times. He sought enlightenment mainly by *nien-fo*, or reciting the Buddha's name, a practice of the Pure Land School. Yung-ming said, "Those who devote themselves to Ch'an and neglect the Pure Land will fail, nine out of ten, to attain enlightenment; but those who devote themselves to the practice of Pure Land will, without exception, have their awakening. Those who practice Ch'an and Pure Land at the same time will be at their best; they will be like tigers wearing horns."
(Chang Chung-Yuan: *Original Teaching of Ch'an Buddhism*). *NOTE:* "Zen master Yung-Ming (q.v.) introduced a development that truly bore fruit only later ... He may be considered a pioneer of the unification movement between Zen and the Pure Land tradition, a movement that later on was to gain the upper hand in East Asian Buddhism."
Dumou: 234-235 #0776
See also Four Options

◙ **ZAFU**

▸"A round cushion used for sitting meditation."
Batc: 384 #1854

◙ **ZAZEN**

▸Japanese for "Zen sitting," Zen meditation. #2281

◙ **ZEN**
see Zen School

◙ **ZEN AND PURE LAND**
see Zen / Pure Land

◙ **ZEN OF THE PATRIARCHS**
see Patriarchal Zen

◙ **ZEN PATRIARCHS**
see   Twenty-Eight Indian Patriarchs

◙ **ZEN SCHOOL**
Syn: Ch'an; Dhyana; Zen
See also: Zen/Pure Land; North America (Buddhism in); Meditation; Patriarchal Zen; Tathagata Zen; Suzuki, D.T.; Ultimatism; Shouts and Blows; Obaku Zen School

----

▸"The word 'Zen' comes from the Sanskrit dhyana (meditation). The word 'dhyana' was transcribed as Ch'an in Chinese,

and the latter was transcribed as Zen in Japanese."
Dait: 372
In the west, the word Ch'an is far better known by its Japanese name *Zen*. Hence, in this glossary, the word zen is generally used in lieu of Ch'an.
Editor: na
"It is said that one day Brahma, lord of creation, offered the Buddha a flower and asked him to preach the Dharma. When the Buddha held up the flower, his audience was puzzled, except for Kashyapa, who smiled. This is how Zen began. And this is how it was transmitted: with a flower, with a rock wall, *with a shout*." (Red Pine, *The Zen Teaching of Bodhidharma*,, p. xvi.)
I. Generalities
"A school of Mahayana Buddhism in China founded by Bodhidharma (6th century). This school stresses the cultivation of intuitive wisdom. An extremely influential Buddhist school in East Asia."
Chan: 486
"A school which maintains that enlightenment is not to be found in the pursuit of doctrinal studies but only through the direct perception of one's own mind with the practice of meditation.

Bodhidharma (sixth century) is regarded as the founder. The Treatise on the Perception of the True Nature of the Mind, said to be the work of Bodhidharma but probably written by later disciples, describes Zen in these words: 'A special transmission outside the sutras,/ Independent of word and writ,/ Pointing directly to the mind of man,/ Seeing one's true nature and attaining Buddhahood.' According to this school, supreme enlightenment is wordlessly transmitted from mind to mind, and Shakyamuni Buddha is said to have transferred his true enlightenment in this way to his disciple Mahakashyapa. The lineage then passed to the second patriarch Ananda and then finally to the twenty-eigthth Indian patriarch Bodhidharma, who brought the 'wordless tradition' to China where it became known as Ch'an Buddhism, [now far better known by its Japanese name, Zen]. Thereafter, the teaching of Zen was transmitted to the second Chinese patriarch Hui-k'o, the third, Seng-ts'an, the fourth, Tao-hsin, the fifth, Hung-jen, and the sixth patriarch, Hui-neng (638-713). In the days of Hui-neng, the sect divided into the Southern school of Zen, led by Hui-neng, and the Northern school, headed by Shen-hsiu. The Northern school rapidly declined, but the Southern school produced excellent disciples and became the Ch'an. [This southern school eventually subdivided itself into seven schools, of which the better known are the Rinzai (Lin-chi) and Soto (Ts'ao-tung).] ...

In Japan, Zen was established in the early days of the Kamakura period when Eisai went to Sung China and brought back the teachings of the Lin-chi school. Subsequently Dogen also went to Sung China and brought back the Ts'ao-tung school's teachings. During the Kamakura and the Muromachi periods (1336-1573), Zen teachings became connected with bushido or the way of the samurai and greatly prospered. In 1654, Ingen (Chin Yin-yuan) came from Ming China to Japan and later founded the Obaku Zen School (q.v.), [which combines Zen and Pure Land practices]."
Sokk: 516-518

"The critic will be inclined to call Zen absurd, confusing, and beyond the ken of ordinary reasoning. But Zen is inflexible and would protest that the so-called common sense way of looking at things is not final, and that the reason why we cannot

attain to a thoroughgoing comprehension of the truth is due to our unreasonable adherence to a 'logical' interpretation of things. If we really want to get to the bottom of life, we must abandon our cherished syllogisms, we must acquire a new way of observation whereby we can escape the tyranny of logic and the onesidedness of our everyday phraseology ... This is because Zen has come to the definite conclusion that the ordinary logical process of reasoning is powerless to give final satisfaction to our deepest spiritual needs."
Suzuki/58: na

"It is sometimes suggested that Ch'an represents a radically new development, even one which is no longer Buddhist at all. This is an exaggeration. In fact there is almost nothing in Ch'an which cannot be paralleled in earlier Indian Buddhism. The difference is in style rather than content. Ch'an adopted unconventional and unusual forms of expression. Probably the example of Taoism is very important here, especially for its tradition of simplicity and naturalness."
Hinn: 325

"Concerning Zen Buddhism, no one can deny its great contribution in bringing thousands to direct realization. Zen is emptiness in action, the living prajnaparamita. It is hard to find words to praise Zen adequately. The more one studies and practices Dharma, the more one appreciates and admires Zen. However, without proper guidance and sufficient preparation, Zen can also be dangerous and futile. By misconstruing a pseudo-experience as true enlightenment, one may develop an unwarranted self-conceit. Zen can also induce a devil-may-care attitude and one may eventually lose all ground in one's Dharmic efforts." (G.CC. Chang, tr., *A Treasury of Mahayana Sutras*)
Chan: xi

Most ancient masters, including such figures as the Patriarch Dogen, the founder of the Japanese school of Soto Zen, held that only monks and nuns could achieve Enlightenment through Zen. (See Kenneth Kraft, *Zen: Tradition and Transition*, p.186.)
Tam: 319 #0593

II. Main Practice
Seated meditation and Koan Study

"The practice of sitting in

meditation was carried out widely in ancient India and was incorporated into Buddhism by Shakyamuni himself, who sat in meditation when he attained his enlightenment under the Bodhi tree. This practice was introduced into China, where T'ien-t'ai taught it as part of an integrated system of disciplines to perceive the true nature of one's mind. The Ch'an (Jpn./Zen) school attaches great importance to the practice of seated meditation."
Sokk: 515-516

"[The Lin chi/Rinzai school stresses] sudden enlightenment and the use of koans (paradoxical questions for jerking the mind out of its normal patterns into a sudden awareness of the truth). The Ts'ao Tung/Soto school stresses gradual enlightenment and a combination of methods including koans, by relying mainly on the silent illumination of seated meditation (zazen), ending in the realization of the individual's oneness with reality."
Larousse: 495-496

"One of the greatest advantages of the half, or full-lotus sitting posture is that when the hands and feet are brought together in one point with the hands resting on the heels of the feet, pulse, blood pressure, metabolism, and other vital functions are at their quietest. It should be noted, however, that though these physiological functions are greatly quieted, the Zen meditator does not sink into a trance state, unresponsive to the world around him. Rather, electroencephalographic studies have shown that one doing concentrated Zen meditation responds immediately to external stimuli and, in fact, responds each time the same stimulus is repeated, whereas most people lose awareness of such repeated stimuli. Moreover, while the response appears each time on the EEG of one doing zazen, it also very quickly disappears. It can be said, then, that the person seriously practicing Zen meditation is fully aware of what is happening in the world around him yet does not cling to this awareness. These EEG results with Zen meditators contrast sharply with those found among people involved in other disciplines. In Yoga meditation, for example, it was shown that the practitioner is, in a sense, tuned out from the world around him, and does not respond at all to external stimuli. See *Altered States of Consciousness*, ed.

Charles Tart p. 489-506."
Kapl/80: 272
NOTE: Zen/Pure Land
"Zen Master Yung-Ming (q.v.) introduced a development that truly bore fruit only later ... He may be considered a pioneer of the unification movement between Zen and the Buddha Recitation tradition, a movement that later on was to gain the upper hand in East Asian Buddhism."
Dumou: 234-235   #2276

◎ **ZEN / PURE LAND**
See also: Pure Land Buddhism (Summary); Zen School; Yung-Ming; Yin-Kuang; Chu-Hung; Han-Shan

----

▸ *Please read entries "Pure Land Buddhism (Summary)" and "Zen" before the following:*
In the west, Pure Land and Zen, two of the most popular schools of Buddhism are sometimes viewed as different forms of practice, designed for different categories of believers. This is not however the teaching of Patriarchs and Masters in East Asia where Zen and Pure Land are considered complementary -- like the two wings of a bird.
(I) Wisdom and Compassion
"The Dharma was the pride of

T'ang Buddhism (China). From the founding of the dynasty (618) to the An Lu-shun revolt (755), a succession of great minds and the schools they championed laid a philosophical foundation for the future of Mahayana Buddhism. These schools--T'ien-t'ai, Hua-yen, Pure Land, and Ch'an--can also be seen as bringing to maturity different forms of piety, stretching back to Indian origins. It is hard enough to see any unity to Mahayana in India, much less to discern a teleological structure in Sinitic (Chinese) Mahayana. Yet the emergence of these four schools was not a fortuitous event, but accorded with the four optimal poles in Mahayana Buddhology. Buddhas could be either *laukika* or *lokottara* (mundane or transmundane), oriented to either *prajna* or *karuna* (wisdom or compassion)... Early Buddhism knew only the 'historic didactic' Sakyamuni Buddha. The idealization of the Buddha began within the Mahasanghika (q.v.) school, which marked the shift from the historical to the transhistorical. It was with Mahayana that [transcendental, salvific Buddhas such as Amitabha] emerged; *compassion* was given equal status with *wisdom* in a host of new salvific Buddhas and Bodhisattvas. A total rehumanization of the Buddha was accomplished in East Asia." Yoshi/Lai: 331

(II) Easy Vs. Difficult Practice

"The Pure Land school accepted the Zen perspective [on enlightenment] as valid in principle, but questioned how many people could get results by using Zen methods. Pure Land teachers granted that Zen might indeed be the 'supreme vehicle' but insisted that for most people it was too rigorous and demanding to be practical. The Pure Land method of buddha-name recitation was offered as a simpler method by which average people could make progress toward enlightenment..." (J.C. Cleary, *Pure Land, Pure Mind*.) Clear: xxx

(III) Zen is Pure Land

"When Bodhidharma talked about Ch'an, he was directly pointing at the luminous self-nature. The one mind of universality is exactly this luminous self-nature. Even though the two traditions [of Ch'an and Pure Land] use different terms, what they realize is the same mind. Well indeed did Chung-feng say this: 'The dhyana is the dhyana of the Pure Land, and the Pure Land is the Pure Land of Ch'an.' Some people might object by saying that Ch'an does not resort to the written word, whereas the Pure Land advocates the invocation of the name of Amitabha Buddha. But, they do not know that [in the Ch'an tradition] the Dharma is transmitted by a verse of four sentences and the imprinting on the mind is found in the four volumes of the scripture [the *Lankavatara Sutra*]. When these are compared with the four syllables of the name Amitabha, they are indeed far more wordy. As a matter of fact, not to rely on the written word does not mean to annihilate the written word. An enlightened person knows that it really means one should refuse to adhere to the written word and yet, at the same time, not cling to this refusal." Yu: 62

"Zen Master Yung-ming's syncretism went as far as to advocate the religious practice of the Nembutsu (Buddha Recitation) or invocation of the name of Amitabha Buddha. This was by no means a complete innovation, since three disciples of the Fifth Patriarch of Ch'an -- Fa-chih (635-702) and his disciple Chih-wei (646-722), the fourth and fifth patriarchs of the Ox-head school, as well as Chih-shen (609-702) -- had already practiced the nembutsu in addition to Zen meditation... During the Sung period, sometimes with the support of the masters and sometimes against their opposition, the nembutsu made greater and greater inroads into Zen monasteries. This process of mixing religious practices continued through the Yuan period and came to term during the Ming dynasty. The simultaneous practice of Zen and the nembutsu became a matter of common practice. In trying to judge this whole development, we must not forget the inner affinities of the two practices. The psychological effects of the meditative repetition of the holy name are close to the effects of Zen meditation... In China, the syncretistic tendencies and movements during the Sung period went on to meet with widespread success. In Zen monasteries, the invocation of Amitabha was practiced in combination with sitting in meditation. Moreover, during the Ming period we see a complete fusing of all Chinese Buddhists schools and sects. The more intellectually oriented schools of Avatamsaka and T'ien-T'ai as well as the Vinaya school were all cast in the same mold, the shape of which was determined principally by Zen and the Pure Land. Well-known Zen masters contributed to this unification. One of the most effective was the respected monk Chu-hung (1535-1615) who, after being admitted to monastic life by a Zen master, preached the dual practice of Zen and Buddha Recitation. This highly educated man left behind many writings. Han-shan Te-ch'ing (1546-1623), the best known Zen master at the end of the Ming period, also combined Zen practice with devotion to Amitabha Buddha, who, it said, appeared to him while he was invoking the holy name." (H. Dumoulin, *Zen Buddhism: A History/India and China*, p. 286.)

See also the following advice from the eminent 16th century Zen Master Chu Hung to a lay disciple: "This Pure Land Path is the most primal and the most subtle and wondrous. It is also the simplest. Because it is simple, those of high intelligence overlook it. Birth and death are not apart from a single moment of mindfulness. Consequently all the myriad worldly and world-transcending teachings and methods are not apart from a single moment of mindfulness. Right now take this moment of mindfulness, and be mindful of buddha, remember buddha, recite the buddha-name. How close and cutting! What pure essential energy, so solid and real! If you see through where this mindfulness arises, this is the Amitabha of our inherent nature. This is the meaning of the patriarch coming from the West [the meaning of Zen]." (J.C. Cleary, tr., *Pure Land Pure Mind*) Editor/Zen: 3-4

(IV) Note

"Throughout its history Buddhism [in East Asia] has tended to be the preserve of the members of an intellectual, spiritual and social elite, and the focus has almost everywhere been in the monasteries. *Pure Land Buddhism*, however, has more general appeal. It offers an 'easy practice' that can be implemented in the world, without becoming a monk or nun; and it promises salvation to everyone through Amitabha's vows -- to those still tied to the passions, even to those who have committed serious crimes. Profound study and meditation are moreover distrusted as they are seen as leading to intellectual and spiritual arrogance. Pure Land was therefore the first really *democratic form of Buddhism*, stressing humility rather than attainment, and as such became hugely successful among ordinary East Asians. Pious societies were spawned under its auspices, like the White Lotus Society which developed into a sizeable movement... In its heyday, the good works of its devotees included providing public amenities (bath-houses, hostels, mills, etc.), donating cloth, copying sutras and hosting vegetarian banquets. It was unusual in allowing women to play a prominent part in its affairs. Of the various schools that burgeoned in T'ang dynasty China, only Pure Land and Ch'an (Zen) had the vitality to survive the great Persecution of 845 (q.v.). Indeed, in East Asia the methods of both schools were often practiced in tandem for double effectiveness -- 'like a tiger wearing horns.'" (Patriarch Yin-Kuang)

Snell/Elements: 110 #1789

Caveat:

"According to Elder Master Yin Kuang, Pure Land followers should not seek guidance on Pure

Land matters from Zen Masters. This is because the answers of Zen Masters are all directed towards principle and essence, while the Pure Land approach is based on phenomena and marks. This being the case, and considering the different areas of emphasis, beginning Pure Land practitioners who do not yet fully understand essence and marks, noumenon and phenomena, will not only fail to benefit from the answers of Zen Masters, they may develop even greater doubts, perplexity and inconsistent views." (*Buddhism of Wisdom of Faith.*)
Tam: 163

◙ **ZEN LOGIC**
▸"Zen training is a process of transcending thought, for the intellect functions in duality, and the 'moment' of Zen experience is in Non-duality. Normal logic is therefore worse than useless to achieve this experience; it binds the mind in the coils of concepts. Only when it is seen that A is A because A is not-A is the mind set free. This logic is the fruit of Zen experience and not a means to it. It can be stated, therefore, but not be the subject of intellectual argument."
Hump: 223

◙ **ZEN PATRIARCHS**
see Twenty-Eight Indian Patriarchs

◙ **ZENDO**

▸Lit: "meditation hall". Also Japanese name of Shan-tao (q.v.), a famous patriarch of the Pure Land school.   ◙

Although he knows that Buddha lands
Are void like living beings
He goes on practicing the Pure Land
(Dharma) to teach and convert men.

Bodhisattva's practice
Vimalakirti Sutra

Avatamsaka Sutra,
chapter 40:

Practices and Vows of the Bodhisattva Samantabhadra

(Translated into Chinese by the Indian Master Prajna in the eighth century A.D.)

At that time, having praised the exalted merits and virtues of Buddha Vairocana, the Bodhisattva Samantabhadra addressed the assembled Bodhisattvas, along with Sudhana, as follows:

"Good men, even if all the Buddhas of the ten directions were to speak continuously, for as many eons as there are fine motes of dust in an incalculable number of Buddha-lands (worlds), the merits and virtues of the Buddha could never be fully described.

"Those wishing to achieve these merits and virtues should cultivate ten vast and great practices and vows. What are these ten?

First, Pay homage and respect to all Buddhas.
Second, Praise the Buddhas.
Third, Make abundant offerings.
Fourth, Repent misdeeds and evil karmas (actions).
Fifth, Rejoice in others' merits and virtues.
Sixth, Request the Buddhas to teach.
Seventh, Request the Buddhas to remain in the world.
Eighth, Follow the teachings of the Buddhas at all times.
Ninth, Accommodate and benefit all living beings.
Tenth, Transfer all merits and virtues universally."

[After explaining the significance of the first eight vows, the Bodhisattva Samantabhadra continues.]

Ninth Vow

"Sudhana, *to accommodate and benefit all living beings* is explained like this: throughout the oceans of worlds in the ten directions exhausting the Dharma Realm (cosmos) and the realms of empty space, there are many different kinds of living beings. That is to say, there are those born from eggs, the womb-born, the transformationally born, as well as those who live and rely on earth, water, fire, and air for their existence. There are beings dwelling in space, and those who are born in and live in plants and trees. This includes all the many species and races with their diverse bodies, shapes, appearances, lifespans, families, names, and natures. This includes their many varieties of knowledge and views, their various desires and pleasures, their thoughts and deeds, and their many different behaviors, clothing and diets.

"It includes beings who dwell in different villages, towns, cities and palaces, as well as gods, dragons, and others of the Eight Divisions, humans and non-humans alike. Also there are footless beings, beings with two feet, four feet, and many feet, with form and without form, with thought and without thought, and not entirely with thought and not entirely without thought.

"I will accord with and take care of all these many kinds of beings, providing all manner of services and offerings for them. I will treat them with the same respect I show my own parents, teachers, elders, Arhats, and even the Buddhas. I will serve them all equally without difference.

"I will be a good physician for the sick and suffering. I will lead those who have lost their way to the right road. I will be a bright light for those in the dark night, and cause the poor and destitute to uncover hidden treasures.

"The Bodhisattva impartially benefits all living beings in this manner.

"Why is this? If a Bodhisattva accords with living beings, then he accords with and makes offerings to all Buddhas. If he can honor and serve living beings, then he honors and serves the Buddhas. If he makes living beings happy, he is making all Buddhas happy. Why is this? It is because all Buddhas take the mind of Great Compassion as their substance. Because of living beings, they develop Great Compassion. From Great Compassion the Bodhi Mind is born; and because of the Bodhi Mind, they accomplish Supreme, Perfect Enlightenment (Buddhahood).

"It is like a great regal tree growing in the rocks and sand of barren wilderness. When the roots get water, the branches, leaves, flowers, and fruit will all flourish. The regal bodhi-tree growing in the wilderness of Birth and Death is the same. All living beings are its roots; all Buddhas and Bodhisattvas are its flowers and fruit. By benefitting all beings with the water of Great Compassion, one can realize the flowers and fruit of the Bodhisattvas' and Buddhas' wisdom. Why is this? It is because by benefitting living beings with the water of Great Compassion, the Bodhisattvas can attain Supreme, Perfect Enlightenment. Therefore, Bodhi belongs to living beings. *Without living beings, no Bodhisattva could achieve Supreme, Perfect Enlightenment.*

"Good man, you should understand these principles in this way: When the mind is impartial towards all living beings, one can accomplish full and perfect Great Compassion. By using the mind of

Great Compassion to accord with living beings, one perfects the *offering of the Dharma* to the Buddhas. In this way the Bodhisattva constantly accords with living beings.

"Even when the realms of empty space are exhausted, the realms of living beings are exhausted, the karmas of living beings are exhausted, and the afflictions of living beings are exhausted, I will still accord endlessly, continuously, in thought after thought, without cease. My body, speech and mind never weary of these deeds.

Tenth Vow

"Moreover, good man, *to transfer all merits and virtues universally* is explained like this: all the merits and virtues, from the first vow, to pay homage and respect, up to and including the vow to accommodate and benefit all living beings, I universally transfer to all living beings throughout the Dharma Realm (cosmos) and to the limits of empty space. I vow that all living beings will be constantly peaceful and happy without sickness or suffering. I vow that no one will succeed in doing any evil, but that all will quickly perfect their cultivation of good karma. I vow to shut the door to evil destinies and open the right paths of humans, gods and that of Nirvana. I will stand in for living beings and receive all the extremely severe fruits of suffering which they bring about with their evil karma. I will liberate all these beings and ultimately bring them to accomplish unsurpassed Bodhi (Buddhahood). The Bodhisattva cultivates transference in this way.

"Even when the realms of empty space are exhausted, the realms of living beings are exhausted, the karmas of living beings are exhausted, and the afflictions of living beings are exhausted, I will still transfer all merits and virtues endlessly, continuously, in thought after thought without cease. My body, speech and mind never weary of these deeds.

"Good man, these are the Ten Great Vows of the great Bodhisattvas in their entirety. If all Bodhisattvas can follow and abide by these Great Vows, then they will succeed in bringing all living beings to maturity. They will be able to accord with the path of Supreme, Perfect Enlightenment and complete Samantabhadra's sea of conduct and vows. Therefore, good man, you should know the meaning of this ....

"Further, when a person who singlemindedly recites these vows is on the verge of death, at the last instant of life, when all his faculties scatter and he departs from his relatives, when all power and status are lost and nothing survives, when "his Prime Minister, great officials, his inner court and outer cities, his elephants, horses, carts, and treasuries of precious jewels" can no longer accompany him, these Great Vows alone will stay with him. At all times they will guide him forward, and in a single instant he will be reborn in the Land of Ultimate Bliss. Arriving there, he will see Amitabha Buddha, the Bodhisattvas Manjusri, Samantabhadra, Avalokitesvara, Maitreya, and others. The appearance of these Bodhisattvas will be magnificent and their merits and virtues complete. Together they will surround him.

"This person will see himself born from a lotus flower and will receive a prediction of Buddhahood. Thereafter, he will pass through an incalculable number of eons and, with his power of wisdom, he will accord with the minds of living beings in order to benefit them everywhere, throughout the countless worlds of the ten directions.

"Before long he will sit in a Bodhimandala (place of Enlightenment), subdue the demonic armies, accomplish Supreme, Perfect Enlightenment, and turn the wonderful Dharma wheel (preach Buddhism). He will cause living beings in worlds as numerous as the fine motes of dust in Buddha-lands to develop the Bodhi Mind (Mind of Enlightenment).

"According with their inclinations and basic natures, he will teach, transform, and bring them to maturity.

"To the exhaustion of the oceans of future eons, he will greatly benefit all living beings ...."

***

At that time, the great Bodhisattva Samantabhadra, wishing to restate his meaning, contemplated everywhere in the ten directions and spoke in verse.

1 - Before the Buddhas, "Lions Among Men",
   throughout the worlds of the ten directions,
In the past, in the present, and also in the future,
With body, speech and mind entirely pure,
I bow before them all, omitting none.

With the awesome power of Samantabhadra's vows,
I appear at the same time before every Buddha,
And in transformed bodies as numerous as motes of
   dust in all lands,
Bow to Buddhas as numerous as motes of dust in all
   lands.

2 - With oceans of sound I everywhere let fall
Words and phrases, wonderful and endless,
Which now and through all the eons of the future,
Praise the wide, deep sea of the Buddhas' merits and
   virtues.

3 - Flower garlands, supreme and wonderful,
Music, perfumes, parasols, and canopies,

And other decorations rich and rare,
I offer up to every Buddha.

Fine clothing, superior incense,
Powdered and burning incense, lamps and candles,
Each one heaped as high as mount Sumeru,
I offer completely to all Buddhas.

With a vast, great, supremely liberated mind,
I believe in all Buddhas of the three periods of time;
With the strength of Samantabhadra's conduct and vows,
I make offerings to all Buddhas everywhere.

4 - For all the evil deeds I have done in the past,
Created by my body, speech, and mind,
From beginningless greed, anger, and delusion,
I now know shame and repent them all.

5 - I rejoice in the merits and virtues
Of all beings in the ten directions,
From the most humble to the Arhats,
Pratyeka Buddhas, Bodhisattvas and Buddhas.

6 - Before the "Lights of the Worlds" of the
    ten directions,
Who have just accomplished Supreme Bodhi,
I now request and beseech them all
To turn the foremost, wondrous Dharma wheel.

7 - If there are Buddhas who wish for Nirvana,
I request with deep sincerity

That they dwell in the world for a long time,
To bring benefits and bliss to every being.

The good roots gained
From following and rejoicing in merit
    and virtue
And from repentance and reform,
I transfer to living beings and the Buddha Way.

8 - I study with the Buddhas and practice
The perfect conduct of Samantabhadra;
I make offerings to all the Buddhas of the past
And to all present Buddhas throughout the ten directions.

All future "Teachers of Gods and Men"
Whose aspirations and vows have been completed,
I will follow in study throughout the three periods of time
And quickly attain Great Bodhi ...

I vow that every being in all directions
Will be peaceful, happy, and without worry.
May they obtain the proper Dharma's profound aid,
And may all their afflictions be wiped away,
    without exception.

In my practice, striving for Buddhahood,
I will gain the knowledge of my past lives
    in all destinies.
I will always leave the home-life and cultivate
    pure precepts,
Without default, never broken, and without stain.

Be they gods, dragons, yakshas, or kumbhandas,
Humans, non-humans, and the rest,
In the many languages of all such living beings,
With every sound I will speak the Dharma.

I will cultivate the pure Paramitas with vigor,
And never abandon the Bodhi Mind.
I will banish all obstructions and defilements,
And fulfill all wondrous practices.

From all delusions, karmas, and demon-states,
Amid all worldly paths, I will be freed,
As the lotus does not touch the water,
As sun and moon do not stop in space.

9 - Ending the sufferings of the paths of evil,
And to everyone equally bringing joy,
May I for eons like the motes of dust
    in all lands
Ever benefit all in the ten directions.

Always in accord with living beings,
Cultivating through all future eons
The vast conduct of Samantabhadra,
The unsurpassed Great Bodhi will I perfect.

I vow always to meet Buddhas face to face
And the hosts of disciples who gather around them;
I will raise offerings which are vast and great,
Untiring to the end of future eons.

I will hold high the subtly wondrous Dharma
And illuminate all the practices of Bodhi;
I will be ultimately pure in Samantabhadra's way,
Practicing until the end of time.

Inexhaustible blessings and wisdom
I cultivate throughout all worlds;
By concentration, wisdom, skillful means,
*   and samadhis,*
I will gain an endless store of merits and virtues.

In one mote of dust are lands as numerous as motes of
*   dust;*
In each land are incalculable numbers of Buddhas.
In every place where Buddhas dwell I see the host
*   assembled,*
Endlessly proclaiming all the practices of Bodhi.

In ten directions everywhere, throughout the sea of
*   lands,*
Every hair-tip encompasses oceans of past, present and
*   future.*
So, too, there is a sea of Buddhas, a sea of Buddha
*   lands;*
Pervading them all I cultivate for seas of endless time.

The speech of all Buddhas is pure;
Each word contains an ocean of sounds.
According with what beings like to hear,
The Buddhas' sea of eloquence flows forth ...

I can penetrate the future
And exhaust all eons in a single thought.
In a single thought I compress
All eons of the three periods of time.

In one thought I see all "Lions of Men"
Of the past, present, and future;
I constantly fathom the Buddhas' states,
Their magical samadhis and their awesome strength.

On the tip of an extremely fine hair,
Appear jewelled lands of past, present and future;
Lands on hair-tips as numerous as dust motes in all
*   lands of the ten directions,*
I deeply enter, adorn, and purify ...

The sea of lands I everywhere adorn and purify,
And I liberate all living beings, without exception.
With skill I make selections from among the sea of
*   Dharmas*
And enter deeply into the wisdom sea ...

Each Buddha has an elder disciple
Named Samantabhadra, Honored One.
I now transfer all good roots, and I vow
To perform deeds of wisdom identical to his.

I vow that my body, speech and mind will be
*   forever pure,*
And that all practices and lands will be also.
I vow in every way to be identical
To the wisdom of Samantabhadra.

I will wholly purify Samantabhadra's conduct,
And the great vows of Manjusri as well.
All their deeds I will fulfill, leaving nothing undone.
Till the end of time I will never tire.

Infinite and measureless is my cultivation;
Boundless merit and virtue I obtain.
Amid limitless practices I will dwell in peace,
And penetrate the strength of spiritual powers.

10 - Manjusri has wisdom, courage and bravery;
Samantabhadra's conduct and wisdom are the same.
I now transfer all good roots
In order to follow them in practice and in study ...

In the three periods of time, all Buddhas praise
Such vows as these, lofty and great.
I now transfer all good roots, wishing to perfect
The supreme practices of Samantabhadra.

I vow that when my life approaches its end,
All obstructions will be swept away;
I will see Amitabha Buddha,
And be born in his Land of Ultimate Bliss and Peace.

When reborn in the Western Land,
I will perfect and completely fulfill,
Without exception, these Great Vows,
To delight and benefit all beings.

The Assembly of Amitabha Buddha is completely pure;
When from a matchless lotus I am reborn,

I will behold the Buddha's Measureless Light as He
*   appears before me*
To bestow a prediction of Buddhahood.

Receiving a prediction from the Buddha,
I will take countless appearances and forms,
And with wisdom power vast and great, pervade ten directions
To benefit all the realms of living beings.

Realms of worlds in empty space might reach an end,
And living beings, karmas and afflictions be
*   extinguished;*
But they will never be exhausted,
And neither will my vows.

With myriad jewels in boundless lands in all
*   directions,*
I make decorations and offerings to the Buddhas.
For eons as numerous as the motes of dust in
*   all lands,*
I bring the foremost peace and joy to gods and humans.

Yet, if anyone believes in these Great Vows,
As they pass by the ear but a single time,
And in search of Bodhi thirstily craves these vows,
The merits and virtues gained will surpass these
*   offerings.*

With bad advisors forever left behind,
From paths of evil he departs for eternity,
Soon to see the Buddha of Limitless Light
And perfect Samantabhadra's Supreme Vows.

Easily obtaining the blessings of long life,
Assured of a noble rebirth in the human realm,
Before long he will perfect and complete
The practices of Samantabhadra.

In the past, owing to a lack of wisdom power,
The five offenses of extreme evil he has committed;
In one thought they can all be wiped away by reciting
The Great Vows of Samantabhadra.

His clan, race, features and characteristics
With his wisdom are all perfected and complete;
Demons and externalists will have no way to harm him,
And he will be a field of merits in the Triple Realm.

To the regal Bodhi tree he will quickly go,
And seated there subdue hordes of demons.
Supremely and perfectly enlightened, he will turn the
    Dharma wheel,
To benefit all sentient beings.

If anyone can read, recite, receive, and hold high
Samantabhadra's Vows and proclaim them,
His reward only the Buddhas will know,
And he will obtain Supreme Enlightenment.

If anyone recites Samantabhadra's Vows,
I will speak of a portion of his good roots:
In one single thought he can fulfill
The pure vows of sentient beings.

The supreme and endless blessings from
   Samantabhadra's conduct
I now universally transfer;
May every living being, drowning and adrift,
Soon return to the Pure Land, the Land of
   Limitless Light!

***

When the Great Bodhisattva Samantabhadra finished speaking these pure verses on the Great Vows of Samantabhadra before the Buddha, the youth Sudhana was overwhelmed with boundless joy. All the Bodhisattvas were extremely happy as well, and the Buddha applauded saying, "Good indeed, good indeed! ..."

With bad advisors forever left behind,
From paths of evil he departs for eternity,
Soon to see the Buddha of Limitless Light
And perfect Samantabhadra's Supreme Vows.

The Vows of Samantabhadra
Avatamsaka Sutra

Note on
Pure Land Buddhism
by Dr. J.C. Cleary

Buddhism has evolved many, many forms during its long history. Codes of conduct, guidelines for communal life, rituals, meditative practices, modes of teaching, images, fables and philosophies have varied greatly over time and place. According to the fundamental Buddhist principle of skill-in-means, this multiformity is natural and proper, a necessary response to the great variety of circumstances in which Buddhism has been propagated.

Skill-in-means requires that the presentation of the Buddhist Teaching, (sometimes simply called "the Dharma"), be adapted to the mentality and circumstances of the people being taught. According to Buddhist seers, the absolute truth is inconceivable and cannot be captured in any particular formulation. Therefore in Buddhism there is no fixed dogma, only provisional, partial expressions of the teaching, suited to the capabilities of the audience being addressed.

In keeping with this fundamental principle, a tolerant, nonsectarian approach has normally prevailed throughout Buddhist history. Where dogmatic controversies and sectarian partisanship have cropped up in the communities of Buddhist followers, these are distortions of the teaching, and have always been based on misunderstanding and misinformation. In embracing Pure Land Buddhism, therefore, people are not rejecting any of the other streams of the Buddhist tradition -- they have only decided that Pure Land methods are most appropriate and most effective for them.

***

Pure Land Buddhism is a religion of faith, of faith in Amitabha Buddha [and in one's capacity to achieve Buddhahood]. Amitabha Buddha presides over the Pure Land, a "paradise" in the west, the land of ultimate bliss, named "Peaceful Nurturing." In the Pure Land, there is none of the suffering and defilement and delusion that normally blocks people's efforts toward enlightenment here in our world (which the Buddhists named "Endurance.")

The immediate goal of Pure Land believers is to be reborn in Amitabha's Pure Land. There, in more favorable surroundings, in the presence of Amitabha, they will eventually attain complete enlightenment.

The essence of Pure Land practice thus consists of invoking the name of Amitabha Buddha, contemplating the qualities of Amitabha, visualizing Amitabha, and taking vows to be born in the Pure Land.

***

Making a vow to attain birth in the Pure Land signifies a fundamental reorientation of the believer's motivations and will. No longer is the purpose of life brute survival, or fulfillment of a social role, or the struggle to wrest some satisfaction from a frustrating, taxing environment. By vowing to be reborn in the Pure Land, believers shift their focus. The joys and sorrows of this world become incidental, inconsequential. The present life takes on value chiefly as an opportunity to concentrate one's awareness on Amitabha, and purify one's mind accordingly.

The hallmark of Pure Land Buddhism is reciting the buddha-name, invoking Amitabha Buddha by chanting his name. Through reciting the buddha-name, people focus their attention on Amitabha Buddha. This promotes mindfulness of buddha, otherwise known as *buddha-remembrance* [buddha recitation].

In what sense is buddha "remembered"? "Buddha" is the name for the one reality that underlies all forms of being, as well as an epithet for those who witness and express this reality. According to the Buddhist Teaching, all people possess an inherently enlightened true nature that is their real identity. By becoming mindful of buddha, therefore, people are just regaining their own real identity. They are remembering their own buddha-nature.

Buddha as such is a concept that transcends any particular embodiment, such as Shakyamuni Buddha (the historical buddha born in India), or Maitreya Buddha (the future buddha), or Vairocana Buddha (the cosmic buddha) or Amitabha Buddha (the buddha of the western paradise). Buddha exists in many forms, but all share the same "body of reality," the same *Dharmakaya*, which is formless, omnipresent, all-pervading, indescribable, infinite -- the everywhere-equal essence of all things, the one reality within-and-beyond all appearances.

Dharmakaya Buddha is utterly abstract and in fact inconceivable, so buddha takes on particular forms to communicate with living beings by coming within their range of perception. For most people, this is the only way that buddha can become comprehensible and of practical use. The particular embodiments of buddha, known as Nirmanakaya, are supreme examples of compassionate skill-in-means.

Pure Land people focus on buddha in the form of Amitabha, the buddha of infinite life and infinite light. Believers put their faith in Amitabha Buddha and recite his name, confident in the promises he has given to deliver all who invoke his name. All classes of people, whatever their other characteristics or shortcomings, are guaranteed rebirth in the Pure Land and ultimate salvation, if only they invoke Amitabha's name with singleminded concentration and sincere faith.

Buddha-Name Recitation

Buddha-name recitation is practiced in many forms: silently or aloud, alone or in groups, by itself or combined with visualization of Amitabha or contemplation of the concept of buddha, or combined with the methods of Zen. The aim is to concentrate one's attention on Amitabha, and let all other thoughts die away. At first and all along, miscellaneous thoughts intrude, and the mind wanders. But with sustained effort, one's focus on the buddha-name becomes progressively more steady and clear. Mindfulness of buddha -- buddha-remembrance -- grows stronger and purer.

Reciting the buddha-name functions as a powerful antidote to those great enemies of clear awareness that Buddhists have traditionally labeled "oblivion" and "scattering." "Oblivion" refers to the tendency of the human mind when not occupied by its habitual thoughts to sink into a state of torpor and sleepy nescience. "Scattering" is the other pole of ordinary mental life, where the consciousness flies off in all directions pursuing objects of thought and desire.

Through the centuries, those who practice it have found that buddha-name recitation is a much more beneficial use of mind than the ordinary run of hopes and fears that would otherwise preoccupy their minds. Calm focus replaces agitation and anxiety, producing a most invigorating saving of energy. "Mixed mindfulness is the disease. Mindfulness of buddha is the medicine."

According to the Pure Land teaching, all sorts of evil karma are dissolved by reciting the buddha-name wholeheartedly and singlemindedly. What is karma? In Buddhist terms, "karma" means "deeds," "actions." Through sequences of cause and effect, what we do and what those we interact with do determines our experience and shapes our perceptions, which in turn guides our further actions.

Habitual patterns of perception and behavior build up and acquire momentum. Now we are in the grips of "karmic consciousness," so-called because it is a state of mind at once the result of past deeds and the source of future deeds. This is the existential trap from which all forms of Buddhist practice aim to extricate us.

According to the Pure Land teaching, buddha-name recitation is more effective for this purpose than any other practice, and can be carried out by anyone. The key is being singleminded, focusing the mind totally on Amitabha, and thus interrupting the onward flow of karmic consciousness. This is where Zen and Pure Land meet.

All Classes Go to the Pure Land

Buddha-name recitation enables all classes of people to attain birth in the Pure Land, from the most virtuous Buddhist saints, to those who are incapable of meritorious actions and do not develop the aspiration for enlightenment.

In Pure Land terminology, "nine classes" go to the Pure Land. The highest class are those who achieve the traditional goals of Buddhism -- that is, who free themselves from desire, observe the precepts, and practice the six perfections of giving, discipline, forbearance, energetic progress, meditation and wisdom. The lowest class who go to the Pure Land are those who keep on, as wayward human animals, piling up evil karma and committing all kinds of sins: even they can attain birth in the Pure Land, if only they focus their minds and recite the buddha-name.

Buddha-name recitation in itself dissolves away evil karma, no matter how serious – so say the Pure Land teachings. Infinity lies latent in the gaps within moment-to-moment mundanity – in the Zen formulation. But above all it is the power of Amitabha that makes birth in the Pure Land possible for sinners as well as saints, because Amitabha has vowed to save all who faithfully and singlemindedly invoke his name.

The Pure Land

Amitabha's Pure Land is depicted in a way designed to attract believers. In the Pure Land there is no sickness, old age, or death. The sufferings and difficulties of this world do not exist. Those born in the Pure Land come forth there from lotus flowers, not from a woman's womb in pain and blood, and once born they are received and welcome by Amitabha and his assistants. They receive immortal, transformed bodies, and are beyond the danger of falling back into lesser incarnations. They are in the direct presence of Amitabha Buddha and the great bodhisattvas Kuan-yin (Avalokitesvara) and Shih-chih (Mahasthamaprapta), who aid in their ultimate enlightenment.

Those who go to the Pure Land live there among beings of the highest virtue. Beautiful clothing and fine food are provided to them ready-made. There are no extremes of heat and cold. Correct states of concentration are easy to achieve and maintain. There are no such things as greed, ignorance, anger, strife, or laziness.

The Pure Land is described, metaphorically, as resplendent with all manner of jewels and precious things, towers of agate, palaces of jade. There are huge trees made of various gems, covered with fruits and flowers. Giant lotuses spread their fragrance everywhere. There are pools, also made of seven jewels, and filled with the purest water, which adjusts itself to the depth and temperature the bathers prefer. Underfoot, gold covers the ground. Flowers fall from the sky day and night, and the whole sky is covered with a net made of gold and silver and pearls. The Pure Land is perfumed with beautiful scents and filled with celestial music.

Most precious of all, in the Pure Land, we are told, not only the buddha and bodhisattvas, Amitabha and his assistants, but even the birds and the trees (as manifestations of Amitabha) are continuously expounding the Dharma, the Buddhist Teaching.

Pure Land Literature

Pure Land literature offers many stories presented as real-life biographical accounts which corroborate the efficacy of Pure Land practice, and the description of the Pure Land paradise drawn from the scriptures. Like most Buddhist biographies written in China, these accounts are very terse, and focus on the subject's religious life. There are stories of men and women, monks and nuns, nobles and high officials and commoners too, people young and old in various stations of life, all devoted to Pure Land practice.

The stories often relate people's early experience of Buddhism, and note the various practices they took up and the scriptures they studied. In due time, as the stories tell it, their faith in Pure Land is awakened, perhaps by meeting an inspirational teacher, perhaps through a dream or vision, perhaps from hearing the Pure Land scriptures, perhaps from personal acquaintance with a devoted Pure Land practitioner.

The stories always make a point of the zeal and dedication of the true believer in reciting the buddha-name. Here are some typical descriptions:

"He cut off his motivation for worldly things and dedicated his mind to the Pure Land."

"He concentrated his mind on reciting the buddha-name."

"She recited the buddha-name with complete sincerity."

"He set his will on the Pure Land."

"She recited the buddha-name day and night without stopping."

"He recited the buddha-name singlemindedly."

"She developed the mind of faith and recited the buddha-name tirelessly."

"She turned her mind to buddha-name recitation and practiced it wholeheartedly, never slacking off."

"The older he became, the more earnest he was in reciting the buddha-name."

This is the message of the Pure Land life stories.

The climax of a typical Pure Land biography comes in the subject's death scene, when buddha-name recitation is rewarded and the Pure Land teachings are confirmed.

The believer dies peacefully, even joyously, with mind and body composed, in full confidence of rebirth in paradise, reciting the buddha-name. Often the Pure Land devotee is able to predict his or her own death in advance, and calmly bid farewell to loved ones. Sometimes the believer receives reassuring visits from Amitabha in dreams or visions to prepare her or him to face the end.

Various signs give proof that the dying person is about to be reborn in the Pure Land. Uncanny fragrances and supernatural colored lights fill the room. Celestial music is heard. Flowers from the Pure Land appear: yellow lotuses, green lotuses, golden lotuses. The dying person sees Amitabha coming from the west to welcome him, or feels Amitabha's hand on his head, or sees Amitabha accompanied by Kuan-yin and Shih-chih appear to lead him to paradise. The dying person sees visions of the Pure

Land: Amitabha and his companions seated on a jeweled dais, or the seven jewel ponds, or a staircase of gems leading up to the Pure Land.

Those close to the dying believer receive assurances that rebirth in the Pure Land is imminent. In the most frequent motif, the dying person announces to his or her companions, "Buddha is coming to welcome me!" The dying person's relatives dream of a lotus opening in the Pure Land's jewel pond, with their reborn kinsman appearing inside it. Or the relatives see visions of the deceased riding off to the west on a green lotus. Or the dead person visits the survivors in dreams and assures them that she has indeed been reborn in the Pure Land.

After the person dies, the people in the room perceive a magical fragrance and hear celestial music gradually fading away toward the west. A golden lotus might appear on the death bed or on top of the coffin. The dead believer's corpse does not decompose. Auspicious colored clouds hang over the funeral pyre.

With elements like these, the death scenes in Pure Land biographies are meant to prove to the faithful that rebirth in the Pure Land is indeed the guaranteed fate of those who recite the buddha-name.

***

Besides collections of believers' biographies, Pure Land literature includes other types of works designed to promote faith in the Pure Land teachings.

Many commentaries were composed on the sutras basic to Pure Land Buddhism: the *Amitabha Sutra,* the *Contemplation of Amitabha Sutra (Meditation Sutra),* and the *Sutra of Infinite Life (Longer Amitabha Sutra).*

Pure Land adepts also wrote essays to explain Pure Land beliefs in terms of Great Vehicle Buddhism as a whole, and to answer objections to Pure Land teachings and clarify points of doubt.

Some writers linked the Pure Land teaching to the other currents in Buddhism by picking out references to Amitabha's Pure Land and buddha-name recitation contained in the Buddhist scriptures and philosophical treatises not identified with the Pure Land school.

There are many records of talks given by famous Pure Land teachers down through the centuries, and personal letters they wrote, urging people to adopt Pure Land practice as the most effective way to make progress on the Buddhist Path.

Pure Land Associations

For many Pure Land Buddhists, an important means of strengthening their faith has been membership in a group of fellow believers. The faithful join to form Pure Land associations, where they can meet regularly with like-minded people to recite the buddha-name and, if they are fortunate, listen to genuine teachers expound Pure Land texts. Though buddha-name recitation can of course be done alone in private, many people have found group recitation very powerful in helping them to focus their attention. Being part of a community with shared beliefs helps to reinforce the dedication of the individual and his belief that Pure Land is a correct application of the Dharma that really works for people of that place and time. When methods are being applied correctly, the group also provides the individual believer with living examples of the mental strength and unshakable serenity acquired by longterm practitioners of buddha-name recitation.

Pure Land adepts often founded teaching centers where people could gather to recite the buddha-name and hear the Pure Land doctrine. They enrolled believers in religious associations dedicated to buddha-remembrance, with their own bylaws for membership, scheduled meetings, and guidelines for practice. Though many monks and nuns practiced buddha-name recitation, and many lay Buddhists pursued Pure Land practice on their own, the typical institutional form of Pure Land Buddhism was the voluntary association of laypeople, sometimes, but not always, led by monks and nuns.

On a purely social level, Pure Land associations could evolve into communities that offered their members not only ideological companionship and a sense of belonging, but also tangible material support in the form of mutual aid and a network of people who could be trusted and relied on. In many times and places, Pure Land societies have had their own facilities and funds. Under oppressive conditions, where the local social structure offered little security and much institutionalized violence and exploitation, popular religious groupings might become the real locus of loyalty and community feeling.

Pure Land Buddhism as Other-worldly

Among the many varieties of Buddhism, the Pure Land teaching most deserves the epithet "other-worldly," often erroneously applied to Buddhism as a whole. Pure Land doctrine teaches that this world is an arena of unavoidable suffering and frustration, and holds out the vivid prospect of rebirth in another, better world, where sickness, pain and death do not exist. This world is a hopeless trap, from which we can escape only by the power of Amitabha. Unless we attain rebirth in the Pure Land, peace and happiness, to say nothing of enlightenment, are beyond reach ...

From a Buddhist perspective, it is the modern "this-worldly" orientation to life that is a form of unrealistic escapism and unwarranted pessimism about human possibilities. It is unrealistic because it seeks the meaning of life in gratifications that can only be temporary and partial: it seeks escape from mortality in transient pleasures. It is unnecessarily pessimistic because it ignores or denies the transcendental capacity inherent in humankind: "turning one's back on enlightenment to join with the dusts."

Pure Land Buddhism within the Buddhist Spectrum

What was the relationship between Pure Land and the other forms of Buddhism in East Asia?

Pure Land teaching incorporated many of the standards and perspectives that were basic in popular

Buddhism as a whole, deriving from the Buddhist scriptures. Pure Land teachers urged their listeners to observe the basic Buddhist moral code, to refrain from killing, stealing, lying, sexual excess, and intoxication. Strict vegetarianism was encouraged, as a corollary to the precept against taking life. Pure Land people were to give their allegiance to the "Three Jewels," that is, the enlightened one (Buddha), the teaching of enlightenment (Dharma), and the community of seekers (Sangha).

Pure Land teachers adopted the usual Buddhist moral perspective of cause and effect, of rewards and punishments according to one's actions. Pure Land people were taught to accumulate merit by good works, such as giving charity to the needy, helping widows and orphans, maintaining public facilities, supporting monks and nuns, contributing money and supplies for ceremonies and rituals, and making donations to Buddhist projects like building temples, casting statues and painting images, and copying and printing scriptures. Many Pure Land believers, in addition to reciting the buddha-name, studied and chanted various Buddhist scriptures, like the *Lotus Sutra*, the *Diamond Sutra*, and the *Flower Ornament (Avatamsaka) Sutra*. All these merit-making activities were viewed as auxiliary to the main work of reciting the buddha-name.

Pure Land theorists were faced with the task of clarifying their teaching of salvation through faith in Amitabha, given the mainstream scriptural Buddhist view of salvation as the reward for eons of diligent effort at self-discipline and purification and refinement of perceptions. By holding out the prospect of rebirth in the Pure Land through buddha-name recitation even to sinners, the Pure Land teaching appears to depart from a strict rule of karmic reward, which emphasizes the individual's own efforts as the decisive factor in spiritual attainment.

The Pure Land teachers explained this apparent anomaly by appealing to the infinite compassion of Amitabha Buddha (as an expedient embodiment of the infinitely pervasive Dharmakaya Buddha), who promises that all who invoke his name will attain birth in his Pure Land. The pioneers of the Pure Land teaching indeed took the position that for people in the later ages, the arduous path of self-restraint and purification proposed in the old Buddhist scriptures was no longer feasible. For average people, the only hope of salvation would be to rely on another power than their own, the power of Amitabha Buddha [in addition to their own personal effort].

The Pure Land practice of reciting the buddha-name bears a family resemblance to the chanting of mantras that plays a major role in esoteric Buddhism. As the Pure Land master Chu-hung said, "Reciting the buddha-name is equivalent to upholding a mantra. After you have gained power by reciting the buddha-name, you will be able to face objects with equanimity." According to the Pure Land teaching, invoking the buddha-name brings into play the vows of Amitabha Buddha, whose supernatural powers bring those who invoke him rebirth in the Pure Land. The key element is faith in Amitabha, and the Pure Land teaching is propounded as an easy path open to everyone.

***

Reciting the buddha-name and chanting mantras can be seen to operate in similar ways, from the point of view of the analysis of the workings of the human mind taught by Yogacara Buddhism and adopted by the Zen school.

Both practices in effect suspend the operation of the discriminating intellect, the faculty of the internal dialogue through which people from moment to moment define and perpetuate their customary world of perception. As the Yogacara bodhisattvas pointed out, people ordinarily are not in touch with phenomena themselves, but rather with mental representations projected onto phenomena. What we ordinarily perceive is not the world itself, but a description of the world that we have been conditioned to accept. The internal dialogue of the intellect holds in place these representations, which make up the world of delusion.

By focusing on the sounds of the mantra or the syllables of the buddha-name invocation, the internal dialogue is stopped. Once its grip is loosened, the description it perpetuates is suspended. Then other descriptions of reality, other worlds, can come into view (such as Amitabha and the Pure Land, or the interplay of deities visualized in esoteric Buddhism, or the infinite vistas of the *Avatamsaka Sutra*).

***

Operating in East Asia, Pure Land teachers had to reconcile their views with the perspective of Zen Buddhism. While Pure Land was the most widespread popular form of Buddhism in East Asia, Zen was the form that was intellectually preeminent.

According to the Zen school, since all people inherently possess buddha-nature, the potential for enlightenment, enlightenment equal to the buddhas can be attained in this lifetime by a properly directed and executed effort to break through the barriers of delusion. Rather than venerating the Buddhist scriptures as sacred but unattainable standards, the Zen people went to great lengths to apply the perceptions revealed in the sutras in practice. Generations of enlightened Zen adepts "appeared in the world" to demonstrate a freedom from worldly bonds and a mastery of the Buddha Dharma that proved that liberation was not an unattainable goal. Through their personal example and the unparalleled originality of their utterances, the Zen masters made a great impact on East Asian high culture in the realms of religion, philosophy, and aesthetics. The prestige of Zen was such that the other schools of Buddhists, and Confucians and Taoists as well, all had to answer to its perspectives.

***

The Pure Land school accepted the Zen perspective as valid in principle, but questioned how many people could get results by using Zen methods. Pure Land teachers granted that Zen might indeed be the "direct vehicle," but insisted that for most people it was too rigorous and demanding to be practicable. The Pure Land method of buddha-name recitation was offered as a simpler method by which average people could make progress toward enlightenment. The Pure Land teachers pointed out that many who scorned Pure Land methods as simplistic, and who proudly claimed allegiance to the Zen school, actually achieved nothing by stubbornly clinging to Zen methods. "With Zen, nine out of ten fail. With Pure Land, ten thousand out of ten thousand succeed."

The Zen school itself came to make room for Pure Land methods. From the time of Yung-ming Yen-shou in tenth century China, who was a master of scriptural Buddhism, Pure Land, and the Zen school, the synthesis of Zen and Pure Land figured prominently in the teachings of many Zen adepts.

In the Zen understanding of Pure Land, Amitabha Buddha represents the enlightened essence of our own true identity, while the Pure Land is the purity of our inherent buddha mind. Buddha-name recitation is effective as a means to cut through the deluded stream of consciousness and focus the mind on its true nature. "Being born in the Pure Land" means reaching the state of mental purity where discriminating thought is unborn and immediate awareness is unimpeded.

The synthesis of Zen and Pure Land methods was epitomized by the "buddha-name recitation meditation case" taught by many Zen masters. "Meditation cases" (koans) in Zen are generally short sayings or question-answer pairs or dialogues or action-scenes which were designed for use as focal points in meditation. They were designed with multiple levels of meaning that interact with the mind of the person meditating to shift routine patterns of thought and open up deeper perceptions. Sustained concentration on the meditation point provides the opportunity for direct insights beyond the level of words.

Examples of meditation cases are: "What was your original face before your father and mother gave birth to you?" "The myriad things return to one: what does the one return to?" "What is the Dharmakaya? A flowering hedge." "What is every-atom samadhi? Water in the bucket, food in the bowl." Sayings like these were everyday fare in the Zen school. The Pure Land master Chu-hung put together a detailed compendium of how to meditate with koans.

In the buddha-name recitation meditation case, the person intently reciting the buddha-name asks himself or herself, "Who is the one reciting the buddha-name?" "Who is the one mindful of buddha?" The question is answered when the practitioner comes face to face with his or her own buddha-nature. The one mindful of buddha is the buddha within us. This is the Zen rationale for Pure Land practice.

The Last Rites

(Excerpted from *Buddhism of Wisdom and Faith*
by Dharma Master Thích Thiên Tâm)

Preparations on the Eve of Death

Preparation of External Conditions

The ancients had a saying:

> We see others die, and our hearts ache. We ache not
> because others die, but because soon it will be our turn!

There is no greater sadness, no greater tragedy in the
world than the separation of death. However, it is
something no one in the world can escape. Therefore,
those who aspire to be of benefit to themselves and others
should be prepared and ready for it. In truth, the word
"death" is a misnomer, because it is merely the end of a
period of retribution. When we leave this body, because
of the connecting undercurrent of karma, we will be

reborn into another body. Those who do not know the Dharma are resigned to being under the sway of karma. Those who know the Pure Land method should practice Buddha Recitation with Faith and Vows and prepare their "personal provisions," so that they may be reborn in peace and harmony. Only in this way can they hope to achieve an early escape from the illusory suffering of Birth and Death and attain the true joy of ever-dwelling Nirvana.

Furthermore, the Pure Land practitioner should not be concerned about himself alone, but should be filial and compassionate toward parents, relatives and friends as well, enjoining them all to practice Buddha Recitation. He should also assist them when they are seriously ill – and at the time of death. These altruistic practices also create merits and good conditions for himself in the future.

There are many details connected with the last rites. I will first speak about external conditions. The Pure Land practitioner should, while still in good health, prepare himself and seek friends of like practice, particularly among neighbors, for mutual devotional help in cases of serious illness and at the time of death. Such preparations are crucial because we generally have heavy karma and even if we have striven to the utmost, it may be difficult to maintain right thought at such times. This is due to the emergence of karma accumulated from time immemorial, which weakens the body and perturbs the mind. Without the assistance of others, it is difficult to escape the cycle of Birth and Death. Is this not wasting an entire lifetime of cultivation? This is the first important point.

Secondly, when a Pure Land practitioner sees his strength ebbing, he should settle all his worldly affairs, so that he will not be preoccupied at the time of death. If he is a monk, he should turn over the affairs of the temple to his disciples and designate his successor. If he is a layman, he should divide his wealth and property in a suitable manner and make all other necessary arrangements. He should also instruct his family and relatives that should he be gravely ill or on the verge of death, they should not weep and lament or otherwise show their grief. Rather, if they care for him, they should calmly recite the Buddha's name on his behalf, or assist him in other ways to achieve rebirth in the Pure Land. This would be true concern and love.

Spiritual Preparations

In addition to the external preparations just described, the Pure Land practitioner should prepare himself spiritually. What do these preparations entail? On the way to liberation, the practitioner should have a transcendental bent of mind, realizing that wealth and property, as well as family, relatives and friends, are all illusory conditions. Relying in life on an illusory realm, he will die empty-handed. If he fails to understand this truth, family and possessions will certainly impede his liberation. In extreme cases, he may even be reborn in the animal realm -- as a dog or a snake, for example, to watch over his former houses and properties. There are many instances of individuals unable to let go of family and possessions, who experience difficulty at the time of death. They cannot close their eyes and die peacefully.

***

When this author was still a novice, attending to his Master and serving him tea late at night, he overheard an elder monk relate an anecdote. The main lines of the story are as follows.

Once, in times past, there were two monks who cultivated together. One liked the high mountain scenery, while the other built himself a hut on the banks of a brook, near a forest. Years went by. The monk who resided by the brook passed away first. Learning the news, his friend went down to visit his grave. After reciting sutras and praying for his friend's liberation, the visiting monk entered samadhi and attempted to see where his friend had gone -- to no avail. The friend was nowhere to be found, neither in the heavens nor in the hells, nor in any of the realms in between. Emerging from samadhi, he asked the attending novice, "What was your Master busy with every day?" The novice replied, "In the last few months before his death, seeing that the sugar cane in front of his hut was tall and green, my Master would go out continually to apply manure and prune away the dead leaves. He kept close watch over the cane, and seemed so happy taking care of it."

Upon hearing this, the visiting monk entered samadhi again, and saw that his friend had been reborn as a worm inside one of the stalks of sugar cane. The monk immediately cut down that stalk, slit it open and extracted the worm. He preached the Dharma to it and recited the Buddha's name, dedicating the merit to the worm's salvation.

This story was transmitted by word of mouth; the author has not found it anywhere in sutras or commentaries. However, if we judge it in the light of the Dharma, it is not necessarily without foundation. Buddhist sutras actually contain several similar accounts.

For example, there is the story of a novice who was greedy for buttermilk and was reborn as a worm in the milk pot. There is also the anecdote of a layman who was a genuine cultivator, adhering strictly to the precepts, but, being overly attached to his wife, was reborn as a worm in his wife's nostrils. As she cried her heart out by the side of the coffin, she tried to clear her nose, and the worm was expelled onto the floor. Greatly ashamed, she was on the verge of stamping it with her foot. Fortunately, the whole scene was witnessed by an enlightened monk, who stopped her and told her the causes and conditions of the worm. He then preached the Dharma to the worm, seeking its liberation.

There is also the story of a sea merchant's wife so attached to her own beauty that upon her death, she was reborn as a worm crawling out of her nostrils and wandering all over her own pallid face.

Thus, the Pure Land cultivator should keep his mind empty and still and meditate day in and day out, severing the mind of greed rooted in attachment and lust. He should resolutely direct his thoughts to the Pure Land, so that at the time of death, he will not be hindered and led astray by his evil karma.

Elder Master Tzu Chao once said:

The Pure Land practitioner on the verge of death usually faces Three Points of Doubt and Four Narrow Passes which obstruct his rebirth in the Pure Land. He should be prepared, reflecting on them in advance to eliminate them.

The Three Points of Doubt are:

1) Fearing that his past karma is heavy and his period of cultivation short, and that therefore, he may not achieve rebirth in the Pure Land;

2) Fearing that he has not yet fulfilled his vows and obligations or severed greed, anger and delusion, and that therefore, he may not achieve rebirth in the Pure Land;

3) Fearing that even though he has recited the Buddha's name, Buddha Amitabha may not come, and that therefore, he may not achieve rebirth in the Pure Land.

The [two main] Narrow Passes are:

1) Because of suffering due to illness, he may come to malign the Buddhas as ineffective and unresponsive;

2) Because of love-attachment, he may chain himself to his family, unable to let go.

Once aware of the doctrine of the Three Doubts and the Four Narrow Passes, the wise can ponder and find a solution. The author shall merely summarize a few points below. Fellow cultivators can expand on them according to their own backgrounds and understanding.

a) Overcoming the Three Doubts

1. Previous heavy karma, present perfunctory practice.

Amitabha Buddha is renowned for his Eighteenth Vow: not to attain Buddhahood unless sentient beings who sincerely desire to be reborn in the Pure Land, and who singlemindedly recite His name, are reborn there. The Buddhas do not engage in false speech, and therefore the practitioner should believe in them. Ten utterances or thoughts represent a very short cultivation period, yet the practitioner can still achieve rebirth in the Pure Land.

We who have recited the Buddha's name many times over should, therefore, eliminate all doubts.

Moreover, no matter how heavy the karma of sentient beings is, if they sincerely repent and rely upon Amitabha Buddha, they will all be welcomed and guided back to the Pure Land. Do we not recall that the *Meditation Sutra* teaches:

> If anyone who has committed the Five Grave Offenses or Ten Evil Deeds sees an evil omen appear as he is on the verge of death, he needs only recite the Buddha's name one to ten times with all his heart, and Buddha Amitabha will descend to welcome and escort him back to the Pure Land.

In the commentary *Accounts of Rebirth*, there are cases of individuals who throughout their lives were slaughtering livestock, breaking the precepts and engaging in all manner of evil conduct. Nevertheless, on their deathbeds, when the "marks of hell" appeared and, desperate, they singlemindedly recited the Buddha's name, they immediately saw Amitabha Buddha arriving to welcome them. Why should we, who are not that sinful or deluded, worry about not achieving rebirth in the Pure Land?

2. Unfulfilled vows; non-severance of greed, anger and delusion.

Cultivators' vows can be divided into two categories: religious and mundane.

Religious vows: Some practitioners have vowed to build a temple, practice charity or recite various sutras or mantras a certain number of times, etc. However, they have not completely fulfilled their vows when it is time for them to die. These cultivators should think: reciting the Buddha's name in all earnestness will earn them rebirth in the Pure Land, where they will have ample opportunity to achieve immeasurable merits and virtues. Their present vows to build temples and recite sutras are merely secondary matters. The fact that they may not have fulfilled them should be of no great concern.

Mundane vows: These include family obligations such as caring for sick, aging parents or helpless wives and young children, as well as business debts to be paid or certain other commitments to be fulfilled. Faced with these worries, the practioners should think: on our deathbed, there is nothing that can be done, whether we worry or not. It is better to concentrate on Buddha Recitation. Once we are reborn in the Pure Land and Buddhahood is achieved, all vows, wishes and debts can be taken care of, as we will be in a position to rescue everyone, family and foes alike.

The *Questions of King Milinda Sutra* contains the following parable:

A minute grain of sand, dropped on the surface of the water, will sink immediately. On the other hand, a block of stone, however large and heavy, can easily be moved from place to place by boat. The same is true of the Pure Land practitioner. However light his karma may be, if he is not rescued by Amitabha Buddha, he must revolve in the cycle of Birth and Death. With the help of Amitabha Buddha, his karma, however heavy, will not prevent his rebirth in the Pure Land.

We can see from this passage that thanks to "other-power," the Pure Land method can benefit the practitioner, however heavy his karma may be. The huge block of stone represents the weight of heavy karma, the boat symbolizes the power of Amitabha Buddha's Vows. Therefore, the cultivator should not think that residual greed, anger and delusion will prevent him from achieving rebirth in the Pure Land. This example should also resolve doubts concerning past heavy karma, as in doubt number one above.

3. Despite recitation, Amitabha Buddha may not come, after all.

At the time of death, the Pure Land practitioner will see, depending on his virtues, Amitabha Buddha, the Bodhisattvas or the Ocean-Wide Assembly come to welcome him. Sometimes he may not see anything, but, thanks to the power of his vows and the "gathering in" power of Amitabha Buddha, he will be reborn in the Pure Land all the same. The difference lies in his level of cultivation, whether subtle or gross, transcendental or mundane. What is most important at the time of death is to recite the Buddha's name in all earnestness and not worry about anything else. Any doubts at that time will give rise to obstructions and impediments.

In summary, at the time of death, the practitioner should not be concerned about whether or not he witnesses auspicious signs. He should just concentrate on reciting the Buddha's name in all earnestness until the very end.

b) Overcoming the Narrow Passes

These "passes" can be described as follows:

- Slandering the Buddhas because of suffering and disease;
- Binding and chaining oneself to family and friends through love-attachment.

Sincere practitioners who meet with accidents, disease and disaster should reflect that these are sometimes due to virtues accrued through cultivation. Either the heavy karma (which he should have endured) has been commuted to light karma (which he is now enduring), or else, future karma has been transformed into current karma, giving him the opportunity to repay karmic debts before achieving rebirth in the Pure Land. Should he doubt this and speak ill of the Dharma, he would lack faith and understanding, display ingratitude toward the Buddhas and bring evil karma upon himself.

Among the rebirth stories, we find instances where this "bunching and compressing of karma" has allowed cultivators to hasten their rebirth in the Pure Land. Therefore, when Pure Land cultivators encounter such instances, they should be aware and understand them thoroughly.

Furthermore, this body is illusory and provisional. Depending on his merit or bad karma, the practitioner's life will be long or short, happy or filled with hardship. He should systematically rely on the Buddhas and firmly believe in the law of cause and effect.

When ill or in bad health, the practitioner should direct his thoughts toward Amitabha Buddha exclusively. He should not seek the help of externalist gurus, shamans or healers. Nor should he listen to those who do not yet understand the Dharma and revert to a non-vegetarian diet, drink alcoholic beverages, etc. Our bodies are truly full of filth; the sooner we return to the Pure Land, the better. It is like casting off a smelly, ragged garment and donning a beautiful, fragrant outfit. What is there to worry about?

***

Concerning the danger of love-attachment at the time of death, as indicated earlier, the practitioner should think thus: family members, including parents, brothers, sisters, husbands, wives and children, are temporarily gathered together in this life as a result of previous causes and conditions, such as karmic debts or love and hatred, accumulated from time immemorial. When these causes and conditions come to an end, we all part and go our separate ways. If we truly care for them, we should endeavor to be reborn in the Pure Land, so as to be able to save everyone, friend and foe alike. Although we may have attachments to family and friends, when death approaches, there is nothing we can bring along or do, as even our very body disintegrates and returns to dust. If we harbor thoughts of attachment and love, not only will we fail to achieve rebirth in the Pure Land, we will not escape the endless cycle of Birth and Death.

The practitioner should ponder and clearly recall the Three Doubts and Four Narrow Passes to prepare himself. His mind will then be calm and undisturbed at the time of death.

Critical Importance of the Moment of Death

Seeking Guidance from Spiritual Advisors

The Pure Land practitioner should take medicine when he falls ill and his condition is not desperate, but he must persevere in reciting the Buddha's name. When his condition is hopeless, he may refuse further medication.

A well-known Elder Master, gravely ill, responded with the following gatha, when his disciples sought his approval to send for a physician:

> The Honored Amitabha Buddha
> Is the foremost king of physicians.
> If we forget this and fail to heed Him,
> We are indeed deluded!
> One utterance of the Buddha's name
> Is the wonderful panacea,
> If we forget this and fail to take it,
> We are truly and greatly mistaken!

We must remember that when death is impending, the practitioner should let go of everything around him, including his own body and mind, and concentrate singlemindedly on reciting the Buddha's name, earnestly seeking rebirth in the Pure Land. By so doing, if his life span has come to an end, he will surely achieve rebirth there. On the other hand, if his life span is not yet over, even though he seeks rebirth, his condition will improve, thanks to his sincere and steadfast mind (as part of his bad karma will have been dissipated in the process). Acting otherwise, he will forfeit rebirth in the Pure Land if his lifespan has come to an end (as he was only seeking recovery, not rebirth). If his lifespan is not yet over, he will aggravate his illness through worry and fear.

When they fall gravely ill, some Pure Land practitioners are not encouraged to practice Buddha Recitation, as their family members lack understanding of Buddhism. On the other hand, their kin spare no time or effort seeking out all kinds of charlatans and quacks. Some families even go to such lengths as making offerings to various deities in the hope of obtaining a quick cure. Thus, the patient not only does not receive the benefit of "supportive recitation," his mind is divided and disturbed. He cannot, therefore, be reborn in the Pure Land. The entire process is sometimes motivated by a sense of filial obligation or the desire for a good name, aimed at neighbors and friends. Little do they know that the Buddhas and sages are not deceived, and that a filial, sincere mind does not depend on external factors! Such behavior only makes the wise smile in pity.

When the patient is gravely ill but still conscious, his close family members should invite good spiritual advisors to preach the Dharma and enlighten him. If no monk or nun can be found, a knowledgeable lay person should be invited over to comfort the patient and preach the Dharma to him. The spiritual advisor should remind and enjoin the patient's relatives to be compassionate and ensure that everything is conducted according to the Way, so that the patient may enjoy the benefit of rebirth in the Pure Land.

***

In general, the spiritual advisor should follow the guidelines set out below.

1. Remind the patient of the sufferings of the Saha World and the joys of the Pure Land, so that he may develop a mind of devotion and attraction to the Pure Land. The good advisor should also enumerate and praise the patient's good deeds, merits and virtues in cultivation. This will make him happy and free of doubts, certain that when the time comes to die, he will, thanks to his good deeds, be reborn in the Pure Land.

2. If the patient has any doubts, the advisor should, depending on the circumstances, explain the Three Points of Doubt and the Four Narrow Passes discussed earlier. A critical detail to bear in mind here: the dying person should be reminded to eliminate all regret over wealth and property, as well as attachment to close family and relatives.

3. If the patient has a will, so much the better, but if not, the advisor should counsel against all inquiries in this regard. He should also advise everyone to refrain from useless chitchat that could rekindle the patient's love-attachment to the world, which is detrimental to rebirth in the Pure Land.

4. When relatives and friends come to visit, they should be discouraged from standing before the patient, inquiring about his health in a sad, piteous way. If they come out of true concern, they should merely stand on the side, reciting the Buddha's name aloud for a moment. If, lacking understanding of the Dharma, the visitors act

conventionally [crying, etc.], they are in effect pushing the dying person into the ocean of suffering -- a most regrettable occurrence indeed!

5. The patient should be counselled to practice charity and give away his personal effects to the needy. Or, better still, in accordance with the *Ksitigarbha (Earth Store Bodhisattva) Sutra*, he should use the proceeds from the sale of his personal possessions to purchase Buddhist images or sutras for free distribution. All this helps the patient increase his stock of merits and eliminate bad karma, thus facilitating rebirth in the Pure Land.

The good advisor should keep these general guidelines in mind, but be ready to improvise according to the situation.

Conducting "Supportive Recitation"

Family members and relatives of a dying patient should remain calm, without weeping or lamenting, from the time he becomes gravely ill until his last moments. Some people, while not crying, still show sorrow and emotion on their faces. This, too, should be avoided, because, at this juncture, the dying person has reached the crossroads which separate the living from the dead, and the mundane from the transcendental. The critical importance and danger of this moment can be compared to standing under a sword -- his fate is determined by a hair's breadth!

At this time, the most important thing is to practice supportive recitation. Even though a person may have set his mind on rebirth in the Pure Land, if family members weep and lament, thus arousing deep-seated feelings of love-attachment, he will certainly sink into the cycle of Birth and Death, wasting all his efforts in cultivation!

When a patient on the verge of death wishes to bathe, dress in different garments, or change his position or sleeping quarters, we may comply, while exercising caution and acting in a gentle, careful manner at all times. If the patient refuses, or cannot give his consent because he has become mute, we certainly should not go against his wishes. This is because the patient on the verge of death is generally in great physical pain. If he is forced to move, bathe or change clothing, he may experience even greater pain. There are numerous cases of cultivators who had sought rebirth in the Pure Land but failed to achieve this goal because their relatives moved them around, disturbing them and destroying their right thought. This unfortunate development occurs very often.

There are also cases of individuals who might have achieved rebirth in the higher realms. However, out of ignorance, others made them suffer physically (by rearranging the positions of their hands and feet, for instance), making them irritated and angry. Because of this one thought of anger, they immediately sank into the evil realms. As an extreme example, King Ajatasatru had earned numerous merits and blessings through cultivation. However, at the time of death, one of his attendants dozed off and inadvertently dropped a paper fan onto the king's face. He became so furious that he expired on the spot -- to be reborn, it is said, as a python! This example should serve as a warning to us all.

At the time of death, the cultivator himself should either lie down or sit up, according to what comes naturally, without forcing himself. If he feels weak and can only lie down, forcing himself to sit up, for appearances' sake, is dangerous and should be discouraged. Likewise, even though, according to Pure Land tradition, he should lie on his right side facing west, if, because of pain, he can only lie on his back or on his left side facing east, he should act naturally and not force himself. The patient and his family should understand all this and act accordingly.

***

Supportive recitation by family members or Dharma friends is most necessary when a patient is on the verge of death. This is because, at that time, he is weak in body and mind and no longer master of himself. In such trying circumstances, not only is it difficult for those who have not cultivated in daily life to focus on Amitabha Buddha, even individuals who have regularly recited the

Buddha's name may find it difficult to do so in all earnestness -- unless there is supportive recitation.

Such recitation should closely follow the guidelines set out below.

1. Respectfully place a standing Amitabha Buddha statue in front of the patient, so that he can see it clearly. Place some fresh flowers in a vase and burn light incense with a soft fragrance. This will help the patient develop right thought. A reminder: the incense should not be overpowering, to avoid choking the patient and everyone around.

2. Those who come to practice supportive recitation should take turns ... It should be remembered that the patient, in his weakened state, requires a lot of fresh air to breathe. If too many persons come and go or participate in the recitation session, the patient may have difficulty breathing and become agitated, resulting in more harm than benefit. Therefore, participants should consult their watches and silently take turns reciting, so that recitation can continue uninterrupted. They should not call to one another aloud. Each session should last about an hour.

3. According to Elder Master Yin Kuang, the short recitation form (Amitabha Buddha) should be used, so that the patient can easily register the name in his Alaya consciousness, at a time when both his mind and body are

very weak. However, according to another Elder Master, we should ask the patient and use the form he prefers (short or long), to conform to his everyday practice. In this way, the patient can silently recite along with the supportive recitation party. To go counter to his likes and habits may destroy his right thought and create an offense on our part. Furthermore, we should not practice supportive recitation in too loud a voice, as we will expend too much energy and be unable to keep on for very long. On the other hand, neither should we recite in too low a voice, lest the patient, in his weakened state, be unable to register the words.

Generally speaking, recitation should not be too loud or too low, too slow or too fast. Each utterance should be clear and distinct so that it can pass through the ear and penetrate deep into the patient's Alaya consciousness. One caveat: if the patient is too weak [or is in a coma], he will not be able to hear "external" recitation. In such a case, we should recite into the patient's ear. This helps the patient keep his mind clear and steady.

4. With regard to percussion instruments, it is generally better to use the small hand bell, instead of the wooden fish gong with its bass tone. The hand bell, with its clear, limpid sound, can help the patient develop a pure and calm mind. However, this may not apply in all cases. For instance, an Elder Master once taught, "It is best to recite the Buddha's name by itself without musical accompaniment, but since each person's

preferences are different, it is better to ask the patient in advance. If some details do not suit him, we should adapt to the circumstances and not be inflexible."

The above are some pointers to keep in mind with regard to supportive recitation.

After Death

Between Death and Burial

When a person has just died, the most important thing is not to rush to move him. Even if his body is soiled with excrement and urine, we should not hasten to clean it. We should wait about eight hours -- or a minimum of three hours -- before cleaning the body and changing its clothes. Relatives should not weep and wail immediately before and after the actual death. Doing so is not only useless, it can be harmful, as this can cause the deceased to develop thoughts of attachment, which may prevent him from achieving liberation. To be of true benefit to the patient, we should concentrate on reciting the Buddha's name in all earnestness, without crying until at least eight hours have passed. Why is this necessary? It is because although the patient has stopped breathing, his Alaya consciousness has not yet left his body. If, during this period, we move the body, clean it, change its clothes, or weep and lament, the deceased may still experience feelings of pain, sadness, anger or self-pity, and descend upon the Evil Paths. This is a crucial point -- a critical one -- that relatives should note and remember well.

**

The practice of touching the body of the deceased to locate the last warm spot and deduce his place of rebirth is grounded in the sutras and commentaries. However, we should not be inflexible. If the patient had sincere, earnest faith and vows in normal times and clearly exhibits right thought at the time of death, this is sufficient evidence of rebirth in the Pure Land. Some persons who are not careful keep "feeling" the body, touching one spot after another, disturbing the deceased. This can cause great harm.

After the patient has expired, the persons who came to recite the Buddha's name should continue doing so for another three hours. After that, the body should be left alone, free of all disturbances, for another five hours (or a total of eight hours), at which time it can be bathed and given a change of clothing. If, during the entire eight-hour period, someone, or a group of persons, can remain near the deceased reciting the Buddha's name, so much the better. Except for recitation, nothing should be done. A reminder and caveat: during this period, the "deceased" may still have consciousness and feelings.

After the eight-hour period, if the limbs have grown stiff and cannot move, we should put a towel soaked in hot water around the joints. After a while, the body can be repositioned.

***

Funeral arrangements should be kept simple, not accompanied by superfluous ceremonies occasioning unnecessary expenses. Another caveat: only vegetarian food should be served. No non-vegetarian food should be provided as offerings or to entertain guests -- for to take life is to sadden the departed with more karmic obstructions and "heavy baggage," making his liberation that much more difficult. Even if he has already been reborn in the Pure Land, his grade of rebirth may be lowered as a result.

Some time ago, this author, along with other monks and nuns, attended an elaborate funeral for the stepmother of one of his friends, a high-ranking Master in Long An province, southern Vietnam. Throughout the funeral, only vegetarian food was served. After congratulating his friend, the author inquired about this and was told, "the serving of vegetarian food is due partly to my recommendation; however, the major impetus was an event which took place not long ago in a nearby village:

"After a prosperous elder had passed away, his son ordered a huge quantity of livestock slaughtered to feed relatives and friends for several days. (In his lifetime, the elder, a good-natured, benevolent man who practiced

Buddha Recitation and was vegetarian several days a month, had had many friends and associates.) The very evening after the funeral, his eldest grandson suddenly had a fit in front of everyone. His face all red, he suddenly jumped onto the wooden plank bed in the living room, sat squarely upon it, and slapped his hand against a nearby desk. Calling his father by his given name, he scolded him loudly: *'Right up until my death*, I practiced charity and accumulated merits; without any heavy transgressions, I should have been reborn wealthy and into a good family. Instead, because of you and the heavy karma of killing you created on my behalf, I, as *your father*, am now confined and forced to look after a herd of cows, as well as pigs, chickens and ducks. I have to run back and forth barefoot through mud and thorns. My sufferings are truly beyond description!'"

After recounting the story, the Master smiled and said, "This event, which occurred only a few months ago, is known to the entire village and is believed and dreaded by my relatives. For precisely this reason, when I suggested vegetarian food, the idea was immediately accepted."

The *Ksitigarbha Sutra* [ch. VII] goes into detail about the harm associated with slaughtering animals to serve guests at funerals. Buddhist followers should take heed and bear this in mind.

***

When performing follow-up good deeds on behalf of the deceased, we should dedicate the merit and virtue to all sentient beings in the Dharma Realm. In this way, these merits and virtues will be multiplied many times over, and so will the benefits accrued to the deceased.

These preparations for the time of death have been taken from the teachings of Elder Masters of the past. The last moments of life are the most crucial ones. If the "provisions for rebirth" are not ready and adequate, the patient cannot avoid extreme fright and bewilderment. At that time, too late to seek help and faced with the simultaneous appearance of all kinds of bad karma accumulated over countless lifetimes, how can he achieve liberation? Therefore, while we may rely on others for support and assistance at the time of death, we ourselves should strive to cultivate during normal times. Only then will we feel free and at peace.

I beg you all, fellow Pure Land practitioners, to take heed and be prepared, so that we may all be reborn in the ocean-wide Lotus Assembly!

Success and Failure in Supportive Recitation

1. Story of LCL

The layman LCL was a legislator and an official early in life. As he had affinities with Buddhism, he contributed to such good works as restoring a local temple, donating land to it and inviting an Elder Master to head it. He was also diligent in raising funds to build a statue of the Bodhisattva Avalokitesvara, which was about one hundred feet high.

In 1933 he took refuge with the Triple Jewel under the Patriarch Yin Kuang. He resolved to be a vegetarian six days a month and took up the practice of Buddha Recitation. In the years that followed, however, because of his heavy schedule, his practice, while sincere, was irregular.

In 1938, he fell gravely ill. As time went by and his condition did not improve, he made large donations to worthwhile activities, in the hope of expunging some of his bad karma. He also became a full time vegetarian. The following year, as his illness took a turn for the worse, his wife and sons, realizing the importance of the last moments, hurriedly invited monks from the local temple to recite the Buddha's name at his bedside.

On the 19th of January of that year, LCL, sensing that his end was near, asked to be taken out to the courtyard to breathe fresh air. After speaking to his brothers and sisters, he requested his son to kneel down to hear his will. As he was speaking, LCL's countenance suddenly changed. Seeing this, his wife and son helped him back into the house and placed a statue of a standing Amitabha Buddha before him. They then began to recite aloud, together with the monks. For several months, LCL's left arm had been paralyzed, but when he saw the statue, he managed to regain the use of his arm. With palms joined, he began to recite the Buddha's name, his face radiant and beaming with joy. At that moment, he seemed to have forgotten all pain and suffering, as he recited along with the others for a while, before dying peacefully, at the age of sixty-one.

The layman LCL had practiced Buddha Recitation sincerely during the last part of his life. At his deathbed, thanks to supportive recitation, a number of auspicious signs appeared. These included stable faculties, right thought and a peaceful death, as though in samadhi. We can therefore deduce that he certainly achieved rebirth in the Pure Land.

While the layman's rebirth was due to his maturing good roots, it was also helped by the supportive recitation he received when on his deathbed. Thus, Pure Land practitioners should recognize the particular importance and urgency of supportive recitation just before death.

2. Story of DH

The laywoman DH was the wife of a certain man in the city of Yangchow. As she could not bear children, her husband took a concubine, which made it difficult for her to remain in the conjugal home. Therefore, she went to live with her stepmother, another lay Buddhist, who loved her as her own daughter. They supported and relied on one another, and two years passed as though they were but one day.

The laywoman DH was a vegetarian who earnestly practiced Buddha Recitation day and night. She and her stepmother realized that they had scant merits and few good conditions in this life, and no one else to rely on in case of need, as their relatives were dead or far away. They therefore wholeheartedly helped one another, as Dharma friends along the Way. From the point of view of faith and daily cultivation, DH far surpassed LCL of our previous story. Unfortunately, however, because of heavy residual karma and unfavorable conditions, she always met with adverse circumstances and her mind was never at peace.

In 1938, sensing that a major upheaval was impending, mother and daughter immediately left Hong Kong, where they had been staying, to seek refuge back on the mainland. At that time, the cost of living was skyrocketing. Renting a place to live was dificult, while staying in hotels for any length of time was both costly and inconvenient. Fortunately, a local abbot took pity on the women and set aside a small area of his temple for them and three other refugees.

Around March of the following year, DH suddenly contracted typhoid fever. The illness lasted for over a month, with no signs of recovery. At that time, the temple was very busy and space was at a premium. If she were to die there, it would cause a great deal of inconvenience. Therefore, with great reluctance, her stepmother decided to bring her to the local hospital.

The hospital followed Western medical practice, making it difficult to engage in supportive recitation freely and in an appropriate manner. On the 18th of August, after two or three days in the hospital, with no one practicing supportive recitation at her bedside and in a confused state of mind, the laywoman DH died. She was fifty-one years of age at the time.

We can see that the laywoman DH was truly a woman of faith, who had practiced in earnest. If, at the time of death, she had had the benefit of adequate supportive recitation, auspicious signs of rebirth in the Pure Land should have appeared, no fewer than in the case of LCL. Such was not, unfortunately, the case. Because of adverse circumstances, she died in a coma, unattended by Dharma friends. She probably did not achieve rebirth in the Pure Land, but merely managed to sow the seeds of Enlightenment for future lives. What happened to her was regrettable, but demonstrates that supportive recitation at the time of death is truly of crucial importance.

3. Story of DLH

The layman DLH was from a poor merchant family. Well-mannered and courteous, he had a good grasp of worldly affairs. In 1922, following the example of a friend, he took refuge with the Triple Jewel, and along with others, vowed to develop the Bodhi Mind, to rescue himself and others.

A few years later, because of a serious illness, he abandoned vegetarianism and began to drift away from his Buddhist friends. In July of that year, his illness grew more severe, and everyone feared the worst. Realizing that his end was near, DLH sincerely repented his past transgressions, let go of everything and concentrated all his time and effort on Buddha Recitation. Fellow cultivators, fearing that his practice was still shallow, were continuously at his bedside.

Supportive recitation itself began on the 12th of July. Three days later, the layman DLH suddenly experienced a surge of strength, feeling fresh and well. On the 17th, he told everyone that in a dream, he had seen an aura of light as bright as five or six electric bulbs. That evening, his complexion appeared to be normal. His fellow cultivators continued their recitation until the wee hours and were preparing to leave, when DLH suddenly said, "I have not yet reached the Pure Land. Please continue reciting all day."

The group gladly complied, and recitation went on,
with DLH mostly remaining silent. He was smiling
calmly, his face radiant, as though he had received some
news that was good beyond expectation. This continued
for some time, until he became still and immobile, his
gaze fixed on the standing Amitabha statue facing him.
His eyes then began to cloud over and his breathing
subsided. He passed away at five o'clock that morning.

The cultivators took turns reciting, interspersing
recitation with words of encouragement and exhortation,
until his body was completely cold. His next of kin had
been warned not to weep or wail. At ten a.m., one of the
practitioners touched DLH's body and discovered that it
was cold all over except for the crown, which was as hot
as boiling water.

The sutras contain a stanza:

The crown stands for sainthood, the eyes rebirth in a
    celestial realm,
The heart indicates the human realm, the belly stands
    for the ghostly,
The knees are tantamount to animality, the soles of the
    feet stand for the hells.

When the cultivator's body is completely cold except
for the crown, that person has been reborn in the realm
of the saints, or of the Buddhas. When his eyes are the

last to remain warm, he has been reborn in the celestial realms; warmth in the area of the heart means rebirth among human beings. If the abdominal area retains warmth after the body has grown cold, he has been reborn among hungry ghosts. The knees represent rebirth among animals, while the soles of the feet indicate the hellish realms. Thus, the last warm spot represents the place where the consciousness of the deceased escaped the mortal body.

The fact that DLH's crown was the last warm spot shows that he achieved rebirth in the Pure Land -- his very goal in the last years of his life.

The layman DLH was not above violating the precepts. His cultivation was shallow and wanting as well. His rebirth in the Pure Land, therefore, was largely due to the supportive recitation of his fellow cultivators. Here again, we can see the importance of supportive recitation at the time of death. That time was the 18th of July 1924 -- and DLH was thirty years old!

Realms of worlds in empty space might reach an end,
And living beings, karma and afflictions be extinguished;
But they will never be exhausted,
And neither will my vows.

The Vows of Samantabhadra
Avatamsaka Sutra

Mudras of Rebirth
in Amitabha's Pure Land

Middle and Lower Grades (Classes)

AMIDAS OF THE MIDDLE AND LOWER CLASSES

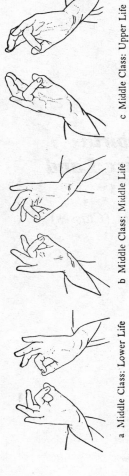

a Middle Class: Lower Life

b Middle Class: Middle Life

c Middle Class: Upper Life

d Lower Class: Lower Life

e Lower Class: Middle Life

f Lower Class: Upper Life

"Wherever the Buddha's teachings have been received, either in cities or countrysides, people would gain inconceivable benefits. The land and people would be enveloped in peace. The sun and moon will shine clear and bright. Wind and rain would appear accordingly, and there will be no disasters. Nations would be prosperous and there would be no use for soldiers or weapons. People would abide by morality and accord with laws. They would be courteous and humble, and everyone would be content without injustices. There would be no thefts or violence. The strong would not dominate the weak and everyone would be settled at their proper place in society."

❀ *The Sutra of Amitabha's Purity,*
   Equality, and Understanding

A PATH TO TRUE HAPPINESS

True Sincerity
towards others
Purity Of Mind
within
Equality
in everything we see
Proper Understanding
of ourselves and our environment
Compassion
helping others in a wise and unconditional way

See Through
to the truth of impermanence
Let Go
of all wandering thoughts and attachments
Freedom
of mind and spirit
Accord With Conditions
go along with the environment
Be Mindful Of Amitabha Buddha
*wishing to reach the Pure Land and follow in
His Teachings*

DEDICATION OF MERIT

May the merit and virtues
accrued from this work,
Adorn the Buddha's Pure Land,
Repaying the four kinds
of kindness above,
and relieving the sufferings of
those in the Three Paths below.

May those who see and hear of this,
All bring forth the heart of
Understanding,
And live the Teachings for
the rest of this life,
Then be born together in
The Land of Ultimate Bliss.
Homage to Amitabha Buddha!

NAMO AMITABHA

Reprinted and Donated for free distribution by
The Corporate Body of the Buddha Educational Foundation
11 F., 55 Hang Chow South Road Sec 1, Taipei, Taiwan, R.O.C.
Tel: 886-2-23951198 , Fax: 886-2-23913415
Email: overseas@budaedu.org.tw
Printed in Taiwan
1998 July, 30000 copies
EN103-1340